Christians have been commissioned by Jesus to "proclaim the good news" and to "make disciples of all nations." But does that mean that every individual Christian is called to be an evangelist? That is very often the impression given in the church, and we are pointed to various verses in the Bible that are supposed to show that. Alternatively, do some Christians have that particular gift and calling, with others of us being called more simply to be salt and light in the world, witnessing to the Lord in that way? In this careful and scholarly study the Korean scholar Dr Bo Young Kang engages carefully with relevant texts in Paul's letters, relating Paul's teaching to that of Jesus, bringing out major themes, and helping us think constructively about what is still the great commission of the Lord to his church.

David Wenham, PhD
Associate Tutor in New Testament
Trinity College, Bristol, UK

Heralds and Community

An Enquiry into Paul's Conception of Mission
and Its Indebtedness to the Jesus-Tradition

Bo Young Kang

MONOGRAPHS

© 2016 by Bo Young Kang

Published 2016 by Langham Monographs
an imprint of Langham Creative Projects

Langham Partnership
PO Box 296, Carlisle, Cumbria CA3 9WZ, UK
www.langham.org

ISBNs:
978-1-78368-901-9 Print
978-1-78368-062-7 Mobi
978-1-78368-063-4 ePub
978-1-78368-064-1 PDF

Bo Young Kang has asserted his right under the Copyright, Designs and Patents Act, 1988 to be identified as the Author of this work.

All rights reserved. No part of this publication may be reproduced, stored in a retrieval system or transmitted, in any form or by any means, electronic, mechanical, photocopying, recording or otherwise, without the prior written permission of the publisher or the Copyright Licensing Agency.

British Library Cataloguing in Publication Data
A catalogue record for this book is available from the British Library

ISBN: 978-1-78368-901-9

Cover & Book Design: projectluz.com

Langham Partnership actively supports theological dialogue and a scholar's right to publish but does not necessarily endorse the views and opinions set forth, and works referenced within this publication or guarantee its technical and grammatical correctness. Langham Partnership does not accept any responsibility or liability to persons or property as a consequence of the reading, use or interpretation of its published content.

Contents

Abstract xi
Acknowledgements xiii
Abbreviations xv
Chapter 1 1
   General Introduction
     1.1. Paul's Conception of Mission and the Issue of His
        Missio-Ecclesial Understanding 1
        1.1.1. Paul's Mission and Paul's Conception of Mission 1
        1.1.2. Renewed Interest: The Issue of Paul's Missio-Ecclesial
            Understanding 3
     1.2. Current Contour of the Debate 7
        1.2.1. The Issue of Mission-Continuity between Paul and the
            Church 8
        1.2.2. The Question of Mission Continuity and Discontinuity
            between Paul and the Church: W.-H. Ollrog's Study of the
            Co-Workers 11
        1.2.3. The Question of the Background for Paul's Conception
            of Mission 13
        1.2.4. Other Scholars in the Debate 18
        1.2.5. Conclusion 22
     1.3. Objectives and Methodological Considerations 24
        1.3.1. Focal Points 24
        1.3.2. Definition of Mission in Discussing Paul's Conception
            of Mission 25
        1.3.3. Question of the Origins of Paul's Conception of Mission
            within Paul's Jewish-Christian Thought World 31
     1.4. Summary 52

Chapter 2 55
   Silence or Non-Silence? An Exegetical Study of Pauline Texts Having
   Possible Relevance to the Church's Proactive Verbal Proclamation
   of the Gospel
     2.1. Selecting the Relevant Pauline Passages 56
        2.1.1. Individual vs Community 56

  2.1.2. Direct / Active Verbal Engagement vs Passive / Indirect
    Witness to the Message 57
  2.1.3. Community Accession vs Community (re)Production 57
 2.2. Paul's Positive Recognition of the Church's Proactive
 Gospel-Proclamation? 59
  2.2.1. 1 Thessalonians 1:8 59
  2.2.2. Philippians 1:5 65
  2.2.3. Philippians 1:14 77
 2.3. Paul's Exhortation for Proactive Congregational Evangelism? 86
  2.3.1. Philippians 1:27–30 86
  2.3.2. Philippians 2:16 98
 2.4. Texts from the Disputed Letters 110
  2.4.1. Ephesians 6:15 110
  2.4.2. Ephesians 6:17b 120
 2.5. Conclusion: Paul's Consistent Silence about Congregational
 Evangelism 125

Chapter 3 129
*Heralds and Community: Paul's Conceptualization of Mission as a
Bifurcated Eschatological Event*
 3.1. Paul's Jewish Eschatology and His Conception of Mission 129
  3.1.1. Paul's Jewish Eschatology and His Persecution of
    the Church 130
  3.1.2. Paul's Jewish Eschatological Worldview and the
    Proclamation of the Gospel 137
 3.2. Paul's Conception of Mission as an Inaugurated
 Eschatological Event 141
  3.2.1. Paul's Conception of Mission within His Inaugurated
    Eschatological Framework 141
  3.2.2. Paul's Conception of Mission and the Eschatological
    Ingathering of the Gentiles 142
  3.2.3. Conclusion: Paul's Conception of Mission as a
    Bifurcated Eschatological Event of the Restoration of Israel
    and the Incoming of Gentiles 157
 3.3. The Gospel Heralds as an Eschatological Event in Paul 158
  3.3.1. Paul's Commission as One of the Eschatological
    Heralds of the Gospel 158
  3.3.2. The Scope of the Gospel Heralds in Paul 165
  3.3.3. Conclusion 179
 3.4. The Community of the People of God as an Eschatological
 Event in Paul 181

3.4.1. Paul's Missio-Ecclesial Understanding within His
Conception of Mission 181
3.4.2. Ἐκκλησία as an Eschatological Event in Relation to the
Eschatological Heralds 184
3.4.3. The Vocation of the Church in Paul's Thought 191
3.4.4. Conclusion 222
3.5. Conclusion: Paul's Conception of Mission as a Bifurcated
Eschatological Event as the Primary Reason for His Silence
about the Church's Evangelism 222

Chapter 4 225
Paul's Mission-Conception of the Eschatological Heralds and the Jesus-Tradition

4.1. Paul's Conception of the Eschatological Heralds and the
Jesus-Tradition of the Mission Discourse 226
  4.1.1. Paul's Knowledge of the Context and the Contents of
  the Mission Discourse 226
  4.1.2. Paul's Conception of the Eschatological Heralds as
  the Extension of the Pre-Easter Sending of the Disciples
  of Jesus 232
  4.1.3. Conclusion 240
4.2. The Jesus-Tradition as a Historical Corroboration of Paul's
Apostleship 241
  4.2.1. The Subjectivity Problem with Paul's Apostleship 241
  4.2.2. Paul's Subjectivity Problem and the Apostleship of the
  Pre-Easter Disciples 243
  4.2.3. Paul's Appeals to Other Apostles 246
4.3. Conclusion 252

Chapter 5 255
Paul's Mission-Conception of the Eschatological Community and the Jesus-Tradition

5.1. The Question of the Influence of the Jesus-Tradition on
Paul's Missio-Ethical Understanding 255
  5.1.1. The Influence of the Teachings of Jesus on Paul's
  Ethical Understanding 255
  5.1.2. Paul's Missio-Ecclesial Vision in Philippians in
  Comparison with the Sermon on the Mount 260
5.2. Paul's Dependence for His Missio-Ethical Understanding in
Philippians 1:6–11 / 1:27–2:18 on the Jesus-Tradition in
Matthew 5:14–16 263

  5.2.1. Correspondence in the Function of the Jewish
    Apocalyptic Eschatological Duality 263
  5.2.2. Conceptual and Linguistic Agreement in Regard to
    the Function of "Good Works" between Philippians 1:6–11
    and Matthew 5:16b..268
  5.2.3. The Collocation of Verbal and Thematic Parallels 271
 5.3. Conclusion: The Influence of Jesus' Missio-Ethical Teaching
  on Paul's Conception of the Mission of the Eschatological
  Community 282

Chapter 6 285
Summary and Conclusions
 6.1 Summary of Conclusions..286
 6.2 Conclusion and Implications 289

Appendix A 291
Paul's Conception of Universal Evangelism?
 A.1. "Χριστὸς καταγγέλλεται" in Philippians 1:18, a Theological
  Axiom of Unlimited Evangelism? 291
  A.1.1. Does Paul's εἴτε . . . εἴτε Construction Always Come
    as a Universal Statement? 292
  A.1.2. Paul's Use of εἴτε . . . εἴτε Construction with
    Universal Statement 293
  A.1.3. Is "Χριστὸς καταγγέλλεται," a Theological Axiom of
    Unlimited Evangelism?..297
 A.2. Conclusion...299

Appendix B 301
The Origin of the Pauline (or Christian) Apostolate
 B.1. Pre-Pauline Nature of Apostolate...301
 B.2. Ἀπόστολος Χριστοῦ and Jesus' שליחים..306

Appendix C 311
The Scope of Apostles in Paul's Thought
 C.1. The Question of the Scope of Apostles in Paul's Thought........311
  C.1.1. Paul's Apostleship as a Unique Category? 311
  C.1.2. Paul, One among Many Christian Missionary
    Apostles Apart from the Twelve?...................................312
  C.1.3. Paul, One of the Apostles Commissioned by the
    Risen Lord, Who Can Elect Apostles Even Today? 314

    C.2. Paul's Use of the Appellation Apostle..315
        C.2.1. Andronicus and Junia(s) (Rom 16:7) 315
        C.2.2. Silvanus and Timotheus (1 Thess 2:7) 319
        C.2.3. Apollos (1 Cor 3:5–4:13)..323
        C.2.4. Barnabas (1 Cor 9:6, cf. Acts 14:4, 14) 328
        C.2.5. James (Gal 1:19; 1 Cor 15:5–7) 329
    C.3. Conclusion...337

Bibliography.. 339
Reference Index... 375
Author Index... 393

Abstract

This study aims to explore the shape and nature of Paul's conception of mission explaining his understanding of the church's mission in relation to his understanding of his own mission as an apostle, and also to show the influence of the Jesus-tradition on the apostle's conception. The thrust of the thesis is encapsulated in its title – *Heralds and Community: An Enquiry into Paul's Conception of Mission and Its Indebtedness to the Jesus-Tradition*. This reflects a conviction that constructing a plausible conceptuality of mission as understood by Paul and considering influential factors, particularly the Jesus-tradition, are essential for understanding Paul's ecclesial understanding and its relationship to his self-conception.

The findings and positions taken in this study are as follows: (1) Scholars have exaggerated the *functional* continuity between the apostle and the church in terms of evangelistic mission by using exegetically unsustainable arguments; in fact, Paul's letters are silent about proactive verbal evangelism by the church *qua* the church. (2) Paul's silence about congregational evangelism is due to his particular two-pronged (bifurcating) conception of mission, one prong being the event of eschatological heralds, the other prong being that of eschatological community. (3) In this conception of mission Paul maintains that God's inaugurated and ongoing salvation is to be implemented by proactive *proclamation* of the gospel by the heralds on the one hand, and by ontological / ethical *actualization* of the gospel by the community of the people of God on the other hand. (4) Jewish scriptures and traditions are formative for Paul's conception of mission, but Paul shows at various points his deep indebtedness to the Jesus-tradition, particularly to the context and contents of the synoptic mission discourse (for his concept of the heralds) and the Sermon on the Mount (for his concept of the community).

Acknowledgements

Several people have participated in the successful completion of this study. First I would like to give thanks to my teachers. My supervisor at Trinity College in Bristol, Rev Dr David Wenham, has been instrumental in guiding me throughout the entire research process, helping me grasp important ideas, providing many helpful comments, encouraging me to complete the project. Throughout my research, he was not just an academic expert but also a good Christian shepherd. I am also indebted to Rev Dr John Nolland, Rev Dr Pieter Lalleman, Dr Robert Dutch, Dr Stephen Travis and Rev Dr Steve Finamore. As I underwent upgrade examinations and the final viva they provided very useful comments. Rev Dr Christopher Wright, who was my principal at All Nations Christian College, has been a big influence on my biblical and missiological thoughts. He kindly read my dissertation and encouraged me to publish it.

I am also very grateful to those who helped me practically. I received help with English expressions and various practical helps from Dr John Gwyther and Mrs Julia Gwyther. They have always been good friends to my family and me. I also wish to thank the staff of Trinity College, Su Brown, Hazel Trapnell, Merry Carol Schoberg, Diana Dodson Lee and Sam Hands, and Vivian Doub at Langham Partnership International for their kind help regarding books, administration and all the publication process.

Last but not least, I want to express my love and thanks to my family. My wife Kyoungmi, and two children Sungeun and Dongwoo have been so good in supporting me with love and prayers throughout this long lasting project.

Having counted all these people and the blessings through them, I must now confess that it is God who has brought all these to me!

Incheon, March 2016

Bo Young Kang

Abbreviations

1. General

AD	Anno Domini
C	Century
DSS	Dead Sea Scrolls
LXX	Septuagint
LXE	English Translation of the LXX by L. C. L. Brenton
MT	Masoretic Text of the OT
NIV	New International Version
NJV	New King James Version
NT	New Testament
OT	Old Testament
Q	Quelle or "Sayings" source common behind Matthew and Luke
RSV	Revised Version

2. Periodicals, Reference Works and Serials

AB	Anchor Bible
ABD	D. N. Freedman, ed., *Anchor Bible Dictionary* (6 vols; New York: Doubleday, 1992)
ANTC	Abingdon New Testament Commentary
ARSHLL	Acta Reg. Societatis Humaniorum Litterarum Lundens
ATR	*Anglican Theological Review*
AYB	The Anchor Yale Bible

BAGD	W. Bauer, W. F. Arndt, F. W. Gingrich and F. W. Danker, *A Greek-English Lexicon of the New Testament and Other Early Christian Literature,* 2nd ed. (Chicago: University of Chicago Press, 1979)
BDAG	W. Bauer, W. F. Arndt and F. W. Gingrich, *A Greek-English Lexicon of the New Testament and Other Early Christian Literature,* 3rd ed., rev. and ed. F. W. Danker (Chicago: University of Chicago Press, 2000)
BDF	F. Blass and A. Debrunner, *A Greek Grammar of the New Testament and Other Early Christian Literature,* trans. and rev. R. W. Funk (Chicago: University of Chicago Press, 1961)
BJRL	*Bulletin of the John Rylands University Library of Manchester*
BNTC	Black's New Testament Commentary
BTB	*Biblical Theology Bulletin*
CBQ	*Catholic Biblical Quarterly*
CECNT	Critical and Exegetical Commentary on the New Testament
CTJ	*Calvin Theological Journal*
DJG	J. B. Green, S. McKnight and I. H. Marshall, eds., *Dictionary of Jesus and the Gospels* (Downers Grove: InterVarsity Press, 1992)
DNTB	C. A. Evans and S. E. Porter, eds., *Dictionary of New Testament Background* (Downers Grove: InterVarsity Press, 1993)
DPL	G. F. Hawthorne and R. P. Martin, eds., *Dictionary of Paul and his Letters* (Downers Grove: InterVarsity Press, 1993)
EBC	Expositor's Bible Commentary
EKKNT	Evangelisch-katholischer Kommentar zum Neuen Testament
ERT	*Evangelical Review of Theology*
ETL	*Ephemerides theologicae lovanienses*
ExpTim	*Expository Times*
FAT	Forschungen zum Alten Testament
FRLANT	Forschungen zur Religion und Literatur des Alten und Neuen Testaments

HTKNT	Herders theologischer Kommentar zum Neuen Testament
IBS	*Irish Biblical Studies*
ICC	International Critical Commentary
IDB	*Interpreter's Dictionary of the Bible*
JAC	*Jahrbuch für Antike und Christentum*
JBL	*Journal of Biblical Literature*
JETS	*Journal of the Evangelical Theological Society*
JGRChJ	*Journal of Greco-Roman Christianity and Judaism*
JHC	*Journal of Higher Criticism*
JSJSup	Journal for the Study of Judaism in the Persian, Hellenistic and Roman Period Supplement Series
JSNT	*Journal for the Study of the New Testament*
JSOT	*Journal for the Study of the Old Testament*
JSNTSup	Journal for the Study of the New Testament Supplement Series
JSP	*Journal for the Study of the Pseudepigrapha and Related Literature*
JTS	*Journal of Theological Studies*
JTSA	*Journal of Theology for Southern Africa*
KD	*Kerygma und Dogma*
KEKNT	Kritisch-exegetischer Kommentar über das Neue Testament
LNTS	Library of New Testament Studies (formerly JSNTSup)
MM	J. H. Moulton and G. Milligan, *The Vocabulary of the Greek Testament: Illustrated from the Papyri and Other Non-literary Sources* (London: Hodder and Stoughton, 1930)
NCBC	New Century Bible Commentary
Neot	*Neotestamentica*
NICNT	New International Commentary of the New Testament
NIGTC	New International Greek Testament Commentary
NovT	*Novum Testamentum*
NovTSup	Novum Testamentum Supplement Series
NTL	New Testament Library
NTS	*New Testament Studies*
RAC	T. Klauser et al (ed.), *Reallexikon für Antike und Christentum* (Leipzig: Hiersemann Verlag, 1941–)

RB	*Revue biblique*
RevExp	*Review and Expositor*
RHPR	*Revue d'histoire et de Philosophie Religieuses*
SBL	Society of Biblical Literature
SBLDS	Society of Biblical Literature Dissertation Series
SBLMS	Society of Biblical Literature Monograph Series
SBS	Stuttgarter Bibelstudien
SEÅ	*Svensk exegetisk årsbok*
SHBC	Smyth & Helwys Bible Commentary
SNTS	Society for New Testament Studies
SNTSMS	Society for New Testament Studies Monograph Series
StBT	*Studia Biblica et Theologica*
StTh	*Studia theologica*
VTSup	Vetus Testamentum Supplements
TB	*Tyndale Bulletin*
TDNT	G. Kittel and G. Friedrich, eds., *Theological Dictionary of the New Testament* (10 vols.; Grand Rapids: Eerdmans, 1964–1976)
THKNT	Theologischer Handkommentar zum Neuen Testament
THNTC	Two Horizons New Testament Commentary
TNTC	Tyndale New Testament Commentary
USQR	*Union Seminary Quarterly Review*
WBC	Word Bible Commentary
WMANT	Wissenschaftliche Monographien zum Alten und Neuen Testament
WTJ	*Westminster Theological Journal*
WUNT	Wissenschaftliche Untersuchungen zum Neuen Testament
ZNW	*Zeitschrift für die Neutestamentliche Wissenschaft*
ZTK	*Zeitschrift für Theologie und Kirche*

3. OT Apocrypha, Pseudepigrapha, Dead Sea Scrolls and Rabbinic Works

1, 2 Esdr	1 and 2 Esdras
1, 2 Macc	1 and 2 Maccabees

Abbreviations

Bar	Baruch
Jdt	Judith
Pr Azar	Prayer of Azariah
Sir	Sirach
Tob	Tobit
Wis	Wisdom
1, 2 Enoch	*Ethiopic, Slavonic Enoch*
2 Bar.	*Syriac Apocalypse of Baruch*
4 Ezra	*The Fourth Book of Ezra*
3, 4 Macc	*3 and 4 Maccabees*
Jub.	*Jubilees*
Pss. Sol.	*Psalms of Solomon*
Sib. Or.	*Sibylline Oracles*
T. Asher	*Testament of Asher*
T. Ben.	*Testament of Benjamin*
T. Gad	*Testament of Gad*
T. Jos.	*Testament of Joseph*
T. Judah	*Testament of Judah*
T. Mos.	*Testament of Moses*
T. Zeb.	*Testament of Zebulon*
CD	Damascus Document
1QH^a	Thanksgiving Hymns^a
1QM	War Scroll
1QpNah	Pesher / Commentary on Nahum
1QS	Community Rule
1QSa	Rule of the Congregation
4Q181	Ages of Creation
4Q521	Messianic Apocalypse
11Q13	Melchizedek Document
b. Pesah.	*Pesahim in the Babylonian Talmud*
b. Shab.	*Shabbat in the Babylonian Talmud*
m. 'Abot	*'Abot in the Mishnah*
m. Rosh Hash.	*Rosh Hashanah in the Mishnah*
Tg. Isa.	*Targum of Isaiah*

4. Classical, Hellenistic and Early Christian Writers and Sources

Did.	*Didache*
1, 2 Clem.	*1 and 2 Clement*
Arist.	Aristotle
Op. Omnia	*Opera Omnia*
Pol.	*Politica*
Diod. Sic.	Diodorus Siculus
Diog. Laert.	Diogenes Laertius
Josephus	Flavius Josephus
War	*The Jewish War*
Ant.	*Jewish Antiquities*
Life	*The Life of Flavius Josephus*
Philo	Philo of Alexandria
Mos.	*The Life of Moses*
Laws	*The Special Laws*
Man	*Every Good Man*
Plato	Plato
Prot.	*Protagoras*
Thuc.	Thucydides
Hist.	*The History of the Peloponnesian War*
Xen.	Xenophon
Cyr.	*Cyropaedia*
Aug.	Augustine
Con.	*Confessions*
Ign.	Ignatius
Magn.	*Letter to the Magnesians*
Trall.	*Letter to the Trallians*
John Chrys.	John Chrysostom
Hom. Phil	*Homilies on Philippians*
Justin	Justin Martyr
Dial.	*Dialogue with Trypho*
1 Apol.	*1 Apology*

CHAPTER 1

General Introduction

1.1. Paul's Conception of Mission and the Issue of His Missio-Ecclesial Understanding

1.1.1. Paul's Mission and Paul's Conception of Mission

It is relatively recently that modern NT scholarship has begun to pay attention to Paul's mission with a proper recognition of its context and relation to his theology. Until the mid-twentieth century,[1] though there was interest in Paul as a missionary, Paul's mission tended to be dealt with in terms of him as a model of Christian piety[2] or part of a biographical description of

---

1. Scholars often point to Johannes Munck's publication of *Paulus und die Heilsgeschichte* (Copenhagen: Ejnar Munksgaard, 1954) - *Paul and the Salvation of Mankind* (ET; London: SCM Press, 1959) - as a major contribution to the shift. Cf. K. Stendahl, "Preface" to the English Translation of Munck's *Christ and Israel: An Interpretation of Romans 9-11* (Philadelphia: Fortress, 1967), vii; Stendahl, "The Apostle Paul and the Introspective Conscience of the West," in *Paul Among Jews and Gentiles* (Philadelphia: Fortress, 1976), 78–96; E. P. Sanders, *Paul and Palestinian Judaism* (London: SCM, 1977), 442; M. Hengel, *Between Jesus and Paul: Studies in Earliest History of Christianity* (London: SCM, 1983), 49–53; D. Senior and C. Stuhlmueller, *The Biblical Foundations for Mission* (London: SCM, 1983), 161–165; T. L. Donaldson, *Paul and the Gentiles: Remapping the Apostle's Convictional World* (Minneapolis: Fortress, 1997), 20; W. Campbell, *Paul and the Creation of Christian Identity* (London: T. & T. Clark, 2008), 17–23. Cf. D. J. Bosch, *Transforming Mission: Paradigm Shifts in Theology of Mission* (New York: Orbis, 1991), 124, who suggests P. Wernle, *Paulus als Heidenmissionar* (Freiburg: B. Mohr, 1899) as the first serious scholarly attempt to look at Paul from the perspective of his missionary calling and ministry. However, R. L. Plummer, *Paul's Understanding of the Church's Mission: Did the Apostle Paul Expect the Early Christian Communities to Evangelize?* (Carlisle: Paternoster, 2006), 13, suggests, as a counterbalance to Bosch's view, C. von Weizsäcker, *The Apostolic Age of the Christian Church* (London: Williams and Norgate, 1894–1895).

2. E.g. J. Warneck, *The Living Forces of the Gospel: Experiences of a Missionary in Animistic Heathendom* (Edinburgh: Oliphant, Anderson & Ferrier, 1909).

those who were vital to the expansion of Christianity[3] or in terms of his evangelistic methods.[4] In short, Paul's mission was generally approached either as practice to be emulated / narrated / compared or as a mere backdrop against which Paul's other important theologies were construed.[5]

However, what N. A. Dahl regarded as "something wrong," namely this separation between Paul's orthopraxy and orthodoxy and understanding Paul's mission only in terms of the former,[6] seems to have been gradually remedied in Pauline scholarship over the past several decades. Paul's mission is today approached not merely as an isolated external / practical aspect of the apostle's life, but as of utmost significance for explaining the basis of the apostle's entire life and theology. Balancing the two aspects seems to have come about because of the increase of scholarly interest in Paul's conception of mission rather than Paul's practice of mission.[7]

---

3. E.g. C. von Weizsäcker, *The Apostolic Age of the Christian Church* (London: Williams and Norgate, 1894–1895); A. von Harnack, *The Mission and Expansion of Christianity in the First Three Centuries* (Gloucester: Peter Smith, 1972, [1902]).

4. E.g. R. Allen, *Missionary Methods: St. Paul's or Ours?* (London: World Dominion Press, 1962 [1912]). Additional bibliography in this regard can be found in R. Riesner, *Paul's Early Period: Chronology, Mission Statement, Theology* (Grand Rapids: Eerdmans, 1998), 254–255, n.104.

5. Cf. W. P. Bowers, "Mission," *DPL*, 608, who finds such a "deficiency" still present in contemporary Pauline scholarship. See also E. J. Schnabel, *Early Christian Mission*, vol. 1 (Downers Grove: IVP; Leicester: Apollos, 2004), 6.

6. N. A. Dahl, *Studies in Paul: Theology for the Early Christian Mission* (Minneapolis: Augsburg, 1977), 70.

7. E.g. J. Knox, "Romans 15:14–33 and Paul's Conception of His Apostolic Mission," *JBL* 83 (1964): 1–11; F. Hahn, "Paul's Conception of Mission," in *Mission in the New Testament* (London: SCM, 1965), 95–110; W. P. Bowers, "Studies in Paul's Understanding of His Mission," (PhD dissertation, Cambridge University, 1976); G. Bornkamm, "The Missionary Stance of Paul in 1 Corinthians 9 and in Acts," in *Studies in Luke-Acts*, eds. E. Keck and J. L. Martyn (Philadelphia: Fortress, 1980), 194–207; D. Zeller, "Theologie der Mission bei Paulus," in *Mission Im Neuen Testament*, ed. K. Kertelge, Quaestiones Disputatae 93 (Freiburg: Herder, 1982), 164–189; D. O. Brotherton, "An Examination of Selected Pauline Passages concerning the Vocational Missionary: An Interpretive Basis for Critiquing Contemporary Missiological Thoughts," (PhD dissertation, Southwestern Baptist Theological Seminary, 1986); C. K. Barrett, "Paulus als Missionar und Theologe," *ZTK* 86 (1989): 18–32; W. S. Campbell, "Paul's Missionary Practice and Policy in Romans," *IBS* 12 (1990): 2–25; A. J. Dewey, "ΕΙΣ ΤΗΝ ΣΠΑΝΙΑΝ: The Future and Paul," in *Religious Propaganda and Missionary Competition in the New Testament World: Essays Honoring Dieter Georgi*, SNT, eds. L. Bormann, K. D. Tredici and A. Standhartinger (Leiden: Brill, 1994), 321–349; O. Hofius, "Paulus-Missionar und Theologe," in *Evangelium, Schriftauslegung, Kirche: Festschift Für Peter Stuhlmacher Zum 65. Geburtstag*, eds. J. Ådna, S. J. Hafemann and O. Hofius (Göttingen: Vandenhoeck & Ruprecht, 1997), 224–237; A. J. Hultgren, *Paul's Gospel and Mission: The Outlook from his Letter to the Romans* (Philadelphia: Fortress

1.1.2. Renewed Interest: The Issue of Paul's Missio-Ecclesial Understanding

Such recognition of the apostle's mission as the "*Sitz im Leben* of Pauline theology,"[8] and the significance of his conception of mission, seems to have facilitated renewed interest in Paul's mission in recent Pauline scholarship. One notable issue that has attracted scholar response is the question of the relation of Paul's conception of his own mission to his ecclesial understanding: what was Paul's understanding of the role of the church, if mission was so fundamental to the apostle? In what way did Paul relate the church to his own mission? Did he think that the mission was a responsibility of the church *as a whole* or was it the responsibility of selected specialists like himself? Did he conceive of or develop any theological framework in which his mission and the work of the church were interrelated?

However, the relationship of the apostle's mission and the work of the church is not entirely a new issue. In Robert Plummer's estimation, at least until the last century there was a generally agreed assumption by many that Paul expected the churches to engage in active missionary work.[9] He also cites a few pre-1950s scholars who held a contrary conclusion to the general assumption.[10] However, it seems that the issue in this period did not form a scholarly debate:[11] in most cases, Paul's expectations for the church in relation to his mission were assumed as a natural corollary either

---

Press, 1985); J. B. Polhill, "Paul: Theology Born of Mission," *RevExp* 78 (1981): 233–247; D. J. Bosch, "Mission in Paul: Invitation to Join the Eschatological Community," in *Transforming Mission: Paradigm Shifts in Theology of Mission* (Maryknoll: Orbis, 1991), 123–178; K. Stendahl, *Final Account: Paul's Letter to the Romans* (Minneapolis: Fortress, 1995); M. Barram, *Mission and Moral Reflection in Paul* (New York: Peter Lang, 2006); P. Barnett, *Paul, Missionary of Jesus* (Grand Rapids: William B. Eerdmans, 2008); T. J. Burke and B. S. Rosner, *Paul as Missionary: Identity, Activity, Theology and Practice* (London: T. & T. Clark, 2011).

8. E.g, Hengel, *Between Jesus and Paul*, 49–53.

9. R. L. Plummer, "A Theological Basis for the Church's Mission in Paul," *WTJ* 64 (2002): 253; Plummer, *Paul's Understanding*, 2–3.

10. Ibid., 16–22.

11. Cf. J. P. Dickson, *Mission-Commitment in Ancient Judaism and in the Pauline Communities: The Shape, Extent and Background of Early Christian Mission* (Tübingen: Mohr Siebeck, 2003), 2; Plummer, *Paul's Understanding*, 7, n.13, cites Gustav Warneck's criticism (*Evangelisch Missionslehre: Ein missionstheoretischer Versuch* [Gotha: Friedrich Andreas Perthes, 1892–1903]) on liberal scholars such as Ernst Troeltsch who limits the church's mission to moral and humanitarian concerns. However, the scholarly interaction was on Christian mission theology in general but not particularly on "Paul's understanding

of Paul's preoccupation with an expectation of the imminent *parousia* of Christ that prevented him from envisioning an ongoing mission of the church[12] or of an introspective understanding of the Christian community not as a mission agent but a place for moral regeneration.[13]

The problematic nature of the issue of congregational evangelism in Paul's thought began to be recognized as scholars noted the inadequacy in the use of materials other than Paul's own accounts to construe any of his conceptions and as they recognized the scanty evidence for the view that Paul expected the church to evangelize.[14] But it seems to have been W. Paul Bowers whose argument brought the issue to a real scholarly debate at least for the English-speaking Pauline scholarship. In his 1976 Cambridge PhD dissertation (which was never published as a monograph), Bowers discussed Paul's "conception" of his own mission.[15] How his study diverged from most of the other studies on Paul's mission was in its focus not on "what Paul did," but on "what he *thought* he was doing" and "the sort of

---

of the church's mission" (cf. E. Troeltsch, *The Absoluteness of Christianity and the History of Religions* [Westminster: John Knox Press, 2005]).

12. E.g. E. Renan, *Saint Paul* (Paris: Calmann Lévy, 1883), 562; W. Wrede, *Paul* (London: P. Green, 1907), 47–48; See also recently Hultgren, *Paul's Gospel and Mission*, 134–144.

13. E.g. P. Wernle, *The Beginnings of Christianity*, vol. 1 (London: Williams & Norgate, 1903), 191.

14. We may cite some continental scholars who reflect these considerations in their treatment of the issue: e.g. H. Greeven, "Die missionierende Gemeinde nach den Apostolischen Briefen," in *Sammlung und Sendung – Vom Auftrag der Kirche in der Welt: Eine Festgabe für D. Heinrich Rendtorff zu seinem 70. Geburtstag am 9. April 1958*, eds. J. Heubach and H.-H. Ulrich (Berlin: Christlicher Z-Verlag, 1958), 66; P. Lippert, *Leben als Zeugnis: Die werbende Kraft Christlicher Lebensführung nach dem Kirchenverständnis neutestamentlicher Briefe* (Stuttgart: Katholisches Bibelwerk, 1968), 127–128, 171, 175–176; H.-W. Gensichen, *Glaube für die Welt: Theologische Aspekte der Mission* (Gütersloh: Gerd Mohn, 1971), 165–186. W.-H. Ollrog, *Paulus und seine Mitarbeiter: Untersuchungen zu Theorie und Praxis der paulinischen Mission* (Neukirchen-Vluyn: Neukirchener Verlag, 1979), 130–132. With the awareness of the problem but in the defense of traditional approach, e.g. D. van Swigchem, *Het missionair karakter van de Christelijke gemeente volgens de brieven van Paulus en Petrus* (Kampen: Kok, 1955), 15–23, 40–77, 109–240; H. Ridderbos, *Paul: An Outline of His Theology* (Grand Rapids: Eerdmans, 1975), 432–435, who endorses Swigchem's view. See also J. P. Ware, *The Mission of the Church in Paul's Letter to the Philippians in the Context of Ancient Judaism* (Leiden: Brill, 2005), 4; Plummer, *Paul's Understanding*, 22–23.

15. W. P. Bowers, "Studies in Paul's Understanding of His Mission," (PhD dissertation, Cambridge University, 1976).

activity which Paul took to be implied by his vocation."[16] This approach certainly reflects the necessity of correcting earlier approaches to Paul's mission merely in terms of his practice, since his conception of mission generally provides an explanation or rationale for practice of mission.

However, it was neither his divergent approach to the issue of Paul's mission nor his general thesis (i.e. the "scope" of Paul's conception of his mission that includes his ongoing pastoral ministry for established community as well as initial evangelism) that caused scholarly interest in him. While it seems that his distinction between the concept of mission and the practice of mission has not been sufficiently recognized,[17] it was Bowers' conclusion in the second study in the dissertation[18] and his repeated assertion in one of his subsequent articles[19] where he deals with Paul's ecclesiological understanding in relation to his conception of mission that evoked most response from other scholars.[20] This debate, now well recognized by scholars of Pauline mission, is the subject that the current study seeks to explore.

With regard to (the role of) the church in Paul's concept of mission, Bowers observes that in most cases missionary activity by the church "lies somewhere in the conceptual background" but is not clearly in view in the Pauline texts, and concludes that "a concept of the church at mission"

---

16. Ibid., 2–6, 81–82 (original emphasis).

17. A notable appreciation of the point is found in J. P. Dickson, *Mission-Commitment*, 6, who, even if the focus is rather on the relation of Paul's conception (Pauline expectations) to the church's mission and the actual practice of the church, is rightly aware of the difficulty to discern whether such expectations corresponded to any real practice among members of the community. See also Barram, *Mission and Moral Reflection*, who devotes his entire study to confirming and developing Bowers' focus on Paul's conception of his own vocation. He rightly notes that the distinction between Paul's thought and Paul's mission practice raises a crucial methodological issue (12).

18. Bowers, "Studies," 18–80.

19. Bowers, "Church and Mission in Paul," *JSNT* 44 (1991): 89–111.

20. E.g. P. T. O'Brien, *Gospel and Mission in the Writings of Paul; An Exegetical and Theological Analysis* (Carlisle: Paternoster, 1995), 53–77, 83–138; I. H. Marshall, "Who Were the Evangelists?" in *The Mission of the Early Church to Jews and Gentiles*, WUNT, eds. J. Ådna and H. Kvalbein (Tübingen: Mohr Siebeck, 2000), 253–264; J. P. Ware, *The Mission of the Church*, 2–8, 270–271; Schnabel, *Early Christian Mission*, 2. 1454; Dickson, *Mission-Commitment*, 1–2; R. L. Plummer, "A Theological Basis for the Church's Mission in Paul," *WTJ* 64 (2002): 265; Plummer, *Paul's Understanding*, 24–25; D. Chae, "Paul," in *Dictionary of Mission Theology: Evangelical Foundation*, ed. J. Corrie (Nottingham: IVP, 2007), 277–278; M. J. Keown, *Congregational Evangelism in Philippians: The Centrality of an Appeal for Gospel Proclamation to the Fabric of Philippians* (Carlisle: Paternoster, 2008), 1.

in Paul's thought "failed to take any distinct shape."[21] In his 1991 *JSNT* article Bowers repeats the question, "Were those churches meant in turn to focus themselves upon ongoing mission?"[22] After a discussion on the Pauline texts that are often deemed to suggest "churches as instruments of active mission," he draws an exegetical conclusion:

> There is certainly no thought of the churches undertaking any mission themselves . . . [the churches] do not themselves become agents of mission but rather render support to a particular mission, a support which emerges in the circumstances not as a general function of the life of these churches *qua* churches, but as a function of their relationship with Paul, the one who under God has fathered their communities and therefore merits continuing fellowship.[23]

In addition to this exegetical conclusion, he suggests that while Paul had "multiple aspects of his mission" – initiatory evangelism, the founding of churches, and the nurture of those churches towards maturity in Christ[24] – he did not expect the churches that he founded to duplicate "as church" the first and the second aspect of his mission, but independently to duplicate Paul's third aspect of mission, the nurture of the churches as the churches do "self-nurturing."[25] For Bowers this is not to suggest that the apostle opposed churches becoming involved in active independent missionary outreach, nor to indicate that Paul's thought was really inimical to the idea, since there is no such indication.[26] Rather, according to Bowers, while there is much that is conducive to "the idea of the church itself as mission," in Paul's thought the concept of God at work through select

---

21. Bowers, "Studies," 120. Cf. Ollrog, *Mitarbeiter*, 130–131, whose estimation of Pauline references to the church's relation to missionary preaching is similar to that of Bowers: "Soooft Paulus auf die missionarische Verkündigung zu sprechen kommt, ist niemals eine Gemeinde als Ganze Subjekt des Handelns."

22. Bowers, "Church and Mission," 89.

23. Ibid., 102.

24. Ibid., 105. For a detailed argument for this point, see Paul Bowers, "Fulfilling the Gospel: The Scope of the Pauline Mission," *JETS* 30 (1987): 185–198.

25. Bowers, "Church and Mission," 105: "In Paul's understanding, his own missionary role and the role of his churches overlapped one another rather than paralleled one another."

26. Ibid., 109–110.

individuals may well "simply have eclipsed the influence of a concept of God at work through the select community" largely owing to "his highly personal understanding of mission."[27] So, we may summarize Bowers' view as *Paul's individualistic and non-ecclesial understanding of mission*.[28]

1.2. Current Contour of the Debate

Bowers' thesis as such prompted a response from an Australian scholar Peter T. O'Brien,[29] and as a result, the issue received subsequent scholarly responses and became an ongoing dispute among recent NT scholars.[30] A few recent studies have provided useful surveys of various significant works that deal with the issue.[31] Such surveys suggest a *dichotomy* between scholars who argue for Paul's conception of his mission as envisioning the church's active participation in evangelistic mission and those who argue for a conception of mission that restricts the church's participation only to some non/indirect-evangelistic support for Paul's mission (e.g. finance, prayer, ethical apologetic).

While we may appreciate the broad contour of the current debate, however, it seems that the dichotomy is too simplistic to show the inherent complexity of the issue and tends to assume an unnecessary sharp disjunction between the two positions. Thus, we now briefly re-examine the discussions not by focusing on the scholars' conclusions but by observing

---

27. Ibid., 110. See also Bowers, "Fulfilling the Gospel," 198, "Paul's missionary vocation finds its fulfillment in the presence of firmly established churches."

28. Note that Bowers also observes in his dissertation the apostle's geographical (18–80) and eschatological orientation (122–170) which is closely related to the apostle's "peculiar sense of vocation" (13).

29. Dickson, *Mission-Commitment*, 2, notes that it was at the 1992 Annual Moore College Lectures under the topic of "Consumed by Passion: Paul and the Dynamic of the Gospel": the lecture material was published under the same title a year later (Homebush West: Anzea) and republished under the title of *Gospel and Mission in the Writings of Paul: An Exegetical and Theological Analysis* (Carlisle: Paternoster, 1995).

30. Cf. M. F. Bird, *Crossing Over Sea and Land: Jewish Missionary Activity in the Second Temple Period* (Peabody: Hendrickson, 2010), 3, who recognizes the issue as an extended historical question of early Christian mission; E. L. Ochsenmeier, who kindly allowed me to read the proposal of his prospective monograph on early church's evangelism is also concerned about the issue.

31. E.g. Plummer, *Paul's Understanding*, 1–42; Keown, *Congregational Evangelism*, 3–28. See also Ware, *The Mission of the Church*, 1–8.

their diverse approaches and interests that may provide considerations for a fresh way of addressing the issue.

1.2.1. The Issue of Mission-Continuity between Paul and the Church

1.2.1.1. P. T. O'Brien

Apart from Bowers, Peter T. O'Brien is the most frequently quoted scholar in the ongoing debate since his thesis was in general opposite to Bowers' conclusion. His polemic is well summarized in his contention that Bowers' conclusion is "an argument from silence" and that Paul's silence about the matter in his letters cannot prove absence from Paul's thought of any expectation for Christians' involvement in evangelism.[32]

For O'Brien this shortcoming is to be remedied in two ways: (1) by recognizing some passages where Paul is seen to expect not only the church's supportive role for the apostle's missionary work, but also the active evangelistic role (i.e. 1 Cor 10:31–11:1; Phil 1:5, 14–18, 27, 30; 2:16; Eph 6:10–20);[33] (2) by recognizing Paul's theological ground (i.e. Paul's theology of the gospel as the locus of God's salvation-historical intervention) that leads him to a natural assumption of universalistic proclamation of the gospel by believers in the gospel (Rom 1:1–17).[34]

For O'Brien, while the problematic nature of the dearth of Pauline reference to congregational evangelism is acknowledged,[35] such a problem is explainable given Paul's theology of the gospel that is by nature the dynamic marching of God's salvation through God / Christ himself in believers.[36] According to this view, Paul's theology of the gospel as such leads the apostle to speak of the spread the gospel not from the perspective of human agency but from a "divine perspective" (e.g. Col 1:5–6; 1 Thess 1:5; 2 Thess 2:13; 3:1–2).[37] Despite the dearth of Paul's references to congre-

---

32. O'Brien, *Consumed*, 130.
33. Ibid., 105–127. This view is followed by Schnabel, *Early Christian Mission*, 2. 1459–1465; Marshall, "Who Were the Evangelists?" 258–262.
34. O'Brien, *Consumed*, 126–127; O'Brien, *Gospel and Mission*, 53–77. See also Schnabel, *Early Christian Mission*, 2. 1457; Marshall, "Who Were the Evangelists?" 255.
35. O'Brien, *Consumed*, 105; O'Brien, *Gospel and Mission*, 137.
36. Ibid., 53–77, 96–97, 113–114, 127–128.
37. Ibid., 138.

gational evangelism, for O'Brien, Bowers' conclusion, which tends to rule out the significance of ordinary Christians' evangelistic role from Paul's missionary horizon, is theologically and exegetically untenable.

1.2.1.2. R. L. Plummer

O'Brien's thesis is repeated and substantially expanded by a North American Baptist scholar Robert L. Plummer.[38] Basing his argument first on O'Brien's suggestion of Paul's theology of the gospel as the key to understanding Paul's expectation for the church's centrifugal evangelistic mission, Plummer seeks to provide a more detailed rationale for viewing Paul's understanding of the gospel not merely as a message of definable content but also as "a powerful, effective, and dynamic force" that accomplishes God's will (i.e. salvation of the predestined).[39] Then, he goes on to argue that such a dynamic nature of the gospel was the theological ground not only for Paul's understanding of his own apostolic mission, but also for his understanding of the church's mission that is fundamentally in continuity with the apostle's mission.[40]

The approaches and conclusions of the two scholars are very similar to each other, particularly in that they take not only exegetical considerations but also Paul's theological ground for their arguments about Paul's expectation for the church's evangelistic mission. This is certainly an alternative to Bowers' approach that considers Paul's geographical and eschatological aspects (as well as ecclesiological) which he thinks is the essential theological ground for Paul's individualistic conception of mission.[41]

However, what is at stake here is whether Paul's theology of the gospel, as O'Brien and Plummer suggest, did bring about in Paul's thought any notion of universal evangelism. While Paul's understanding of the gospel as a powerful force for one's salvation and God's initiative in such a *nomen actionis* is to be by all means granted as they suggest, it is less clear whether

---

38. See also J. P. Ware, "The Thessalonians as Missionary Congregation: 1 Thessalonians 1.5–8," *ZNW* 83 (1992): 128–129, who endorses O'Brien's view.

39. R. L. Plummer, "A Theological Basis," 255–267; Plummer, *Paul's Understanding*, 50–56.

40. Ibid., 56–64.

41. See n.28. It is noteworthy that Bowers' approach resembles the earlier proposal by Wrede (see n.12). Cf. Ware, *The Mission of the Church*, 6.

Paul's theology of the gospel as the dynamic marching of God's salvation amounts to an expectation for universal evangelism: is the self-diffusive nature of the gospel logically indicative of one's or the church's active engagement with the gospel message?[42] If Paul understood the advancement of the gospel in terms of God's own act, what about God's sovereignty to choose his agent for the implementation for his salvation (e.g. Gal 1:11–17; Rom 10:15–17; 1 Cor 12:28ff, cf. Eph 4:11ff)?

We need to note that to establish such a connection between Paul's theology of the gospel and his expectation for universal evangelism, O'Brien and Plummer also offer the questionable exegetical consideration of Paul envisioning the church's active evangelism (e.g. based on 1 Cor 10:31–11:1; 1 Thess 1:5).[43] Such a mingling of the two considerations (i.e. an exegetical consideration and a theological consideration) makes both vulnerable instead of reinforcing each other.

Nevertheless, it seems that O'Brien and Plummer rightly question the legitimacy of a sharp distinction between proactive / organized / direct propaganda and passive / *ad hoc* / indirect witness to the faith by the church or between propaganda "*qua* churches" and propaganda by many undefined Christian individuals to postulate an absence of expectation for the church's mission work or mission-discontinuity between Paul and the church.[44] Despite the paucity of Paul's overt exhortation to evangelize, if he positively envisioned some missional / evangelistic impact from his converts' Christian life at least, we need to carefully weigh the legitimacy of Bowers' statement that "a concept of the church at mission apparently failed to take any definite shape in Paul's thinking insofar as it is available to us."[45]

---

42. At least Luke's accounts of the early church in Jerusalem in the first eight chapters in Acts do not seem to agree with such an automatism: while the members celebrated life in the Christian community (2:44–47, 6:1ff) proactive proclamation of the gospel was done by only the apostles and perhaps the seven deacons (2:14ff, 3:12ff, 6:8ff, 8:5ff).

43. For a detailed discussion on those passages see below chapter 2.

44. O'Brien, *Consumed*, 106, 130; O'Brien, *Gospel and Mission*, 137; R. L. Plummer, "Imitation of Paul and the Church's Missionary Role in 1 Corinthians," *JETS* 44, no. 2 (2001): 234–235; Plummer, *Paul's Understanding*, 96–105. See also Schnabel, *Early Christian Mission*, 2. 1459, 1465–1472. See also Ollrog, *Mitarbeiter*, 141, who observes a somewhat deliberate missionary effect by the church "*als Ganze*."

45. Bowers, "Church," 110.

1.2.2. The Question of Mission Continuity and Discontinuity between Paul and the Church: W.-H. Ollrog's Study of the Co-Workers

Ollrog's monograph does not seem to know about Bowers and only encompasses a discussion about the historical information ("die historischen Angaben")[46] and the significance ("die Bedeutung")[47] of Paul's co-workers ("Mitarbeiter") in his mission and theology. Nevertheless, it is worth mentioning here since his observations about Pauline texts concerning the church's relation to Paul's missionary proclamation and the role of those co-workers concerning the apostle and the church have received substantial attention by those engaged in the current debate.

Ollrog observes various "Missionsverkündigung" in Paul's letters and suggests that the "Handelndes Subjekt" of the terms is never "eine Gemeinde als Ganze," but always the apostle himself or other individuals – "Mitarbeiter" (e.g. 1 Thess 2:1–12; 3:2; 1 Cor 3:5ff; 4:17; 9:5ff; 16:15f; Phil 1:14–18; 2:22, 25, 30; 4:3; Phlm 13; 2 Cor 1:19; Rom 16:3, 5, 9, 12f).[48] In Ollrog's exegetical point of view, the church appears always "als Objekt, als Empfänger der Botschaft" (e.g. Phil 1:7; 1 Thess 1:8) and is never encouraged or obliged to act as missionaries.[49] For Ollrog this consideration provides a rationale for the lack of request for church's missionary preaching and his consistent description of his communities as a whole as object and recipient of the missionary preaching.[50]

Ollrog's emphasis on the obviousness of the church's passive stance towards missionary preaching in Paul's conception given the frequency of the proclamation language in Paul's letters[51] seems to be close to that of Bowers in that he strongly denies any Pauline idea of the church *qua* church being

---

46. Ollrog, *Mitarbeiter*, 7–108.
47. Ibid., 109–235.
48. Ibid., 130–131. Ollrog's observation includes εὐαγγελίζεσθαι, κηρύσσειν, καταγγέλλειν, λαλεῖν τὸν λόγον, κοπιᾶν, συνεργεῖν, διακονεῖν, and their substantive forms (Ibid., n.80).
49. Ollrog, *Mitarbeiter*, 131.
50. Ibid., 132. This view is substantially shared by Dickson, *Mission-Commitment*, 133–152.
51. Ibid., 131: "Gemessen an der Häufigkeit des Vorkommens der Verkündigungstermini, ist dieser Befund eindeutig."

obliged to carry out missionary preaching. In this regard, there is some justification in seeing Ollrog's thesis as an endorsement of Bowers' view[52] or to include both in the same category of scholars (e.g. those who maintain the "Apostle-Church Mission Discontinuity").[53]

However, it is to be noted that what Ollrog actually offers can be explained neither by a view of Paul as maintaining a non-ecclesial understanding of mission nor by a model of mission-discontinuity between the apostle and the church. Rather, we need to consider carefully the implication of those Mitarbeiter in Paul's mission. Contrary to Bowers, Ollrog thinks that while Paul certainly maintained a functional distinction between the co-workers and the rest of the church,[54] the responsibility of the task of mission was for the whole church since what was done by the co-workers was "Die Mitarbeitermission als Gemeindemission"[55] and the co-workers were delegates / representative of the church "als missionierende Gemeinden."[56] Even if Ollrog does not find any evidence of Paul's expectation for evangelism by the rest of the members of the communities apart from the co-workers, this certainly does not mean a "mission (or evangelism) free" church in the apostle's mind. Rather, according to Ollrog, Paul's missionary task was a shared obligation with the communities and they were "partners" in his missionary work "durch ihre Mitarbeiter."[57]

---

52. Cf. Dickson, *Mission-Commitment*, 2.

53. Plummer, *Paul's Understanding*, 24–25.

54. Ollrog, *Mitarbeiter*, 119–125.

55. Ibid., 119.

56. Ibid., 129: "Die Mitarbeitermission wurde dadurch verstandlich, daß sie als Gemeindemission begriffen werden konnte. In den Mitarbeitern übernahmen die Gemeinden Verantwortung für das paulinische Missionswerk. Auf diese Weise bekundeten sie ihr Selbstverständnis als missionierende Gemeinden. Das Ergebnis der Frage nach der Rolle der Mitarbeiter ist also, daß wir die Rolle der Gemeinden des Paulus anders einzuschätzen haben."

57. Ibid., 132: "Gleichwohl hatten die Gemeinden als Gemeinden Christi Anteil an der Aufrichtung der Weltherrschaft Christi und besaßen deshalb Mitverantwortung für die Mission. Paulus verband beide Anlegen durch den Gedanken der Delegierung und Repräsentation der Mitarbeiter für ihre Gemeinden. Zu Partnern in seinem Missionswerk wurden die Gemeinden durch ihre Mitarbeiter. Zu Partnern in seinem Missionswerk wurden die Gemeinden durch ihre Mitarbeiter. In ihnen beteiligten sie aktiv an seinem Missionswerk; nicht direkt zwar, sondern durch Delegation vermittelt, gleichwohl aber konkret und verbindlich. Somit zeigen die paulischen Gemeinden ein erstaunlich reflektiertes Selbstverständnis, indem sie als Teile um ihre Verantwortung für das Ganze wissen und ihr in der Teilhabe am paulinischen Missionswerk Ausdruck geben." In this

Ollrog's view certainly represents an aspect of the complexity of the current issue that cannot be appreciated through an either / or view (i.e. continuity *or* discontinuity) about the mission-relation of the apostle to the church.[58] And it seems to generate, for a more plausible explanation for Paul's conception of mission, a methodological need for a careful distinction between *functionality* and *intentionality* in the matter of works for salvation (or the gospel), and perhaps an epistemological accountability to the tension between *continuity* and *discontinuity* in the matter of the relation of the apostle to the church.

1.2.3. The Question of the Background for Paul's Conception of Mission

1.2.3.1. J. P. Ware

Despite their contradictory conclusions regarding the relation between the apostle's conception of his own mission and the apostle's expectation of the church, James P. Ware and John P. Dickson deserve our attention under the same heading here, since their approaches to the issue are notably similar to each other and raise an important related issue, the question of the relation of Paul's conception of mission to Second Temple Judaism.

Like O'Brien and others, Ware remains unconvinced by the suggestion that Paul's expectation for the church's involvement in mission was limited to non-verbal and indirect participation.[59] While Ware acknowledges, "Clearly Paul's churches as a whole did not participate in the sort of planned missionary activity. . .," he is undecided about whether in Paul's thought the "spread of the gospel through active verbal mission" was

---

regard, Dickson's estimation of Ollrog's view along with Bowers ("no clear concept of congregational mission-commitment developed in Paul's thinking," *Mission-Commitment*, 312) seems to be unsatisfactory.

58. This seems to have already been reflected in the survey by Keown (*Congregational Evangelism*, 16–17) who diverges from other surveys by allocating Ollrog as corresponding to the view of O'Brien and others ("Those That See the Church as Responsive in Terms of Proclamatory Evangelism").

59. His view first appeared on the basis on his exegesis on 1 Thess 1:8 in the article, "The Thessalonians as Missionary Congregation: 1 Thessalonians 1.5–8," *ZNW* 83 (1992): 126–131.

reserved exclusively for authorized proclaimers or shared in "a large context of active spread of the message by believers generally."[60]

This leads him to the question, "Did Paul envision the self-identity of his churches as involving a divine command to spread the gospel?"[61] and to an exegetical investigation into Philippians.[62] Here, Ware finds in the first two chapters of the letter ample evidence for viewing Paul's expectations for the Philippians' mission participation as not merely something indirect / passive, but as involving the active verbal spread of the gospel: thus (1) Paul envisions active proclamation as a general Christian activity (Phil 1:12–18a);[63] (2) Paul focuses not only on his own apostolic mission, but on the spread of the gospel through his converts' working out their salvation (Phil 1:18b–2:11);[64] (3) Paul expects his converts at Philippi to be functioning as lights in the world by "holding forth the word of life" (λόγον ζωῆς ἐπέχοντες) which clearly indicates verbal proclamation of the gospel by the congregation (Phil 2:12–18).[65]

While Ware's thesis makes some contribution to Philippians study,[66] its contribution to our current debate is that it raises the question of the background for Paul's missio-ecclesial understanding.[67] Ware distances himself from those scholars who include the early Christian missionaries (including Paul) within a broader class of Hellenistic philosophical and religious

---

60. J. P. Ware, *The Mission of the Church in Paul's Letter to the Philippians in the Context of Ancient Judaism* (Leiden: Brill, 2005), 9. The monograph is a revision of his PhD dissertation, "'Holding Forth the Word of Life': Paul and the Mission of the Church in the Letter to the Philippians in the Context of Second Temple Judaism," (PhD dissertation, Yale University, 1996). Ware, *The Mission of the Church*, 9.

61. Ware, *The Mission of the Church*, 10.

62. As his rationale for his focus on Philippians, he states that: "all [the evidences] suggest that Paul does not elsewhere exhort his churches to spread the gospel, not because an active mission of the church had no place in his thought, but in the context of a shared understanding of mission in which the need for explicit exhortation to spread the gospel was not pressing. In Philippians, by contrast, Paul's response to the situation at Philippi brings his theology of the church's mission to fuller expression" (Ibid., 235).

63. Ibid., 171–186.

64. Ibid., 201–236.

65. Ibid., 237–284.

66. He raises the unity issue of Philippians by suggesting that mission is a major concern of the letter (Ibid., 164–171).

67. Ibid., 10: "An important related question involves the background or source of the missionary consciousness of Paul and other Christian proclaimers."

propagandists (among whom the so-called "divine men" tradition was deemed to be playing a significant role for their vocation and practice).[68] Ware, then, sets his study of Paul's conception of mission in Philippians against the background of the interpretive tradition within Second Temple Judaism, particularly the motif of the Servant Songs of Isaiah – in which the conversion of Gentiles was readily envisioned.[69] The main contention is that as the Servant Songs provided a view of Israel as the nation of the eschatological "priests and prophets" for the Gentiles' salvation, Paul's missio-ecclesial understanding is largely indebted to it.[70] Ware further argues that such a Jewish heritage is the cause for Paul's "christological understanding of mission" and comes largely from his reading of the Isaianic Servant figure seen both messianically *and* collectively / ecclesiologically; this led the apostle to the view of the church as well as the apostle himself as verbal proclaimers of the gospel (at least in Philippians).[71] According to him, Paul's missionary consciousness, while not having its origins in the previous Jewish mission (since there was no actual mission despite extensive expectation for eschatological salvation of the Gentiles and an active role of Israel in it), is nonetheless "firmly rooted in Jewish understandings of Gentiles and their conversion."[72]

1.2.3.2. J. P. Dickson

John P. Dickson, while not agreeing with Ware's exegetical conclusions on the texts from Philippians (and other texts as well), therefore, rejecting the suggestion of Paul's expectation for the church's verbal missionary proclamation, basically shares the same interest in the background of Paul's conception of mission. He sets his entire study within the "socio-historical context of Judaism in Paul's era" in order to demonstrate "continuity between Jewish practices designed to 'win' Gentiles and those expected of Paul's converts."[73]

---

68. Ibid., 11–17.
69. Ibid., 57–159.
70. Ibid., 57–159, 224–236, 251–256, 270–282.
71. Ibid., 274–282.
72. Ibid., 290.
73. Dickson, *Mission-Commitment*, 6.

However, the substantial difference between Dickson's view and that of Ware is that Dickson understands the "continuity" of Paul's conception of mission with ancient Judaism not in terms of the traditional Jewish eschatological expectation / understanding of Gentiles' conversion and the role of eschatological Israel, but rather in actual "mission-commitment" that found "two-fold expression amongst Jews in the period leading up to the rise of Christianity."[74]

Following Terrence L. Donaldson's suggestion,[75] Dickson distinguishes the question as to whether Judaism was a missionary religion from whether there was a missionary mindset and also actual missionary activity in ancient Judaism.[76] As for the latter, Dickson observes Jewish literature showing the existence of some Jewish missionaries proselytizing[77] and various mission-commitments by Jewish communities of Palestine and the Diaspora.[78] As Dickson finds in Paul's letters a similar two-fold structure of Pauline mission ("Heralds and Partners"),[79] he concludes that, "Paul's notion of mission-commitment betrays a deep indebtedness to his Jewish heritage."[80]

Therefore, despite the similar interest in ancient Judaism as the most significant background for the apostle's conception of mission, what distances both from each other is not only different exegetical conclusions but also different conclusions about Paul's Jewish heritage. While for Ware ancient Judaism simply existed providing Paul with ideas for his Christian mission, for Dickson it actually provided the apostle with a model of mission conception and practice.

The two approaches reflect the general shape of the recent Pauline scholarship in which the importance of Paul as a Christian Jew (shaped within the thought world of Second Temple Judaism) and the universalist patterns within the spectrum of a diverse Judaism have been regaining prominence.

---

74. Ibid., 11–85 (quotation is from 85).
75. Donaldson, *Paul and the Gentiles*, 59.
76. Dickson, *Mission-Commitment*, 12–13.
77. Ibid., 11–50.
78. Ibid., 51–85. By this he also distances himself from Bowers (Ibid., 312).
79. Ibid., 86–132.
80. Ibid., 313.

While the significance of ancient Judaism to a discussion of the apostle's thought is to be acknowledged, the issue at stake, however, is whether one can *locate* Paul's (or early Christians') conception and practice of mission safely within the socio-historical context of Jewish orientation / practice of proselytism as Dickson attempts. Somewhat problematic is his categorical equating of Jewish proselytism with Paul's mission.[81] More at stake is whether demonstrating the existence of the two-fold mission expression in Judaism (according to one's definition of mission or criteria of missionary religion) can amount to Paul's "indebtedness" to such a two-fold expression of mission. It is doubtful whether one can claim Paul's "indebtedness" to a hypothetical socio-historical context without providing sufficient evidence that Paul was part of it.[82] Moreover, Dickson should also have discussed and showed the inter-relation between proselytizers and Jewish communities and Paul's indebtedness to it regarding the relation between his mission and his communities, if such a two-fold expression of mission was indebted to the alleged Jewish mission expression.

---

81. According to a recently growing consensus, while the existence of Jewish efforts in the period to draw the Gentiles "under the wings of the *Shekhina*" can be attested by various evidences, such efforts did not develop as a recognizable missionary pattern comparable to that of Paul: cf. F. Hahn, *Mission in the New Testament*, 21–25 (despite his affirmation of the existence of pre-Christian Jewish proselytism and its positive preparatory role for the rise of Christian mission); W. P. Bowers, "Paul and Religious Propaganda in the First Century," *NovT* 22, no. 4 (1980): 316–323; S. McKnight, *A Light among the Gentiles: Jewish Missionary Activity in the Second Temple Period* (Minneapolis: Fortress Press, 1991), 56; M. Goodman, *Mission and Conversion: Proselytizing in the Religious History of the Roman Empire* (Oxford: Oxford University Press, 1994), 60–90; R. Riesner, "A Pre-Christian Jewish Mission?" 221–250; Eckhard J. Schnabel, "The Expansion of God's People in Early Jewish Texts," in *Early Christian Mission* (Downers Grove: InterVarsity Press, 2004), 1. 92–173. See also more recently Bird, *Crossing Over Sea and Land*, who, while affirming evidences of actual Jewish efforts to earn proselytes in the period, if not from Palestinian sources (134–148), deals with the issue by making a careful distinction between "mission" within Judaism (some sporadic activities for full incorporation into bona fide Jews) and "mission" of early Christianity (149–156): he concludes that despite the "clear antecedents in Jewish interpretive traditions" and "indebtedness to intra-Jewish debates about pagans, proselytism, and 'God-fearers'" the early Christian mission made notable changes and transformation of which origin is to be found somewhere else other than such antecedents in Judaism (155–156). See also P. Barnett, *Paul: Missionary of Jesus* (Grand Rapids: Eerdmans, 2008), 36–38: "Yet even those who support the notion of a gentile mission are [like Dickson] forced to use qualifying terms like 'informal' and 'sporadic'." It appears, then, that there was not an earlier Jewish mission to the Gentiles that provided a pattern for Paul's later *intentional* mission to the Gentiles, as from circa 47" (38, original emphasis).

82. Note that Dickson, *Mission-Commitment*, 46–49, only suggests Gal 5:11 as the evidence.

1.2.4. Other Scholars in the Debate

Despite similarities to the scholars we mentioned above there are a few others whose discussions merit our further attention.

1.2.4.1. I. H. Marshall

I. Howard Marshall also provides a brief discussion on the issue only partly affirming Bowers' view on Paul's personal understanding of mission as a part of a bigger picture in which it can be sufficiently understood that "the gospel had been proclaimed in a representative kind of way."[83]

However, he is generally opposed to Bowers' exclusion of the church from Paul's missionary horizon.[84] He considers historically "a wider perspective" through the Gospels and Acts suggesting that: (1) while mentioning the (re)commissioning of the Eleven by the risen Lord (Matt 28), the evangelist does not treat the commissioning as something given exclusively to those disciples, but presents it as applicable to the entire church as well; (2) the picture from Acts shows that mission was based on the church; (3) the evangelism done by the dispersed Jerusalem Christians was basically in line with that of the special missionaries like Paul; (4) even if Paul's mission is solely portrayed as independent and essential in his epistles it was due to the apostle's situation where he could establish his position over neither against Jerusalem nor Antioch.[85] Based on this, Marshall concludes that "church-based missions and local evangelism are clearly envisaged in Acts and there is no conflict with the Pauline picture. The two can have existed side by side."[86]

He further suggests some exegetical considerations on several passages that may indicate congregational evangelism (1 Thess 1:8; Phil 2:14–17) and missionary intention of the congregation (1 Cor 7:16; 10:31–11:1; 14:23–25; 2 Cor 5:18–6:2; Titus 2:10).[87] This consideration leads him to explain Paul's dearth of attention to congregational evangelism by locating the apostle in "an early stage in the evolution of missionary consciousness":

---

83. I. H. Marshall, "Who Were the Evangelists?" 254.
84. Ibid., 255–263.
85. Ibid., 256–258.
86. Ibid., 258.
87. Ibid., 258–262.

while at this stage mission was understood in terms of preaching and proclamation carried on primarily by people who had a charisma for the activity, the work also embraces congregations; congregational evangelism was at least present in a "somewhat rudimentary form in Paul."[88]

1.2.4.2. E. J. Schnabel

In his second volume of *Early Christian Mission*, Schnabel observes various missionary works of the Christian communities.[89] While acknowledging the importance of Bowers' careful reading of some Pauline texts that are misleadingly taken as referring to congregational evangelism, he argues against Bowers' wholesale rejection of the individual believers' evangelistic task in Paul's thought.[90]

Schnabel distances himself from Marshall's suggestion of Paul's idea of the church's mission in rudimentary form by contending for Paul's fully developed idea about the church's mission.[91] Nevertheless, his approach is substantially similar to that of Marshall as he first appeals to some "general considerations" that he thinks to be indicating Paul's conception of mission in line with the evangelists' accounts in which mission is not confined to the Twelve (or the Eleven) but extended to the church,[92] and then he goes on to consider some Pauline texts that may indicate Paul's fully developed expectation for the church's various "missionary works" ranging from the congregations' various actions contributive to an evangelistic effect (e.g. 1 Cor 7:16; 10:31–11:1; 14:14–15; 2 Cor 3:3; 1 Tim 1:11–17; 2:1–4; 3:7; Titus 2:3–5; 1 Thess 3:12) to the activity of evangelism (e.g. 1 Thess 1:8; Phil 1:6; 2:14–17; Eph 6:10–20; 2 Tim 4:5).[93]

It seems that the studies by Marshall and Schnabel aptly show that Paul's mission should not be seen in strict isolation from the church and other

---

88. Ibid., 262–263.
89. Schnabel, *Early Christian Mission*, 2. 1451–1475.
90. Ibid., 1455.
91. Ibid., 1455–1456.
92. Ibid., 1456–1457.
93. Ibid., 1459–1472. He further argues that since such a fundamental missionary perspective of Paul's understanding of the nature of the church is underscored in Romans the letter should be seen as a "missionary document" (1472–1475).

missionaries despite the apostle's uniqueness. However, such a common ground of mission for the apostle and the church is conceivable only when the difference between *intentionality* and *functionality* is not considered. For example, as they do not distinguish the two, the mission of the church *by* selecting and sending evangelists (Acts 13:1ff) is largely equated with the mission of the apostle by himself.[94] While the apostle expected the church to be continuous with the apostle himself regarding others' salvation is one thing, whether the function of the church in mission is also continuous with the apostle in the apostle's thought is another and seems solely dependent on how to read some Pauline texts that deal with the issue.

Somewhat related to this, both authors throughout their studies tend to blur the difference between various individual Christians and the church *qua* the church, and do not consider the significant question as to whether such evangelistic works of the congregations should be taken as something *vocationally equivalent* to the apostle's own. Whether rudimentary or fully developed, what Marshall and Schnabel suggest as evidence for the apostle's expectation for the church's missionary involvement needs to be approached with a careful consideration of such distinctions as Ware maintains at least on methodological grounds.[95]

1.2.4.3. M. J. Keown

The most recent treatment on the debate is Keown's study on Philippians. Similarly to Ware's approach, Keown provides an exclusively exegetical study of the letter with the intention to show that "essential to Paul's understanding of evangelistic proclamatory mission, was his desire that the

---

94. Marshall, "Who Were the Evangelists?" 257, 262; Schnabel, *Early Christian Mission*, 2. 1457, 1458f–1459.

95. We may add some inappropriateness in appealing to Matt 28:20 as evidence for mission that is not limited to the Eleven but extended to the church. It is neither exegetically conclusive nor historically provable. Cf. E. Ochenmeier, "The Great Commission (Matt 28.19–20) in History and Today or Why the Great Commission Is Not the Duty of All Believers," Paper Presented at the New Testament Study Group of the Tyndale Fellowship, Cambridge (UK), July, 2011. See also R. Hvalvik, "In Word and Deed," in *The Mission of the Early Church to Jews and Gentiles*, eds. J. Ådna and H. Kvalbein (Tübingen: Mohr Siebeck, 2000), 277–280, who suggests that the Great Commission was understood and quoted as a commission given only to the apostles and never used for encouragement for congregational evangelism in the pre-Constantinian period.

church continue this work in their own towns and regions."[96] Despite the exegetical similarity to Ware's study, Keown argues that Paul's imperative to proclaim the gospel is found not only in the first two chapters of the epistle but the evidences exist explicitly, implicitly and rhetorically in the entire epistle since the apostle makes his imperative intent of proclamatory evangelism "the fabric of Philippians."[97] And for Keown such a responsibility of proclamatory evangelism is not merely for every local congregation but every believer in Paul's thought as the apostle portrays the notion of universal evangelism as an "axiomatic theological statement" (1:18)[98] and his expectation that all members will emulate the evangelistic zeal of official evangelists (e.g. 2:19–30; 4:1–3, 9).[99]

While acknowledging the usefulness of other approaches such as thematic analysis and historical analysis,[100] Keown is methodologically satisfied neither by the comparative study by Ware and Dickson nor by consideration of the Gospels and Acts. In Keown's estimation Ware and Dickson fail to show any actual connection between the apostle and his contemporaries;[101] while "the relationship of Paul to the practice of the early church found in the Gospel-Acts tradition is of more consequence," "establishing the connections here is also highly contentious."[102] Rather, Keown prefers an "emic approach" for an answer to the current question focusing solely on the apostle's own letters since "ultimately only the apostle can answer this."[103]

Keown's study is one of the most extensive exegetical treatments of Philippians in relation to Paul's missio-ecclesial understanding. It does indeed appear to be methodologically preferable to seek to understand Paul in his own terms rather than interpreting him through the lens of non-Pauline NT writings or in terms of our contemporary categories such as

---

96. Keown, *Congregational Evangelism*, 1.

97. Ibid., 1, 187–206.

98. Ibid., 95–102, 281. See also below appendix A: Paul's Conception of Universal Evangelism?

99. Keown, *Congregational Evangelism*, 148–267.

100. Ibid., 280.

101. Ibid., 29–30.

102. Ibid., 31.

103. Ibid., 30.

"mission." It is, however, doubtful if Keown's purely exegetical approach (looking at a single Pauline letter!) can provide a clear picture of the apostle's missio-ecclesial understanding. It is demonstrable (as we will hope to show later) that the texts in Philippians of possible relevance to our current enquiry are to a considerable degree allusive and even equivocal. In such a case, it is conclusions about what is "exegetically improbable" rather than ones based on what is "exegetically possible" that should carry the day. It is suspicious that Keown's study is so heavily dependant on the latter.

Further, as modern and post-modern Pauline scholarship has gradually realized, Paul's "understanding" or "theology" that we can appreciate is not a mere continuum of his written language but thoughts crystallized in his epistles through his historical interaction with his inner and outer world. Considering the situational character of Paul's letters as well, the latter recognition rightly necessitated enquiries into Paul's socio-historical environment, various comparative studies, cross-checks within the Pauline thought world and so on. If it is such a methodology that was found wanting in some presentations of Paul (e.g. the History-of-Religions school's "Hellenistic Paul" or the Tübingen school's "Paul as the Founder of Gentile Christianity"), it is also such a methodology that to a notable extent restored a presentation of Paul and his theology (e.g. Paul's understanding of Torah and Judaism).

Therefore, despite some dissatisfaction in previous deductive approaches, one's exegetical approach to the issue being collaborated with some sound etic approaches (e.g. asking what external factors facilitated Paul's particular missio-ecclesial understanding) will represent an evolution of the current debate.

1.2.5. Conclusion

Our brief observation of the current debate provides some points to be borne in mind. First, while no one denies Paul's consciousness of the church as his partner in the furtherance of the gospel, there is no exegetical agreement on whether the apostle expected the church "as a whole" to participate in proactive verbal evangelism. Second, while no one denies Paul's special place for the furtherance of faith and the substantial difference between his role as a missionary and that of the church, Bowers' denial of Paul's consciousness of the church as an agent for mission is largely rejected, despite the lack of explicit exhortation for congregational evangelism. Third, while scholars generally agree that for the discussion of Paul's conception of mission, "mission" refers to one's or communities' deliberate efforts to spread the gospel aiming at conversion of others, their descriptions of Paul's expectation for the church's role in such a "mission" differ according to how they understand the scope, motive / result or form of such efforts. Fourth, while an exegetical approach to Paul's texts is the primary method for the enquiry into Paul's missio-ecclesial understanding, a consideration of the apostle's theological and socio-historical background emerges as a crucial factor in exploring the issue.

If the commonly assumed definition of mission is granted, the first two points imply that our further discussion is to begin with assuming a certain "mission-continuity" between Paul and the church or at least Paul's missio-ecclesial understanding regarding his understanding of his own mission.[104] This again means that the unsettled exegetical question is not about such a mission-continuity between Paul and the church but about *the nature of such a continuity*. As Ollrog's and Dickson's arguments may suggest, is the mission-continuity perceived by Paul merely in terms of an *intentionality*, or, as O'Brien's and others' arguments suggest, in terms of a *functionality* as well?

On a more fundamental level, the debate seems to be dependant on how one defines the term "mission." It must be emphasized that applying such a modern definition of mission to an ancient figure is inevitably going to be inadequate. This means not only that our discussion needs at least a "good" working definition of mission for a coherent discussion but also that a better explanation for Paul's particular conception of what we like to call "mission" is conditional on the relevance of the term to the apostle. Therefore, it would not be an exaggeration to say that the current debate has more to do with a more plausible description of Paul's *conceptuality* regarding what Pauline scholars have generally called "mission" than simply to explain away the relation between Paul and the church under a given popular definition of mission.

---

104. See also Barram, *Mission and Moral Reflection*, 135–173, who rightly connects Paul's apostolic mission with his communities' right behaviour (e.g. 1 Cor 9:19–23; 10:31–11:1) in terms of "salvific intentionality" (173).

1.3. Objectives and Methodological Considerations

1.3.1. Focal Points

As the present study joins the ongoing debate summarized above, our central question will remain: "Did Paul expect the church as a whole to do proactive verbal evangelism on the ground of its vocational self-understanding?" This will necessitate our study to have an extensive exegetical focus on various debated Pauline texts. And our study will also attempt to identify the most probable background for Paul's particular understanding. However, it is distinct with respect to previous studies in some important focal points.

First, our primary focus will be on "Paul's conception of mission" not in terms of Paul's understanding of the *tasks* that are expected to be completed by the apostle himself and the church for the spread of the gospel and the winning of the converts, but in terms of Paul's more comprehensive framework of reference according to which he understood what is expected to be accomplished, and why, and in what way this is to be done. This approach is different from that of Bowers and others who approach the issue not clearly distinguishing "mission" from "proselytism / conversion" or "vocation." In the previous studies "mission" is, therefore, by and large equated with various forms of activities (or even intentions) aimed at a socio-religious form of "conversion." While we will *not* dispense with such a definition of mission, "mission" will be approached, if not anachronistically applied to Paul,[105] primarily as something that can accommodate not only Paul's understanding of the *contents* of task but also the *context* of task according to which Paul identified his own vocation and that of the church within the fuller divine plan for the salvation of creation. The presupposition of the study, therefore, is that an understanding of the relation of Paul's vocation to that of the church can be reached through a historically and theologically plausible reconstruction of the apostle's "concept of mission" *as his mission-theological framework*.

---

105. Cf. R. Hvalvik, *Struggle for Scripture and Covenant: The Purpose of the Epistle of Barnabas and Jewish-Christian Competition in the Second Century* (Tübingen: Mohr Siebeck, 1996), 279.

Second, while acknowledging the importance of the interpretive tradition of the Jewish Scripture and the socio-historical milieu of Second Temple period for the formation of Paul's concept of mission, our study will focus more specifically on *Jewish restoration eschatology*. It will endeavour to provide a rationale for viewing Paul's mission not merely in terms of evangelistic pattern (i.e. proselytism or conversion of the Gentiles / non-Christians through direct and indirect commitments) but primarily in terms of the *ongoing restoration of Israel*. One of the most important results of this study is the recognition of the importance of the latter motif as a key to appreciating Paul's missio-ecclesial horizon and the relation between the apostle and the church regarding the task of proactive verbal proclamation of the gospel.

Third, the consideration of Jewish restoration eschatology as a specific (prospective) theological background for the apostle's conception of mission raises the further question as to whether Paul's conception of mission as such had any antecedent to which he can be shown to be indebted. In this regard, the present study chooses to focus on some traditions of (or memories about) Jesus: some aspects of his movement can be approached through the lens of the same Jewish eschatological vision, that provides a certain mode / pattern of operation and the traditions of whose sayings and accounts in various degrees, if not great, can be analyzed in terms of the apostle's indebtedness.

1.3.2. Definition of Mission in Discussing Paul's Conception of Mission

1.3.2.1. Problem in the Definition of Mission

As we are engaged in the discussion about Paul's conception of mission, our immediate problem is the confusion raised by the ambiguity and different uses of the term "mission." For instance, Bowers, by suggesting Paul's failure to conceive any idea of "the church at mission,"[106] seems to restrict the meaning of mission to direct, verbal and outward religious propaganda for non-members' conversion. Despite the anachronistic and even artificial nature inherent in the term mission, insofar as Paul's preaching of the gospel

---

106. Bowers, "Studies," 120.

had such a dimension Bowers' use of the term as such is to be affirmed. Nevertheless, the problem is that, as Bowers suggests that Paul's pastoral nurture for the churches as included in the apostle's "understanding of his mission" (or vocation),[107] he expands (self-contradictorily) the range of the meaning of "mission" to a non-evangelistic (according to his former use) and in-community category of activity. Moreover, this again indicates that for his discussion of Paul's conception of mission it is inevitable that Bowers cannot but oscillate between a reference to a task and a reference to one's notion of his or her vocation.[108]

So, Bowers' oscillation seems to be weakening his wholesale rejection of the church as an agent of mission, at least on a logical ground: on what basis should what Paul's mission entails (i.e. the church's behaviour resultant from Paul's mission) be left out of *a* mission? If Paul's teaching for the church is what is willed by God (θέλημα τοῦ θεοῦ) to be entrusted to the churches *through* the apostle (e.g. 1 Thess 4:1–8), then isn't it the case that what is willed by God for the churches anyway, analogous to what is willed by God for Paul (e.g. 1 Cor 1:1)? If what is entrusted to Paul by God's will is to be called "his mission," is it not legitimate to call what is entrusted to the church *a mission*?

It seems that, while a conversionist definition of mission is to be utilized as much as it can account for some important aspects in Paul's mission (and the church's involvement), it is unwise to let the definition have a monopoly in a discussion about Paul's view of his mission. While what we call Paul's mission certainly *included* such a dimension of conversion, it was in no way a self-generated intention or activity but more fundamentally related with his notion of θέλημα τοῦ θεοῦ. This teleological notion of vocation seems to be crucial for understanding the apostle's self-understanding and his ecclesial understanding regarding the specific task of conversion.

Another example is Dickson's attempt to overcome a minimalist definition of mission. While he maintains, following the lead of Scot Mcknight[109]

---

107. Ibid., 105; Bowers, "Fulfilling the Gospel," 185–198.

108. A similar oscillation is observed in Hvalvik's discussion about "consciousness of having a mission" within Judaism in *The Struggle for Scripture and Covenant*, 271ff. Cf. Ibid., 269, in which he largely rejects to use of "mission" as a general reference to vocation or task.

109. McKnight, *A Light among the Gentiles*, 4–5.

and Martin Goodman,[110] that the ultimate goal of mission is universal conversion, he complains about their failure to see the larger goal of winning outsiders in various non-aggressive religious activities suggesting that, "*Information, apologetic, education* and *proselytism* are not so neatly separated. Rather than being distinct types of mission, these categories ought to be viewed as points along a continuum of mission."[111] This leads him to a definition of mission: "The range of activities by which members of a religious community desirous of the conversion of outsiders seek to promote their religion to non-adherents."[112]

As Dickson notes, this definition of mission certainly (and in my opinion rightly) gives a "proper place" to "the real expressions of mission-commitment of a community,"[113] and this aspect is largely ignored in Bowers' study. Nevertheless, despite Dickson's attempt to broaden the scope of mission within Paul's missio-ecclesial horizon, what is actually broadened is the criterion of proper religious propaganda within ancient Judaism as various forms of expressed intention are included in the range of a proper mission.[114] The result is that, while the various forms of expressed intentionality for conversion become comparable to that of the Pauline community, Paul's own mission remains at odds with such a broadened definition of mission.

What we need to note is that such a conversionist definition of mission is devised to answer the question, "what makes a religion a missionary religion?" and reflects scholarly interest in the question as to whether ancient Judaism (and other philosophical and religious groups in the Greco-Roman world) had a missionary character compared to the relatively

---

110. Goodman, *Mission and Conversion*, 6.

111. Dickson, *Mission-Commitment*, 8 (original emphasis).

112. Ibid., 10 (original emphasis). Dickson notes that his definition of mission is a combination of the view of J. Carleton Paget, "Jewish Proselytism at the Time of Christian Origins: Chimera or Reality?" *JSNT* 62 (1996): 65–103, who allows non-aggressive forms of "openness to outsiders" as indication to "missionary religion" (77) and that of Riesner, "A Pre-Christian Jewish Mission?" 223, who requires both "intentionality" and "activity" for a proper definition of mission.

113. Dickson, *Mission-Commitment*, 10.

114. Cf. Riesner, "A Pre-Christian Mission?" 222. See also K. L. Yinger's review on Dickson's monograph in "A Book Review of John P. Dickson, 'Mission-Commitment in Ancient Judaism and in the Pauline Communities . . .'" *JSNT* 27 (2004): 118: "Those utilizing Dickson's position should not overstate the difference to Goodman and McKnight; he nuances rather than overturns them."

obvious missionary orientation of the early Christian movement. It means that, while such a device is concerned with a socio-historically discernable pattern of praxis, it is not generally concerned with one's utmost inner motive or particular worldview that may generate such a pattern. This again means that by ignoring such significant factors and exclusively focusing on a socio-religious aspect of conversion that may be only externally detected in both Judaism and Paul, Dickson's definition of mission notably fails to filter the distinctiveness of Pauline mission from Jewish proselytism.

Perhaps, this consideration of mission is important in a study about the first-century religious activist whose surrounding world was full of propaganda of convictions. However finely mission is defined considering various socio-psycho-religious dimensions, nevertheless, it is still the case that this sort of definition may not be sufficient (and may be anachronistic) when one attempts to examine how a first-century Christian Jew – who had a strong sense of being called to devote himself to such an activity that we call "mission" – conceived of such a phenomenon. Particularly, Paul's notion of *what* and *for what* or *in what way* such a phenomenon should happen may not be accounted for with such a pattern-analytical definition of mission.

Therefore, while benefiting from such a definition of mission in terms of "intentionality" and "activity" toward a proper "conversion,"[115] in this study our use of the term "mission" needs to expand to account for Paul's unique understanding of himself and his surrounding world in relation to the activity of propagation of the faith in Christ.

1.3.2.2. Mission as an Eschatological Event
In this regard, it is helpful to bring the notion of mission in terms of an "event" in which one's rationale for and method of such an activity is

---

115. Cf. Reisner, "A Pre-Christinan Mission?" 221–223.

accounted. The beginning of this approach is seen in scholars such as Oscar Cullmann[116] and Johannes Munck.[117]

On the basis of his reading of 2 Thessalonians 2:6–7, Cullmann believes that the "delaying power" (τό κατέχον) which prevents the advent of Antichrist, who is the sign of the coming of Christ, is none other than the preaching of the gospel to the Gentiles (Mark 13:10 / Matt 24:14); and the one (ὁ κατέχων) who does the role of κατέχον is none other than Paul himself, the apostle to the Gentiles.[118] Since Paul's preaching is the delaying power and opens up the curtains of the messianic drama, for Cullmann, Paul's gentile mission has "le caractère eschatologique."[119]

Munck, by taking this view that Paul's preaching to the Gentiles is τό κατέχον that precedes the Messianic time, notes that Paul's is the "instrument of eschatological plan that comes from God."[120] Recently, Hanna Stettler, on the basis of her reading of Colossians 1:24 ("Paul is filling up the lack of Christ's sufferings to their fullness by his bodily or physical suffering: he does so on behalf of the church which, as a consequence, has to suffer less"), suggests that in Paul's mission theology – while his mission is a delaying factor of the lawless one by providing the opportunity for the full number of the Gentiles to come in – his mission can also be seen from a different angle (from the church's perspective) as a suffering that shortens the period of tribulation for the church.[121]

For these scholars Paul's mission per se is an eschatological event. Whether or not Paul (or a Deutero-Pauline circle) regarded himself as

---

116. O. Cullmann, "Le caractère eschatologique du devoir missionnaire et de la conscience apostolique de S. Paul: Étude sur le katéchon (-ōn) de 2 Thess. 2.6–7," *RHPR* 16 (1936): 210–245, cited in Munck, *Salvation of Mankind*, 36, n.1. The same article in German appears in Cullmann, "Der eschatologische Charakter des Missionsauftrags und des apostolischen Selbstbewußtseins bei Paulus," in *Vorträge und Aufsätze, 1925–1962* (Tübingen: Mohr, 1966), 305–336.

117. Munck, *Salvation of Mankind*, 36–42.

118. Cullman, "Le caractère eschatologique," 224.

119. Ibid., 243.

120. Munck, *Salvation of Mankind*, 41.

121. H. Stettler, "Colossians 1:24 in the Framework of Paul's Mission Theology," in *The Mission of the Early Church to Jews and Gentiles*, eds. J. Ådna and H. Kvalbein (Tübingen: Mohr, 2000), 185–208.

such a central figure for the eschatological schedule,¹²² it is sufficiently sustainable that his missionary activity was in a sense an eschatological event which God himself caused to happen. Paul's preaching of the gospel is not merely his willful activity for others' salvation, but the result of the "necessity" that is imposed on him (1 Cor 9:16: "ἀνάγκη γάρ μοι ἐπίκειται") and a faithful participation in the eschatological drama in which God's eschatological message of salvation is proclaimed and through which the eschatological people of God are being fully gathered before the *parousia* of Christ (Rom 11:25–26, cf. Isa 59:20–21).¹²³

Therefore, the notion of mission as an eschatological event involves not only implementation on the part of Paul, but also the apostle's awareness of a certain eschatological (or even historical) context that prompts his participation.¹²⁴ In this light, while we do not dispense with the popular definition of mission (and indeed we need to employ it at times to engage with the discussion), I differ from Bowers and others by defining mission for Paul, not in terms of activity designed to achieve socio-religious incorporation of people into his faith community, but primarily in terms of his conceptualization of what is expected to happen and of those things that will bring about that happening within God's eschatological drama. This approach to "Paul's mission" will lead us to observe the apostle's teleological perception of himself and the church and take into account the (Pauline) church's unique place regarding Paul's own place within that eschatological event.

As such, our use of the term "eschatology" or "eschatological" needs a little clarification. For our current discussion, it is unnecessary to explore all the complexities of ever-evolving modern and post-modern discussions

---

122. Cf. Bowers, "Mission," *DPL*, 617–618, who, while affirming the eschatological framework for Paul's conception of mission, questions Paul's pivotal role and exclusively futuristic orientation within such an end-time drama.

123. Cf. A. Schweitzer, *The Mysticism of Paul the Apostle* (London: A. & C. Black, 1931), 183; Hahn, *Mission in the New Testament*, 99–100.

124. This consideration also indicates that any idea that Paul's eschatological orientation is purely futuristic or that early Christian mission was a substitution for imminent eschatology is not a satisfactory notion. For Paul mission started as a response to the realization that the end-time drama has already started through the Christ-event. Cf. Bosch, *Transforming Mission*, 41, 141–143; K. Y. Lim, "*The Sufferings of Christ Are Abundant in Us*": *A Narrative Dynamics Investigation of Paul's Sufferings in 2 Corinthians* (London: T. & T. Clark, 2009), 53–58.

of the topic.[125] We will follow a conventional use of the term within recent Pauline studies, using the term "eschatology" to refer to: the cluster of ideas about "the end" and things that are related to it as generally conceived of within Paul's Jewish and Christian thought-world. While scholars tend to reduce it to "existential" or "non-cosmological / temporal" categories,[126] or exclusively to one temporal aspect (i.e. to "purely imminent / futuristic"[127] or "purely realized / present" categories)[128], we will eschew such a reduction as unnecessary. As we will at times explain, "eschatology" in Paul is best approached in terms of so-called "inaugurated eschatology" in which both the present and future dimensions of the "end" are observed in a dialectic tension. Therefore, in our discussion, "eschatology" or "eschatological" will be used generally in relation to Paul's particular view about things that were scripturally and traditionally expected to be caused by God at the final stage of human history towards the final consummation of God's first creation, whether on an individual level, or a national level, or a universal / cosmological level.

1.3.3. Question of the Origins of Paul's Conception of Mission within Paul's Jewish-Christian Thought World

Having stated that our focus is not only on Paul's *conception* of mission (from which his missionary act derives) but also on the most probable causal elements for Paul's conception of mission, our enquiry into the issue can be stated as a discussion of the *origins* of or *background* for Paul's conception of mission. Thus, here, I do not mean origin as the chronological starting point, but rather the most decisive paradigmatic practice or concept that informs or influences one's paradigmatic understanding of one's practice or concept. Therefore, in what follows a careful distinction should

---

125. Cf. H. Schwarz, *Eschatology* (Grand Rapids: Ferdmans, 2000), 26–30.

126. Most notably, R. Bultmann, "History and Eschatology in the New Testament," *NTS* 1 (1954/1955): 139.

127. Schweitzer, *Mysticism*, 52, 182–183.

128. C. H. Dodd, *The Apostolic Preaching and Its Developments: Three Lectures with an Appendix on Eschatology and History* (London: Hodder & Stoughton, 1936), 65; Dodd, *The Mind of Paul: II in New Testament Studies* (Manchester: University Press, 1953), 112–113.

be drawn between the "origin of Paul's mission" and the "origin of Paul's conception of mission."[129]

Given the growing consensus that among various propaganda of cults and philosophies in the Greco-Roman world there is no evidence of the existence of a paradigmatic pattern of mission that may be comparable to that of Paul,[130] I do not intend to consider such propaganda as possible origins of Paul's conception of mission. Rather, as I assume that Paul's life and thought in itself was a struggle with thoroughly Jewish issues even in his gentile mission context, and that the central background of his notion of the church (which is none other than the result and part of his mission) is the Jewish hope for the eschatological people of God,[131] this also leads to an assumption that Paul's contemporary Jewish-Christian thought world is the most appropriate arena to investigate the question of the origin of Paul's thought formation as a missionary.[132]

---

129. For instance, Heikki Räisänen's proposal of the Hellenistic church Paul joined as the starting point of his mission (*Paul and the Law* [Tübingen: Mohr Siebeck, 1987], 251–263) may be regarded as an example of the study of the "origin of Paul's mission." See also M. F. Bird, *Jesus and the Origins of the Gentile Mission* (London: T. & T. Clark, 2006), whose "origin" throughout the study refers to a genetic origin of missionary propagation by the people of God to the Gentiles. Cf. T. L. Donaldson, "Israelite, Convert, Apostle to the Gentiles: The Origin of Paul's Gentile Mission," in *The Road from Damascus: The Impact of Paul's Conversion on His Life, Thought, and Ministry*, ed. R. N. Longenecker (Grand Rapids: Eerdmans, 1997), 62–83, whose "origin" generally refers to a decisive cause for Paul's "gentile convictions."

130. E.g. Bowers, "Paul and Religious Propaganda in the First Century," *NovT* 22, no. 4 (1980): 316–323; Goodman, *Mission and Conversion*, 20–37; T. Engberg-Pederson, "The Hellenistic *Öffentlichkeit*: Philosophy as a Social Force in the Greco-Roman World," in *Recruitment, Conquest, and Conflict: Strategies in Judaism, Early Christianity and the Graeco-Roman World*, eds. P. Borgen, V. K. Robbins, and D. B. Gowler (Atlanta: Scholars, 1998), 16–37; D. E. Aune, "Jesus and Cynics in First-Century Palestine: Some Critical Considerations," in *Hillel and Jesus*, eds. J. H. Charlesworth and L. Johns (Minneapolis: Fortress, 1997), 176–192; Ware, *The Mission of the Church*, 10–17.

131. E.g. K. Stendahl, *Paul among Jews and Gentiles, and Other Essays* (London: SCM Press, 1977); E. P. Sanders, *Paul, the Law, and the Jewish People* (Philadelphia: Fortress Press, 1983); N. T. Wright, *Paul: In Fresh Perspective* (Minneapolis: Fortress Press; London: SPCK, 2005), 108–129.

132. This is by no means to suggest that the Greco-Roman world had nothing to do with Paul's formation as a person. I agree that Paul as a "person" is best described as a man of three worlds: Jewish, Greek and Roman (cf. B. Witherington, *The Paul Quest: The Renewed Search for the Jew of Tarsus* [Leicester: IVP, 1998], 52–88). At any rate, regardless of to what extent Paul's appreciation of Hellenism is to be described (e.g. J. M. G. Barclay's "lower accommodation" in "Paul among Diaspora Jews: Anomaly or Apostate?" *JSNT* 60 [1995]: 92–111, or Jürgen Becker's "near assimilation" in *Paul: Apostle to the Gentiles*

1.3.3.1. Jewish Factors Contributive to Paul's Conception of Mission

Since recent NT scholarship has started to pay more attention to the Jewishness of Paul (and of course of Jesus),[133] scholars are now more ready to consider some Jewish factors that existed within Second Temple Judaism as crucial for his Christian conception of mission.[134] Some suggestions and issues raised by a few recent scholars may provide us with useful (positive and negative) methodological considerations for our enquiry into Paul's conception of mission and its Jewish background.

1.3.3.1.1. Jewish worldview and Paul's conception of mission
Being interested primarily in Paul's Jewish apocalyptic framework as a "coherent centre" (through which Paul's other contingent reflections make coherent sense),[135] J. Christiaan Beker suggests a certain continuity as a missionary between the pre-Damascus Pharisaic Paul and Paul the Christian in terms of Jewish apocalyptic structure of thought:

[Louisville: Westminster John Knox Press 1993], 55), Hellenistic features in Paul are to be admitted (e.g. the high likelihood of his birth in the Hellenistic city of Tarsus, his relatively free use of Greek language, the knowledge and use of Greek philosophy, literature and rhetoric). However, while Paul's familiarity with them is unmistakable it is to be noted that nowhere is there evidence that such a familiarity indicates Paul's profound Hellenization in the matters of his theological thinking (cf. e.g. H. Koester, "Paul and Hellenism," in *The Bible in Modern Scholarship*, ed. J. P. Hyatt [Nashville: Abingdon, 1965], 187–195; E. A. Judge, "St. Paul and Classical Society," *JAC* 15 [1972], 32–33). See also N. T. Wright, *Paul*, 3–12; J. D. G. Dunn, *Beginning from Jerusalem: Christianity in the Making* (Grand Rapids: Eerdmans, 2009), 322–335.

133. E.g. W. D. Davies, *Paul and Rabbinic Judaism: Some Rabbinic Elements in Pauline Theology* (4th ed.; London: SPCK, 1981 [1948]); Sanders, *Paul and Palestinian Judaism*; G. Theissen and D. Winter, *The Quest for the Plausible Jesus: The Question of Criteria* (Louisville: Westminster John Knox Press, 2002).

134. This is not to ignore some earlier contributions such as Schweitzer, *Mysticism*, 177–204; Munck, *Salvation of Mankind*, 36–86, who attempted to locate Paul's mission thoroughly within his Jewish worldview and context. However, these approaches were not fully appreciated until scholars were more ready to see the Christian identity not any more in antithesis to Judaism and not in comparison with various religions in Greco-Roman world. Cf. Campbell, *Paul and the Creation of Christian identity*, 15–32. For the shift of scholarly interest from Paul at Damascus or after Damascus to Paul before Damascus see M. Hengel, *The Pre-Christian Paul* (London: SCM, 1991), xiii, 87.

135. J. C. Beker, *Paul the Apostle: The Triumph of God in Life and Thought* (Philadelphia: Fortress Press, 1980), 11–19, 135–347: "Paul's gospel is formulated within the basic components of apocalyptic" (145).

Paul's apocalyptic conviction was not initiated by his conversion to Christ but formed the background of his Pharisaic worldview. The continuity between Paul the Pharisee and Paul the Christian lies in a different posture toward the relation between the Torah and the messianic promises and not in a change from "legal casuistic Pharisaism" (Paul the Pharisee) to "universalistic apocalyptic thinking" (Paul the Christian). Because Paul had probably been an apocalyptic Pharisaic "missionary" before his conversion, if we can trust Acts 9:1–2, the apocalyptic structure of his thought remains the constant in his Pharisaic and Christian life.[136]

Here, despite his reference to Acts 9:1–2, in what sense Beker speaks of the pre-Christian Paul as an "apocalyptic Pharisaic missionary" remains vague. Whether he has in mind the idea of Jewish delegates as "itinerant missionaries" in Judaism,[137] or whether he simply refers to a religious activist given an authorized task (as a "mission"), or even whether he implies that the Pharisaism in Paul's time operated within a universalistic apocalyptic vision being linked with a certain Jewish mission is not at all clear. While we cannot be sure about how the continuity as a "missionary" is construed, however, Beker's view as such lends us a reasonable notion: worldview is crucial for one's sense of purpose and task if one is a religious activist. If one's structure of convictions about the world remains largely unchanged even after experiencing significant change in convictions, it is reasonable to expect some significant continuity that transcends even the life changing experience. The crucial question for us, then, is "what convictions within such a Jewish worldview transcended Paul's profound reorientation as a Christian activist particularly for his Christian conception of mission?" However, if Beker's thesis has any bearing for our study, it seems to be equally important to ask "what elements were modified in Paul

---

136. Ibid., 144.

137. Cf. K. Kohler, *The Origin of the Synagogue and the Church* (New York: Macmillan, 1929), 160, cited in Riesner, "A pre-Christian Jewish Mission?" 220, n.78.

as a Christian missionary within such a largely continuous convictional structure?"[138]

1.3.3.1.2. The question of the origin of Paul's gentile convictions
Terence L. Donaldson suggests a similar sort of continuity between Paul before and after the Damascus event regarding the basic structure of convictions within the Jewish thought world; not in terms of a Jewish apocalyptic worldview but in terms of Jewish convictions about the Gentiles.[139]

Being dissatisfied with both the traditional explanation for the origin of Paul's gentile convictions (as a corollary of Paul's christological awakening that results in a shift from a particularistic Judaism to a universalistic Christianity) and the model of Paul's gentile mission as a later development

---

138. While Beker, *Paul the Apostle*, 145–146, acknowledges that "apocalyptic undergoes a profound modification in Paul [the Christian]," he accentuates that such a modification "does not affect the intensity of its expectation" (Ibid., 145), and seems to be down playing the significance of Paul's modification in temporal conception of the world and its salvation:
> Paul's modification of apocalyptic should not be exaggerated or be construed in terms of an abstruse dialectic. . . . the distinction between primitive Christianity and Judaism does not lie simply in their different conceptions of salvation, with one viewing it as present reality and the other as a purely future hope. Qumran has demonstrated clearly that the new age is already appropriated as a present reality and is not simply a future expectation. The community knows itself to be the new temple and the new covenant and celebrates the Spirit in its midst. This means that the difference between at least a form of apocalyptic Judaism and Pauline Christianity must not be drawn in terms of temporal distinctions. Rather it raises the question about the mode and quality of the new in the present" (Ibid., 150).

I find this suggestion unconvincing. It is difficult to say that the Qumran community perceived the reality of the world to come in the same way in which Paul the Christian perceived it. While for Paul the reality of the messianic age is not only in intense apocalyptic expectation but primarily based on the historical event of the arrival of the messiah in the near past (e.g. Rom 1:1ff), the Qumran community does not show any such indication. Rather, various texts from the Qumran scrolls, particularly from 1QSa (or Rule of the Congregation) show that the Qumran community lived the present pre-messianic age on the verge of the End of the days anticipating the messianic age that will soon come (cf. L. H. Schiffman, *The Eschatological Community of the Dead Sea Scrolls: A Study of the Rule of the Congregation* (Atlanta: Scholars Press, 1989), while Paul clearly saw his present time as the messianic age (e.g. 2 Cor 5:17; 6:2). If a similarity between Pauline community and the Qumran sect can be spoken of in terms of "the mode and quality of the new in the present" such a mirroring of the future in the present within the two communities seems to be grounded on very different temporal conceptions of the messianic age. I think that such a difference in temporal conception of the messianic age has a very important bearing for Paul's conception of mission particularly in relation to the implication of the notion to the restoration of Israel. We will come back to the point later.

139. Donaldson, *Paul and the Gentiles*, 81–248.

(as Paul's theological deliberation from his Christian situations such as opposition to his law-free mission and failure in Jewish mission),[140] Donaldson more positively considers various Jewish "patterns of universalism" (e.g. covenantal nomism, eschatological pilgrimage of the nations, righteous Gentiles and proselytism) that may indicate the possibility of Paul's gentile convictions being rooted somewhere in Judaism which was not totally legalistic nor purely particularistic.[141] This leads him to conclude, "Paul's gentile convictions are best explained as the reconfiguration, under the impact of his Damascus experience, of convictions formed during his 'earlier life in Judaism.'"[142]

However, according to Donaldson such a reconfiguration is not the result of Paul's adaptation of all such Jewish universalistic patterns – since most of the parallels are merely "surface similarities"[143] – but it is only Jewish proselytism that has a real connection with Paul's gentile convictions and his mission to them.[144] In the view of Paul's theological reflections on the Torah-Christ antithesis, the remaining currency in the significance of Israel and in the categorical distinction between Jews and Gentiles, and Paul's various reflections concerning gentile salvation, Donaldson suggests that "Gentile salvation can be best accounted for in terms of an underlying pattern of convictions in which Gentiles are thought of as proselytes to an Israel reconfigured around Christ."[145]

While Donaldson's major contribution is his cogent explanation of Paul's gentile convictions stemming from his pre-Damascus Jewish disposition, what seems to be particularly helpful for our enquiry is his balanced consideration of Paul's mission both as universalistic (concern for the gentile salvation) and particularistic (concern for the Christ / the

---

140. Ibid., 3–24, 263–272.

141. Ibid., 25–27, 51–78, 273–305; Terence Donaldson, "Proselytes or 'Righteous Gentiles'? The Status of Gentiles in Eschatological Pilgrimage Patterns of Thought," *JSP* 7 (1990): 3–27; "Israelites, Converts, Apostle to the Gentiles," 81–83.

142. Donaldson, *Paul and the Gentiles*, 263.

143. Ibid., 166–169, 187–197, 230–236 (the quotation is from 230).

144. Ibid., 273–307; Donaldson, "Israelite, Convert, Apostle to the Gentiles," 77–79. Note that the theme of pilgrimage of the Gentiles was formerly affirmed in Donaldson's earlier article, "The 'Curse of the Law' and the Inclusion of the Gentiles: Galatians 3.13–14," *NTS* 32 (1986): 94–112, as significant for Paul's gentile mission.

145. Donaldson, *Paul and the Gentiles*, 107–248 (the quotation is from 236).

gospel-defined Israel).¹⁴⁶ This consideration must prevent our discussion about Paul's conception of mission from being biased solely towards its *centrifugal dimension*, which has often been overemphasized as if it is the most distinctive or even exclusive feature in Paul's conception of mission. As Donaldson's thesis aptly shows, the particularistic or centripetal dimension was another significant constituent part of Paul's convictions about his Christian mission, and it seems to be a positive indication for the Jewish character of Paul's conception of mission.¹⁴⁷

1.3.3.1.3. Jewish proselytism as the exclusive conceptual background for Paul's mission?

However, despite Donaldson's question limited only to the issue of the origin of Paul's "gentile convictions," he so stresses Jewish proselytism as the exclusive entry route of Paul's gentile convictions into his gentile mission, that another major Jewish stream of tradition is unduly suppressed as irrelevant to Paul's conception of mission from the outset. For instance, having moved from his former position¹⁴⁸ to a position in which he does not any more view Paul's gentile mission through the lens of Jewish restoration eschatology, Donaldson undercuts any idea that connects Paul's mission with a Jewish eschatological pilgrimage expectation.¹⁴⁹ His primary reason for this is that the eschatological pilgrimage is always conditional

---

146. He argues that while Paul maintained, as a pre-Damascus Jew, Jewish particularism in which the Torah works as the boundary marker not between Jews and the Gentiles but between God's covenantal members (including Gentile proselytes by whom some universalistic characteristic of Judaism can be shown) and the rest, Paul after his conversion maintained a similar sort of particularistic view on the Christian community (i.e. membership only obtained by the Christ-centered gospel). By so doing, he suggests that Paul's gentile mission cannot be accounted for with the model of Paul's conversion in which universalism supersedes particularism (Ibid., 107–164; Donaldson, "The Origin of Paul's Gentile Mission," 68–83). Cf. N. T. Wright, *The Climax of the Covenant: Christ and the Law in Pauline Theology* (Edinburgh: Clark, 1991), 163–164, who suggests that while the Abrahamic covenant is universal (i.e. envisaging "a single family"), the Torah is particularistic (i.e. creates "a plurality by dividing Gentiles from Jews").

147. This again indicates that Paul's ecclesial understanding is connected to his missional horizon, since the centripetal or particularistic dimension of his mission exists only on the assumption of a community, the people of God with a new self-conception. This naturally leads to a supposition that Paul maintained a framework of reference according to which he understood the matters of his mission and that of the church as something integral rather than as separate sets of ideas (*pace* Bowers, "Studies," 120).

148. Donaldson, "The 'Curse of the Law'," 94–112.

149. Donaldson, *Paul and the Gentiles*, 187–197.

on the restoration of Israel and will imply an "anomaly" in Paul if he bases gentile salvation not on the restoration of Israel but on their failure (Rom 11:12, 15).[150]

While an argument against this position will be made later, at least one question is to be asked here: do we really need to think that such a particularistic *and* universalistic pattern in Paul's mission is due to Jewish proselytism *exclusively*? In my opinion, the positive tension between a universalistic and particularistic Jewish stance towards the Gentiles is not necessarily to be seen as an exclusive pattern of Jewish proselytism. Jewish eschatological expectation for the incoming of the Gentiles, if not following the line of "righteous Gentiles" concept or the "two covenants" theory, is a good model for such a feature, a combination of both particularistic and universalistic aspects.[151] Thus, if such a pilgrimage motif was part of Paul's pre-conversional disposition, and if Paul's Damascus experience allowed him to realize that the time for the gentile salvation is ripe (as the advent of the Jewish messiah signals the arrival of the end-time and the restoration of Israel),[152] it is sufficient to expect Paul to be led to such a stance toward the Gentiles without linking Paul's former connection with the pattern of Jewish proselytism.

To substantiate his argument Donaldson further suggests that "attitudes and activities" that are similar to those of the forceful advocate of circumcision "Eleazar" (*Ant.* 20.43) characterized Paul the "preacher of circumcision" prior to the Damascus event (Gal 5:11).[153] Despite his careful disclaimer lest it suggests unnecessary implications,[154] such a suggestion inevitably implies the exclusive role of Jewish proselytism for the formation

---

150. Ibid., 192–193. As an indication to the improbability of Paul's dependence on the motif of eschatological pilgrimage of the Gentiles, he further argues that the motif is absent from Paul's letters (Ibid., 194–195).

151. Note that Donaldson makes a counter claim in favour of Jewish proselytism: "parallels between Paul's Israel-centered view of the gentile mission and Jewish patterns of universalism are by no means restricted to eschatological pilgrimage expectations" (Donaldson, *Paul and the Gentiles*, 195).

152. Cf. Munck, *Salvation of Mankind*, 255–278; N. T. Wright, *Climax*, 150–151.

153. Donaldson, *Paul and the Gentiles*, 277–284.

154. Ibid., 283–284.

of Paul's missionary thought, since (it is argued) not only did Paul *know* the pattern of Jewish proselytism but he also *was* a part of it.[155]

Dickson's thesis, mentioned above, is based on Donaldson's position as such.[156] Dickson's further suggestion is that such an ancient Jewish proselytism found two-fold expression and to such a pattern Paul's two-fold structured expression is indebted, not simply theologically but also socio-historically.[157]

It seems that both scholars are correct that Eleazar the Galilean who insisted on the circumcision of Izates the king of Adiabene aptly indicates that ancient Judaism had a certain type of advocate of circumcision for God-fearing Gentiles.[158] Moreover, no one can rule out Galatians 5:11 as an exegetically possible case of Paul speaking of his pre-Damascus career as an advocate of circumcision.[159] Nevertheless, I do not think that these two cases amount to an evidence for a recognizable socio-historical context by which the pre-Damascus Paul's career is construed or of which he was a part. As our extent sources from the NT, Jewish, and pagan literature[160] do not provide us with a uniform *modus operandi* of Jewish proselytism with any clarity,[161] we have no means of comparison by which we can identify the pattern and location of Paul's former κηρύσσειν περιτομὴν against the

---

155. Note that the title of the article that abstracts his thesis is "Israelite, Convert, Apostle to the Gentiles: The Origin of Paul's Gentile Mission."

156. Dickson, *Mission-Commitment*, 33–49.

157. See above 2.3.2.

158. Donaldson, *Paul and the Gentiles*, 59; Dickson, *Mission-Commitment*, 12–13. Cf. Bird, *Crossing Over Sea and Land*, 97–98. See also n.81.

159. It seems to be unlikely that ἔτι in Paul's retort (εἰ περιτομὴν ἔτι κηρύσσω) simply refers to his opponents' word. Considering Paul's affirmative attitude towards Jewish Christians living according to their tradition (1 Cor 7:17–20, 19:19–23, cf. Acts 16:3), his clear sense of vocation for circumcision-free gospel (Gal 2:8ff), and his Christian stance towards the meaninglessness of circumcision as the means of securing membership in Christ (Gal 5:6), it is unlikely that κηρύσσειν περιτομὴν refers to Paul's advocating circumcision in a similar sense to "preaching Christ" after his conversion. What is the warranted meaning seems to be Paul's certain stance / activity concerning circumcision before his conversion. Cf. e.g. R. N. Longenecker, *Galatians* (Dallas: Word Books, 1990), 232–233.

160. For a comprehensive selection and treatment of the sources see R. Riesner, "A Pre-Christian Jewish Mission?" 220–235.

161. Cf. Bird, *Crossing Over Sea and Land*, 149: "What evidence does exist for it is either ambiguous (like what happened to trigger the expulsions of Jews from Rome), spasmodic (like the activity of Jewish Christian proselytizers), or exceptional (like Ananias and Eleazar in Adiabene)."

background of such Jewish efforts to draw the Gentiles "under the wings of the *Shekhina*" (*b. Shab.* 31a).[162]

While Dickson exclusively bases his thesis on the assumption of Jewish proselytism as a socio-historical background for Paul's mission, his further discussion of Jewish background for Paul's self-conception seems to betray the weakness of his prior assumption. As Dickson (in my opinion rightly) thinks that Paul's self-conception as the authorized eschatological herald of the gospel is best explained by his indebtedness to the traditional Jewish eschatological herald motif running down from Isaiah to the apostle,[163] his focus inevitably turns away from Jewish proselytism. While he fails to observe whether such a herald motif is connected with a socio-historical context in which Jewish proselytism operated,[164] he observes various Jewish texts inspired by the Isaianic eschatological herald motif including texts from the Qumranites (1QH^a 22:10–15; 11Q13; 4Q521)[165] and from the Jesus-traditions (Matt 11:2–6 / Luke 7:18–23; Mark 1:14–15; Luke 4:17–18).[166] What is interesting is that the Jewish socio-historical context from which the two sets of texts stemmed seems to have little to do with Jewish prosleytism but arguably more to do with Jewish hope for the restoration of Israel (cf. e.g. Matt 10:5–6; 15:24), of which the vision was often expressed even in an anti-missionary fashion (e.g. 1QM 1:9–10; 4:12; CD 1:4–10; 2:6–7).[167] This indicates that while Dickson aptly shows Paul's theological indebtedness for his particular self-conception to the Jewish traditional hope for the restoration of Israel, his overall consideration of the

---

162. Cf. Barnett, *Paul: Missionary of Jesus*, 125, who rightly observes that whether or not Eleazar's insisting on the circumcision of Izates implies proseytism or anti-proselytism (i.e. hindering Izates from becoming a proselyte on Ananias' circumcision free terms) is not at all clear.

163. Ibid., 165–173. See also "Paul as an Eschatological Herald," in *Paul as Missionary*, eds. T. Burke and B. Rosner (London: T & T Clark, 2011), 9–24.

164. Note that blessings for Gentiles and proselytism are often mentioned in apologetic explanation for the dispersion of God's people among the Gentiles (e.g. Tob 13:3–6; *b. Pesah.* 87b; *b. Shab.* 31a; *2 Bar.* 1:4; 41:4; Philo, *Mos.* 1.149). Cf. Hvalvik, *The Struggle for Scripture and Covenant*, 273–276.

165. Ibid., 156–158.

166. Ibid., 156–165.

167. Cf. Riesner, "A Pre-Christian Jewish Mission?" 225.

socio-historical context of Jewish proselytism seems to have little to offer in this matter.

The weakest point in viewing Paul's mission exclusively through the lens of Jewish proselytism is its minimalist view of Paul's mission (as if it is a concern and activity for the Gentiles' salvation) and the failure to consider Paul's ongoing concern for the salvation of Israel as his *mission agenda*.[168] As is obvious in Donaldson's study, the framework of Jewish proselytism presupposes two antithetical axes: Israel and the Gentiles. The prerequisite for such a bipolar structure is the ultimately safeguarded status of the former through covenantal relationship to God and the ultimate nature of the latter as the sinful and the lost.[169] Thus, while Donaldson allows no room for Israel's own ontological issue within the framework, he by analogy assumes Paul's mission to be operating between the two similar axes: reconfigured Israel and the Gentiles.[170]

However, as hinted in Romans 9–11 (particularly 11:11–12, 25–27), Paul's mission seems to have a certain triadic structure (the apostle and / or the church - the Gentiles - Israel "κατὰ σάρκα") rather than a bipolar structure. While such a structure may bear various implications, what seems to be probable here is that it stems from his notion of the people of God in a *dialectic* tension between the church and physical Israel (e.g. Gal 6:16; Rom 2:28–29; 9:1–8; 11:13–32).[171] If this consideration is sound, it is difficult to locate Paul's mission within a framework in which the obdurate Israel is awkwardly put aside from consideration. Moreover, even if Paul affirms the church's being right with God in Christ not by the Law (e.g. Rom 3:21ff; 8:1ff), such a relation of redefined Israel to God still comes with the stern warning of the danger of "will be cut off" (ἐκκοπήσῃ, Rom

---

168. Cf. S. Kim, *The Origin of Paul's Gospel* (Tübingen: Mohr Siebeck, 1984), 97.

169. Donaldson, *Paul and the Gentiles*, 52; "Perhaps the most consistent way that Israel's covenantal self-understanding could be extrapolated to the situation of the Gentiles was to see the covenant as a kind of Noah's ark outside of which there was no salvation . . . Gentiles could avail themselves of the possibility of climbing into the ark by means of proselytism."

170. Donaldson, *Paul and the Gentiles*, 236–260.

171. I find L. T. Johnson's "a dialectic within history" ("Paul's Ecclesiology," in *The Cambridge Companion to St Paul*, ed. J. D. G. Dunn [Cambridge: Cambridge University Press, 2003], 202) the most satisfactory description for Paul's perception of the relation of the two.

11:18–22).[172] Here Paul does not base his notion of the people of God on an optimistic covenantal framework,[173] but allows a possibility of God's judgment on his own covenantal people according to their sins.[174] Instead of viewing Paul's mission through the framework of Jewish proselytism in which the status of the people of God is by and large taken for granted, it seems to be more reasonable to compare Paul's mission with the framework of Jewish restorationism, the vision of which generated not only the hope for the restoration of the nation (that will condition the destiny of the nations) but also often dovetailed with various forms of recognition of a certain tension or rupture between the ideal people of God and the current Israel in failure or incompleteness or even under judgment.[175]

Despite the existence and the verisimilitude of Paul's pre-Damascus connection to it, Jewish proselytism in ancient Judaism is found wanting when considered as the background for Paul's mission. While it provides a superficial and partial correspondence in terms of Paul's concern

---

172. Note that other NT uses of the verb (Matt 3:10; 5:30; 7:19; 18:8; Luke 3:9; 13:7; Rom 11:24; 2 Cor 11:12) converge to mean the act of amputation and discarding.

173. Cf. E. P. Sanders, *Paul and Palestinian Judaism*, 75, 422, who suggests a "covenantal nomism" as the fundamental characteristic of Palestinian Judaism in Paul's time in which the matter of "staying" in the covenantal relationship is by and large guaranteed through obedience to Torah while "getting" in the covenantal relationship is understood as purely the matter of God's grace and election.

174. Cf. J. M. Scott, *Paul and the Nations: The Old Testament and Jewish Background of Paul's Mission to the Nations with Special Reference to the Destination of Galatians* (Tübingen: Mohr Siebeck, 1995); Scott, "Restoration of Israel," *DPL*, 799–805; R. B. Hays, *Echoes of Scripture in the Letters of Paul* (New Haven: Yale University Press, 1989), 160–164; N. T. Wright, "The Messiah and the People of God: A Study in Pauline Theology with Particular Reference to the Argument of the Epistle to the Romans," (PhD dissertation, University of Oxford, 1980), 218, who reads some Pauline texts in terms of Paul's Deuteronomic perspective in viewing Israel (Deut 32). Particularly, J. M. Scott ("Restoration of Israel," 797) seems to be correct in criticizing Sanders by pointing that too much emphasis on "continuity in the covenantal relationship between God and his people, and readily available atonement for sin" fails to notice "another major stream of tradition in Palestinian Judaism, which emphasizes prolonged discontinuity in the relationship as punishment for sin." This tendency seems to be not unrelated to Donaldson's thesis as it assumes that Paul was a covenantal nomist (see n.169).

175. E.g. Sir 22:13; 36:13; 1 Macc 1:43–53, 62–64; 3:15–19; 7:9, 22; 9:5–6, 23–27, 51; *4 Ezra* 3:11–17, 36; 7:22–24, 50–61; 8:2–3, 14–18; 9:8–12; *1 Enoch* 5:6–9; 10:16; 80:2–8; 81:7–9; 83:8; 89:73; 90:26–30; 94:4; 99:10; *2 Bar.* 8:33; 24:1–25:24; 29:3–30:3; 41:3; 77:2–6; *T. Mos.* 4:8; *Jub.* 15:34; 23:19; *Pss. Sol.* 8:15–20; 10:6, 9; 12:6; 13:5–10; 17:26–46; CD 1:3–5; 1:12–2:12; 3:19–20; 1QM 10:9; 13:8; 14:8–9; 1QS 4:11–14; 5:22; 8:4; 1QSa 1:6; 1QH 6:7–8; 15:18–21; 1QpNah 3:2–3; 4Q181.

for Gentiles, his self-conception and ecclesial aspects of his mission agenda seem to have more to do with Jewish eschatological hope for the restoration of Israel and its closely related motif of the pilgrimage of the Gentiles. In this regard, we opt to pay more positive attention to the possibility of such a Jewish eschatological hope in our enquiry into Paul's conception of mission and its Jewish background.

However, this will not necessitate an extensive comparative study of Jewish literature of eschatological hope with Paul's missionary idea. Rather, as increasingly appreciated in recent NT scholarship (and particularly among scholars of the historical Jesus),[176] we will assume that one of the most distinctive features of Second Temple Judaism was various aspirations and expressions of the nation's restoration / deliverance by God's decisive eschatological act, of which patterns can be summarized in the expression "Jewish restoration eschatology." And we particularly pay attention to the fact that the Gentiles' fate, if not by all strands of ancient Judaism, was envisioned positively or at least inextricably interwoven with the fate of Israel.[177] With such an assumption, we will simply utilize the pattern of Jewish restoration eschatology for our attempt to build a hypothesis of Paul's conception of mission asking whether his idea is patterned after the Jewish eschatological hope.

1.3.3.2. Conversion and Post-Conversion Factors Contributive to Paul's Concept of Mission

If (the pre-Christian Saul / Paul) Paul's contemporary Jewish environment is important for the question of the background of his conception of mission, factors that radically changed Paul from the zealous persecutor of the messianic sect to the preacher of their faith or that emerged

---

176. Cf. B. F. Meyer, *The Aims of Jesus* (London: SCM, 1979); E. P. Sanders, *Paul, the Law, and the Jewish People* (Philadelphia: Fortress Press, 1983); Meyer, *Jesus and Judaism* (London: SCM, 1985); N. T. Wright, *The New Testament and the People of God* (London: SPCK, 1992); Wright, *Jesus and the Victory of God* (*Christian Origins and the Question of God*; London: SPCK, 1996); J. M. Scott, *Restoration: Old Testament, Jewish and Christian Perspectives* (Leiden: Brill, 2001); S. M. Bryan, *Jesus and Israel's Traditions of Judgment and Restoration*, SNTSMS (Cambridge: Cambridge University Press, 2002); J. Knight, *Jesus: An Historical and Theological Investigation* (London: T. & T. Clark, 2004); B. Pitre, *Jesus, the Tribulation, and the End of the Exile: Restoration Eschatology and the Origin of the Atonement* (Tübingen: Mohr Siebeck, 2005); Bird, *Jesus and the Origins of the Gentile Mission*.

177. Cf. Bird, *Jesus and the Origins of the Gentile Mission*, 26–29.

for his Christian formation process are also very important considerations, since he explicitly talks about the sharp contrast between his former life in Judaism as an outstanding zealous Jew and the revelation of the Son in him that led to his life and ministry in Christ (Gal 1:13–16; Phil 3:5–9): this may mean that Paul experienced a sort of conversion, if not a kind of change of religion,[178] and factors for his missionary thought formation, if not all, cannot be construed purely in terms of a continuity with his former life in Judaism.

In various scholarly discussions with regard to Paul's Christian formation at least three routes are considered: (1) the Damascus road event; (2) the *Sitz im Leben* of pre-Pauline Christian communities; and (3) the memory of Jesus' teaching and work – the Jesus-tradition. If these functioned as constitutive routes for Paul's Christian formation, can Paul's conception of mission also be explained *via* these routes?

1.3.3.2.1. The Damascus event and its impact on Paul's conception of mission

Interpretation of Paul's experience *en route* to Damascus (Gal 1:15–16; 1 Cor 9:1–2; 15:8–11; 2 Cor 4:6; Phil 3:7–8, cf. Acts 9:1–9; 22:4–11; 26:9–18)[179] has been undertaken in a variety of ways, and it would take us too far off course to attempt to consider the whole range of issues related to Paul's conversion / call experience. However, insofar as such an experience had a life-changing impact on the Pharisaic zealot (Phil 3:5–9), and since he specifically connects it with his sense of being called by God (Gal 1:15–16), it is necessary to consider the likely impact of that Damascus experience on his missionary thought and practice in our enquiry.

In earlier discussions (traditional and academic) Paul's Damascus experience was often interpreted psychologically: as the decisive event through

---

178. See below n.187, 188.

179. Even if a few 18th century sceptical scholars attempted to explain Paul's autobiographical references as "overheated imagination" which has nothing to do with the event outside Damascus (e.g. G. Lyttelton, *Observations on the Conversion and Apostleship of St. Paul: By Lord George Lyttelton; with an Introductory Essay by Henry Rogers* [London: R. Dodsley, 1747]), most recent scholars agree in that Paul's biographical references to the revelation of Jesus Christ to him or his having seen Jesus our Lord correspond with Luke's accounts of Paul's Damascus encounter with the risen Jesus. Cf. Dunn, *Beginning from Jerusalem*, 346.

which Paul's troubled conscience in a legalistic Judaism was settled down by his religious conversion into the liberating faith in Christ.[180] Similarly, Paul's universalistic mission (being closely related to such a sense of conversion) was understood in terms of his compensatory outworking of an uneasy psyche by breaking with an exclusivist or particularistic Judaism.[181] However, considering the inappropriateness of the description of Judaism as a wholesale legalistic religion,[182] the inadequacy of psychological approaches to historical data,[183] and Paul's "robust conscience" regarding his pre-Christian Jewish upbringing,[184] this psychological consideration of Paul's Damascus experience and universalistic mission seems to be unsatisfactory[185] and offers little for our enquiry.

Such an introspective reading of Paul's Damascus experience was challenged earlier by Munck.[186] But it was Krister Stendahl who substantially influenced scholars in this regard. Instead of the traditional definition of conversion, Stendahl suggested rather a direct and constituent link between Paul's gentile mission and his experience on the road to Damascus.

---

180. E.g. Aug. *Con.* 8:12; A. D. Nock, *Conversion: The Old and the New in Religion from Alexander the Great to Augustine of Hippo* (Oxford: Clarendon Press, 1933); W. James, *The Varieties of Religious Experience* (New York: Coller MacMillan, 1961). For additional bibliography see Dunn, *Beginning from Jerusalem*, 356, n.159.

181. E.g. A. Deissmann, *St. Paul: A Study in Social and Religious History* (London; Hodder & Stoughton, 1912); J. Klausner, *From Jesus to Paul* (London: Allen & Unwin, 1946); J. S. Stewart, *A Man in Christ: The Vital Element of St. Paul's Religion* (London: Hodder & Stoughton, 1947).

182. E.g. Davies, *Paul and Rabbinic Judaism*; E. P. Sanders, *Paul, the Law, and the Jewish People* (Philadelphia: Fortress Press, 1983). However, it is often noted that both scholars mention Paul's "uneasy conscience" (Davies, *Paul and Rabbinic Judaism*, 63) or "secret dissatisfaction" (Sanders, Ibid., 152) as his pre-conversional Jewish predisposition concerning the issue of law and Gentiles.

183. E.g. W. G. Kümmel, *Römer 7 und die Bekehrung des Paulus* (Leipzig: Hinrichs, 1929); B. R. Gaventa, *From Darkness to Light: Aspects of Conversion in the New Testament* (Philadelphia: Fortress Press, 1986). See also Beker, *Paul the Apostle*, 3-5.

184. E.g. K. Stendahl, *Paul Among Jews and Gentiles, and Other Essays* (Philadelphia: Fortress, 1976), 14-15; Donaldson, *Paul and the Gentiles*, 265.

185. Cf. R. H. Bell, *The Irrevocable Call of God: An Inquiry into Paul's Theology of Israel* (Tübingen: Mohr Siebeck, 2005), 40, n.9. For lasting but modified examples of the psychological approach see G. Theissen, *Psychological Aspects of Pauline Theology* (Edinburgh: T. & T. Clark, 1987), 177-265; D. Boyarin, *A Radical Jew: Paul and the Politics of Identity* (Contraversions; Berkeley: University of California Press, 1994), 39-44, who interprets Paul's conversion and mission in terms of his Hellenistic / universalistic resolution of his troubled conscience within particularistic Judaism.

186. Munck, *Salvation of Mankind*, 11-35.

He argued that what Paul experienced on the road to Damascus was not a conversion (i.e. neither a change of religion nor a resolution of his inner guilt) at all, but a specific call to be the apostle to the Gentiles and a decisive momentum that initiated in him a theological quest for the meaning of the arrival of the messiah for the relationship between Jews and Gentiles.[187] Even if his dismissal of the concept of conversion is challenged by those who argue for the validity of the conversional interpretation of the event,[188] Stendahl rightly illuminates the centrality of the divine calling in the Damascus event and its close connection to Paul's mission-theological reflection.

Subsequent scholarly discussions of Paul's Damascus experience and its relation to his mission-theological reflection have considered other related issues such as: (1) the temporal point at which Paul's sense of calling for gentile mission first entered his mind (e.g. S. Kim,[189] J. D. G. Dunn,[190] F. Watson[191]); (2) the *Sitz im Leben* of the early Christian Paul, whose entry into a Hellenistic Christian community and his nurture within it as a missionary thinker and activist were decisively occasioned by the event (e.g.

---

187. Stendahl, *Paul among Jews and Gentiles*, 7–23. See also Stendahl, "The Apostle Paul and the Introspective Conscience of the West," 78ff.

188. E.g. Kim, *Origin, passim*; A. F. Segal, *Paul the Convert: The Apostolate and Apostasy of Saul the Pharisee* (New Haven: Yale University Press, 1990), 72; J. M. Everts, "Conversion and Call of Paul," *DPL*, 161–162; C. Wanamaker, "'Like a Father Treats His Own Children': Paul and the Conversion of the Thessalonians," *JTSA* 92 (1995): 46–55; most recently Dunn, *Beginning from Jerusalem*, 353–357.

189. Kim, *Origin*, 137–232, 268; Kim, *Paul and the New Perspective: Second Thoughts on the Origin of Paul's Gospel*, (Tübingen: Mohr Siebeck, 2002), 22. He sees it not only as an immediate and inseparable notion from the soteriological formulation of the gospel that comes directly from the event but also as a straightforward result of a verbal commission by the risen Lord (Kim, *Paul and the New Perspective*, 35–37).

190. J. D. G. Dunn, *Jesus, Paul and the Law: Studies in Mark and Galatians* (London: SPCK, 1990), 97–98; Dunn, "'A Light to the Gentiles': The Significance of the Damascus Road Christophany for Paul," in *The Glory of Christ in the New Testament: Studies in Christology in Memory of George Bradford Caird*, eds. L. D. Hurst and N. T. Wright (Oxford: Clarendon Press, 1987), 91–98. He differs from Kim in that Paul's call for the gentile mission is rather an immediate corollary to Paul's recognition of the christophany as God's initial restoration to the situation of Adamic humanity being manifested in Jesus' crucifixion and resurrection.

191. F. Watson, *Paul, Judaism and the Gentiles: A Sociological Approach* (Cambridge: Cambridge University Press, 1986), 28–38, who regards Paul's concern for the Gentiles and the mission to them as a later or secondary development being derived from his initial preaching to Jews and its failure due to their rejection.

H. Räisänen,[192] A. F. Segal[193]); (3) the effect of the event on Paul's pre-Damascus Jewish ideas of universalism, including that of the pilgrimage of the Gentiles into Zion,[194] and openness towards "righteous Gentiles / God-fearers,"[195] and proselytes.[196]

In summary, for those who regard what Paul experienced on the road to Damascus as an immediate call to be the apostle to the Gentiles, the notion that the Damascus event was the origin of Paul's gentile mission is either a straightforward one or a natural corollary. But for those who regard the Damascus event basically as a *driving force* in Paul for his change of communities or for re-configuration of his Jewish predisposition, the event outside Damascus per se is not the origin of Paul's mission since it has more to do with the effect than the cause.

For our current purpose these diverging discussions do not necessarily elicit our either / or response. Rather, we have some light on how to relate the impact of the Damascus event on Paul and his conception of mission. It seems that, on the one hand, the Damascus experience *precipitated* Paul's practice of (gentile) mission in one way or another, but, on the other hand, it is less likely that the immediate impact of the "revelation of the Son" gave Paul a *comprehensive map of mission* from the outset other than an *imperative or necessity of gentile mission*. Even if one may agree or disagree with the hypothesis of Paul's mission-theological reflection within his religious contexts before and after the Damascus event, at least the underlying presumption seems to be agreeable: the impact of the Damascus event was not only formational but also causal so that it touched various areas in and around Paul taking various indirect routes and resulted in more profound effects on Paul's missionary horizon than the immediate effect of the event itself.

---

192. Räisänen, *Paul and the Law*, 251–163.

193. Segal, *Paul the Convert*, xii, 11, 26, 205.

194. E.g. E. P. Sanders, *Paul, the Law, and the Jewish People*, 171; N. T. Wright, *Climax*, 141–151.

195. E.g. L. Gaston, *Paul and the Torah* (Vancouver: University of British Columbia Press, 1987); P. J. Tomson, *Paul and the Jewish Law: Halakha in the Letters of the Apostle to the Gentiles* (Assen [Netherlands]: Fortress Press; Minneapolis: Van Gorcum, 1990).

196. E.g. Donaldson, *Paul and the Gentiles*, 107–164.

1.3.3.2.2. *Paul's conversion and his re-evaluation of the pre-Easter Jesus*

If such a consideration of the impact of the Damascus event is sound, what else can we think of – apart from the direct commission of Paul as the apostle among the Gentiles and the suggested theological and situational corollaries of the event – as decisive factors that might have had a profound, if not a direct, influence on the apostle's conception of mission? Particularly on our question for Paul's missio-ecclesial understanding and its relationship to his own mission does the event have any bearing?

In my opinion, one likely but notably ignored consideration is a scenario in which the Damascus event (and the subsequent period within the Christian context) occasioned Paul's re-evaluation / appreciation of Jesus' teaching and ministry decisively influencing his self-conception as the apostle to the Gentiles and his missio-ecclesial understanding.

It is important to note that, while Paul's missionary theology and practice is adequately dealt with as related directly or indirectly to Paul's Damascus experience, the impact of such an experience regarding his mission-theological reflection about Jesus often tended to be dealt with as if it is exclusively governed by Paul's christological re-evaluation on Jesus of Nazareth as the exalted Christ and the Lord and its implication for the terms of gentile salvation (e.g. Christ-Torah antithesis that leads to a Torah-free membership); aspects of the activities of Jesus, particularly as the leader of a Jewish restoration movement are hardly considered to be influential on Paul's missionary thought and practice.[197]

This tendency seems to have some justification considering that Paul's autobiographical references and Luke's accounts on Paul's conversion all highlight the glorious, heavenly nature of the Son whom Paul encountered.[198] Moreover, Paul's letters exhibit a notable dearth of references to

---

197. Even by one who positively values the influence of the Jesus-tradition on Paul: e.g. S. Kim, *Second Thoughts*, 43, considers, for instance, Paul's learning of some Jesus-traditions about Jesus' attitude toward the rules of the covenant and the food laws that might have affected his law-free gospel and the issue of gentile inclusion. However, Kim does not consider any formational aspect of the Jesus-tradition for Paul's missionary thought and practice, but only as aspect confirming what is christologically derived from Paul's experience at the Damascus event.

198. Cf. Dunn, *Beginning from Jerusalem*, 350.

his dependence or knowledge or allusion to the traditions of the pre-Easter Jesus, while they are full of Paul's mammoth theological reflection on the post-Easter Jesus who is the exalted Christ.[199] Since Rudolf Bultmann regarded these features as indicating that Pauline mission / theology was exclusively interested in the "Easter faith" at the cost of "the historical Jesus,"[200] a vast number of modern and post-modern scholars even among those who do not necessarily agree with Bultmann have a tendency (arguably misleading) to draw a sharp distinction between the exalted Christ in faith or the post-Easter Christ and the Jesus of history or the pre-Easter Jesus, as if the former always eclipses the latter in Paul's thought.

Perhaps, at some different level, scholars' disinterest in the connection between Paul's mission and the ministry of the pre-Easter Jesus seems to be not unrelated to a hard and fast conceptual differentiation of the two movements: Paul's mission in a common scholarly view being conceived to be the matters about gentile conversion (mission in a proper sense of the word)[201] regarding the Jesus movement in the dominant view being conceived to be first and foremost a Jewish movement aimed at the restoration of Israel rather than the salvation of the Gentiles (not mission in a proper sense of the word).[202]

---

199. Cf. W. Wrede, "The Task and Methods of '"New Testament Theology'," in *The Nature of New Testament Theology: The Contribution of William Wrede and Adolf Schlatter*, ed. and trans. R. Morgan (London: SCM, 1973), 104, 105, who claims that Paul's letters contains no *ipsissima verba*.

200. Cf. e.g. R. Bultmann, *Primitive Christianity in Its Contemporary Setting* (London: Thames and Hudson, 1956), 79–92. His assumption of Paul's thorough indifference in the pre-Easter Jesus and the exclusive emphasis on the Easter faith as the heart of Pauline theology stems from a reading of 2 Cor 5:16 as Paul's refusal of knowing Christ "according to flesh" in terms of "the historical Jesus" (e.g. Bultmann, *Glaube und Verstehen* [Tübingen: Mohr Siebeck, 1933], 190ff) and an interpretation of Gal 1:11ff as Paul's denial of his dependence on any Jesus-tradition (deemed to be mediated by a human agent) and the insistence on his apostolic authority solely on the revelation of the risen Christ (e.g. Bultmann, *Theology of the New Testament* [New York: Scribner, 1951–1955], 1:292ff).

201. See above *3.2.1.* and *3.3.1.3*.

202. Cf. J. Jeremias, *Jesus' Promise to the Nations* (London: SCM, 1958), *passim*; Sanders, *Jesus and Judaism*, 218–219; J. P. Meier, *A Marginal Jew: Rethinking the Historical Jesus*, vol. 2 (New York: Doubleday, 1994), 315; J. D. G. Dunn, *Jesus Remembered* (Christianity in the Making; Grand Rapids: Eerdmans, 2003), 539; P. Fredriksen, *Jesus of Nazareth, King of the Jews: A Jewish Life and the Emergence of Christianity* (New York: Vintage Books, 2000), 94.

With the growing consensus regarding the "Jewishness" of both Jesus and Paul,²⁰³ however, the dichotomy between the two figures seems to have waned and is giving way to a new explanation for the two figures' utmost ministerial aims in terms of a Jewish issue of the restoration of Israel.²⁰⁴ If Paul's mission were not only about gentile salvation but also more profoundly about Israel's restoration, a strict categorical differentiation between Paul's mission from the ministry of the pre-Easter Jesus from the outset would lose its justification.

Moreover, as numerous scholars admit today, it is impossible to deny Paul's knowledge about some of the Jesus-tradition and even thought-*relationship* to the pre-Easter Jesus.²⁰⁵ It is widely agreed that Paul, at the very least, uses some materials about Jesus' teaching and life elsewhere in his letters, and it is no less certain that Paul obtained, at some points (or periods) after his conversion, the church's memory of Jesus, *the Jesus-tradition*.²⁰⁶ The ongoing question is how much about the Jesus-tradition Paul knew

---

203. See above n.133.

204. See above n.176.

205. The scholars form a broad spectrum of opinions ranging from those who consider Paul's obvious quotations of several isolated dominical sayings – e.g. N. Walter, "Paul and the Early Christian Jesus-Tradition," in *Paul and Jesus*, ed. A. J. M. Wedderburn (London: T. & T. Clark, 1989), 51–80 – to those who consider Jesus-Paul thought connection in various plausible cases where Paul seems to be alluding to or echoing the Jesus-traditions – most notably D. Wenham, *Paul: Follower of Jesus or Founder of Christianity* (Grand Rapids: Eerdmans, 1995). It is often noted, however, that Paul's thought connection to the dominical tradition does not necessarily amount to his thought connection to the pre-Easter Jesus, since the dominical tradition may or may not be in touch with the historical Jesus. Cf. M. D. Hooker's review "'*Paul: Follower of Jesus or Founder of Christianity?* by D. Wenham," *JBL* 115 (1996): 758; M. W. Yeung, *Faith in Jesus and Paul: A Comparison with Special Reference to "Faith That Can Remove Mountains" and "Your Faith Has Healed / Saved You"* (Tübingen: Mohr Siebeck, 2002), 6. Other scholarly quarters often dispense with the theory of transmission of the Jesus-tradition (whether oral or written) and tend to limit the connection between Paul and the gospel materials only to the Pauline influence on the evangelists – e.g. K. Wegenast, *Das Verständnis der Tradition bein Paulus und in den Deuteropaulinen* (Neukirchen Vluyn: Neukirchener Verlag, 1962), 91–92; M. Goulder, *Midrash and Lection in Matthew* (London: SPCK, 1974), 153–170; D. C. Sim, "Matthew and the Pauline Corpus: A Preliminary Intertextual Study," *JSNT* 31 (2009): 401–422. The recognized difficulties indicate that Paul's thought connection to the pre-Easter Jesus involves not only the issue of Paul's knowledge of the dominical materials but also of the authenticity of the materials.

206. Cf. J. D. G. Dunn, "The Relationship between Paul and Jerusalem according to Galatians 1 and 2," *NTS* 28 (1982): 461–478; most recently Dunn, *Beginning from Jerusalem*, 369.

or to what extent and in what way Paul's use of the Jesus-tradition can be detected (including the issue of dominical authenticity in such traditions). Therefore, while Paul's reticence to mention the Jesus-tradition needs to be accounted for,[207] any explanation which minimizes the significance of the pre-Easter Jesus in Paul's thought and ministry would be perverse.[208]

These factors, then, should allow us to ask whether Paul's conversion / call experience had a crucial impact on Paul's attitude toward Jesus (whether as a Jesus in history or in dominical tradition) who is exalted, revealed and present in one's confessional existence, but also as one who pursued his own mission in a tangible matrix of orthodoxy and orthopraxy, to which, at the very least external level, Paul's own pattern of missionary thought and practice is comparable.[209]

Actually, there are a few attempts (if not interested in the impact / implication of Paul's conversion / call experience) to compare Paul's ministry

---

207. For a systematic review of the history of scholarship on the issue see most recently F. Holzbrecher, *Paulus und der histrische Jesus: Darstellung und Analyse der bisherigen Forschungsgeschichte* (Tübingen: Francke, 2007).

208. Cf. A. J. M. Wedderburn, "Paul and the Story of Jesus," in *Paul and Jesus*, ed. A. J. M. Wedderburn (London: T & T Clark International, 2004), 179: "That such an appeal [to the Jesus-tradition] is for the most part implicit rather than explicit may stem from the fact that it was simply assumed at that stage that Christian beliefs were in fact shaped or to be shaped by that historical reality. In other words there was then no question or possibility envisaged of cutting loose from that foundation story, nor was there any conception that Christian tradition had in any way loosened its hold upon that story."

209. The rationale for the assumption may be stated as follows: (1) Paul's encounter with the risen Jesus had primary significance in his re-evaluation of Jesus of Nazareth. In other words, it was not only about Paul's encounter with one who is exalted and is to come, but also with the one who had already existed in history (cf. e.g. Gal 1.4; 4:4; 1 Cor 9:5; 11:23-25; Rom 1:3; 9:5; 15:8); (2) Paul's recognition of Jesus as the messiah of Israel is directly connected with his missionary preaching. For instance, the reference to Paul's preaching of "the crucified Christ," which is a "stumbling block to Jews" (1 Cor 1:23) self-evidently reflects Paul's own previous evaluation of the pre-Easter Jesus, who was crucified before other Jews as a sinner (cf. Gal 3:1, 13ff; Deut 21:23); (3) if the re-evaluated crucified Jesus as the true messiah of Israel is a part of his preaching and resultant from none other than his unique experience, it is unlikely that such a re-evaluation was limited only to his crucifixion as the messiah: it is more likely that his re-evaluation included every aspect about Jesus that had been known to Paul; (4) if Paul's re-evaluation of Jesus included Jesus' teaching and life and not just his crucifixion, it is unlikely that he ditched or forgot them at the expense of Jesus' crucifixion, resurrection, and appearance to him. Rather, it is likely that he valued and included them in his new or re-oriented understanding and practice after his conversion / call; (5) if some information about Jesus' own thought and practice (rather than the odd isolated sayings) was known to Paul, it is unlikely that Paul disregarded it as irrelevant for his missionary thought and practice (cf. 1 Cor 4:17, 9:14, 11:1).

with that of Jesus in terms of "parallels / correspondences"[210] or a "family resemblance,"[211] focusing on the attitudinal / stylistic similarities of ministry conducted between the two figures. However, any continuity or thought-relation between the two figures in terms of "conception" of ministry / mission or missio-ecclesial understanding seems to be largely untouched. This lead us to a hypothetical consideration of Paul's re-evaluation / appreciation of Jesus' ministry being decisively occasioned by his conversion / call experience and to a particular question of whether Paul's appreciation of the pre-Easter Jesus' thought and practice affected his particular conception of mission.

1.4. Summary

To sum up, in this introductory chapter (1) we have identified the issue of Paul's missio-ecclesial understanding *in relation to* his conception of his own apostolic mission as a reemerging and ongoing debate; (2) by surveying recent scholarly approaches and conclusions regarding the issue, we have identified three areas which require our further investigation: (a) the question of Paul's expectation for congregational evangelism; (b) the question of Paul's conception of mission; (c) the question of the background to Paul's conception of mission; and finally (3) for our further discussion in what follows, we have observed the methodological adequacy / usefulness in defining Paul's mission in terms of an eschatological event, and have postulated the necessity to consider the Jesus-tradition as a background for Paul's conception of mission.

Having stated our focal points and some considerations for method, we will proceed with this study in order to provide a plausible description of Paul's conception of mission that explains what the apostle expected the role of the church to be in relation to his own mission and to identify

---

210. C. Wolff, "Humility and Self-denial in Jesus' Life and Message and in the Apostolic Existence of Paul," in *Paul and Jesus*, ed. A. J. M. Wedderburn (London: T & T Clark International, 2004), 145–160; Wedderburn, "Paul and the Story of Jesus," 180.

211. J. W. Drane, "Patterns of Evangelization in Paul and Jesus: A Way Forward in the Jesus-Paul Debate?" in *Jesus of Nazareth: Lord and Christ: Essays on the Historical Jesus and New Testament Christology*, eds. J. B. Green and M. Turner (Grand Rapids: Eerdmans, 1994), 281–296.

dominical influence in it. This will be pursued first, in chapter 2 by observing various relevant texts from Paul's letters in order to evaluate how Paul understands the church's missional role particularly regarding its evangelistic function: it will be specifically asked whether or not Paul envisions the church being proactive in evangelism; second, in chapter 3 by utilizing the exegetical conclusion drawn from chapter 2 and by considering other relevant Pauline texts and external factors vital to Paul's missiological thought in order to delineate the shape and nature of Paul's conception of mission; and finally, in chapters 4 and 5 by investigating the probable and plausible influences of the Jesus-tradition on Paul's missiological thought in order to elucidate the apostle's indebtedness to dominical ideas and practices which may not be seen purely as common Jewish traits.

So, now we must move on to investigate how Paul understands the church's evangelistic function.

CHAPTER 2

Silence or Non-Silence? An Exegetical Study of Pauline Texts Having Possible Relevance to the Church's Proactive Verbal Proclamation of the Gospel

The aim of this chapter is to investigate exegetically various Pauline texts' interpretation of which may hint at Paul's conception of mission, particularly regarding his idea of the relation between his own apostolic mission and his expectations about the church's missional role.[1] As we have already noted, the examination is to be made regarding whether such a mission relationship between Paul and the church was envisioned by Paul not only in terms of sharing the same *evangelistic intention* but also in terms of sharing the same *evangelistic function*. It is our opinion that for such an

---

1. This aim presupposes (1) that Paul's own letters are the only primary sources for our enquiry into Paul's conception of mission, and (2) that the so called the "Pauline corpus" includes some letters whose epistolary authenticity is under dispute. Regarding Acts, I do not think it relevant to our current aim in this chapter which seeks Paul's own conception. Nevertheless, I do not rule out its usefulness at times in our study at least as a secondary source for the external features of the apostle's missionary practice. Regarding the disputed letters I am sympathetic to the view that they are Pauline in some significant sense, but my concern for pure methodology prefers the undisputed letters over the disputed letters as our relevant sources. As Barram rightly points out (*Moral Reflection*, 13), if a plausible case can be made using only the undisputed letters for methodological purposes, "the subsequent addition of corroborating evidence from Acts and / or the disputed letters would serve only to make the proposal more convincing." In this regard, we will deal with various texts from Paul's generally undisputed letters first, and then texts from the disputed letters will be discussed in addition in order to see whether or not the epistolary authenticity issue affects our exegetical conclusion.

examination we need at least to ask whether there is any clearly recognizable indication in Paul's letters that he intends his evangelistic role to be transferred to the church. This inevitably makes our exegetical treatment of Paul's letters a matter of deciding a "silence" or a "non-silence" in regard to the church's proactive verbal proclamation of the gospel.

2.1. Selecting the Relevant Pauline Passages

For the discussion of the issue, scholars generally consider Paul's texts at least in five different categories: (1) Paul's strategic (geographical) conception of mission assuming further evangelism in the hinterlands by the local communities planted by the apostle; (2) Paul's implicit inclusion of the church's evangelistic responsibility in his exhortation for his converts to imitate himself; (3) Paul's teaching about the church in the use of body / building metaphors which may indicate the church's numeric growth through evangelism; (4) Paul's referencing the church's evangelism with approval; and (5) Paul's explicit / implicit exhortation for the church to evangelize. However, as we need to further define our exegetical aim, not all these alleged cases seem to require our investigation here.

2.1.1. Individual vs Community

First, we need to consider that the continuity of the evangelistic task between the apostle and the church may not be established by some individual church members' ad hoc evangelism. Where a Pauline reference explicitly mentions some individual members' proclamation of the gospel this cannot serve as a criterion for a *functional continuity* between Paul and the church. This will constitute at best some *intentional continuity* between the apostle and the church only where there is a clear indication that such a proclamation is under the aegis both of the church and the apostle. Therefore, to be valid evidence for either silence or non-silence our exegesis should be able to discern if the text provides a clear indication that the evangelism is not only by individual members but also by a local church's concerted aim that derives from an identifiable expectation on Paul's part.

2.1.2. Direct / Active Verbal Engagement vs Passive / Indirect Witness to the Message

Even if a certain activity of the church as a whole such as a community meeting for worship and teaching could have served as the means of sharing of the message of Christian salvation (e.g. 1 Cor 14:23–25), this case does not establish the functional continuity of the evangelistic task between the apostle and the church.[2] Even if this dynamic is certainly assumed by the apostle (1 Cor 14:25), what is assumed is a mere corollary of the community's mature practice of the spiritual gifts, which exposes the essence of the Christian message. Moreover, this exposure of the message in such an indirect manner cannot be equated with Paul's own (or even others missionaries') direct verbal engagement with the gospel message.

2.1.3. Community Accession vs Community (re)Production

Strictly speaking, the continuity of the evangelistic task with Paul is established only when the effect of the message is the same, whether it is a direct evangelism or indirect witness to the message, or whether the church as a whole or individuals. As we have seen in Bowers' argument, Paul's evangelistic task was ultimately aimed at creating a community and bringing it to its full maturity through a few discernibly different evangelistic and nurturing processes (rather than merely a dissemination of the gospel),[3] the continuity of the evangelistic task between Paul and the church (or even any other missionary) cannot be construed simply on the basis of an apparent model of evangelism.[4] If one wants to argue for any functional continuity between Paul and the church, then one will need to show that we have exegetically clear evidence of Paul's expectation for the church's concerted ministry aimed at *community production* rather than merely community accession (and edification). However, such a sharp distinction between production and accession would perpetuate a gulf not only between the apostle and the church but also between him and other early Christian

---

2. Cf. Schnabel, *Early Christian Mission*, 2. 1459.
3. Bowers, "Church and Mission in Paul," 105. See also Ibid., 89; Bowers, "Fulfilling the Gospel," 185–198.
4. Cf. Barram, *Moral Reflection*, 1–9.

missionaries. Therefore, the two previous considerations will be sufficient for our current purpose.

Considering these, passages put forward for cases (1) (Rom 15:19ff) and (2) (1 Cor 11:1; 2 Cor 5:20; Phil 4:9; 1 Thess 1:6; 2:14–16) may be invalid for our current test. In case (1), it can be countered by an ongoing proactive evangelism not necessarily by a whole church activity but by individuals. Even if the congregation's evangelistic role is granted,[5] whether Paul means a concerted proactive evangelism or some sort of indirect witness to the gospel is not discernible at all by the texts.[6] Similarly, in case (2), even if the congregation's evangelistic role as the implication of imitating Paul's model is granted,[7] no decision can be made about the exact nature of such an evangelistic role. In regard to the implication of Paul's body / building metaphor in case (3) (Eph 2:19–22; 4:16), I am sympathetic to those who see the motif of growth / maturity in terms of Paul's (or Deutero-Pauline) missio-ecclesial understanding.[8] But it seems apparent that such a motif of growth / maturity as the body of Christ is primarily an ontological concern rather than the church's outward activity (evangelism?).[9] While these passages are invalid or insufficient for our current test, some passages suggested for the cases (4) and (5), namely 1 Thessalonians 1:8; Philippians 1:5; 1:14; 1:27–30; 2:16; Ephesians 6:15, 17b remain valid material to investigate. They are usually deemed to be Paul's clear references to an evangelism not by individuals but by the church, and the church's evangelistic function not merely indirectly but also directly and proactively. Our test must be directed to these passages.

---

5. Cf. Harnack, *Mission and Expansion*, 74.

6. Cf. Bosch, *Transforming Mission*, 131–138, 168, who seems to suggest the church's ongoing mission to hinterlands is not through a direct evangelism but through attraction to the gospel.

7. Cf. O'Brien, *Consumed*, 105; Plummer, *Paul's Understanding*, 81–92.

8. E.g. E. Schweizer, "The Church as the Missionary Body of Christ," *NTS* 8 (1961–1962): 1–11; G. K. Beale, *The Temple and the Church's Mission: A Biblical Theology of the Dwelling Place of God* (Downers Grove: InterVarsity Press; Leicester: Apollos, 2004), 245–292.

9. Cf. Bowers, "Church and Mission," 95–97. See also R. J. Banks, *Paul's Idea of Community: The Early House Churches in Their Cultural Setting* (Peabody: Hendrickson, 1994), 63–64. For my explanation of the use of "ontological" in the current study, see below chapter 3, n.206.

2.2. Paul's Positive Recognition of the Church's Proactive Gospel-Proclamation?

2.2.1. 1 Thessalonians 1:8

Various exegetes have recognized 1 Thessalonians 1:8 as the most evident reference to a wider diffusion of the gospel by local congregations (at least in Thessalonica).[10] Such an interpretation is based on at least two things: (1) verse 8a which reads "ἀφ' ὑμῶν γὰρ ἐξήχηται ὁ λόγος τοῦ κυρίου" may be read as "the gospel of Christ / God has been proclaimed by the church in Thessalonica"; (2) verse 8b, c which reads "οὐ μόνον ἐν τῇ Μακεδονίᾳ καὶ [ἐν τῇ] Ἀχαΐᾳ, ἀλλ' ἐν παντὶ τόπῳ ἡ πίστις ὑμῶν ἡ πρὸς τὸν θεὸν ἐξελήλυθεν, ὥστε μὴ χρείαν ἔχειν ἡμᾶς λαλεῖν τι" may indicate Paul's admiration of the Thessalonians' powerful and effective proclamation of the gospel that reached the regions of Macedonia and Achaia, and even beyond, so that he finds no need for a further evangelism in those regions by himself.

2.2.1.1. A Consideration of the Context in Verses 6–10

However, such a reading lacks firm exegetical ground. As the connective γὰρ (v. 8a and v. 9a) naturally indicates, it would be unwise to read the verse in isolation from verses 6–7 and verses 9–10. In verses 6–7 Paul's primary referent is to what had happened to the Thessalonians: the fact that they became (ὥστε γενέσθαι) a model or example (τύπος) to all the believers in Macedonia and Achaia. Verse 6 seems to explain how they are such a τύπος: despite affliction (ἐν θλίψει) they became imitators of Paul (and his colleagues) and the Lord by their reception of the word with the joy of the Holy Spirit. In verses 9–10 Paul restates the *contents* of their example

---

10. E.g. Allen, *Missionary Methods*, 125–26; Van Swigchem, *Het Missionair Karahter*, 260; F. F. Bruce, *1 & 2 Thessalonians*, WBC (Waco: Word Books, 1982), 16; E. Best, *The First and Second Epistles to the Thessalonians*, BNTC (London: A & C Black, 1986), 80; L. Morris, *The First and Second Epistles to the Thessalonians*, NICNT (Grand Rapids: Eerdmans, 1991), 50–51; Ware, "Missionary Congregation," 126–131; O'Brien, *Gospel and Mission*, 111; E. J. Richard, *First and Second Thessalonians* (Collegeville: The Liturgical Press, 1995), 70; Marshall, "Who Were the Evangelists?" 259; G. L. Green, *The Letters to the Thessalonians*, PNTC (Grand Rapids: Eerdmans; Leicester: Apollos, 2002), 101–105; A. J. Malherbe, *The Letters to the Thessalonians*, AB (New York: Doubleday, 2000), 117; Plummer, *Paul's Understanding*, 63; Schnabel, *Early Christian Mission*, 2. 1459–1460.

(perhaps for the purpose of encouragement) in the manner of quoting the report (ἀπαγγέλλουσιν) heard from the believers (αὐτοί) whom Paul met and / or is now with, and whom he has already mentioned in verse 7. It includes (1) how they received / welcomed Paul's (and his colleagues') entrance (εἴσοδος); (2) how they returned (ἐπεστρέψατε) from idols to God; and (3) their anticipation of the *parousia* of the Son. Despite the change of language, it seems apparent that the report mentions basically the same as what was mentioned in verses 6–7 (i.e. their conversion by receiving the word from the apostle and their firm faith in [the coming of] Christ).

Regarding the manner in which the Thessalonians were a τύπος to other believers, a few suggested that Paul's "imitators" language in verse 6 implies an inclusion of his evangelistic role.[11] Dickson rejects this view by pointing out that, if such an evangelistic role is included in the Thessalonians' exemplary faith, Paul's restatement of it in verses 9–10 should have included some indication of their dissemination of the gospel to the Greeks.[12]

In favour of Dickson's view, I do not think that one can recognize such an evangelistic intent from the Thessalonians' exemplary faith. Since the Thessalonians' being imitators of Paul and Christ and thus becoming an example to other believers is explicitly connected to their reception of the word (δεξάμενοι τὸν λόγον, v. 6), it is much more reasonable to regard the imitation primarily in the ontological sense (i.e. becoming like Paul and Jesus in terms of their understanding of / relationship to God, albeit still as Gentiles)[13] and to think of their being a model or example simply in terms

---

11. O'Brien, *Gospel and Mission*, 83–107; Ware, "Missionary Congregation," 127; Plummer, *Paul's Understanding*, 60.

12. Cf. Dickson, *Mission-Commitment*, 99: "Why, if the reputation of the Thessalonians were two-fold in v. 8 (mission and faith), does the report about the Thessalonians in v. 9 concern only one aspect of this reputation, namely, the sort of reception the missionary team experienced?"

13. Note that Paul here uses a noun μιμητής rather than a verb μιμέομαι. Perhaps, it would be too strict to discriminate the meaning between the noun and the verb. However, it is to be noted that while Paul's "imitation" language in the undisputed letters is always in the noun form (e.g. μιμηταί γίνεσθε: 1 Cor 4:16; 11:1; 1 Thess 1:6; 2:14, cf. Eph 5:1), we have only two occurrences in the verbal form in 2 Thess 3:7, 9. This may indicate that Paul's imitation language is primarily concerned with ontological aspect of those in Christ that should condition their further behavioural aspects.

of their change of identity and the fidelity to the message that caused such a change (and presumably entailed adversity, cf. 2:14). In the context of verses 6–10, while the effect the message had on the Thessalonians is the primary concern, what they do for the message itself (i.e. evangelism to non-believers) is not in view.[14]

Considering the above, the second part of the evangelistic reading (i.e. "ὥστε μὴ χρείαν ἔχειν ἡμᾶς λαλεῖν τι" [v. 8c] in the sense of a thorough evangelism that left no need for the apostle's further evangelism) seems to turn out immediately to be very improbable: since Paul could realize that the report about the faith of the Thessalonians was well spread among the believers (cf. Rom 1:8), he did not feel any need to speak about it to them.[15] So an evangelistic reading by scholars of the passage seems to be a reading between the lines of verse 8a detached from the context.

2.2.1.2. The Meaning of "From You the Word of the Lord Has Rung Abroad"

The consideration of the context in verses 6–10 leads some to oppose the evangelistic reading. For instance, Bowers concludes that "The 'sounding out' of the 'word of the Lord', whatever the initial impression, may then actually denote not the spreading gospel but instead the spreading report on the gospel's triumph at Thessalonica."[16] Similarly, Wanamaker maintains that ὁ λόγος τοῦ κυρίου is not to be regarded as the message of the gospel but "the report concerning what the Lord has done among you [Thessalonians]."[17]

---

14. Cf. G. D. Fee, *The First and Second Letters to the Thessalonians*, NICNT (Grand Rapids: Eerdmans, 2009), 44. See also V. P. Furnish, *1 & 2 Thessalonians*, ANTC (Nashville: Abingdon, 2007), 46.

15. *Pace* Green, *Thessalonians*, 104.

16. Bowers, "Church and Mission," 99.

17. C. A. Wanamaker, *The Epistles to the Thessalonians: A Commentary on the Greek Text*, NIGTC (Exeter: Paternoster Press; Grand Rapids: Eerdmans, 1990), 83. See also most recently, Fee, *The First and Second Letters to the Thessalonians*, 44.

Apart from the consideration of the context of verses 6–10, such a reading of ὁ λόγος τοῦ κυρίου is suggested by a consideration of the syntactic structure of verse 8 in terms of A-B-A′:

A ἐξήχηται ὁ λόγος τοῦ κυρίου
    B οὐ μόνον ἐν τῇ Μακεδονίᾳ καὶ [ἐν τῇ] ’Αχαΐᾳ, ἀλλ’ ἐν παντὶ τόπῳ
A′ ἡ πίστις ὑμῶν ἡ πρὸς τὸν θεὸν ἐξελήλυθεν

For instance, Dickson finds a chiasmus structure in the verse and concludes that ὁ λόγος τοῦ κυρίου and ἡ πίστις ὑμῶν ἡ πρὸς τὸν θεὸν "contain a synonymous reference to a 'message.'"[18] For Gordon Fee, the two expressions "should be viewed as in near apposition to each other."[19]

However, such an equating or approximation of the two expressions is not convincing. As scholars (who usually adapt the evangelistic reading) rightly point out, Paul would hardly describe the report about someone's conversion as the contents of the "word of the Lord."[20] Even if ὁ λόγος τοῦ κυρίου is not Paul's favourite expression to refer to the message of the gospel,[21] he has already used ὁ λόγος in the sense of his missionary message (therefore the gospel message) in verse 6.[22] And later in 4:15 he mentions "ἐν λόγῳ κυρίου" in the sense of solemn message about / from the Lord or a

---

18. Dickson, *Mission-Commitment*, 100:

Movement of message	A¹ ἐξήχηται
The message itself	B¹ ὁ λόγος τοῦ κυρίου
Place of report	C¹ οὐ μόνον ἐν τῇ Μακεδονίᾳ καὶ [ἐν τῇ] ’Αχαΐᾳ
Place of report	C² ἀλλ’ ἐν παντὶ τόπῳ
The message itself	B² ἡ πίστις ὑμῶν ἡ πρὸς τὸν θεὸν
Movement of message	A² ἐξελήλυθεν

19. Fee, *The First and Second Letters to the Thessalonians*, 44.
20. E.g. Ware, "Missionary Congregation," 327–328; Marshall, "Who Were the Evangelists?" 259; Plummer, *Paul's Understanding*, 88; Schnabel, *Early Christian Mission*, 2. 1459–1460.
21. There is only one occurrence in 2 Thess 3:1 in the sense of the message of the gospel.
22. This may suggest that Paul knew the expression as a conventional reference to the gospel message as Luke did (Acts 8:25; 12:34; 13:44, 48; 15:35, 36; 19:10).

reference to dominical authority.²³ But in 3:6 he describes Timothy's report of the faith of the Thessalonians as "εὐαγγελισαμένου" not bringing "the word of the Lord." This may suggest that while Paul could use εὐαγγέλιον /εὐαγγελίζεσθαι to convey the general sense of (heralding) "good news" as well as the solemn sense of the "good news of Christ," the word of the Lord is always used to convey the solemn sense. Thus, considering all these, "ὁ λόγος τοῦ κυρίου" here is to be read as the gospel message or at least some authoritative message from / about the Lord.²⁴

However, this point does not necessarily undermine our previous point that the Thessalonians' proclamation of the gospel for unbelievers is not in view in the context. Rather, while ἐξήχηται ὁ λόγος τοῦ κυρίου is best understood as referring to the furtherance of the gospel message,²⁵ for several reasons we may think that the active instrument for the furtherance of the gospel is not the Thessalonians but Paul and his colleagues. First, regarding the meaning of ἀφ' ὑμῶν, as Milligan correctly observes, if Paul intended the Thessalonians' "instrumental role" in the furtherance of the gospel, δι' ὑμῶν or ὑφ' ὑμῶν would have been the more natural choice: the most natural rendering of ἀπό here is the "point of departure."²⁶ Second, considering the geographical dimension of Paul's mission in which he continuously

---

23. The meaning of ἐν λόγῳ κυρίου in 1 Thess 4:15 is disputed. While I am inclined to see it as a dominical tradition indicator (cf. J. Jeremias, *Unknown Sayings of Jesus* [London: SPCK, 1964], 81–83; D. Wenham, *Follower*, 305–316), there are other views (cf. M. W. Pahl, D, *Discerning the "Word of the Lord": The Word of the Lord in 1 Thessalonians 4:15*, LNTS [London: T. & T. Clark, 2009], 5–34, 169–171). However, our point is still supported.

24. In this sense, it seems that whether τοῦ κυρίου is a genitive subjective or a genitive objective is not crucial.

25. Cf. 2 Thess 3:1 where ὁ λόγος τοῦ κυρίου clearly refers to Paul's missionary message.

26. G. Milligan, *St. Paul's Epistles to the Thessalonians: The Greek Text with Introduction and Notes* (London: Macmillan, 1908), 32. Cf. Dickson, *Mission-Commitment*, 99. Note that in Gal 1:1 (Παῦλος ἀπόστολος οὐκ ἀπ' ἀνθρώπων οὐδὲ δι' ἀνθρώπου) Paul clearly exhibits his careful distinction between the two prepositions ἀπό and διά. One may suggest 2 Cor 7:13, which reads ὅτι ἀναπέπαυται τὸ πνεῦμα αὐτοῦ (Titus') ἀπὸ πάντων ὑμῶν, as an example in which Paul could use ἀπό instead of the instrumental ὑπό (cf. R. P. Martin, *2 Corinthians*, WBC [Waco: Word Books, 1986], 241). However, such an expectation misses out the point that what gave Titus rest was the Corinthians' positive response to Paul's rebuking letter (vv. 8–9). If the refreshing factor were their direct act or word of comfort to Titus, it would be more natural to have an instrumental preposition than ἀπό. Therefore, it is here grammatically and logically correct for Paul to use ἀπό purely in terms of departure to refer to such a refreshing factor that comes *from* them. Paul's over all usage of ἀπό (occurring 104 times throughout the disputed and undisputed letters) never confuses

made a move from (ἀπό) one place to another, ἀφ' ὑμῶν here is very likely to refer to Paul and his colleagues' further move from Thessalonica to other untouched areas.[27] Third, if one considers Luke's accounts of Paul's mission in Thessalonica (Acts 17:1–10) seriously, it is likely that ἀφ' ὑμῶν here has something to do with Paul and his colleagues' untimely departure from the Thessalonians. This consideration fits well with the Thessalonians' situation which Paul alludes to in the next chapter concerning their suffering at the hands of their own countrymen (v. 14) and Paul's departure from them which made him feel like an orphan ("ἀπορφανισθέντες ἀφ' ὑμῶν," v. 17). This situation suggests that while Paul and his colleagues' departure *from them* (ἀφ' ὑμῶν) was inevitable for their further evangelism in other places (cf. Acts 17:5–10), Paul leaves with an anxiety concerning the faith of the Thessalonians who are left behind. Here, there is little room for Paul thinking of their active evangelism (that even preceded his evangelism in other regions!).[28]

Then, Paul's recall of such a situation aptly explains why Paul juxtaposes in 1:8 his evangelism and the report about the faith of the Thessalonians in such a laudatory way, particularly locating the two reports in the same starting point (ἀφ' ὑμῶν) with the very similar verbs of a great resonance (ἐξήχηται, v. 8a; ἐξελήλυθεν, v. 8c). It is very likely that in verse 8 Paul's rhetoric states how such an anxiety (brought about by his untimely departure from the Thessalonians) was nicely resolved and provided him a ground for thanksgiving. Verse 8a, b states that as he departed from them his message of the gospel was rung out marching powerfully to the regions

---

its usual meaning (i.e. "away from," "out of [separation / departure / origin]" but not "through" or "by" in the sense of a direct subject of the action).

27. Cf. Phil 4:15: "ἐν ἀρχῇ τοῦ εὐαγγελίου, ὅτε ἐξῆλθον ἀπὸ Μακεδονίας"; Rom 15:19b: "ἀπὸ Ἰερουσαλὴμ καὶ κύκλῳ μέχρι τοῦ Ἰλλυρικοῦ πεπληρωκέναι τὸ εὐαγγέλιον τοῦ χριστοῦ." For the geographical dimension of Paul's mission see e.g. Bowers, "Studies in Paul's Understanding of His Mission," 18–80; Riesner, *Paul's Early Period*, 245–253; Schnabel, *Early Christian Mission*, 2. 1294–1300. While whether Paul pursued a systematic geographical plan is an ongoing debate, that Paul's mission was geographically orientated and intended to reach untouched areas is unmistakable (Rom 15:20ff).

28. In Acts 17–18 Luke is silent about any mission that preceded Paul's mission in Macedonia and Achaia. Rather he mentions some Diaspora Jews coming from Thessalonica to persecute Paul's mission (17:13). It is not difficult to imagine that if those Jews from Thessalonica could stir up the local people at Berea to persecute Paul, it would have been much easier for them to stir up local people at Thessalonica to persecute the believing Thessalonians.

of Macedonia / Achaia and beyond (with the help of the Spirit);[29] and verse 8c states his realization / amazement that it is not only his gospel message that was powerfully sounded out but also in the same manner the faith of the Thessalonians (cf. Rom 1:8) whom he thought to be left behind. What is stressed here is the same manner by which the two *different* reports are sounded forth under the *same* divine aegis that transcends human limits.[30] Such rhetorical words would certainly function as a great encouragement for the Thessalonians whose surroundings are hostile to their faith. But it is primarily Paul's expression of his gratitude to God who never allows his itinerant ministry to be in vain (2:1), since his itinerant mission does not merely leave vulnerable young Christians behind him but actually creates a community of the people of God whose fidelity to the word accompanies him for the challenge and benefit of others' faith.

In summary, from 1 Thessalonians 1:8 we are not given any indication that Paul had a positive recognition of the Thessalonians' congregational evangelism, but rather only his amazement at the powerful furtherance of the gospel itself whether preached through his itinerant evangelism or lived out by a local Christian community.

2.2.2. Philippians 1:5

In Philippians 1:3–8 Paul offers his thanksgiving to God in regard to the Philippians. Particularly in verse 5, Paul mentions the Philippians' "sharing in the gospel" (ἐπὶ τῇ κοινωνίᾳ ὑμῶν εἰς τὸ εὐαγγέλιον) as the / a ground for his thanksgiving. The meaning of the phrase can be understood in several different senses: (1) the Philippians' incorporation into what the gospel means for them (e.g. salvation);[31] (2) their monetary involvement in Paul's

---

29. Paul has previously stated that his gospel preaching had come to Thessalonica ἐν δυνάμει (v. 5). So Dickson, *Mission-Commitment*, 102. Cf. Rom 10:18 in which the heralds' voice (that sounds out the ῥῆμα of Christ) reaches the end of the world.

30. Cf. Furnish, *1 & 2 Thessalonians*, 47.

31. Usually by taking the εἰς as a periphrasis for the genitive (cf. e.g. Rom 1:8; 1 Thess 2:3; Phlm 5–6). E.g. H. Seesemann, *Der Begriff* KOINΩNIA *im Neuen Testament* (Giessen: Verlag von Alfred Toepelmann, 1933), 73–76, 79; F. Hauck, "κοινός," *TDNT* 3. 789–821 (805). For more scholars in this regard see Ware, *The Mission of the Church*, 167, n.11; Keown, *Congregational Evangelism*, 211, n.28.

apostolic proclamation of the gospel;[32] (3) their own active evangelistic involvement.[33] In regard to our primary investigation, what particularly draws our attention is view (3), which may lead one to posit a sort of congregational evangelism.[34]

2.2.2.1. A Linguistic Consideration of ἡ κοινωνία ὑμῶν εἰς τὸ εὐαγγέλιον

Perhaps, one of the reasons for the exegetically unsettled discussion of the phrase is Paul's unique construction κοινωνία + εἰς in the NT, and that κοινωνία εἰς τὸ εὐαγγέλιον appears only in Philippians 1:5.[35] Nevertheless, at the same time, Paul frequently employs the noun κοινωνία, the verb κοινωνέω, and their cognates throughout his letters.[36] And there are nu-

---

32. E.g. J. B. Lightfoot, *Saint Paul's Epistle to the Philippians: A Revised Text with Introduction, Notes, and Dissertations* (4th ed. with slight alterations; London: Macmillan, 1898), 81–83; R. P. Martin, *Philippians*, TNTC (Leicester: IVP; Grand Rapids: Eerdmans, 1991), 49; I. J. Loh and E. A. Nida, *A Translator's Handbook on Paul's Letter to the Philippians* (London: United Bible Societies, 1977), 11; D. E. Garland, "Philippians 1:1–26: The Defense and Confirmation of the Gospel," *RevExp* 77 (1980): 329–330; G. F. Hawthorne, *Philippians*, WBC (Waco: Word Books, 1983), 19–20; F. F. Bruce, *Philippians*, NIBC (Peabody: Hendrickson Publishers, 1989), 31; P. T. O'Brien, *The Epistle to the Philippians*, NIGTC (Grand Rapids: Eerdmans: Bletchley: Paternoster, 1991), 62–63; G. D. Fee, *Paul's Letter to the Philippians*, NICNT (Grand Rapids: Eerdmans, 1995), 60–61; G. W. Peterman, *Paul's Gift from Philippi: Conventions of Gift-Exchange and Christian Giving*, SNTSMS (Cambridge: Cambridge University Press, 1997), 100; M. Bockmuehl, *A Commentary on the Epistle to the Philippians*, BNTC (London: Black, 1997), 58; Schnabel, *Early Christian Mission*, 2. 1460; Plummer, *Paul's Understanding*, 73–74; Keown, *Congregational Evangelism*, 212–213. Cf. J. A. Fitzmyer, "The Letter to the Philippians," in *The Jerome Biblical Commentary*, eds. R. E. Brown, J. A. Fitzmyer, and Roland E. Murphy (Englewood Cliffs: Prentice-Hall, 1968), 249, who limits it to material sharing. So Dickson, *Mission-Commitment*, 125–129, while leaving the possibility of a direct evangelistic contribution (125–126), prefers an exclusively material interpretation.

33. E.g. C. J. Ellicott, *A Critical and Grammatical Commentary on St. Paul's Epistle to the Philippians, Colossians, and to Philemon with a Revised Translation* (London: J.W. Parker, 1861), 21; Silva, *Philippians*, 47; J. Gnilka, *Der Philipperbrief*, HTKNT (Freiburg: Herder, 1968), 44–45; Fee, *Philippians*, 82–84; Hawthorne, *Philippians*, 19–20; Bruce, *Philippians*, 31; O'Brien, *Philippians*, 63; Michael, *Philippians*, 62; Loh and Nida, *Philippians*, 11; Peterman, *Paul's Gift*, 101; Bockmuehl, *Philippians*, 60–61; Ware, *The Mission of the Church*, 170; Schnabel, *Early Christian Mission*, 2. 1460; Keown, *Congregational Evangelism*, 207–216.

34. Cf. Keown, *Congregational Evangelism*, 206–232: "[κοινωνία here] includes active congregational evangelism from the Philippian church (1:27c; 2:16; 4:2–3)" (210).

35. Not identical, yet another similar construction in Phil 4:15: ἐκοινώνησεν εἰς λόγον.

36. κοινωνέω: Rom 12:13; 15:27; Gal 6:6; Phil 4:15, cf. 1 Tim 5:22; συγκοινωνέω: Phil 4:14, cf. Eph 5:11; κοινωνία: Rom 15:26; 1 Cor 1:9; 10:16; 2 Cor 6:14; 8:4; 9:13; 13:13; Gal 2:9; Phil 1:5; 2:1; 3:10; Phlm 6; noun / substantive adjective κοινωνός: 1 Cor

merous instances of τὸ εὐαγγέλιον with three other occurrences of εἰς τὸ εὐαγγέλιον in his letters.[37] This may give us some useful, if not conclusive, linguistic hints for Paul's use of the expression in question.

2.2.2.1.1. The active evangelistic sense of εἰς τὸ εὐαγγέλιον (v. 5)

One crucial consideration in understanding the phrase in question is the meaning of εἰς τὸ εὐαγγέλιον. As mentioned above, it was often suggested that εἰς τὸ εὐαγγέλιον here refers to the Philippians' incorporation into the message of the gospel.[38] The implication of such a view is that Paul gives thanks to God because the Philippians' life is harmonious with what the gospel calls for.

Actually, such a passive sense of the gospel is emphatically stressed elsewhere in the same letter (cf. μόνον ἀξίως τοῦ εὐαγγελίου τοῦ Χριστοῦ πολιτεύεσθε, 1:27).[39] However, it is doubtful whether the current εἰς phrase, at least linguistically, denotes such a sense. Rather, it is more likely that the phrase εἰς τὸ εὐαγγέλιον here refers to an active evangelistic sense of the furtherance of the gospel for the following reasons. First, all of the other three instances of εἰς τὸ εὐαγγέλιον (2 Cor 2:12; 9:13; Phil 2:22) are best understood as "for the furtherance / advancement of the gospel."[40] Second, in his thanksgiving section (v. 7) συγκοινωνούς μου τῆς χάριτος is

---

10:18, 20; 2 Cor 1:7; 8:23; Phlm 17; συγκοινωνός: Rom 11:17; 1 Cor 9:23; Phil 1:7, cf. κοινωνικός: 1 Tim 6:18.

37. 2 Cor 2:12; 9:13; Phil 2:22. Cf. Phil 1:12: εἰς προκοπὴν τοῦ εὐαγγελίου.

38. See n.31.

39. Cf. O'Brien, *Philippians*, 147–148.

40. The meaning of 2 Cor 9:13b is often construed in terms of the nature / function of the genitive τῆς ὁμολογίας ὑμῶν (either subjective genitive or objective genitive or epexegetic genitive) or what syntactical end εἰς τὸ εὐαγγέλιον is connected (either to τῇ ὑποταγῇ or to ὁμολογίας or appositionally to both). It is widely construed, however, that in any case the meaning is similar since obedience / subjection and acknowledgement are closely related to each other in Paul's mind – cf. V. P. Furnish, *II Corinthians*, AB (Garden City: Doubleday, 1984), 445 – signifying together the Corinthian's faithfulness to the gospel. Thus, the reading of the verse in a strict syntactical connection of the three phrases ἐπὶ τῇ ὑποταγῇ + τῆς ὁμολογίας + εἰς τὸ εὐαγγέλιον as "a set" produces similar renderings: "for the obedience of the acknowledgement of the gospel of Christ," viz while the passive and confessional sense of the gospel is evident, the active and promotional sense of the gospel, if not ruled out, is not clear. Cf. R. C. H. Lenski, *The Interpretation of St Paul's First and Second Epistles to the Corinthians* (Minneapolis: Augsburg Publishing House, 1963), 1184–1185; C. K. Barrett, *A Commentary on the Second Epistle to the Corinthians*, BNTC (London: Black, 1986, c1973), 240–241; R. P. Martin, *2 Corinthians*, WBC (Waco: Word Books, 1986), 293; F. F. Bruce, *1 and 2 Corinthians*, NCB (London: Oliphants, 1971), 228;

related to Paul's suffering and ministry for the proclamation of the gospel (ἔν τε τοῖς δεσμοῖς μου καὶ ἐν τῇ ἀπολογίᾳ καὶ βεβαιώσει τοῦ εὐαγγελίου).[41] Third, in the adjacent self-report section (v. 12) Paul again clearly mentions the progress of the gospel (εἰς προκοπὴν τοῦ εὐαγγελίου ἐλήλυθεν).[42] Considering these, it is probable that the referent of εἰς τὸ εὐαγγέλιον is in the first instance to the active evangelistic progress of the gospel.

2.2.2.1.2. *The linguistic referent of* ἡ κοινωνία ὑμῶν εἰς τὸ εὐαγγέλιον

What, then, does Paul mean by the phrase ἡ κοινωνία ὑμῶν by combining it with εἰς τὸ εὐαγγέλιον in Philippians 1:5? Because of the active sense of εἰς τὸ εὐαγγέλιον, it is probable that ἡ κοινωνία ὑμῶν denotes the Philippians' certain involvement that results in the advancement of the gospel. In this sense, Lightfoot and other scholars seem to be correct in suggesting that the

---

S. J. Kistemaker, *Exposition of the Second Epistle to the Corinthians*, NTC (Grand Rapids: Baker Book House, 2002), 320.

However, some scholars such as M. E. Thrall, *A Critical and Exegetical Commentary on the Second Epistle to the Corinthians*, vol. 2, ICC (Edinburgh: T. & T. Clark, 2000), 590, and Dickson, *Mission-Commitment*, 129–130 are hesitant to take ὁμολογίας / ὁμολογέω as syntactically connected with εἰς τὸ εὐαγγέλιον. Instead Dickson suggests that "Paul may mean that the Corinthians' 'submission to their confession' is 'for the sake of the gospel of Christ'" (Dickson, *Mission-Commitment*, 129). See also B. Witherington, *Conflict and Community in Corinth: A Socio-Rhetorical Commentary on 1 and 2 Corinthians* (Grand Rapids: Eerdmans, 1994), 71: "obedience to their confession."

In favour of this alternative suggestion, I would suggest that even ὑποταγή is abrupt with the εἰς + the accusative construction in the sense of "subjection to." In two other instances of ὑποταγῇ / ὑποταγή (1 Cor 15:28; Gal. 2:5) the indirect object of the action of submission is the dative. This may indicate that εἰς τὸ εὐαγγέλιον in 2 Cor 9:13 is not syntactically connected with the preceding but only signifies its result. In other words, Paul had already signified by ἡ ὑποταγὴ τῆς ὁμολογίας ὑμῶν the Corinthians' passive obedience to what they confess (according to the gospel) as a set of ideas, and by εἰς τὸ εὐαγγέλιον he indicates, as another set of ideas, the active, but indirect effect of such a passive obedience to the gospel (their almsgiving for the Jerusalem saints).

41. Cf. Keown, *Congregational Evangelism*, 212, who observes that Paul uses the term "the gospel" in the active sense in the thanksgiving sections of other letters (Rom 1:9; 1 Thess 1:5; Col 1:5–6).

42. We may also positively consider scholars' appeal to the notable proportion of the noun εὐαγγέλιον in the sense of "a noun of agency" (e.g. O'Brien, *Philippians*, 62; Dickson, *Mission-Commitment*, 124) or the term's almost "personified" character (e.g. Gnilka, *Der Philipperbrief*, 44) in this direction.

phrase refers to the Philippians active "participation in" or "co-operation in" or "partnership in" the furtherance of the gospel.[43]

However, while we may readily accept such a derivative sense of κοινωνία,[44] it would be misleading if one understands the phrase as if εἰς τὸ εὐαγγέλιον is like a "realm" in which the furtherance of the gospel is actively sought by Paul, and he is delighted by the Philippians' active participation in that realm becoming like the apostle in *function* not only in *intention*. It is to posit a one-to-one correspondence between "your participation / cooperation" and ἡ κοινωνία ὑμῶν, and between "in [the furtherance of] the gospel" and εἰς τὸ εὐαγγέλιον. This is akin to washing away the detail of the linguistic function of κοινωνία / κοινωνέω and the significance of the implication of the language employed in the letter (and particularly in the thanksgiving section).

It is unmistakable that the basic meaning of such κοινωνία / κοινωνέω language is the action of sharing.[45] And the action naturally requires two things: the direct object that is shared and the co-actor that shares the direct object together with the main actor.[46] Therefore, the language, even in the derivative sense "participation" or "cooperation," always retains the

---

43. Lightfoot, *Philippians*, 81: "co-operation in the widest sense, their participation with the apostle"; O'Brien, *Introductory Thanksgivings in the Letters of Paul*, NovTSup (Leiden: Brill, 1977), 25. "active participation"; O'Brien, *Philippians*, 62: "your cooperation [in promoting] the gospel"; Plummer, *Paul's Understanding*, 73: "The Philippians' partnership in the gospel's advance"; Keown, *Congregational Evangelism*, 211: "your active participation in the gospel mission."

44. It is widely held that κοινωνία / κοινωνέω is a derivative of κοινός which means "common" or "mixed / shared / profane," hence perhaps the sense of two parties which mix together or share something together. Cf. Hauck, "κοινός," 789–809; MM, 350; BDAG, 824.

45. See n.43.

46. Thus, for example, in Gal 6:6 the action of sharing has "all the good things" as the direct object and "the instructor of the word" as the co-actor. At times Paul does not clearly specify the two with the noun but the context always aptly shows what the two are. For instance, in 1 Cor 1:9, while God's calling the Corinthians into the fellowship of Christ is the primary referent, the context of the immediately following verses aptly shows that the action of sharing (κοινωνία) in v. 9 has "his Son Jesus Christ" as the direct object (*viz*, the objective genitive) and the Corinthians, despite their party spirit, are the co-sharers with each other of the one Son and the Lord. In the case of δεξιάς κοινωνίας in Gal 2:9 the act of sharing right hands (the direct object) with each other, *viz* Peter and Paul (the indirect object) is clearly implied by the context.

sense of "sharing something in common with some one or others."[47] The question is, then, what is the direct object of the Philippians' action of sharing, presumably with Paul (as the co-actor of the sharing, συγκοινωνούς μου, v. 7)? Can one take εἰς τὸ εὐαγγέλιον, if it signifies the furtherance of the gospel, as if it is the object of sharing or the common ground Paul and the Philippians stand on together as a συγκοινωνός to each other?

However, it seems that it is not the case here. For Paul the specificity of the direct objective of the action of sharing always comes with the genitive case modifier (as the objective genitive).[48] Besides, if the object that is shared is derivatively understood in terms of "realm" (a realm of fellowship and participation) it comes with the dative.[49]

In contrast to these cases, Romans 15:26 (as well as 2 Cor 9:13), often cited as comparison,[50] well illuminates a different linguistic function of εἰς + accusative construction in connection with κοινωνία. Here the function of the εἰς and what follows is clear: simply the result of the sharing or the destination to which the result of the action of sharing reaches. The context clearly shows that the direct object of the action of sharing on the part of the Macedonians and Achaians is the monetary service to help the saints in Jerusalem (διακονεῖν τοῖς ἁγίοις, v. 25),[51] rather than οἱ πτωχοί themselves.[52] And the co-actor (or more precisely the original actor) of the sharing is Paul who primarily holds the ministry (v. 25). While the sharing takes place

---

47. Cf. Hauck, "κοινός," 797: "[κοινωνέω means] to share with someone (to be κοινωνός) in something which he has . . . or to have a share with someone (to be fellow) in something which he did not have." See also Witherington, *Paul's Letter to the Philippians: a Socio-Rhetorical Commentary* (Grand Rapids: Eerdmans, 2011), 56.

48. Rom 11:17; 1 Cor 1:9; 9:23; 10:16; 2 Cor 8:4; 13:14; Phil 1:7; 2:1; 3:10; 4:15; Phlm 6.

49. Rom 12:13; 15:27; Gal 6:6.

50. O'Brien, *Philippians*, 62.

51. Cf. 2 Cor 9:12–13 where the financial aids to the Jerusalem saints (προσαναπληροῦσα τὰ ὑστερήματα τῶν ἁγίων) is clearly stated as the "ministry of the service" (ἡ διακονία τῆς λειτουργίας ταύτης), and the proof of the Corinthians' sharing of such a service (ἡ δοκιμὴ τῆς διακονίας ταύτης) that results in the glorification of God (δοξάζοντες τὸν θεὸν) is grounded on (ἐπὶ τῇ) the sincerity / simplicity of the Corinthians' sharing of such a ministry / service for the sake of them and all (ἁπλότητι τῆς κοινωνίας εἰς αὐτοὺς καὶ εἰς πάντας). Here again, the direct object of sharing is the ministry to help the Jerusalem saints rather than the saints themselves.

52. It is very abrupt if εἰς τοὺς πτωχοὺς is taken as the direct object of the action of sharing.

between Paul and the Gentile Christians, only the benefit (money) of such a sharing of the ministry goes to the Jerusalem Christians.[53]

The linguistic referent of κοινωνία εἰς in Romans 15:26 is exactly the same as that of Philippians 1:5. As verse 7 in the same thanksgiving section clearly indicates (συγκοινωνούς μου), the action of κοινωνία takes place between the Philippians and Paul as the co-actor. However, the direct object of the Philippians' sharing with Paul is not immediately indicated (yet to be unpacked in the latter section of the letter, 4:10ff),[54] while the result of such a κοινωνία is clearly indicated in εἰς τὸ εὐαγγέλιον, the furtherance of the gospel.[55] Therefore, εἰς τὸ εὐαγγέλιον per se, despite its clear indication to the active advancement of the gospel, does not linguistically function to define the nature of the Philippians' κοινωνία in Philippians 1:5.[56]

On what ground, then, can one expect that the Philippians' κοινωνία with Paul for the furtherance of the gospel is to be understood "in the widest sense" even including their "congregational evangelism"? It is surely not on the linguistic ground but possibly on a consideration of the context / contents of the letter.

---

53. It may be said that κοινωνία, *viz* the sharing of money or even fellowship, is made between the Gentiles and the Jerusalem Christians. But it is at best mediated *via* the action of sharing of the monetary service between the Gentiles with the apostle.

54. It is probable that in v. 7 the direct object of the action of sharing between Paul and the Philippians is partly alluded to in ἔν τε τοῖς δεσμοῖς μου καὶ ἐν τῇ ἀπολογίᾳ καὶ βεβαιώσει τοῦ εὐαγγελίου, συγκοινωνούς μου τῆς χάριτος πάντας ὑμᾶς ὄντας.

55. Cf. Dickson, *Mission-Commitment*, 125: "O'Brien's case would be stronger had Paul used κοινωνία followed by the noun εὐαγγέλιον in the genitive or dative case. As it is, κοινωνία + εἰς with εὐαγγέλιον distances the subjects slightly from the activity denoted by 'gospel'. Paul is saying that the Philippians' 'partnership' was for the preaching of the gospel, not in the task of preaching itself."

56. Our suggestion, then, raises a question against O'Brien's critique on Seesemann's and others' treatment of the phrase (O'Brein, *Philippians*, 61–62). While O'Brien's critique is rightly directed to Seesemann's near equating the phrase with "your faith," it is doubtful that Seesemann is wrong because he reads the κοινωνία passively (Ibid., 61) – and because he connects it with what is construed from v. 6 (Ibid., 62). Since the active sense of "your participation in" does not come directly from the noun κοινωνία per se, but rather from the combination of it with εἰς τὸ εὐαγγέλιον, it is more reasonable to think that Paul can regard the Philippians' κοινωνία, whether their passive incorporation into the gospel or their active contribution to it, as the active contribution to the spread of the gospel (cf. 2 Cor 9:13). However, in what way for Paul such a passive incorporation into the gospel can serve for the furtherance of the gospel requires an explanation. For a further discussion see chapter 3.

2.2.2.2. *The Nature of the Philippians'* κοινωνία εἰς τὸ εὐαγγέλιον

2.2.2.2.1. Κοινωνία *as a financial contribution*

What we clearly have as the explanation of such κοινωνία is only found in the latter part of the letter (4:10–20), particularly in 4:14–18. Here Paul's κοινωνία language once used in 1:5, 7 is resumed (συγκοινωνήσαντές μου, 4:14 / συγκοινωνούς μου, 1:7; ἐκοινώνησεν εἰς λόγον, 4:15 / ἐπὶ τῇ κοινωνίᾳ ὑμῶν εἰς τὸ εὐαγγέλιον, 1:5). In the light of Paul's clear mentioning of the common ancient Greek business phrase "giving and receiving" (εἰς λόγον δόσεως καὶ λήμψεως, v. 15, cf. εἰς λόγον ὑμῶν, v. 17),[57] the Philippians' sending to him "for the needs" (εἰς τὴν χρείαν μοι ἐπέμψατε, v. 16),[58] "gift" (τό δόμα) in contrast with "fruit" (ὁ καρπός), and receiving what is sent from the Philippians from Epaphroditus (δεξάμενος παρὰ Ἐπαφροδίτου τὰ παρ' ὑμῶν, verse 18, cf. 2:25), it is unmistakable that the Philippians' κοινωνία refers to their financial contribution to the apostle's ministry. What is more striking is that the resumption of the κοινωνία language comes with the resumption of the various attached qualifiers (τῇ θλίψει, 4:14 / ἕν τε τοῖς δεσμοῖς μου, 1:7; ἐν ἀρχῇ τοῦ εὐαγγελίου ὅτε ἐξῆλθον ἀπὸ Μακεδονίας, 4:15 / ἀπὸ τῆς πρώτης ἡμέρας ἄχρι τοῦ νῦν, 1:5).[59] This strongly suggests that Paul does not simply recall the motif of κοινωνία in the sense of "whatever it may be," but rather *unpacks* what is less clearly indicated in 1:5, 7.

---

57. Cf. J. H. Moulton and G. Milligan, *The Vocabulary of the Greek Testament: Illustrated from the Papyri and Other Non-literary Sources* (London: Hodder and Stoughton, 1930), 186–187, who observe the connection between Phil 4:15 and Papyri Oxy II 275.19 in terms of the function of εἰς which denotes the account into which money is paid. For the well-attested commercial use of the phrase in the ancient Greek literature and the papyri, see Moulton and Milligan, 106; Kittel, "λογος," *TDNT* 4. 104; BGAD, 240–205, 478; P. Marshall, *Enmity in Corinth: Social Conventions in Paul's Relations with the Corinthians*, WUNT (Tübingen: Mohr Siebeck, 1987), 157–164.

58. Cf. Rom 12:13 where ἡ χρεία is used in the material sense with the verb κοινωνέω.

59. For more comprehensive verbal and thematic parallels between 1:3–7 and 4:10–20 see G. W. Peterman, "Giving and Receiving in Paul's Epistles: Greco-Roman Social Conventions in Philippians and in Other Pauline Writings," (DPhil dissertation, King's College, London, 1992), 107–110; Peterman, *Paul's Gift*, 91–92.

While most exegetes agree that the nature of the κοινωνία in 1:5 is aptly elucidated by 4:14–18,⁶⁰ many maintain that the financial sharing is only a part of what Paul means by κοινωνία in Philippians 1:5.⁶¹ For instance, Keown opines that because the contents of the letter include the references to Paul's encouragement of the Philippians' active evangelism (1:27c; 2:16; 4:2–3) κοινωνία in 1:5 is inclusive of their evangelism.⁶² However, it seems that, whether such passages refer to congregational evangelism or not is one thing (and we will come back to this later) and whether by κοινωνία in 1:5 Paul intends to include congregational evangelism is another. This leads us to consider some aspects of the thanksgiving section.

2.2.2.2.2. ἐπὶ πάσῃ τῇ μνείᾳ ὑμῶν (v. 3) as Paul's first ground for thanksgiving

Many exegetes and English translations (e.g. NIV, RSV) read verses 3–4 as the introduction to his first ground for thanksgiving in verse 5, as they read τῇ μνείᾳ ὑμῶν (v. 3b) in the sense of "Paul's remembrance of the Philippians" (ὑμῶν as the objective genitive) and / or ἐπὶ πάσῃ as "every time" or as "every occasion" (ἐπί in the temporal / occasional sense).⁶³

In support, Paul's almost formulaic expression "μνείαν ὑμῶν ποιοῦμαι" in his other thanksgiving sections (e.g. Rom 1:9; 1 Thess 1:2; Phlm 4, cf. Eph 1:16; 2 Tim 1:3)⁶⁴ and the three other constructions of ἐπὶ πάσῃ + dative noun(s) + ὑμῶν which may be rendered as "at the time / occasions of all our . . ." (2 Cor 1:4; 7:4; 1 Thess 3:7)⁶⁵ are often pointed to. However, there are an increasing number of exegetes who prefer an alternative causal

---

60. See n.32.
61. See n.33.
62. Keown, *Congregational Evangelism*, 210–215. Similarly O'Brien, *Philippians*, 63, but only pointing to 1:27, 28.
63. E.g. Gnilka, *Der Philipperbrief*, 42–43; G. P. Wiles, *Paul's Intercessory Prayers: The Significance of the Intercessory Prayer Passages in the Letters of St Paul*, SNTSMS (Cambridge: Cambridge University Press, 1974), 205, n.4; Hawthorne, *Philippians*, 15–17; Fee, *Philippians*, 78–80; Bockmuehl, *Philippians*, 58; U. B. Müller, *Der Brief des Paulus an die Philipper*, THKNT (2ⁿᵈ ed.; Liepzig: Evangelische Verlagsanstalt, 2002), 39; P. A. Holloway, *Consolation in Philippians: Philosophical Sources and Rhetorical Strategy*, SNTSMS (Cambridge: Cambridge University Press, 2001), 88–80.
64. J.-F. Collange, *The Epistle of Saint Paul to the Philippians* (London: Epworth Press, 1979), 43.
65. Cf. BAGD, 287 (II, 2); BDAG, 367 (18, b).

reading of the phrase based on the possibility of reading the ὑμῶν in verse 3 as the subjective genitive, *viz* ἐπὶ πάσῃ τῇ μνείᾳ ὑμῶν as "for all your (the Philippians) remembrance [of me] (Paul)."[66]

Despite the wide acceptance of the temporal reading, there are a few reasons to prefer the alternative causal reading. First, there is no reason to believe that Paul's formulaic use of μνείαν ὑμῶν ποιοῦμαι (in terms of his action of remembering his converts) exhausts his use of the word μνεία.[67] Rather, as in 1 Thessalonians 3:6 Paul certainly recalls Timothy's report about the Thessalonians having always a good memory of Paul and his colleagues (ὅτι ἔχετε μνείαν ἡμῶν ἀγαθὴν πάντοτε), it is most probable that μνεία, like κοινωνία, is a relational term for Paul.[68] Second, despite some instances of the ἐπί + dative constructions possibly in a temporal sense in Paul's letters, in 1 Thessalonians 3:9 Paul uses the ἐπὶ πάσῃ phrase in the causal sense,[69] in particular, with his thankfulness to God (τίνα γὰρ εὐχαριστίαν δυνάμεθα τῷ θεῷ, v. 9a).[70] This context makes a good thematic

---

66. E.g. P. Schubert, *Form and Function of the Pauline Thanksgivings* (Berlin: Alfred Töpelmann, 1939), 74; W. Schenk. *Die Philipperbriefe des Paulus: Kommentar* (Stuttgart: W. Kohlhammer, 1984), 94; R. Jewett, "The Epistolary Thanksgiving and the Integrity of Philippians," *NovT* 12 (1970): 50; Martin, *Philippians*, 61; O'Brien, *Philippians*, 59–61; Peterman, *Gift from Philippi*, 93–99; B. Witherington, *Friendship and Finances in Philippi: The Letter of Paul to the Philippians* (Valley Forge: Trinity Press International, 1994), 38; Dickson, *Mission-Commitment*, 123; J. Reumann, *Philippians: A New Translation with Introduction and Commentary*, AYB (New Haven, Conn: Yale University Press, 2008), 102–103.

67. O'Brien, *Philippians*, 60, rightly distinguishes between "remembrance" as the meaning of μνεία when used in an ἐπί prepositional phrase and "mention" as the connotation of it when used with the verb ποιοῦμαι. See also Reumann, *Philippians*, 102–103. O'Brien also points to Bar 5:5 where the genitive can qualify the causal dative μνείᾳ as the subjective genitive "χαίροντας τῇ τοῦ θεοῦ μνείᾳ" (rejoicing upon God's remembrance [of the Israelites]). So Dickson, *Mission-Commitment*, 123. Pace M. R. Vincent, *A Critical and Exegetical Commentary on the Epistles to the Philippians and to Philemon*, ICC (Edinburgh: T. & T. Clark, 1897), 6.

68. Cf. Witherington, *Paul's Letter to the Philippians: a Socio-Rhetorical Commentary* (Grand Rapids: Eerdmans, 2011), 56.

69. It reads "Τίνα γὰρ εὐχαριστίαν δυνάμεθα τῷ θεῷ ἀνταποδοῦναι περὶ ὑμῶν, ἐπὶ πάσῃ τῇ χαρᾷ ᾗ χαίρομεν δι' ὑμᾶς ἔμπροσθεν τοῦ θεοῦ ἡμῶν."

70. See also 1 Cor in which ἐπί + dative in the thanksgiving section is used in the causal sense. O'Brien, *Philippians*, 59, observes that it is only when ἐπί is followed by the genitive that it is used in a predominantly temporal sense in the opening Pauline thanksgivings (Rom 1:10; Eph 1:16; 1 Thess 1:2; and Phlm 4).

and verbal parallel with that of Philippians 1:3.[71] Third, and most importantly, if ἐπὶ πάσῃ τῇ μνείᾳ ὑμῶν is read in the casual sense, it immediately provides the reason for Paul's thanksgiving (εὐχαριστῶ τῷ θεῷ μου) – the reason for which is not immediately clear when the ἐπί phrase is read in the temporal sense.[72] This means that the Philippians' remembrance of Paul was the first ground for his thanksgiving, making their κοινωνία εἰς τὸ εὐαγγέλιον in verse 5 the second.[73]

2.2.2.2.3. μνεία and κοινωνία as the expression of the Philippians' concern for Paul

If what we have considered above is sound, we now have the two relational nouns μνεία (v. 3) and κοινωνία (v. 5) in a neat parallel. They both are the causes of Paul's thanksgiving. And they both refer to what the Philippians did concerning Paul. But, more importantly, they both prompt Paul's reflections in return concerning the Philippians (v. 4 and v. 6):[74]

Ground 1   A   ³ἐπὶ πάσῃ τῇ μνείᾳ ὑμῶν

Reflection 1   B   ⁴πάντοτε ἐν πάσῃ δεήσει μου ὑπὲρ πάντων ὑμῶν μετὰ χαρᾶς τὴν δέησιν ποιούμενος

Ground 2   A′   ⁵ἐπὶ τῇ κοινωνίᾳ ὑμῶν εἰς τὸ εὐαγγέλιον ἀπὸ τῆς πρώτης ἡμέρας ἄχρι τοῦ νῦν

Reflection 2   B′   ⁶πεποιθὼς αὐτὸ τοῦτο ὅτι ὁ ἐναρξάμενος ἐν ὑμῖν ἔργον ἀγαθὸν ἐπιτελέσει ἄχρι ἡμέρας Χριστοῦ Ἰησοῦ

---

71. Cf. O'Brien, *Philippians*, 59: "Indeed, when ἐπί with the dative is used after εὐχαριστέω it always expresses the ground for thanksgiving; I know of no instance in the extrabiblical Hellenistic sources where ἐπί τινα after εὐχαριστέω indicates anything other than the cause for thanksgiving."

72. Cf. Witherington, *Philippians*, 56: "Why would Paul tell the Philippians he is thankful to God that he has remembered them? . . . It is rhetorically more likely then that Paul is thankful for their remembrance of him here."

73. Dickson, *Mission-Commitment*, 123, n.121: "This would make for a neat syntactical and thematic balance with v. 5 in which Paul offers his second ground for thanksgiving."

74. O'Brien, *Philippians*, 63, regards v. 6 as Paul's third ground for thanksgiving. However, this reading seems to downplay the parallel between v. 4 and v. 5 and the thought connection between v. 5 and v. 6. Rather, it is to be noted that ἄχρι and ἡμέρας in v. 5 are repeated in v. 6 and πεποιθὼς αὐτὸ τοῦτο is more naturally connected with the following ὅτι clause than the preceding clause. See also Fee, *Philippians*, 85; Dickson, *Mission-Commitment*, 127; Keown, *Congregational Evangelism*, 216.

The importance of this observation is that what we have here are rhetorically stressed exchanges made between the two parties. Regardless of what the nature of the relation of the two nouns is, or what the exact meanings and implications of the two nouns are (often expected to be widely inclusive!), μνεία and κοινωνία here function as intermediation between the Philippians and Paul for their exchange of concerns for each other before God.

The nature of such an exchange of concerns seems to be clear from the context of 4:10ff. As most commentators agree, Paul mentions in 4:10 the Philippians' resumed material support brought by Epaphroditus (cf. 2:25) as the expression of their ongoing concern (φρονεῖν) for Paul.[75] While this makes an unmistakable parallel with 1:3,[76] it aptly shows that Paul's two grounds for thanksgiving are reiterated in the latter section of 4:10–20, not separately, but as one theme, namely the Philippians' financial gift for Paul particularly for his need while he is in chains (4:14–18).[77] As Paul receives their concern expressed in the material support, he first expresses his concern in return for them in his ceaseless entreaty in joy for all of them (v. 4) and then his conviction about God's ultimate completion of his "good work" (ἔργον ἀγαθόν) commenced in the Philippians (v. 6).[78] The mutual concern between the apostle and his congregation, thus, is exchanged in

---

75. Cf. 1 Thess 3:6–9.

76. Since ὅτι which starts 4:10 is causal for Paul's rejoicing in the Lord, and the cause for the joy is the Philippians' revived expression of concern for the apostle. Cf. Dickson, *Mission-Commitment*, 126.

77. Peterman, *Paul's Gift*, 92: "Paul's response to the Philippians' gift is not an afterthought. Though the message of 4.10–20 is more concrete and specific, that message is basically a reiteration of the thought found in 1:3–11."

78. The meaning of ἔργον ἀγαθόν here is interpreted generally in three different ways: (1) God's own redemptive work (e.g. Martin, *Philippians*, 63; Loh and Nida, *Philippians*, 12; Silva, *Philippians*, 52; O'Brien, *Philippians*, 64–65: "new creation"; Witherington, *Philippians*, 60: "internal sanctification"); (2) God's work by human means (e.g. Hawthorne, *Philippians*, 21; Bockmuehl, *Philippians*, 62; J. M. Gundry Volf, *Paul and Perseverance: Staying In and Falling Away*, WUNT (Tübingen: Mohr, 1990), 34; (3) Works for the proclamation of the gospel (e.g. Ollrog, *Mitarbeiter*, 70–75, 171; "missionswork"; Dickson, *Mission-Commitment*, 127–128; Keown, *Congregational Evangelism*, 218–-219: "dual reference" to God's redemptive work and the gospel work (with the emphasis on the later). While I am inclined to the second view, there seems to be no overriding reason to reject any of them, since the three seem to be all closely related. However, the third option seems to be prone to blurring the difference between direct proclamation and indirect witness to the gospel.

terms of "giving and receiving" (4:15) of the material gift and the spiritual blessing (cf. 4:17–19).

As Peterman and others rightly point out, however, this reciprocity is not to be seen as a mere typical feature of an ancient friendship letter in which one's expression of friendship often appears as a money transaction entailing one showing favour in return.[79] Rather, Paul's focus is on his joy in the implication or the result of such reciprocity, namely the furtherance of the gospel. Nevertheless, it is undeniable that the participation language per se refers to the Philippians' material support.

In summary, while by no means may we rule out the possibility of the Philippians' being active in evangelism, it is doubtful that such an active evangelism is implied by Paul in his use of κοινωνία in Philippians 1:5. Our consideration of the linguistic referent of κοινωνία ὑμῶν εἰς τὸ εὐαγγέλιον and the rhetorical implication of 1:3–6 in light of 4:10–20 narrows down the scope of the Philippians' κοινωνία. And it is in the first instance material sharing with Paul. While such an ongoing friendship in material sharing (κοινωνία, 1:5b; 4:15–18) for Paul's ministry and suffering (1:7c; 4:18) is recognized as a praiseworthy contribution (καλῶς ἐποιήσατε, 4:14, ὀσμή εὐωδίας δεκτή εὐάρεστος τῷ θεῷ, 4:18) to the furtherance of the gospel (εἰς τὸ εὐαγγέλιον, 1:5) prompting his thanksgiving to God (1:3), neither Paul's κοινωνία language nor the context of his thanksgiving gives a clear indication of the Philippians being actively involved in evangelism. The Philippians' evangelistic contribution that we can identify in Philippians 1:5 is one made *via* the apostle, or one made *via* what they did εἰς τὸν Παῦλον.

2.2.3. Philippians 1:14

Many exegetes read Philippians 1:14 as referring to multiple Christians' evangelism in the city of Paul's imprisonment, not in terms of individual Christian preachers in particular but the Christians in general or a

---

79. Peterman, *Paul's Gift*, 121–162. He particularly rejects J. P. Sampley's case for Paul's relationship with the Philippians in the pattern of the Roman consensual *societas* (*Pauline Partnership in Christ: Christian Community and Commitment in Light of Roman Law* [Philadelphia: Fortress Press, 1980]). See also e.g. Bockmuehl, *Philippians*, 263–267; Witherington, *Philippians*, 18–19; O'Brein, *Philippians*, 534–535.

congregation in the city.⁸⁰ This exegetical ground provides a few scholars with a launching pad from which they develop an argument for the "church's mission" or "congregational evangelism" – functionally identical with Paul's own evangelism – not least as the contents of Paul's expectation for the church's κοινωνία εἰς τὸ εὐαγγέλιον (1:5).⁸¹

2.2.3.1. οἱ ἀδελφοί as a Congregation or Individual Christians?

Often emphasized and favoured, under exegetical consideration, is the inclusive nature for the term οἱ ἀδελφοί in Paul's letters. For instance, while affirming that οἱ ἀδελφοί can refer to a more restricted group of persons when they need distinction from other Christians in general (e.g. Rom 16:14; Phil 4:21; Gal 1:2; 2 Cor 11:9), Ware observes that "in all such cases the precise nature of the restriction is expressly defined within the context."⁸² Ware goes on to remark that "Paul's use of the term ἀδελφός with reference to specific co-workers does not function as an official title, but reflecting the egalitarian character of early Christian missionary language, describes them as fellow believers belonging to the Lord."⁸³ This

---

80. E.g. Lightfoot, *Philippians*, 88; Vincent, *Philippians*, 17–18; Martin, *Philippians*, 186; Fee, *Philippians*, 115; O'Brien, *Philippians*, 94; Michael, *Philippians*, 33; Hawthorne, *Philippians*, 35; A. Motyer, *The Message of Philippians: Jesus Our Joy* (2ⁿᵈ ed.; Leicester: IVP, 1997), 69–70; H. C. G. Moule, *The Epistle of Paul the Apostle to the Philippians* (Cambridge: Cambridge University Press, 1923), 19–20; Bockmuehl, *Philippians*, 76; Loh and Nida, *Philippians*, 21; Garland, "Defense," 332; F. B. Craddock, *Philippians* (Atlanta: John Knox Press, 1985), 25; Silva, *Philippians*, 78 (with a reservation, 69); W. Hendrickson, *Philippians*, NTC (Edinburgh: Banner of Truth, 1962), 70; J. H. Houlden, *Paul's Letters from Prison: Philippians, Colossians, Philemon and Ephesians* (Harmondsworth: Penguin, 1970), 56; L. G. Bloomquist, *The Function of Suffering in Philippians*, JSNTSup (Sheffield: JSOT Press, 1993), 149; Witherington, *Friendship*, 45; F. W. Beare, *Philippians* (London: Black, 1959), 59; T. Hawthorne, "'Philippians i.12–19.' With special reference to vv. 15.16.17," *Expository Times* 62 (1950–1951): 316–317; H. A. Kent Jr., "Philippians," in *EBC*, ed. F. Gaebelein, vol. 11/12 (Grand Rapids: Zondervan, 1978), 111; Ware, *The Mission of the Church*, 181–182; Schnabel, *Early Christian Mission*, 2. 1460; Plummer, *Paul's Understanding*, 73; Keown, *Congregational Evangelism*, 81; Reumann, *Philippians*, 173.

81. Ware, *The Mission of the Church*, 170, 175–186: "The language of the thanksgiving period itself would imply that the Philippians' partnership for the gospel involved more than their financial support of Paul's mission, and this is confirmed by 1:12–14, where Paul is interested in the advancement of the gospel through the direct missionizing activity of Roman Christians." See also Keown, *Congregational Evangelism*, 73–86, 210.

82. Ware, *The Mission of the Church*, 182.

83. Ibid. See also C. Forbes, "Prophecy and Inspired Speech in Early Christianity and Its Hellenistic Environment," (PhD dissertation, Macquarie University, 1987), 301.

leads him to conclude that "used apart from such delimitations, the term in the context of Philippians 1:12–14 must refer to Christians generally, in 1:12 (ἀδελφοί) to the Christians at Philippi and in 1:14 (τῶν ἀδελφῶν) to the Christians at Rome."[84] Similarly, Keown argues that οἱ ἀδελφοί of verse 14 "should be taken inclusively of all Christians in the church (including co-workers) in Paul's context who were inspired into proactive evangelism by his presence in prison."[85]

On the contrary, some others regard οἱ ἀδελφοί as the technical term for a group of specialized evangelists (e.g. "Mitarbeiter") and maintain that Philippians 1:14 is one case.[86] E. Ellis, for example, pays attention to the definite article which consistently accompanies the plural ἀδελφοί whenever it refers to co-workers in distinction from the Christians in general and the anarthrous use of the vocative ἀδελφοί being used for its collective sense.[87] In favour of Ellis' case, Dickson stresses "the statistical weight of evidence" of twenty-four times for οἱ ἀδελφοί in the sense of "Paul's colleagues" out of forty-six occurrences of the expression, concluding that "οἱ ἀδελφοί is most naturally read as a technical designation – like διάκονος and σύνδουλος – for a recognized co-worker in the Pauline mission."[88]

Ellis and Dickson's case is plausible but not probable. It is more natural to think that the consistent appearance of an article is purely grammatical (i.e. Paul uses it not necessarily because "the brothers" are missionaries but because of the specific identity of the brothers in contrast to the rest of congregation, whether the brothers are missionaries or not [cf. e.g. 1 Cor 8:12; 1 Thess 4:10]). What we can safely say from Paul's use of (οἱ) ἀδελφοί is that the term describes the familial relationship of Christians toward all their fellow believers.

---

84. Ware, *The Mission of the Church*, 182.

85. Keown, *Congregational Evangelism*, 73, 81.

86. E. Ellis, "Paul and Co-workers," *NTS* 17 (1971): 446; Gnilka, *Der Philipperbrief*, 59; R. Jewett, "Conflicting Movements in the Early Church as Reflected in Philippians," *NovT* 12 (1970): 369; Ollrog, *Mitarbeiter*, 194–196; Dickson, *Mission-Commitment*, 144–152.

87. Ellis, "Paul and Co-workers," 445–448. So Dickson, *Mission-Commitment*, 145–147.

88. Dickson, *Mission-Commitment*, 145–147.

However, our point does not necessarily support Ware's and others' case for Philippians 1:14, arguing against the possibility of "the brothers" being some other individuals apart from the church. While it cannot be argued that οἱ ἀδελφοί here refers to missionary colleagues because it is a technical term for the meaning, we must allow the possibility that οἱ ἀδελφοί at least here is referring to a group of Christians in distinction from the congregation simply because of the specificity given from the article and their practice of evangelism. Even if the specificity of οἱ ἀδελφοί in verse 14 does not follow as in Romans 16:14–15 or Philippians 4:21–22 etc., this cannot automatically indicate that οἱ ἀδελφοί is used here inclusively as if it is equivalent to οἱ ἅγιοι or ἡ ἐκκλησία.[89] It is also to be noted that while οἱ ἅγιοι and ἡ ἐκκλησία are always used to convey the collective sense, namely Christians as a congregation or the church,[90] it is evident in Philippians 4:21b that Paul can use οἱ ἀδελφοί to refer to individual Christians in distinction from a community (v. 22a). And Paul certainly prefers the two collective terms to οἱ ἀδελφοί when he clearly refers to the entire congregation in contrast to specific brothers (e.g. Rom 16:15; Phil 4:22; Gal 1:2; 1 Cor 16:19; 2 Cor 11:8). It may be worth asking, therefore, if Paul wanted to mention the brothers at the place of his chains in terms of the church or a congregation, why did he not employ one of his preferred terms? And why did he even modify οἱ ἀδελφοί with οἱ πλείονες rather than οἱ πάντες (cf. 1 Cor 16:20)?[91]

2.2.3.2. ἐν κυρίῳ Modifying οἱ ἀδελφοί or πεποιθότας?

Another exegetical ground for the argument for congregational evangelism is the function of ἐν κυρίῳ in verse 14. Following many exegetes who

---

89. Ware, *The Mission of the Church*, 181, n.63. While Ware notes the similar function of οἱ ἀδελφοί and οἱ ἅγιοι as the general designations referring to all Christians or to all Christians in a given locality, he does not consider the difference between the two terms in Paul's usage.

90. οἱ ἅγιοι: e.g. Rom 1:7; 12:13; 15:25; 15:26; 15:31; 16:2; 16:15; 1 Cor 1:2; 6:1, 2; 14:33; 16:1, 15; 2 Cor 1:1; 8:4; 9:1, 12; 13:12; Phil 1:1; 4:21, 22; 1 Thess 3:13; 5:26, 27. ἡ ἐκκλησία: e.g. Rom 16:1–5, 16, 23; 1 Cor 1:2; 6:4; 7:17; 10:32; 16:19; 2 Cor 1:1; 8:1; Gal 1:2, 13, 22; Phil 3:6; 4:15; 1 Thess 1:1; 2:14; 2 Thess 1:1; Phlm 2.

91. Cf. O'Brien, *Consumed*, 115, who is one of the proponents of reading the phrase as "the Christians in general" even remarks that "[the brothers] appear to be individual Christians, rather than a church as a church, who were engaged in this praiseworthy endeavour."

favour the syntactic link between ἐν κυρίῳ and πεποιθότας,[92] Ware contends that God's activity expressed in the phrase ἐν κυρίῳ "has an instrumental force" and "identifies the increased courage of the believers as the work of God."[93] The implication of this reading is reminiscent of O'Brien's thesis, as we have mentioned earlier, that the source of evangelism is the spirit of Christ / God: evangelism, therefore, is for every one in the Lord. It again implies for Ware that the Philippians' missionizing partnership with Paul is through sharing the same direct evangelism, since Paul mentions in Philippians 1:12–14 the Roman Christians' direct evangelism (according to Ware's estimation) is not merely as "apologetic" but "rather paradigmatic and paraenetic."[94] While such a function of the Lord for the Christian's bold evangelism has some theological justification, it is doubtful that it is a Pauline idea or that one should read Philippians 1:14 in that way.

2.2.3.2.1. οἱ ἀδελφοί ἐν κυρίῳ as a Pauline expression

We need to note that scholars do not provide overriding reasons for why ἐν κυρίῳ here modifies the participle rather than οἱ ἀδελφοί. For instance, Fee rules out οἱ ἀδελφοί ἐν κυρίῳ as improbable Pauline language since he thinks that ἐν κυρίῳ would be a "redundancy" if it modifies οἱ ἀδελφοί, which already refers to Christians in general.[95] Lightfoot observes a few instances of ἐν Χριστῷ / ἐν κυρίῳ modifying ὁ ἀδελφός in two disputed letters (i.e. Col 1:2; 4:7; Eph 6:21), and concludes that "the brothers in the Lord" does not stand out as Pauline language.[96]

In light of our previous discussion, Fee's estimation seems to be hasty since the inclusive nature of οἱ ἀδελφοί here is not conclusive. It is true that we have no exact parallel elsewhere in the undisputed Pauline letters. However, considering Paul's general use of ἐν κυρίῳ stressing the

---

92. E.g. Lightfoot, *Philippians*, 88; Ellicott, *Philippians*, 32; H. von Soden, "ἀδελφός," *TDNT* 1. 144, n.1; Gnilka, *Der Philipperbrief*, 59, n.29; Hawthorne, *Philippians*, 35; Garland, "Defense," 332; O'Brien, *Philippians*, 94–95; Silva, *Philippians*, 68–70; Bruce, *Philippians*, 42; Bockmuehl, *Philippians*, 76; Loh and Nida, *Philippians*, 21; Craddock, *Philippians*, 25; Ware, *The Mission of the Church*, 178–179.
93. Ware, *The Mission of the Church*, 179.
94. Ibid., 185.
95. Fee, *Philippians*, 115–116.
96. Lightfoot, *Philippians*, 88.

particularity of Christian existence, life and ministry,[97] there seems to be no reason for Paul to eschew ἐν κυρίῳ to modify Christians, whether collectively or individually, as a redundancy.[98] Rather, Paul in Romans 16:11 calls those belong to Narcissus' household (οἱ ἐκ τῶν Ναρκίσσου) "ὄντες ἐν κυρίῳ." This seems to be not far from calling them οἱ ἐκ τῶν Ναρκίσσου ἐν κυρίῳ. If this is the case for Philippians 1:14, viz οἱ ἀδελφοί [οἱ ὄντες] ἐν κυρίῳ, it would well make sense as a typical Pauline expression. This should alert one not to rashly rule out the case of ὁ ἀδελφός ἐν κυρίῳ in the disputed letters as un-Pauline language.

2.2.3.2.2. πεποιθότας τοῖς δεσμοῖς μου

In favour of ἐν κυρίῳ + πεποιθότας, Fee further points to Philippians 2:24; Galatians 5:10; Romans 14:14; and 2 Thessalonians 3:4, where ἐν κυρίῳ qualifies the verb to mean "to have confidence in the Lord."[99] It is true that Paul in the verses clearly mentions a confidence "in the Lord." It is doubtful, however, that such cases are applicable to ἐν κυρίῳ πεποιθότας in Philippians 1:14.

While Paul clearly uses πείθω + ἐν κυρίῳ to refer to a conviction in the Lord, he always does so in regard to his own conviction in the Lord. While Paul once negatively uses πείθω + ἐν dative construction to refer to "having confidence in the flesh" (Phil 3:3, 4),[100] πείθω + ἐν κυρίῳ is never used in relation to others. Besides, Paul's conviction in the Lord always denotes the definiteness and clarity of his idea regarding the truth or the matter of his apostolic ministry being always accompanied by a ὅτι clause to specify

---

97. Rom 14:14; 16:2, 8, 11ff, 22; 1 Cor 1:31; 4:17; 7:22, 39; 9:1f; 11:11; 15:58; 16:19; 2 Cor 2:12; 10:17; Gal 5:10; Phil 1:14; 2:19, 24, 29; 3:1; 4:1f, 4, 10; 1 Thess 3:8; 4:1; 5:12; Phlm 16, 20. Cf. 2 Thess 3:4; Col 3:18, 20; 4:7, 17; Eph 2:21; 4:1, 17; 5:8; 6:1, 10, 21. Cf. Oepke, "ἐν," *TDNT* 2. 541, who reads οἱ ἀδελφοί in Phil 1:14 in connection with ἐν κυρίῳ for the meaning of "membership" in the church.

98. Dickson, *Mission-Commitment*, 148, critiques Fee's view by pointing that Paul makes a similar redundancy by adding ἐν Χριστῷ to the "saints" (Phil 1:1).

99. Fee, *Philippians*, 116.

100. Phil 3:3: "... οἱ πνεύματι θεοῦ λατρεύοντες καὶ καυχώμενοι ἐν Χριστῷ Ἰησοῦ καὶ οὐκ ἐν σαρκὶ πεποιθότες." The location of ἐν σαρκὶ modifying from before πεποιθότες is a stylistic inversion. Besides the sense of πέποιθα is more about "trusting" or even "boasting" than "being emboldened."

the contents of such a conviction.[101] This seems to suggest that Paul uses πείθω + ἐν κυρίῳ in the sense of the Lord's illumination and direction in his own apostolic ministry rather than the Lord's emboldening and encouraging power.

Another difficulty in reading ἐν κυρίῳ πεποιθότας in the sense of the Lord as the source or instrument of evangelistic zeal is a syntactical one. While some scholars resort to dual instrumental modifiers from before (ἐν κυρίῳ) and after (τοῖς δεσμοῖς μου) the verb or the ἐν κυρίῳ as a sphere in which the Christians gain confidence to preach through Paul's chains,[102] the result is an unusual location of ἐν κυρίῳ with an abrupt function of the phrase τοῖς δεσμοῖς μου which immediately follows the verb.[103]

Of course, no one can rule out the possibility that what we have in Philippians 1:14 is Paul's unusual expression with an unnatural word order. However, the problem in such a reading is not only a linguistic or syntactical one but also a logical one. As Dickson rightly points out, if Paul wanted to mention a conviction to proclaim as being emboldened by the Lord or by being in the sphere of the Lord, one must explain how Paul in verses 15–18 could mention the preachers who were ill-motivated (τινὲς . . . διὰ φθόνον καὶ ἔριν . . . οἱ ἐξ ἐριθείας . . . οὐχ ἁγνῶς οἰόμενοι θλῖψιν ἐγείρειν τοῖς δεσμοῖς μου).[104]

Considering the positive estimation of οἱ ἀδελφοὶ ἐν κυρίῳ as a Pauline expression and the deficiency in ἐν κυρίῳ + πεποιθότας, it seems more natural to read the perfect participle πεποιθότας as being modified only by the following dative τοῖς δεσμοῖς μου. This reading well accords with the

---

101. See also Rom 8:38; 15:14; 2 Cor 2:3; Phil 1:6, 25 where πέποιθα with a ὅτι clause refers to Paul's own conviction in terms of his definiteness about something.

102. E.g. Reumann, *Philippians*, 174; Ware, *The Mission of the Church*, 178–179; Keown, *Congregational Evangelism*, 73.

103. Fee, *Philippians*, 116, argues, in support of his reading ἐν κυρίῳ modifying backward, that "all the other modifiers in this clause also stand in emphatic first position," viz ἐν κυρίῳ before πεποιθότας, περισσοτέρως before τολμᾶν, and ἀφόβως before λαλεῖν. However, this structure, if granted, is quite notably disturbed by τοῖς δεσμοῖς μου. It seems to be more reasonable to count two emphatic first position adverbial phrases, namely (a) περισσοτέρως τολμᾶν and (b) ἀφόβως . . . λαλεῖν, as the participle πεποιθότας is clearly modified by τοῖς δεσμοῖς μου from behind.

104. Dickson, *Mission-Commitment*, 148, n.61. Considering the immediate mention of the preachers in the contrasting motives (v. 15), it seems to be improbable that the preachers in v. 14 and those in v. 15ff are different groups. Cf. Reumann, *Philippians*, 173.

context of verses 12–18. Paul repeatedly mentions οἱ δεσμοί μου (1:7, 13, 17), which is an important topic in the self-report section. In verse 12 Paul hopes for the Philippians to know that "things happened to me" (τὰ κατ' ἐμέ) have turned out rather "for the progress of the gospel" (εἰς προκοπὴν τοῦ εὐαγγελίου). It is most probable that, as most commentators agree, τὰ κατ' ἐμε generally refers to, or at least includes οἱ δεσμοί Παύλου.[105] In this light of οἱ δεσμοί μου as the cause for the progress of the gospel and the latter mentioning of the two groups of preachers in verses 15–18, it seems to be very likely that Paul mentions his imprisonment in verse 14 as the cause for the multiple brothers' motivation, whether pure or impure (vv. 15–17), for the proclamation that at any rate resulted in the progress of the gospel (v. 18).

2.2.3.3. A Certain Degree of Specificity in οἱ πλείονες τῶν ἀδελφῶν ἐν κυρίῳ

Considering the previous points, it seems best to take οἱ πλείονες τῶν ἀδελφῶν ἐν κυρίῳ as a single construction, which is a logical subject-phrase[106] descriptive of a group of Christians and πεποιθότας τοῖς δεσμοῖς μου περισσοτέρως τολμᾶν ἀφόβως τὸν λόγον λαλεῖν as a logical predicate-clause, which is mainly descriptive of their action (λαλεῖν). On this syntactical ground, we may see, particularly because of the modifying ἐν κυρίῳ and the comparative substantive adjective οἱ πλείονες, that οἱ ἀδελφοί Paul mentions in verse 14 is not as general as others regard it to be.

The modifier ἐν κυρίῳ may refer basically to the brothers' membership to the church, as Oepke has noted.[107] But in the light of Romans 16 where Paul uses ἐν κυρίῳ to specify Christian individuals, and Colossians 4:7 and Ephesians 6:21 where Tychicus is specifically called ὁ ἀδελφός ἐν κυρίῳ, a certain specificity or even delimitation in the phrase οἱ ἀδελφοί ἐν κυρίῳ, if not a separation from the rest of the church, seems to be unmistakable.

---

105. Cf. O'Brien, *Philippians*, 89–90.

106. I use "logical" here in distinction from "grammatical," thus, I mean by "logical subject-phrase" an actual actor / subject part within a long sentence, while the actual "grammatical" subject is Paul, the subject of the verb βούλομαι of v. 12. Cf. M. A. K. Halliday, *Introduction to Functional Grammar* (London: Arnold, 1985), 31–37, who distinguishes three different categorical functions within a complex sentence: "grammatical," "psychological," and "logical."

107. Oepke, "ἐν," 541.

Even if the delimitation is not given in a clear contrast to the entire congregation as is in Romans 16:14; Philippians 4:21; Galatians 1:2; and 2 Corinthians 11:9, it is certainly identifiable by the high probability of the two differently motivated groups of preachers (vv. 15–18) to be none other than the brothers mentioned in verse 14.

As discussed above, Paul's presentation of his own imprisonment as the cause of the proclamation (v. 12, 14, 17) is to be taken as an exegetical key to understanding the identity of the brothers of verse 14 and the preachers of verses 15–18. It seems very likely that Paul mentions the same brothers throughout the self-report section: it was Paul's chains that are responsible for the emboldened evangelism by the brothers in the Lord (vv. 12–14), whose identity the Philippians may or may not recognize, yet among whom, on the one hand, some were positively motivated (v. 16) by Paul's confinement, on the other hand, others were negatively motivated (v. 17).[108] If οἱ πλείονες τῶν ἀδελφῶν ἐν κυρίῳ refers to "the majority of the Christians in the city of Paul's chains," one needs to envisage the church or the house churches where most of the members responded to Paul's adversity through evangelism with a particular motive, positive or negative. While this is not entirely impossible, it is more likely that such a vibrant evangelism as the response to Paul's adversity either in good will or in opposition would be expected from those who had a similar position or role to Paul's own within a Christian community.[109]

In this estimation of the identity of ὁ ἀδελφός ἐν κυρίῳ in verse 14, the substantive adjectival οἱ πλείονες is not to be taken as indicative to the majority of the brothers at the city as the Christians in general (in the sense of ἡ ἐκκλησία or οἱ ἅγιοι).[110] Whether it means the superlative sense

---

[108]. See Hawthorne, *Philippians*, 36; Fee, *Philippians*, 118; Michael, *Philippians*, 37; O'Brien, *Philippians*, 98; Reumann, *Philippians*, 197–201. *Pace* e.g. Bruce, *Philippians*, 19; Vincent, *Philippians*, 18; Gnilka, *Der Philipperbrief*, 60, who see vv. 15–18 as referring to a different group from those in v. 14.

[109]. See R. Jewett, "Conflicting Movements," 369. In this regard, Dickson's suggestion that "it is probable that Paul has, in fact, sought to distinguish between the anarthrous 'brothers' of v. 12 (the recipients of the letter) and 'the colleagues' of v. 14 by the modifying phrase ἐν κυρίῳ ('in / for the Lord')" (*Mission-Commitment*, 148) is weighty, even if it cannot be proved.

[110]. *Pace* Plummer, *Paul's Understanding*, 73; Keown, *Congregational Evangelism*, 85, n.77.

"the most / majority of" (e.g. 1 Cor 10:5; 15:6) or purely the comparative sense "the increased number of" (e.g. 2 Cor 4:15),[111] it most likely refers to the multiplicity of those Christian individuals within the loosely defined group of those specifically motivated to speak the word of the Lord publicly. Furthermore, if Paul's stress on the paradoxical result of his adversity (i.e. the progress of the gospel, v. 12, 18) is rightly appreciated, the purely comparative sense of οἱ πλείονες, namely "more and more brothers in the Lord," makes more sense than the superlative sense.

In summary, without necessarily resorting to Ellis' hypothetical technical term οἱ ἀδελφοί, our observation shows that the brothers who vibrantly preached the gospel in the city of Paul's confinement are less likely to be the Christians in general. A certain specificity suggested by the expression οἱ πλείονες τῶν ἀδελφῶν ἐν κυρίῳ and the consideration of the context of 1:12–18 aptly indicate that what Paul mentions in Philippians 1:14 is not a wider scale of diffusion of the gospel by a congregation being emboldened by the Lord, but, somewhat paradoxically, yet obviously as the mark of God's grace (1:13, 29), the progress of the gospel through the increased number of the Christian brothers who wanted to speak the word more boldly in public.

2.3. Paul's Exhortation for Proactive Congregational Evangelism?

2.3.1. Philippians 1:27–30

A number of scholars have pointed to Philippians 1:27–30 as a section where Paul's evangelistic exhortation for the community is in view.[112] For instance, O'Brien takes Paul's exhortation in 1:27 (μόνον ἀξίως τοῦ

---

111. For the comparative sense of οἱ πλείονες see e.g. BDAG, 824; C. F. D. Moule, *An idiom book of New Testament Greek* (2nd ed.; Cambridge: University press, 1959), 108; R. G. Bratcher. *A Translator's Guide to Paul's Second Letter to the Corinthians* (London: United Bible Societies, 1983), 47, 48; Martin, *2 Corinthians*, 82, 91; NIV; NRS. Cf. Barrett, *Second Epistle to the Corinthians*, 136, 144, who reads it superlatively.

112. E.g. D. van Swigchem, *Her Missionair Karakter*, 260; O'Brien, *God and Mission*, 116–117; O'Brien, *Philippians*, 148; V. C. Pfitzner, *Paul and the Agon Motif: Traditional Athletic Imagery in the Pauline Literature*, NovTSup (Leiden: Brill, 1967), 116–120, 152; Ware, *The Mission of the Church*, 216–223; Keown, *Congregational Evangelism*, 109–124.

εὐαγγελίου τοῦ Χριστοῦ πολιτεύεσθε) primarily in terms of Paul's reminding the Philippians of "the prior action of God in their midst" for their life "wholly committed to the advance of the gospel, that is, its dynamic onward march, they will walk worthily of the gospel by holding fast to it, preaching and confessing it in spite of opposition and temptation."[113] The implication of such a reading of the verse is that, by ἀξίως τοῦ εὐαγγελίου τοῦ Χριστοῦ, Paul does not simply expect the community's life to be faithful to what the gospel of Christ means to them (i.e. in terms of *fidelity* to the contents / message of the gospel),[114] but also their active and outward effort for the cause of the faith of the gospel (i.e. its spread and growth), the task of which is the same as that of Paul.[115]

In his subsequent publication,[116] O'Brien points to three considerations in support of his evangelistic interpretation: (1) the meaning of the imperative, πολιτεύεσθε is encompassing the whole dimension of Christian life which includes evangelism; (2) the meaning of the participle, συναθλοῦντες is to be interpreted through its athletic metaphor which Paul uses for contending for his apostolic gospel-proclamation; (3) Paul's connection in verse 30 of his own struggle (ἀγών), which is for the furtherance of the gospel, with that of the Philippians.[117]

Following O'Brien's lead, Keown stresses the importance of the participial clause συναθλοῦντες τῇ πίστει τοῦ εὐαγγελίου (v. 27c) as the key to understanding Philippians 1:27–30.[118] Preferring τῇ πίστει as a "dative of interest or advantage," thus, to mean "to promote belief in the message of the Lord,"[119] Keown reads the clause to be referring to the Philippians'

---

113. O'Brien, *Philippians*, 148.

114. Cf. Rom 16:2; 1 Thess 2:12; Eph 4:1; Col 1:10; 3 John 6.

115. O'Brien, *Philippians*, 152: "The Philippians were to stand united in their struggle for the cause of the faith – its spread and growth, the same goal that was set before all of Paul's work."

116. O'Brien, *Gospel and Mission*, 116–117.

117. See Ware, *The Mission of the Church*, 216–218; Keown, *Congregational Evangelism*, 103–104, 117–123. Cf. Pfitzner, *Paul*, 82–129.

118. Keown, *Congregational Evangelism*, 108–109. See also Ware, *The Mission of the Church*, 216.

119. Keown, *Congregational Evangelism*, 113–114. See also e.g. BDAG, 964; Pfitzner, *Paul*, 116; Vincent, *Philippians*, 34; Gnilka, *Der Philipperbrief*, 99; Fee, *Philippians*, 166; Hawthorne, *Philippians*, 57; O'Brien, *Philippians*, 152; Bockmuehl, *Philippians*, 99; Reumann, *Philippians*, 268. See also Dickson, *Mission-Commitment*, 105–106, who, while

corporate struggle in "all manner of contending for the faith of the gospel including evangelism."[120]

Even if Ware finds in Paul's exhortation in verse 27 no indication to "active verbal mission," he thinks that the Philippians are exhorted to spread the message "through conduct and suffering motivated by a missionary purpose."[121] Ware further contends that Paul expected the Philippians' mission through conduct and suffering (v. 27) to be "complemented by an active mission of verbal proclamation" (1:28).[122] In support, he argues that Paul had already provided a "paradigm" in 1:12–26, in which the Roman Christians' evangelism (1:14) and his own mission (1:19–20) are identified in terms of courageous speaking of the gospel in the face of opposition, and this paradigm is practically applied in verse 28 to the Philippians to "display their own fearlessness through bold confession and proclamation of the gospel."[123]

2.3.1.1. ἀξίως τοῦ εὐαγγελίου τοῦ Χριστοῦ

The first issue at stake is whether Paul's emphatic exhortation μόνον ἀξίως τοῦ εὐαγγελίου τοῦ Χριστοῦ πολιτεύεσθε can be interpreted as an imperative of the Philippians' active proclamation of the gospel. O'Brien's interpretation of verse 27a involves taking πολιτεύεσθαι ἀξίως τοῦ εὐαγγελίου to refer to the Philippians' conduct *beneficial to* the gospel. This seems to be ignoring the usual semantic function of the adverb ἀξίως which primarily signifies the authoritative nature in what follows the adverb (normally as a genitive case, similarly to κατὰ + accusative) and the subordinate nature in the verb which is qualified by ἀξίως. Thus, its usual meaning "in a manner worthy of" or "in conformity to"[124] is not in the sense of the consequence of an action (of the verb) directed *towards* what follows ἀξίως, but rather in the sense of an authority of what follows ἀξίως to control or define the preceding verb to have a desirous contents and consequence.

---

preferring the dative of advantage, rightly points to the significant difference between the advancement of "the gospel itself" and that of "the faith of the gospel."

120. Keown, *Congregational Evangelism*, 116.
121. Ware, *The Mission of the Church*, 217.
122. Ibid., 220.
123. Ibid., 219–220 (220).
124. Cf. BDAG, 94.

Therefore, what O'Brien contends for is to *redirect* the consequence of the verb πολιτεύεσθαι towards "the gospel of Christ" as the beneficiary of the action. In the light of other biblical cases and other Paul's own cases where ἀξίως never makes what follows it a beneficiary of the conduct,[125] O'Brien's case here is an ingenious idea.

It is no exception in Philippians 1:27a, where ἀξίως τοῦ εὐαγγελίου functions as the authoritative control for the verb πολιτεύεσθαι. The immediate and obvious referent of ἀξίως τοῦ εὐαγγελίου is to the role of the gospel of Christ as the source or authority for the Philippians' proper conduct expressed in the imperative πολιτεύεσθε. The emphatic concern (μόνον, cf. Gal 2:10) in Paul's exhortation is, then, not the Philippians' contribution to the spread of the gospel, but the imperative for the community's right mode of life as *informed by* the good news of Christ. Therefore, πολιτεύεσθε is not simply a case of all encompassing reference to any possible behaviour (including evangelism), but the word Paul had carefully chosen stresses primarily the Philippians' identity as the citizens of the community of the gospel, whose communal life is to be governed by the gospel of Christ, and whose citizenship is not in the Roman territory but in heaven (3:20).[126]

Considering such a primary sense of the imperative as the *fidelity to* the message that the Philippians had already embraced (i.e. the gospel),[127] O'Brien's redirection of the consequence of the fidelity to the gospel towards the furtherance of the gospel seems to be derived primarily not from exegetical, but theological,[128] grounds.

---

125. Cf. Wis 7:15, 16:1; Sir 14:11; Rom 16:2; 1 Thess 2:12; Eph 4:1; Col 1:10; 3 John 6.

126. It is often suggested that πολιτεύεσθαι is almost equivalent to the more usual verb περιπατεῖν "to walk" (Rom 6:4; 8:1, 4; 13:13; 14:15; 1 Cor 3:3; 7:17; 2 Cor 4:2; 5:7; 10:2f; 12:18; Gal 5:16; Phil 3:17f; 1 Thess 2:12; 4:1, 12. Cf. 2 Thess 3:6, 11; Col 1:10; 2:6; 3:7; 4:5; Eph 2:2, 10; 4:1, 17; 5:2, 8, 15). Cf. BGAD, 649. While the similarity between the two verbs in Paul is to be acknowledged, the particular appropriateness of the former within the letter is unmistakable. Cf. Bockmuehl, *Philippians*, 98; Fee, *Philippians*, 162.

127. Cf. Witherington, *Philippians*, 96.

128. O'Brien, *Philippians*, 62, 148: "[in Phil 1:27a] Paul draws attention once again to that dynamic personal entity (εὐαγγελίον) to which he has referred so often in the chapter, in which Christ is mighty at work in its proclamation (for when the gospel is preached he is the one who speaks) and which at the same time has him as the centre of its contents" (Ibid., 148).

2.3.1.2. τῇ πίστει *as the Dative of Location and Instrument*

The further issue, then, is whether the primary sense of the imperative πολιτεύεσθε is complemented by Paul's extended idea in the clause ὅτι στήκετε ἐν ἑνὶ πνεύματι μιᾷ ψυχῇ συναθλοῦντες τῇ πίστει τοῦ εὐαγγελίου (v. 27c) as a more explicit evangelistic exhortation, namely the Philippians' corporate contending "for the furtherance of the faith of the gospel."

Due to its unusual construction, it is very difficult to know the exact meaning of τῇ πίστει τοῦ εὐαγγελίου in verse 27c. Some have taken the dative as an instrumental dative, as in "through / by means of the faith,"[129] or as a dative of association, as in "together / in concert *with* the faith" (as a personified entity).[130] More exegetes, including O'Brien, prefer the dative as one of "interest" or "advantage."[131]

It is important to note, however, that O'Brien's rendering provides no reason for endorsing the evangelistic interpretation of verse 27c. As parallel to "contending for the faith," O'Brien and others point to Jude 3, which reads ". . . ἀνάγκην ἔσχον γράψαι ὑμῖν παρακαλῶν ἐπαγωνίζεσθαι τῇ ἅπαξ παραδοθείσῃ τοῖς ἁγίοις πίστει" (. . . I felt the necessity to write to you exhorting you to contend for the faith that was once passed on to the saints).[132] It is reasonable to take the dative τῇ . . . πίστει as a dative of interest or advantage as long as the faith is the direct interest of the fighting (ἐπαγωνίζεσθαι). It is to be noted, however, that the interest in τῇ πίστει here primarily refers to the interest in the Christians' preservation of and their fidelity *to* the faith, which was at once soundly passed on to them, and now is put into danger of contamination by those who secretly crept into the community (v. 4). While the interest in outwardly spreading the faith is not in view, it is clear that the faith is to be soundly maintained among

---

129. J. Calvin, *The Epistles of Paul the Apostle to the Galatians, Ephesians, Philippians, Colossians*, trans. T. H. L. Parker (Grand Rapids: Eerdmans; Carlisle: Paternoster Press, 1996), 27; BDF #195.

130. BDF #193; Lightfoot, *Philippians*, 105; E. Lohmeyer, *Der Brief an die Philipper*, KEKNT (Göttingen: Vandenhoeck & Ruprecht, 1964), 75–76. Michael, *Philippians*, 66–67, in opposition to the view, argues that there is no parallel of personified faith in Paul's view and the view downplays the cooperation on the part of the Philippians.

131. See n.119.

132. O'Brien, *Philippians*, 152; V. C. Pfitzner, *Paul*, 116; Beare, *Philippians*, 66; Gnilka, *Der Philipperbrief*, 99; Loh and Nida, *Philippians*, 40.

the members of the community by their contending *for it* against the threat which undermines the faith (v. 4) and their community (v. 12, 19).

Despite the significant difference between the two texts / letters (authors, audiences and contexts), the manner of the Christians' contending for the faith is strikingly similar. They, in both the communities, are exhorted to contend so that the *orthodoxy* of the faith remains sound among them, either by fighting against false teaching (or a teacher) that undermines their faith (Jude 3) or by contending together against the external adversaries who threaten their faith (Phil 1:27c, 28), so that they can continue to live in the sound *orthopraxy* of the faith, by "building themselves upon their most holy faith" (τῇ ἁγιωτάτῃ ὑμῶν πίστει ἐποικοδομοῦντες ἑαυτούς, Jude 20), or by "standing firm on the faith of the gospel" (στήκετε ἐν ἑνὶ πνεύματι μιᾷ ψυχῇ συναθλοῦντες τῇ πίστει τοῦ εὐαγγελίου, Phil 1:27c).[133]

What is important in this observation is that the interest or advantage expressed in the dative does not exhaust the intended sense of ἡ πίστις in Philippians 1:27c. Rather, it is probable that τῇ πίστει τοῦ εὐαγγελίου is intended to qualify the main verb στήκετε as well as a dative of location / sphere,[134] or even instrument,[135] and thus as the authority or means for sound orthopraxy in the Philippians' communal life. Without resorting to non-Pauline sources like Jude, we may consider some Pauline support. First, Paul's conception of πίστις in his letters emphatically displays its causative character in the course of salvation (cf. Gal 2:16; Rom 1:5–17; 3:22–30; 4:9–20; 5:1–2; 9:30–32; 10:9; 11:20).[136] Second, Paul often exhibits his understanding of the faith to be functioning to bring firmness or cause for steadfastness in Christians' life (e.g. διὰ τῆς πίστεως . . . νόμον

---

133. Witherington, *Philippians*, 104; Dickson, *Mission-Commitment*, 106, draw a sharp distinction between orthodoxy and orthopraxy of the gospel in favour of the latter. Cf. Hawthorne, *Philippians*, 57, who favours orthodoxy here. This seems to be an unnecessary dichotomy.

134. Cf. Rom 14:1; 2 Cor 13:5; Phil 3:9; Col 1:23; 2 Tim 3:10; Titus 1:13; 2:2; 2 Pet 1:5; Acts 6:7. See also 1 Chr 9:22; 14:22.

135. Cf. Rom 4:20; 5:2; 11:20; 1 Cor 16:13 (location is also possible); Col 2:7; Heb 4:2; 1 Pet 5:9; Acts 15:9; 16:5 (location is also possible).

136. Even if Paul can use the faith as an object of proclamation (cf. Gal 1:23: εὐαγγελίζεσθαι τὴν πίστιν ἥν ποτε ἐπόρθει), the faith always serves as the means for one who holds or lives by it to maintain a proper relationship with God (e.g. Rom 1:5, 16:26: εἰς ὑπακοὴν πίστεως; Gal 2:16; Rom 3:20, 26; 5:1; 9:30: ἡ δικαιοσύνη ἐκ πίστεως).

ἱστάνομεν, Rom 3:31. Cf. 2 Cor 1:24; Rom 5:2; 11:20). Third, Paul uses in 1 Corinthians 16:13 and 2 Corinthians 1:24 the verbs στήκω and ἵστημι in direct connection with the dative (ἐν) τῇ πίστει, which is best understood as a dative of location / sphere (or instrument).[137]

Considering the above observations, it would be hasty for one to conclude that the likely rendering of τῇ πίστει in Philippians 1:27c as a dative of interest or advantage indicates the Philippians' corporate outward verbal proclamation of the gospel. Rather, while no one can be certain whether συναθλοῦντες τῇ πίστει τοῦ εὐαγγελίου refers to the Philippians' corporate action in the interest of such an outwardly spread of the gospel, there is plenty of room for us to take it as a corporate struggle for the faith of the gospel, primarily for the Philippians themselves as something *ontological*, namely their contending for the faith in terms of ongoing maintenance and sound actualization of the faith for their life in the community.

The latter case is well elucidated by Paul's mentioning in verse 28 of the adversaries (οἱ ἀντικείμενοι) and his hope that the Philippians would not be frightened by them. Despite the obscurity in the identity of the opponents and the nature of the persecution and suffering,[138] scholars often persuasively illumine the opposition that might have led the Philippians to the point of giving up their faith,[139] not necessarily imagining a full scale persecution from the Roman authorities, but more adequately, the experiencing of a great deal of difficulties through discrimination, ostracization, and enmity from their local civic communal systems, religio-socio-econo-political.[140]

---

137. Cf. Phil 4:1: "οὕτως στήκετε ἐν κυρίῳ ἀγαπητοί"; 1 Thess 3:8: "ὅτι νῦν ζῶμεν ἐὰν ὑμεῖς στήκετε ἐν κυρίῳ."

138. The view that the adversity and suffering of the Philippians was from a Jewish source (i.e. false Christian teachers) – e.g. J.-F. Collange, *The Epistle of Saint Paul to the Philippians* (London: Epworth, 1979), 71–72 – is challenged by the view of the non-Christian gentile source (e.g. economic problems under the Roman or Gentile civic patronage system) – e.g. P. Oakes, *Philippians: From People to Letters*, SNTSMS (Cambridge: Cambridge University Press, 2001), 84–98.

139. Cf. G. W. Hansen, *The Letter to the Philippians*, PNTC (Grand Rapids: Eerdmans: Nottingham: Apollos Press, 2009), 95.

140. C. S. de Vos, *Church and Community Conflicts: The Relationships of the Thessalonian, Corinthian and Philippian Churches with their Wider Civic Communities*, SBLDS (Atlanta: Scholars, 1997), 263–286; C. Osiek, *Philippians, Philemon*, ANTC (Nashville: Abingdon Press, 2000), 50; Witherington, *Philippians*, 104.

In such a situation, Paul's injunction not to be panicked, with the preceding exhortation to contend together for the faith, seems to have more to do with the Philippians' corporate striving for the maintenance and right exercise of their faith in the face of opposition, in which the members of the nascent community were prone to abandonment of the faith in Christ (1:28–29) or misexercise of the faith (cf. 2:3, 4, 14; 3:2; 4:2). The community's outward witness to the faith, then, would be the highest level of expectation on the part of Paul. However, it would be more urgent and practical for him to exhort them to "stand firm" (στήκετε) on the ground of what they had first received (τῇ πίστει τοῦ εὐαγγελίου, thus, the dative as a dative of location / sphere, cf. οὕτως στήκετε ἐν κυρίῳ ἀγαπητοί, 4:1), forming a united front to endure the opposition (ἐν ἑνὶ πνεύματι μιᾷ ψυχῇ συναθλοῦντες), for their own progress in the faith of the gospel (τῇ πίστει τοῦ εὐαγγελίου, thus, the dative of a dative of interest or advantage, cf. εἰς τὴν ὑμῶν προκοπὴν καὶ χαρὰν τῆς πίστεως, v. 25).[141]

2.3.1.3. Semantic Consideration in Verse 27

However, we need to admit that our suggestion immediately above meets with a syntactical difficulty. Since in verse 27c the two catch phrases ἑνὶ πνεύματι[142] and μιᾷ ψυχῇ[143] separate στήκω and τῇ πίστει τοῦ εὐαγγελίου, so it is not surprising that the majority of commentators draw a syntactic break between the two phrases, *viz* στήκετε ἐν ἑνὶ πνεύματι and μιᾷ ψυχῇ συναθλοῦντες τῇ πίστει τοῦ εὐαγγελίου.[144] This syntactic break seems to be sound as the καί + participial phrase naturally follows.

It is to be noted, however, that this syntactic consideration is not fully satisfactory. As we have seen already, it is probable that στήκω the main verb of the ὅτι clause (v. 27c) is semantically connected with τῇ πίστει τοῦ εὐαγγελίου, despite the apparent syntactic connection between τῇ πίστει

---

141. Cf. Rom 1:17: "δικαιοσύνη γὰρ θεοῦ ἐν αὐτῷ ἀποκαλύπτεται ἐκ πίστεως εἰς πίστιν."

142. Most commentators agree that πνεῦμα here is not the Holy Spirit but the human πνεῦμα (cf. 1 Thess 5:23).

143. The expression is often regarded as one of friendship language. Cf. S. K. Stowers, "Friends and Enemies in Politics of Heaven: Reading Theology in Philippians," in *Pauline Theology*, ed. J. M. Bassler, vol. 1 (Minneapolis: Fortress, 1991), 110–113.

144. Cf. Lightfoot, *Philippians*, 106, who also stresses the difference between [human] "spirit" and "soul."

τοῦ εὐαγγελίου and συναθλοῦντες. Moreover, considering that the other occurrences of the verb στήκω / ἵστημι elsewhere in Paul's undisputed letters are always associated with God / Lord / Christ / faith as a divine cause / sphere of standing,[145] "stand firm in one spirit" is unusual.[146] Rather, the cardinal sense of "oneness" or "unity" in the three consecutive ἐν ἑνὶ πνεύματι, μιᾷ ψυχῇ, and συναθλοῦντες strongly suggests that they are a single semantic unit as a manner of "standing firm in / by the faith of the gospel." This consideration should allow us to appreciate the semantic relation between verse 27a and verse 27c as follows:

A ²⁷<u>μόνον ἀξίως τοῦ εὐαγγελίου τοῦ Χριστοῦ</u>   B <u>πολιτεύεσθε</u>
   [ἵνα εἴτε ἐλθὼν καὶ ἰδὼν ὑμᾶς εἴτε ἀπὼν ἀκούω τὰ περὶ ὑμῶν]
B' [ὅτι] **στήκετε**   B" ἐν ἑνὶ πνεύματι μιᾷ   A' <u>τῇ πίστει</u>
                      ψυχῇ **συναθλοῦντες**   <u>τοῦ εὐαγγελίου</u>
                   B''' ²⁸καὶ μὴ **πτυρόμενοι** ἐν μηδενὶ ὑπὸ
                      τῶν ἀντικειμένων

In this rough chiastic semantic structure, we can clearly see that the dative τῇ πίστει is more aptly understood as a dative of location and even instrument, in which and by which the Philippians' footing is to be fixed and their life should be directed. And such a sense well accords with verse 27a, where τὸ εὐαγγέλιον τοῦ Χριστοῦ functions as an authoritative standard in which or according to which (ἀξίως) the Philippians should live their lives (πολιτεύεσθε).

Moreover, some ambiguity arising from Paul's unusual combination of τῇ πίστει with the genitive τοῦ εὐαγγελίου can be removed by the parallel **A**. As τοῦ εὐαγγελίου τοῦ Χριστοῦ (v. 27a) carries a locative or instrumental character for the verb πολιτεύεσθε, so does τοῦ εὐαγγελίου (v. 27c) for στήκετε. Thus, the genitive τοῦ εὐαγγελίου in verse 27c is best taken as the genitive of origin (the faith that is in or comes from the gospel) rather than

---

145. Rom 14:4; 1 Cor 16:13; Gal 5:1; Phil 1:27; 0; 1 Thess 3:8.

146. This is not to suggest that "standing in one sprit" cannot be a Pauline idea, but only that its unusual nature may suggest a different semantic flow in the sentence as I suggest here.

of apposition (the faith that is the gospel)[147] or of object (the faith in the gospel).[148] The meaning of verse 27c, then, would be "stand firm in / by the faith which is or is shown in the gospel," and this perfectly fits into the idea of verse 27a, where the suitability (ἀξίως) for which the gospel of Christ requires the Philippians is no other than their life / conduct in *this faith*.

2.3.1.4. The Meaning of the Gospel in Verse 27

If our observation so far is sound, the two clauses containing the gospel terminology, ἀξίως τοῦ εὐαγγελίου τοῦ Χριστοῦ (v. 27a) and τῇ πίστει τοῦ εὐαγγελίου (v. 27c) should be taken to be exhibiting Paul's logic that the gospel of Christ *provides* the Philippians with a basis or model for appropriate conduct in the face of opposition and suffering (vv. 28–30) and the danger of self-centeredness that threatens the church's identity and unity (2:1–4). A critical corollary of this logic, then, is the question as to which aspect of the gospel of Christ did Paul have in mind that provided the Philippians with their ground to conduct themselves suitably or faithfully? And what is the exact meaning of "the faith that is in the gospel"?

As the nature of the gospel, then, two suggestions are possible: (1) Paul speaks of the gospel as the *kerygma* from which an appropriate attitude is emotionally or rationally derived in gratitude for or with confidence in that the Philippians are saved in Christ; or (2) Paul speaks of the gospel as a *reference to* Christ's career as a faithful Son / Servant to God known to the Philippians through Paul's teaching, so that they could take it as their reference for appropriate conduct.

---

147. Cf. Gal 1:22 (νῦν εὐαγγελίζεται τὴν πίστιν ἥν ποτε ἐπόρθει) where Paul certainly uses the "faith" as the object of the action of proclamation. However, it may not follow that the faith is the gospel, since it is not certain here whether he means by the faith a "message" in the sense of the gospel or "religious adherence" to a certain faith system or simply "faith in Jesus Christ." In light of ἥν ποτε ἐπόρθει it is more likely that the faith refers to the latter two cases.

148. The suggestion of an objective genitive is not convincing, since Paul and other NT writers always use a dative qualifier for such a sense (cf. Gal 3:26; Rom 3:25; Eph 1:15; Col 1:4, and particularly Mark 1:15: πιστεύετε ἐν τῷ εὐαγγελίῳ). Therefore, Paul would have written τῇ πίστει ἐν τῷ εὐαγγελίῳ to mean "the Philippians' faith in the gospel." Cf. R, B. Hays, "ΠΙΣΤΙΣ and Pauline Christology: What Is at Stake?" in *Pauline Theology Vol. 4: Looking Back, Pressing On*, eds. E. E. Johnson and D. H. Hay (Atlanta: Scholars Press, 1997), 59, who strictly distinguishes Paul's verbal use of the word (πιστεύω) from substantial use (e.g. πίστις or πίστεως) in Galatians arguing that there are no cases in Galatians where the noun unambiguously denotes the human act of believing.

Considering our observations so far, option 2 is preferable. If Paul did not have in mind any particular aspect of the gospel and the faith from which the Philippians would benefit, then, the gospel and the faith are too loosely put. And on a linguistic and logical basis, "by the faith that is in the gospel" requires at least a subject or an actor that performs the faith or demonstrates what this faith is within the world of the gospel. Therefore, my suggestion is to paraphrase τῇ πίστει τοῦ εὐαγγελίου with "by following the exemplary faith of Jesus Christ, whom the gospel speaks of," or "by having faith in Jesus Christ whom the gospel presents as the model of faithfulness to God."[149]

Moreover, some further considerations give good reason to consider the gospel language in verse 27 as connected to some ethical connotations which may not be satisfactorily appreciated by a purely *kerygmatic* sense of the gospel as suggested in option 1. First, the idea of the verb στήκετε is clarified by the specific attitude ἐν ἑνὶ πνεύματι (in one spirit) and μιᾷ ψυχῇ συναθλοῦντες (contending together in one mind). Second, the attitude appears to be ethical behaviour as indicated by the reappearance of the phrase in the adjacent section (τὸ αὐτὸ φρονῆτε, τὴν αὐτὴν ἀγάπην ἔχοντες, σύμψυχοι, τὸ ἓν φρονοῦντες, 2:1–4) that is clearly intended for the exhortation for ethical conduct among the community members. Third, the ethical demand is closely connected with the attitude of Christ (v. 5), which is powerfully expressed in the so called "Christ-Hymn" (vv. 6–11).[150] Fourth, and most importantly, the Christ-Hymn, which is not

---

149. I must admit here that I am methodologically indebted to R. B. Hays' actantial analysis of πίστις Χριστοῦ in *The Faith of Jesus Christ* (2nd ed.; Grand Rapids: Eerdmans, 2002); Hays, "ΠΙΣΤΙΣ and Pauline Christology," 35–60. For the weakness in such an actantial analysis see J. H. Lee, "Against Richard B. Hays's 'Faith of Jesus Christ'," *JGRChJ* 5 (2008): 51–80. Despite the inconclusive nature of the debate (cf. e.g. P. J. Achtemeier, "Apropos the Faith of/in Christ: A Response to Hays and Dunn," in *Pauline Theology*, eds. E. Johnson and D. Hay [Minneapolis: Fortress Press, 1991–1197], 82–92), and Paul's clear notion of the Christians' "having faith in Christ Jesus" (ἡμεῖς εἰς Χριστὸν Ἰησοῦν ἐπιστεύσαμεν, Gal 2:16), Christ as the actor of having faith or being faithful is also an unmistakable feature particularly in the "Christ-Hymn."

150. Considering the emphatic τοῦτο that is reflective of the previous thought (v. 5), the connection between Paul's demand for the Philippians' ethical behaviour (vv. 1–4) and the Christ Hymn (vv. 6–11) is unmistakable. Cf. G. D. Fee, "Philippians 2:5–11: Hymn or Exalted Pauline Prose?" *BBR* 2 (1992): 36: "The use of the verb φρονεῖτε in v. 5 demands that Paul is still concerned with the issue of vv. 1–4; otherwise, the use of language becomes nearly meaningless. Furthermore, the points made about Christ in vv. 6–8 are precisely

least a narrative presenting by and large the entire career of Christ not only as the preexistent and exalted one but also as the incarnate one (i.e. historical Jesus), probably provides the entire paraenesis of 1:27–2:18 (or even of the entire letter) with a prime model for how to live *ethically* in the community.[151]

These considerations seem to strengthen our proposal that Paul in verse 27 uses the term "the gospel of Christ" and "the faith that is in the gospel" in the sense of a basis or a model according to which the Philippians are to conduct themselves (not in the sense of the objective to which the Philippians are to contribute). And if our estimation of the nature and function of the Christ-Hymn in the *paraenesis* is sound, we cannot miss the impression that Paul presents the Christ-Hymn as the gospel referred in verse 27 and Jesus Christ in that gospel as the model of the faith. We may further take this as evidence that Paul shows a dual understanding of the gospel: (1) Christ's redemptive work as the *kerygma* (cf. Phil 1:5, 7, 12, 16; 2:22; 4:3, 15) to which his apostolic calling is devoted; and (2) what is narrated (or remembered or taught) about the entire career of Jesus on which his further pastoral concern for the maturity of his converts is focused, namely by providing the model of Christ as the imperative to his community to be in conformity with it (πολιτεύεσθε ἀξίως τοῦ εὐαγγελίου τοῦ Χριστοῦ!).

In summary, our close examination of Philippians 1:27–30 and the adjacent verses shows that the proponents of the evangelistic interpretation of the text have little exegetical ground. Rather, Paul's emphasis is laid on the Philippians' life in conformity with what their Lord had shown.

---

those of vv. 3–4 – selflessness and humility. Indeed, the key sentence (v. 8) includes the two key words."

151 Cf. L. W. Hurtado, "Jesus as Lordly Example in Philippians 2:5–11," in *From Jesus to Paul: Studies in Honour of Francis Wright Beare*, eds. P. Richardson and J. C. Hurd (Waterloo: Wilfrid Laurier University Press, 1984), 113–126; S. E. Fowl, *Philippians*, THNTC (Grand Rapids; Eerdmans, 2005), 108–113. Pace E. Käsemann, "A Critical Analysis of Philippians 2:5–11," in *God and Christ: Existence and Province*, JTC 5, eds. R. W. Funk and G. Ebeling (New York: Harper, 1968), 45–88 (83–84); R. P. Martin, *Carmen Christi: Philippians II 5–11 in Recent Interpretation and in the Setting of Early Christian Worship* (Grand Rapids: Eerdmans, 1983, c1967), xii. As Fee rightly notes ("Philippians 2:5–11," 37), however, this position notably ignores the significant connection between Christ's selflessness and humility (vv. 6–8) and what Paul mentions in vv. 1–4 at the expense of Christ's incarnation and vindication that cannot be ethically imitated by human beings.

As unanimously agreed, it is Christ's self-lowering, servantship and obedience as the mark of God's ultimate will and vindication. If Paul had in mind anything evangelistic in his exhortation as such, it would be the Philippians' life per se shaped by Christ's character and example, as the citizens of heaven, whose vindication in God will definitely be recognized by all at Christ's *parousia*, but also whose *proleptic* vindication may currently be recognized by other Philippians' eyes (cf. Phil 2:11).[152] This suggestion will be supported by our further discussion of another text from Philippians below.

2.3.2. Philippians 2:16

In Philippians 2:15 Paul admonishes the Philippians to be (ἵνα γένησθε) "faultless and pure as the children of God without blemish in the midst of a crooked and perverse generation," strongly recalling the language of Deuteronomy 32.[153] This admonition is extended by parenthetical or ad-

---

152. Ware, *The Mission of the Church*, 224–235, contends that, because of the link between Phil 2:6–9 (the suffering Messiah) and the fourth Servant Song (Isa 52:14–53:12) and the connection between Phil 2:10–11 (the vindication of the Messiah) and the LXX Isa 44:18–25 (the universal eschatological homage to God among all the peoples), and particularly because of the clear "invitation to conversion directly addressed to Gentiles" (Isa 45:22) (227–230), Phil 2:10–11 is "strongly evocative of the gentile mission, and portrays the conversion of Gentiles through this mission as both the purpose of the humiliation and exaltation of Christ Jesus described in the hymn (2:6–9), and inauguration of the universal lordship of Christ Jesus which will be consummated at his advent" (230). He, then, remarks that "The hymn's portrayals of the eschatological exaltation of the Servant as inaugurated in the gentile mission, is in turn reflected in the hortatory function of the Christ-hymn within the wider letter" (231), and "the Christ hymn prepares the way for the direct exhortation to mission activity which follows in 2:12–18" (236). This suggestion seems to aptly illuminate the eschatological character of the Christ-event and its close connection with Paul's conception of mission. And Ware brings a fresh look at the hortatory function of Phil 2:6–11 in relation to Paul's missio-ecclesial understanding. Ware's direct connection of Isa 45 with the emphasis on the Philippians' active role in mission, however, shows little sensitivity to the fact that in Jewish eschatological vision gentile salvation is envisioned only as a corollary of the restoration / vindication of Israel. Rather, it is more likely that the Christ-hymn is connected to Paul's hortatory end in the letter exactly in the same way in which the Jewish interpretive tradition of the Scriptures put priority on Yahweh's own elect people, whose vindication / restoration would entail the streaming in of the Gentiles.

153. Cf. F. F. Bruce, "St. Paul in Macedonia: 3. The Philippian Correspondence," *BJRL* 63 (1981): 159. Despite the ἵνα + the subjunctive γένησθε an imperatival sense is unmistakable, since a direct connection with the explicit imperative, πάντα ποιεῖτε in v. 14 is strongly suggested by the typological and theological unity in regard to its OT background of Israel "grumbling" about God in the wilderness and God's negative verdict on them (cf. Deut 32:5–20). The connection may be extended to the imperative πολιτεύεσθε of 1:27 which is the beginning of the paraenesis.

ditional clauses, "among whom [you are] seen as lights in the world" (ἐν οἷς φαίνεσθε ὡς φωστῆρες ἐν κόσμῳ) and "taking hold / holding forth of word of life" (λόγον ζωῆς ἐπέχοντες). Considering the Philippians' luminosity among the world,[154] and its linguistic and thematic similarity to the LXX Daniel 12:3,[155] it is often suggested that Paul here expresses the *missional responsibility* of the Christian community for the rest of the world.[156] As Paul's paraenetical focus is the Philippians' obedient life without blemish in the midst of a corrupt generation, this missional emphasis is primarily concerned about witness through a Christian's behaviour and attitude.[157]

However, for some scholars this missional responsibility of the Philippians is not merely socio-ethical but includes the church's proactive verbal engagement with the gospel, since, according to them, the second additional clause λόγον ζωῆς ἐπέχοντες of verse 16b is to be taken as Paul's explanation of how this missional responsibility is to be accomplished and this is by the church spreading the gospel through proactive evangelism. For instance, Ware regards the clause as "extremely significant" since the meaning of the verb ἐπέχω in Philippians 2:16 is not "hold fast" but best taken as "hold forth" which indicates Paul's explicit command for the church at Philippi to spread the gospel, whereas in no other letter does Paul explicitly command his congregation to preach the gospel.[158] In support, he provides a detailed study of the use of the verb in ancient Greek literature and concludes that, while the verb can have generally two distinguishable senses (1) "hold back" / "refrain" and (2) "holding forth," "extension" of an object (transitively), "spread" / "extension" of the subject (intransitively), "hold

---

154. See also e.g. Isa 9:2–7; 42:6–7; 49:6; 58:8–10; Matt 5:14–16; John 1:4–5; 8:12; 9:5; 12:46.

155. E.g. Fee, *Philippians*, 246; Beare, *Philippians*, 92; Michael, *Philippians*, 106; Martin, *Philippians*, 120; Bockmuehl, *Philippians*, 158; Marshall, *Philippians*, 64; Gnilka, *Der Philipperbrief*, 153; Schenk, *Die Philipperbriefe*, 222; Ware, *The Mission of the Church*, 254–256.

156. E.g. Silva, *Philippians*, 147; Fee, *Philippians*, 247; O'Brien, *Philippians*, 292–296; Martin, *Philippians*, 120; Hendriksen, *Philippians*, 125. Bruce, *Philippians*, 85. *Contra* Dickson, *Mission-Commitment*, 111, who rules out the missional implication of the text.

157. Cf. Schenk, *Die Philipperbriefe*, 222–223.

158. Ware, *The Mission of the Church*, 270. So Plummer, *Paul's Understanding*, 74–77. Cf. Marshall, "Who Were the Evangelists?" 260; Schnabel, *Early Christian Mission*, 2. 1461; Keown, *Congregational Evangelism*, 136–139.

fast" / "hold" as the meaning of the verb are not attested in ancient Greek literatures of any period.[159]

Contrary to Ware, Keown acknowledges that "hold fast" is well attested as a possible meaning of ἐπέχω in extra biblical literature,[160] and Paul could have been intentionally ambiguous allowing both meanings.[161] He, however, prefers the extensive sense of "hold forth" as the meaning of the verb of Philippians 2:16, on the ground that: (1) the use of the verb in the NT slightly supports an extensive interpretation; (2) κατέχω is a more likely choice of the verb if Paul clearly intended to say "holding," "holding onto" or "hold fast" (e.g. 1 Cor 11:2; 15:2; 2 Cor 6:10; 1 Thess 5:21);[162] (3) considering Paul's general varied use of the MT and the LXX, Daniel 12:3 is likely background and could have given Paul the active sense of the verb (i.e. "those who lead the many to righteousness").[163] According to Keown, λόγος ζωῆς recalls other uses of gospel and parallels in Philippians (Phil 1:5, 7, 12, 14, 15, 16, 17, 18, 27; 2:22; 4:3, 15)[164] and this leads him, with the previous point and some other contextual considerations, to conclude that "it seems best to read 2:16a as an explicit appeal for evangelism."[165]

While some evangelistic connotation in Philippians 2:16a is unmistakable, the attempt to read the text in terms of a direct and verbal proclamation of the gospel by the church seems to be questionable. I would, rather,

---

159. Ware, *The Mission of the Church*, 267–269.

160. Keown, *Congregational Evangelism*, 136–137.

161. Ibid., 146.

162. On this point Keown follows Hendriksen, *Philippians*, 126. Cf. Dickson, *Mission-Commitment*, 110, n.76, who suggests that κατέχω (1 Cor 15:2) and ἐπέχω (Phil 2:16) are synonymous in Paul to mean "retaining" as attested by John Chrys. *Hom. Phil* 62.244.

163. Keown, *Congregational Evangelism*, 36–139.

164. Ibid., 139–140: His contextual considerations include that: (1) evangelism is emphasized in the whole letter to the point of 2:16 (1:3–11, 1:12–18a, 22, 27–30, 2:5–11); (2) Timothy's example is not steadfastness but evangelism (2:19–23); (3) the problem in Philippi in 2:14 is unified evangelism rather than steadfastness; (4) the eschatological concern of 2:16b ("so that in the day of Christ I may have cause to glory because I did not run in vain nor toil in vain") can be understood "evangelistically," since the Philippians' evangelism may add more ground of boasting and can be included in the orb of global imitation (4:9).

165. Ibid., 145. Keown goes on to remark that his conclusion "further weakens the view that Paul understood the church's mission as merely centripetal. Certainly proponents of the view are right to emphasize community, unity and relationships as central, but these are to be understood in the context of evangelistic mission" (147).

argue that whether Paul intended this sort of evangelism by the Philippians or not cannot be decided by the passage, while non-verbal and indirect evangelistic influence on the lost is clearly in view.[166]

2.3.2.1. The Meaning of ἐπέχοντες of Philippians 2:16a

While the meanings "holding fast" and "holding forth" are both possible, the verb ἐπέχω elsewhere in the NT (Luke 14:7; Acts 3:5, 19:22; 1 Tim 4:16) helps little in deciding the meaning of ἐπέχοντες in Philippians 2:16.[167] The verb is either used intransitively to denote "hold one's attention" (Luke 14:7; Acts 3:5; 1 Tim 4:16) or used transitively to mean "to hold time / to stay" (Acts 19:22).[168] Moreover, any lexical argument for the meaning of the verb in Philippians 2:16 based on a particular use of the verb in ancient Greek texts seems to be methodologically indecisive, since ἐπέχω has a wide range of lexical meanings.[169] While Ware's observation is contributive to the discussion about the meaning of Philippians 2:16 by providing some convincing evidence for "holding forth" as a possible meaning of the verb,[170] his wholesale rejection of "holding fast" as a possible rendering of ἐπέχοντες is seriously misleading.[171] In fact, there are ample occurrences of the verb with a direct object which is simply taken hold or maintained by the subject without any implication of the object being offered to or extended (e.g. Josephus, *War* 2.462; 3.487; 4.442; 5.186, 303, 543; 6.180;

---

166. I am slightly reluctant to employ "evangelistic" and tend to prefer "missional" in this argument, since insofar as the primary idea of "evangelism" or "evangelistic" is dealing with one's reception of the gospel message in a verbal communication, while "missional" can be understood as including various aspects and influence of the gospel message. However, insofar as indirect and non-verbal influence of the gospel can result in one's reception of and obedience to the gospel, "evangelistic" may not be excluded. Cf. Barram, *Moral Reflection*, 149–152, who considers Paul's understanding of the "Evangelistic Function of Christian Behaviour" which is not verbal and proclamatory.

167. Cf. Bowers, "Church and Mission," 100, who finds only one occurrence in D (the Codex Bezae) Luke 4:42 where ἐπέχω replaces κατέχω meaning "hold fast."

168. *Pace* BAGD 285; O'Brien, *Philippians*, 297, who take the verb in Acts 19:22 as intransitive. On semantic grounds this is possible (in the sense of "stay"), but the accusative χρόνον as the object of the action must not be ignored.

169. For a balanced presentation of a variety of meanings of the verb in extra biblical literature see Dickson, *Mission-Commitment*, 108–110.

170. Ware, *The Mission of the Church*, 259–267.

171. Ibid., 267–270.

Ant. 2.101; 20.145).[172] In this regard, deciding the meaning of ἐπέχοντες of Philippians 2:16a cannot rely on any simple lexical argument but has more to do with its literary context and Paul's general ecclesial reflection available in the letter.

It seems that exegetes, if not all, are generally divided into two groups in deciding the meaning of the verb as if "holding fast" and "holding forth" are mutually exclusive. To my mind, however, it is misleading to take the two possible meanings of the verb as mutually antithetical as if Paul could have intended only one or the other meaning. I would rather argue that Paul could have intended both of the senses in his use of the verb. How can, then, the two meanings be reconciled in Paul's single use of the verb? I would suggest that "holding fast" is Paul's *primary intention*, whereas "holding forth" is his *corollary intention*.[173]

2.3.2.2. Holding Fast as the Primary Intention

It is to be noted that τὴν ἑαυτῶν σωτηρίαν κατεργάζεσθε of 2:12 functions as the prime admonition of the paraenetic section of 2:12–18, as all commentators agree. Here, Paul's first concern is the Philippians' salvation that is to be completed by the day of the Lord (2:16b, cf. 1:6, 9–11), while that of outsiders is left untouched for a moment.

This is specifically expounded by "without grumblings and disputes" (χωρὶς γογγυσμῶν καὶ διαλογισμῶν) in verse 14, of which the language and idea are very likely to be derived from the OT references to the wilderness generation of Israelites (Num 11:1–6; 14:1–4; 20:2; 21:4–5).[174] Deuteronomy 32:5 recalls this "crooked and perverse generation" (γενεὰ σκολιὰ καὶ διεστραμμένη) of Israelites with the sentence that they are οὐκ αὐτῷ τέκνα (cf. τέκνα θεοῦ ἄμωμα, Phil 2:15). What we need to observe is that the behavior, grumblings and disputes that led the Israelites to defection are employed to admonish the believing community of the Philippians, whereas "γενεὰ σκολιὰ καὶ διεστραμμένη" – who are not

---

172. Cf. BGAD, 285; BDAG, 362; O'Brien, *Philippians*, 297; Dickson, *Mission-Commitment*, 109–110; Keown, *Congregational Mission*, 136–137.

173. By "corollary" I do not mean "ancillary" or "secondary" to the primary, but rather "obviously expected" or "mutually reinforcing." Cf. Martin, *Philippians*, 121–122: "The two meanings of the verb happily dovetail."

174. Bruce, *Philippians*, 59; O'Brien, *Philippians*, 290.

God's children – is applied to the non-believing Philippians (γενεᾶς σκολιᾶς καὶ διεστραμμένης). So, the echo of the defection of the Israelites and the negative admonitions ("χωρὶς γογγυσμῶν καὶ διαλογισμῶν"; "ἵνα γένησθε . . . τέκνα θεοῦ ἄμωμα") directed to the Philippians certainly indicate Paul's deliberate connection of the fate of the disobedient Israelites and the Philippians.[175] This again indicates Paul's implicit concern about the salvation-threatening danger of certain behaviour within the Philippians: complaints and disunities. Thus, obedience and working out one's salvation in verse 12 is expounded in verse 14 in terms of the Philippians' proper conduct that secures their own salvation.

This salvation-threatening danger has already been alluded to in Philippians 1:28: οἱ ἀντικείμενοι, *the external threats*. Since this could threaten the Philippians' life in salvation (v. 28), Paul needs to admonish them to have fidelity to the gospel (v. 27),[176] and not to be terrified by the opponents, as the sign of their salvation (ἔνδειξις ὑμῖν δὲ σωτηρίας). Now in 2:12–15 Paul pays his attention in turn to the *internal danger* that could threaten the Philippians' salvation with their blemish (i.e. γογγυσμῶν καὶ διαλογισμῶν), which is to be found only among those who are not the children of God.

On this ground Paul in verse 12 urges the Philippians to "accomplish"[177] their salvation, which is not automatically guaranteed, but to be completed by obedient behaviors as the proper children of God.

Paul's other employment of the OT text of Daniel 12:3a in Philippians 2:15c in a direct connection with the Deuteronomic expression supports this view. Even if Paul in verse 15c fails to employ "those who understand (or are wise)" (οἱ συνιέντες/הַמַּשְׂכִּלִים) from Daniel 12:3a, his citation in a close connection with the Deuteronomic indictment about the wilderness generation of Israelites, who are "foolish people" (Deut 32:6), who cannot

---

175. Cf. 1 Cor 10:1–13 in which Paul similarly relates the Corinthians with the Israelites in the desert.

176. On this point see above 3.1.

177. The imperative κατεργάζεσθε of v. 12, while denoting a state of accomplishment or completion, certainly assumes incompleteness of something by suggesting the necessity of an act toward that state. Cf. Phil 3:8–12, where Paul speaks of his ongoing effort to be found in Christ and incompleteness of his goal in relation to resurrection. The nuance is not merely ministerial but also salvific.

"understand" their past (v. 7) and future (v. 29), certainly illuminates that Paul had in mind this motif of "the wise."[178] As in Daniel 12:3 it is only those who "understand" that shall shine the eschatological (resurrectional)-celestial luminosity, the straightforward connection of the Deuteronomic indictment (as the negative example) and the luminosity of the people of God in Daniel 12:3a (as the positive example) is possible only under the assumption in verse 15c that the Philippians are (to be) the eschatological people of God, who can (or are wise enough to) "understand" God's salvific will for themselves.

Paul's going back to the OT themes regarding Israel's fate, negative and positive in his paraenesis for the Gentile converts, indicates two important points: (1) Paul regards the church of the Gentiles as the *eschatological* and *covenantal* people of God; (2) Paul is concerned about the *covenantal faithfulness* of Israel to its creator God. The contrast set between the failure of the wilderness generation and the glorious luminosity of the eschatological people of God cannot be explained without traditional Jewish covenantal theology and Paul's contemporary eschatological interpretation of the theology: the covenantal faithfulness of God and Israel's faithfulness to the covenantal charter, the Torah.

In this light, λόγος ζωῆς reflects well Paul's appropriation of Daniel 12:2–3 where "some shall awake to everlasting *life*" (ἀναστήσονται οἱ μὲν εἰς ζωὴν αἰώνιον/יָקִיצוּ אֵלֶּה לְחַיֵּי עוֹלָם) is connected (*not* juxtaposed) with "those who understand," and is best read as "the word that gives life."[179] Even if Paul does not bother to employ the LXX Daniel 12:3b (οἱ κατισχύοντες τοὺς λόγους μου), λόγος ζωῆς of verse 16a clearly reflects the idea and language of Daniel 12:2 and particularly the LXX 12:3b. That λόγον ζωῆς ἐπέχοντες immediately follows this skilful conflation of the OT themes strongly suggests that the expression should be understood

---

178. Note that Paul's rare use of the verb always refers to the OT understanding of God's will for man's salvation or the wisdom of Christ: Rom 3:11 (Ps 14:2, 53:2); 15:21 (Isa 52:19); 2 Cor 10:12. Cf. Eph 5:17.

179. H. A. W. Meyer, *Critical and Exegetical Handbook to the Epistles to the Philippians and Colossians*, CECNT (Edinburgh: T. & T. Clark, 1875), 117; Loh and Nida, *Philippians*, 71. Cf. O'Brien, *Philippians*, 298.

primarily in terms of the Philippians' final salvation by their comprehension of (שָׂכַל/συνίημι) and faithfulness to (κατισχύω) the word of life.[180]

Therefore, Paul's eschatological boasting which follows immediately in verse 16b is best understood in this way, and the connotation of outward evangelism seems to have little to do with it.[181] Even if what Paul wants is to depart (from his bodily life) and to be with Christ (1:23), he knows (οἶδα) that he will be released from the chains (1:19) having the conviction (καὶ τοῦτο πεποιθὼς) that this is because the Philippians need his further bodily life and presence among them for their progress and joy in the faith (1:25). Paul, then, speaks of his revisit to the Philippians in connection with their ground of boasting (τὸ καύχημα ὑμῶν) which he wishes to be abundant in Christ (v. 26). What is certain from the logic here is that τὸ καύχημα of the Philippians is based on Paul's further apostolic ministry for the Philippians' "progress and joy of the faith" rather than simply on his release from the chains and visit to them. This "progress and joy of the faith" is elucidated by the following exhortation, μόνον ἀξίως τοῦ εὐαγγελίου τοῦ Χριστοῦ πολιτεύεσθε (1:27), which Paul will continue to give in his presence with them, yet at the moment only through his letter while he is absent (εἴτε ἐλθὼν καὶ ἰδὼν ὑμᾶς εἴτε ἀπών, v. 27b).

What is to be noted from this observation is that the Philippians' boasting is mentioned in terms of their faithfulness to the gospel. It seems that in 2:16b Paul reiterates the same motif, but in the setting of the *parousia* of Christ, in which the reciprocity of his own apostolic boasting and his converts' boasting will meet at one final point.[182] It will be a great joy and

---

180. Cf. Silva, *Philippians*, 136–137; Bockmuehl, *Philippians*, 136–137; Witherington, *Friendship*, 71.

181. Cf. Witherington, *Friendship*, 73, who maintains that evangelism is in Phil 2:16 referred to only in the context of seeking unity. It seems that Witherington by "evangelism" here does not mean an outward preaching of the gospel but only an indirect witness to Christ through the unity of the community. Pace Ware, *The Mission of the Church*, 271: "The relationship of the Philippians' extension of the gospel to Paul's ministry is highlighted in Philippians 2:16b–18"; Keown, *Congregational Evangelism*, 139–140: "The eschatological concern of 2:16b can be understood evangelistically" (140).

182. The eschatological reciprocity between Paul's apostolic boasting and that of his converts in relation to proper conduct clearly appears in 2 Cor 1:12–15: ὅτι καύχημα ὑμῶν ἐσμέν, καθάπερ καὶ ὑμεῖς ἡμῶν, ἐν τῇ ἡμέρᾳ τοῦ κυρίου Ἰησοῦ (v. 14). It is strikingly similar to Phil 1:25–26 and 2:15–16b in that: (1) the Corinthians' ground of boasting of the apostle is explicated in terms of the testimony of the apostle's (moral) conscience (τὸ μαρτύριον τῆς συνειδήσεως ἡμῶν) that in proper godly conduct (ὅτι ἐν ἁπλότητι καὶ

cause for boasting for the Philippians if they are found faithful until the end for which the apostle will have faithfully laboured. It will be a great regret for the apostle if any of those who received the message of the gospel fail to complete faithfully their salvation in the day of the Lord (cf. Phil 1:6, 9–11).[183]

This observation of the context should lead us to see that Paul's primary intention in the expression λόγον ζωῆς ἐπέχοντες is fidelity to the message of the gospel rather than spreading of the gospel to others. What is admonished in the participial clause is the Philippians' obedient life by *sticking to* or *staying in* or *taking hold* what is preached to them: the message of life,[184] which guides them to the final salvation in the midst of persecution and danger which threaten their salvation externally (Phil 1:28) and internally (Phil 2:14). This idea of sticking to the message of the gospel as the way to salvation is well attested by 1 Corinthians 15:2.[185] While this teaching is related to the Corinthians' theological misunderstanding of the resurrection (1 Cor 15:12, 35) and its consequential effect on their behaviours (15:32–58), this idea is now applied in a different context of the community of the Philippians whose fidelity to the message of the gospel is to be strengthened, since their improper attitudes and the tangible opposition from outside could undermine their salvation.

εἰλικρινείᾳ τοῦ θεοῦ) lived out in the world and toward the Corinthians (v. 12); (2) Paul's ground of boasting of the Corinthians is based on his conviction that the Corinthians will completely "understand" (ἐπιγνώσεσθε) the apostolic teaching until the day of the Lord (v. 13); 3) due to this conviction (καὶ ταύτῃ τῇ πεποιθήσει) Paul plans to revisit the Corinthians (vv. 15–16).

183. Bowers, "Church and Mission," 100; O'Brien, *Philippians*, 298; Martin, *Philippians*, 121–122; Dickson, *Mission-Commitment*, 110–111.

184. Dickson is reluctant to read λόγος ζωῆς here as the gospel, while preferring "principle" or "fact" of life itself (*Mission-Commitment*, 113–114). He argues that only 3 occurrences out of the 20 anarthrous uses of λόγος in Paul refer to the message of salvation, and the flexible use of the term in Greek warrants a caution. This view is not satisfactory. While the lexical support is weak, the contextual support from 1:27a, c is unmistakable, since, even as Dickson himself agrees (113), it is most probable that 1:27 is thematically connected to 2:16. See also Keown, *Congregational Mission*, 140–145.

185. On the thematic and verbal similarity between Phil 2:16 and 1 Cor 15:2 see Dickson, *Mission-Commitment*, 110, n.76. He notes that the theme of a Christian's "holding fast" of "the gospel" guaranteeing "salvation" appears in both references. A similarity can be seen in Phil 1:27–28.

In this regard, λόγον ζωῆς ἐπέχοντες is nearly a reiteration of 1:27a: ἀξίως τοῦ εὐαγγελίου τοῦ Χριστοῦ πολιτεύεσθε. By both Paul refers to the only suitable way to Christian salvation, namely the life that is in conformity to the gospel of Christ (1:27a),[186] or the life that is holding fast the message of life (2:16b).

2.3.2.3. Holding Forth as the Corollary Intention

Nevertheless, the above conclusion must not weaken the co-existent or at least corollary sense "holding forth" in the verb ἐπέχω.

As often (rightly) suggested, Paul's direct combination of the verb φαίνομαι with ὡς φωστῆρες ἐν κόσμῳ strongly indicates that the LXX Daniel 12:3a (φανοῦσιν ὡς φωστῆρες τοῦ οὐρανοῦ) is behind Philippians 2:15c. This leads Dickson to argue for Paul's exclusive use of the LXX in Philippians 2:15–16a, and to rule out the sense of "holding forth" which may be supported by the Hebrew version of Daniel 12:3b which reads "and those who lead the many to righteousness" (וּמַצְדִּיקֵי הָרַבִּים).[187]

But I would doubt this view and suggest that Paul did intend "holding forth" as well as "holding fast" with some reason. First, as M. Silva and others rightly observe, the decision about Paul's OT textual source for his citation / allusion is very tangled due to his masterly freedom and the lack of uniformity in his pattern,[188] and λόγον ζωῆς ἐπέχοντες of verse 16a is probably one such case. If Paul did stick exclusively to the LXX Daniel 12:3 for Philippians 2:15c and 2:16a, why did he not choose to use the same verb κατισχύω from the LXX Daniel 12:3b? While λόγον ζωῆς, as mentioned previously, may support the LXX wording for its textual background, Paul's choice of an ambiguous verb may not conclusively support this. It seems less likely that the choice of ἐπέχω – which can certainly mean "hold out / forth" – instead of κατισχύω or κατέχω – which exclusively means "hold fast" – is accidental or due to his dependence on his rough memory of the LXX text. Rather, it is more likely that he deliberately chose the verb while substantiating it in the original Hebrew text, which is in his mind also relevant to his intention. It is quite probable that Paul could appreciate the

---

186. Or the life that is standing "in the faith of the gospel" (1:27c).
187. Dickson, *Mission-Commitment*, 112.
188. M. Silva, "Old Testament in Paul," *DPL*, 630–642.

corollary relationship between faithful staying in the word of life and the effect of its exposure.

Second, Paul's ἐν κόσμῳ is at any rate not identical to τοῦ οὐρανοῦ of the LXX. It is possible that it is Paul's unconscious alteration, which is not crucial, but not very probable. It is more likely that Paul had different sources and / or a theological reason to do so. Actually, there is a strong likelihood that Daniel 12:3 is not the only textual background of Philippians 2:15c. As often rightly pointed out,[189] the Jesus-tradition of the "light of the world" captured later in Matthew 5:14a could also have given Paul the idea and the language of the luminosity of the people of God for Philippians 2:15.[190] Moreover, that the lights are located in the κόσμος in the dominical saying (ὑμεῖς ἐστε τὸ φῶς τοῦ κόσμου) coincides with Paul's expression. Since it is very likely that Paul knew the Hebrew version of Daniel 12:3 which clearly speaks of the *beneficial role of the wise*, if Paul knew the Jesus-saying "you are the light of the world," it is very likely that he understood it in this manner (cf. Matt 5:14b–16).

Third, the previous point is strengthened when we consider that for his exhortation Paul significantly alters his traditional and contemporary Jewish apocalyptic motif of the vindication of the people of God (who will have been through suffering) *at the Eschaton* into what is (to be) happening *now*. While in all the other Jewish texts exegetically influenced by Daniel 12:3 (e.g. *1 Enoch* 38:1–4; *2 Enoch* 66:7; *2 Bar.* 51:3; *T. Mos.* 10:9; *4 Macc* 17:5; *4 Ezra* 7:97, [124] 125) and for Daniel 12:3 itself as well, this luminosity of the people of God as their final vindication is described only in terms of the apocalyptic-futuristic event, in which they "shall shine" (φανοῦσιν) like the stars of the sky, the Philippians are now (to be) the luminaries (φαίνεσθε) among (μέσον/ἐν οἷς) the world.[191] In this shifted eschatological view (the end time having already arrived), the world (not heaven) still includes the crooked and perverse generation as the co-inhabitants with the pure and innocent. Considering this, it seems likely that

---

189. Beare, *Philippians*, 92; Bruce, *Philippians*, 85; D. Wenham, *Follower*, 254; Martin, *Philippians*, 121; Bockmuehl, *Philippians*, 158.

190. We will discuss in detail in chapter 5 Paul's likely dependence on the Jesus-tradition of the light saying in Phil 1–2.

191. Cf. Ware, *The Mission of the Church*, 155, who correctly observes this.

Paul regards the luminosity of the Philippians not merely as the proleptic glory of the people of God which sharply contrasts them with the doomed disobedient, as often so described in the apocalyptic parables,[192] but rather as a beneficial light as in Matthew 5:14–16.[193]

Considering these points, it seems that, while Paul quite clearly intended in Philippians 2:16a the sense of "holding fast" of LXX Daniel 12:3b, he also intended the verb to be conveying the sense of the beneficial role of the wise as in the original Hebrew text, the meaning of which was widely lost in his contemporary popular interpretations, but well recovered in the Jesus-tradition: "You are the light of the world" signifies the eschatological luminosity of the people of God here and now as a guiding light for others. In this sense, "holding forth" may also have been intended.

However, it may be seriously misleading to understand ἐπέχοντες which legitimately connotes "holding forth" as if it denotes Christians' direct and verbal evangelistic action to lead many into the righteousness, as Fee, Ware, Keown and others contend. While the close connection in Philippians of the eschatological reign of God, God's activity of the spread of the gospel in Paul's evangelism, and the Philippians' partnership in that mission to each other,[194] "holding forth" in the active sense of an exhortation to "spread the gospel" (as Paul himself does) is a rather unfortunate illogical leap.[195] Rather, the sense of "holding forth" is to be seen as a natural corollary of the Philippians' faithful "holding fast" of the word of life. This is to be observed again from the literary context in which Paul uses such language.

While the imperatival force primarily resides in the two previous clauses, πάντα ποιεῖτε χωρὶς . . . (v. 14) and ἵνα γένησθε . . . (v. 15a) requiring specific behaviour, the two verbs φαίνεσθε and ἐπέχοντες simply state the fundamental implication of the Philippians' behaviour as such in the world as the children of God.[196] Perhaps the participial ἐπέχοντες is best rendered as the explanation of the manner of the present middle indicative

---

192. Notably *1 Enoch* 38:1–4.

193. Cf. Isa 9:2–7; 42:6–7; 49:6; 58:8–10; Matt 4:16; Luke 1:78–79; John 8:12.

194. Cf. Ware, *The Mission of the Church*, 237.

195. Ibid., 271.

196. Neither φαίνεσθε nor ἐπέχοντες constitutes an imperatival force. Cf. O'Brien, *Philippians*, 297. *Pace* Hawthorne, *Philippians*, 103, who argues that the ἐπέχοντες is an imperatival participle which signals a new beginning. This is not convincing, since the

φαίνεσθε.[197] From this observation one may infer that: (1) the luminosity of the Philippians signifies the Philippians' right conduct (cf. 1:6: ἔργον ἀγαθὸν) as the sign (cf. 1:28: ἔνδειξις) of their being the children of God rather than any direct evangelistic act; (2) the right conduct – as the result of the Philippians' "holding fast" the word of life – as it is visualized (φαίνεσθε) rather than verbally reported, may deliver or extend (thus, "holding forth") the message of salvation (or life) to the world, namely, rather than through gospel-proclamation but through gospel-actualization. While the missional implication of the church right in the middle of the world is unmistakable in Philippians 2:15b, c–16a, Paul's explicit exhortation for the Philippians to conduct a proactive evangelistic mission is not in view in the text as Ware, Keown and others contend.

2.4. Texts from the Disputed Letters

2.4.1. Ephesians 6:15

The final part of the exhortation to the Ephesians (6:10–20) focuses on the spiritual battle that the Christians are to fight against the evil spiritual powers, not beings who are of flesh and blood (v. 12).[198] The point of the exhortation is to put on the full armour of God to be able to "stand" (στῆναι)[199] against the schemes of the devil (v. 11, 13). For those who argue

---

objectival λόγον ζωῆς clearly indicates its thematic continuity with "the wise" of Dan 12:3a which is a direct motif of Phil 2:15c.

197. Cf. Loh and Nida, *Philippians*, 71.

198. The identity of those principalities, authorities, world rulers of this darkness, and evil spiritual beings in the heavenly realms are debated. E.g. H. Berkhof, *Christ and the Powers* (Scottdale: Herald Press, 1953); G. B. Caird, *Principalities and Powers: A Study of Pauline Theology* (Oxford: Clarendon Press, 1956); C. E. Arnold, *Powers of Darkness: A Thoughtful, Biblical Look at an Urgent Challenge Facing the Church* (Leicester: IVP, 1992); A. N. S. Lane, ed., *The Unseen World: Christian Reflections on Angels, Demons and the Heavenly Realm* (Cumbria: Paternoster Press, 1996); W. Wink, *The Powers That Be: Theology for a New Millenium* (Garden city: Doubleday, 1998); P. T. O'Brien, "Principalities and Powers: Opponents of the Church (20th-century Interpretations)," *ERT* 16 (1992): 353–384; C. Forbes, "Pauline demonology and/or cosmology? Principalities, powers and elements of the world in their Hellenistic context," *JSNT* 85 (2002): 51–74; W. Carr, *Angels and Principalities: The Background, Meaning and Development of the Pauline Phrase hai archai kai exousiai*, SNTSMS (Cambridge: Cambridge University Press, 2005). However the identity is interpreted our discussion is not affected.

199. See also v. 14: "στῆτε."

for the author's explicit exhortation for the church to engage in evangelistic proclamation, the third and the sixth items "having the feet shod" ἐν ἑτοιμασίᾳ τοῦ εὐαγγελίου τῆς εἰρήνης (v. 15) and "taking up" τὴν μάχαιραν τοῦ πνεύματος, ὅ ἐστιν ῥῆμα θεοῦ (v. 17) are important supporting evidence for their view.

2.4.1.1. ἐν ἑτοιμασίᾳ τοῦ εὐαγγελίου τῆς εἰρήνης

In Ephesians 6:15, the noun, ἑτοιμασία, is used in the dative case following the instrumental or locational ἐν (cf. v. 14) and qualified by τοῦ εὐαγγελίου τῆς εἰρήνης. For many commentators what matters in the interpretation of the phrase is primarily how to render the NT *hapax* noun ἑτοιμασία. It was often taken as the act of "preparation," or the result of the act, "preparedness" or "readiness for good works" (cf. the use of cognate words in Titus 3:1; 2 Tim 2:21; 1 Pet 3:15).[200] By taking this meaning of the noun, the phrase, ἐν ἑτοιμασίᾳ τοῦ εὐαγγελίου τῆς εἰρήνης is often interpreted as "readiness" or "preparedness" to proclaim the gospel of peace (i.e. τοῦ εὐαγγελίου τῆς εἰρήνης as a genitive of object).

For instance P. T. O'Brien, by pointing to the LXX Psalm 9:38 (τὴν ἑτοιμασίαν τῆς καρδίας αὐτῶν) reads ἑτοιμασία as signifying "a state of being ready for action."[201] With his typical emphasis on Paul's use of εὐαγγέλιον as *nomen actionis*, he takes the qualifying τοῦ εὐαγγελίου as a genitive of objective that is the message to be proclaimed by one in ἑτοιμασία.[202] To support his connection of the readiness of verse 15 with one's act of proclamation of the gospel of peace, he points to Isaiah 52:7 and Ephesians 2:17. According to him, while Isaiah 52:7 lacks such a language of readiness "the messenger's preparedness to announce the good tidings to Zion is obvious" and Ephesians 2:17 focuses upon "the proclamation of the gospel of peace

---

200. For the earlier interpretations of the noun in terms of readiness, see M. Barth, *Ephesians*, vol. 2, AB (Garden City, N.Y: Doubleday, 1974), 797, n.214. He mentions that Calvin and Abbott read ἑτοιμασία as "readiness for service" which is established by the gospel but not towards the mission for the gospel since preparation to preach the gospel is not ordinary Christians' business. Cf. Friedrich, "εὐαγγέλιον," *TDNT* 2. 706; BDAG, 401.

201. P. T. O'Brien, *The Letter to the Ephesians*, PNTC (Leicester: Apollos, 1999), 475–479.

202. Ibid., 477.

to those for whom this reconciliation has been won."²⁰³ To strengthen his congregational evangelistic interpretation of Ephesians 6:15, he points to Colossians 4:6 which he believes to be paralleling the verse in question by addressing the congregation's verbal activity to outsiders. These considerations and the conclusion are maintained essentially intact by E. J. Schnabel,²⁰⁴ and notably by R. L. Plummer²⁰⁵ and M. J. Keown.²⁰⁶ What is at stake in this view for our further discussion is: (1) Is the traditional rendering of ἑτοιμασία (readiness or preparedness) satisfactory? (2) In relation to ἑτοιμασία, what is the function of the genitive construction τοῦ εὐαγγελίου τῆς εἰρήνης? (3) If Isaiah 52:7 and Ephesians 2:17 have something to do with Ephesians 6:15, to what extent is this the case?

2.4.1.2. The Meaning of ἑτοιμασία

The traditional view of ἑτοιμασία of Ephesians 6:15 as readiness is sometimes challenged.²⁰⁷ For instance, Markus Barth suggests another reading of the verb which emphasizes "solidity" and "stability" on the grounds of three points: (1) the authors of the LXX take the ἑτοιμ-word group as having been derived from the Hebrew verb כּוּן ("to be or stand firm," "taut," "well found" or "establish") or the cognate noun מָכוֹן ("established place" or "foundation"); (2) the author of the Ephesians by implying the Roman battle footwear "caliga" might not have meant speedy mobility from them but rather "a solid stance" for long marches or prevention from "sliding"; (3) feet with such a mobility are often related with evil doers as the object of condemnation (Isa 59:7; Rom 3:15) not knowing the way of peace

---

203. Ibid. To strengthen his congregational evangelistic interpretation of Eph 6:15, O'Brien adds Col 4:6 which he believes to be Paul's exhortation for congregational verbal evangelism.

204. Schnabel, *Early Christian Mission*, 2, 1464.

205. Plummer, *Paul's Understanding*, 78–80.

206. Keown, *Congregational Evangelism*, 288–292. See also C. E. Arnold, *Ephesians: Power and Magic; the Concept of Power in Ephesians in Light of Its Historical Setting*, SNTSMS (Cambridge: Cambridge University Press, 1989), 120.

207. M. R. Vincent, *Word Studies in the New Testament*, vol. 3 (Peabody: Hendrickson, 1888), 409; A. F. Buscarlet, "The 'Preparation' of the Gospel of Peace," *ExpTim* 9, no. 1 (1897): 38–40; Barth, *Ephesians*, 798–799; E. D. Roels, *God's Mission: The Epistle to the Ephesians in Mission Perspective* (Franeker: T. Wever, 1962), 218; E. Best, *A Critical and Exegetical Commentary on Ephesians*, ICC (Edinburgh: T. & T. Clark, 1998), 599–600; Dickson, *Mission-Commitment*, 118–120.

(Rom 3:17). And in Isaiah 52:7 while footwear is not in view it is the feet of the messenger of good tidings of peace that receives the admiration. These considerations lead him to conclude that the verse does not use the messenger imagery (Rom 10:14–18) but rather speaks of the "equipment"[208] provided by God which makes Christians able to "stand" and "resist."

With some others J. P. Dickson suggests "fixedness" as the meaning of the noun to confirm Barth's view by observing the eleven instances of the noun ἑτοιμασία in the LXX. He, admitting that there is one exception in Wis 13:12 (εἰς ἑτοιμασίαν τροφῆς: "for the preparation of food"), suggests that ἑτοιμασία throughout the LXX consistently refers to the place upon which or manner in which something is fixed. This leads him to read ἐν ἑτοιμασίᾳ as adverbially meaning, "securely fastening one's shoes" and τοῦ εὐαγγελίου τῆς εἰρήνης as a genitive of origin (i.e. security comes from the gospel), or alternatively, ἑτοιμασία as a reference to "boots as sturdy foundation" so that τοῦ εὐαγγελίου τῆς εἰρήνης is appositional to the footwear.[209]

Against this attempt to undermine "readiness" or "preparation" as the meaning of the verb in question, Andrew T. Lincoln points again to the LXX (and other classical literature as well) to argue that the word nowhere means "firm footing" and the more usual sense is "readiness," "preparedness," or "preparation."[210] Nevertheless, for him, Isaiah 52:7, Romans 10:15, and Ephesians 6:15 are not connected in terms of proclamation but only in relation to "feet,"[211] he does not go in the direction which O'Brien's camp pushes. Rather, he suggests that the readiness is not for the proclamation of the gospel but for the battle that the gospel of peace bestows.[212] In a similar fashion, R. L. Plummer opines that in all the instances [in the LXX], preparedness of the position or foundation is still determinative.[213] In opposition to Barth's refusal of mobility at the cost of stability, Keown appeals to "the general notion of a soldier" who is always ready to move and

---

208. Cf. Roels, *God's Mission*, 218, who also mentions "equipment" or "foundation" for the meaning of the noun; Best, *Ephesians*, 599–600.

209. Dickson, *Mission-Commitment*, 118–120.

210. A. T. Lincoln, *Ephesians*, WBC (Dallas: Word Books, 1990), 448–449.

211. Ibid., 448.

212. Ibid., 449.

213. Plummer, *Paul's Understanding*, 78 (original emphasis). Also see Schnabel, *Early Christian Mission*, 2. 1464.

implied in Paul's own ministry, and is led to opt for the traditional rendering of "readiness or preparedness."[214]

Even if it is to be admitted that neither "fixedness" nor "steadfastness" is found as the direct meaning of ἑτοιμασία in the LXX, and the act of preparing is always assumed in the noun, I think that the noun ἑτοιμασία of Ephesians 6:15 is best rendered as "foundation" rather than "readiness" or "preparedness."

First, while the act or intent of the act of preparing (i.e. preparation) is a possible rendering of ἑτοιμασία (e.g. Wis 13:12), it is doubtful that the author of Ephesians 6:15 handles the noun in that fashion as if the implied Christian soldier is to be the actor of the action or the bearer of the quality of preparedness. Actually, the Christian's readiness for the spiritual battle is all assumed in the imperative verbs and participles: στῆτε (v. 14); περιζωσάμενοι (v. 14); ἐνδυσάμενοι (v. 14); ὑποδησάμενοι (v.15); ἀναλαβόντες (v. 16); and δέξασθε (v. 17). It seems redundant to mention preparatory alacrity for Christian service or battle as the quality of a specific item of footwear.

Second, it is to be noticed that, even if ἑτοιμασία in the instrumental dative construction is in a neat syntactical parallel with verse 14a, namely ἐν ἀληθείᾳ, it is rather the qualifier τῆς εἰρήνης that is in a neat semantic parallel receiving the real significance as the third item proper (i.e. the footwear). This point is to be supported by the syntactic structure and the parallelism of other qualifiers of the direct objects of all the acts of armouring in the surrounding verses:

14a περιζωσάμενοι τὴν ὀσφὺν ὑμῶν **ἐν ἀληθείᾳ**

14b ἐνδυσάμενοι τὸν θώρακα **τῆς δικαιοσύνης**

15 ὑποδησάμενοι τοὺς πόδας ἐν ἑτοιμασίᾳ τοῦ εὐαγγελίου **τῆς εἰρήνης**

16 ἀναλαβόντες τὸν θυρεὸν **τῆς πίστεως**

17a τὴν περικεφαλαίαν **τοῦ σωτηρίου** δέξασθε

---

214. Keown, *Congregational Evangelism*, 289–290. This idea is untenable, since mobility and fixedness are not mutually exclusive in the notion of Christian spiritual warfare. Rather, as Eph 6:13, 14 suggests, fixedness or stability on a firm ground is a necessary condition to stand and to proceed with the ongoing march.

Silence or Non-Silence?

In verse 14 although the armour (or belt) for the loin is only implicit in the instrumental dative ἐν ἀληθείᾳ, it is certain that ἀλήθεια per se is the proper armour as the genitive qualifier τῆς δικαιοσύνης appositionally signifies another armour ὁ θώραξ.[215] As two other items in verses 16–17a are also signified by the appositional genitive qualifiers, τῆς πίστεως and τοῦ σωτηρίου, τῆς εἰρήνης in verse 15 is sufficiently to be seen as the identity of the third armour for Christian feet.[216] While a juxtaposition of all the other divine gifts or qualities with the NT *hapax* ἑτοιμασία is awkward, a juxtaposition with εἰρήνη makes a natural parallel. This observation makes it very likely that the writer uses ἑτοιμασία just as a package description of the following double genitive construction τοῦ εὐαγγελίου τῆς εἰρήνης, namely "what is ready" that is the gospel of peace.

Third, and more importantly, it is doubtful that the usual use of ἑτοιμασία in the LXX is "preparation" for an active service as Lincoln and others suggest. While it is to be admitted that the active sense of "preparing" by an actor is certainly assumed, it is also to be noted that in the LXX, the quality of the preparing act or intent in ἑτοιμασία is usually limited to the causer of the result or the actor of the action, and the force of being prepared or ready is therefore always passive rather than active. For instance, in the LXX Psalm 9:38[217] (MT Ps 10:17),[218] whereas the verb προσέσχεν is used for the original hiphil תַּקְשִׁיב (cause to hear) making the sense clear that it is God's *ear* that has the active function of hearing,[219] the translator chooses the noun ἑτοιμασία instead of any Greek verb (e.g. ἑτοιμάζω) for

---

215. It seems highly likely that the writer of Ephesians echoes the LXX Isa 59:17; 11:5 and Wis 5:17–20 for the use of some divine gifts or attributes as if they are items to put on (e.g. ἐνεδύσατο δικαιοσύνην ὡς θώρακα). On this see e.g. Lincoln, *Ephesians*, 436. For the unlikelihood of 1QM; 1QH 3:24–39; 6:28–35 as the background see Lincoln, *Ephesians*, 438; Arnold, *Power and Magic*, 109–110.

216. If Wis 5:17–20 were a background of Eph 6:11–17, the appositional relationship may also be attested by Wis 5:18: ἐνδύσεται θώρακα δικαιοσύνην (he will put on a breastplate that is righteousness). Cf. T. Moritz, *A Profound Mystery: The Use of the OT in Ephesians*, NovTSup (Leiden: Brill, 1996), 193–194; Roels, *God's Mission*, 218; Dickson, *Mission-Commitment*, 119, n.108; O'Brien, *Ephesians*, 481, n.180.

217. τὴν ἐπιθυμίαν τῶν πενήτων εἰσήκουσεν κύριος
τὴν ἑτοιμασίαν τῆς καρδίας αὐτῶν
προσέσχεν τὸ οὖς σου

218. תַּאֲוַת עֲנָוִים שָׁמַעְתָּ יְהוָה תָּכִין לִבָּם תַּקְשִׁיב אָזְנֶךָ

219. Cf. The LXX Ps 114:2.

the hiphil תָּכִין as the active sense of preparing. By encapsulating the action and the result in the single noun ἑτοιμασία, the translator makes the two senses of "God's preparing act" and "what is prepared" (or established) co-existent. However, this is a clear indication that their hearts (αἱ καρδίαι αὐτῶν/לִבָּם) are not the active actors of preparation but only the result of God's act of preparation (so that they are only made ready to be mercifully dealt with by God).[220] This reference certainly militates against O'Brien's and others' view that ἑτοιμασία is primarily rendered as "readiness" or "preparation" for an active service. Even in Wis 13:12 in which the act of preparing is most clearly exhibited in εἰς ἑτοιμασίαν τροφῆς (for the preparation of food) the noun either signifies the actor's (i.e. woodworker) act of preparing itself or food's readiness to be consumed: the passive service. In all other cases, the noun denotes a state or status of being prepared or established by either God or persons but does not carry any ongoing sense of act of preparing for an active service as if the noun per se contains such a force. The force of act of preparing is all consumed by the assumed actors and what the noun carries is the result of the act to be used (cf. Ezra 2:68; 3:3; Ps 64:10; 88:15; Zech 5:11; Dan 11:7; 11:20–21). In short, ἑτοιμασία as "readiness" or "preparedness" for an active service is not attested by the LXX and its usual meaning is rather passive in sense (i.e. a thing that is ready to be used).[221]

Considering this observation, it is most likely that the author of Ephesians 6:15 uses ἑτοιμασία in the common LXX sense of "foundation" or "ground" that is made ready to be built on or stood on or more aptly for the literary context, *to be shod with*.[222] Its "readiness" maintained in ἑτοιμασία, then, is not something to be imposed or transposed to the

---

220. Nah 2:4 is a possible case for this, since ἐν ἡμέρᾳ ἑτοιμασίας αὐτοῦ can be translated as "on the day of his (the Lord's) muster." In this case, the verb כון is replaced by the noun ἑτοιμασία which may mean either the Lord's act of muster (in the sense of preparation for battle) or the chariots mustered in array by the order of the commander in chief (in the sense of what is established by the command).

221. One possible support for this passive sense of ἑτοιμασία is the traditional Christian art of the "ἑτοιμασία" which refers to the image of "empty-throne" which is ready to be occupied by Christ at the *parousia*. Cf. J. Beckwith, *Early Christian and Byzantine Art* (2nd ed.; New Haven: Yale University Press, 1986), 116–118.

222. So E. D. Roels, *God's Mission*, 218; Dickson, *Mission-Commitment*, 119.

Christians for their active and wilful service but rather a thing's availability for the Christians' use. Therefore, the sense of "stability" or "fixedness" may be sustained as a derivative sense of the noun.

2.4.1.3. The Function of τοῦ εὐαγγελίου τῆς εἰρήνης

If the previous point is sound, what is the thing that is ready to be used by the Christian soldiers? As already touched on, it is most likely that it is ἡ εἰρήνη. This, then, may mean none other than that ἑτοιμασία and ἡ εἰρήνη are appositional. A clue for this interpretation is given in the writer's earlier teaching about the specific implication of Christ's sacrifice that had brought the Gentile Ephesians the reconciling power "the peace (ἡ εἰρήνη)" not only with God but also with the Jews (2:13–14). The writer again clearly states that what Christ preached is none other than ἡ εἰρήνη that destroys enmity and alienation and creates new family relationships vertically and horizontally (vv. 17–19). The motif of εἰρήνη that is to be celebrated between Jews and Gentiles in God is again presented as the revealed contents of the mystery that prompted the apostle's ministry and even suffering (3:1–13). Then, the connection between ἡ εἰρήνη and the "foundation" on which the Ephesians are "built" (v. 20: ἐποικοδομηθέντες ἐπὶ τῷ θεμελίῳ) must be clearly seen. Even if some syntactic and semantic difficulty arises from the qualifying genitive construction τῶν ἀποστόλων καὶ προφητῶν regarding whether the writer implies the apostles and prophets being the foundation itself (as appositional genitive),[223] what is unmistakably in view in these verses is that Jesus Christ and the apostles and (the) prophets are primarily the *bringers* of the message of peace,[224] that gives the Ephesians

---

223. Positively e.g. A. T. Robertson, *A Grammar of the Greek New Testament in the Light of Historical Research* (3rd ed.; New York: Hodder & Stoughton, 1919), 498; R. Schnackenburg, *The Epistle to the Ephesians* (Edinburgh: T. & T. Clark, 1991), 122–123; F. F. Bruce, *Epistles to the Colossians, to Philemon, and to the Ephesians*, NICNT (Grand Rapids: Eerdmans, 1984), 304; Lincoln, *Ephesians*, 153; Best, *Ephesians*, 280; O'Brien, *Ephesians*, 213; Banks, *Paul's Idea*, 48. Negatively H. A. W. Meyer, *Critical and Exegetical Handbook to the Epistle to the Ephesians and the Epistle to Philemon*, CECNT (Edinburgh: T. & T. Clark, 1895), 142; K. O. Sandnes, *Paul - One of the Prophets?: A Contribution to the Apostle's Self-Understanding*, WUNT (Tübingen: Mohr Siebeck, 1991), 229.

224. Cf. O'Brien, *Ephesians*, 216, who explains the apostles and prophets being the foundation through their normative teaching that is the right foundation.

the foundation on which they can celebrate the vertical and the horizontal reconciliation (2:11–19).²²⁵

This idea reappears in the whole phrase ὑποδησάμενοι τοὺς πόδας ἐν ἑτοιμασίᾳ τοῦ εὐαγγελίου τῆς εἰρήνης of 6:15 in the form of an injunction. Since the worldly power threatens the peace that the Ephesians now celebrate, they should stand firm on the ground so that the peace shall not be taken away. As Lincoln rightly observes, it is "paradoxical" that the peace "produced by the gospel" is the armour with which the Ephesians are to fight "against the alienating and fragmenting powers of evil."²²⁶

Then, we may take the genitive construction τοῦ εὐαγγελίου τῆς εἰρήνης as a whole epexegetical to ἑτοιμασία, or τοῦ εὐαγγελίου as a genitive of origin (or subjective) to both ἑτοιμασία and ἡ εἰρήνη: the proclaimed message of peace that is the foundation or the proclaimed message that brings peace that is the foundation. In this regard, it is difficult to see the gospel as the objective of ἑτοιμασία as O'Brien and others contend. While τοῦ εὐαγγελίου may be taken as the noun of agent or as an indication to its character as a *nomen actionis*, the actor of the proclamation of the gospel is basically the bringer of the message to the Ephesians (2:17–20: Christ and the apostles and prophets) and the primary focus of the proclamation is the facilitation of the foundation that is or brings peace *among* the Ephesians (cf. 2:21–22). Contrary to those who argue for the Ephesians' evangelistic role in the expression, τοῦ εὐαγγελίου τῆς εἰρήνης only serves as the origin or identity of the armour.

2.4.1.4. The Extent to which Isaiah 52:7 and Ephesians 2:17 Are Related to Ephesians 6:15

Considering the use of πόδες in relation to εὐαγγελ-language (i.e. εὐαγγελιον) and εἰρήνη in Ephesians 6:15 the link with the messenger imagery of the LXX Isaiah 52:7 is unmistakable. And as the εὐαγγελ-language and εἰρήνη are directly connected in 2:16, the link between 2:17 and 6:15 is strong. Then, can we deduce from the obvious links that the writer expects οἱ πόδες of the Ephesians to be shod *as the messengers* of the gospel of peace as the Isaianic εὐαγγελιζόμενος and Christ both are?

---

225. Cf. Lincoln, *Ephesians*, 449.
226. Ibid.

Some considerations make this deduction improbable. First, as the εὐαγγελ-language and εἰρήνη are connected in terms of the messengers' proclaiming act that brings εἰρήνη for the hearers' benefit in Isaiah 52:7 and Ephesians 2:17, οἱ πόδες of the Ephesians who are the beneficiaries of the proclaiming act are fundamentally different from οἱ πόδες εὐαγγελιζομένου who are the actors of the proclaiming act. The correspondence between the eulogized πόδες εὐαγγελιζομένου and οἱ πόδες of the Ephesians is *heterogeneous* and *reciprocal* rather than *homogeneous* and *transitional*. Second, as touched on previously, Christ's proclamation of peace (Eph 2:17) and its foundational significance for the Ephesians (2:20, 3:17) are emphatically expounded in terms of the Ephesians' transplantation from this world of death to the heaven of life (2:1–6), from the realm of alienation and fragmentation to the realm of reconciliation with God and his people (2:11–19). In light of this such a transplantation or change of footing of the Ephesians is frequently related to their edification (2:20, 21), their maturity to the fullness of God in Christ (3:14–19; 4:13–16), and their new way of life by "putting on the new man" in contrast to outsiders (4:17–24), it is most likely that οἱ πόδες of the Ephesians of 6:15 has little to do with their service or mobility in or for the world but a connotation of footing on the ground for change, growth or firmness. Third, as the author of Ephesians emphasizes the unique role of Christ, the apostles and prophets (including Paul) as the heralds (2:17), foundation (2:20), and the revealers of the mystery of Christ that has been long sealed (3:1–13), the messenger language (i.e. εὐαγγελιζομένος) is hardly transposable to the community of the Ephesians but rather remains as the mark of those special ministers of the gospel.[227]

While the ideas and language in Isaiah 52:7 and Ephesians 2:17 are all related to Ephesians 6:15, to link οἱ πόδες of the Ephesians directly to the act of proclamation either by Christ or the Isaianic herald is no more than an arbitrary endeavour.

---

227. Cf. Rom 10:15 where Paul borrows the Isaianic messenger language from the LXX Isa 52:7. By pluralizing the term, Paul extends the scope of the group of the divinely authorized heralds, but not to put all the believers into the same category, but only the twelve and himself. This point will be discussed more in detail in chapter 4.

In summary, as a very similar exhortation in Colossians 1:23 more clearly does,²²⁸ the author of Ephesians 6:15 wants to bring two things in the phrase: (1) the heralds of Christ, the apostles and the prophets brought the gospel to the Ephesians for their peace; (2) the gospel that generated the peace between the Ephesians and God and other people of God (Israel) should be their firm ground for their ongoing spiritual battle. Whether or not the author encourages the community to spread the gospel cannot be decided by the text.

2.4.2. Ephesians 6:17b

2.4.2.1. Congregational Evangelism as Spiritual Warfare?

Along with the "helmet of salvation" (ἡ περικεφαλαία τοῦ σωτηρίου) Ephesians 6:17 requires the Ephesians to take (δέξεσθαι) the "sword of the spirit" (ἡ μάχαιρα τοῦ πνεύματος) which is the "word of God" (ῥῆμα θεοῦ). C. E. Arnold suggests that in the verse the writer of Ephesians by making ῥῆμα refer to "the gospel" (cf. Rom 10:8) "goes beyond the readiness of the Christian warrior to make known the gospel (v. 15) to a mention of the dynamic which makes the gospel successful – the Spirit."²²⁹ By pointing to the writer's use of the sword as the last weapon to be enumerated, he goes on to argue that in verse 17b "the preaching of the gospel is depicted as the most aggressive manoeuvre against the realm of the devil and his hosts."²³⁰ Fee maintains similar position. He takes the sword as an offensive weapon that is given by or belonging to the Spirit.²³¹ By taking ῥῆμα of Ephesians 6:17 with the emphasis on "speaking" of a message at a given point rather than on the message itself, he reads the verse in question "speaking forth" of the message, inspired by the Spirit.²³² According to him, the implication of

---

228. The striking thematic similarity of Col 1:23 to Eph 6:15 is unmistakable: (1) primary exhortatory point is the Colossians' fidelity to the gospel; (2) the fidelity is expounded in terms of their being firmly grounded in the faith (τῇ πίστει τεθεμελιωμένοι καὶ ἑδραῖοι) and not moving away from the hope of the gospel; (3) the gospel was proclaimed to them by the minister of the message, the apostle Paul.

229. Arnold, *Power and Magic*, 111.

230. Ibid., 120.

231. G. D. Fee, *God's Empowering Presence: The Holy Spirit in the Letters of Paul* (Peabody: Hendrickson Publishers, 1994), 728, reads τοῦ πνεύματος as the genitive of source or possession.

232. Ibid., 728–729.

this proclaiming of the word "under the empowering of the Spirit of God" is not only "some *ad hoc* word directed at Satan" but also that "men and women might hear and be delivered from Satan's grasp."[233]

Similarly, O'Brien pays attention to the sword of the spirit as a weapon of aggression, which is identified with the word of God, by which Paul often signifies the gospel (Rom 10:17).[234] According to him, Paul draws attention to the "ongoing warfare with evil powers in the heavenlies" and a "weapon carried by the Messiah" by alluding to Isaiah 11 which portrays the future smiting of the nations by the Messiah – on whom the Spirit of the Lord rests, smiting the earth with his word of his mouth and destroying the wicked with the breath of his lips (v. 4, cf. Rev 19:15). This weapon, he argues in favour of Fee's interpretation, is also "available for Christians to use" for proactive evangelism.[235] Based on these views, Keown argues that the spiritual warfare is both defensive / apologetic and offensive / proactive and this "necessarily implies a proclamatory dynamic": "the authentic Pauline believer is to be prepared to go and proclaim the gospel as led by the Spirit of God."[236]

Even if this evangelistic interpretation of Ephesians 6:17b does not appear as a consensus, the aggressive nature of the sword as the word of God in terms of proclamatory connotation and the Spirit's role as the generative or empowering source for Christians' use of the weapon of the message of the gospel are widely held.

2.4.2.2. The Meaning of the Sword

It is to be noted, however, that while in Ephesians 6:14–17a the identity of the pieces of armour are signified by the appositional qualifiers of the divine gifts, ἡ μάχαιρα τοῦ πνεύματος of verse 17b may not be seen in this

---

233. Ibid., 729. Cf. Lincoln, *Ephesians*, 451; Schnabel, *Early Christian Mission*, 2. 1464–1465.

234. O'Brien, *Ephesians*, 481–482.

235. Ibid., 482. O'Brien follows Fee's note almost intact: "What is in view here is not some ad hoc word addressed to Satan, as though what we speak against him will defeat him. Rather, it is the faithful speaking forth of the gospel in the realm of darkness, so that men and women held by Satan might hear this liberating and life-giving word and be freed from his grasp." See also O'Brien, *Gospel and Mission*, 125.

236. Keown, *Congregational Evangelism*, 293, 295.

way.[237] Most commentators correctly point out that τοῦ πνεύματος cannot be appositional to ἡ μάχαιρα, but rather qualifies the sword as a genitive of source[238] or possession[239] to provide the weapon its penetration (cf. 1 Thess 1:5; Heb 4:12) or authorship[240] to cause the sword to function.[241] But this leads most of them to read the following ῥῆμα θεοῦ as referring back to the entire ἡ μάχαιρα τοῦ πνεύματος. This reading is not satisfactory and causes the unnecessary over interpretation that the weapon to wield (ἡ μάχαιρα) is Spirit-empowered proclamation of the gospel (ῥῆμα).

The most likely connection of Isaiah 11:5 with Ephesians 6:14 must allow one to expect some further connection between Ephesians 6:17b and Isaiah 11.[242] The LXX Isaiah 11:4 depicts the Messiah as one who will strike (πατάξει) to slay (ἀνελεῖ) the wicked of the earth "with the word" (τῷ λόγῳ) of his mouth and "with breath" (ἐν πνεύματι) through the lips. It is to be noted that the connection between the motif of the Messiah's smiting of the wicked and the Christian's armouring and weaponry to fight against the evil power is not only in terms of ideas (in the sense of the Messiah transferred to the Christians), but also in terms of language. With regard to the instruments to punish the wicked, while the MT Isaiah 11:4 has שֵׁבֶט (rod or club) the LXX employs λόγος which pairs with πνεῦμα as the rendering of רוּחַ. Here the word and the breath of the Messiah are simply juxtaposed to signify their co-identity as divine instruments and the co-effect of destruction of the wicked. Their interrelationship is not in view but their shared function is the focus. Even if Ephesians 6:17b has ῥῆμα

---

237. *Pace* H. Conzelmann, "Die Brief an die Epheser," in *Die briefe an die Galater, Epheser, Philipper, Kolosser, Thessalonicher und Philemon*, eds. J. Becker, H. Conzelmann, and G. Friedrich (Göttingen: Vandenhoeck & Ruprecht, 1990), 91.

238. Ibid., 482; Fee, *Empowering Presence*, 728; Schnackenburg, *Ephesians*, 279; Lincoln, *Ephesians*, 451.

239. F. W. Beare, *The Epistle to the Ephesians, in Interpreter's Bible* 597–749; Keown, *Congregational Evangelism*, 293; Fee, *Empowering Presence*.

240. Cf. T. K. Abbott, *A Critical and Exegetical Commentary on the Epistles to the Ephesians and to the Colossians*, ICC (Edinburgh: T &T. Clark, 1899), 187; Barth, *Ephesians*, 776; Mitton, *Ephesians*, 227.

241. *Contra* Lincoln, *Ephesians*, 451, who suggests that the Spirit does not provide the sword but only God who can provide its cutting edge.

242. Cf. O'Brien, *Ephesians*, 482; Lincoln, *Ephesians*, 451.

instead of λόγος, the synonymous nature of the words sustains the relatedness of the language of the two texts.

A similarity can be observed in the LXX Isaiah 59:17–21, where the divine warrior – who also put on the armour of the divine gifts or attributes (v. 17) – will bring vengeance against the enemies (vv. 18–19) yet be the Redeemer for Zion (v. 20), and reconstitutes a covenant that the Spirit and the word shall not depart from the covenantal people and their descendants forever.[243] Here again, the Spirit (τὸ πνεῦμα) and the word (τὰ ῥήματα) are juxtaposed to signify their equal value as the divine gifts that sustain the covenantal relationship with the Lord.[244] This observation should inform one's interpretation of ἡ μάχαιρα τοῦ πνεύματος ὅ ἐστιν ῥῆμα θεοῦ, namely, the relationship of the three ἡ μάχαιρα, τὸ πνεῦμα and ῥῆμα θεοῦ.

First, as it is highly likely that the idea and language of the Spirit and the word in the Isaianic references are the background of Ephesians 6:17b, it is again very likely that the parallel relationship between the Spirit and the word is maintained in the use of τὸ πνεῦμα and ῥῆμα θεοῦ of Ephesians 6:17b. Even if τὸ πνεῦμα and ῥῆμα θεοῦ may not be identical in *nature*, they are identical in *function*: yielding destruction on the enemies. Thus, ὅ ἐστιν ῥῆμα θεοῦ is better described as referring back only to τὸ πνεῦμα that yields its cutting edge (i.e. the sword) as ῥῆμα θεοῦ does the same.[245] Then, the meaning of ἡ μάχαιρα in the phrase becomes clearer: the effect (the cutting edge) of both the divine Spirit and Word – as the smiting and slaying power comes from them.

Second, in light of the previous point, it may be that the writer of Ephesians implies, two items to take (δέξεσθαι), rather than one, which may function as aggressive weapons to defeat the evil power. Just as other commands to dress in the previous verses are all focusing on the divine gifts that explain the nature of the garments, δέξασθε of Ephesians 6:17b also focuses on the divine gifts: the Spirit of God *and* the word of God (of the

---

243. The LXX Isa 59:21: "... τὸ πνεῦμα τὸ ἐμόν ὅ ἐστιν ἐπὶ σοί καὶ τὰ ῥήματα ἃ ἔδωκα εἰς τὸ στόμα σου οὐ μὴ ἐκλίπῃ ἐκ τοῦ στόματός σου καὶ ἐκ τοῦ στόματος τοῦ σπέρματός σου ..."

244. Cf. Dickson, *Mission-Commitment*, 121.

245. Even if the Greek relative pronoun ὅ does not exclusively refer to the immediately preceding word in the same gender, it is still more natural to expect it to do so here (i.e. the neuter ῥῆμα corresponds only to the neuter τὸ πνεῦμα rather than the feminine ἡ μάχαιρα).

gospel). Here, the relation of the two in the Christian battle is not causative / derivative but simply complementary in yielding an effect (the sword). Then, the meaning of τὸ πνεῦμα and ῥῆμα θεοῦ and the relationship of the two must not be arbitrarily over interpreted as if the writer of the letter implies "proclamation of the gospel" or "spirit-led proclamation" as Fee and others contend. As Dickson correctly observes, δέχομαι in the Pauline letters (including the disputed ones) is almost always associated with a passive sense denoting reception or acceptance of a person or message.[246] If the imperative verb focuses on two divine gifts to be taken, the aggressiveness is not implied in terms of Christians' wielding of the weapon under the Spirit's empowerment (e.g. speaking forth of the message being inspired by the Spirit) as, but in terms of intrinsic nature of the divine Spirit and word. What is exhorted in the command δέξασθε for the Ephesians is not the proclamatory act of the word of God, but faithful holding on or fidelity to what is given: the Spirit of God and the message of salvation that yield the defeat of Satan.

Third, the previous point is attested by the Ephesians' focus on the role of the Spirit and the word. In 5:18 the Ephesians are commanded not to be drunk but to be filled with the Spirit (πληροῦσθε ἐν πνεύματι). This Spirit-filledness is directly connected to their praiseful and thankful communal life (vv. 19–20) and ushers it into obedient, sacrificial and loving caring Christian familial and social relationships according to Christ's model or will (5:21–6:9). Moreover, the role of the word for the sanctity of the church (καθαρίσας τῷ λουτρῷ τοῦ ὕδατος ἐν ῥήματι) is directly connected with this spiritual maturity of the Christian community (5:26). Here the Spirit and the word of God (or Christ) complementarily sanctify and mature the body of Christ. They are not described as something to be proclaimed for the outsiders. To be sure, the writer of Ephesians repeats this theme in the pericope of the divine armour, since there are enemies (6:12) that hate this happening. The sword, therefore, is not viewed as the means for the spread of the gospel, but in the first instance for the combat that fights against the evil attack and ultimately defeats Satan as the church becomes mature and holy by the Spirit and the word.

---

246. Dickson, *Mission-Commitment*, 121: 1 Thess 1:6; 2:13; 1 Cor 2:14; 2 Cor 6:1; 8:17; 11:4; Gal 4:14; Col 4:10; 2 Thess 2:10.

2.5. Conclusion: Paul's Consistent Silence about Congregational Evangelism

The above exegetical study demonstrated that there is no conclusive exegetical evidence that Paul mentions or expects congregational evangelism in the often-suggested Pauline passages. It was observed that the passages often suggested as Paul's positive mentioning of the church's proactive evangelism are either the reference to Paul's own apostolic mission or some Christian individuals' evangelism, but there is no indication of congregational evangelism. It was also observed that the passages often deemed to be Paul's exhortation indicative to or inclusive of the church's active spread of the gospel do not provide any syntactic, semantic and contextual ground for such an interpretation, while their hortatory stress is always on the Christians' socio-ethical life in fidelity to the gospel or their life in fixidity to the message of the gospel.

It was, however, also shown that, while the church's proactive evangelism is not voiced, the apostle clearly stresses that all the members of the church are partakers of his evangelistic mission by expecting them to be contributive to the furtherance of the gospel through various non-direct evangelistic means, which may either strengthen Paul's own mission or give the witness to the gospel.

How, then, do we have to take the observation, particularly about the silence? For Ware, who argues for Paul's apparent "voice" regarding congregational evangelism at least from Philippians, the problem of Paul's notable silence about congregational evangelism elsewhere in his letters is aptly solved by the situational character of Paul's letters, in which "the need for explicit exhortation to spread the gospel was not pressing."[247] Contrary to this, our exegetical discussion here indicates that the problem is never solved, but rather intensified by Paul's consistent silence about congregational evangelism even in Philippians. Thus, while the situational character of Paul's letters is again relegated to a mere possibility for the explanation for his consistent silence, the possibility is further weakened by Paul's apparent voice about the church's missio-ecclesial connection (through

---

247. Ware, *The Mission of the Church*, 235.

indirect evangelistic participation) to his own apostolic mission, even more intensifying the problem: why is Paul silent about the church's proactive evangelism, while he certainly recognizes it as the partaker of his apostolic proclamation of the gospel?

While we need to allow all the possible explanations for the silence, it is much easier to think and very likely that the consistent silence is a natural result from Paul's conception of mission which makes him fail to mention the church's role in such an evangelistic task. In this regard, Dickson seems to be right on target to propose a "two-dimensional view of mission" in Paul, who envisioned two functionally different but intentionally related mission entities: "authorized heralds and their partners."[248] While we may employ Dickson's two-dimensional interpretation of Paul's conception of mission for our further discussion, however, we may not hastily assume the "nature and extent" of Paul's conception of mission on the basis of Paul's particular silence on congregational evangelism as if such a silence informs the shape of Paul's mission-ecclesial understanding.[249]

Rather, the limitation of our exegetical conclusion is to be borne in mind. Since the discussion that led to our exegetical conclusion has only covered some generally suggested Pauline passages, it cannot and must not pretend to be "conclusive." Furthermore, if our conclusion is made by appealing to "Paul's silence" rather than his apparent "voice," our conclusion is intrinsically prone to the weakness of an argument from silence: since *a silence never amounts to an absence.*[250]

---

248. Dickson, *Mission-Commitment*, 176–177.

249. Note that Dickson takes the conclusion of his exegetical study (Dickson, *Mission-Commitment*, 86–177) as the basis for his further lengthy discussion of the "nature and extent of congregational missionary partnership" (178–308). While he provides an excellent discussion on the issue, which has been generally ignored or at best superficially dealt with, that the study is suggested as the "second dimension of Paul's view of mission" to the "first dimension" as if the two constitute "Paul's view of mission" is unsatisfactory. By doing so Dickson relegates Paul's missio-ecclesial understanding to a secondary place to Paul's "first dimension," *viz* his own or other eschatological heralds' mission.

250. Cf. D. Wenham, "The Story of Jesus Known to Paul," in *Jesus of Nazareth: Lord and Christ: Essays on the Historical Jesus and New Testament Christology*, eds. J. B. Green and M. Turner (Grand Rapids: Eerdmans, 1994), 291, who remarks on the danger in an argument appealing to "silence" on the part of Paul about something: "Had the Corinthian church not had acute problems over the observation of the Lord's Supper, we might have discovered that the Supper was unknown in the Pauline churches; had the Corinthians not

That being the case, we eschew a hard and fast judgment on Paul's missio-ecclesial understanding as if our exegetical conclusion indicates that he never expected the church's proactive evangelism. Rather, what we have found, namely Paul's consistent silence about congregational evangelism, while certainly and frequently voicing the church's fidelity to the gospel, is to serve as a preliminary data for our further attempt to construe a plausible description of Paul's conceptuality of mission that may explain why Paul fails to mention the church's proactive evangelism.

---

had mixed-up ideas about the resurrection of the dead, we would not have discovered the extent of Paul's knowledge of the resurrection traditions."

CHAPTER 3

Heralds and Community: Paul's Conceptualization of Mission as a Bifurcated Eschatological Event

The aim of this chapter is to provide a plausible answer to the question posed by our previous exegetical study: why is Paul silent about the church's proactive evangelism, while he certainly recognizes the church as a partaker in his apostolic proclamation of the gospel? As we have assumed that such a silence is most likely due to Paul's conception of mission, we intend to verify this assumption by investigating in what way Paul conceptualized "mission," hoping to show that his conception of mission explains his silence about congregational evangelism.

3.1. Paul's Jewish Eschatology and His Conception of Mission

If Bowers is correct to note that what Paul thinks he should be doing (i.e. his concept of *his* mission / vocation) is crucial for what he does (i.e. Paul's implementation of his mission / vocation),[1] we may think further that what shapes Paul's pattern of thinking, his worldview, is crucial for what he thinks he should be doing. As we have mentioned, J. C. Beker, having suggested that Jewish apocalyptic worldview is the "coherent centre" of Pauline thought,[2] notes the unmistakable connection between the coherent

---

1. Bowers, "Studies," 2–6, 81–82.
2. Beker, *Paul the Apostle*, 135–181.

centre and Paul's mission.³ Whether or not "apocalyptic" can be taken as the centre of the apostle's convictions even after his conversion,⁴ it seems right at any rate to suggest that one's thought and practice are by and large governed by the one's worldview, all the more so for someone operating within a life-governing and action-provoking "ism," such as Paul's own, namely Judaism (Gal 1:13–14) or Pharisaism (Phil 3:5, cf. Acts 23:6; 26:5).

In this regard, to discuss the likely worldview that Paul held before his conversion and what particular aspect of the worldview is related to his sense of purpose and action may be a good starting point for our further discussion of how the worldview in Paul, as the Christian apostle, was related to his conception of mission.

3.1.1. Paul's Jewish Eschatology and His Persecution of the Church

What we know most clearly about Paul's pre-conversion career is the fact that he persecuted the church (Gal 1:13; 1 Cor 15:9; Phil 3:6, cf. Acts 8:3; 9:1–2). The reason for his persecution of the early followers of Jesus may be explained in various ways.⁵ A common explanation is to consider the external factors, namely "what provoked Paul to persecute."⁶ For a fuller

---

3. Ibid., 144.

4. Cf. R. N. Longenecker, "The Nature of Paul's Early Eschatology," *NTS* 31 (1985): 85–95, who, in response to Beker's thesis, argues for "functional Christology" as the central conviction in the post-Damascus Paul.

5. For a summary of various views on the reason for Paul's persecution, see R. N. Longenecker, *Paul, Apostle of Liberty*, (New York: Harper & Row, 1964), 21–64; E. J. Schnabel, *Early Christian Mission*, 2. 927–928.

6. The explanation is usually concerned with what was happening in relation to those in the sect of the Nazarenes and particularly the message of the Hellenist Jewish Christians (e.g. Stephen) from the sect (i.e. their profession and proclamation of the faith in the crucified Jesus as the Messiah and the blasphemous criticism regarding the two undergirding pillars of the Judaism: the law and the Temple, cf. Acts 6:8–8:3). Cf. M. Hengel, *The Pre-Christian Paul* (London: SCM; Philadelphia: Trinity Press International, 1991), 72–84; Kim, *The Origin of Paul's Gospel*, 44–50; A. J. M. Wedderburn, "Paul and Jesus: Similarity and Continuity," in *Paul and Jesus*, ed. A. J. M. Wedderburn (London: T & T Clark), 123–124; D.-A. Koch, "Crossing the Border: The Hellenists' and Their Way to the Gentiles," *Neot* 39 (2005): 306–307. See also most recently, Barnett, *Paul, Missionary of Jesus*, 45–53, who suggests that "the addition of many priests (who offered *sacrifices* in the Temple)" to the Christian community at Jerusalem (Acts 6:7) was the "catalyst" of a series of events (vv. 5–13) in which particularly Stephen and the "Hellenist disciples" became opposed to the "Hebrew" disciples. He further suggests that such a tension within the nascent Christian community is responsible for Stephen's radical preaching about the

explanation, however, we need to go deeper and to identify his internal reasoning. While a psychological explanation would be futile, we need to consider as one of the reasons for the violent persecution of the sect of the Nazarenes the most vital part of Paul's pre-Christian worldview, namely, his Jewish eschatology.

3.1.1.1. Jewish Worldview and Restoration Eschatology

Many scholars agree that first-century Judaism was often expressed in terms of Jewish restorationism (i.e. aspirations and hopes for the deliverance of the Jewish nation as God's covenant people from their sin and obduracy which had led to the exile, and from ongoing affliction, bondage and disgrace under pagan rulers even after their returning from the exile).[7]

Such aspirations were by no means expressed in monolithic terms but involved various conceptions, such as "a new Temple," "the return of the Lord to Zion," "the advent of messianic figure(s)," "the renewal of the covenant," "the establishment of righteous people / the restoration of the twelve tribes," "the restoration of the Davidic / Solomonic territory of Israel," "the ultimate destruction of the wicked including both unrepentant Israelites and the nations," "the pilgrimage of the nations into Zion," and "the renewal of creation."[8]

Christopher Rowland identifies two major traditions of interpretation within Second Temple Judaism: (1) those who might be called pragmatists

---

Temple, and it eventually led Paul as a Hillelite Pharisee to change his tolerant stance toward the sect of the Nazarenes and to turn to persecution.

7. E.g. G. W. E. Nickelsburg, *Jewish Literature Between the Bible and the Mishnah: A Historical and Literary Introduction* (Philadelphia: Fortress Press, 1981), 18; C. Rowland, *Christian Origins: An Account of the Setting and Character of the Most Important Messianic Sect of Judaism* (2nd ed.; London: SPCK, 2002), 86–91; E. Schürer, *The History of the Jewish People in the Age of Jesus Christ* (New English version; Edinburgh: T. & T. Clark, 1986), 514–47; H. W. Hollander and M. de Jonge, *The Testaments of the Twelve Patriarchs* (Leiden: Brill, 1985), 39–40, 53–56; E. P. Sanders, *Jesus and Judaism*, (London: SCM, 1985), 77–119; Sanders, *Judaism: Practice and Belief, 63 BCE–66 CE* (London: SCM; Philadelphia: Trinity Press International, 1992), 289–298; Wright, *People of God*, 299–338; Wright, *Jesus and the Victory of God* (London: SPCK, 1996), 616–623; Dunn, *Jesus Remembered*, 393–396; J. M. Scott, ed., *Restoration: Old Testament, Jewish and Christian Perspectives*, JSJSup (Leiden: Brill, 2001); Scott, "Restoration," *DPL*, 796–805; M. Bird, *Jesus and the Origins*, 28–45; P. T. Gadenz, *Called from the Jews and from the Gentiles: Pauline Ecclesiology in Romans 9–11*, WUNT (Tübingen: Mohr Siebeck, 2009), 41–63.

8. For relevant canonical and pseudepigraphical references, see e.g. Dunn, *Jesus Remembered*, 393–396; Bird, *Jesus and the Origins*, 28–45.

or "activists," who sought God's deliverance by obedience and readiness to fight a holy war for the Lord (Num 25:6ff; Judg 6); (2) those who could be seen as "quietists" living in hope, who understood God's salvation only in terms of quiet trust and faith in God (e.g. Exod 15; Ps 18:7ff; Isa 10:16; 28:14ff; 29:5ff; 59:15ff).[9] James M. Scott suggests two strands of tradition in relation to Jewish interpretation of the post-exilic situation: (1) the "theocratic stream" that understood somewhat optimistically the restoration of Israel as having already occurred in the reestablishment of Jerusalem Temple cult and reinforcement of Israel's covenantal faithfulness to God; (2) the "eschatological stream" that regarded Jewish post-exilic situation as an ongoing exile which will be dealt with in terms of the ultimate restoration of the nation through God's eschatological vindication of the nation.[10]

While these different types or streams of Jewish traditions may elucidate the range of Jewish restorationism and people's different inclinations and emphases, we need to note that all these features (even though inharmonious with each other at times) are not wholly unrelated ideas but represent different presentations / interpretations of the *story of Israel* undergirding particular expectations and worldviews.[11]

We further need to note that the "eschatological" elements in such Jewish worldviews were not only relevant to a small fringe apocalyptic group of Judaism, but rather represented one of the most prominent, if not predominant, contemporary Jewish understandings of themselves and the world.[12] The world was often conceived through a dualistic frame of the two contrasting worlds, namely the current unsatisfactory world vs the world behind / beyond the tapestry of the current world and / or the world in the (near) future, that will be revealed or arrive by a decisive divine

---

9. Rowland, *Christian Origins*, 97.

10. Scott, "Restoration," 797–799.

11. Cf. M. Bird, *Jesus and the Origins*, 27: "Jewish restoration eschatology, then, is the attempt to tell a story about Israel, God and the future. 'Story' is perhaps the most characteristic expression of world-view."

12. Cf. J. J. Collins, *The Apocalyptic Imagination: An Introduction to the Jewish Matrix of Christianity* (New York: Crossroad, 1984), 7. See also Wright, *People of God*, 244–279, who suggests that the most fundamental tenets (beliefs) of Judaism (i.e. monotheism and election), inevitably precipitate an eschatology.

intervention.[13] Very often it was expressed in typical Jewish apocalyptic eschatological language of two ages: "This Age" (e.g. of Israel's obduracy or / and of suffering under evil pagan rule) will end with the arrival of "the (Messianic) Age to Come."[14] Even if this sort of doctrine of the two antithetical ages most clearly appears in post-70 AD literature (cf. e.g. *4 Ezra* 7:50, 112–119; 8:1; *m. 'Abot* 4:1), the concept of the "termination of this Age" (cf. *1 Enoch* 16:1) is already apparent at the latest in the pre-Maccabean or the Hasmonean period. And the expectation for the restoration in contemporary and subsequent literature of the Second Temple period largely presupposes this apocalyptic eschatological framework of the two ages – whether or not the literature is to be properly labelled as one of the "apocalypses."[15]

Scholars often emphasize the present aspect of the transpiration of the heavenly / future things, minimizing the distinction between the "apocalyptic" and "eschatological" characteristic of the worldview.[16] While "This

---

13. This is not to suggest that the Jewish apocalyptic eschatology is limited to conceptions of temporal / cosmological duality. In fact the Jewish apocalyptic eschatology includes a psychological / microcosmic duality or a forensic form of apocalyptic eschatology as well (e.g. *4 Ezra* 3:5–7; 20–21; *2 Bar.* 17:2–3; 1QS 1:18–24; 3:17–4:1; 1QM 13:9–12; *T. Judah* 20:1–5; *T. Asher* 1:3–5, cf. 2 Cor 5:17; Gal 5:16). Cf. M. C. de Boer, "Paul and Apocalyptic Eschatology," in *The Encyclopedia of Apocalypticism Vol. 1: The Origins of Apocalypticism in Judaism and Christianity*, ed. J. J. Collins (London: Continuum, 2000), 359–336. However, this sort of duality is largely framed within a temporal / cosmological duality (e.g. *2 Bar* 17:4: the free will to choose the law instead of Adam's way in the present age is to prepare the coming glorious age; 1QS 4:18–19: the destruction of the spirit of error within the children of righteousness by God at the eschaton, cf. Rom 6:6; the status of a self according to different aeons).

14. D. S. Russell, *The Method & Message of Jewish Apocalyptic, 200 BC–AD 100* (Old Testament Library; London: SCM, 1964), 269. Even if in *Apocalypse of Weeks* (*1 Enoch* 91–104) Jewish history is divided into "ten weeks (ages)" (91:11–17; 93:3–10), the presentation of each week largely reflects a two-fold scheme (seven weeks of this worldly concept vs three weeks of transcendental perspective). Whether the eighth week refers to the temporal messianic age is debated. Cf. L. R. Helyer, "The Necessity, Problems, And Promise of Second Temple Judaism for Discussions of New Testament Eschatology," *JETS* 47, no. 4 (2004): 603–605, who is opposed to Russell's scepticism on the temporal messianic period.

15. Cf. P. D. Hanson, "Apocalypse, Genre" and "Apocalypticism," in *IDB: Supplementary Volume*, (Nashville: Abingdon, 1976), 27–34; Rowland, *Christian Origins*, 54–56; J. J. Collins, *The Apocalyptic Imagination: An Introduction to Apocalyptic Literature* (2nd ed.; Grand Rapids: Eerdmans, 1998), 2; de Boer, "Paul and Apocalyptic Eschatology," 353.

16. E.g. Beker, *Paul the Apostle*, 145–146; See also J. D. G. Dunn, *Unity and Diversity in the New Testament: An Inquiry into the Character of Earliest Christianity* (3rd ed.; London: SCM, 2006), 337–371, whose use of "apocalyptic" is more adequately applicable to the so

Age" and the "Age to Come" are not necessarily conceived as consecutively connected,[17] what is clear in this sort of Jewish apocalyptic worldview, however, is that the restoration of Israel is seen as a historically future event climaxing at the end of this age. Even among the Qumranites for whom the end time is to be visible in their present communal life (e.g. 1QSa), their ritual purity in a thorough separation from the rest of Israel only signifies the foretaste of or the readiness for the arrival of the messianic era but not its *historical* arrival or inauguration.[18] Although the intensity and the practice were different from that of the Qumran sect, a similar anticipation of future restoration of Israel seems to be applicable to the Pharisees among whom Paul once was a member.

3.1.1.2. Pharisaic Expectation of the Restoration of Israel and Paul's Persecution

While our extant source materials do not give us a clear picture of the exact nature and the agenda of the Pharisees,[19] there is no compelling reason to doubt that the Pharisees shared a Jewish apocalyptic eschatological

---

called "inaugurated eschatology." Cf. C. Rowland, *The Open Heaven: A Study of Apocalyptic in Judaism and Early Christianity* (London: SPCK, 1982), 355.

17. Dunn, *Unity and Diversity*, 340–345.

18. See my argument in chapter 1, n.138. Note that the Jewish authors of some texts such as *Jub.* 23:26–29 and *1 Enoch* 93 (+ 91:12–17) could mention an eschatological timetable as if it had already begun in their time of composition. Cf. D. C. Allison, "The Eschatology of Jesus," in *The Encyclopedia of Apocalypticism Vol. 1: The Origins of Apocalypticism in Judaism and Christianity*, ed. J. J. Collins (London: Continuum, 2000), 1. 272–273. Nevertheless, it would be an over-reaction to lump these texts with so-called inaugurated eschatology. As G. Macaskill, *Revealed Wisdom and Inaugurated Eschatology in Ancient Judaism and Early Christianity*, JSJSup (Leiden: Brill, 2007), 45, rightly notes, judgment and restoration are still thoroughly unrealized, and the reversal of history is in the imminent future, but in the future nonetheless.

19. The selection of the source material is debated. While generally agreed source materials include Josephus, *War*, *Ant.*, the NT texts, and the early rabbinic literature (cf. A. J. Saldarini, "Pharisees," *ABD* 5.289–303; S. Manson, "Pharisees," *DNTB*, 782–787), J. Neusner, *The Rabbinic Traditions about the Pharisees before 70* (3 vols.; Leiden: Brill, 1971), limits them to the rabbinic sources. Some other scholars include *The Psalms of Solomon* (e.g. J. L. Trafton, "The Psalms of Solomon: New Light from the Syriac Version?" *JBL* 105 [1986]: 227–237] and / or the texts from the DSS such as 4QpNah (e.g. A. I. Baumgarten, "Rivkin and Neusner on the Pharisee," in *Law in Religious Communities in the Roman Period: The Debate over Torah and Nomos in Post-biblical Judaism and Early Christianity*, SCJ, eds. P. Richardson and S. Wilfrid [Waterloo: Published for the Canadian Corporation for Studies, 1991], 117; Saldarini, "Pharisees," 301, as a general reference including the Pharisees; Wright, *People of God*, 181–182).

worldview that anticipated the eschatological restoration of Israel as one of the central issues.

From the consideration of a few generally agreed features of Pharisaism,[20] it may be inferred that, while the Qumranites' anticipated the restoration of Israel through a radical ritual separation from the rest of the Israelites, the Pharisees, as a sort of reformist group,[21] sought the intensification of ritual purity not only within themselves but also in the entire nation.[22] Their pattern of ostracizing the ungodly (cf. Mark 2:16 and par.) probably indicates their belief that the arrival of God's future vindication is conditional on the maintenance of the nation's ritual purity and its delay is due to the impurity of the nation because of the ungodly.[23]

If this is the case for Paul who once was a Pharisee, it seems likely that his persecution of the Nazarene sect indicates not only that he saw the sect as seriously challenging what the Pharisees held as vital, according to their ancestral traditions (Gal 1:14) transmitted *from the past*, but he also considered that it was a movement whose members must be ostracized and

---

20. (1) They were generally lay experts in the Law with a special emphasis on tithing, ritual purity, and Sabbath according to their own traditional living code in addition to the biblical Law; (2) even if they were not as a group of a ruling class they struggled to gain power seeking to influence the entire society; (3) they maintained some apocalyptic eschatological views, *viz* believing in God's eschatological vindication / judgment responsive of human decision / action, the bodily resurrection, and the afterlife.

21. For the view of the Pharisees in the first century AD as a political revolutionist group whose agenda and influence were related to anti-Roman liberation ideology, see Wright, *People of God*, 181–203; Wright, *Victory of God*, 369–442. For a critique of Wright's view, L. T. Johnson, "A Historiographical Response to Wright's Jesus," in *Jesus and the Restoration of Israel: A Critical Assessment of N. T. Wright's Jesus and the Victory of God*, ed. C. C. Newman (Carlisle: Paternoster, 1999), 212–216.

22. Cf. J. Neusner, *From Politics to Piety: The Emergence of Pharisaic Judaism* (Englewood Cliffs: Prentice-Hall, 1973), 83, who suggests that such ritual purity of the Pharisees was due to their priestly self-conception (Exod 19:6). See Sanders, *Jewish Law from Jesus to the Mishnah: Five Studies* (London: SCM; Philadelphia: Trinity Press International, 1990), chapter 3, who is opposed to Neusner's suggestion of the significance of the purity code for the Pharisees and their non-political priestly self-conception. Cf. Wright, *People of God*, 188, who, while acknowledging the significance of purity code for the Pharisees towards the entire nation (186–188), but only through the "symbolic relationship to the wider political agenda" (187). See also J. Bowker, *Jesus and the Pharisees* (Cambridge: University Press, 1973), 17; C. Blomberg, *Contagious Holiness* (Downers Grove: IVP, 2005), 25–26.

23. Cf. J. Klausner, *The Messianic Idea in Israel: From Its Beginning to the Completion of the Mishnah* (London: Allen and Unwin, 1956), 404, who notes that the Pharisees of the day saw sins (impurity according to the law) as a delaying factor of the eschatological redemption.

which itself needed to be destroyed (πορθέω, Gal 1:13), because it was a disturbing influence and because it was seen as an obstacle to the nation's purity, that being the condition for God's decisive intervention for the nation's ultimate restoration *in the future*.[24]

In this regard, Paul's pre-Christian understanding of the restoration of Israel seems to be located within the "eschatological stream" according to Scott's classification, and more within the "activists" stream than the "quietists" stream, according to Rowland's categorization.

3.1.1.3. Questions for Paul's Conception of His Post-Conversion Mission

Our consideration above shows that Paul, at least before his conversion, appears to be a person whose perception of the world played a decisive role in his sense of purpose and his determination of action. This should lead us to ask whether it is still the case for Paul the *preacher*, rather than the *persecutor*, of the Christian faith, particularly regarding his conception of mission that had undergone a radical turn from his former Pharisaic convictions.

Of particular importance in our consideration of Paul's pre-Christian worldview is that his ultimate purpose that determined his action (i.e. persecution) was the futuristic hope for the nation, that is, the eschatological restoration of Israel. If the issue was so crucial even prompting Paul to militant action, we need to ask what happened to such a crucial issue after his conversion. Did the issue become irrelevant to Paul's conception of mission as he received the divine commission to announce the Son to the Gentiles (Gal 1:16)? Or did it become at any rate futile as a new ideal about the people of God emerged in Paul (Gal 6:16; Rom 9:8) or as he renounced his former Jewish grounds (Phil 3:7–8)? Or was it still understood as something

---

24. We need to note that the similarities between Paul's eschatological language and ideas in 1 Cor 15:23–28 (i.e. the advent of the Messiah / messianic kingdom, the schematization of eschatological time, the final judgment and consummation of all things at the time of ultimate end) and that of some texts from the pseudepigraphical literature (e.g. *1 Enoch* 37–71; 91:12–17; 93:1–10; *Jub.* 1:27–29; 23:26–31; *4 Ezra* 13; *2 Bar.* 29–30; 40; 72–74) indicate that Paul's eschatological understanding should by and large be located within a matrix of Jewish expectations for the messianic age and the final consummation. Cf. L. J. Kreitzer, *Jesus and God in Paul's Eschatology*, JSNTSup (Sheffield: JSOT Press, 1987), 93–170; Kreitzer, "Eschatology," *DPL*, 256–262.

to be awaited according to Jewish eschatological time scheme but only as a corollary of Paul's gentile mission (Rom 11:25ff)? Whatever the answer is, it would be incongruous if Paul conceived of his post-conversion mission dissociated from the issue, despite his apparent self-conception as the apostle among the Gentiles (Gal 2:7–9).

3.1.2. Paul's Jewish Eschatological Worldview and the Proclamation of the Gospel

3.1.2.1. Paul's Post-Conversion Mission in Eschatological Framework

Scholars seem to answer, if not fully, the first question posed immediately above. Despite the radical break with his former life as a Pharisaic Jew, scholars often recognize that Paul's post-conversion mission was still governed by his Jewish eschatological framework. A. Schweitzer provided a seminal idea. According to him, Paul maintained an eschatological conviction that the end will come only when the number of the elect from among the Gentiles has been completed, and being alone in apprehending such a necessity to preach the gospel to the Gentiles, he felt himself under compulsion to carry the gospel into the whole world.[25] As we have mentioned already, Cullman, Munck and Stettler took this line of thought and further stressed the pivotal role of the apostle's mission that will lead up to or even hasten the *parousia*.[26]

Of particular importance in Schweitzer and others' insight is that it provides a crucial idea that Paul conceptualized his mission within his eschatological framework.[27] As we have considered in the introductory chapter, this rightly leads us to approach Paul's conception of mission in terms of an eschatological event, complementing our necessary consideration of Paul's mission in terms of "task" or "contents."

However, while Schweitzer and others' insight certainly benefits our further discussion of Paul's conception of mission, it is to be noted that their estimation of Paul's eschatological framework is biased toward a

---

25. Schweitzer, *Mysticism*, 183.
26. See chapter 1, *3.2.2*.
27. Bowers, "Mission," *DPL*, 618.

purely futuristic dimension, making Paul's conception of mission exclusively *parousia*-oriented and *apostle*-centred.[28] This again inevitably relegates, whether permanently or temporarily, the issue of Israel out of Paul's conception of mission, while the eschatological ingathering of the Gentiles is viewed as if it exclusively occupies the apostle's conceptuality of mission.

It seems after all that a partial view of Paul's eschatological framework entails a partial view of Paul's conception of mission. Therefore, a more adequate construction of Paul's conception of mission requires a fuller consideration of his eschatological framework. In this regard, we are required to consider: (1) in what way is Paul's conception of mission "eschatological" (i.e. whether or not Paul maintained his Jewish apocalyptic eschatology even after his conversion / call); (2) chronologically at what point did Paul's eschatological convictions become a framework for his conception of mission (i.e. whether or not it was Paul's pre-conversional Jewish predisposition); (3) to what extent does his eschatological framework serve in Paul's conception of mission (i.e. whether it covers only Paul's own self conception as a missionary – as Schweitzer and others all seem to assume – or it covers something more than Paul's own vocation, namely that of others and of the church).

3.1.2.2. The Pre-Eschaton Paul and Paul of the Eschaton

Sometimes the "Jewish apocalyptic Paul" is overly emphasized leaving no difference between the "pre-Damascus Paul" and the "post-Damascus Paul" regarding his eschatological perspective. For example, Schweitzer located Paul (obviously the one after the Damascus event) within the world of "late

---

28. See above chapter 1, n.123, 124. Cf. Bowers, "Mission," *DPL*, 617–618, who, while pointing out Munck's indifference to the "collaborative" nature of Paul's mission at the expense of his pivotal role and his overemphasis on the future eschatological dimension, still stresses Paul's individualistic conception of mission: "it would appear that in that eschatological self-understanding we are nevertheless provided central explanatory sources for Paul's thinking on mission. Paul's theology of mission is a theology of his own mission, and he understood that mission as an eschatological event" (618).

Jewish Eschatology,"[29] and claimed that Paul's (apocalyptic) eschatology was future-oriented and future-dominated.[30]

However, this interpretation of Paul's eschatology is seriously (and rightly) challenged by many on the ground that post-Damascus Paul does not show in his letters a monolithic eschatological perspective: on the one hand, Paul's letters exhibit various aspects of his first-century Jewish apocalyptic worldview and some futuristic orientation (e.g. 1 Thess 1:9f; 4:13–5:11; 1 Cor 7:7–40; 15:20–23; 51–52; Rom 6:4–5; Phil 4:5), on the other hand, his Jewish apocalyptic eschatology appears to be a worldview that underwent significant adaptation in the light of the already happened and now happening Christ-event in the history of the world (e.g. Gal 1:4; 2:20; 6:15; 1 Cor 2:6; 7:29–31; 10:11; 2 Cor 5:1–10, 17; Rom 6:1–11; Phil 1:21, 23; 2:12–16). Thus, it is widely agreed now that while Paul maintains his ardent expectation for the Lord's appearing in a pattern corresponding to Jewish apocalyptic expectation, his theology is largely grounded on the recent past (i.e. the historical Christ-event) which signifies the realized aspect of the Age to Come and the present reality (i.e. Christian communities in Christ); this entails the current necessity of form of life (e.g. new creation) appropriate for the New Age, which has already dawned but not yet having fully eclipsed "This Age."[31] For Paul, while the Jewish apocalyptic duality provides a framework (in which temporal / spatial distinction or duality is maintained), the sharpness of the distinction is greatly blurred,

---

29. Schweitzer, *Mysticism*, 11. He means by "the late Jewish Eschatology" the Jewish apocalyptic eschatology, the world of which was conceived of by the authors of *1 Enoch*; the Psalms of Solomon; *2 Baruch*; *4 Ezra*; *Jubilees*; the *Testaments of the Twelve Patriarchs*; *Assumption*; the earlier and later canonical prophets (Ibid., 54–55). Cf. M. C. de Boer, "Paul and Apocalyptic Eschatology," 347.

30. Schweitzer, *Mysticism*, 52: "From the first letter to his last Paul's thought is always uniformly dominated by the expectation of the immediate return of Jesus, of the Judgment, and the Messianic glory."

31. E.g. W. Baird, "Pauline Eschatology in Hermeneutical Perspective," *NTS* 17 (1971): 314–327; L. E. Keck, "Paul and Apocalyptic Theology," *Interpretation* 38 (1984): 231; R. N. Longenecker, "The Nature of Paul's Early Eschatology," *NTS* 31 (1985): 85–95; Beker, *Paul the Apostle*, 145–146; V. P. Branick, "Apocalyptic Paul?" *CBQ* 47 (1985): 664–675; I. H. Marshall, "A New Understanding of the Present and the Future: Paul and Eschatology," in *The Road from Damascus*, ed. R. N. Longenecker (Grand Rapids: Eerdmans, 1997), 43–61; B. Witherington, *Jesus, Paul, and the End of the World: A Comparative Study in New Testament Eschatology* (Exeter: Paternoster Press, 1992), 15–35; N. T. Wright, *Paul in Fresh Perspective*, 50–57.

and the temporal focus is largely grounded on the proleptic reality of already / now that awaits the full consummation.[32]

Of course the explanation of Paul's eschatological perspective is still a huge area of debate regarding its proper description of the matter (i.e. is it apocalyptic or eschatological?) and about where to put the stress within the proleptic reality (i.e. whether on "already" or on "not yet").[33] Nevertheless, there is no doubt that Paul's Christian eschatological framework is not future dominated but rather contains serious concerns for the present due to his view shifted to the inaugurated nature of the end.

This shift made within Paul's eschatological framework, however, gives rise to various scholarly explanations. The difference is often regarded as showing that Paul's mind changed or developed regarding eschatological matters within his Christian career, the changes being identified either on the basis of some traceable Pauline chronology[34] or judgments about the authenticity of a letter (e.g. ambivalence in conceiving the timing of Christ's *parousia* between 1 and 2 Thess and between 1 and 2 Cor).[35] However, this developmental approach tends to over-interpret the change that happened within Paul's Christian career as a total change or radical break from the previous Christian view, and fails to take into account the basic coherence and consistency in Paul's writings both earlier and later on the matter.[36]

---

32. Cf. D. E. Aune, "Eschatology (Early Christian)," *ABD* 2. 602; Marshall, "A New Understanding," 49. One example of Paul's specific shift from future to past / present can be seen in Phil 1:15b, where Paul's allusion to the LXX Dan 12:3 alters the future φανοῦσιν to the present φαίνεσθε.

33. Cf. Beker, *Paul the Apostle*, 149, who, while acknowledging the "reduction of apocalyptic terminology and the absence of apocalyptic speculation" as the sign of the strong modification of normal apocalyptic thought due to the Christ-event and the "age to come" already present (145), warns against exaggerating such a modification stressing the eventual but not yet realized aspect, *viz* "Triumph of God" (355–360); Beker, *Paul's Apocalyptic Gospel: The Coming Triumph of God* (Philadelphia: Fortress Press, 1982), 40.

34. E.g. Dodd, *The Mind of Paul*, 67–82, 83–128; C. L. Mearns, "Early Eschatological Development in Paul: The Evidence of I and II Thessalonians," *NTS 27* (1981): 137–157.

35. E.g. Schweitzer, *Mysticism*, 42; Cf. P. J. Achtemeier, "An Apocalyptic Shift in Early Christian Tradition: Reflections on Some Canonical Evidence," *CBQ* 45 (1983): 231–248; J. C. Beker, *Heirs of Paul: Paul's Legacy in the New Testament and in the Church Today* (Minneapolis: Fortress, 1991), 67.

36. Cf. P. Woodbridge, "Did Paul Change His Mind? – An Examination of Some Aspects of Pauline Eschatology," *Themelios* 28, no. 3 (2003): 5–18. See also Witherington, *Jesus, Paul and the End of the World*, 23–35, who rightly observes that the "imminent language" that scholars think to be attached particularly to Paul's earlier letters is not in

Rather, it seems more natural to think that the most profound shift in Paul's eschatological framework had already taken place at the Damascus event. If what was revealed to or seen by Paul at the event was Jesus the Messiah (Gal 1:16; 1 Cor 9:1; Rom 1:2–5),[37] it could only mean for Paul, formerly a Pharisee, that the awaited Eschaton had indeed arrived.[38] This, then, should lead us to see the contrast of the eschatological perspectives between the pre-Damascus Paul and the post-Damascus Paul not between the apostle earlier and later.

Our observation here indicates that if Paul conceptualized his mission within his eschatological framework he did it as a "Paul of the Eschaton" rather than as the "pre-Eschaton Paul." The radical contrast between the pre-Eschaton Paul and Paul of the Eschaton, then, appears to be on his sense of purpose. While the pre-Eschaton Paul, as we have seen in his persecution of the church, feels a future-oriented necessity to facilitate the arrival of the Eschaton, Paul of the Eschaton, rather feels a present-oriented necessity to bring Jews and Gentiles "under Christ's law" who had already become the present reality (cf. 1 Cor 9:16–22).

3.2. Paul's Conception of Mission as an Inaugurated Eschatological Event

3.2.1. Paul's Conception of Mission within His Inaugurated Eschatological Framework

Our observation above shows that, while Paul's conception of mission is to be approached in terms of an eschatological event, the eschatological framework is to be characterized as an inaugurated eschatology. In this regard, I would argue that what we call "Paul's mission" is to be understood not only as his implementation of what he thought as his vocation or calling (Gal 2:2), but also as what he thought as a more or less broad

---

fact clearly indicative of Paul's specific conviction about the imminent *parousia* but rather signifies only the implication that the *parousia* "might be soon" (24), *viz* "as a means of producing moral seriousness in his audience" (33).

37. Cf. S. Kim, *Origin*, 56, 104.

38. Cf. Bosch, *Transforming Mission*, 127; Senior and Stuhlmueller, *The Biblical Foundation*, 169.

event God brings (or more precisely had been bringing since the event of Christ) into the inaugurated new world and towards its consummation: an inaugurated eschatological event, an event into which Paul's own vocation / implementation has a place.

Therefore, a distinction is to be made between "thinking of Paul's own vocation / implementation per se as an eschatological event" and "thinking of Paul's conception of mission as an eschatological event." As touched on above, previous scholars' observation tended to exclusively focus on Paul's own vocational conception and its significance within the eschatological drama that still awaits its final curtain to be drawn, Paul's vocation / implementation itself is equated with an / the eschatological event per se. This may inevitably result from their scope of observation, and Paul's mission per se at any rate should be seen as an eschatological event. However, my suggestion is that it is better to include Paul's (conception of his) missional vocation / implementation within his broader conception of an eschatological event that engages more than one eschatological participant and stretches its temporal scope to "already" as well as "not yet": an eschatological event that Paul came to perceive as having being inaugurated by the most decisive act of God in / with the Christ-event.

3.2.2. Paul's Conception of Mission and the Eschatological Ingathering of the Gentiles

3.2.2.1. The Implication of Inaugurated Eschatology for Restoration Eschatology

If through his encounter with the risen Lord Paul came to perceive his world in terms of inaugurated eschatology, what implication had his new picture of the world for other matters? More specifically, if, as we have discussed above, "restoration eschatology" was a decisive reason for his particular socio-religious pattern of behaviour under the old perception of the world (i.e. notably his persecuting), what did the changed worldview mean to his particular framework of thought within which he sought the restoration of his nation?

I would argue that the implication of his changed worldview was that he believed two things to be happening: (1) the inauguration of the restoration of Israel and (2) subsequently the inauguration of the incoming of the Gentiles. In my opinion, Paul's notion of the inauguration of the dual eschatological event played a decisive role for him and provided him with a framework within which he conceived of *his* mission.

With increasing scholarly appreciation of the universalistic aspects of Second Temple Judaism despite its general Jewish particularism,[39] it is often recognized that Paul's gentile mission generally is patterned after the Jewish scriptural (prophetic) and traditional (apocalyptic eschatological) expectation of the eschatological ingathering of the Gentiles into Zion that is precipitated by the eschatological restoration of Israel (e.g. Ps 47:6–9; 68:30–32; Isa 2:2–4; 11:6–10; 18:7; 19:23; 25:6–10a; 42:1–12; 45:14; 56:6–8; 60:11, 14; 66:18–20; Jer 3:17; 16:19; Hag 2:7; Zech 8:20–23; 14:16; Mic 4:1–3; 7:17; Tob 13:11–13; 14:6–7; *1 Enoch* 10:21; 48:5; 53:1; 90:33; *T. Ben.* 9:2; *2 Bar.* 68:5; *Sib. Or.* 3:702–731; 767–795; *Pss. Sol.* 17:31; *4 Ezra* 13:12; 1QS 11:13–14; 1QM 12:13–14; *Tg. Isa.* 16:1).[40] For instance, E. P. Sanders maintains that Paul's entire work had its "setting in the expected pilgrimage of the Gentiles to Mount Zion in the last days."[41] C. H. H. Scobie suggests that Paul's tremendous urgency in the missionary task (1 Thess 1:9–10) presupposes "the conviction that with the Christ event the New Age has dawned" and "the Old Testament concept of the eschatological ingathering of the Gentiles."[42]

---

39. Cf. J. D. G. Dunn, "Was Judaism Particularist or Universalist?" in *Judaism in Late Antiquity*, eds. J. Neusner and A. J. Avery-Peck, Part 3, vol. 2 (Leiden: Brill, 1995), 57–74. See also chapter 1, *3.3.1.* and n.194, 195 and 196.

40. E.g. Schweitzer, *Mysticism*, 177–187; Munck, *Salvation of Mankind*, 255–278; H. J. Schoeps, *Paul: The Theology of the Apostle in the Light of Jewish Religious History* (London: Lutterworth Press, 1961), 219; Hahn, *Mission*, 108–109; Bowers, "Studies," 172; M. Barth, *The People of God*, JSNTSup (Sheffield: JSOT, 1983), 43; Sanders, *Paul, the Law, and the Jewish People*, 171; J. D. G. Dunn, *Romans 9–16*, WBC (Nashville: Thomas Nelson, 1988), 575, 682; C. H. H. Scobie, "Jesus or Paul? Origin of the Universal Mission," in *From Jesus to Paul*, eds. P. Richardson and J. C. Hurd (Waterloo: Wilfrid Laurier University Press, 1984), 51–52; R. D. Kaylor, *Paul's Covenant Community* (Atlanta: John Knox, 1988), 7, 37; R. B. Hays, *Echoes of Scripture in the Letters of Paul* (New Haven: Yale University Press, 1989), 36–37, 71, 162; Wright, *Climax*, 150–151, 245; B. W. Longenecker, *Eschatology and the Covenant: A Comparison of 4 Ezra and Romans 1–11*, JSNTSup (Sheffield: JSOT, 1991), 264; J. M. Scott, "Paul's Use of Deuteronomic Tradition," *JBL* 112 (1993): 645; A. J. Köstenberger and P. T. O'Brien, *Salvation to the Ends of the Earth: A Biblical Theology of Mission* (Leicester: Apollos, 2001), 164–165; Ware, *The Mission of the Church*, 228; A. J. Hultgren, *Paul's Letter to the Romans: A Commentary* (Grand Rapids: Eerdmans, 2011), 418.

41. E. P. Sanders, *Paul, the Law, and the Jewish People*, 171.

42. C. H. H. Scobie, "Jesus or Paul?" 51–52.

3.2.2.2. First Gentiles Then Jews?

While the scholars agree that Paul's pattern of mission followed the Jewish universalistic expectation for the eschatological inclusion of the Gentiles, their presentation of that particular pattern of mission varies according to their understanding of Paul's eschatology. For example, Schweitzer's exclusive focus on the futuristic aspect of Paul's eschatology (by appealing to *the Apocalypse of Ezra* which talks about the "completion of the number of the Elect" leading to the arrival of the messianic kingdom) leads him to understand Paul's gentile mission ("in the analogy of Jewish [Pharisaic] missionary activity among Gentiles") as squarely fitting into the pattern of Jewish expectation – the completion of the number of the gentile elect that preconditions the *parousia*.[43] While finding such an aspect indeed in Paul's mission, others consider Romans 11:25 and following as indicating that Paul made a significant modification to his Jewish view, since for him the restoration of Israel does not precede the incoming of the Gentiles, but rather follows the completion of the incoming of the Gentiles, this idea would mean the "inversion" of the order in God's redemptive plan,[44] and / or the large-scale conversion of ethnic Jews at the end of this age, the *parousia*.[45]

This attempt to account for Paul's gentile mission as being patterned, though modified, after the eschatological pilgrimage of the gentile tradition is rigorously criticized by Donaldson (at the cost of another Jewish pattern of universalism, namely proselytism). His criticism is based on

---

43. Schweitzer, *Mysticism*, 182–183.

44. E.g. Munck, *Christ and Israel: An Interpretation of Romans 9–11* (Philadelphia: Fortress Press, 1967), 18–19, 120–125; Stendahl, *Paul, among Jews and Gentiles*, 28–29; Sanders, *Paul, the Law, and the Jewish People*, 123; Stendahl, *Jesus and Judaism*, 93–94; Dunn, *Romans 9–16*, 682; Scobie, "Jesus or Paul?" 52; W. S. Campbell, "Israel," *DPL*, 445; J. R. Wagner, *Heralds of the Good News: Isaiah and Paul "in Concert" in the Letter to the Romans*, NovTSup (Leiden: Brill, 2002), 292–293; Witherington, *Paul's Letter to the Romans: A Socio-rhetorical Commentary* (Grand Rapids: Eerdmans, 2004), 274–276.

45. E.g. Munck, *Salvation of Mankind*, 275–281; Munck, *Christ and Israel*, 139–141; Käsemann, *Commentary on Romans* (Grand Rapids: Eerdmans, 1980), 314–315; C. K. Barrett, *The Epistle to the Romans*, BNTC (Peabody: Hendrickson, 1991), 206; O. Hofius, "'All Israel Will Be Saved': Divine Salvation and Israel's Deliverance in Romans 9–11," *PSB*, Supplementary Issue 1 (1990): 19–39; D. J. Moo, *The Epistle to the Romans*, NICNT (Grand Rapids: Eerdmans, 1996), 722–729; J. A. Fitzmyer, *Romans: A New Translation with Introduction and Commentary*, AB (New York: Doubleday, 1993), 619–620; P. Stuhlmacher, *Paul's Letter to the Romans: A Commentary* (Edinburgh: T. & T. Clark, 1994), 172.

several points: (1) the eschatological dimension of Paul's mission alone is not sufficient to connect Paul with the tradition of the eschatological ingathering of the Gentiles;[46] (2) the reversal of the end-time scenario is not a modification but its "evisceration," since in the Jewish traditional expectation the ingathering of the Gentiles "follows" the restoration of Israel "as a matter not simply of *sequence* but of *consequence*";[47] (3) it is an anomaly for Paul to describe his gentile mission as grounded on Israel's stumbling, defeat, and rejection (Rom 11:12–15), if Paul understood it as grounded on the eschatological pilgrimage tradition;[48] (4) Paul does not appeal to the scriptural authority that might have supported his gentile mission in connection with the tradition as such;[49] (5) despite Paul's firm conviction of the equality of Jew and Gentile in both plight and salvation, Paul's ongoing distinction between Jews and Gentiles may not be easily explained on eschatological pilgrimage terms;[50] and (6) there are other parallels between Paul's Israel-centred gentile mission and a Jewish pattern of universalism such as Jewish proselytism.[51]

Donaldson's criticism reveals some inadequacy in attempts by scholars to connect Paul's gentile mission with the eschatological pilgrimage tradition. Nevertheless, I do not think that his criticism can rule out Paul's basic adaptation of the tradition per se. Rather, I argue that, while some necessary correctives are required, there are some unmistakable indications that Paul's gentile mission is generally patterned after the eschatological pilgrimage tradition.

3.2.2.2.1. *The restoration of Israel as an inaugurated eschatological event*

As a necessary corrective to Schweitzer's line of thought, we need to note that Paul conceives the correlation of the salvation of Israel and the Gentiles not merely towards the coming of the messianic age, but also in terms of its inaugurated fulfillment in God's graceful redemptive act. In Romans

---

46. Donaldson, *Paul and the Gentiles*, 188.
47. Ibid. (original emphasis).
48. Ibid., 193.
49. Ibid., 194–195.
50. Ibid., 195.
51. Ibid., 195–196.

11:1–17 Paul makes it clear that Israel's rejection is only partial (cf. v. 25)[52] and the redemption of Israel is also partly fulfilled in a "remnant" (λεῖμμα, v. 5) who is / are the "elect" (ἐκλογή, v. 7).[53] Even if the full restoration of Israel is something still to be awaited (v. 12), such a people of God "in the present time" (ἐν τῷ νῦν καιρῷ) is / are the one(s) who already have "obtained" (ἐπέτυχεν) what Israel seeks: the redemption of God (v. 7), while the rest of Israel "became hard hearted" (ἐπωρώθησαν, v. 7).[54] Even if it is not immediately expounded how this Jewish elect functions for the salvation of the Gentiles since Paul directly connects the salvation of the Gentiles in terms of the stumbling and rejection of the rest of Israel (vv. 11–12, cf. vv. 30–31), it becomes clear in verses 16–17 that Paul regards the Jewish remnant (as he describes them as the whole batch attached to the first part of dough offered as ἀπαρχή, and the branches connected to ῥίζα) as the *channel* of the richness (πιότης) (of the first fruit or the root) for the salvation of the Gentiles who were grafted (ἐνεκεντρίσθης) to them (cf. Rom 15:27).[55] Paul's emphatic mentioning of his being an "Israelite" (ἐγὼ Ἰσραηλίτης εἰμί, v. 1), then, may be seen in this direction. What is to be noted is that God's redemptive act, the election of the remnant, and the salvation of the Gentiles are all described in terms of "already" and their

---

52. Whether in v. 25 μέρος qualifies Israel or insensibility / hard heart is debated. Even if I am inclined to the former view (part of Israel) since Paul's general argument in vv. 1–12 supposes the two parts of Israel, it does not affect our discussion. Cf. Munck, *Christ and Israel*, 132; C. E. B. Cranfield, *The Epistle to the Romans*, ICC (2 vols.; Edinburgh: T. & T. Clark, 1975), 574; Dahl, *Studies in Paul*, 152–153; Käsemann, *Romans*, 313; Barrett, *Romans*, 206; J. R. Robinson, "ΠΩΡΩΣΙΣ and ΠΗΡΩΣΙΣ," *JTS* 3 (1902): 83; Wright, *Climax*, 247; Wagner, *Heralds*, 278; L. E. Keck, *Romans*, ANTC (Nashville: Abingdon Press, 2005), 279; B. Byrne, *Romans* (Collegeville: Liturgical Press, 1996), 354. *Pace* e.g. BDAG, 633 (1. c); K. L. and M. A. Schmidt, "πωρόω," *TDNT* 5. 1027; U. Wilckens, *Der Brief an die Römer*, vol. 2, EKKNT (3rd ed.; Zürich: Bebziger Verlag, 1993), 254; Gaston, *Paul*, 143; Dunn, *Romans 9–16*, 679; Beker, *Paul the Apostle*, 333; Fitzmyer, *Romans*, 621; Hofius, "All Israel Will Be Saved," 34, n.86; Stuhlmacher, *Romans*, 172; Hultgren, *Romans*, 417.

53. Cf. ὑπόκατάλειμμα (Rom 9:27), cf. שְׁאָר (Isa 10:22).

54. Cf. J. G. D. Dunn, *The Theology of Paul the Apostle* (Edinburgh: T. & T. Clark, 1998), 521, who perceives this contrast as "eschatological tension of Israel" in which the remnant of Israel stands for "now already" over against the "not yet of the rest of Israel."

55. Cf. M. D. Nanos, *The Mystery of Romans: The Jewish Context of Paul's Letter* (Minneapolis: Fortress, 1996), 252, who correctly notes that "The 'rich root of the olive tree,' which appears to signify the remnant of restored Israel that Paul in his ministry to the Gentiles represents (cf. vv. 1–10), 'supports' all the branches, both the Gentiles who are grafted in from a 'wild olive tree' and the natural branches of the 'cultivated olive tree.'"

correlation is defined in terms of a chronological and lineally causal relationship. This seems to suggest that Paul perceived at least the beginning (or "already" part) of God's redemption of the world and his implementation of vocation in terms of an inaugurated fulfillment of the eschatological expectation of the ingathering of the Gentiles into the eschatological elect of Israel. And it must be seen in line with what Paul mentions in Romans 1:16 (cf. 2:10).[56]

3.2.2.2.2. Lack of evidence for a chronological correlation

As a necessary corrective to the view concerning Paul's "inversion" of the traditional redemptive order (Rom 11:25–27), it is to be noted that despite the notable modification there is no firm ground to allow such a notion of inversion in Paul's argument. If the final salvation of the whole of Israel is understood as chronologically correlative to the final salvation of the full number of the Gentiles, Donaldson's criticism may be justified: the inversion of the redemptive order is not just a modification but its "evisceration." However, this criticism (on those who maintain that Paul carried out his mission according to the pattern of the eschatological pilgrimage despite his inversion of the redemption order) is not necessary since Paul did not invert nor eviscerate the traditional redemptive order in his understanding of the consummation of the salvation of Israel and the Gentiles.

As the previous point suggests, if Paul already saw in the election of the remnant of Israel and the Gentiles grafted to them the inauguration of God's redemption according to the traditional order (first in the Jewish remnant then the Gentile believers), why did he need to invert the traditional order for the final stage of God's redemption? Does the "mystery" (v. 25) that Paul mentions as the explanation of the Gentiles' salvation in place of the heart-hardened part of Israel suggest any chronological correlation between the final salvation of the Gentiles and that of Israel in the subsequent stage of Paul's mission?[57] If one believes so, a logical problem is also

---

56. It seems to me that πρῶτος denotes temporal priority of Israel's redemption. Cf. Sanders, *Paul, the Law and the Jewish People*, 118; Cranfield, *Romans*, 1. 91; J. D. G. Dunn, *Romans 1–8*, WBC (Nashville: Thomas Nelson, 1988), 40.

57. Cf. Hultgren, *Romans*, 419, who remarks that "if the Jewish people will be saved by their acceptance of the gospel within history, there is no 'mystery' (or secret) to speak of at all. Moreover, the 'mystery' is not Israel's ultimate salvation but 'the way in which Israel will achieve that ultimate salvation.'"

at stake. If this is the case for Paul, it should follow that all ethnic Israelites must remain hard-hearted until the end since until the final salvation of the Gentiles there is no room for Israel's salvation. Or one must explain how the temporarily stumbling Israel as a whole or as individuals can perceive and get envious (Rom 10:19, 11:11, 14) about the moment of the fulfillment of the salvation of the Gentiles. Is such a momentous eschatological time perceivable to the human mind? If such a time could be signaled by an obvious eschatological event (e.g. the *parousia* of Christ) as some like to suggest,[58] why does Paul need to speak particularly of Israel's jealousy towards the Gentile believers (as the means for their salvation) which seems pointless before such an obvious triumph of Christ? What is more natural and imperative than a simple confession along with obedience to him (cf. Phil 2:10ff; Isa 45:23ff)?[59]

3.2.2.2.3. Interdependence between Gentiles' salvation and Israel's restoration

Some further exegetical considerations militate against the chronological correlation between the final salvation of the Gentiles and that of Israel:

(1) Even if ἄχρι of verse 25b may suggest a certain temporal sense between the hardening of hearts in part of Israel (πώρωσις ἀπὸ μέρους τῷ Ἰσραὴλ γέγονεν) and the full and final incoming of the Gentiles (τὸ πλήρωμα τῶν ἐθνῶν εἰσέλθῃ), the temporal sense cannot be understood as if the cessation of the hardening of hearts will *occur* and the restoration of the rest of Israel will *start* only when the incoming of the Gentiles is completed.[60] Rather, this sort of temporal sequence mediated by the adverbial preposition ἄχρι that signifies the cessation of the former event and the occurrence of a new phase by the arrival of the latter event is possible only

---

58. See n. 44.
59. Cf. Nanos, *Mystery*, 257.
60. Cf. Dunn, *Romans 9–16*, 680, who, while seeing ἄχρι οὗ as certainly suggesting a temporal sequence ("until the time when") between the incoming of the full number of the Gentiles and the cessation of Israel's blindness, does not think it to be indicating the final events in strict sequence. While Dunn sees a certain "degree of complementarity between Jew and Gentile within the eschatological assembly of God's people," he does not further attempt to explain in what precise way all Israel will be saved by pointing to the sufficiency in Paul's "apocalyptic" word of "fullness" (691). *Pace* Cranfield, *Romans*, 2. 574–575: "[Rom 11:25b–26a] should be understood as simply indicating three successive stages in the divine plan of salvation" (575).

when one of the events is clearly (or grammatically) negative. For instance, in 2 Macc 14:10 which reads "ἄχρι γὰρ Ιουδας περίεστιν ἀδύνατον εἰρήνης τυχεῖν τὰ πράγματα (for as long as Judas lives, it is not possible to attain peace for the matters)" the (logical and temporal) former event is clearly negative (ἀδύνατον εἰρήνης τυχεῖν τὰ πράγματα). What is clear is that only when the temporarily latter event happens (naturally the killing of Judas) can a new situation (possible to attain peace) come.

It is doubtful if Romans 11:25 is such a case. First, the two events are juxtaposed as grammatically positive statements: "hardness[61] has come upon part of Israel"; (until) "the fullness of the Gentiles has come in." Second, since Paul does not provide any indication, it is doubtful that the cessation (as the perfect tense γέγονεν and the ἄχρι naturally enough suggest) of the hardened heart indicates an initiation to a next step. Rather, it seems to me that the use of ἄχρι in Romans 11:25b is very similar to that of Galatians 3:19 which reads "[ὁ νόμος] τῶν παραβάσεων χάριν προσετέθη, ἄχρι(ς) οὗ ἔλθῃ τὸ σπέρμα ᾧ ἐπήγγελται ([the Law] was added because of the transgressions, until the seed should come to whom the promise was made)": while the ἄχρι clearly indicates the cessation of the former event (the end of the service of the Law) at the point of the latter event (the coming of the seed, Christ, cf. Rom 10:4), a further stage for the Law is impossible since it ceased to be in service. In this direction, I propose that while the temporal sense of ἄχρι of Romans 11:25 denotes the continuation of the period of the hardened heart (for its mysterious function for the Gentiles' inclusion, 11:11–12, 17ff)[62] until the point of the incoming of the fullness of the Gentiles is completed, and connotes a gradual diminution of Israel's insensibility until its zero point, which per se means the fulfillment of Israel's salvation,[63] as the fullness of the Gentiles is to be

---

61. It is possible to read πώρωσις as "insensibility" which in English functions similarly to "impossibility." Then, one may like to regard the event of hardening of hearts as negative event as the case of ἀδύνατον εἰρήνης τυχεῖν τὰ πράγματα of 2 Macc 14:10. However, this could be a very arbitrary comparison since the grammatical and semantic function of πώρωσις is to be compared with εἰρήνη rather than ἀδύνατος.

62. Cf. Nanos, *Mystery*, 247–255, 264–265.

63. Cf. Wright, *Climax*, 249: "Paul is envisaging a steady flow of Jews into the church."

expected to have come (εἰσέλθῃ) in a similar temporal fashion: a gradual increase of the incoming until its fullest point.[64]

(2) The previous point is supported by a more adequate reading of καὶ οὕτως of verse 26. While the grammatical function of the adverbial phrase is explained in several ways,[65] exegetes are often divided regarding whether the phrase indicates any temporal sequence between the full incoming of the Gentiles (v. 25b) and the salvation of the whole Israel (v. 26a)[66] or not.[67]

Even if, as Van der Horst has shown, such a temporal sense in καὶ οὕτως is a grammatical possibility in here (e.g. 1 Cor 11:28), however, the usual sense of καὶ οὕτως (i.e. "and in this manner") is to be favoured here.[68] Paul has explained the election of the remnant "in the same way then (οὕτως

---

64. Cf. Ibid.: "During this period of time, the Gentiles are to come in to the people of God: and that is how God is saving 'all Israel.'" However, the latter point seems unsatisfactory. Despite Paul's overall emphasis on the unity between the two believing ethnic groups and the implication of the church representing a "single worldwide family," it seems unlikely that Paul moves to this point from his overall argument throughout Rom 11 for God's covenantal faithfulness to empirical Israel (i.e. all Israel = the remnant of Israel + currently obdurate Israel) vis-à-vis the Gentile believers in Romans. Even if Wright is well aware of the problem of the thought of the church as supplanting Israel (249–251), his reading of "all Israel" of v. 26a seems to be contradictory to what he previously argued. Cf. P. Richardson, *Israel in the Apostolic Church*, SNTSMS (Cambridge: Cambridge University Press, 1969), 131–206; J. Jervell, "The Might Minority," *StTh* 34 (1980): 25; Nanos, *Mystery*, 256.

65. There are generally four different grammatical explanations: (1) modal; (2) consecutive; (3) correlative; and (4) temporal. Cf. J. A. Weaver, *Theodoret of Cyrus on Romans 11:26: Recovering an Early Christian Elijah Redivivus Tradition* (New York: Peter Lang Publishing, 2007), 9.

66. E.g. Barrett, *Romans*, 223; Käsemann, *Romans*, 313–314; B. Corley, "The Jews, the Future and God," *SJT* 19 (1976–1977), 51; T. R. Schreiner, *Romans*, BECNT (Grand Rapids: Baker, 1998), 621; N. A. Dahl, "The Future of Israel," in *Studies in Paul: Theology for the Early Christian Mission* (Minneapolis: Augsburg, 1977), 152–153; Cranfield, *Romans*, 2. 576; M. N. A. Bockmuehl, *Revelation and Mystery in Ancient Judaism and Pauline Christianity* (Tübingen: Mohr Siebeck, 1990), 173; Stuhlmacher, *Romans*, 172; C. Talbert, *Romans*, SHBC (Macon, Smyth & Helwys, 2002), 264; P. W. van der Horst, "Only Then Will All Israel Be Saved: A Short Note on the Meaning of *kai houtōs* in Romans 11.26," *JBL* 119 (2000): 521–525; Witherington, *Romans*, 274–275.

67. E.g. G. Vos, *The Pauline Eschatology* (Grand Rapids: Eerdmans, 1979 [1953]), 89; Ridderbos, *Outline*, 358; Beker, *Paul the Apostle*, 334; Wright, *Climax*, 249–250. Cf. Fitzmyer, *Romans*, 622; Hofius, "All Israel Will Be Saved," 35; S. Kim, *Origin*, 83–84; Sanders, *Paul the Law and the Jewish People*, 193–194, who, while do not find the temporal sense, read the adverb as denoting a sequential consequence / conclusion.

68. Rom 5:12; 1 Cor 7:17, 36; 14:25; 15:11; Gal 6:2; 1 Thess 4:17. Cf. Witherington, *Romans*, 274, who, following Horst, sees the case of 1 Thess 4:17 as denoting a temporal sequence.

οὖν καὶ)" of God's election of the seven thousand (vv. 4–5); he emphasizes Gentiles' salvation purely in terms of God's own mercy, and he goes on to stress that the dynamic of Israel's salvation is to be understood "in this manner (οὕτως καὶ)" (i.e. solely God's own mercy, vv. 30–31). Thus, it seems very likely that Paul does mean the same in the use of the adverb in verse 26 as he stresses the divine initiative in Israel's salvation (v. 26a). In this regard, I propose to take the three occasions of οὕτως in Romans 11 as all referring to God's sovereignty in his act of election and his covenantal faithfulness that never abandons his people (v. 29) and even reaches to "no people" (v. 11, cf. 10:19). Paul mentions about the gradual increase of the incoming Gentiles in verse 25. In a similar fashion he mentions his conviction of the final salvation of Israel to the point of its fullness. Here, in no way can one conclusively construe a temporal sequence between the final salvation of the Gentiles and that of Israel. What can be inferred from their relationship, as Beker rightly puts it, is that it is more or less "interdependence" rather than chronologically / lineally sequential.[69]

(3) The context of Romans 11 does not necessarily envisage the salvation of the temporarily stumbling Israel as something to be initiated only at some point in the definite future (presumably after the full incoming of the Gentiles), but rather as an event that may happen currently or very near future. By reading "ζωὴ ἐκ νεκρῶν" of verse 15 literally as denoting the eschatological resurrection that ushers the messianic age, some see it as an indication of Israel's "acceptance" as purely a futuristic eschatological event that is closely linked to the eschatological resurrection.[70] However, this reading is not conclusive. As Paul can speak of "as ones alive out of the dead (ὡς ἐκ νεκρῶν ζῶντας)" in Romans 6:13 in the metaphorical sense, a strong claim for a literal reading cannot be made for Paul's reference here.[71] It is still too general to mean the eschatological resurrection.

---

69. Beker, *Paul the Apostle*, 334, notes that καὶ τότε is more adequate if Paul intended any temporal sequence.

70. E.g. Munck, *Christ and Israel*, 126–127; Käsemann, *Romans*, 294; Cranfield, *Romans*, 2. 563; D. Zeller, *Juden und Heiden in der Mission des Paulus: Studien zum Römerbrief* (Stuttgart: Katholisches Bibelwerk, 1973), 242–243; Dunn, *Romans*, 658; Beker, *Paul the Apostle*, 153; Moo, *Romans*, 274, 695–696; Witherington, *Romans*, 274–275.

71. Cf. Wright, *Climax*, 248, who sees the resurrection motif metaphorically in a paralleling way of referring to the Gentiles' salvation as a *creatio ex nihilo* in Rom 4:17.

Rather, we need to pay attention to verse 14 where the verb παραζηλόω (to provoke to jealousy) is used to denote the intended result of Paul's gentile mission so that he might save (σώσω) "some" of his fellow Jews. What is to be noted is that the salvation induced by jealousy here does not envision the eschatological totality of the restoration of Israel, but only a part of it.[72] If the salvation induced by the jealousy in Israel (cf. 10:19; 11:11) is to be understood only in terms of a large-scale eschatological conversion provoked by the full accomplishment of the incoming of the Gentiles, how can we understand this sort of partial coming out from those obdurate Israelites through their jealousy? This verse clearly shows that while Paul envisages the final stage of the definite future in which the restoration of Israel will culminate with its totality, for Paul God's "mysterious" provoking of Israel to jealousy by salvation among the Gentiles is already initiated in current time.[73]

(4) The immediately previous point should shed some light in a text critical consideration of the second νῦν in verse 31 (e.g. ℵ B D*,C). If Paul envisages "some" of the Jews coming into the salvation not in the definite future but currently or in near indefinite future, the second νῦν well fits with this and there is no reason to go for P[46] or other authorities which lack it (e.g. A D² F).[74] Then, Paul's careful rhetorical arrangement for the correlation of the salvations of the two parties may not be seen as presenting their chronological relation but rather their simple interdependence:

ὥσπερ γὰρ ὑμεῖς ποτε ἠπειθήσατε τῷ θεῷ
       νῦν δὲ ἠλεήθητε τῇ τούτων ἀπειθείᾳ
οὕτως καὶ οὗτοι νῦν ἠπείθησαν τῷ ὑμετέρῳ
ἐλέει ἵνα καὶ αὐτοὶ νῦν ἐλεηθῶσιν

---

72. *Pace* Käsemann, *Romans*, 306–307.
73. Cf. Barrett, *Romans*, 199.
74. Cf. Morris, *Romans*, 425.

3.2.2.3. The Inauguration of the Restoration of Israel as the Starting Point of Ongoing Salvation for Jews and Gentiles

Does this absence of chronological correlation between the consummation of the Gentiles' salvation and that of Israel, then, mean Paul's abandonment of the traditional Jewish view of the pilgrimage of the Gentiles? It is unlikely.

3.2.2.3.1. A bifurcation of the two salvations in the "Not Yet"

As for Paul the beginning of the Gentiles' salvation was firmly grounded according to the traditional redemptive order, God's ongoing redemptive plan moves towards its culmination in a bifurcation of the two salvations for Jews and Gentiles. Perhaps, it is a striking change to an ordinary contemporary Jewish eye that the final restoration of Israel is not expected any more to precede that of the Gentiles but will be accomplished alongside. Nevertheless, this significant change may be seen not as an evisceration of the Jewish tradition from Paul's conception of mission but rather as a modification. The change is made only in the "not yet" part that envisions the culmination of God's eschatological redemption, and the "already" part is firmly grounded on the Jewish scriptural / traditional order of salvation history.

3.2.2.3.2. Pattern of Jewish redemptive order in the "Not Yet"

Even in the "not yet" part of the eschatological horizon, in which Paul's understanding of the scriptural texts about the eschatological salvation of Israel (and the Gentiles) is inevitably modified, the typical beneficiary role of the salvation of Israel for the forthcoming salvation of "no people" is maintained. In Romans 11:26 Paul professes his conviction about the salvation of the rest of Israel (who are temporarily obdurate). Here Paul uses a citation from Isaiah 59:20 in which the original ἕνεκεν Σιων/לְצִיּוֹן (to Zion) is altered into ἐκ Σιὼν (from Zion).[75] The original text plainly envis-

---

75. Contrary to B. Schaller, "'ΞΕΙ ΕΚ ΣΙΟΝ Ο ΡΥΟΜΕΝΟΣ' Zur Textgestalt von Jes 59:20f. in Röm 11:26f," in *De Septuaginta: Studies in Honour of John William Wevers on His Sixty-Fifth Birthday*, eds. A. Pietersma and C. Cox (Toronto: Benben, 1984), 201–206, viz "EK" as an mistransmission of "ΕΙΣ," Paul's almost precise verbatim (ἥξει ἐκ Σιὼν ὁ ῥυόμενος, ἀποστρέψει ἀσεβείας ἀπὸ Ἰακώβ, cf. ἥξει ἕνεκεν Σιων ὁ ῥυόμενος καὶ ἀποστρέψει ἀσεβείας ἀπὸ Ἰακώβ, the LXX Isa 59:20) and the context of Paul's argument in

ages the redeemer's coming *to Zion* for the restoration of Israel. For Paul this original vision is now fulfilled in the remnant, and the Redeemer is with them now (v. 11). Thus, the ongoing process until the consummation of the salvation of Israel is now differently envisioned: the redeemer will now come *from* (or *via*) *Zion*, the remnant of Israel (and those Gentiles grafted into them) to the rest of Israel (and the rest of the Gentiles as well).[76]

What is to be noted here is that the eschatological salvation of those who are currently "not the people of God" from Paul's perspective (including Jews and Gentiles)[77] is envisioned through the existence of those who are the people of God. Despite Paul's alteration of the definition of the people of God and the modified eschatology (the dialectic tension between already and not yet), neither the inversion of the Jewish traditional redemptive order nor abandonment of the eschatological pilgrimage tradition can be construed. Rather, the expectation of the consummation of the whole of Israel (and implicitly that of the Gentiles) still rests within the framework of the traditional eschatological redemption scheme in which the restoration of the people of God precipitates the salvation of those who are not currently the people of God.

Therefore, Paul's explanation of the salvation of the Gentiles in terms of Israel's failure rather than its restoration is not such an anomaly as Donaldson supposes. It simply belongs to God's sovereignty that has been already portrayed in Scripture (Rom 11:11ff, cf. 9:6–29). As touched on

---

the entire Rom 11 (see below) strongly suggest that ἐκ instead of ἕνεκεν is not an erroneous transmission of the scripture but rather a deliberate alteration to signify a certain change in view of the manner in which God's eschatological redemption comes to Israel. Cf. C. D. Stanley, "'The Redeemer Will Come ἐκ Σιών' Romans 11.26–27 Revisited," in *Paul and the Scriptures of Israel*, JSNTSup, eds. C. A. Evans and J. A. Sanders (Sheffield: JSOT Press, 1993), 118–142, who argues for Paul's citation from a non-Christian Judaistic oral tradition which already included the alteration as such.

76. *Pace* e.g. Moo, *Romans*, 728–729; Witherington, *Romans*, 276, who see the "Zion" as new Jerusalem in heaven (Gal 4:26) from which the deliverer will come at the *parousia*. This view is unlikely, since the original OT text (Isa 50:20) clearly refers to the earthly realm where the people of God dwell and Paul's another use of Zion in adjacent Rom 9:33 refers to the same. This point will be addressed more in detail later.

77. As Paul exhibits his deep appreciation of the Song of Moses (Deut 32) – cf. Hays, *Echoes*, 84–164 – it seems very likely that Paul could think of the obdurate Jews in his time as temporarily "not children of God" (Deut 32:5, 21, cf. Rom 10:19, Phil 2:15) or equivalent to Gentiles as "no people" (cf. Rom 2:28–29) despite his firm conviction of God's ultimate faithfulness to the empirical Israel.

in our first point, since Paul's main argument is that the Gentile believers should not boast over the non-believing Jews, οἱ κλάδοι ἐξεκλάσθησαν, even if what is highlighted is the relationship between the believing Gentiles and the rejection of the rest of Israel, the rejection of Israel does not exhaust Paul's rationale for the incoming of the Gentiles as he clearly indicates the lineally defined correlation between the two believing ethnic groups (Rom 11:17–18). As Paul puts it, that part belongs to "this mystery" that had not been easily comprehended. Here, Paul's point is not about explaining things that had been well (or even over) appreciated by the Jews (the Gentiles will be saved only in terms of the restoration of Israel) or endorsing things that could have been erroneously construed by the Gentile believers (Israel's place is now taken over by the Gentile believers), but the thing to be comprehended thenceforth (by the believers Jews and Gentiles): the interrelationship (or interdependence) between Israel and the Gentiles in the course of their salvation towards its culmination, since the fulfillment of the traditional expectation is already inaugurated and it provides the ongoing pattern in which the salvation of those who are not the people of God (Jews and Gentiles) can be expected through the existence of the restored people of God (Jews and Gentiles).

Even if such an interdependence does not appear in the Jewish tradition of the eschatological pilgrimage of the Gentiles, the mystery comprehended by Paul as such is possible only when he realized that the fulfillment of the expectation of the restoration of Israel (in the election of the remnant of Israel) and the ingathering of the Gentiles (in the inclusion of the Gentiles in the place of those who missed the blessing!) is inaugurated just as the Jewish expectation had envisioned. Such an interdependence is a natural corollary of the extended eschatological horizon where the promise of the restoration of Israel and the incoming of the Gentiles is already fulfilled.

3.2.2.4. Presence of the Theme of the Eschatological Gathering in Paul

Donaldson's argument for the "virtual absence of eschatological pilgrimage texts" in Paul is unconvincing.[78] As even he himself admits,[79] in Romans

---

78. Donaldson, *Paul and the Gentiles*, 195.
79. Ibid., 194.

15:12 Paul cites Isaiah 11:10 which is one of the most vivid descriptions of the eschatological ingathering of the Gentiles. The citation appears in the "climax" section (15:7–13) of Romans 14:1–15:13,[80] where it serves as Paul's rationale for the unity between Jewish Christians and Gentile Christians along with other scriptural citations (Ps 18:49; Deut 32:43; Ps 117:1). According to Donaldson, since the citation indicates Paul's mere practice of some sort of rabbinic keyword pattern of argument by appealing to each part of the *Tanakh* and the citation of Isaiah 11:10 merely denotes the connection of the salvation of the Gentiles with the work of the Messiah, the citation itself cannot be evidence for the view that Paul carried out his gentile mission within an eschatological pilgrimage.[81]

This conclusion is a *reductio ad absurdum*. Insofar as Isaiah 11:10 is cited in the context where Paul talks about the inclusion of the Gentiles into the people of God (15:8–9) and Paul has already in Romans 9–11 argued his point in the framework of the traditional redemption order, Paul's citation from a clear eschatological pilgrimage tradition should clarify that the redemption order maintained by himself has much to do with the eschatological pilgrimage tradition per se. Moreover, there are indirect indications that Paul understood his mission largely being framed by the tradition. One of the possible justifications for Paul's alteration of ἕνεκεν Σιων/לְמַעַן צִיּוֹן to ἐκ Σιών in Romans 11:26 is Isaiah 2:2–3,[82] which depicts the eschatological gathering of the nations to the mountain of the Lord's house, the symbol of the restoration of Israel (v. 2). In 2 Corinthians 6:2 Paul's ground for his claim that "now is the acceptable time, now is the day of salvation [of the Corinthians]" is Isaiah 49 which depicts the promise of the eschatological restoration of Israel (v. 8) through the Lord's servant who is the light to the nations (v. 6). Even if the explicit appeal to scriptural support is scanty and the connection is rather implicit, Paul's conviction about the salvation of the Gentiles is certainly presented within the scriptural background, which envisages the lineally causal correlation of the eschatological salvation of Israel and that of the Gentiles.[83]

---

80. Cf. Wright, *Climax*, 235.
81. Donaldson, *Paul and the Gentiles*, 194–195.
82. Cf. Wright, *Climax*, 250.
83. Cf. Wagner, *Heralds*, 294, n. 227.

3.2.3. Conclusion: Paul's Conception of Mission as a Bifurcated Eschatological Event of the Restoration of Israel and the Incoming of Gentiles

By the way of an endorsement of E. P. Sanders and others with some modification, the discussion so far leads to the idea that Paul's understanding of his mission is firmly grounded on his notion of God's faithful fulfillment of his promise of the restoration of Israel and the ingathering of the Gentiles. We have shown that the new element which the Christian Paul introduced into the traditional framework of Jewish restoration eschatology (Israel first and then Gentiles) was not an "inversion" of redemptive order (Gentiles and then Israel) but a modification necessitated by the inauguration of the restoration of Israel in the first generation of Jewish believers (Jewish remnant first and then Gentiles / obdurate Israel).

However, particularly important for our purpose is not merely Paul's pattern of gentile mission as such, but that his notion of mission is shaped in terms of a God-driven eschatological event already inaugurated yet to be consummated. As the fulfillment of this expectation was inaugurated in the Christ-event and the election of the remnant of Israel with Gentile participants ("already"), Paul's apostolic mission among the Gentile world is best understood as *his ongoing participation into the God-brought / bringing eschatological event* that calls for his implementation for the *continuation* of (1) the restoration of Israel and (2) the ingathering of the Gentiles until its final stage.

If this observation answers the question of *what* (not in the sense of "what to do" but more precisely "what has been / is happening" or "what is to happen": What is to be continued until the culmination of the end time-process is the incoming of the Gentiles and the restoration of Israel) in Paul's conception of mission, at least two further significant points arise: (1) our discussion of Paul's conception of mission is not to be limited to his own eschatological apostolic vocation of the preaching of the gospel among the Gentiles, but should be extended to a wider subjective framework which can accommodate or account for the entire process of the eschatological event that God brings about for the continuation of the already inaugurated fulfillment;[84] and (2) we still need to answer a further question in terms of *how*: What is Paul's understanding of *the way of implementation* (by God) in which the restoration of Israel and the ingathering of the Gentiles will continue until its final completion?

3.3. The Gospel Heralds as an Eschatological Event in Paul

How, then, did Paul perceive God's implementation for the continuation of the restoration of Israel and incoming of the Gentiles? One obvious answer from Paul's letters is God's election of the heralds for the announcement of the good news, the apostolic message that God has restored his people Israel in the remnant marked by the faith in / of his Son, and now the Gentiles are welcome to share the same faith (e.g. Rom 1:1–6, cf. e.g. Gal 1:15–16a; 2 Cor 6:1–10; Rom 10:5–13).

3.3.1. Paul's Commission as One of the Eschatological Heralds of the Gospel

3.3.1.1. Paul, Prophets, and the Servant of the Lord

For the background of Paul's understanding of this divine election / sending for the proclamation of the good news – most probably to have entered into Paul's convictional world after his encounter with Christ outside Damascus – scholars often point to Paul's appeal to the OT prophets such as Jeremiah and Isaiah, whose calling was based on their special divine election before their birth (Jer 1:5; Isa 49:5), and to whom Paul's apostolic affliction may be comparable.[85]

---

84. In this sense, Paul's conception of mission may be seen as analogous to the modern / post-modern missiologists' notion of "*missio Dei*": mission not as the act of individuals or the church but God's own act for the redemption of creation, within which various "sub-missions" are in view.

85. E.g. E. Lohmeyer, *Grundlagen Paulinischer Theologie* (Beiträge Zur Historischen Theologie; Tübingen, 1929), 201; Rengstorf, "ἀπόστολος," *TDNT* 1. 438–441; Y. K. Fung, *The Epistle to the Galatians*, NICNT (Grand Rapids: Eerdmans, 1988), 63–64; C. A. Evans, "Paul and the Prophets," in *Romans and the People of God: Essays in Honor of Gordon D. Fee on the Occasion of His 65th Birthday*, eds. S. V. Soderlund and N. T. Wright (Grand Rapids: Eerdmans, 1999), 115–128; *idem*, "Prophet, Paul as," *DPL*, 762–765. For extensive studies on the apostle's self-conception and ministry in relation to Jewish scriptural and traditional

However, it seems that, while the calling of the prophets in the OT texts certainly provides Paul with a parallel to and corroboration of his own special divine commission as one of the apostles, such a parallel does not provide anything further, apart from how Paul perceived his own vocation in relation to the opposition he was faced with. What is to be noted is that such a corroboration by appealing to the OT prophetic calling appears only either in a polemical situation regarding (the genuineness of) his apostleship (Gal 1:11–2:10) or a context of suffering and opposition (1 Thess 2:2–4; 3:4).[86]

What we need to keep in mind is that Paul conceived his mission not simply as a divinely commissioned one but in a broader picture a participation in God's implementation of the eschatological redemption.[87] And, even if Paul is aptly explained in terms of a "prophetic figure" (i.e. spirit-filled seer and authoritative messenger / teacher / interpreter of God's word, cf. e.g. 2 Cor 12:1–10; 1 Cor 14:6ff), Paul's understanding of (Christian) prophets and prophecy is notably different from that of the OT prophets.[88] But elsewhere in his letters (and particularly in Romans which is less polemical in character than Galatians regarding his apostleship) in relation to his gentile mission Paul frequently quotes or alludes to the Deutero-Isaianic texts which are about God's eschatological implementation for the restoration of Israel and the incoming of the Gentiles through the eschatological "Ebed Yahweh" figure (Isa 42:1–9; 49:1–6; 50:4–9; 52:13–53:12) and the eschatological "messenger of the good news" (Isa 52:7).[89] In this

---

understanding of prophets see e.g. W. A. Grudem, *The Gift of Prophecy in 1 Corinthians* (Lanham: University Press of America, 1982); Sandnes, *Paul One of the Prophets?*

86. Cf. C. A. Evans, "Prophet, Paul As," *DPL*, 763.

87. Cf. M. Hengel and A. M. Schwemer, *Paul between Damascus and Antioch: The Unknown Years,* trans. J. Bowden (London: SCM, 1997), 95: "For Paul the eschatological "apostolic" sending by God or Christ is oriented on the sending of the prophets of the Old Covenant, indeed it surpasses these. Now the sending relates to the eschatological final salvation and therefore to decision."

88. Cf. B. Witherington, *The Paul Quest: The Renewed Search for the Jew of Tarsus* (Leicester: IVP, 1998), 135, who, while generally following D. Aune (*Prophecy in Early Christianity and the Ancient Mediterranean World* [Grand Rapids: Eerdmans, 1983], 203–211), points out: (1) the political setting and nature of much OT prophecy is missing from Paul's letters; (2) they were by and large prosecutors of the covenant lawsuit.

89. Rom 10:15 (Isa 52:7); 10:16 (Isa 53:1); 11:34 (Isa 40:12); 15:21 (Isa 52:15); Gal 4:27 (Isa 54:1); 2 Cor 6:2 (Isa 49:8); Phil 2:16 (Isa 49:4).

sense, while Paul's self conception certainly has to do with his idea of the OT prophetic calling and ministry, another aspect that considers the "Ebed Yahweh" motif,[90] in my opinion, is weightier and must supplement our understanding of the background of the apostle's self-conception.

However, the eschatological "Ebed Yahweh" motif may not exhaust the background that explains Paul's understanding of his special divine commission, since in Romans 15:20–21 Paul, on the one hand, closely connects his mission to Gentiles with the ministry of the Servant in Isaiah 52:15[91] (cf. 2 Cor 6:1–10;[92] Phil 2:16b[93]), and on the other hand, clearly takes the Servant figure messianically, that is as Jesus Christ, the embodiment of the good news (vv. 20–21),[94] as other early Christians did.[95] If Paul

---

90. E.g. A. Kerrigan, "Echoes of Themes from the Servant Songs in Pauline Theology," *Studiorum Paulinorum Congressus 1961* (Rome: Pontifical Biblical Institute, 1963), 217–228; P. Dinter, "Paul and the Prophet Isaiah," *BTB* 13 (1983): 48–52; R. B. Hays, "Who has believed our message?: Paul's Reading of Isaiah," *SBL 1998 Seminar papers* (Atlanta: Scholars Press, 1998), 216–217; S. Kim, "Isaiah 42 and Paul's Call," in *Paul and the New Perspective*, ed. S. Kim (Grand Rapids: Eerdmans, 2001), 101–127; Kim, "Paul as an Eschatological Herald," in *Paul as Missionary: Identity, Activity, Theology, and Practice*, eds. T. J. Burke and B. S. Rosner (London: T & T Clark, 2011), 13–18; Riesner, *Paul's Early Period*, 245–253; Stettler, "Colossians 1:24," 194; J. R. Wagner, "The Heralds of Isaiah and the Mission of Paul: An Investigation of Paul's Use of Isaiah 51–55 in Romans," in *Jesus and the Suffering Servant: Isaiah 53 and Christian Origins*, eds. W. H. Bellinger and W. R. Farmer (Harrisburg: Trinity, 1998), 193–222; Wagner, *Heralds of the Good News: Isaiah and Paul "in Concert" in the Letter to the Romans* (Leiden: Brill, 2002); Köstenberger and O'Brien, *Salvation*, 165–166, 170; Ware, *The Mission of the Church*, 275.

91. Cf. Wagner, "Isaiah in Romans and Galatians," 128–129; Wagner, "The Heralds," 195–202.

92. Cf. Wilk, "Isaiah in 1 and 2 Corinthians," 151–152.

93. Cf. E. Larsson, *Christus als Vorbild: eine Untersuchung zu den paulinischen Tauf- und Eikontexten* (Uppsala: C. W. K. Gleerup, 1962), 272–273, who observes Paul's similar connection of his gentile mission in Phil 2:16b with the second Servant Song (Isa 49:1–6) in terms of the fear about "laboring for nothing."

94. Paul's equation of Christ with the Servant is explicit in that Paul employs περὶ αὐτοῦ (the LXX Isa 52:15) that refers to the Servant (Isa 52:13) in the context where he speaks of "the gospel of Christ" (v. 19b) and "Christ was named" (v. 20a). Cf. Wagner, "The Heralds," 198. See also e.g. Rom 4:25–5:1; 1 Cor 15:3; Phil 2:5–11.

95. Cf. Matt 8:17; 20:28; Mark 10:45; John 1:29; 12:38; Acts 3:13; 8:32–35; *1 Clem.* 16; Justin *Dial.* 13.32; *1 Apol.* 50–51. For a discussion on the messianic interpretation of Isa 53 in Jesus and within the early Christianity, see M. Hengel, "Jesus, the Messiah of Israel: The Debate about the 'Messianic Mission' of Jesus," in *Crisis in Christology: Essays in Search of Resolution*, ed. W. R. Farmer (Livonia: Dove Booksellers, 1995), 217–240; O. Betz, "Jesus and Isaiah 53," in *Jesus and the Suffering Servant: Isaiah 53 and Christian Origins*, eds. W. H. Bellinger, Jr. and W. R. Farmer (Harrisburg: Trinity, 1998), 70–87; O. Hofius, "Das vierte Gottesknechtslied in den Briefen des Neuen Testaments," in *Der leidende Gottesknecht:*

saw the Servant figure as such, one must explain how Paul could boldly relate the Messiah's election / commission (cf. בְּחִירִי/ὁ ἐκλεκτός μου, Isa 42:1; יְהוָה מִבֶּטֶן קְרָאָנִי מִמְּעֵי אִמִּי הִזְכִּיר שְׁמִי/κύριος ἐκ κοιλίας μητρός μου ἐκάλεσεν τὸ ὄνομά μου, Isa 49:1) to his own election / commission (Gal 1:15–16b).[96] Moreover, one needs to explain Paul's obvious awareness of other missionaries (e.g. 1 Cor 3:5–10; 9:5; Gal 1:8) to whom he seems to attribute a full legitimacy as missionaries alongside himself. However, it is not at all clear whether such a Servant figure can be connected to them. In this regard, to connect Paul' conception of his vocation and mission with that of the Servant, as if Paul saw himself as the Servant, is misleading.[97]

3.3.1.2. Paul, the Messiah, the Servant of the Lord, and the Gospel Herald

In my opinion, the connection of Paul's gentile mission with that of the Servant of the Lord should be explained in terms of *Paul's perception of the Messiah (or the Servant of the Lord) as the messenger of the good news* – as well as the embodiment of the good news – and himself (and presumably other individuals) as one of subsequent messengers who are divinely (or by the Messiah) authorized.[98]

At least in the book of Isaiah in its final form (to which Paul most likely had access) the Servant figure in the first song appears to be a sort of eschatological proclaimer of God's law ("his teaching" [תּוֹרָתוֹ], Isa 42:4, cf. Isa 2:3) as well as the embodiment of a covenant of and a light to the nations (42:6) and an agent of God's eschatological rule (42:7–9). Again in the second song of the Servant, he is depicted as a verbal agent for God's glory ("and he made my mouth like a sharp sword . . . [you are my servant,

---

Jesaja 53 und seine Wirkungsgeschichte, FAT, eds. B. Janowski and P. Stuhlmacher (Tübingen: Mohr Siebeck, 1996), 107–127; D. J. Bingham, "Justin and Isaiah 53," *Vigiliae Christianae* 54 (2000): 248–261. *Pace* M. D. Hooker, *Jesus and the Servant* (London: SPCK, 1959), who argues for a minimal influence of the Servant motif on the NT writers and no evidence of Jesus' mission being influenced by the motif. See also Bultmann, *Theology of the New Testament*, 31–33.

96. Cf. Köstenberger and O'Brien, *Salvation*, 166; Wagner, *Heralds*, 222.

97. *Contra* P. Dinter, "Paul and the Prophet Isaiah," 48–52. Cf. J. R. Wagner, "The Heralds of Isaiah," 222; Köstenberger and O'Brien, *Salvation*, 166, who correctly point out the misleading connection.

98. For the divine authorization (for the speech of the good news) in the interpretative tradition of the Isaianic texts, see J. P. Dickson, *Mission-Commitment*, 153–176.

Israel, in whom] I will be glorified," 49:2–3) and the restoration of the nations as well as Israel as the "light to the nations." Moreover, the first Servant song (42:1–9) and the fourth song about the suffering Servant immediately follow the motif of the מְבַשֵּׂר/εὐαγγελιζόμενος whom God sends to Zion/Jerusalem to announce that God's reign has arrived (41:27f; 52:7f, cf. 40:1–9; 61:1). This may indicate that at least the final form of the book of Isaiah suggests *the close connection of the eschatological gospel herald with the Servant of the Lord* or *the eschatological gospel herald as another aspect of the Servant of the Lord*.[99]

If we consider that in Second Temple Judaism, at least the Qumranites often read the Isaianic gospel herald *messianically* (e.g. 11Q13; 4Q521),[100] it would not be a *novum* for Paul who could identify Jesus the Messiah with the suffering Servant of the Lord (Isa 52:13–53:12) to further identify him with the eschatological herald.[101] Moreover, if we accept the rather tentative conclusion that Paul read the Isaianic texts as such, it becomes easier to understand Paul's rather enigmatic explanation of his (geographically sensitive pioneering) mission to the Gentiles in Romans 15:16–20 in a close association with the ministry of the Servant (Isa 52:15b), whom he obviously identifies with Jesus the Messiah. Even if Paul could not take up the role of the Servant in terms of the Messianic role ontologically, which *inaugurates* the fulfillment of God's promise as the embodiment of God's redemptive act in the vicarious suffering / death / vindication on behalf of God's people and the Gentiles or as the light to the nations per se, Paul could see his mission as an extension or a continuation of the ministry of the Messianic Servant on the basis that both the Messiah and the apostle himself are the eschatological heralds whom God raises as his implementation.[102]

---

99. C. A. Evans, "The Function of Isaiah in the New Testament," 659.

100. A. Chester, "Jewish Messianic Expectations," 20–27, 55–56; Dunn, *Romans 9–16*, 622. Cf. Dickson, *Mission-Commitment*, 157, who argues that the eschatological herald in Isa 52:7 and 61:1 is elevated to a messianic figure in 1QH[a] 22:10–15. However, the text is too fragmentary to discern the exact import and whether it alludes to the Isaianic passage.

101. Cf. See also Stuhlmacher, *The Pauline Gospel*, 142–153, who observes the second century Rabbi Jose identifying מבשר of Isa 52:7 with the Messiah.

102. Cf. Dunn, *Romans 9–16*, 865–866.

3.3.1.3. Plurality of מְבַשֵּׂר/εὐαγγελιζόμενος in Paul

Elsewhere in the Pauline letters other evidences that Paul saw himself as an eschatological מְבַשֵּׂר/εὐαγγελιζόμενος is emphatic.[103] However, his notion about מְבַשֵּׂר/εὐαγγελιζόμενος is not limited to himself being closely associated with the Servant, but frequently expands to other individuals. Particularly in Romans 1:1–6, his focus is not simply his special quality as an apostle which patterned after the OT prophets or the eschatological Servant of the Lord in terms of the divine election from their birth, but *his location* within the divine eschatological implementation for the fulfillment of the promise of redemption. For instance, in Romans 1:5 Paul's gentile mission appears to be his response to or participation into God's "grace" and "apostleship" that was given to *certain individuals* through the Messiah (δι' οὗ ἐλάβομεν).[104] Here, it appears that those who received apostleship through the Messiah constitute God's decisive eschatological implementation "for the obedience of faith among all nations (πᾶσιν τοῖς ἔθνεσιν)"[105] among whom the Romans also belong. The more fundamental divine implementation that is effectively summarized in the "good news of God" (εὐαγγέλιον θεοῦ, v. 1), namely that God fulfilled his promise (which had already been given to his prophets) in his Son the Messiah Jesus (vv. 2–4), is facilitated by a further divine implementation of the election / commission in those who received apostleship (v. 5), among whom Paul belongs. This carefully crafted opening sentence manifests Paul's self-conception as one of those who are divinely entrusted for the cause of the εὐαγγέλιον θεοῦ.[106]

---

103. κῆρυξ (1 Tim 2:7; 2 Tim 1:11) seems to carry a similar sense considering Paul's frequent use of the verb κηρύσσω in e.g. Rom 10:8, 14, 15; 1 Cor 15:11–12; 2 Cor 1:19; 4:5; Gal 2:2; Phil 1:15; 1 Thess 2:9.

104. This may not be an epistolary plural. *Contra* Morris, *Romans*, 48.

105. Πας certainly makes the phrase referring not to the Gentiles but to all nations including the Jewish nation.

106. While, as we have observed above, Paul never attributes the noun (or substantive adjective) εὐαγγέλιον to a receiving community / individual in the sense of an agent for direct evangelism but only in the sense of the receiver's fidelity / accountable life to the gospel, Paul almost always uses εὐαγγέλιον to refer to either his own / his colleagues' or other apostles' activity for the cause of the gospel (1 Thess 1:5; 2:2, 4, 8, 9; 3:2; 1 Cor 4:15; 9:12–23; 15:1; Gal 1:11; 2:2, 7; 2 Cor 2:12; 4:3; 8:18; 10:14; 11:4, 7; Rom 1:1, 9; 2:16; 15:16–20; 16:25; Phil 1:5–7, 12, 16; 2:22; 4:3, 15; Phlm 1:13, cf. Eph 6:19; Col 1:23; 1 Tim 1:11; 2 Tim 1:8, 11; 2:8).

Again, in Romans 10:5–21, when Paul argues that righteousness and salvation are not through the law but through faith so that Jews and the Gentiles alike have access (cf. Rom 2:24; 3:9) and that this message was indeed preached to Israel (vv. 18–21), Paul identifies these messengers with the one who is prefigured in Isaiah 52:7 (מְבַשֵּׂר/εὐαγγελιζόμενος) by quoting the text.[107] As Paul's contemporary Jewish exegetical tradition interpreted the text as a reference to the eschatological messianic age,[108] for Paul, who is "at / of the Eschaton" the advent (or sending) of the eschatological herald is *an event in the present time*.[109] What is to be noted here is that Paul modifies the original singular מְבַשֵּׂר/εὐαγγελιζόμενος to a plural οἱ εὐαγγελιζόμενοι.[110] Seen in the light of the previous point, it is not surprising that Paul uses the plural substantive participle: such a plurality in Paul's quotation of the Isaianic eschatological herald indicates Paul's notion of the advent of the eschatological heralds as God's eschatological implementation for the restoration of Israel and incoming of the Gentiles through the gospel that is preached by those gospel heralds; and at least indirectly signifies his conscious / unconscious inclusion of himself among those eschatological heralds (cf. vv. 8, 14–16).[111] And this must explain Paul's frequent employment of the verb εὐαγγελίζεσθαι to refer to not only his own apostolic ministry (e.g. 1 Cor 1:17; 9:16, 18; 15:1; Gal 1:11, 16; 4:13; 2 Cor 11:7; Rom 1:15; 10:15; 15:20), but also the same or at least

---

107. Cf. Wagner, "The Heralds of Isaiah," 207.

108. Wagner, *Heralds*, 170–186.

109. Cf. Käsemann, *Romans*, 294: "[the quotation] shows that the sending on which all else depends has taken place and does take place."

110. The modification seems to be Paul's own since the Jewish interpretive tradition uniformly reads the singular here. Cf. Wagner, "The Heralds," 207, n.46.

111. Cf. J. R. Wagner, "The Heralds of Isaiah," 207, n.47, who correctly observes the verb ἀποστέλλω in v. 15 to be intended to remind his readers of the apostle's own call; Wagner, "Isaiah in Romans and Galatians," in *Isaiah in the New Testament: The New Testament and the Scriptures of Israel*, eds. S. Moyise and M. J. J. Menken (London: T. & T. Clark, 2005), 119.

externally similar activity of other individuals (e.g. Gal 1:8–9; 2 Cor 10:16; Rom 15:20b, cf. Eph 2:17[112]).[113]

3.3.2. The Scope of the Gospel Heralds in Paul

How should we, then, understand this plurality of the eschatological heralds that occurs elsewhere in Paul's letters? In other words, who were these eschatological heralds for Paul? As Paul saw himself and multiple individuals as eschatological heralds who are sent alongside or by Christ as God's eschatological implementation for the cause of the gospel, what exact scope did Paul maintain for these gospel heralds?

3.3.2.1. The Church as Eschatological Herald of the Gospel?

If, as we have touched on above, those scholars who focus exclusively on Paul's own mission as an eschatological outworking of the Deutero-Isaianic texts is one extreme position that does not seriously consider the plurality, another extreme position is a view that over emphasizes the plurality as if it includes all believers (i.e. the church) in Paul's thought.

One example is J. P. Ware's thesis. As we have seen, Ware devotes his study of Philippians to elucidating the close connection between Paul's own mission and the role of the church within his Jewish eschatological perspective. Ware suggests that this "plurality of the proclaimers" in Romans 10:15 and elsewhere should be explained by Paul's understanding of the Isaianic Servant figure in a collective sense as well as messianic sense.[114] According to him, Paul applies some scriptural texts (i.e. Dan 12:3; Wis 2:19) that reflect the Jewish exegetical tradition, which interprets the Isaianic Servant figure in a collective sense (as the persecuted righteous remnant of Israel), to the believers in Philippi (Phil 1:27–29; 2:15b; 4:5).[115] He further argues that, as Paul explicitly connects his mission with the Servant figure,

---

112. The author of Ephesians describes Christ as one who proclaimed peace (εὐηγγελίσατο εἰρήνην, cf. Isa 52:7; 57:19). This may indicate that, as we propose, Paul viewed that the Messiah (the Isaianic Servant) is none other than the Isaianic eschatological herald, and that the author faithfully preserves the Pauline idea.

113. This point is also to be elucidated by Paul's use of the noun form. This will be discussed later.

114. Ware, *The Mission of the Church*, 276–277.

115. Ibid., 217, 219–220, 254–256.

the same connection is also in view (Phil 2:16b–18) between the church's mission (as a parallel mission of the community of priests and prophets to that of Paul, Phil 1:17–18)[116] and that of the Servant figure.[117] For Ware, the tension between the collective sense and the messianic sense of the Isaianic Servant figure in Paul is, thus, reconciled in Paul's "christological understanding of mission as the activity of Christ": Paul "understood the risen Christ at work to fulfill his mission as God's messianic Servant, not only in Paul's own apostolic mission, but also in the mission activity of his churches."[118] This conclusion implies nothing less than the equation of the church, the entire body of people of God with the מְבַשֵּׂר/εὐαγγελιζόμενος.

I find Ware's point that Paul saw the church as an eschatological entity into which the eschatological Servant of the Lord is incorporated attractive. This view is certainly suggestive of Paul's tendency to see Christ himself as the personification / representative of Israel, in whom the restoration of Israel is achieved (e.g. Gal 3:10–14; Rom 9:4f),[119] Paul's explicit / implicit connection of the Gentile Christian community with Israel (e.g. 2 Cor 6:2;[120] Phil 2:14–16[121]; cf. 1 Cor 10:1–13; 2 Cor 3:7–18; Gal 4:21–31), the Jewish concept of "corporate personality" (e.g. 1 Cor 15:22, 45; Rom 5:12–21), or even his metaphor of the church as the body of Christ (e.g. 1 Cor 10:17; 11:29; 12:12ff; Rom 12:4–5, cf. Col 1:18; Eph 4:12).

Nevertheless, it seems that Paul seeing his community of converts as a manifestation of the Messiah is one thing and Paul seeing them *specifically* as a collective entity of the Servant figure who had a particular mission as מְבַשֵּׂר/εὐαγγελιζόμενος is another. Paul's allusion to some scriptures which had been interpreted in other strands of Judaism as viewing the eschatological Israel in the sense of a collective entity of the suffering Servant does not

---

116. Ibid., 114–141, 271–274.

117. Ibid., 274–279.

118. Ibid., 279–282 (quotations in 280, 281). Note that the concept of Paul's Christological understanding of mission that is naturally transposed to the entire body of believers is reminiscent of O'Brien's view.

119. Particularly, Wright, *Climax*, 141, 146, 150–151, 196, 245.

120. See below 4.2.3.

121. See my argument above 3.2. Cf. Ware, *The Mission of the Church*, 217, 219, suggests a connection between Phil 1:29; 4:5 and Wis 2:12–5:13 in terms of a missiological implication of the "persecuted righteous figure" whose gentleness is known to all.

necessarily warrant the view that Paul had the same interpretation. While Paul clearly connects his ministry with the Servant's ministry in terms of מְבַשֵּׂר/εὐαγγελιζόμενος, this sort of direct connection is never applied to his community of converts. Rather, as we will discuss below, Paul's employment of the motif of the Isaianic Servant figure in relation to communities of converts is always made *indirectly*, only *through* the Messiah and his envoys.[122] Despite Paul's concern for the missional / evangelistic effect of the church on outsiders (e.g. Phil 2:15),[123] this indirect connection of the community of converts with the Servant figure cannot constitute any indication to Paul's inclusion of the community in his plural εὐαγγελιζόμενοι. Rather, the connection only indicates that the community of converts is related to the Servant *as an ongoing object of the ministry of the gospel heralds* who are closely associated with the Servant, the Messiah.

3.3.2.2. Paul's Use of εὐαγγελ-Language

The previous point can be elucidated by considering Paul's use of εὐαγγελ-language in his letters.[124] Scholars discuss various aspects regarding Paul's use of εὐαγγελ-language. One of the most widely appreciated aspects of Paul's use of the language is that for Paul εὐαγγελ-language primarily denotes the announcement of God's salvation in the event of Christ. Scholars

---

122. A theological connection between of מְבַשֵּׂר/εὐαγγελιζόμενος and שליח/ἀπόστολος in Paul's thought will be discussed later.

123. Ware, *The Mission of the Church*, 276, insists that Paul uses the Servant motif "in the context of an exhortation to active mission [of the church]." This leads him to nearly equate Paul's mission with that of the church in terms of proclaiming the gospel. However, this view is wrongly grounded on an unconvincing exegesis of Phil 2:15–16.

124. For this point, I presuppose, following the scholarly consensus, that Paul's (or the Christians') use of the gospel-language most probably derived from the Jewish scriptural and exegetical tradition of מְבַשֵּׂר/εὐαγγελιζόμενος: e.g. M. Burrows, "The Origin of the Word Gospel," *JBL* 44 (1925); 21–33; Friedrich, "εὐαγγελίζω," *TDNT* 2. 707–737; Stuhlmacher, *Das paulinische Evangelium*, 82–92; Dunn, *Theology*, 163–181; Bowman, "Gospel and its Cognates in Palestinian Syriac," 54–67; Hengel-Schwemer, *Between Damascus and Antioch*, 92; O'Brien, *Gospel and Mission*, 77–81; Broyles, "Gospel (Good News)," 282–286; Cf. Dickson, *Mission-Commitment*, 153–174, who generally follows the consensus, yet reserves the Greco-Roman provenance to be providing Christian use of the language a "significant context" in which Christians use it for a "significant announcement" (153–154, n.1, 175–176).

such as R. Bultmann[125] and V. P. Furnish[126] note that Paul regularly uses the noun εὐαγγέλιον in the sense of *nomen actionis*: the activity of preaching of the gospel contents as well as the content of the message per se.[127] J. P. Dickson persuasively argues that while the language in Paul is used in a complex meaning,[128] the linguistic reality accords with the Judaeo-Greco-Roman use of εὐαγγελ-language that primarily points to an announcement of news and an authorization of the messenger.[129]

What is significant about this aspect in our discussion is that, as we have shown in the previous chapter, Paul never attributes the language to his community members in general or an entire community in a way in which he does to himself and some other individuals. It is again noteworthy that scholars' attempts to read εὐαγγέλιον in Pauline texts in terms of the church's direct verbal proclamation has no sound exegetical grounds. This may be an indication that Paul conceived a well-defined distinction between the eschatological heralds and the community members in general (as congregations or the church) in relation to the task of verbal communication of the gospel message. However, to avoid any danger of an argument from silence, it is necessary to observe whether Paul's use of that particular language elucidates the silence in that way.

D. Litfin[130] suggests that whenever Paul talks about his commission as an apostle almost without exception εὐαγγελ-language appears.[131] We saw in the previous section that Paul perceived his calling as an apostle in

---

125. Bultmann, *Theology of the New Testament*, 87.

126. V. P. Furnish, "Prophets, Apostles and Preachers: A Study of the Biblical Concept of Preaching," *Interpretation* 17, no.1 (1963): 48–60, 52–53.

127. Cf. Dodd, *The Apostolic Preaching*, 9–10; J. I. H. McDonald, *Kerygma and Didache: The Articulation and Structure of the Earliest Christian Message*, SNTSMS (Cambridge: Cambridge University Press, 1980), who observes the two-fold aspect (preaching and teaching) of the Christian's communication of the gospel message.

128. The complexity involves a question as to whether Paul uses the language also in the sense of "secondary" communication of the gospel with already believing members of a Christian community (e.g. Rom 1:15; Eph 3:8). This issue will be touched on later.

129. Dickson, *Mission-Commitment*, 88–91, 153–176.

130. D. Litfin, *St. Paul's Theology of Proclamation: 1 Corinthians 1–4 and Greco-Roman Rhetoric* (Cambridge: Cambridge University Press, 1994), 188. See Dickson, *Mission-Commitment*, 88.

131. 1 Thess 2:4; Gal 1:15–16; 1 Cor 1:17; 9:14; 15:9–11; 2 Cor 4:1–5; Rom 1:1, 9; 1:14–15; 15:17–20; Col 1:23–27.

terms of his participation into God's implementation through those eschatological εὐαγγελιζόμενοι, so it is not surprising for him to conclude that: "[εὐαγγελίζεσθαι] constituted his apostolic calling."[132] Similarly, Dickson remarks that "the language of εὐαγγελ- takes us to the heart of Paul's self-identity as a 'missionary.'"[133]

As our previous exegetical study has shown, in Paul's letters the connection of the language with the church is detected only in terms of the church's financial and spiritual partnership with Paul's mission or their fidelity to the gospel message, but the same or at least analogous connection that is found between Paul's missionary self-conception and the language is found explicitly in Paul's understanding of / attitudes to his co-workers or other missionaries.[134] In various places Paul clearly attributes to his co-workers the εὐαγγελ-language in the analogous sense that is attached to the apostle himself by including them to his missionary preaching.[135]

For instance, it is widely agreed that in 1 Thessalonians 1:5 the first person plural ἡμῶν that qualifies τὸ εὐαγγέλιον is not an epistolary plural but a direct indication that Paul includes his co-workers, Silvanus and Timothy in the same category as the heralds of the gospel.[136] It is still arguable as to whether the two co-workers are apostles in the same sense as Paul's perception of his own apostleship (cf. "ὡς χριστοῦ ἀπόστολοι" 2:6).[137] Nevertheless, the expression "τὸ εὐαγγέλιον ἡμῶν" (cf. 2 Cor 4:3; 2 Thess 2:14) certainly indicates that in Paul's thought they all belonged to οἱ εὐαγγελιζόμενοι.[138] What is to be noted here is that the ἡμῶν does not simply include the two co-workers in the gospel heralds but also

---

132. Litfin, *St. Paul's Theology*, 88.

133. Dickson, *Mission-Commitment*, 91.

134. For a detailed study of Paul's co-workers, see Ollrog, *Mitarbeiter*, 130–132; Ellis, "Paul and His Co-Workers," 437–452.

135. εὐαγγέλιον: 1 Thess 1:5; 2:2–4, 8–9; 3:2; Gal 1:6–9; 2:7; 1 Cor 9:1–14; 15:3–11; Rom 10:15–16. Cf. 2 Thess 2:14; 2 Tim 1:8. εὐαγγελίζομαι / εὐαγγελίζεσθαι: Gal 1:8–9; 2 Cor 10:16; Rom 15:20b, cf. Eph 2:17.

136. Cf. Richard, *Thessalonians*, 109–110; Best, *Thessalonians*, 99–100; Bruce, *Thessalonians*, 31; Dickson, *Mission-Commitment*, 91.

137. In my opinion, Paul's mentioning of the plural apostles does not indicate that the two co-workers had the same apostleship that Paul attributed to himself. We will discuss this point later.

138. *Pace* Green, *Thessalonians*, 94, n.27, who notes that "we should not understand the "Gospel" here as the act of proclamation."

effectively contrasts the gospel heralds with the Thessalonians as the recipients of the gospel message (εἰς ὑμᾶς). This pattern is repeated in 1 Thessalonians 2:2–4 (ἐπαρρησιασάμεθα . . . τὸ εὐαγγέλιον – πρὸς ὑμᾶς) and in verse 9 (ἐκηρύξαμεν . . . τὸ εὐαγγέλιον – εἰς ὑμᾶς).[139] Whether this contrast is accidental or intended is not at all clear. And one may even suspect the contrast set between the first person plural and the community in general to be too general or irrelevant to be an issue in our discussion, since Paul's point is simply that the communication of the gospel is made between the two parties, the heralds and the community.

Nevertheless, a consideration of Paul's careful distinction between exclusive use of second person plural pronouns (as the pronoun referring to Paul's apostolic band) from inclusive use of them (as the pronoun referring to Christian existence) or plural "you" (referring to recipients of apostolic ministry / epistles) elsewhere in his letters[140] may lead one to the belief that this distinction is not accidental or customary but more likely to be theological. For instance, in the second letter to the Corinthians the apostle wants the Corinthians to understand his apostolic message and ministry more fully (1:12–14) - in a difficult situation most likely due to some Corinthians' preference for other leaders rather than Paul (e.g. Apollos) and the accusation from certain intruders - Paul repeatedly presents to the Corinthians the characteristics of his and his co-workers ministry as (genuine) gospel heralds with the first person plural pronoun ἡμεῖς throughout 2:14–7:4.[141] In this context, even if God's inauguration of his reign encompasses "all things" (γέγονεν καινὰ τὰ πάντα, 5:17; τὰ πάντα ἐκ τοῦ θεοῦ, v. 18) making God's righteousness in Christ for all who believe, presumably

---

139. Cf. 2 Thess 2:14 (διὰ τοῦ εὐαγγελίου ἡμῶν- ἐκάλεσεν ὑμᾶς).

140. E.g J. J. Kijne, "We, Us and Our in I and II Corinthians," *NovT* 8 (1966): 171–179; J.-F. Collange, *Enigmes de la deuxième épître de Paul aux Corinthiens: étude exégétique de 2 Cor. 2:14–7:4*, SNTSMS (Cambridge: Cambridge University Press, 1972), 271. *Contra* M. Carrez, "Le 'Nous' en 2 Corinthiens," *NTS* 26 (1979–1980): 474–486.

141. Cf. S. Kim, "Paul as an eschatological Herald," 14, who observes another example of Paul's exclusive use of "us" in 2 Cor 1:21–22. He effectively argues against any inclusive reading of "us" in the verses (e.g. reading the verses as a baptismal confession) by observing: (1) such a reading cannot satisfactorily explain the remarkable χρίσας (21b); (2) it is less likely that Paul suddenly turns from the context of defending his apostolic behaviour to a general affirmation about the baptismal experience of himself and the Corinthians; (3) having specifically separated "you" from "us" in 21a, it is less likely that the immediately following "us" include "you"; (4) the "us" and "our" in v. 22 must to do the same.

including the Corinthians as well as the gospel heralds (5:15, 21),[142] the first person plurals associated in the expressions "we are the aroma of Christ" (2:15), "our gospel" (4:3), "we have this treasure in clay jars" (4:7) and "we are ambassadors of Christ" (5:20)[143] are all primarily signifying the ministry of the gospel heralds set in contrast to object of God's redemption through their ministry in the world including the Corinthians (ἐν τοῖς σῳζομένοις καὶ ἐν τοῖς ἀπολλυμένοις ἐν τοῖς σῳζομένοις, 2:15; ἐν τοῖς ἀπολλυμένοις, 4:3; παρακαλοῦντος δι' ἡμῶν δι' . . . καταλλάγητε, 5:20b, c).

What is particularly significant about this exclusive "we" set in contrast to the Corinthians is that it reflects Paul's consciousness of God's implementation for his eschatological redemption through his Servant whose ministry reaches not only the remnants of Israel but also the Gentile nations (Isa 49:1–13).[144] In 6:1 Paul repeats again (implicitly but quite clearly)

---

142. Cf. Kijne, "We, Us and Our," 178–179;

143. S. E. Porter "Paul's Concept of Reconciliation, Twice More," in *Paul and His Theology*, ed. S. E. Porter (Leiden: Brill, 2006), 134–144; Porter, "Reconciliation as the Heart of Paul's Missionary Theology," in *Paul as Missionary*, eds. T. J. Burke and B. S. Rosner (London: T & T Clark, 2011), 172–176, suggests that Paul's language of reconciliation in 2 Cor 5 indicates that "we all are ambassadors for or on behalf of Christ (2 Cor 5:20), including Paul, his companions, and the Corinthian believers." This suggestion is weak since Paul's logic of 5:20 clearly makes the role of ambassadors apply only to those eschatological heralds ("we") while the Corinthians ("you") are the object of such ministry of the ambassadors through whom God makes the appeal for reconciliation in Christ to the Corinthians. While the reconciliation is given to all (universally) who are in Christ (5:18b, cf. Rom 5:11) the *recipients of the ministry of reconciliation* (v. 18c) is to be understood in light of v. 20. In 2 Cor 5:16–20 what is expected from the Corinthians is to know their new existence in Christ (v. 16–17) and what God had done in / through Christ and his envoys (v. 18–19), and "therefore (οὖν)" what they should do: *not the ministry of reconciliation but to "reconcile themselves to God"* (δεόμεθα ὑπὲρ Χριστοῦ, καταλλάγητε τῷ θεῷ, v. 20). If Paul's point in mentioning reconciliation was about the universality of the ministry of ambassador / reconciliation, Paul's imperative should have been "do the ministry of reconciliation" rather than "be reconciled to God." Similarly, in Eph 6:20 the ministry of ambassador is attributed to Paul alone and Paul (or the writer) does not ask the Ephesians to share such a role but only expects their prayer for Paul's successful implementation of such a ministry. Thus, it is inappropriate to take Paul's mentioning of the reconciliation given to all who are in Christ as an indication of universality of the ministry of ambassadors or reconciliation. While such a reconciliation is to be celebrated universally, for Paul, divinely authorized heralds are selected to work as ministers of reconciliation ("to us," v. 18c) for the celebration of such reconciliation given to those in Christ ("us," v. 18b). See also C. Wolff, "True Apostolic Knowledge of Christ: Exegetical Reflections on 2 Cor 5.12ff," in *Paul and Jesus*, ed. A. J. M. Wedderburn (London: T & T Clark, 2004), 92–97.

144. According to some writers the Isaianic text does not refer to the salvation of the Gentiles but only to the ingathering of the dispersed remnants of Israel from the nations (e.g. F. H. Holmgren, *With Wings as Eagles: An Interpretation* [Chappaqua: Biblical Scholars

the contrast between the exclusive "we" as God's co-workers (συνεργοῦντες δὲ καὶ παρακαλοῦμεν)[145] and the Corinthians as the object (ὑμᾶς) of their ministry. And then, immediately (v. 2) quotes Isaiah 49:8a[146] to underscore that "now" is the time in which God's promise of eschatological salvation is being fulfilled. However, the fact that he goes back immediately to focus on God's co-workers in their perseverance under affliction and hardship (vv. 3–10) indicates that his point of quotation resides not in the timing of the eschatological salvation, but in that Paul and his co-workers are indeed the legitimate associates of the eschatological Servant envisioned in the Scripture to be working in the time of eschatological salvation (Isa 49:6–13).[147] The agony of the Servant (ἐγὼ εἶπα κενῶς ἐκοπίασα καὶ εἰς μάταιον καὶ εἰς οὐδὲν ἔδωκα τὴν ἰσχύν μου) in Isaiah 49:4a must be reflected in Paul's concern about his mission being "not in vain" (μὴ εἰς κενὸν) in 6:1 and the immediate vindication of the Servant in Isaiah 49:4b must be behind Paul's description of the paradoxical joy and glory in the midst of affliction and hardship in verses 8b–10.[148]

It is worth repeating here that Paul's connection in Romans of his own apostolic mission with that of the Isaianic Servant figure is possible through his notion that the Servant is none other than the Herald. Then, the same holds true in Paul's connection of "we" with the Servant in 2 Corinthians: his colleagues are also the co-heralds with the Servant, the Messiah (cf. 5:20; 6:1; 1 Cor 3:9a). What is to be noted here is that the Servant figure

---

Press, 1973], 54–59; N. H. Snaith, "A Study of the Teaching of the Second Isaiah and Its Consequences," in *Studies on the Second Part of the Book of Isaiah*, eds. H. M. Orlinsky and N. H. Snaith [Leiden: Brill, 1977], 155–157). But Paul's use of the text in his gentile mission context certainly indicates that Paul read the text as referring to the Gentiles' salvation as well as that of the remnant of Israel.

145. The identity of the complement of the participle συνεργοῦντες is debated. However, the most convincing view is that Paul means "working together with God" as Paul's entire argument in the letter suggests. Cf. R. P. Martin, *2 Corinthians*, 164–165.

146. The quotation employs the exact verbatim from the LXX Isa 49:8a (καιρῷ δεκτῷ ἐπήκουσά σου καὶ ἐν ἡμέρᾳ σωτηρίας ἐβοήθησά σοι) except a minor modification (οὕτως λέγει κύριος to λέγει γάρ).

147. This implies, considering 6:1 (cf. 5:20–21), in Paul that the Corinthians' turning away from him would imply abandoning the grace of God. Cf. F. Wilk, "Isaiah in 1 and 2 Corinthians," in *Isaiah in the New Testament*, eds. S. Moyise and M. J. J. Menken (London: T. & T. Clark, 2005),151–152.

148. Cf. Wilk, "Isaiah in 1 and 2 Corinthians," 152, who further observes Paul's echo of Isa 49:4–8 in 2 Cor 5:17–6:2.

is not incorporated into the community of the converts but only to the gospel heralds who minister to the community. Rather, the community is an ongoing object of the ministry of the gospel heralds.

Even if Paul alone is considered, in Philippians 1:16b a similar observation can be made. As we have touched on above, while Paul's language "οὐδὲ εἰς κενὸν ἐκοπίασα" clearly reflects his conscious connection of his ministry to the Servant's ministry (Isa 49:4),[149] the community of the Philippians is, rather than the co-ministers with the Servant and the apostle (as J. P. Ware contends), an ongoing object (until the *parousia*) of Paul's ministerial concern (vv. 14–16a) as a gospel herald *to them*.

3.3.2.3. Paul's Use of εὐαγγελίζομαι in Romans 1:15

This distinction between the gospel heralds and the community of converts is more clearly in view in Paul's use of the verb εὐαγγελίζομαι in Romans 1:15. In the hope of visiting the Christians in Rome, Paul uses the infinitive aorist "εὐαγγελίσασθαι" to refer to his intention to share his apostolic teaching with them. However, this point often meets with objections. Scholars such as Zeller[150], Klein[151], C. A. Evans[152] and Litfin[153] argue that for Paul εὐαγγελίζομαι always refers to the fixed meaning of the first time proclamation for conversion and not his pastoral activity for the benefit of the congregation.[154] For some exegetes Paul's such a willingness to proclaim the gospel is not the current one but only that of the past as he now simply refers back to it as the aorist infinitive εὐαγγελίσασθαι suggests.[155] Some others read ὑμεῖς to be Paul's reference to the addressees not as Christians

---

149. Cf. Larsson, *Vorbild*, 272–273.

150. D. Zeller, *Juden und Heiden in der Mission des Paulus: Studien zum Römerbrief* (Stuttgart: Katholisches Bibelwerk, 1973), 55–58.

151. G. Klein, "Paul's Purpose in Writing the Epistle to the Romans," in *The Romans Debate*, ed. K. P. Donfried (Edinburgh: T. & T. Clark, 1991), 47.

152. C. A. Evans, "Preacher and Preaching: Some Lexical Observations," *JETS* 24, no. 4 (1981): 315–322.

153. Litfin, *St. Paul's Theology*, 195–197.

154. See also Dickson, *Mission-Commitment*, 89, who points to the inappropriateness of the idea of εὐαγγελίζεσθαι applying to the believers once the gospel is preached and believed.

155. Käsemann, *Romans*, 20; Byrne, *Romans*, 50–51; Dickson, *Mission-Commitment*, 89.

but as simply ones in Rome.¹⁵⁶ For N. Turner, the verb is another expression of "tell."¹⁵⁷ In my opinion, all these explanations are unsatisfactory, since: (1) οὕτως in the beginning of verse 15 signifies Paul's currently resumed intention. If he simply referred back to the past unsuccessful intention (vv. 13–14), verse 15 is redundant; (2) grammatically, the aorist infinitive εὐαγγελίσασθαι has no particular temporal sense of "past";¹⁵⁸ (3) having clarified that his recipients are all the saints in Rome in an adjacent verse (v. ß: πᾶσιν τοῖς οὖσιν ἐν Ῥώμῃ ἀγαπητοῖς θεοῦ, κλητοῖς ἁγίοις), it is very unnatural for Paul again to blur his point in his second person plurals in verses 13–15; and (4) in response to Turner, that in the immediately following verse Paul mentions the gospel as the power of God for salvation signifies εὐαγγελίσασθαι as a verbal communication none other than that of the gospel message.

Rather, as in Romans 1:5 and 16:26 Paul describes the function of the apostleship in terms of the cause of the "obedience of faith" (εἰς ὑπακοὴν πίστεως) among all nations through the preaching of the gospel (cf. Rom 15:18) and as his paraenetic thrust is frequently expressed in ὑπακούω/ὑπακοῇ [to the gospel or Christ] by existing Christians (2 Cor 7:15; 10:5–6; Rom 6:12, 16; 10:16; 16:17, 19, 26; Phil 2:12; Phlm 21; cf. 2 Thess 1:8; 3:14), it is not satisfactory to restrict the verb εὐαγγελίζομαι to the act of initial evangelism for non-believers.

Considering all these it is more natural to see εὐαγγελίζομαι in Romans 1:15 as signifying Paul's communication of the further gospel message with the community of the converts in Rome.¹⁵⁹ This, on the one hand, indicates that Paul's εὐαγγελ-language includes various aspects as well as the primary proclamation, all of which come from his life long vocation as one of the gospel heralds (cf. 1 Cor 1:17),¹⁶⁰ on the other hand, signifies that

---

156. F. Godet, *Commentary on St Paul's Epistle to the Romans*, vol. 1 (Edinburgh: T. & T. Clark, 1892), 148; L. Morris, *Romans*, 65; Watson, *Paul, Judaism and the Gentiles*, 103.

157. N. Turner, *Grammatical Insights into the New Testament* (Edinburgh: T. & T. Clark, 1965), 92.

158. Schreiner, *Romans*, 53.

159. Cf. Bowers, "Fulfilling the Gospel," 196; Barram, *Moral Reflection*, 84–85.

160. Dunn, *Romans 1–8*, 34: "It is simply that if any one verb sums up his lifelong obligation it is this one – "to preach the gospel" – so that its use can embrace the whole range of his ministry, including his explication of the gospel, as in this very letter." He further points to 1 Thess 3:6 as a sufficient evidence that Paul's use of εὐαγγελίζεσθαι was

communities of converts were ongoing objects of those εὐαγγελ-ministries of the εὐαγγελ-ministers.

3.3.2.4. Community's Responsibility to Support Gospel-Workers

It seems that this distinction between the gospel heralds and the community as the object of their ministry is not Paul's unreflected practice for his ad hoc explanation of the interrelationship between the apostle and the community. Rather, it appears to be his established notion that comes from a more fundamental tradition and / or his reflection on how God implements the continuation of the restoration of Israel and incoming of the Gentiles.

In 1 Corinthians 9:14 Paul mentions "those who proclaim the gospel" (τοῖς τὸ εὐαγγέλιον καταγγέλλουσιν). Here, despite Paul's renunciation of it (v. 15), the gospel preachers' right to the congregation's financial support is affirmed by the apostle by grounding it on "the Lord also commanded" (οὕτως καὶ ὁ κύριος διέταξεν)[161] as well as scriptural authority, traditional maxims, and contemporary socio-religious convention (vv. 7–13). What is striking about this is two-fold: (1) the expression τοῖς τὸ εὐαγγέλιον καταγγέλλουσιν emphatically recalls מְבַשֵּׂר/εὐαγγελιζόμενος;[162] and (2) those gospel preachers are clearly set in contrast with Christian communities in general who are presumably to support (financially) those gospel

---

not narrowly fixed. Cf. O'Brien, *Gospel and Mission*, 62, who correctly argues that "[Paul's εὐαγγελ-language covers] the whole range of evangelistic and teaching ministry," but considers the point as an indication that Paul's gospel language includes the communities' various activities for the communication of the gospel. However, this conclusion is not convincing considering our exegesis in the previous chapter. Rather, the point only strengthens our case that the gospel is primarily an authorized speech of the gospel heralds not only to non-believers but also to Christian community.

161. It is widely agreed that Paul here alludes to the Jesus-tradition of the Mission discourse – e.g. J. P. Brown, "Synoptic parallels in the Epistle and Form History," *NTS* 10 (1963): 27–48; D. Dungan, *The Sayings of Jesus in the Churches of Paul: The Use of the Synoptic Tradition in the Regulation of Early Church Life* (Oxford: B. Blackwell; Philadelphia: Fortress Press, 1971), 1–80; B. Fjärstedt, *Synoptic Tradition in 1 Corinthians*: Themes and Clusters of Theme Words in 1 Corinthians 1–4 and 9 (Uppsala, 1974), 66–94; D. Wenham, *Follower*, 190–199. This point is extremely significant in our primary discussion of the origin of Paul's concept of mission. This issue will be discussed later.

162. In v. 18 Paul explicitly uses the participle εὐαγγελιζόμενος to denote his ministry.

preachers (cf. 1 Tim 5:18).¹⁶³ The particular appeal to such authorities certainly shows that his distinction as such is not an ad hoc one, nor a mere common sense, but rather a well established theological notion.¹⁶⁴

To sum up, our considerations over Paul's use of εὐαγγελ-language and its related ideas strongly speak against the direction taken by J. P. Ware. Paul's apostolic self-conception that is understood through the motif of the Isaianic Servant figure does not involves the church as his co-herald of the gospel. Rather, he clearly makes the community of converts an ongoing recipient / object of his and his co-workers' activity of gospelization.¹⁶⁵ This certainly indicates that the scope of the plurality of the מְבַשֵּׂר/ εὐαγγελιζόμενος that is in view in Romans 10:15 only includes Paul himself

---

163. Cf. Dickson, *Mission-Commitment*, 93. Ellis in his study on "the brothers" in 1 Thess and 2 Thess ("Co-Workers," 449–451) observes a similar distinction between gospel preachers and the Thessalonians in general regarding financial support. He argues that the recipients of 2 Thess might be a group of Christian workers and those brothers are already alluded to in 1 Thess 4:11f and 5:14. According to him, that the general recipients of 2 Thess are strongly admonished to leave "all those idle brothers" and, following Paul's model and to be willing to forgo the Christian workers' right to be supported (2 Thess 3:6–15. Cf. 1 Thess 4:11–12) strongly suggests that the recipients of 2 Thess are not the Thessalonian congregation in general but those brothers devoted to Christian ministry. Perhaps, Paul had written his first letter to the congregation in general expecting some brothers staying among them may read 4:11f (cf. Ibid., 448–449), knowing that some other "brothers" who were evangelizing neighbouring areas might have missed the chance to read or listen to the letter. This conjecture well explains Paul's need to write the second letter and its repetitive nature; moreover, the rather abrupt adjuration to read out the letter to "all the holy brothers" in 1 Thess 5:27 well explains Paul's concern that his message might not reach them; then, Paul's salute-request combined with τοὺς ἀδελφοὺς πάντας in 5:26 (cf. πάντα ἅγιον ἐν χριστῷ Ἰησοῦ, Phil 4:21) can be explained in this way as well: Paul simply does not want any of the brothers to miss the holy kiss; again, the brotherly love given to πάντα τοὺς ἀδελφοὺς τοὺς ἐν ὅλῃ τῇ Μακεδονίᾳ in 4:10 may not be simply mutual Christian affection but the Thessalonian Christians' support for the brothers who work for Christ in a similar way to that of Paul. Even if his suggestion seems inconclusive regarding the identity of the brothers and the recipient of the second letter, the existence among the congregation of the gospel workers who naturally expected financial support from the congregation is very probable.

164. Even if such an appeal to other authorities and explicit use of εὐαγγελ-terminology are lacking from Gal 6:6, Paul's use of the two singulars "the one who is taught (ὁ κατηχούμενος)" and "the one who teaches (ὁ κατηχῶν)" in a direct connection to the theme of Christian community's material support to such a teacher of the word (cf. R. N. Longenecker, *Galatians*, 279) may recall such a distinction and right / duty relationship in 1 Cor 9:14.

165. The term I employ here is indebted to M. F. Bird, *A Bird's-Eye View of Paul: The Man, His Mission and His Message* (Nottingham: IVP, 2008), 162, who uses "gospelization" – and "gospelize" (25) – in the sense of Paul's further communication of the gospel with his converts for the purpose of discipleship.

and those individuals whom Paul thought to be set aside for the cause of the faith in the gospel not only among non-believers but also among the church.

3.3.2.5. Apostles, Prophets and Teachers as Types of the Eschatological Heralds in Relation to the Church (1 Cor 12:28)

From our discussion we may more specifically suggest that it is not only those known as apostles before Paul, plus Paul himself and his named missionary co-workers, who were responsible for the teaching of the gospel within established communities (as well as evangelistic preaching), but that others also fall into the category of the eschatological heralds whom Paul refers to in different ways (e.g. ὁ κατηχῶν, Gal 6:6; διάκονοι, 1 Cor 3:5; 2 Cor 6:4; Rom 16:1; συνεργοί, 1 Cor 3:9, cf. e.g. οἱ κοπιῶντες ἐν λόγῳ καὶ διδασκαλίᾳ, 1 Tim 5:17b).

However, it should be emphasized that Paul does not provide us with a list of those who fall into this category. Nor indeed does he explicitly refer to his co-workers as "eschatological heralds." Often the designations he gives to Christian individuals are quite general and do not say anything positive (or negative) about their possible status as eschatological heralds (e.g. ἀγαπητός, Rom 16:5ff; συστρατιώτης, Phil 2:25; Phlm 2; συγγενής, Rom 16:7; οἰκονόμος, 1 Cor 4:1; λειτουργός, Phil 2:25).[166] This makes it difficult to identify the exact range of which designations or categories might point to people being eschatological heralds.

Nevertheless, Paul seems to provide at least a clue in 1 Corinthians 12:28 where, discussing the Spirit's giving of different charisms within the church, he introduces three types of people, "apostles," "prophets" and "teachers." Despite the context in which the focus is emphatically on spiritual unity and mutual love among church members as one "body" (vv. 12–27), these three groups of people receive a certain descriptive differentiation from the rest of charisms: while "apostles," "prophets" and "teachers" are enumerated with the adverbial qualifiers "first," "second" and "third" respectively

---

166. Cf. Ellis, "Co-Workers," 437, n.3., who considers Paul's use of ἀδελφή (Phlm 2) as "general" while regarding οἱ δελφοί *passim* as "technical."

(whether in the sense of chronology or order in significance or both),[167] the remainder of the charisms are enumerated with "thereupon" (ἔπειτα) in a group except for δύναμις.[168] Moreover, while the former groups are not simply gifts but persons, the latter are all spiritual gifts (vv. 28–30).[169]

Some considerations suggest that there is something more than a mere stylistic matter behind such a descriptive difference. First, Paul's earlier enumeration of different spiritual gifts (vv. 8–10) has a similar descriptive differentiation between gifts with regard to "word" (i.e. "λόγος σοφίας," "λόγος γνώσεως," v. 8) and the remainder (vv. 9–10) by "ἑτέρῳ," while each gift is enumerated with "ἄλλῳ" within each group. Second, as commentators unanimously agree, "apostles, prophets and teachers" refer to those with special place for the preaching and teaching of the gospel / word within the church, while other charisms do not necessarily have such functions. Third, the author of Ephesians mentions in 4:11 a very similar list: apostles, prophets, evangelists, pastors and teachers, whose tasks are clearly described as something in relation to the church, in other words, "equipping the saints" for their work of service and building up the body of Christ (v. 12).

The above considerations suggests a Pauline view in which those who have tasks of preaching and teaching of the gospel / word have a certain distinctive position in relation to the church. It may be that the category of the eschatological heralds generally corresponds with such types of people (i.e. apostles, prophets and teachers). "Teachers," for Paul, probably embraces a variety of ministries, though all closely related to one another in terms of the ministry of the gospel / word, whether itinerant preaching or

---

167. Cf. G. D. Fee, *The First Epistle to the Corinthians*, NICNT (Grand Rapids: Eerdmans, 1987), 619–620, who, while being reluctant to see any different significance between the three groups, finds a certain difference in relation to one's "precedence over the other in the founding and building up of the local assembly" (620).

168. Ibid., 618.

169. Ibid., 619. For Fee such a difference, however, is of minimal significance since Paul's enumeration is about "ministries" rather than "offices" held by certain persons in the local church.

stationary teaching, and in terms of "reward" (μισθός) of such ministries (1 Cor 3:8, cf. e.g. 1 Cor 9:14; Gal 6:6; 1 Tim 5:18).[170]

This is not to suggest, however, that Paul sees the eschatological heralds as a *supra*-church structure. Rather, the particular phrase "ἐν τῇ ἐκκλησίᾳ" in 1 Corinthians 12:28a suggests that Paul sees even those gospel heralds who have foundational significance for the formation of the Christian communities (i.e. "apostles," Rom 1:5ff, cf. e.g. Eph 2:20; *Did.* 11:4 in which prophets have a similar significance) as having their ecclesial place *within* Christian communities *as a part of God's people* along with other non-foundational gospel workers and church members.

3.3.3. Conclusion

In this section I have argued that for Paul the advent / sending of the multiple gospel heralds (prefigured in the Isaianic Servant Songs) was in itself an eschatological event that God was bringing into his world, and his *how* in which he implements the ongoing restoration of Israel and incoming of the Gentiles. We have further observed that while Paul finds in this event a place along with other individuals who are closely associated with the Messiah, who is the Suffering Servant and the eschatological herald of the good news, the apostle locates, as well as the non-believing world, the believing communities as an ongoing object of the ministry of these eschatological heralds of the gospel.

From this observation one may infer, as an answer to our primary question (why does Paul fail to mention the church's proactive evangelism?), that such a task εὐαγγελίζεσθαι is never understood as transferable to the church. Since for Paul it is not merely a communication / dissemination of the gospel contents (or *kerygma*), but a specialized / authorized task that requires both *heralding* and *elucidating* the message of God's universal salvation for the church as well as the world, it is understood as assigned only to the multiple εὐαγγελιζόμενοι.

Such a suggestion is plausible but not conclusive. As we did in the previous chapter, we need to eschew taking Paul's failure to mention the

---

170. Ellis, "Co-Workers," 440–441. Perhaps, a certain tension between similarity and dissimilarity between "apostles / prophets" (e.g. *Did.* 13) and "teachers" underlies the Deutero-Pauline terms "evangelists" and "pastors."

church as one of the εὐαγγελιζόμενοι in his letters as an indication of an absence of such expectation from the apostle's thought. Rather, we need to pay attention to Paul's conception of the εὐαγγελιζόμενοι (and his use of εὐαγγελίζεσθαι) as crucial information for the apostle's conception of mission. Our observation here at least indicates a certain inadequacy in the widespread scholarly and ecclesial tendency to recognize Paul's conception of mission purely in terms of the apostle's (even more misleadingly, the church's) socio-religious effort for the propagation of the gospel message towards those who do not belong to the community of converts. Rather, as Paul perceived the advent / election of the eschatological gospel heralds as God's implementation for the initiation and continuation of the eschatological redemption which is yet to be consummated with the incoming of the fullest number of the Gentiles and the fullest restoration of Israel (Rom 11:25b–26), Paul's conception of mission is approached not only in terms of the *inclusion of non-members* but also in terms of *bringing about the full restored-ness of the community of converts* among whom God's redemption is to be fully actualized until the day of Jesus Christ (e.g. 1 Thess 5:1–8; 1 Cor 1:8; 2 Cor 1:14; 2:6; Phil 1:6, 10; 2:16. cf. 2 Thess 1:10; 1 Cor 3:13; 5:5; Rom 2:16; Eph 4:30; 2 Tim 4:8).

If the church is the ongoing object of the mission of the εὐαγγελιζόμενοι and Paul's eschatological horizon envisions the full restoration of Israel in and through the church, without any particular indication of the church's co-heraldship, do we really need to identify the eschatological significance and role of the church only in terms of what usually defines Paul's own vocation? If for Paul the church has any eschatological significance and purpose that is still to be completed as God wills, and Paul is devoted to this purpose, is not this purpose of the church part of Paul's own conception of mission regardless of what he thinks he himself should do? This necessitates our further discussion about the implication of Paul's ministry among / towards the communities of converts in relation to his conception of mission.

3.4. The Community of the People of God as an Eschatological Event in Paul

3.4.1. Paul's Missio-Ecclesial Understanding within His Conception of Mission

From our discussion so far it may be said that the community of converts, which comprises the remnant of Israel and the Gentiles who are reckoned as being right with God through the faith in / of Christ, in some measure, is an outcome or a product of the ministry of the eschatological heralds of the gospel. This aspect is also well brought out in Paul's metaphors such as farmer / builder in relation to field / building (1 Cor 3:6–9, cf. Gal 2:18; 2 Cor 10:8; 12:19; 13:10; Rom 11:6; 15:20) or father in relation to children (1 Cor 4:15); these metaphors point to the church's dependence on Paul.[171] In this regard, the existence (or activity) of the heralds is at least logically prior to the existence of the communities.

Can this relationship to the apostle, however, mean that Paul has any notion of the church's secondary or ancillary significance to his own mission as a gospel herald to non-believing individuals? Or, put a bit differently, can it further indicate that Paul has any notion that the community of converts *teleologically* exists for the same or similar task that is entrusted to the apostle? Indeed, this line of thought can be seen in scholarly discussions.

Some scholars maintain that, since Paul's pastoral ministry is rather a subsidiary work or inevitably forced on him due to his successful proactive missionary preaching, Paul regarded his ministry in and for communities as a peripheral or even hindering element to his own apostolic vocation proper (as a missionary apostle for the Gentiles).[172] The consequence is two-fold: (1) a dichotomy between "Paul the missionary (or apostle)" and "Paul the

---

171. Cf. E. Best, *Paul and His Converts: The Sprunt Lectures 1985* (Edinburgh: T. & T. Clark, 1988), 140.

172. E.g. Knox, "Romans 15:14–33," 1–11; G. Bornkamm, *Paul* (London: Hodder and Stoughton, 1971), 54–55; O. Hofius, "Paulus-Missionar und Theologe," in *Evangelium Schriftauslegung Kirche: Festschrift Für Peter Stuhlmacher Zum 65. Geburtstag*, eds. J. Ådna, S. J. Hafemann, and O. Hofius (Göttingen: Vandenhoeck, 1997), 224–237.

pastor" – or a dichotomy between Paul's theology and Paul's ethics;[173] and (2) a relegation of the church as a secondary agent of mission to the apostle (or at worst depriving the church of its missional significance). It seems that the misleading dichotomy is rightly remedied by a number of scholars' attempts to reconcile the two distinct aspects within Paul's single framework of reference.[174] However, it is to be noted that the latter problem is still lurking in the recent discussions of Paul's missio-ecclesial understanding that we have mentioned in the introductory chapter.[175] They are loosely based on the assumption that the church's "mission" is to be understood as the same or at least of a similar sort to Paul's own mission as if Paul had such a notion of "mission" purely in terms of a religious propaganda.

A further implication of understanding the church's mission in this fashion is the *relegation of Christian ethics to a secondary position, evangelism being primary*. It may be redundant to cite the various attempts to emphasize the missional place of the moral / ethical life of the Christian community or the connection between Paul's mission and the church's moral / ethical life, but the mission is always understood in terms of a nonbeliever's conversion / salvation and the moral / ethical life as a contributive force (centripetally) for it. One of the most recent attempts is Michael Barram's work. He complains that it is an "inadequate manner" in which scholars tend to neglect the connection between Paul's mission and the church's ethical / moral behaviour from the Pauline texts which lack any explicit evangelistic implications, while identifying such connections only from texts in which Paul specifically mentions the evangelistic effect (e.g.

---

173. E.g. M. Dibelius, *A Fresh Approach to the New Testament and Early Christian Literature* (*The International Library of Christian Knowledge*; London: Nicholson & Watson, 1936), 143–144, 217–220; H. D. Betz, *Galatians: A Commentary on Paul's Letter to the Churches in Galatia* (Philadelphia: Fortress Press, 1979), 292.

174. E.g. V. P. Furnish, *Theology and Ethics in Paul* (Nashville: Abingdon Press, 1968); W. Dennison, "Indicative and Imperative: The Basic Structure of Pauline Ethics," *CTJ* 14 (1979): 55–78; J. Eckert, "Indikativ und Imperativ bei Paulus," in *Ethik Im Neuen Testament*, ed. Kal Kertelge (Freiburg: Herder, 1984), 168–189; M. Parsons, "Being Precedes Act: Indicative and Imperative in Paul's Writing," in *Understanding Paul's Ethics: Twentieth Century Approaches*, ed. B. S. Rosner (Carlisle: Paternoster Press, 1995); R. B. Hays, *The Moral Vision of the New Testament: Community, Cross, New Creation* (San Francisco: Harper, 1996); B. Rosner, "Paul's Ethics," in *The Cambridge Companion to St. Paul*, ed. J. D. G. Dunn (Cambridge: Cambridge University Press, 2003), 212–223.

175. See chapter 1, 2.1–2.5.

1 Cor 7:16; 14:22–25).[176] According to Barram, Paul's moral reflection for his community of converts or their entire (moral) behaviour / life being encouraged by every thing that he writes, thinks, and does is constitutive of Paul's comprehensive understanding of mission since Paul understood that a Christians' moral behaviour always has "salvific function" for others (1 Cor 9:19–23; 10:31–11:1).[177] For him, "'mission' is an appropriate and necessary rubric" for interpreting Paul's moral instructions,[178] which are "*missional* events if they are not strictly *evangelistic*."[179]

This attempt is helpful and indeed valid insofar as the evangelistic implication of the ethical dimension of the church is rightly considered in relation to Paul's conception of mission. Nevertheless, it seems not fully to remedy the inadequacy in scholarly discussion of Paul's mission in relation to his ethical reflection. While it is right to see the crucial connection between Paul's mission and the evangelistic implication of the church's ethical behaviour, such an understanding of mission as a "rubric" under which Paul's moral reflection is expounded still makes the church's ethical / moral existence at best secondary / subordinate / sub-category to initial evangelism.

Considering Paul's eschatological framework of reference (i.e. now as the time for the continuation of the restoration of Israel and the incoming of the Gentiles into God's inaugurated salvation) and his understanding of the unique role of the eschatological heralds within it, it is doubtful that Paul maintained such a perspective towards the vocation of the church in relation to that of his own. Rather, in this section we will argue that, through a careful consideration of Paul's ecclesiological ideas within his eschatological framework, the community of converts per se appears to be a constituent part of his broader concept of mission with a wholly equal weight and independent significance to the enterprise of the eschatological heralds; and that this surely is the primary reason for Paul's total silence about the church's gospel preaching activity.

---

176. Barram, *Moral Reflection*, 8–9.
177. Ibid., 9, 42–77, 142–147.
178. Ibid., 147.
179. Ibid., 148. Cf. Dickson, *Mission-Commitment*, 262–292, who partly deals with the same issue.

3.4.2. Ἐκκλησία as an Eschatological Event in Relation to the Eschatological Heralds

The question of which ground Paul's view of the communities of converts rests on is approached in different ways. One common approach is to consider Paul's central theological issue such as salvation / freedom in Christ[180] that emphatically and frequently appears throughout his letters. Another common approach is to consider a central issue of Paul's pastoral concern such as the stability or integrity of a community, issues of which prompted Paul to pen his correspondence.[181] These approaches are valid and helpful and are to the benefit of our discussion. However, what we need to do in this section is to consider Paul's ecclesiological understanding firsthand through / within Paul's eschatological framework so that the eschatological significance of the church in Paul's thought can be more adequately observed,[182] particularly alongside his notion of the eschatological event of the gospel heralds.

3.4.2.1. Ἐκκλησία as a Concrete Localized Assembly of Converts in Paul

Our first attention should be given to the eschatological significance in Paul's most frequent designation for the communities of converts, ἐκκλησία.[183] It is often considered whether Paul's use of ἐκκλησία reflects: (1) the LXX's translation of various assemblies of Israelites particularly קָהָל before the Lord, the gathering of Israel to listen to God's word (e.g. Num 1:3; Deut 4:10; 23:1–3; Josh 9:2; Ps 21:22);[184] (2) and / or an assembly of the Greco-Roman citizens called out by a herald to make important political / civil decision for their welfare;[185] (3) and / or Judaeo-Graco-Roman voluntary clubs and associations with various purposes for gathering in a context of

---

180. E.g. Banks, *Paul's Idea*, 15–25.

181. E.g. L. T. Johnson, "Paul's Ecclesiology," in *The Cambridge Companion to St Paul*, ed. J. D. G. Dunn (Cambridge: Cambridge University Press, 2003), 200–201.

182. Cf. Furnish, *Theology and Ethics*, 214; Hays, *Moral Vision*, 19–27.

183. It occurs 44 times in the undisputed letters and 18 in the disputed letters.

184. See also Josephus, *Ant.* 4.35, 309; *Life* 268; *War* 1.654, 666.

185. E.g. Thuc. *Hist.* 1.187, 139; 6.8; 8.69; Philo, *Laws* 2.44; *Man* 138 *et al*; Acts 19:32–41.

oikonomia increasingly popular in the late Hellenistic period.[186] Because of all these pre-Pauline Jewish and Hellenistic usages of the word and the existence of pre-Pauline Christian communities that included Greek-speaking members at the very early stage, it is very unlikely that the Christian use of the term is Pauline coinage.

Whether or not these are all reflected in Paul's designation, what is widely agreed about Paul's use of ἐκκλησία is that it refers *primarily to an actual localized assembly / gathering* that is continuously held by those who are being made right with God through the faith in / through the Christ-event, being distinguished from others in the cities / regions (e.g. 1 Thess 1:1; Gal 1:2, 22; 1 Cor 7:17; 11:6, 18; 12:28;[187] 14:33–34; 16:19; 2 Cor 8:1, 19–24; 11:8, 28; 12:13, cf. 1 Cor 11:18; 14:35; Acts 8:3).[188] Some less concrete local sense of the church (i.e. "the church of God") appearing in Paul's retrospective accounts of his persecution (1 Cor 15:9; Gal 1:13; Phil 3:6) does not negate this point. It is most likely that Paul refers to the assembly of Christians that gathered in Jerusalem at the time of his persecution and dispersed around Judaea later.[189] Even the Deutero-Pauline notion of the high Christology / ecclesiology – which depicts the heavenly,

---

186. Cf. Banks, *Paul's Idea*, 7–14; Johnson, "Paul's Ecclesiology," 200–201.

187. The sense of ἐν τῇ ἐκκλησίᾳ of 1 Cor 12:28 is often taken as primarily the universal church as the plural "apostles" better implies plurality of assemblies rather than many apostles within a single community and as only allowing the sense of a single localized assembly within that universal sense (e.g. R. P. Martin, *Studies in 1 Corinthians* 12–15; Ridderbos, *Outline*, 328–330). Some others maintain that the sense is limited to the local assembly at Corinth (e.g. Dunn, *Jesus and the Spirit*, 262–263; Dunn, *The Theology of Paul the Apostle*, 540–541. Cf. Banks, *Paul's Idea*, 35–37; O'Brien, "Church," *DPL*, 124). It seems to me, following Fee, *1 Corinthians*, 618, n.13, that, while it is difficult to exclude some collective sense of other local assemblies, the primary sense is the local assembly at Corinth since the logic and the linguistic connection of v. 28 with v. 27 (ὑμεῖς δέ ἐστε σῶμα Χριστοῦ) is hardly mistakable. Moreover, the plural "apostles" does not necessarily imply apostles *vis-à-vis* or *in* the universal church, but rather signifies their significance within and accessibility to any local community as co-founders (despite indirectness) of the church (cf. e.g. Rom 1:5; *Did*. 11:4). Cf. D. E. H. Whiteley, *The Theology of St. Paul* (Oxford: Blackwell, 1964), 187.

188. E.g. A. Fridrichsen, "Eglise et Sacrement dans le Nouveau Testament," *RHPR* 17 (1937): 345; K. L. Schmidt, "ἐκκλησία," *TDNT* 3. 508; D. Guthrie, *New Testament Theology* (Leicester: IVP, 1981), 743; Banks, *Paul's Idea*, 28–36; O'Brien, "Church," *DPL*, 124; Dunn, *Theology*, 540; Beker, *Paul the Apostle*, 322–323. The difference between the assembly itself and the members that gather is very minimal.

189. Cf. Banks, *Paul's Idea*, 30, who rightly cites Gal 1:22 ("the churches of Judaea") to support the view. *Pace* Whiteley, *Theology*, 188.

cosmological reality of the church as the body whose head is the pre-existent, exalted Christ (Col 1:18; Eph 1:22) points to Christ's cosmological headship that is proleptically present in a concrete local gathering here and now rather than the sum total of those assemblies or their members (cf. Col 2:18–19; Eph 4:1–16).[190] Even if some collective or even universal sense cannot be thoroughly denied from Paul's thinking about the church since the sense is implicit already in Paul's body of Christ language or saints language,[191] Paul's ἐκκλησία is not used merely as a concept or a metaphor that refers to some sense of togetherness / connectedness of the churches and their members regardless of time and space but the primary referential point is a concrete assembly that entails every aspect of a real-life situation here and now within the community and towards the surrounding regions.

3.4.2.2. Ἐκκλησία as an Eschatological Event in Paul

What is significant about Paul's use of the term as such? It is to be answered through Paul's eschatological framework that conceives of the inauguration of the restoration of Israel in terms of the Christian community of the Jewish remnant and the Gentile associates whose ontological / teleological

---

190. This is not to deny the possible conception of the universalistic character of the church as the body of the pre-existent / exalted Christ, that is developed particularly in Eph 1:22–2:22. However, this universalistic communion or horizontal unification (between the Jewish Christians and the Gentile Christians, Eph 2:14–19) is rather a corollary of a vertical unification between God and humanity by Christ' cross (Eph 2:13, 16, cf. Col 1:20–22) and can be celebrated only when the heavenly / cosmological eminence of Christ truly governs a local dimension of a community (cf. Eph 6:10–19). Cf. Dunn, *Theology*, 541: "Its reality and vitality as church depended more immediately on its own direct continuity through Christ and its founding apostle with the assembly of Yahweh." Therefore, any timeless and spaceless association of the churches or of the believers into the universal community under Christ's cosmological headship (which is rather distant from Paul's firsthand use of ἐκκλησία) can be actualized only when the body of Christ is not merely a metaphor of an ideal but a reality in a concrete local community situation. As such, the heavenly reality of the church is stressed, but the point that authors of Eph and Col want to make does not fall upon the universalistic communion of the believers but again on the very Pauline thought that *a* community is *the* body of Christ therefore it must conform itself to its head. Therefore, the difference between the ecclesiologies in the undisputed letters and the disputed two letters in some measure may be put in terms of a perspective in a different angle (i.e. not from body to head but from head to body) rather than in terms of development in conception or a extension in scope. Cf. Guthrie, *New Testament Theology*, 743; E. Schweizer, *Church Order in the New Testament* (London: SCM, 1961), 105ff. *Pace* C. L. Mitton, *The Epistle to the Ephesians* (Oxford, 1951), 18; D. E. Nineham, "The Case against the Pauline Authorship" in *Studies in Ephesians*, ed. F. L. Cross (London: Mowbray, 1956), 32.

191. Cf. Whiteley, *Theology*, 188–189.

identity is to be found in the Jewish concept of the people of God (e.g. Rom 9:24–26; 11:1ff; 15:7–12).[192] More importantly, as we have already touched on, this notion of the church as the eschatological community of the people of God is not to be isolated but to be considered together with the notion of the eschatological heralds. As Paul's quotation of Isaiah 49:8 in 2 Corinthians 6:2 clearly indicates, God's inclusion of the Gentiles in the promised salvation for his remnant is happening currently. Even if this community of salvation is mediated by the eschatological heralds who work on behalf of Christ (5:19–20; 6:1), the emphasis on the promised salvation that is to be celebrated "now" by the Corinthian community (ἰδού, νῦν καιρὸς εὐπρόσδεκτος, ἰδού, νῦν ἡμέρα σωτηρίας) signifies Paul's view of ἐκκλησία as an actual eschatological event in which accountability to its God-given teleological mark (i.e. a community of the people of God or of salvation) is to be continuously actualized (cf. 5:20b; 6:1); equally as Paul saw the advent / sending of the eschatological heralds as an actual event happening currently so that the specific task is to be continuously fulfilled for the world and the communities.

It seems that the eschatological significance of the church paralleling that of the apostle is not merely rhetorical, since it is further elucidated by Paul's use elsewhere of the verb (εκ)καλέω and the noun κλῆσις that are certainly related to Paul's use of ἐκκλησία.[193] Such invitation language in Paul's letters is almost exclusively used to refer either to God's own eschatological act of calling of those to whom he wants to give salvation in Christ, more specifically a letter-receiving community in Christ,[194] or to the gospel heralds (1 Cor 15:9; Gal 1:15, cf. 2 Tim 1:9).[195] This may mean that for

---

192. Cf. Davies, *Paul and Rabbinic Judaism*, 101ff; Davies, *The Gospel and the Land*, 182; Guthrie, *New Testament Theology*, 750. For our use of "ontological" see n.206.

193. Cf. Schmidt, "ἐκκλησία," *TDNT* 3. 530–531; J. Gnilka, *Theologie des Neuen Testaments* (Freiburg: Herder, 1994), 111. Pace Dunn, *Theology*, 537, who is cautious about the links of the language since Paul refrains from such an interplay of ideas.

194. καλέω: Rom 4:17 (in the sense of God's fundamental act of creation / salvation that is to be applied to God's eschatological salvation through faith in Christ, cf. v. 16), 8:30; 9:7, 12, 24–26; 1 Cor 1:9; 7:15, 17–18, 20–22, 24; 10:27; Gal 1:6; 5:8, 13; 1 Thess 2:12; 4:7; 5:24, cf. Eph 4:1, 4; Col 3:15; 2 Thess 2:14; 1 Tim 6:12. κλῆσις: Rom 11:29; 1 Cor 1:26; 7:20; Phil 3:14. cf. Eph 1:18; 4:1, 4; 2 Thess 1:11.

195. The only exception is 1 Cor 10:27 which only refers to non-believers' invitation to a pagan feast.

Paul the Christian community is not a mere corollary of the ministry of the eschatological heralds, but more properly and fundamentally an eschatological event that God himself brings into being in the present time and space. And it further indicates that for Paul God's eschatological calling / invitation includes at least *two discernable entities*: the eschatological heralds and the eschatological communities.

3.4.2.3. Two Vocations: Juxtaposition of ἐκκλησία with the Apostle

Despite the common ground through / into which both the apostle (or the gospel heralds) and a community of converts are called, namely God's grace and mercy (cf. 1 Cor 1:24; Rom 8:28), the paralleling eschatological significances of the two parties are unmistakable in Paul's *juxtaposition* of the two in a *contrasting manner* (rather than including in one category) in terms of "κλητός" (one who is called to be).

This juxtaposition exists in Paul's two opening verses of the first letter to the Corinthians. In verse 1 Paul describes himself as "one who is called to be an apostle of Christ Jesus" (Παῦλος κλητὸς ἀπόστολος Χριστοῦ Ἰησοῦ) and in verse 2 juxtaposes his addressees (τῇ ἐκκλησίᾳ τοῦ θεοῦ τῇ οὔσῃ ἐν Κορίνθῳ, ἡγιασμένοις ἐν Χριστῷ Ἰησοῦ) by describing them as "to ones who are called to be saints" (κλητοῖς ἁγίοις). Despite the slight distance between the two phrases,[196] the same juxtaposition appears in Romans 1:1–7a. In verse 1 while Paul describes himself, quite similarly to 1 Corinthians 1:1, "one who is called to be an apostle set apart for the gospel of God" ([δοῦλος Χριστοῦ Ἰησοῦ] κλητὸς ἀπόστολος ἀφωρισμένος εἰς εὐαγγέλιον θεοῦ), he again describes his addressees in Rome as "to ones who are called to be saints" (κλητοῖς ἁγίοις).

Certain considerations will prevent us from seeing this juxtaposition of the two callings (κλητός vis-à-vis κλητοί) as a mere stylistic / rhetorical practice, or an unreflectively / customarily made distinction for an addressor / addressee / blessing block common in epistles in those days. Rather, we need to recognize that Paul implicitly but quite clearly stresses *two*

---

196. This distance should not be regarded as real, since vv. 1–6 is the addressor part with a parenthetical list of descriptions while v. 7a is the addressee part, both of which belong to a salutation section still in one sentence.

eschatologically significant callings in his greeting, namely an eschatological herald in relation to an eschatological assembly of the saints.

First, Paul's use of κλητοὶ ἅγιοι in 1 Corinthians 1:2 in apposition to ἡ ἐκκλησία is important since it indicates the nature of ἡ ἐκκλησία. Here, Paul seems to use the full formulation "the church(es) of God" + locality + "in Christ" (cf. 1 Thess 2:14) which is often varied (e.g. 1 Thess 1:1 – "the church" + locality + "in God and Christ") or abbreviated (e.g. Gal 1:13; 1 Cor 10:32; 11:22; 15:9; 2 Cor 1:1: "the church(es) of God") or shortened as more simply "the church" (e.g. 1 Cor 16:1, 19; 2 Cor 8:1; Gal 1:2).[197] This full formulation associates the existence of a localized community with God as its source and with Christ as its mediator. When this association is considered with the assembly's eschatological character and particularly with γιοι language which Paul fairly frequently uses as a collective designation for the believers,[198] it strongly recalls the eschatological people of the Most High prefigured in the Danielic texts such as Daniel 7:13–27 where the eschatological elect, who are given the kingdom and dominion when the one like the Son of Man comes, are called קְדִישִׁין/οἱ ἅγιοι (cf. e.g. *Pss. Sol.* 17:26; 1QS 5:13; 8:17–23; *1 Enoch* 38:4–5).[199] As we have already observed, if Paul in Philippians 2:16 could associate the community of converts with the Danielic eschatological people of God (Dan 12:3), it is

---

197. Cf. O'Brien, "Church," *DPL*, 126.

198. It is noteworthy that, while Paul customarily uses "brother / sister" language to refer to Christians both for collective sense with the plural and individual sense with the singular (e.g. Rom 14:10ff, 16:23; 1 Cor 1:1; 5:11; 6:5; Phil 2:25. cf. Col 1:1; Eph 6:21), he never uses ἅγιος in this manner. The word is always used in the collective sense, as the masculine plural, to refer to either a local community or a notable portion of a community or all believers regardless of locality. Cf. Rom 1:7; 8:27; 12:13; 15:25–26, 31; 16:2, 15; 1 Cor 1:2; 14:33; 16:1, 15, 20; 2 Cor 1:1; 8:4; 9:1, 12; 13:12; Phil 1:1; 4:21, 22; Phlm 5, 7, cf. 2 Thess 1:10; Col 1:2, 4, 12, 26; 3:12; Eph 1:1, 15, 18; 2:19; 3:1, 8; 4:12; 5:3; 6:18; 1 Tim 5:10. 1 Thess 3:13 is also a possibility (cf. 1 Thess 4:13–14). However, Paul's language seems to be alluding to the LXX Zech 14:5 in which οἱ ἅγιοι are celestial beings rather than the eschatological people of God (cf. Deut 33:2; Ps 89:5, 7; Dan 4:13; 8:13; Matt 13:41, 49; Mark 8:38; 13:27; 2 Thess 1:7; Jude 14–15). Note that the word is exceptionally used in Eph 3:8 to refer to the apostles and prophets but in this case the adjective carries the ordinary sense of holiness rather than the sense of the people of God.

199. It is most likely that the OT references such as "holy assembly" (Ex 12:16), "holy nation" (Ex 19:6), "holy people to God" (e.g. Deut 7:6) or "holy ones" (Ps 15:3) provided the Jewish apocalyptic eschatological interpretative tradition during the Second Temple period with a background for קְדִישִׁין/οἱ ἅγιοι language to refer to those elect in the messianic age. Cf. O. E. Evans, "New Wine in Old Skins: XIII. The Saints," *ExpTim* 86 (1975): 196–200; Fee, *1 Corinthians*, 32–33; Dunn, *Romans 1–8*, 19–20.

not difficult to speculate that Daniel 7 might have the same effect for Paul's ecclesiological thought within his eschatological framework. Together with this, Paul's use of οἱ ἅγιοι in 1 Corinthians 6:2 in the sense of the church judging (κρίνω) the world and even celestial beings (v. 3) strongly suggests that such a Danielic people of God who emerge at the Eschaton is behind Paul's understanding of the identity of ἐκκλησία (cf. κρίσις, Dan 7:22).[200] Then, κλητοὶ ἅγιοι in juxtaposition with κλητὸς ἀπόστολος does not simply bear a literary function (i.e. stating who the addressees are) but also states the eschatological significance of the addressees, the eschatological people of God in relation to the eschatological herald.

Second, since in 1 Corinthians 1:2b Paul states that the Corinthians "had been made holy in Christ Jesus" (cf. Eph 1:4; Col 3:12), κλητοὶ ἅγιοι will be redundant had Paul not intended to put any significance in the particular expression κλητοί.[201] Considering the perfect tense of the participle ἡγιασμένοι, κλητοὶ ἅγιοι must not be seen as an unreflective redundancy but an important indication that the church's primary *teleological significance* (calling or vocation) is to maintain its holiness in the "already–not yet" tension.[202] Similarly, in Romans 1:6 Paul depicts the ones in whom the apostles brought about the obedience of faith as "ones who are called to be of Jesus Christ" (κλητοὶ Ἰησοῦ Χριστοῦ), and then in the immediately following verse he calls his addressees κλητοὶ ἅγιοι. It seems that the genitive Ἰησοῦ Χριστοῦ in verse 6 may be a genitive of subject (in the sense of one who calls and / or possesses)[203] but more likely a genitive of dependence,[204] or a locative genitive similarly to Paul's technical dative ἐν Χριστῷ.[205] In this sense, ἅγιοι in the immediately following verse hints at the meaning of "of Jesus Christ" (or *vice versa*) and the purpose / consequence of the

---

200. Fee, *1 Corinthians*, 233. At the same time, I agree with P. Stuhlmacher, *Biblische Theologie des Neuen Testaments* I (Göttingen: Vandenhoeck & Ruprecht, 1992), 301, who suggests a relation between 1 Cor 6:2 and the Jesus-tradition preserved in e.g. Matt 19:28 / Luke 22:28-30. Cf. D. Wenham, *Follower*, 129.

201. Cf. Fee, *1 Corinthians*, 32.

202. This point is significant since it hints at Paul's understanding of the purpose of the church. This will be discussed later.

203. E.g. Barrett, *Romans*, 22; Cranfield, *Romans*, 1. 68.

204. So Dunn, *Romans 1–8*, 19.

205. Cf. A. Deissmann, *Light from the Ancient East*, trans. by L. R. M. Strachan (New York: George H. Doran Co., 1927), 377; BDF, 183; Morris, *Romans*, 52.

calling. The recurring κλητοί with such a clear teleological mark as his designation for his addressees well signifies that it is the eschatological significance of God's calling that is to be juxtaposed with that of Paul's calling as an eschatological herald.

Moreover, it should be noted that what is self-evident in the whole range of uses of the language ἐκκλησία/καλέω/κλῆσις/κλητοί is that Paul understood being called into a community of converts per se in terms of *vocation* and in this sense he had a strong self-understanding. Therefore, it is to be seen that for Paul ἐκκλησία was not simply a product of the ministry of the gospel heralds or extraneous to his missional horizon but rather it was to be understood as an eschatological event that emerges *alongside* the advent / sending of the eschatological gospel heralds, both of which are to implement the *respective two vocations* for the ongoing divine purpose.

3.4.3. The Vocation of the Church in Paul's Thought

If Paul considered the two parallel vocations to be implemented by the apostle and the church respectively, it is inappropriate to put the two in a single monolithic category that explains the intrinsic nature of the eschatological heralds. However, it would be less appropriate to employ another heterogeneous category to encapsulate or isolate just the church's vocation since the parallel vocations arise from one eschatological horizon that envisions the culmination of the restoration of Israel and the incoming of the Gentiles. Perhaps, then, we need to expand the meaning of the term "mission," if we still want it to refer to the church's vocation, so that it can accommodate each implication of the two parallel vocations conceived by the apostle. However, in what *shape* the expansion of the meaning of mission is to be made is decidable only after we identify the vocation that Paul thought to be given to the church and the relation of the church's vocation as such in relation to Paul's own vocation.

3.4.3.1. Ontological and Ethical[206] Understanding of the Vocation of the Church

It is assumed in numerous scholarly discussions about the early church that Christian propagation to those outside the church was a *raison d'être* for the early church as a substitution for a "thoroughgoing eschatology,"[207] or as the solution to the "cognitive dissonance" caused by the delay of the *parousia*,[208] or as the faithful extension or substantiation of the historical Jesus who could have been the antecedent,[209] or the initiator[210] of the church's on-going mission. This view of the church's self-conception in terms of its

---

206. In the Pauline scholarship, particularly German, there is a certain epistemological tendency to regard "ontological" and "ethical" in Paul's thought as opposing each other – e.g. H. Schlier, *Der Brief an die Galater*, KEKNT 12 (Göttingen: Vandenhoeck & Ruprecht, 1962), 173ff; A. Kehl, "Gewand (de Seele)," *RAC* 10 (1978): 1008ff, 1019ff; U. Schnelle, *Gerechtigkeit und Christusgegenwart: vorpaulinische und paulinische Tauftheologie* (Göttingen: Vandenhoeck & Ruprecht, 1983), 193. However, with Hengel-Schwemer (*Between Damascus and Antioch*, 294), I think the distinction is artificial and unnecessary in Paul's thought world which often reflects the Jewish flexibility between forms and matters. Moreover, as I apply the adjective "ontological" (not in the sense of "relating to the philosophical query of being" – e.g. "ontological argument" – but in the sense of "focused on meaning / idea / purpose residing in oneself") to a community, "ethical" can be accommodated by "ontological" naturally denoting "intra-community ethics." Another common usage of "ontological" in the biblical discussion in the sense of "realistic" in opposition to "metaphorical" – e.g. A. Richardson, *An Introduction to the Theology of the New Testament* (London: SCM), 256–257, n.1 – must be distinguished from my use here. Perhaps, "ontological" applied to a community may be seen as a nuanced version of "introverted Church" as appearing in J. Blauw's argument, *The Missionary Nature of the Church: A Survey of the Biblical Theology of Mission* (Guildford: Lutterworth Press, 1974), 28 (though he argues against it!), if the negative connotation (e.g. "selfish" or "indifferent to others") can be removed.

207. E.g. A. Schweitzer, *The Quest for the Historical Jesus: A Critical Study of Its Progress from Reimarus to Wrede* (2nd ed.; London: Adam and Charles Black, 1911), 369; S. G. Wilson, *The Gentiles and the Gentile Mission in Luke-Acts*, SNTSMS (Cambridge: Cambridge University Press, 1973), 18–20. Cf. B. F. Meyer, *The Early Christians: Their World Mission and Self-Discovery* (Wilmington: Michael Glazier Inc., 1986), who undertakes the study of the universal / world mission of the early Christianity in terms of its "self-definition."

208. E.g. C. K. Barrett, "The Gentile Mission as an Eschatological Phenomenon," in *Eschatology and the New Testament: Essays in Honor of George Raymond Beasley-Murray*, ed. H. Gloer (Peabody: Hendrickson Publishers, 1988), 71; J. G. Gager, *Kingdom and Community: The Social World of Early Christianity* (Englewood Cliffs: Prentice-Hall, 1975), 38–39.

209. E.g. Hengel, *Between Jesus and Paul*, 60–64; Sanders, *Jesus and Judaism*, 68, 220–221; Sanders, *Historical Figure*, 192; Sanders and Davies, *Synoptic Gospels*, 305; Scobie, "Jesus or Paul?" 47–60.

210. E.g. Schnabel, *Early Christian Mission*, 1. 57–58, 384–386; Schnabel, "Beginnings of the Mission to the Gentiles," in *Jesus of Nazareth: Lord and Christ: Essays on the Historical Jesus and New Testament Christology*, eds. J. B. Green and M. Turner (Grand Rapids: Eerdmans), 1994, 37–58; Bird, *Jesus and the Origins*, 125–172.

teleological vocation / service for outsiders' conversion, however, must be profoundly nuanced with Paul's view on the vocation of the church.

As our previous discussions demonstrate, the church in Paul's letters is not expected or exhorted to carry out the role of the gospel workers, while such an evangelistic task in Paul's letters is generally attributed to those gospel heralds. This is not to deny that there is an evangelistic *effect* in some aspects of the church. To use J. P. Dickson's words various "mission-commitments" of the Pauline communities, if not direct gospel-proclamation, were "accorded salvific significance."[211] As Barram rightly concludes, Paul calls for appropriate behaviour as the church's "missional," if not "missionary," function for the salvation of others.[212] Nevertheless, I would argue that such a commitment or function is not the church's primary purpose or *raison d'être* but only a by-product of a more fundamental mission / vocation of the church.[213]

As we concluded in the previous section, it is necessary to approach Paul's conception of mission not only in terms of the inclusion of non-members but also in terms of the inducement of restored-ness of the Christian community of converts until the day of Jesus Christ. This restored-ness is already assumed as being present in the Christian community (e.g. 2 Cor 5:17). However, what is explicit in Paul's letters (including the disputed letters) is that this restored-ness is to be consummated at the *parousia* of Christ (e.g. 1 Thess 5:1–8; 1 Cor 1:8; 2 Cor 1:14; 2:6; Phil 1:6, 10: 2:16. cf. 2 Thess 1:10; 1 Cor 3:13; 5:5; Rom 2:16; Eph 4:30; 2 Tim 4:8) through the church's ongoing effort of self-building (i.e. "edification") on the model of Christ's death and resurrection. As Paul's metaphor of the body of Christ (1 Cor 12:12–27; Rom 12:4–5, cf. 1 Cor 6:15; Col 1:18, 24; 2:19; Eph 1:23) or edifice (1 Cor 3:9–17; 2 Cor 6:16, cf. 2 Cor 4:16–5:5; Eph 2:19–22) effectively signifies, the intrinsic teleological nature of the church occupies Paul's primary concern for the church.

In this regard, my contention is that the church's *raison d'être* or teleological significance or vocation should be distinguished from the way Paul expected it to function, and, therefore, it should be found primarily in

---

211. Dickson, *Mission–Commitment*, 178–308, 313.
212. Barram, *Moral Reflection*, 175–179.
213. Cf. Banks, *Paul's Idea*, 90.

its *ongoing ontological task* to become God's eschatological people rather than what the eschatological people are rightly expected to do. Thus, I would argue that Paul's ethical demand, particularly for the edification of the church, is the vocation intrinsic in the eschatological event of the community that parallels the vocation intrinsic in the eschatological event of the gospel heralds.

There has been much discussion of Paul's ethics and his ideas on edification during the modern and the postmodern eras and a further discussion here would be superfluous. Nevertheless, for our deliberation here, we need to look at some Pauline texts where Paul's ontological / ethical demand on the church displays the church's intrinsic vocation *within* the apostle's eschatological horizon, or in relation to the apostle's own vocation. In this section we will inspect some texts in Galatians and Romans looking for (1) Paul's understanding of the church's ontological / ethical vocation to be the *family of God*, that signifies the qualitative sense of the restoration of Israel manifest among the eschatological people of God; and (2) Paul's understanding of the church's ontological / ethical vocation in his eschatological horizon that envisions the fullest (quantitatively as well as qualitatively) restoration of Israel, that may explain the relationship between the two vocations.

3.4.3.2. The Family of God as the Restored People of God in Paul

Robert Banks seems correct in noting that Paul's household metaphor for the church has received less scholarly attention compared to the metaphor of the body or temple, since the household language (i.e. οἱ οἰκεῖοι) that explicitly denotes the church appears comparatively rarely in Paul's letters, undisputed and disputed (Gal 6:10; Eph 2:19; 1 Tim 3:15).[214]

However, there are ample reasons to believe that Paul's conception of the church in terms of a household whose head is God is the most prominent feature in his ecclesiological horizon: (1) the most prominent self-identity of Christians, Jews and Gentiles, is as the children of God (υἱοί / τέκνα θεοῦ),[215] who are adopted into the Father-Son relationship between God

---

214. Banks, *Paul's Idea*, 48–49. Cf. e.g. R. N. Longenecker, *Galatians*, 283.
215. Gal 3:26; 4:6(x2); 7(x2); Rom 8:14, 16, 19, 21, 29; 9:8; Phil 2:15.

and his Christ through the Spirit of Christ (e.g. Gal 4:6; Rom 8:12–17, cf. Rom 8:29);[216] (2) Paul's favorite formula "God our father (θεός πατήρ / πατρός ἡμῶν)"[217] / "God the father (θεός πατήρ / πατρός)"[218] in a concrete community situation reflects such a Christian identity as the children of God; (3) Paul's language to describe his relationship to the Christian community is primarily a family relationship language such as "brother(s) / sister(s)";[219] (4) Paul's designations for himself and his co-workers in the service for the Christian community often reflect the concept of household personnel who are responsible for a household's affairs;[220] (5) apart from the brethren language to denote Paul's relationship to the community and its individual members, Paul sometimes uses "father / children" language;[221] (6) it is very likely that the context of the church per se was very often of a household situation.[222] In this regard, even if the explicit metaphor appears only sparsely, the concept of the church as the household of God is the most fundamental ecclesiological idea that permeates every aspect of the life and the nature of the church in Paul's thought.

---

216. Note that Paul uses "heir (κληρονόμος)" which is also a household language to denote the corollary Christian identity as the children of God (Rom 8:17; Gal 3:29, cf. Rom 4:14; Titus 3:7).

217. 1 Cor 1:3; 2 Cor 1:2; Rom 1:7; Phil 1:2; Phlm 3. Cf. Col 1:2; Eph 1:2; 2 Thess 1:1–2; 1 Tim 1:2.

218. 1 Thess 1:1; 1 Cor 8:6; Gal 1:1, 3; Phil 2:11. Cf. Eph 6:23; 2 Tim 1:2; Titus 1:4.

219. 1 Thess 1:4; 2:1, 9, 14, 17; 3:2, 7; 4:1, 6, 10, 13; 5:1, 4, 12, 14, 25ff; 1 Cor 1:10, 11, 26; 2:1; 3:1; 4:6; 5:11; 6:5, 6, 8; 7:12, 15, 24, 29; 8:11, 12, 13; 9:5; 10:1; 11:33; 12:1; 14:6, 20, 26, 39; 15:1, 6, 31, 50, 58; 16:11f, 15, 20; Gal 1:2, 11, 19; 3:15; 4:12, 28, 31; 5:11, 13; 6:1, 18; 2 Cor 1:8; 2:13; 8:1, 18, 22f; 9:3, 5; 11:9; 12:18; 13:11; Rom 1:13; 7:1; 8:12, 29; 10:1; 11:25; 12:1; 14:10, 13, 15, 21; 15:14–15, 30; 16:14, 17, 23; Phil 1:12, 14; 2:25; 3:1, 13, 17; 4:1, 8, 21; Phlm 1, 7, 16, 20. cf. 1 Tim 4:6; 5:1; 6:2; 2 Tim 4:21; Col 1:1f; 4:7, 9, 15; Eph 6:21, 23. Paul's frequent use of the term to refer to his co-workers (1 Thess 3:2; 1 Cor 1:1; 16:12; 2 Cor 1:1; 2:13; 8:18; Rom 16:1, 23; Phil 2:25; Phlm 2) – despite a certain special sense attached to the co-workers, cf. Ellis, "Co-workers," 445–452 – and his calling Rufus' mother as his own mother (Rom 16:13) may be an extension of this use of the language.

220. "Steward (οἰκονόμος)": 1 Thess 3:2; 1 Cor 4:1–2; 9:17; Rom 16:23, cf. Titus 1:7; Col 1:25; Eph 3:2. "minister (διάκονος)": Rom 16:1; 1 Cor 3:5; 2 Cor 3:6; 6:4; 11:15, 23; Phil 1:1, cf. Gal 2:17; Rom 15:8; 1 Tim 3:8, 12, 4:6; Col 1:7, 23, 25; 4:7; Eph 3:2, 7; 6:21). Cf. Banks, *Paul's Idea*, 50.

221. 1 Cor 4:15; Phil 2:22; Phlm 10.

222. 1 Cor 1:16; 11:22, 34; 14:35; 16:15, 19; Rom 16:5; Phil 4:22; Phlm 2, cf. 1 Tim 3:4, 5, 12; 5:4, 13; 2 Tim 1:16; 3:6; 4:19; Titus 1:11; Col 4:15. Cf. Dunn, *The Theology of Paul the Apostle*, 541–542; P. H. Towner, "Households and Household Codes," *DPL*, 417.

Then, what is the implication of the understanding of the church in terms of God's family? As scholars aptly point out,[223] the implication is primarily about the members' intra-community relationship and obligation to one another rather than the community's or its members' relationship to the outside world. This is again not to suggest that the latter is not Paul's concern. Paul makes it clear elsewhere in his letters that it is not his idea that the community should indulge in world-negating escapism or separatism (e.g. 1 Thess 4:12; 5:15; 1 Cor 5:10; Gal 6:10a; Rom 12:18). Nevertheless, we need to note that Paul's conception of the church as the household of God entails primarily intra-community ethics rather than the universality of Christian ethics towards the world.

First, Paul's frequent exhortation for familial affection is almost always given with the reciprocal pronoun ἀλλήλων (one another): to love "one another" (1 Thess 3:12; 4:9; Rom 12:10) or to serve (δουλεύω) in love "one another" (Gal 5:13) or to bear the burdens "of one another" (Gal 6:2) or to build up "one another" (1 Thess 5:11) etc. This reciprocal pronoun cannot be understood in terms of a general reciprocity simply assumed between two different parties as if it can denote the Christian's stance in relation to non-Christians.[224] In fact, except for only four cases (cf. 1 Cor 7:5; Rom

---

223. E.g. C. J. H. Wright, "Family," *ABD* 2.768; Towner, "Households and Household Codes," 417–418; Banks, *Paul's Idea*, 50.

224. It is often assumed in terms of inter-church reciprocity rather than of intra-church reciprocity interpreting the "burden" of Gal 6:2 as the financial burden of the Jerusalem saints (e.g. J. G. Strelan, "Burden-Bearing and the Law of Christ: A Re-Examination of Galatians 6.2," *JBL* 94 [1975]: 266–276) or "household of the faith" of Gal 6:10 as the Jerusalem church (e.g. L. W. Hurtado, "The Jerusalem Collection in Galatians," *JSNT* 5 [1979]: 46–62). It is possible that Paul had in mind such a collection from the Galatians when he wrote the letter since he explicitly mentions elsewhere about his exhortation to the Galatians for the collection (1 Cor 16:1) and their actual practice (Rom 15:26). Nevertheless, the meaning of the burden that is to be shared (v. 2) and the identity of οἱ οἰκεῖοι τῆς πίστεως (v. 10) cannot be interpreted only in that direction. As Paul's concern in the immediately preceding section (5:13–26) is best understood to be reflecting the problems caused to the Galatians by the agitators who intruded into the community (2:4), 6:1–10 is also best understood in terms of an antidote to that problem and thus the reciprocity of intra-community rather than of inter-community (cf. E. M. Young, "'Fulfill the Law of Christ': An Examination of Galatians 6.2," *StBT* 7 [1977]: 31–42; R. N. Longenecker, *Galatians*, 238; Witherington, *Grace in Galatia*, 418–438, see also my argument below). It is not to deny the significance of the inter-community reciprocity in Paul's mind since the Jerusalem collection represents the eschatological significance of Paul's mission (cf. K. F. Nickle, *The Collection: A Study in Paul's Strategy* [London: S.C.M. Press, 1966], 138; Munck, *Christ and Israel*, 120–121) and various exchanges between the local

1:27; 2:15; Eph 5:21) the thirty-four occurrences of the pronoun in the Pauline letters (undisputed and disputed) denote a family like relationship / obligation in intra-community reciprocity.[225] Of course, it may be said that it is the letters' intrinsic nature as the responses to the in-community matters that makes Paul's ἀλλήλων appear exclusively as intra-community reciprocity. However, this is not a valid criticism since Paul uses such language commanding intra-community love in a straightforward juxtaposition with a universal ethical concern: (ἀλλὰ πάντοτε τὸ ἀγαθὸν διώκετε [καὶ] εἰς ἀλλήλους καὶ εἰς πάντας, 1 Thess 5:15, cf. Gal 6:10). If Paul's attitude is as such, then Paul's almost exclusive use of ἀλλήλων in the intra-reciprocal sense must not be neglected. Rather, the frequency and the ubiquity of such language is better understood in terms of his fundamental ecclesiological understanding that leads him to approach God's eschatological people primarily in terms of *their intra-community relationship*.

Second, Paul's explicit use of the familial analogy in Galatians 6:10b to denote the Christian community as "the household of the faith (οἱ οἰκεῖοι τῆς πίστεως)" is immediately conjoined with the idea of the *priority* of intra-reciprocal ethics of the church to the universality of the church's ethical and social responsibility.[226] Hans D. Betz observes the significance of

---

churches seem necessary in Paul's mission. However, such an inter-community reciprocity is also to be seen as intra-community reciprocity if the notion of universal church is employed.

225. Rom 1:12; 12:5, 10 (x2), 16; 13:8; 14:13, 19; 15:5, 7, 14; 16:16; 1 Cor 11:33; 12:25; 16:20; 2 Cor 13:12; Gal 5:13, 15 (x2), 17, 26 (x2); 6:2; Eph 4:2, 25, 32; Phil 2:3; Col 3:9, 13; 1 Thess 3:12; 4:9, 18; 5:11, 15; 2 Thess 1:3; Titus 3:3.

226. *Pace* Hurtado, "The Jerusalem Collection in Galatians," 55–56, who argues that the expression refers to the Jerusalem saints and concludes that Gal 6:1–10 is penned to encourage the Galatians to participate in the collection, since: (1) the language used in the argument of vv. 6–8 recalls Paul's encouragement of the Jerusalem collection; (2) there is a possibility that οἱ οἰκεῖοι was originally used to refer to the saints in Jerusalem (Eph 2:19). Despite a certain possibility for such a conjecture, however, it is highly unlikely that Paul's οἱ οἰκεῖοι τῆς πίστεως of Gal 6:10 particularly denotes the Jerusalem community: (1) the similarity of the "sowing and reaping" in Gal 6:7–8 and 2 Cor 9:6ff is superficial since that of Gal 6 is about various (contrasting) consequences according to what to sow in an ethical sense and whereas that of 2 Cor is about the assurance of reaping by sowing; and as the maxim in v. 7 suggests the agricultural imagery itself is too general to recall that of 2 Cor 9; (2) Hurtado fails to explain why, if so, the Galatians backed out of the collection so that he needed to exhort them to do it. It seems less likely that they backed out of it but rather did not need to be exhorted since if James' influence reached the Galatians independently of Paul (2:12) it is more plausible to believe that the brothers from James collected the money from them (cf. Hengel-Schwemer, *Between Damascus and Antioch*, 302–303, cf. Witherington, *Grace in Galatia*, 435, n.57, who explains Paul's silence about the collection

πρὸς πάντας of the verse of ethical exhortation along with the other occurrences in Galatians 2:16; 3:8, 22, 26–28 and stresses the expression as signifying the universal character of God's redemption that "corresponds to the universality of Christian ethical and social responsibility." This apt observation, however, fails to further consider the special significance attached to the following phrase μάλιστα δὲ πρὸς τοὺς οἰκείους τῆς πίστεως as he regards it merely as one "appended" to the former.[227] So, for Betz the μάλιστα phrase is a "typical Pauline paradox."[228]

In my opinion, however, the μάλιστα phrase is neither an appendage to the former nor a paradox. As the adverb μάλιστα is best rendered as "most of all" or "above all," it denotes urgency or priority of a thing in relation to other things. Then, μάλιστα δὲ πρὸς τοὺς οἰκείους τῆς πίστεως is not simply added to the former, but rather highlighted by the sense of primacy or urgency over the former. At the same time, the adverb μάλιστα never contrasts the preceding and the following as if the preceding is to be relegated to insignificance but rather assumes general significance wherever mentioned.[229] Therefore, while for Paul both the intra-reciprocal ethics of the church and the universality of the church's ethical / social responsibility belong to the same significant function that fulfills the law of Christ (6:2), Paul certainly stresses the urgency / priority of the former.

Why, then, does Paul attach such a special significance to intra-reciprocal ethics among the Galatians? Witherington suggests that the reason for the special significance attached to the former is that as the Galatians were in the early stages of the Christian life they needed to establish "a pattern of behaviour that would be a good witness" in their pagan environment, since it would be a real paradox if they claim Christ's universal concern

---

on the grounds that Galatians preceded 1 Corinthians); (3) considering that Paul's juxtaposition is between πρὸς πάντας (most likely "to the believers and non-believers alike") and πρὸς τοὺς οἰκείους τῆς πίστεως (to those of a / the believing community), it is highly unlikely that the latter denotes the particular community in Jerusalem (cf. Witherington, *Grace in Galatia*, 435: "Had Paul said do good to all Christians, and especially to the house of faith, then Hurtado's suggestion might have more plausibility.").

227. H. D. Betz, *Galatians: A Commentary on Paul's Letter to the Churches in Galatia* (Philadelphia: Fortress Press, 1979), 311. Similarly R. N. Longenecker, *Galatians*, 283.

228. Betz, *Galatians*, 311.

229. Cf. Phil 4:22; Phlm 16, cf. 1 Tim 4:19; 5:8, 17; 2 Tim 4:13; Titus 1:10; 2 Pet 2:10.

without showing their own intra-community concern.[230] This view seems a more apt explanation for the relationship between the church's universal concerns in relation to their special concern for their own intra-community matters and points out well where the real paradox arises.

Regretfully, however, the view does not seriously consider the Galatians' own context from which Paul's polemic, argument and exhortation of the letter arise. In my opinion, even if such an evangelistic effect / function intrinsic within the intra-reciprocal love can be demonstrated in other Pauline letters, such a conclusion has little grounding in the letter to the Galatians itself. Moreover, as Galatians 6:10 is Paul's final remark of the section 5:13–6:10 given as an antidote to the so-called "the Galatians' problem(s)," it is vital to approach Paul's employment of the particular household terminology (which in my opinion seems not unreflectively employed) and the specially emphasized significance by considering the fundamental problem that Paul perceived to be at stake within the community.

In my view, Paul's particular employment of the household language and the special significance and urgency attached to the intra-community ethics in Galatians 6:10 have a more fundamental reason apart from any practical concern. My contention is that such a language / idea is in itself polemical, reflecting the *clash of the two conflicting concepts of the people of God* between Paul and his agitators. And this further indicates that what is at stake is not simply a dialectic relationship between the universality of the church's ethics and its intra-community ethics but more fundamentally the issue of "who are the real people of God?" and "what is the real mark of such a people of God?" In this regard, I propose that Paul's conception of the church as the household of God is not merely a description of the church reflective of its family-like nature but serves as an indictment upon a Jewish concept of the people of God (that was postulated by a Judaizing theology) by pointing out that it fails to enable the "Israel" to maintain their real identity / vocation as the household of Israel (e.g. בֵּית יִשְׂרָאֵל/ὁ οἶκος Ἰσραήλ) due to the alienating effect of their self-centred adherence to the law apart from Christ. If this is the case in Paul's language of the household in Galatians 6:10b, it can be further argued that the intra-community

---

230. Cf. Witherington, *Grace in Galatia*, 437.

ethics is not simply stressed over anything but suggested by the apostle as the fundamental purpose (or vocation) of the people of God, for which vocation a concept of the people of God through a Judaizing theology is not after all successful. This can be elucidated by the following arguments.

First, we need to note that even if Paul's polemic against the teaching of the agitators in Galatia is made *externally* about the role and the nature of the law in relation to one's status in the covenantal people of God (Gal 2:16ff; 3:1ff; 3:15ff; 4:1ff; 4:21ff; 5:2ff), what is at stake is not only the question as to "what brings one a complete membership into the people of God?" but also and more fundamentally "who are the people of God?" The latter question is often ignored, however, as the most extensively undertaken approach to Paul's polemic in Galatians is to focus solely on Paul's understanding of the law for one's status in the people of God. Particularly for those who view Paul as a covenantal nomist, the latter question has largely receded as they discuss how Paul differs from or is similar to his opponents in understanding the observance of the law for "getting in" or "staying in" God's covenantal people, as if a monolithic understanding of the people of God is shared by Paul and his agitators.[231]

If we pay due consideration to the latter, we realize that Paul's polemic is not simply about the law but also about the two conflicting conceptions of the people of God. The two conflicting concepts of the people of God, particularly as the household of God, between Paul and his agitators (or the misled Galatians) can be construed (though at best through a careful mirror reading) from Paul's polemic in terms of "who is the seed of Abraham?" (3:6ff, 29). As David Daube insightfully reconstructs, Paul's argument in Galatians 3:6ff, 3:23ff, 4:21ff for the law critical gospel particularly in relation to Abraham and the Abrahamic covenant strongly suggests that the message of the agitators among the Galatians was about the OT scriptural basis for the people of God (e.g. Gen 17:4–14).[232] With Robert Jewett, I think, if this is the case for the message of the agitators in Galatia, that it is less likely that they attempted to deny or substitute Paul's message of salvation in Christ but only "supplemented" what they thought Paul's

---

231. E.g. Sanders, *Paul, the Law, and the Jewish People*, 4.
232. D. Daube, *The New Testament and Rabbinic Judaism* (London: Athlone Press, 1956), 141–150.

gospel was lacking: the observance of the law as the necessary and essential part for the right way to become the rightful people of God.[233] This may indicate that the agitators simply operated within the traditional Jewish concept of the people of God, to which they thought Paul would not have any particular objection.[234]

In this regard, the apostle opposes not only the idea about the law but also the agitators' naïve inclusion of the apostle in their perception of the people of God. As Paul maintains, the meaning of the Jewish scriptural / traditional expression "the seed of Abraham," intact as a nomenclature for the people of God, conflicts with that of the agitators (Christ and those who belong to him, cf. 6:15 vs the covenantal descendants of Abraham, Israel and the nations, through circumcision, cf. Gen 17:10). Thus, Paul's polemic in this regard does not only deal with a different understanding of the role of the law in relation to God's people, but involves also a fundamentally irreconcilable conflict (cf. 1:7ff; 5:2ff; 6:15–16) between two concepts of the people of God.[235]

Second, Paul's use of "the Israel of God (Ἰσραὴλ τοῦ θεοῦ)" in the final benediction (6:16) may serve as an indication that a conflict between two concepts of the people of God is behind the whole argument and exhortation of the letter. As Ernest Burton suggests, the composition of the sentence of verse 16[236] seems to be suggesting at least a linguistic distinction between "upon the Israel of God" and the preceding "upon them" by the separate use of "peace" and "mercy" (rather than a more logically natural and often appearing order "mercy and peace"), two separate uses

---

233. R. Jewett, "The Agitators and the Galatian Congregation," *NTS* 17 (1971): 207; G. Howard, *Paul: Crisis in Galatia: A Study in Early Christian Theology*, SNTSMS (Cambridge: Cambridge University Press, 1979), 1–19.

234. It seems to me that Paul's mentioning of "if I still preach circumcision" in Gal 5:11 indicates the agitators' naïve assumption about Paul's ongoing traditional Jewish conception of the people of God. Cf. R. N. Longenecker, *Galatians*, 232–233. Pace Donaldson, *Paul and the Gentiles*, 192–193; Dickson, *Mission-Commitment*, 46–48.

235. Note that Paul's decisive arguments are made more in terms of "who are the people of God?" than "what makes one a complete member of the people of God": e.g. "οἱ ἐκ πίστεως, οὗτοί εἰσιν υἱοί Ἀβραάμ," 3:7, "Εἰ δὲ ὑμεῖς χριστοῦ, ἄρα τοῦ Ἀβραὰμ σπέρμα ἐστέ, καὶ κατ' ἐπαγγελίαν κληρονόμοι," 3:29, "οὐκ ἐσμὲν παιδίσκης τέκνα, ἀλλὰ τῆς ἐλευθέρας," 4:31.

236. v. 16 reads καὶ ὅσοι τῷ κανόνι τούτῳ στοιχήσουσιν εἰρήνη ἐπ' αὐτοὺς καὶ ἔλεος καὶ ἐπὶ τὸν Ἰσραὴλ τοῦ θεοῦ.

of ἐπί before the respective groups, and the double use of καί before and after ἔλεος.[237] Faithful to the linguistic suggestion many read the Ἰσραὴλ τοῦ θεοῦ as denoting another Jewish group apart from the former group.[238] However, some others, while appreciating such a distinction as present in Paul's argument elsewhere, argue that the particular expression within the context of argument in Galatians – that sharply condemns a separation of one from the other – cannot be seen as denoting a separated Jewish group.[239]

In my view, such a tension between the separation that tends to emerge from Paul's linguistic side and the integration from Paul's theological side is not only an accidental by-product from a modern scholarly debate, but also one that indeed existed in Paul's thought as he penned the last section of the letter reflecting the nature of his polemic in the use of the particular expression. As R. N. Longenecker observes, we need to consider that Paul's expression is a *hapax* in his letters and does not appear elsewhere in the extant literature of Second Temple Judaism or later rabbinic Judaism.[240] This may indicate that this terminology is employed in an *ad hoc* fashion, perhaps from his agitators who might have used it as their self-designation in promoting their own message regarding the "real" people of God (allegedly Torah observant people).[241]

Even if we have no way to prove it, our previous consideration about the two conflicting conceptions of the people of God in Paul's polemic makes Longenecker's suggestion more than a possibility. The language that Paul uses with the two phrases side by side and apparently referring to two

---

237. E. de W. Burton, *A Critical and Exegetical Commentary on the Epistle to the Galatians*, ICC (Edinburgh: T. & T. Clark, 1921), 357–358.

238. Cf. G. Schrenk, "Der Segenwunsch nach der Kampfepistel," *Judaica* 6 (1950): 170–190; D. W. B. Robinson, "The Distinction between Jewish and Gentile Believers in Galatians," *ABR* 13 (1965): 29–44, who see the expression as referring to non-Judaizing Jewish Christians in Galatia. Cf. Mussner, *Galaterbrief*, HTKNT (Freiburg: Herder, 1974), 417; Bruce, *Galatians*, 275, who see it as referring to the totality of Jews who will be saved at the eschaton. See also P. Richardson, *Israel in the Apostolic Church*, SNTSMS (Cambridge: Cambridge University Press, 1969), 74–84, who argues that "Israel" was never applied to the church until the post-NT period.

239. E.g. R. N. Longenecker, *Galatians*, 297–299; J. A. D. Weima, "Gal. 6:11–18: A Hermeneutical Key to the Galatian Letter," *CTJ* 28 (1993): 90–107; Witherington, *Grace in Galatia*, 453.

240. Longenecker, *Galatians*, 299.

241. Ibid.

groups reflects the understanding of his opponents, who distinguish themselves as the Israel of God from the Gentile Christians; but though there is that dichotomy at the linguistic level, there is no such split for Paul at a theological level, as the "Israel of God" cannot for him be limited to Israel "κατὰ σάρκα" (cf. 1 Cor 10:18), but embraces all who "follow this rule" (ὅσοι τῷ κανόνι τούτῳ στοιχήσουσιν) regardless of their ethnicity.[242] So, Paul's use of the Ἰσραὴλ τοῦ θεοῦ with such a tension / ambiguity in his benediction attests the seriousness of the clash between the two concepts of the people of God.

Third, Paul's employment of the οἱ οἰκεῖοι in Galatians 6:10b cannot be seen as isolated from the clash of the two conflicting conceptions of the people of God. Of course, the concept of God as the father and members of a community as brethren is not at all a Christian *novum*: in Paul's Judeo-Christian / Greco-Roman milieu such a familial analogy had a prominence in describing any socio-religio-political unit.[243] Not least the OT often describes God as father and the people of God as his children.[244] In the OT "brother" (אָח/ἀδελφός) is sometimes used to refer to the Israelites' intra-relationship.[245] Moreover, the OT frequently calls the people of God "the house of Israel" (בֵּית יִשְׂרָאֵל/ὁ οἶκος Ἰσραήλ).[246] Perhaps, as L. Gaston[247] and L. W. Hurtado[248] suggest, the early church in Jerusalem could have quite naturally inherited this traditional nomenclature of בֵּית יִשְׂרָאֵל as their self-conception / designation as the eschatological Israel and the household of God (cf. Eph 2:19). In this regard, it is quite natural to expect both Paul

---

242. Cf. N. A. Dahl, "Der Name Israel: Zur Auslegung von Gal 6,16," *Judaica* 6 (1950): 161–170. See also Moo, *Romans*, 574, n.21, who supports the view by pointing to Paul in Rom 11:6–13 "emphasizes the inclusion of Gentiles in the new people of God."

243. For a brief comparison of various familial analogies in antiquity with Paul's idea see Banks, *Paul's Idea*, 54–56.

244. E.g. Ps 2:7; Hosea 11:1; Isa 45:10–11; 63:16; 64:7; Sir 4.10.

245. E.g. Lev 19:17; Deut 15:3, 11, 12; 17:15; 22:1; 24:10.

246. E.g. Exod 16:31; Lev 10:6; Num 20:29; Ruth 4:11; 1 Sam 7:2f; 2 Sam 1:12; 6:15; 12:8; 16:3; 1 Kgs 12:21; Ps 115:12; 135:19; Isa 5:7; 14:2; 46:3; 63:7; Ezek 37:11, 16; 39:12, 22f, 25, 29; 40:4; 43:7, 10; 44:6, 12, 22; 45:6, 8, 17; Hos 1:6; 5:1; 6:10; 11:12; Amos 5:1, 3f, 25; 6:1, 14; 7:10; 9:9; Mic 1:5; 3:1, 9; Zech 8:13.

247. L. Gaston, *No Stone on Another: Studies in the Significance of the Fall of Jerusalem in the Synoptic Gospels* (Leiden: Brill, 1970), 191–192.

248. Hurtado, "Jerusalem Collection," 55.

and his agitators to conventionally employ such a household language / idea for their concept of the people of God.

However, there are some good reasons for viewing Paul's particular employment of the household language not merely as a choice from convention but as one carefully chosen to reflect his polemic against the agitators' theology regarding the concept of the people of God: (1) as Paul's "faith" terminology is almost exclusively used in a polemic against the agitators,[249] it seems that the genitive qualifier "of the faith" (τῆς πίστεως) does not simply denote a Christian community but also connotes that the Christian community is not consonant with the agitators' Judaizing theology but with Paul's message of the faith in / of Christ; (2) as 6:10 is Paul's final exhortation for the Galatians being given as the antidote to their problems (3:1–5; 4:8–11; 4:21; 5:1–12; 5:13–6:10) caused by the agitators' teaching (1:7, 3:1), it is less likely that the exhortation stands on its own;[250] (3) as it is very likely that Paul recaptures his exhortatory point of 5:1–6:10 (or even the entire letter) in the summary statements of 6:12–16,[251] the appearance of a concept of the people of God (i.e. the family of faith) at the end of the exhortation (6:10) seems to parallel the traditional nomenclature of the people of God (i.e. in Israel of God) that appears at the end of the statement: if this is the case, the implication of the expression οἱ οἰκεῖοι τῆς πίστεως can be seen in the same manner as that of the Ἰσραὴλ τοῦ θεοῦ which implies the apostle's linguistic continuity and theological discontinuity with the agitators' conception of the people of God.

Fourth, and most importantly, as οἱ οἰκεῖοι τῆς πίστεως of Galatians 6:10b is to be seen as such, the special emphasis particularly on the intra-community ethics attached to the expression is also to be understood as polemic against the agitators' misleading concept of the people of God and as the antidote to the problems caused by the concept.

---

249. Gal 2:16(x2), 20; 3:2, 5, 7, 8, 9, 11, 12, 14, 22, 23(x2), 24, 25, 26; 5:5, 6.

250. In this statement I assume continuity between Paul's exhortation in Gal 5:13–6:10 and his arguments in the earlier chapters. Cf. R. B. Hays, "Christology and Ethics in Galatians: The Law of Christ," *CBQ* 49 (1987): 268–290; J. M. G. Barclay, *Obeying the Truth: Paul's Ethics in Galatians* (Edinburgh: T. & T. Clark, 1988), 147–155, 178–182, 216–220. For various views disregarding the continuity see Barclay, *Obeying the Truth*, 9–26.

251. Cf. Weima, "Gal. 6:11–18," 90–107, who provides a useful analysis of the structure of Galatians through the final statements of 6:11–18.

There appears to be at least two distinguishable problems among the Galatians in Paul's estimation: the danger of a legalistic / nomistic life style (3:1–5; 4:8–11; 4:21; 5:1–12);[252] and the misuse of freedom (5:13–6:10). As widely agreed today, it seems that the former was caused by certain Judaizing Christians, and the latter reflects the ongoing influence of the paganism on the Galatians even after their conversion. What is to be noted is, as Jewett rightly observes,[253] that Paul does not treat them as separate problems but deals with them as if they are one in character by prescribing a single antidote to them: the Christian love that replaces the law (5:22–23) or fulfills the law of Christ (6:2). This clearly shows that for Paul, loveless libertinism is inseparable from the legalism / nomism, if postulated by the agitators. We have no clear clue as to how these two are related in Paul's thought. Nevertheless, it could be inferred that what concerned the agitators was not simply Paul's law-free gospel that was allegedly unlike that of the Jerusalem apostles,[254] but the Gentile Christians' law-free lifestyle presumably meant it was ethically immoral to a pious Jew.[255] If the law observance was offered not only as a necessary requirement for full membership in the people of God but as a solution to the immoral life, it seems plain that for Paul such a lifestyle is a sliding back to slavery by the impotent and beggarly elements (4:9) and a self-entrapment in the fundamentally impotent attempt to observe the entire requirement of the law (5:3).

What is important in our discussion is that for Paul the failure in such a lifestyle is not simply the impotence to do (ποιέω) the whole law but the much worse result on the lifestyle in the people of God "ὑπὸ νόμον": (1) the alienation of themselves from God's eschatological grace in his Messiah (5:4, cf. Rom 11:7ff); and (2) the alienation of one from another (5:15, 20, 26, cf. 6:1, 2, 6, 10). That Paul's final exhortation focuses on the Galatians' intra-community ethics that can fully implement (ἀναπληρόω)

---

252. Despite my inclination to the view that holds the both legalistic (3:1–18) and nomistic (3:19–29) problems at stake in Paul's polemic (e.g. Longenecker, *Galatians*, 159), the question of the nature of Paul's polemic on the law does not necessarily affect our discussion here.

253. Jewett, "Agitators," 210.

254. Cf. Bruce, *Galatians*, 26.

255. Cf. Barclay, *Obeying the Truth*, 60–68.

the law of Christ (6:2) shows that Paul's concern is focused more on the latter problem.

While such an alienation of one, who is under the law apart from Christ, from the eschatological grace of God in Christ, is an apprehensible idea, the reason for Paul's direct connection of law-observing lifestyle with such an alienation of one from another is not immediately clear.[256] Nevertheless, Paul seems to give a rationale for such a direct connection by his employment of the particular household language. As we touched on above, οἱ οἰκεῖοι suggests a Jewish heritage in Paul's understanding of the people of God. Despite the obvious similarity / continuity, however, Paul's conception of the church in terms of a household must be distinguished from the OT concept of God and Israel with similar familial analogies through a couple of considerations: (1) as D. Guthrie and R. P. Martin rightly point out, the OT familial analogies to the relationship of God and Israel are at best adumbrative, and the fully formulated idea of the people of God in an intimate father-son relationship in a concrete household situation in Paul's thought (and in the NT) must be distinguished from them;[257] (2) the fundamental difference between them is not only about the clarity of the idea, but also about the scope: as C. J. H. Wright observes, while the OT formulation בֵּית יִשְׂרָאֵל/ὁ οἶκος Ἰσραήλ broadly implies the extended kinship of Israel including the concept of "tribe (שֵׁבֶט/מַטֶּה),"[258] "clan (מִשְׁפָּחָה),"[259] and "family / father's house (בֵּית-אָב),"[260] Paul's concept of the church as the household of God seems to fit with the narrower concept of the Greek term οἶκος equivalent to בֵּית-אָב.[261]

---

256. It can be said that Paul simply states the Galatians' ongoing or potential libertine tendency regardless of the Judaizing theology that has no power to stop it. However, as we considered above, it is more likely that Paul speaks of the loveless and self-centered libertinism as part and parcel of the result of the Judaizing attempt.

257. D. Guthrie and R. P. Martin, "God," *DPL*, 357.

258. E.g. Exod 31:2; Num 1:4; Deut 1:23; Jos 1:12; Judg 18:1; 1 Sam 9:21 *et al.*

259. E.g. Gen 10:32; 12:3; 24:38; Exod 6:14; Lev 20:5; Num 1:2; Deut 29:17; Josh 6:23 *et al.*

260. E.g. Gen 12:1; Lev 22:13; Num 2:2; Deut 22:21; Josh 2:12; Judg 6:15; 1 Sam 2:31 *et al.*

261. C. J. H. Wright, "Family," *ABD* 2. 768. The Johannine description of Jesus who speaks of ἡ οἰκία τοῦ πατρός μου as having many dwelling places for the disciples (John 14:2ff) certainly is reminiscent of Paul's concept of the church as the household of God.

If the household analogy was also the agitators' way to refer to the people of God, insofar as it was defined in terms of a legalistic / nomistic lifestyle, it is less likely that the referent of the family is to the kind of בֵּית־אָב. Rather, it is more likely that it referred to the extended Abrahamic family that simply includes law-keeping Gentile converts as its para-Israelites. Within such a wide conception of the house of Israel, what connects the members as a family is not the intrinsic relationship of a family but certain external factors (e.g. circumcision, Gal 5:2ff) that largely demarcate the members of the extended family from the rest of the world.[262] Thus, what is emphasized is the sheer belongingness to the extended covenantal people of God – but the actual quality relationship as a member of the family is lost. In this regard, it is not at all surprising that Paul can relate such an alienation from one another within the community not only with the loveless libertine behaviour but also (perhaps more) with the legalistic/nomistic lifestyle.

Contrary to this, Paul's concept of the church as the household of God emphasizes primarily the intrinsic relationship of the members to one another as they belong to the most intimate single-family unit בֵּית־אָב/οἶκος. Christ is not simply a boundary marker for the demarcation of a member from a non-member, but more profoundly the enabler for the believer to obtain and entertain genuine sonship with regard to God (Gal 4:4ff; 4:21ff) through his Spirit (Gal 3:2; 5:5, 16–26; cf. Rom 8:14ff). For Paul while the works of the law are a mere loveless and self-centred fleshly strife that lends at best a mere demarcation of one group from the rest of the world, at worst a fatal alienation from God and from one another (5:1–4), the outpouring of the Spirit of Christ through faith (3:2) enables the community to implement their being the genuine family of God through their mutual brotherly love (5:13–6:10).

Thus, Paul's sudden employment of the household language with the particular emphasis on the intra-community ethics is fully explicable only when Paul's dissatisfaction with the concept of the people of God according to the agitators' teaching is considered in this way. Usage by Paul of such language within the particular exhortation, therefore, is on the one

---

262. Cf. Rom 9:32; Gal 2:16; 3:2, 5, 10.

hand an explicit antidote to all the alienations caused by the misleading concept of the people of God, and on the other hand an implicit indictment of the failure of the people of God under the law (or Israel according to flesh) to form a loving community as God's household.

In summary, we have argued that Paul's particular employment of the household language and the special significance and urgency attached to the intra-community ethics in Galatians 6:10 are reflective of the *clash of the two conflicting concepts of the people of God* between Paul and his agitators. Particularly Paul's emphasis on the intra-community ethics of the church signifies exactly where Israel according to flesh failed to implement their being the people of God as the household of Israel: *their resulting alienation* due to their adherence to the law apart from Christ, they fundamentally fail to form a loving community as the household of God.

This observation may entail further important implications: (1) if it is a *qualitative failure* of Israel according to the flesh to form a loving community that is to be restored in the church as the loving family of God, it shows that Paul understands the restoration of Israel *qualitatively* as well as *quantitatively* (or numerically) (e.g. πᾶς Ἰσραὴλ σωθήσεται, Rom 11:26);[263] (2) if such a qualitative failure of Israel in the flesh is to be remedied through the revitalized family of God through faith of / in Christ within the church, it implies that Paul understands the church not only as the locus of the restoration of Israel but also as *the means to achieve* the restoration of Israel, at least qualitatively, through its intrinsic nature rather than its external activity. This consideration provides a strong rationale for viewing the church's vocation in Paul's thought primarily in terms of an ontological / ethical one for the manifestation of the restored quality of Israel within and beyond the church.

---

263. In my opinion, when Paul speaks of the "fullness (πλήρωμα)" of Israel in comparison with Israel's current failure (11:12) or the "fullness of the Gentiles has come in" (11:25) he means by πλήρωμα the totality in quality as well as quantity (cf. Munck, *Christ and Israel*, 133–135). However, πᾶς Ἰσραὴλ in 11:26 seems to refer to primarily the numerical side of the totality of the salvation of Israel since the context of Rom 11 largely contrasts it with the currently small number of the remnants. As most scholars agree, I do not think "πᾶς Ἰσραὴλ" as "spiritual Israel" or "each and every Israelite" or "limited number of the elect Jews" but in the sense of a nation as a numeric whole with some exceptions of individuals. Cf. Dunn, *Romans 9–16*, 681.

3.4.3.3. The Church's Ontological / Ethical Vocation and the Full Restoration of Israel

Another important implication of Paul's ontological / ethical demand on the church is to be found in Paul's grand hope for the restoration of "all Israel." If Paul's reflection on intra-community ethics implies the qualitative restoration of Israel currently manifested in the church and he still expects *quantitative or numeric completion* of such a restoration of Israel in Romans 11:25 and following, in what way will this quantitative restoration of Israel be achieved, and what is the relationship of the qualitative restoration to the quantitative restoration? And more importantly, what is the church's role in Paul's grand expectation for the full restoration of Israel?

In Romans 11:25 and following, Paul mentions "this mystery" (τό μυστήριον τοῦτο) which should prevent the Gentile believers in Rome from being arrogant towards the non-believing Jews by unfolding God's gracious and faithful dealings with Israel in relation to the Gentiles (particularly the believing ones). What is to be noted is that while Paul's confidence in Israel's full restoration is largely dependent on God's might (v. 23b),[264] faithfulness to his covenantal people (vv. 26b–29), and unfathomable wisdom (vv. 33–35), *how* God will accomplish it is expressed in terms of God's mysterious economy in which a certain dynamic of the relationship of the two parties has the key to their path to the "fullness (πλήρωμα)."

However, while such a dynamic is key to "God's how" is quite explicit in Paul's manner of revealing the mystery, what Paul refers to in such a dynamic is not immediately clear. By *what* the "unbelief (ἀπιστία, v. 23)" of the temporarily obdurate Israel will end so that they will be grafted again into the original tree is only vaguely hinted at by their "jealousy" towards the Gentiles who became God's people (10:19; 11:11, 14; cf. Deut 32:21). Moreover, Paul's quotation of the OT texts (Isa 59:20–21; Isa 27:9) about the Redeemer's ministry to Jacob (26b) immediately after mentioning his confidence seems to raise more questions than answers (at least in the scholarly debates).

As already touched on, often suggested explanations tend to be based on the view of a temporal sequence between the completion of the Gentiles'

---

264. δυνατὸς γάρ ἐστιν ὁ θεὸς πάλιν ἐγκεντρίσαι αὐτούς.

salvation and that of Israel in verses 25–26b. According to how verses 26b–27 are interpreted, however, conclusions are very different one from another. Some suggest that, since for Paul "the Redeemer" in verse 26b would be understood as the eschatological Messiah or Christ, then Paul expects the full restoration of Israel in terms of an eschatological mass-conversion at the return of Christ in a similar way to Paul's own conversion through the christophany on the way to Damascus.[265] Some others suggest that Paul envisaged a "special way" (*Sonderweg*), a way of salvation which bypasses the gospel and faith in Christ for the historical Israel, since while he refers to the eschatological Redeemer's ministry to Israel he does not bring any explicit conversion language with a christological base for their salvation.[266] As we have touched on above, however, the correlation of the two parties is one of interdependence, rather than chronological sequence, in the course of their salvation towards the eschatological culmination. However one would like to interpret Paul's quotation, these two explanations seem to miss out on Paul's reference to the dynamic between the two parties.

There are some further important considerations which may counter the often suggested explanations. Mark Nanos points out the triple failure in the way of explaining Israel's salvation through an eschatological miracle: (1) it fails to account for Paul's intention to address such a mystery to his addressees, the Gentile believers in Rome by ignoring Paul's desire to provoke jealousy in Israel through his ministry as the motivational stimulus; (2) it is another kind of triumphalism ("we will win in the end!"), which fails to combat the arrogance of the gentile assumptions ("Jews had lost their place"); (3) it suggests that the gospel is not effective in the end, which would have been cause for Paul to abandon his ongoing concern

---

265. E.g. Munck, *Christ and Israel*, 136–138; Hofius, "'All Israel Will Be Saved'," 19–39; Moo, *Romans*, 727–729.

266. E.g. F. Mussner, "Ganz Israel wird gerettet werden (Röm 11. 26)," *Kairos* 18 (1976): 245–253; J. G. Gager, *The Origins of Anti-Semitism: Attitudes toward Judaism in Pagan and Christian Antiquity* (New York: Oxford University Press, 1985), 261–262; L. Gaston, *Paul and the Torah* (Vancouver: University of British Columbia Press, 1987), 130–150. Cf. K. Stendahl, *Meanings: The Bible as Document and as Guide* (Philadelphia: Fortress Press, 1984), 233–244.

with a Jewish mission, or to be ashamed of the power of the gospel, positions he certainly denied (1:16).[267]

Dissatisfaction with the "Sonderweg" theory can be similarly stated. Reidar Hvalvik and many others criticize the Sonderweg theory as it seems to ignore Paul's emphatic emphasis on the gospel that is God's power both for the Jews and the Gentiles (Rom 1:16) and that faith of / in Jesus Christ is the only way for one to be right with God (Rom 3–10).[268] As Nanos rightly points out, a special way, if it was Paul's point, "would not raise much more than indifference towards Israel from them."[269]

Thus, it seems to me that an explanation that considers Paul's own mission to Gentiles as crucial or indirectly causal for the full restoration of Israel is the most probable one.[270] However, this way of explaining regretfully tends to over emphasize Paul's mission per se and pay less, if not little or no, attention to the community of the Gentile believers the significance of whose life is implicit in Paul's key term "jealousy." While, as scholars rightly stress, Paul's eschatological significance for the salvation of Israel must be upheld in his *indirect* influence on the Jewish people, whose hearts are temporarily hardened, by "the initiatory revelation and its progressive unfolding,"[271] or in a more nuanced view that Paul is not only the apostle to the Gentiles but more properly "the apostle to the Gentiles *for the sake of Israel*" (Gal 1:15; Isa 49:1ff),[272] in what way such an indirect influence for the sake of Israel through Paul's mission to the Gentiles can be expected to result in the salvation of all Israel is still to be elucidated.

---

267. Nanos, *Mystery*, 257: "what impact does that have on gentile presumption toward the "stumbling"?"

268. R. Hvalvik, "A 'Sonderweg' for Israel: A Critical Examination of a Current Interpretation of Romans 11.25–27," *JSNT* 38 (1990): 87–107. Cf. E. P. Sanders, "Paul's Attitude toward the Jewish People," *USQR* 33 (1978): 180–183; P. Stuhlmacher, "Interpretation," 562–564; W. S. Campbell, "Salvation for Jews and Gentiles: Krister Stendahl and Paul's letter to the Romans," *Studia Biblica* III (1978): 65–72; Segal, *Paul the Convert*, 130–133; P. Richardson, "Paul, God, and Israel," 189–192; Wright, *Climax*, 254; Moo, *Romans*, 726; Dunn, *Romans*, 683.

269. Nanos, *Mystery*, 258.

270. E.g. F. F. Bruce, *Paul: Apostle of the Heart Set Free* (Grand Rapids: Eerdmans, 1991 [1977]), 335; Wright, *Climax*, 250–251; Nanos, *Mystery*, 281–284; Campbell, "Israel," *DPL*, 445; Cf. Sanders, *Paul, the Law, and the Jewish People*, 194.

271. Bruce, *Paul*, 335.

272. Campbell, "Israel," 445.

In this regard, my contention in this section is that without a consideration of the existence of the church (i.e. the believing community consisting of the Jewish remnant and the Gentile converts) Paul's indirect influence on the salvation of Israel cannot be satisfactorily elucidated, since Paul expects the church to implement their vocation (i.e. the continuation of the gospel generated ontological / ethical demand to become the restored people of God) so that such a visible restored-ness manifest among them might have the effect (more directly than the apostle's own mission per se) of persuading the Jews to positively re-evaluate the gospel leading eventually to the conversion / restoration of "all Israel."

3.4.3.3.1. Implication of "jealousy"

First, we need to look at the implication of the "jealousy" that Paul expects to be provoked through his mission to the Gentiles (11:14, cf. 11:11, 10:19). Even if Nanos pays due attention to the significance of the life of the Gentile believers (who are the result of Paul's mission), for the forthcoming full restoration of Israel,[273] he stresses Paul's primary role in God's mystery for the restoration of Israel's salvation by arguing that the jealousy in Israel is not provoked over the salvation of the Gentiles but towards Paul's mission:

> Strangely, interpreters assume that Paul expects Jews to be jealous of the *salvation* of Gentiles . . . In spite of this common assumption, Paul does not say that Jews will be jealous of Gentiles being saved, which would be but the other side of the exclusivistic triumphalism he is confronting among Christian Gentiles. He explicitly says it is *his ministry* that will be the cause of jealousy for some of them, which is a very different point. It suggests exactly the opposite of the usual view, namely, that Paul assumes his fellow Jews will see in his success among the Gentiles that their own Jewish universalistic hopes are being fulfilled, albeit somehow without their coparticipation in this fantastic privilege as they have expected. Hence

---

273. Nanos, *Mystery*, 240, 260–279, 284.

they would be jealous of Paul's ministry and reconsider his declaration that the hope of Israel has come in Christ Jesus.[274]

I find this suggestion unconvincing. It seems to downplay, at the cost of the Jewish universalism, the Jewish nationalistic enmity towards the Gentiles concerning their threat to the solidarity of the Torah-shaped people of God. If Paul's preaching of the gospel to the Gentiles was law-free or critical, it would be enmity rather than jealousy that would be provoked by it. If anything universalistic rather than nationalistic / particularistic is to be done on the part of Jews being provoked by Paul's ministry among the Gentiles, it would not be a re-evaluation of what Paul preached (righteousness in Christ apart from the Law) but more likely a counter mission that promotes / intensifies the Torah among the Gentiles. Can this be what Paul intends in his mission and his particular expectation for the jealousy aroused in Israel?

Moreover, it seriously ignores Paul's manner of bringing the idea of jealousy in Israel from his source, the Song of Moses in Deuteronomy 32:21.[275] In 10:19, despite minimal alteration of pronouns, Paul faithfully follows the original wording and logic of the LXX Deuteronomy 32:21: "ἐγὼ (God) παραζηλώσω ὑμᾶς (Israel) ἐπ' οὐκ ἔθνει, ἐπ' ἔθνει ἀσυνέτῳ παροργιῶ ὑμᾶς (Israel)." As the double use of ἐπί emphatically points out, it is the Gentile nations (not God's messenger), that is the object of Israel's jealousy that is provoked by God. Even if no one can deny that Paul has in mind himself or his apostleship to the Gentiles as God's agent for the salvation of the Gentiles (as clearly stated in 11:13), what is at hand throughout Paul's argument in Romans 11 is Israel with their hearts hardened in relation to the existence of the Gentile believers, rather than the apostle. Therefore, Paul's mentioning of his vocation as the apostle to the Gentiles in 11:13 and his hope to save "some" of his compatriots through provoking jealousy in 11:14 must be mediated through a believing community (of Jews and Gentiles) rather than his mission per se.

---

274. Ibid., 249 (emphasis is original).
275. Cf. R. Hays, *Echoes of Scripture in the Letters of Paul* (New Haven: Yale University Press, 1989), 164; H. Hübner, *Gottes Ich und Israel: zum Schriftgebrauch des Paulus in Römer 9–11*, FRLANT (Göttingen: Vandenhoeck & Ruprecht, 1984), 107.

For those who maintain that the traditional order of salvation history (the pilgrimage of the Gentiles as the second stage to Israel's eschatological restoration) is "inverted" in Paul's thought, such jealousy in Israel could mean Israel's emotional response to their realization of such "inversion."[276] However, as we have already demonstrated above, this inversion cannot be Paul's own perspective particularly for the "not yet" part of his eschatology, such an implication of the jealousy is unlikely. Moreover, in such a situation, if granted, jealousy would be inappropriate and not necessary.[277] In Paul's thought Christ's eschatological vindication at the *parousia* seems to only involve the immediate culmination / judgment of disobedience of this age and Christ's eternal presence with his people (e.g. 1 Thess 4:13ff; 5:1ff; Rom 2:5ff, 14:10ff; 1 Cor 3:13; 2 Cor 5:10; Phil 2:16). Such a situation (the *parousia*) would hardly necessitate a second stage where the obdurate Israel will realize that the Gentiles have fully come in God's salvation and to be abruptly provoked to jealousy so that they will join the salvation.

In this regard, I propose that this jealousy can hardly refer to the Jews' envy at the apostle's gentile mission or a Jewish mass-emotion towards the eschatological consummation of the Gentiles' salvation, but the envious emotion of Paul's contemporary Jewish people being provoked by God's *Shekinah* (δόξα) dwelling in the church through the works of the Spirit (e.g. Rom 2:29; 7:6; 8:1–27; 12:11; 14:17; 15:19, cf. 1 Cor 3:16–17) and the actualization of the spirit of the Torah (Rom 2:17ff; 14:13–18; 15:1–13; 15:25–28, cf. Gal 5:14; 6:2) which may signify the restored-ness of Israel.

In Romans 9–11 Paul readily follows, to borrow James Scott's expression, "Deuteronomic tradition" which bases the history of Israel on their whole long history of persistent rebellion and obduracy to God envisaging the national restoration through God's covenantal faithfulness (cf. 1 Thess 2:15–16; Gal 3:10).[278] Considering the relatively fixed framework of such a Deuteronomic view of the present situation of Israel in Paul's

---

276. Cf. Cranfield, *Romans*, 2. 576.

277. *Pace* Campbell, "Israel," 445, who, while acknowledging jealousy as the key issue in Paul's indirect influence on Israel's full restoration, maintains the inverted salvation historical order.

278. J. M. Scott, "Paul's Use of Deuteronomic Tradition," *JBL* 112, no. 4 (1993): 645–665; Scott, "Restoration of Israel," *DPL*, 799–805.

contemporary Jewish scriptural interpretive tradition,[279] it is not surprising that Paul could expect such a response ("jealousy") from his fellow Jewish brothers and sisters in the face of the manifest reality that is to be described none other than the (sign of the) restoration of Israel among a Yahweh-worshipping / glorifying Gentile community (Deut 32:21, 43). And again it would be no surprise that Paul could expect that they would be stirred up and led to a re-evaluation and emulation of the way that led the Gentiles to such a restoration.[280]

3.4.3.3.2. Meaning of "from Zion"

Second, only under the light of the previous consideration can we fully understand the implication in the alteration of the original לְצִיּוֹן/ἕνεκεν Σιων to ἐκ Σιών in Paul's quotation of the LXX Isaiah 59:20 (and another conflated text, the LXX Isa 27:9). Discussion by scholars of the alteration largely revolves around the questions as to whether it is Paul himself who makes this alteration or it is already pre-Pauline (whether Judaistic or Christian) coinage,[281] or as to whether such an alteration, whether Pauline or pre-Pauline, indicates God's redemption of his people in Christ's first advent or second advent.[282]

Even if such inquiries and suggestions might elucidate Paul's implication of ἐκ Σιών rather than לְצִיּוֹן/ἕνεκεν Σιων, I do not think that any of the suggestions can demonstrate a radically different implication to which Paul refers by ἐκ Σιών from that by the original לְצִיּוֹן/ἕνεκεν Σιων. What is clear in Paul's citation whether it is his own alteration or of pre-Pauline

---

279. Pollution of the Temple: e.g. Dan 3:38; Sir 36:14; *1 Enoch* 89:73, 90:28–33; *Tob* 14:5; *T. Levi* 16:1 5; 17:10 11; *2 Bar.* 68:5–7; *T. Moses* 4:8. Israel's plight: e.g. Dan 9:4–19; Ezra 9:6–15; Neh 9:5–37; Bar 1:15–3:8; Pr Azar; Sir 36:1–17. Continuing exile: e.g. Dan 9:24, Continuing national sin: e.g. Bar 1:15–3:8; 1 Esdr 8:73–74; 2 Esdr 9:7; *Jub.* 1:12; *1 Enoch* 89:51. Hope for Israel's restoration: e.g. Bar 2:34–35.

280. As we have already discussed above, Paul's contrasting of the two parties, the currently believing Gentiles and the currently obdurate Israel in vv. 30–31 must be seen in this light. Cf. Wright, *Climax*, 249.

281. For various discussions on Paul's citation in Rom 11:26b 27 see C. D. Stanley, *Paul and the Language of Scripture: Citation Technique in the Pauline Epistles and Contemporary Literature* (Cambridge: Cambridge University Press, 1992), 166–171; Stanley, "The Redeemer Will Come ἐκ Σιών," in *Paul and the Scriptures of Israel*, JSNTSup, eds. C. A. Evans and J. A. Sanders (Sheffield: JSOT Press, 1993), 118–142.

282. Cf. F. Refoulé, ". . . Et ainsi tout Israël sera sauvé": Romains 11.25–32 (Lectio Divina 117; Paris: Le Cerf, 1984), 56–61.

Christian or non-Christian / Judaistic, is that it stresses God's initiative and faithfulness for the restoration of all Israel: God will finally restore all Israel. This point is undeniable however the alteration is understood, even with the original לְצִיּוֹן/ἕνεκεν Σιων. But what is more important is simply why Paul in this particular literary context appeals to the Jewish scriptural authority that speaks of the Redeemer's future coming "from Zion" rather than "to Zion." As Nanos rightly reminds us, *what* God will do is simply obvious so that it cannot be a mystery, but *how* God will restore all Israel is the focus of the mystery. Moreover, if the how is only God's eschatological act independent of Paul's addressees, the citation would be rather pointless here. I do not think that this is the case. Rather this consideration would indicate: (1) that it is unlikely that Paul's reference in the citation is to Christ's *parousia* (as we have already touched on above) which makes Paul's addressees irrelevant; and (2) that the reference of Σιών is made to a *metaphorical locality* shared by Paul's addressees as rightful members of the people of God along with the Jewish remnant (v.5ff, 17ff, 24) rather than the heavenly Jerusalem.

To read Σιών in this way must be supported by reference to the original לְצִיּוֹן/ἕνεκεν Σιων and the usual sense in the Jewish scriptural tradition, namely the people of God or Israel who inhabit the city of Jerusalem or parts surrounding it or the country of which the city is the capital (e.g. Ps 9:14; 133:3; 2 Sam 5:7; 1 Chr 11:5; 1 Kgs 8:1; Isa 40:9; 52:7; Mic 4:8; Lam 2:8) or God's earthly dwelling such as the Jerusalem Temple (e.g. Ps 2:6; 9:11; 50:2; 76:2; Isa 8:18; 18:7; 28:16; Joel 3:17).[283] The Σιών in Isaiah 59:20 clearly indicates the earthly realm where the people of God dwell rather than the heavenly realm from which the Redeemer comes. Moreover, Paul's other use of Σιών in Romans 9:33 in the citation of Isaiah 8:14, 28:16 refers to the same.[284] It seems to me, therefore, that in verse 26b Paul's idea of the people / children of God particularly according to the faith in / of Christ (cf. 9:8, 24ff, 33b) is recaptured in Σιών, the common traditional Jewish nomenclature of the people of God or God's earthly dwelling place.

---

283. Cf. W. H. Mare, "Zion," *ABD* 4. 1096–1097.
284. Isa 52:7 that Paul cites includes "Zion" that denotes the same.

In my opinion, the primary referent of Σιών to the earthly locality in Romans 11:26 is often ignored in scholarly discussion,[285] and rashly connected to the future coming of the Redeemer (ἥξει ὁ ῥυόμενος) thereby concluding that ἐκ Σιών implies Christ's heavenly origin or the heavenly Jerusalem from which the eschatological appearance of Christ will be made.[286] However, such a conclusion tends to overlook the significant modifications in Paul's Jewish eschatology: he pays special attention to the inaugurated nature of the future event, particularly the Messiah's coming and the inclusion of the believing Gentiles in the people of God, on the basis of what he has argued in Romans 9:6–10:13.

Thus, the earthly locality of Σιών in verse 26b is very significant when considered together with "from (ἐκ)" rather than "on behalf of (ἕνεκεν)." If the Redeemer is expected to come from the people of God rather than the heavenly Jerusalem at the *parousia*, what can this imply in Paul's particular literary context, namely his revelation of the mystery that his addressees are to understand? N. T. Wright suggests that, since in the OT the eschatological blessing could be thought of in terms of the Torah going out to the nations (e.g. Mic 4:2ff) and for Paul what the Torah could not do is now done in Christ and the Spirit, Paul refers to in the citation "not the *parousia* but the gentile mission."[287] I am not entirely opposed to this view since it is Paul's gentile mission that precipitates the Gentile believers who are the rightful members of the people of God (e.g. Rom 1:5) and, thus, legitimately called Σιών. Nevertheless, it is not satisfactory since the direct reference of the citation is to the restoration of "Jacob" rather than of the Gentiles while Paul's mission is not directly to Israel but only through the preaching to the Gentiles (e.g. 11:13–14, cf. Gal 2:8). E. P. Sanders correctly expresses the problem:

---

285. As exceptions cf. Fitzmyer, *Romans*, 624; U. Wilckens, *Der Brief an die Römer*, EKKNT (3rd ed.; Zürich: Bebziger Verlag, 1993), 257, who maintain that "Zion" refers to Jesus' Jewishness (cf. Rom 9:5).

286. E.g. Schreiner, *Romans*, 619; Dunn, *Romans, 9–16*, 682; Moo, *Romans*, 728–729; P. Stuhlmacher, "Zur Interpretation von Römer 11.25–32," in *Probleme Biblischer Theologie: Gerhard Von Rad Zum 70. Geburtstag*, ed. H. W. Wolff (München: Kaiser, 1971), 561; Witherington, *Romans*, 276.

287. Wright, *Climax*, 250. Cf. Nanos, *Mystery*, 284.

> But the proof-texts which Paul quotes to establish the fact that all Israel will be saved has nothing to do with the gentile mission... Although Paul three times in Romans 11 connects the salvation of Israel with his own mission to the Gentiles, the quotation in 11:26b–27 assigns that salvation to the Redeemer; that is, it puts it outside the bounds of the apostolic missions altogether. Paul treats the quotation in 11:26b–27 as if it proves the point that the Jews will be saved as the result of the gentile mission, but it does not do so.[288]

In this regard, it seems to me that it is not the *parousia*, nor the apostle's mission per se, but the community of the people of God, who are obviously brought about by the apostle's mission, that Paul refers to in his citation. As already touched on earlier on in this chapter, I propose that ἐχ Σιών of Romans 11:26b is Paul's deliberate alteration in order to signify the current dwelling of the Redeemer (whether God or his Christ) *among his people* (Zion, the "currently obeying") and his continuous coming "from them" to the rest of Israel (Jacob, the "currently disobeying") towards the culmination of his eschatological salvation. So, the futuristic coming (ἥξει) of the Redeemer seems to suggest, rather than Israel's mass conversion at the *parousia*, the strong persuasion that *will* follow on from the obedience of the currently faithful people of God to lead the currently obdurate Israel to the same obedience. Nanos seems to provide a more balanced view on the implication of Paul's citation:

> The pattern that Paul is employing to this end necessarily involves the inclusion of the Gentiles (they will also hear the good news), and it even necessarily includes a proper understanding of these matters on the part of the Romans addressed, for their "proper behaviour" is crucial for success. They are also involved in this process as their "obedience of faith" wins respect among the children of Jacob who are not so quickly persuaded of the message, rather than blasphemy of their "good things."[289]

---

288. Sanders, *Paul, the Law, and the Jewish People*, 194.
289. Nanos, *Mystery*, 284.

This interpretation of the citation should shed some light on the unsettled discussion regarding the interpretation of verses 30–31 and must receive complementary support from it.

3.4.3.3.3. Meaning of "by mercy given to you"

Concerning the clear inner chiasmus between "you obtained mercy through their disobedience" (ἠλεήθητε τῇ τούτων ἀπειθείᾳ) and "they disobeyed for / through your mercy" (ἠπείθησαν τῷ ὑμετέρῳ ἐλέει) and the ἵνα clause that follows the dative τῷ ὑμετέρῳ ἐλέει, some exegetes read τῷ ὑμετέρῳ ἐλέει as a dative of advantage ("for your mercy") that corresponds only to the preceding, and the ἵνα clause as not specifically connected to τῷ ὑμετέρῳ ἐλέει but generally what proceeds it.[290]

However, this is unnecessary and even inappropriate. To confine τῷ ὑμετέρῳ ἐλέει only to such a chiasmus is to ignore Paul's intention to reveal the mystery which is particularly to be understood by the obedient (v. 25) since the suggested chiasmus between ἠλεήθητε τῇ τούτων ἀπειθείᾳ and ἠπείθησαν τῷ ὑμετέρῳ ἐλέει is no more than repeating a single point that "Israel's disobedience has a hidden purpose for the Gentiles' salvation." It seems to me that this redundancy is improbable for Paul in his letters as his rhetorical strategy is usually very compact. Rather, as Paul is most probably indicating by "from Zion the Redeemer will come" God's ongoing implementation of his eschatological salvation for the currently obdurate Israel *via* the currently obeying, it seems very likely that through τῷ ὑμετέρῳ ἐλέει Paul is again depicting such a mediatorial role of those who have obtained mercy for the sake of the salvation of those Israelites who are currently disobeying.[291] In this regard, the dative τῷ ὑμετέρῳ ἐλέει seems to be corresponding to the ἵνα clause as one of instrumental, or alternatively (in my opinion, more favourably) corresponding to both the preceding and the following as of advantage *and* instrument ("for and by your mercy").

What we have argued so far is, therefore, that throughout Paul's explication of the mystery in 11:25 and following, while affirming God's

---

290. E.g. Käsemann, *Romans*, 303; H. Schlier, *Der Römerbrief. Kommentar*, HTKNT (Freiburg im Breisgau: Herder, 1977), 343; Dunn, *Romans*, 688.

291. Cf. Munck, *Christ and Israel*, 140; Cranfield, *Romans*, 2. 585; Morris, *Romans*, 425; Nanos, *Mystery*, 261; RSV; NIV; NJV. The adjective ὑμέτερος here is emphatic as the stress is on "your" rather than "mercy."

merciful and faithful initiative and somewhat indirect significance of his gentile mission within it, Paul stresses the present existence of the Gentile believers as a more direct significance for the full restoration of Israel. Even if in Romans 11 what is juxtaposed or contrasted with the currently obdurate Israel is expressed in terms of the believing Gentiles, we should notice that Paul's argument at a deeper level is not simply between the two ethnic groups but more precisely between those who are currently the people of God and those who are not. Therefore, what is unmistakable is that it is the church, the eschatological community of the people of God, that is constantly assumed behind Paul's revelation of the mystery so that it functions as the key to *how* God will save "all Israel" (and by implication the fullness of the incoming of the Gentiles as well).

3.4.3.3.4. Outsider conscious community ethics in Romans 12–15 as the indirect means for the salvation of others

The mode of address changes as Romans 12 begins as Paul's focus is shifted from Israel's unmistakable salvation to the conduct of the church(es) at Rome. However, Paul's unpacking of the mystery is not exhausted by the end of Romans 11 but continues as he provides an emphatic *paraenesis* (παρακαλῶ οὖν ὑμᾶς) for the community in Rome. This continuity is indicated by the οὖν (v. 1a) and Paul's repetition of the theme of the divine mercy that made the Romans God's own (cf. "νῦν δὲ ἠλεήθητε"; "τῷ ὑμετέρῳ ἐλέει," 11:30–31) in ἀδελφοί διὰ τῶν οἰκτιρμῶν τοῦ θεοῦ (v. 1).[292] What is important in this is that what follows further explains the *how* that has already been unpacked in the preceding section: if the church is the key to the *how*, what is given as the imperative to the church cannot be separated from God's mystery for the salvation of all (11:32–36) including Israel.

This observation is important since the following imperative is not a mere collection of ethical reflections (as earlier scholars often assumed) that

---

292. There are two more possible renderings: (1) to read διὰ τῶν οἰκτιρμῶν τοῦ θεοῦ as corresponding to παρακαλῶ as if Paul's appeal is on the ground of God's mercy (cf. e.g. Morris, *Romans*, 433; NIV); (2) to read διὰ τῶν οἰκτιρμῶν τοῦ θεοῦ as corresponding to the following infinitive παραστῆσαι. However, a more natural and balanced rendering is to consider the emphasized significance of the mercy obtained by the Romans in the adjacent verses (11:30–31) and the usual sense of the divine mercy that is frequently connected with the remission of sin or salvation (e.g. 2 Sam 24:14; 1 Kgs 8:50; Neh 1:11; Ps 68:17; Col 3:12).

is irrelevant to Paul's theological reflection that was set out in the preceding parts of the letters. Rather, for Paul in Romans how the church is to conduct itself stems from how he *theologically* perceived the eschatological drama of all things (11:36) and how the church is to accord to this drama. Therefore, the *paraenesis* of Romans deals with the church's vocation as the eschatological people of God.

What is striking, then, is that the following imperative is not an action aimed at those outside the church (e.g. evangelism) but *a community ethic*, an exhortation for desirable life and behaviour that builds the Christian community per se (12:1–15:7). Even if Paul includes a notable portion of the community's behaviour in relation to outsiders of the community (12:14–13:7), presumably including the dispersed who are the children of "Jacob" (11:26b), the church as a whole is not exhorted to go out and persuade them with the gospel message. But rather their behaviour and attitude to the world is simply the extension of what they are expected to do towards each other (εἰς ἀλλήλους) within their own community: the love command (12:4–13; 13:8–10; 14:1–15:13). Behaviour based on loving and receiving each other according to what Christ had done and would expect (13:14; 14:1–18; 15:3, 5, 8),[293] on the one hand edifies the community (14:19; 15:2), and on the other hand earns approval from men (14:18, cf. v. 16).[294] What is unmistakable is that, while the ontological / ethical demand to build the community is what Paul suggests as the church's fundamental calling, the approval from men clearly recalls what has been previously brought about in his revelation of the mystery of God in Romans 11: the restoration of Israel is mediated by the existence of the church as it stands as the restored people of God.

3.4.4. Conclusion

We have in this section discussed Paul's missio-ecclesial understanding in terms of an ontological / ethical demand to form a community of the

---

293. Several scholars suggest that such Pauline texts are possibly influenced by the Jesus-traditions such as the love command and the voluntary slavery to all in the kingdom of God. Cf. M. Thompson, *Clothed with Christ: The Example and Teaching of Jesus in Romans 12.1–15.13*, JSNTSup (Sheffield: JSOT Press, 1991), 163; Dunn, *Romans 9–16*, 824; D. Wenham, *Follower*, 256, 261–267, 404.

294. Cf. Nanos, *Mystery*, 261.

people of God among whom the restoration of Israel is realized. While the evangelistic or missional function in such a vocation is unmistakable, the vocation stressed is the church's ongoing edification of the community as the family of the faith in which the community's prime concern is members' intra-community ethics that should be like Christ's attitudes. As this outsider-conscious community ethics appear in Paul's thought to be the vocation of the eschatological people of God, such a vocation seems to be located along with the vocation of the eschatological heralds within Paul's broad eschatological envisioning of the full restoration of Israel and the incoming of the Gentiles.

3.5. Conclusion: Paul's Conception of Mission as a Bifurcated Eschatological Event as the Primary Reason for His Silence about the Church's Evangelism

This chapter has not sought to establish or to deny that "Paul did not expect his church to engage in active missionary work." Rather, it has aimed to discover how Paul conceptualized issues regarding his apostolic mission and the church's relation to it, hoping to explain Paul's failure to mention the proactive evangelistic mission by the church.

(1) It was argued that Paul's inaugurated eschatological framework enabled him to maintain a certain framework of reference, in which he recognized the ongoing restoration of Israel and the incoming of the nation into it as the *contents* and *context* of "mission." (2) It was observed that within such a conception of mission, as a God-brought eschatological event, Paul envisioned a *bifurcation* of God's two ongoing implementations of his purpose, namely the salvation for the whole world (i.e. Jews and Gentiles) through the *gospelization* by his eschatological heralds on the one hand and the *actualization of the gospel* by the eschatological community of his people on the other. (3) It was particularly proposed that, since for Paul both the eschatological events of εὐαγγελιζόμενοι and ἐκκλησία constitute a single coherent framework for Paul's missional thought (both for his self-conception and missio-ecclesial understanding), Paul's conception of mission must not be limited to a proselytism but is to be approached as

something that includes the church's implementation of its ontological / ethical vocation as the restored people of God.

This view, then, provides an important alternative to the previous proposals of Paul's conception of mission given as an explanation for why Paul fails to mention the church's proactive evangelism. While Bowers explains that it is Paul's self-focused conception of mission that totally eclipses his having any expectation of mission by the church, Dickson explains that it is Paul's two-dimensional view of mission that has only a limited expectation of some indirect evangelistic forms of mission-commitment from the church that makes Paul silent about the issue in question. Such explanations presuppose Paul's mission as a proselytism category and assume Paul's silence about the church's active evangelistic role to be an "absence" from the apostle's mind. In the light of our discussion, however, Paul's conception of mission was neither self-concentrated nor limited to a proselytism category. Rather, we may propose that, without necessarily assuming / imposing an absence of the notion of congregational evangelism from Paul's expectation, it was Paul's well-developed missio-ecclesial understanding primarily in terms of an ontological / ethical vocation, namely the *actualization of the gospel* as the church's mission proper that consistently pressed the apostle for mentioning it instead of the church's *gospelization*.

Having constructed a plausible conceptuality of mission (i.e. two-pronged or bifurcated) as understood by Paul, thus providing an explanation for Paul's silence regarding congregational evangelism, now we must move to the issue of the background for Paul's conception of mission as such.

CHAPTER 4

Paul's Mission-Conception of the Eschatological Heralds and the Jesus-Tradition

Our discussion so far has been concerned with the nature and shape of Paul's conception of mission. We will henceforth be concerned with the background for it. The issue was touched on partly when we saw that Paul's conception of mission is indebted to the Jewish eschatological worldview in general and to the Jewish scriptural and traditional restorative expectation for the future of Israel and the nations in particular. For the remainder of the study our focus will move to post-conversion factors contributing to Paul's conception of mission, particularly paying attention to the Jesus-tradition probably known to Paul.

In support of the legitimacy of the enquiry, we have already drawn attention to the current terrain of NT scholarship with the perception of a dichotomy between Jesus and Paul waning and giving way to a new recognition of the two figures' theologies and ministerial aims as reflecting Jewish ideas of the restoration of Israel.[1] Moreover, we observed that Paul's

---

1. One notable development in this direction, particularly for the connection between the historical Jesus and the early Christians' mission (including the Pauline mission) is a study by Bird, *Jesus and the Origins of the Gentile Mission*, who persuasively links the early Christians' gentile mission with the historical Jesus' mission programme for the restoration of Israel:

"Jesus linked the salvation of the Gentiles with the restoration of Israel and probably envisaged a continuing preaching mission that would include the Gentiles. That is not to say that he conceived of a gentile mission independent of a continuing mission to Israel, or as a sequel to a failed Jewish mission. And there is no clear indication that a preaching mission to Gentiles would have a *Torah*-free basis. What does seem clear is that, as the mission to Israel continues in the future, Gentiles

understanding of his apostleship as one of an εὐαγγελιζόμενος was not simply inspired by the Isaianic Servant motif, but was also an extension of his perception of the Messiah (i.e. Jesus) as the eschatological εὐαγγελιζόμενος. Such a notion does not merely indicate Paul's christological understanding of Jesus as the eschatological Messiah, but may further hint at his self-conception – in view of the pre-Easter Jesus as the preacher of the eschatological salvation (cf. e.g. Luke 7:22–23//Matt 11:4–6).[2]

In light of such positive indications of the connection between the pre-Easter Jesus and Paul's ministerial self-understanding, our discussion of the background for Paul's conception of mission begins appropriately with an investigation into whether Paul's conception of εὐαγγελιζόμενος reflects his indebtedness to Jesus' pre-Easter mission that is remembered in the Jesus-tradition.

4.1. Paul's Conception of the Eschatological Heralds and the Jesus-Tradition of the Mission Discourse

4.1.1. Paul's Knowledge of the Context and the Contents of the Mission Discourse

We have already paid attention to the similarity between Paul's idea of εὐαγγελιζόμενοι and what Paul in 1 Corinthians 9:14 attributes to a dominical saying (οὕτως καὶ ὁ κύριος διέταξεν τοῖς τὸ εὐαγγέλιον καταγγέλλουσιν ἐκ τοῦ εὐαγγελίου ζῆν, cf. Luke 10:7//Mark 10:10).[3] Since, in terms of the right (ἐξουσία) to financial support, Paul makes a *de facto* equating (vv. 4, 12) between himself (and Barnabas) and those to whom (τοῖς τὸ

---

will also have the message of the kingdom announced to them and will be given an opportunity to respond. A gentile mission rests upon a continuing Jewish mission and does not supersede or replace the witness to Israel" (177).

2. Cf. E. P. Weadors, *Jesus the Messianic Herald of Salvation*, WUNT (Tübingen: Mohr Siebeck, 1995), 162–166, who rightly points out that the historicity of the Q presentation of Jesus as the eschatological messianic herald figure is supported by 4Q521.

3. It is improbable that what Paul mentions as the Lord's command refers to a prophetic utterance given to missionaries from the risen Lord. Cf. Brown, "Synoptic Parallels," 37; D. Wenham, *Follower*, 192, n.70. It is equally unlikely that it refers to an agraphon. Cf. D. G. Horrell, "'The Lord Commanded . . . But I Have Not Used . . .' Exegetical and Hermeneutical Reflections on 1 Cor 9.14–15," *NTS* 43 (1997): 594.

εὐαγγέλιον καταγγέλλουσιν, v. 14) the Lord's command is directed, this aptly indicates a certain degree of connection between Paul's conception of εὐαγγελιζόμενοι and his knowledge of the tradition about Jesus.

While such an indication in Paul's argument is unmistakable, to what extent and in what way his thought is derived from the dominical tradition is notably complicated by two facts: (1) Paul's wording which is thought to be an allusion to Jesus' own word is different from the wording of the so called Q logion; and (2) Paul eventually relinquishes (vv. 12, 15, 18) what he has affirmed as a dominical instruction.[4] Scholars often regard the former as evidence that Paul only knew an isolated Jesus' aphoristic saying (which is in fact not peculiar to Jesus) out of its original context.[5] The latter is often viewed as indicating that Paul felt free to relativize the dominical instruction at the expense of a particular theological / contextual demand or even deliberately disobeyed it.[6] For some critics these features further suggest poor preservation of or uncontrolled tradition.[7] These considerations, if granted, seem to suggest that the similarity between Paul's idea

---

4. Despite his renunciation, it is self-evident that Paul's arguments in 1 Cor 9:4–14 affirm the missionaries' prerogative to claim their financial support from the church. Cf. Fee, *1 Corinthians*, 392. Pace W. L. Willis, "An Apostolic Apologia? The Form and Function of 1 Corinthians 9," *JSNT* 24 (1985): 33–48 (35), who rules out an apologetic intention from Paul's argument at the expense of an exemplary intention.

5. E.g. K. Berger, *Die Gesetzesauslegung Jesu: ihr historischer Hintergrund im Judentum und im Alten Testament* (Neukirchen-Vluyn: Neukirchener Verlag, 1972), 382–384; Conzelmann, *1 Corinthians*, 157; A. E. Harvey, "'The Workman Is Worthy of His Hire': Fortunes of a Proverb in the Early Church," *NovT* 24 (1982): 213; C. M. Tuckett, "Paul and the Synoptic Mission Discourse?" *ETL* 60 (1984): 376–381.

6. E.g. J. Moffatt, *The First Epistle of Paul to the Corinthians* (London: Hodder and Stoughton, 1938, [1930]), 118; Dungan, *Sayings of Jesus*, 3, 20, 37; G. Theissen, *The Social Setting of Pauline Christianity: Essays on Corinth* (Philadelphia: Fortress Press, 1982), 44; Thompson, *Clothed*, 192, n.1, 240; D. G. Horrell, "'The Lord Commanded . . . But I Have Not Used . . .' Exegetical and Hermeneutical Reflections on 1 Cor 9.14–15," *NTS* 43 (1997): 587–603 (599); Dunn, *Beginning*, 564, while affirming Paul's notable knowledge of and interest in the Jesus-tradition, regards 1 Cor 9:15ff as the indication of Paul's through deviation from the dominical logion cited in v. 14: "What caused him to ignore a dominical command so completely?"

7. Cf. Holzbrecher, *Paulus und der historischer Jesus*, 160: "Weiterhin aussagekräftig ist dagegen *1 Kor 9,14 im Kontext* weil Paulus dort wirklich explizit von einer Jesustradition abweicht und gegen die Anweisung eines Jesuswortes etwas eigenes setzt. Das belegt in jedem Fall die These von Berger, Theißen und Schüssler-Fiorenza, dass Paulus zumindest gelegentlich und wenn es ihm in seiner missionarischen Praxis geboten schien, kein wortgetreuer oder inhaltsgetreuer "Diener" des irdischen Jesus war und widerlegt zumindest ein Stück weit die These von der gepflegten Tradition."

of εὐαγγελιζόμενοι and the particular dominical instruction is at best a mere superficiality.

However, there are some reasons to believe differently, and to conclude that Paul's idea of εὐαγγελιζόμενοι is more deeply influenced by the particular dominical tradition than scholars often estimate.

4.1.1.1. Fjärstedt's Proposal of Paul's Allusions to a Lukan Type of the Mission Discourse

The first consideration is that it is highly likely that Paul's knowledge about the dominical tradition was not limited to the particular isolated logion but included its original context and other related contents, which are preserved in the synoptic mission discourse.

It is B. Fjärstedt who made a critical challenge to the scholarly position that in 1 Corinthians 9 only an isolated (or context-less) dominical maxim is in view.[8] Fjärstedt pays attention to some "focus words" functioning as places of association within a main theme, and a "cluster of theme words" through which a unity of the basic theme or metaphor is maintained.[9] On this understanding he goes on to look for common collocations of the focus words in both a single context in the Pauline texts and a single context in the synoptic texts.[10]

---

8. B. Fjärstedt, *Synoptic Tradition in 1 Corinthians: Themes and Clusters of Theme Words in 1 Corinthians 1–4 and 9* (Uppsala, 1974).

9. Ibid., 65.

10. Ibid., 65–77. The validity and usefulness of this method is to be acknowledged: it helps one prevent a possible literary link between the epistles and the gospels from being discarded simply because of lack of an explicit contextual similarity; it also enables one to examine, if there is one, how broad or narrow the literary dependence is in scope. D. C. Allison, "The Pauline Epistles and the synoptic Gospels: the Pattern of the Parallels," *NTS* 28 (1982): 6, succinctly endorses the validity of the method by showing the unmistakable verbal and thematic correspondence between Ps 23:1–2 and Mark 6:32–44. Moreover, if one, through Fjärstedt's method, can establish a strong literary link between a Pauline text and a synoptic text which is generally known as Matthean / Lukan redaction, and if the direction of influence can hardly be explained as running from Paul to the evangelists, this, then, may indicate an insufficiency in the two source theory at least regarding the particular synoptic text – cf. D. Wenham, *Follower*, 199. C. M. Tuckett, "Paul and the Synoptic Mission Discourse?" *ETL* 60 (1984): 376–381 (376), despite his source / redaction critical view on the synoptics, acknowledges the validity of the method.

While other links Fjärstedt suggests are tenuous due to his uncontrolled use of the method,[11] what he outlines as a cluster of theme words in 1 Corinthians 9 appears indeed to be a striking parallel with that of Luke 10 (including Luke 9:1, 2, 6):

1 Corinthians 9

ἀπόστολος (1, 2), ἀποστολῆς (2), ἀπόστολοι (5), ἐξουσία (4, 5, 6, 12, 18), ἔργον (1), ἐργάζεσθαι (6), ἐργαζόμενοι (13), φαγεῖν (4), ἐσθίειν (7, 13), πεῖν (4), μισθός (17, 18), θερίζειν (11), εὐαγγελίζεσθαι (16, 18), εὐαγγέλιον (12, 14, 18x2), κηρύσσειν (27).

Luke 10 (Luke 9:1, 2)

ἀποστέλλειν (1, 3, 16, Luke 9:2), ἐξουσία (19, Luke 9:1), ἐργάτης (2x2, 7), ἐσθίειν (7, 8), πεῖν (7), μισθός (7), θερισμός (2X3), λέγειν ἤγγικεν ἡ βασιλεία τοῦ θεοῦ (9, 10, 11), εὐαγγελίζεσθαι (Luke 9:6), κηρύσσειν (Luke 9:2)[12]

As Fjärstedt himself rightly evaluates the common collocation of the clusters of no less than seven parallel key words can hardly have come into existence by coincidence: it is probable that there is a certain literary relationship between Paul and Luke.[13] While the possibility of Luke's utiliza-

---

11. Allison, "Pattern of the Parallels," 6–9; Cf. D. Wenham, *Follower*, 30, n.57. Note that Fjärstedt, *Synoptic Tradition*, 77–87, cites other Lukan passages (Luke 17:7–10; 20:9–19; 3:10–14), Matthean passage (Matt 25:14–30) and Johannine passage (John 3:32–36) to which Paul might have alluded in 1 Cor 9.

12. Fjärstedt, *Synoptic Tradition*, 74–76.

13. Ibid., 76. *Pace* Tuckett, "Paul and the Synoptic Mission Discourse?" 378–379, who raises six points to show that Fjärstedt's links are fragile: (1) Paul never relates the fact that he is an "apostle" to the claim that he has been "sent," thus the link between ἀπόστολος in Paul and ἀποστέλλειν in Luke is doubtful. (2) The ἐξουσία link is uncertain because while Paul refers to "apostolic prerogative," Luke means healing and exorcizing power. (3) While the apostolic missionaries in Luke 10 are "workers," Paul and his colleagues are not to be workers since they claim their right not to work. (4) Paul's "eating and drinking" is too general to bear much significance, and Luke's "eating" theme in 10:8 is redactional under the influence of 1 Cor 10:27. (5) While Luke's "harvest" in Luke 10 is an "eschatological harvest" of the mission, 1 Cor 9:11 talks about a "mundane harvesting" of τὰ σαρκικά. (6) Luke's "ἤγγικεν ἡ βασιλεία τοῦ θεοῦ" and Paul's εὐαγγελίζωμαι are not synonymous, and that Luke's εὐαγγελιζόμενοι serves as the source of Paul's εὐαγγελίζωμαι in 1 Cor 9:16 is refuted by consideration of the strong Pauline nature of εὐαγγελ-word group and Luke's redactional activity of κηρύσσειν (Luke 9:2) and εὐαγγελιζόμενοι (Luke 9:6) on the basis

tion of 1 Corinthians 9 when penning the mission discourse cannot be ruled out, it seems implausible that Luke's wording is due to Paul's words which are spread in the extended argument in such an allusive way. Rather, it seems best to infer that the parallel is due to the two writers' respective dependence on similar sources.

In this light of Paul's knowledge of the context and the contents of a Lukan type of the mission discourse, Paul's reproduction of the workman saying in terms of οἱ τὸ εὐαγγέλιον καταγγέλλουσιν makes perfect sense. Since Paul knew, according to the tradition, that "worker" (ἐργάτης) refers to those who work for the good news, he can paraphrase the saying accordingly.

4.1.1.2. Paul's Understanding of the Lord's Command in 1 Corinthians 9:14

How, then, should we understand Paul's renunciation of the worker's right? Despite the significance of the dominical tradition for his idea of εὐαγγελιζόμενος, did Paul after all disobey the Lord's command? Gerhardsson suggests that "Paul classified Jesus' commandment [in 1 Cor 9:14] as a permission (ἐξουσία, רשות) for the Apostles, not as an obligation (ὀφείλημα, חובה)."[14] However, while such a classification can be made between the Lord's command and that of the apostle (cf. 1 Cor 7:10, 12) whether Paul can make the same distinction between different commands from the Lord is unclear.[15]

We may explain it slightly differently in that Paul from the outset understood the workman saying not as the Lord's command per se but only

---

of Mark 6:12. However, Tuckett's estimation is not satisfactory: (1) he fails to consider the nature of one's literary "echo" or "allusion," whether conscious or unconscious, which does not necessarily "duplicate" exactly the context and contents of the primary text; (2) he fails to consider the possibility of Luke having an independent source apart from 1 Cor, Mark and Q. Cf. M. Goulder, *Luke: A New Paradigm*, JSNTSup (Sheffield: JSOT Press, 1989), 190; D. Wenham, *Follower*, 195–196, n.78.

14. B. Gerhardsson, *Memory*, 319. He further suggests that in this way Paul felt free to abstain from such a commandment, and this further indicates that "the demand that Gentile Christians should be taught to keep all that Jesus had commanded [Matt 28:20] was not confined to some "legalistic" groups in early Christianity" (319). Similarly Bruce, *Paul*, 107–108; Kim, *Paul and the New Perspective*, 261. Cf. Fee, *1 Corinthians*, 413, n.93: "The command is not given *to* the missionaries, but *for* their benefit."

15. Cf. Dungan, *Sayings of Jesus*, 20.

as *what the Lord's command permits*. It is to be noted that Fjärstedt's case of a Lukan type of the mission discourse may not exhaust Paul's knowledge of the contents of the mission discourse. As D. Wenham suggests, the unmistakable link between "free of charge" (ἀδάπανος, 1 Cor 9:18) and "without payment" (δωρεάν, Matt 10:8b) may indicate Paul's further familiarity with a Matthean type of logion ("You received without payment; give without payment").[16] Form critics often regard the saying in Matthew 10:8b as Matthew's redaction, reflecting the redactor's intention to resolve the early church's situation where the "workman saying" was abused by missionaries.[17] While such a situation seems to be a historical reality in the early church (cf. *Did.* 11–13), there is no overriding reason to believe that the saying was not an original part of the mission discourse. Rather, if the non-preparation instruction (Matt 10:9–10a; Luke 9:3, 10:4, cf. Mark 6:9) belonged to the original mission discourse, the sense of the saying well accords with the injunction since they both require the heralds' total reliance on God and full devotion to their mission.[18]

If this is seriously considered, it becomes clearer that Paul's renunciation of the right to support and boast in the proclamation of the gospel "free of charge" is not to be understood as his disobedience to a dominical command at the cost of another command of the Lord. Rather, as Paul knew and understood the *entire* tradition of the mission discourse as the Lord's command,[19] and as a call to radical devotion to the task of the proclamation of the gospel, he never disobeys but faithfully follows it.[20]

If Paul's point in verses 15 and following is as such, why does he not clearly state that his policy is from the Lord's saying as well? Why does he

---

16. D. Wenham, *Follower*, 199–200. Note that the exactly same word δωρεάν is used in 2 Cor 11:7 in which Paul speaks of the same situation as 1 Cor 9:3ff.

17. E.g. Davies and Allison, *Matthew*, 2, 170; Dungan, *Sayings of Jesus*, 69; Horrell, "The Lord Commanded," 597–598.

18. Cf. J. Nolland, *Gospel of Matthew: A Commentary on the Greek Text*, NIGTC (Grand Rapids, Eerdmans; Bletchley: Paternoster, 2005), 417–418.

19. Note that Matt 11:1 uses the same verb διατάσσω to denote the entire instruction given to the disciples.

20. D. Wenham, *Follower*, 200: "[Paul] quite strenuously seeks to defend his apparent failure to obey the Lord, not by making light of the Lord's words, but on the contrary by interpreting them (as giving authority, but not requiring wooden compliance) and by explaining his actions in terms of gospel principles and, indeed, in terms of other sayings of the Lord."

not make clear that the Lord's command is about the gospel, not about the right? In my opinion, Paul actually did that at least partly in his reproduction of the dominical logion, but in a careful way. While the Q logion itself is no more than a worker's right to reward / food, Paul's altered wording betrays the radical nature of the gospel workers' vocation for the sake of the gospel.[21] This point is more clearly expounded in verse 15 and following: he even relinquishes his right for the sake of his calling as a herald of the gospel (cf. 1 Cor 1:17). It is quite likely that while Paul is alluding to the saying behind Matthew 10:8b, in 1 Corinthians 9:18 he deliberately eschews an appeal to dominical authority since such an appeal was his opponents' means (cf. 1 Cor 9:3; 2 Cor 11:7). If misuse of the Lord's teaching was characteristic of his opponents, further argument over interpretation of the Lord's words on the part of Paul would have caused more trouble.[22]

4.1.2. Paul's Conception of the Eschatological Heralds as the Extension of the Pre-Easter Sending of the Disciples of Jesus

4.1.2.1. Paul's Eschatological Past: Cross or Cradle?

In the previous chapter, we pointed out the problem of scholars' overemphasis on the futuristic dimension of Paul's eschatology.[23] We stressed that for Paul, particularly for his conception of mission, there is the Christ event in the *past*, the most decisive eschatological event, and the *already* happening eschatological experience. On this point Bowers correctly points out:

> He [Paul] conceived of his gentile mission as eschatological in nature principally not by virtue of some connection with a yet future event but by virtue of its evident connections with a past one . . . Paul in his mission is much more demonstrably working *from* an eschatological event than *toward* one.[24]

---

21. The emphatic double occurrence of the εὐαγγέλιον may indicate such an implication.
22. Cf. Wedderburn, "Continuity," 190, 189–203, who explains Paul's general silence about the Jesus-tradition in terms of Paul's perception of the Jesus-tradition that was generally in "enemy hands."
23. See chapter 3, *1.2.2.*
24. Bowers, "Mission," *DPL*, 618.

This consideration to some extent can account for Paul's historically understood self-conception. However, the more important question for our further discussion is still to be asked: *to what* does Paul's eschatological *past* point in regard to his self-conception as a gospel herald? It is unanimously, and in no doubt rightly, agreed that the "cross" or the "resurrection" is the decisive or central historical point in Paul's thought. Nevertheless, the significance of the *pre-Easter* Jesus and his ministry in Paul, particularly regarding his apostleship, must not be lost by too narrowly focusing on Jesus' redemptive ministry in his passion and resurrection.[25] N. Walter is correct in this regard: "[b]ut we should also be clear that neither here nor anywhere else does Paul lay any weight on the distinction which we are wont to draw between the 'earthly' and the 'exalted' *Kyrios*."[26]

Thus, it is to be noted as well, while the resurrection (and the Cross) of Christ is central to Paul, it is obvious that Paul can see the *fulfillment* or *decisive start* of the long-awaited salvation in Jesus the Messiah[27] not only after Easter but also before Easter: his birth (Rom 1:3; Gal 3:19, 4:4) and earthly

---

25. Cf. E. B. Allo, *Saint Paul: Second épitre aux Corinthiens*, (2nd ed.; Paris: Études Bibliques, 1956), 179–182, who suggests that εἰ δὲ καὶ ἐγνώκαμεν κατὰ σάρκα χριστόν, ἀλλὰ νῦν οὐκέτι γινώσκομεν in 2 Cor 5:16 indicates Paul's exclusive interest in Christ's redemptive work rather than earthly teaching and ministry thus countering his opponents' appeal to and his co-workers' connection with that aspect (obviously consenting with Bultmann's reading of κατὰ σάρκα χριστόν in the sense of "knowledge about earthly Jesus"). This interpretation is untenable. We know nothing about the nature of Paul's opponents in connection to the earthly Jesus. Moreover, considering Paul's argument in 2 Cor 2 against the opponents' (and many Corinthians') appeal to excellence in flesh which is for Paul antithetical to the spirit of the Cross which might be seen as folly κατὰ σάρκα, the reading of ἐγνώκαμεν κατὰ σάρκα χριστόν as "we have known Christ according to our earthly (or fleshly) perspective of boast" is preferable to "we have known the earthly Jesus." Therefore, the knowledge of the earthly Jesus (or the Jesus-tradition) is thus neither alluded to nor rejected here. Cf. G. N. Stanton, *Jesus of Nazareth in New Testament Preaching*, SNTSMS (London: Cambridge University Press, 1974), 93; P. E. Hughes, *Paul's Second Epistle to the Corinthians: The English Text with Introduction, Exposition and Notes*, NLC (London: Marshall, Morgan & Scott, 1962, c1961), 197; V. P. Furnish, *II Corinthians*, AB (Garden City: Doubleday, 1984), 330; M. E. Thrall, *A Critical and Exegetical Commentary on the Second Epistle to the Corinthians*, vol. 1, ICC (Edinburgh: T. & T. Clark, 1994), 420; C. Wolff, "True Apostolic Knowledge of Christ," in *Paul and Jesus*, ed. Wedderburn (London: T. & T. Clark, 2004), 85–98.

26. N. Walter, "Paul and the Early Christian Jesus-Tradition," in *Paul and Jesus*, ed. Wedderburn (London: T. & T. Clark, 2004), 54.

27. There is a notable objection to reading Paul's Ἰησοῦς Χριστοῦ as Jesus "the Messiah" because of the lack of definite article. However, Paul in the letter to the Romans certainly uses Χριστός in the sense of the Messiah of Israel and the nations (cf. Rom 9:5; 10:4). On this point see Wright, *Climax*, 42–50; D. Wenham, *Follower*, 183–184.

ministry to Israel (Rom 15:1–8; Gal 4:5, cf. Mark 10:43–45).[28] Paul's calling to apostleship to the Gentiles by the risen Christ who is the fulfillment of the expectation of the age to come[29] brings Paul back to the point of the history where God's *Heilsplan* began to be fully revealed, and from there Paul's apostolic ministry starts. For Paul his mission did not simply start from the point of his actual calling (i.e. the Damascus Christophany) or the vindication of Jesus as the Messiah (i.e. the resurrection), but rather touches back to the time of the OT prophets who had been the agents of the promise of the coming of the Messiah from whom all the apostles are given the eschatological apostleship, including Paul (Rom 1:1–6). Even if he joined into this ἀποστολή (Rom 1:5)[30] abruptly after Easter (ὡσπερεὶ τῷ ἐκτρώματι, 1 Cor 15:8), and went to the Gentiles, it is not to be taken as a "struggle with and contradiction to," but of "intended expansion and fulfillment of" (Gal 2:7–8) the first mission given to the pre-Easter apostles by Jesus the Messiah.[31]

4.1.2.2. Paul's Allusion to Jesus' Sending of His Disciples in Romans 10:14–17

This historical and eschatological orientation in Paul regarding his self-conception naturally leads him to connect his own apostleship to the pre-Easter apostles. Even if it does not tell us about an explicit analogy between Paul and the pre-Easter mission of Jesus and his disciples, the case of Romans 10:14–17 shows us that Paul's historical orientation of his self-conception reaches back to the pre-Easter apostleship.

---

28. Cf. Dunn, *Romans 9–16*, 842–847; D. Wenham, *Follower*, 368, n.90.

29. Apart from one occurrence in a disputed letter (Eph 1:21) this apocalyptic language of "the age to come" in Pauline letters is substituted by "καινὴ κτίσις" inaugurated by Christ (2 Cor 5:17; Gal 6:15).

30. The first person plural verb (ἐλάβομεν) which receives the direct object (apostleship) is not to be taken as an epistolary plural (*pace* Harnack, *Mission and Expansion*, 321; Morris, *Romans*, 48) nor as pointing to missionary apostles in Rome (*pace* Dunn, *Romans 9–16*, 24). Rather, it may testify to the apostleship of other apostles along with Paul whose apostleship has its starting point in the apostolate which Jesus the Messiah had established for his pre-Easter mission.

31. Bowers, "Mission," 618; Barnett, *Paul*, 99–117. Cf. Wright, *Fresh Perspective*, 48–49, who connects Paul's mission and Jesus' mission in terms of the implication of the "Jewish Messiah's rule over Israel" as "the Messiah's rule over the world."

4.1.2.2.1. Paul's citation of Isaiah 52:7

While Paul brings different OT references into Romans 10:9–21, of particular interest in our discussion is Paul's purpose for employing Isaiah 52:7[32] in Romans 10:15 and his intentional alteration of the singular מְבַשֵּׂר (MT) / εὐαγγελιζομένου (LXX) into the plural εὐαγγελιζομένων.

Having stated his concern for the salvation of Israel, and their failure regarding the righteousness of God (Rom 1:1–3), Paul in Romans 10:14 and following makes it clear that Israel's rejection[33] of the gospel (vv. 16, 21)[34] will not find an excuse, since God has dealt with them quite fairly (i.e. God has been sending his messengers to Israel). In this logic, Paul's citation of the Isaianic text is not simply to encourage his readers to go and preach the good news (as is often suggested from modern evangelical pulpits), but to stress that the "preaching" of the gospel was indeed made for Israel, since the "sending" of the messengers of the gospel to the Jews indeed had happened.

That the fourth ἐὰν μὴ question (if they are not sent?) is immediately followed by the citation with καθώς certainly indicates that Paul expects the Isaianic text to strengthen his point that it is the dominical "sending" (cf. ἐὰν μὴ ἀποσταλῶσιν) that is the most crucial element in the cause of faith which leads one to salvation *through* the "preaching" of οἱ εὐαγγελιζόμενοι.[35]

---

32. Possibly with an echo of Nah 2:1 (LXX): "ἰδοὺ ἐπὶ τὰ ὄρη οἱ πόδες εὐαγγελιζομένου καὶ ἀπαγγέλλοντος εἰρήνην."

33. Whether Paul meant "πάντες" the nation of Israel or both the Jews and the Gentiles is not immediately clear. Nevertheless, the main thrust of the long section (Rom 9–11) and the specification to the disobedience of Israel indicate the former as more suggestive.

34. Cf. Wright, "The Messiah and the People of God: A Study in Pauline Theology with Particular Reference to the Argument of the Epistle to the Romans," (DPhil dissertation, University of Oxford, 1981), 178–179; Watson, *Paul*, 1986, 166–167; Dunn, *Romans 9–16*, 620, who read Rom 10:14ff as Paul's targeting to Jewish Christians' objection to the universal (gentile) mission.

35. Cf. G. Friedrich, "εὐαγγέλιον," *TDNT* 3. 712; Stuhlmacher, *Romans*, 158; Cranfield, *Romans*, 2. 534. Cf. Dickson, *Mission-Commitment*, 171, who suggests that the citation works for the assertion that gospel-preaching is of a duly authorized kind. While this point is valid, however, it is to be noted that Paul's primary point here is not the heralds' authorized speech but the "dominical action" of "sending" which authorizes the heralds' activity of preaching.

4.1.2.2.2. Preaching from sending

However, what is striking is that, while the motif of the preaching of the multiple heralds sent by God can hardly be derived from the quoted text itself, nor from other similar Isaianic texts such as Isaiah 61:1,[36] the most similar language is found only in Luke 9:2 where the verbs ἀποστέλλω and κηρύσσω are both present.[37]

Luke 9:1 and following has been widely seen as a Markan block. And it is difficult to exclude Luke's redactional activity in Luke 9:2 possibly under Pauline influence.[38] Nevertheless, there is no clear reason to believe that Luke's combination of ἀποστέλλω with κηρύσσω in verse 2 is exclusively from Paul or Mark. First, all the synoptics agree in using the two verbs in their versions of the mission discourse, especially in a part of Matthew's discourse that has high claim to authenticity (Matt 10:5–8). Second, while it may be that Luke alters Mark's ἐκήρυξαν (Mark 6:12) to εὐαγγελιζόμενοι (Luke 9:6), he preserves κηρύσσω in his own non-Markan part (v. 2). Third, the direct combination of ἀποστέλλω with κηρύσσω in the sense of Jesus' commissioning of his disciples to preach the message of God's imminent reign appears in Mark 3:13–19, which is generally seen as a pre-Markan pericope.[39] Therefore, it is quite plausible that the early tradition of the mission discourse included ἀποστέλλω as the starting point of κηρύσσω (and possibly of θεραπεύω), and it was available early, so that Paul and the synoptists could use it for their writings.

However, all this is not to suggest that Paul is now alluding in Romans 10:15 to traditional material preserved in Luke 9:2 – even if it is possible – but only to suggest that his direct link between "sending" and "preaching" may not be indebted exclusively to an Isaianic motif of a divinely authorized preacher, but more likely reflects the Jesus-tradition where the dominical sending and the disciples' preaching are decisive elements

---

36. The combination of "ἀποστέλλω" with "κηρύσσω" in the LXX Isa 61:1 is unlikely to have influenced Paul's direct linking of the two verbs, since the two verbs are simply juxtaposed without any logical sequence.

37. Cf. Matt 10:5, 7; Mark 6:7, 12.

38. Meier, *A Marginal Jew, Vol. 2: Rethinking the Historical Jesus* (New York: Doubleday, 1994), 273, n.10, regards Luke 9:2 as Luke's attempt to link Paul's missionary preaching with that of Jesus and his earliest disciples.

39. R. A. Guelich, *Mark*, WBC (Nashville: Thomas Nelson, 1989), 155.

appearing in sequence. This argument is supported by considering how Paul uses a rhetorical device in Romans 10:13-18 for his point that for Israel there is no excuse for not believing in the gospel (vv. 19-21).

4.1.2.2.3. ἀκοὴ διὰ ῥήματος Χριστοῦ

In verse 13 Paul continues his previous point – that faith that leads one to salvation applies equally to the Jews and the Gentiles –[40] with a citation of Joel 2:32 (3:5 in LXX) with ἐπικαλέω ("to call for") in the sense of "obedient action toward God on the basis of what people come to believe" (v. 14), and develops his argument in a rough parallelism until the end of the chapter:

A: Obedience to the way of salvation

¹³ πᾶς γὰρ ὃς ἂν ἐπικαλέσηται τὸ ὄνομα κυρίου σωθήσεται — *calling*

B: Logical sequence

¹⁴ πῶς οὖν ἐπικαλέσωνται εἰς ὃν οὐκ ἐπίστευσαν — no calling without *faith*

πῶς δὲ πιστεύσωσιν οὗ οὐκ ἤκουσαν — no faith without *hearing*

πῶς δὲ ἀκούσωσιν χωρὶς κηρύσσοντος — no hearing without *preaching*

¹⁵ πῶς δὲ κηρύξωσιν ἐὰν μὴ ἀποσταλῶσιν — no preaching without *being sent*

C: Reference to heralds

καθὼς γέγραπται Ὡς ὡραῖοι οἱ πόδες τῶν εὐαγγελιζομένων ἀγαθά
— as written in Isaiah, the *gospel-heralds* had already been sent to Israel therefore, Israel have already heard the gospel which is the ground for calling!

A′: Disobedience to the way of salvation

¹⁶ ἀλλ' οὐ πάντες ὑπήκουσαν τῷ εὐαγγελίῳ
Ἠσαΐας γὰρ λέγει Κύριε τίς ἐπίστευσεν τῇ ἀκοῇ ἡμῶν

---

40. "πᾶς" here certainly denotes the Jews and the Gentiles (cf. v. 4).

– But Israel *disobeyed* the gospel (by not calling), since they did not have *faith* in what the (Isaianic) missionaries had *reported*

B′: Logical sequence

¹⁷ ἄρα ἡ πίστις ἐξ ἀκοῆς   – *faith* comes
                                      from *hearing*

ἡ δὲ ἀκοὴ διὰ ῥήματος Χριστοῦ

– (hearing and) *preaching* comes through Christ's (*sending*) *word*

C′: Reference to heralds

¹⁸ ἀλλὰ λέγω μὴ οὐκ ἤκουσαν μενοῦνγε
εἰς πᾶσαν τὴν γῆν ἐξῆλθεν ὁ φθόγγος αὐτῶν
καὶ εἰς τὰ πέρατα τῆς οἰκουμένης τὰ ῥήματα

But, I say. Have they not heard? Indeed they have.
(since) their heralds' voice and words (the gospel)
have already reached all the world beyond Israel

Seen in the light of the parallelism B and B′, verse 17 is certainly a repetition of Paul's argument of the logical sequence from "sending" to "believing" in verses 14–15a. Thus, it is reasonable to read ἀκοή in verse 17b as "communication of message" including both ἀκούω and κηρύσσω.[41] More importantly, it is again reasonable to read διὰ ῥήματος Χριστοῦ as "through Christ's *word of sending*"[42] – Χριστοῦ as genitive subjective and ῥήματος as meaning specifically "πορεύεσθε καὶ κηρύσσετε" (Matt 10:6–7, cf. Acts 5:20; 9:15).

This reading of ῥῆμα is not weakened by the use of the same word ῥῆμα as "kerygma" in verse 18 (and v. 8) since Paul is certainly making a shift in the use of ῥῆμα in verse 18 as seen in the light of the parallelism between C and C′. While Paul talks about the sequence "from the Lord's sending of messengers to believer's faith" in B and B′, he now refers to the missionaries

---

41. Paul's previous citation of Isa 53:1 (τίς ἐπίστευσεν τῇ ἀκοῇ ἡμῶν) has ἀκοή in the sense of "what is preached to their ears" that ended up with the rejection to believe.

42. Stuhlmacher, *Romans*, 158, similarly reads ῥήματος based on other NT use of it as "das Befehlswort" (Luke 1:38; 5:5; Heb 1:3; 11:3; 2 Pet 3:2). So Munck, *Christ and Israel*, 94, 135; Morris, *Romans*, 392; Dickson, *Mission-Commitment*, 172–173. *Contra* Käsemann, *Commentary on Romans* (London: SCM, 1980), 295.

(εὐαγγελιζόμενοι) and their *message* of the gospel (ὁ φθόγγος αὐτῶν / τὰ ῥήματα αὐτῶν).

As P. Stuhlmacher suggests,[43] it is likely that Paul's alteration of the singular מְבַשֵּׂר/εὐαγγελιζόμενος in Isaiah 52:7 into the plural εὐαγγελιζόμενοι indicates Paul's conscious reflection on the Jewish eschatological tradition of a "host of eschatological heralds" (e.g. εὐαγγελιζόμενοι in the LXX Joel 3:5 as the rendering of שְׂרִידִים [survivors]) to which Paul finds himself belonging as he understands the eschatological heralds (and their preaching of the eschatological message) as the sign of the coming of God's reign. However, if we consider Paul's allusion to the Jesus-tradition of the missionary charge in such a literary context (i.e. the irony of Israel's obduracy in spite of the messengers of the Lord), what is also and even more likely is that for Paul such a Isaianic herald tradition is actualized in Jesus' sending of his disciples and these multiple εὐαγγελιζόμενοι are none other than those who were sent by Jesus the Lord.

What is significant in this observation is that Paul understands the Jewish scriptural / traditional Isaianic herald motif which provides him with a theological background for his apostolic calling to the Gentiles in the light of the particular Jesus-tradition of the mission discourse. Thus, this may further indicate that for Paul the historical axis of his eschatological concept of his own apostleship is set at the point of the time of the pre-Easter sending of the disciples of Jesus looking backwards to the time of the OT prophets and Jesus' earthly ministry (cf. Rom 1:1–6; 15:8–19) and forwards to the time of *parousia* (cf. Rom 11:25–32).

Paul's eschatological perspective on his own calling and mission takes him back to the past when his apostleship was established by Jesus the Messiah as well as to the future when he expects the Lord's coming and the final consummation. Paul could certainly connect his being sent as an apostle to the Gentiles and his preaching of the message of salvation of God in his Messiah to the historical event of the sending of the pre-Easter

---

43. P. Stuhlmacher, *Das paulinische Evangelium*, FRLANT 95 (Göttingen: Vandenhoeck & Ruprecht, 1968), 148–150; Stuhlmacher, *Romans*, 158–159; Stuhlmacher, "The Pauline Gospel," in *The Gospel and the Gospels* (Michigan: Eerdmans, 1991), 156–165; J. L. Martyn, *Galatians*, AB (New York: Doubleday, 1997), 133–134; Dunn, *Romans 9–16*, 621–622; Dickson, *Mission-Commitment*, 172. Cf. 11Q13 (Melch) 18 which interprets מבשר as "the anointed of the spir[it]" as Daniel said about him (Dan 9:25).

apostles of Jesus. For Paul his apostleship (and ministry) was an extension of that of the pre-Easter apostles. It is likely that Paul's experience of the revelation of the Son of God and the calling to the apostleship to the Gentiles on the road to Damascus was understood at least by Paul as the same event as the event that the disciples of Jesus had experienced when the pre-Easter Jesus appointed them for the mission to Israel, which might have been known to Paul in the form of the church tradition (cf. 1 Cor 15:3)[44] or possibly by the mouth of Peter who was the one of the disciples of the pre-Easter Jesus (Gal 1:18).[45]

4.1.3. Conclusion

Our observations in this section sufficiently suggest that Paul knew the Jesus-tradition of the mission discourse, and that his knowledge of the particular tradition had a profound influence on his conception of the εὐαγγελιζόμενοι and his self-conception as one of the apostles. What is clear from the observed parallel and Paul's argument in 1 Corinthians 9 is that Paul equates himself and Barnabas with those who were entitled to the legitimate workers' reward by the Lord. And it is also clear that these workers are understood primarily in terms of preachers of the gospel. Most importantly, despite a certain degree of reservation (εἰ ἄλλοις οὐκ εἰμὶ ἀπόστολος, v. 2a), Paul claims an apostleship (ἀπόστολος, v. 1; ἀποστολή, 2b) with a relatively clear intention to be compared with those whom the pre-Easter Jesus "sent" (ἀπέστειλεν) into a mission.[46] Again in Romans 10:14–17 Paul echoes the Jesus-tradition of the pre-Easter Jesus' sending of his disciples in a close connection with the Isaianic εὐαγγελιζόμενος motif. This strongly suggests that in Paul שליח/ἀπόστολος and מְבַשֵּׂר/εὐαγγελιζόμενος are closely interwoven for his conception of the eschatological heralds as he envisions the eschatological expectation for the Isaianic heralds for the proclamation of God's reign having been actualized in the earthly Jesus' sending of his disciples and being continuously actualized in the exalted Lord's sending of his messengers among whom Paul finds a place.

---

44. Gerhardsson, *Memory*, 288–323.
45. D. Wenham, *Follower*, 395–397. Cf. Hengel and Schwemer, *Between Damascus and Antioch*, 205–222, who suggests the possible influence on Paul from Barnabas who had a notable history in Jerusalem.
46. See below 2.3.

But one may rightly question why Paul is not explicit in connecting his conception of the eschatological heralds with the pre-Easter apostleship if he has every reason to do so. The issue was briefly touched on earlier in relation to Paul's implicit appeal to dominical logia (cf. Luke 10:7; Matt 10:8b) in 1 Corinthians 9:14 and 18, and we now turn to discuss the issue further.

4.2. The Jesus-Tradition as a Historical Corroboration of Paul's Apostleship[47]

In this section I am going to show how Paul's understanding of himself as an apostle has its roots, not just in the resurrection traditions of Jesus, but also in the pre-resurrection traditions of Jesus' calling of his apostles. The key text for this is 1 Corinthians 9:1.

4.2.1. The Subjectivity Problem with Paul's Apostleship

Even if Paul not only knew the tradition of Jesus' mission charge to the Twelve but also understood his own apostleship as the extension of the pre-Easter apostleship by relating his apostleship to that of the pre-Easter apostleship in the tradition, he does not explain this explicitly or in any detail. Rather, Paul uses the Jesus-tradition as *implicit corroboration* for his unmediated apostleship, which he sees as the same apostleship as that of the Twelve. This is due to the nature of Paul's apostolic calling, which is very *peculiar* and *personal*. Paul himself, and Luke agrees, that Paul's experience on the road to Damascus gave him a strong sense of being sent by Christ. But the sense of being sent or the compulsion (cf. 1 Cor 9:16) to preach the gospel to the Gentiles given to Paul was through a very subjective process.[48] Even if scholars correctly point out that Paul's apostolic

---

47. For the origin, nature, and scope of "apostle(s)" in Paul's thought see appendix B: The origin of the Pauline (or Christian) Apostolate and appendix C: The Scope of Apostles in Paul's Thought. Particularly regarding the scope of apostles, I argue that there is no indication that Paul regards authorized missionaries as apostles as often suggested by proponents of broad conception of apostleship in Paul's thought.

48. Even if in Luke's narrative Ananias plays a certain role in this process (Acts 9:10–17; 22:12–16), his role may have not created any objectivity of Paul's experience of the Christophany. Paul's total silence regarding him may be due to this reason rather than the fictitious nature of Ananias.

conception was initiated or originated from this Damascus experience (Gal 1:15ff) and underwent theological strengthening process through reflection on the OT, e.g. the "Ebed Yahweh" motif in Isaianic texts (Isa 49:1, 4, 6; 42:6–7);[49] prophetic calling from "mother's womb" (Jer 1:5; Isa 49:5);[50] or the LXX's rendering of the calling of the prophets in Isaiah 6:7 and Ezekiel 2:3 ("ἀποστέλλω σε"),[51] this theological process still remains in the realm of subjectivity (as Paul's self conception). For Paul, his apostolic title and quality certainly originated from the Lord, but for others it was not *a prima-facie*-case and still required corroboration.

Perhaps, the difficulties that the primitive Christians had because of the lack of objectivity in Paul's claim for his apostolic origin may at least partly explain the continuous polemical situations regarding Paul's claim to his apostleship.[52] But, scholars' explanation for this polemical situation has been often made in terms of the "fluidity"[53] or "vacancy"[54] or "contest"[55] of the apostolic conception at the time of Paul's ministry. To some extent, these explanations seem plausible when we consider that at the time of Paul's ministry particularly in Achaia people had doubts concerning Paul's

---

49. E.g. L. Cerfaux, *Christ in the Theology of St. Paul* (New York: Herder and Herder, 1959); Kim, *Second Thoughts*, 101–127; Riesner, *Early Period*, 236–237.

50. Fung, *Galatians*, 63–64; Evans, "Paul and the Prophets," 115–128.

51. Sandnes, *One of the Prophets?*, 17–20.

52. The tension between Paul's law-free gospel and the Judaizers' law–observant gospel has been one major explanation for Paul's polemical situations. But the identity of Paul's opponents and the Paul *versus* Jerusalem relationship are still open to debate. See I. J. Elmer, *Paul, Jerusalem and the Judaisers: The Galatian Crisis in Its Broadest Historical Context*, WUNT (Tübingen: Mohr Siebeck, 2009); D. J. Downs, *The Offering of the Gentiles: Paul's Collection for Jerusalem in Its Chronological, Cultural, and Cultic Contexts*, WUNT (Tübingen: Mohr Siebeck, 2008); S. Porter, ed., *Paul and His Opponents* (Leiden: Brill, 2005); N. Taylor, *Paul, Antioch and Jerusalem: A Study in Relationships and Authority in Earliest Christianity*, JSNTSup (Sheffield: JSOT, 1992); J. L. Sumney, *Identifying Paul's Opponents: The Question of Method in 2 Corinthians*, JSNTSup (Sheffield: JSOT, 1990); P. J. Achtemeier, *Paul and the Jerusalem Church: An Elusive Unity* (Eugene: Wipf & Stock, 1987); D. Georgi, *The Opponents of Paul in Second Corinthians: A Study of Religious Propaganda in Late Antiquity* (Philadelphia: Fortress Press, 1986).

53. R. Schnackenburg, "Apostles Before and During Paul's Time," in *Apostolic History and the Gospel*, eds. W. W. Gasque and R. P. Martin (Grand Rapids: Eerdmans, 1970), 287–303 (289).

54. H. Mosbech, "Apostolos in the New Testament," *StTh* 2 (1948): 188–199 (191).

55. W. Seufert, *Der Ursprung und die Bedeutung des Apostolates in der christlichen Kirche der ersten zwei Jahrhunderte* (Leiden: Brill, 1887), 47–48, cited in W. Schmithals, *The Office of Apostle in the Early Church* (London: SPCK, 1971), 232.

apostleship and Paul had to deal with the problem in some way; so he tries to prove his apostleship by the work he did and by the way in which he did it (1 Cor 9:1–2; 15:9f; 2 Cor 12:12). Paul does not appear to suggest or even seem interested in proposing objective criteria of apostleship.

However, this does not mean that Paul had no idea about apostolic criteria. As discussed above, for Paul his apostleship is made possible through its *dominical origin*. And he appeals to other apostles concerning his dominical connection (1 Cor 9:1; 15:5–10). This certainly indicates that "what makes an apostle?" is a very important issue for Paul. Moreover, Paul connects the last resurrection appearance of Christ, which was seen by him, with his apostleship in a manner such that his apostleship is *lastly* given by the resurrected Jesus Christ.[56] Yet his position as a true apostle still needed to be corroborated by the results of his work, though he is the least among them (1 Cor 15:8–12, cf. 1 Cor 9:2). Here, we meet with Paul's sense of not being sufficient (οὐκ εἰμὶ ἱκανὸς, 1 Cor 15:9) to be called an apostle since he persecuted the church of God. But in no way does he feel the lack of the qualities of an apostle. He certainly has the full quality of an apostle even more than any other (2 Cor 11:5; 12:11). What he finds insufficient is a proper *recognition* of his apostleship.

Paul's difficulty, then, when his apostolic authority is in doubt or in need of emphasis, lies in the subjectivity of his experience and leads him to attempt consciously and unconsciously to corroborate the unmediated nature of his apostleship by increasing objectivity, which he sought through various means. Here, our suggestion is that Paul appeals to the OT prophetic figures who owned unmediated divine appointment like his own and sometimes to the visible outcomes of apostolic work, but all those means fall short of sufficiently corroborating the unmediated dominical origin of his apostleship.

4.2.2. Paul's Subjectivity Problem and the Apostleship of the Pre-Easter Disciples

The subjectivity problem in Paul's apostolic conception has sometimes been explicitly and implicitly considered by scholars. For example,

---

56. Jones, "Paul the Last Apostle," 11–28. Cf. P. Barnett, "Apostle," *DPL*, 48. Cf. Kirk, "Apostleship since Rengstorf," *NTS* 21 (1974–1975): 249–264 (264).

Harnack argues that Paul needed to increase or create the recognition that the Twelve were *the original apostles* in his concern for his own recognition.[57] Even if Harnack does not specify Paul's concern for his own recognition of apostleship in terms of the subjectivity problem, he certainly recognizes Paul's appeal to the apostolic authority of the Twelve as Paul's intended literary activity coming from his concern over his lack of apostolic recognition by others. However, Harnack fails to give any reasonable explanation for Paul's "creation" of the apostolic conception for the Twelve in an absolute and rigid sense in order to increase his own apostolic recognition, since Paul in Harnack's view sees himself as an apostle in a more general broader sense. But Harnack simply describes it as brought about by the apostle "paradoxically enough."[58]

W. Seufert certainly recognizes Pauline "subjectivism" in his apostolic conception.[59] He suggests that this subjectivity was not dealt with by Paul himself, but rather by the Jerusalem community in a strong reaction against the successful gentile mission of Paul. He argues that by pulling back to the recognition of the Twelve as apostles externally instituted, the Jerusalem community expected that Paul's apostolic right, which was subjectively based, could be denied.[60]

However, such suggestions necessitate a presupposition of a sharp tension between Paul and the Jerusalem community similar to F. C. Baur's construction of the primitive Christian history, in which Paul and the Judaists struggle over apostolic recognition. While it is certain that Paul's opponents constantly attempted to undermine the legitimacy of Paul's apostleship, such a sharp division between Paul and the Jerusalem church even generating conflicting concepts of apostleship is not attested by our extant sources. While it is probable that there was no uniform concept of apostles (cf. e.g. 2 Cor 11:13), in view of the significance of the dominical tradition of the pre-Easter disciples of Jesus, particularly their commission and sending, it is more plausible to think that both Paul and the Jerusalem

---

57. Harnack, *Mission and Expansion*, 323.
58. Ibid.
59. Seufert, *Ursprung*, 44.
60. Ibid., 47–48.

community regarded the pre-Easter disciples as apostles in a solemn sense (1 Cor 9, cf. Acts 1:21ff).

Schmithals has suggested that Paul never regarded the Twelve (of Jerusalem) as apostles – since Paul always puts them in distinction from ἀπόστολοι whom Schmithals believed to be the earliest missionary apostles in Antioch;[61] he drew his apostolic conception from the "the earthly redeemer-figure" found in the missionary office of Jewish or Jewish Christian Gnosticism whose home land is not Jerusalem but Syria.[62] In this argumentation, Schmithals does not use the word "subjectivity." Nevertheless, he actually understands the Pauline apostolate in terms of "subjectivity" by perceiving it purely in terms of Gnosticism, which is by nature subjective.[63] For Schmithals Pauline subjectivity had no reason to bother with any inner or outer tension in relation to the Jerusalem apostolate, since he believes that Paul's struggle with his opponents (i.e. other Gnostic apostles) was about transplanting the office of Gnostic apostleship into the Pauline ecclesiastical context,[64] and the apostolate attributed to the Twelve was a post-Pauline development, even coming after the composition of the gospel of Mark and Matthew.[65]

The above scholars, even if they differ in degree and direction, illustrate our point that Paul's apostolic conception could be perceived as purely subjective. What follows then is the question of whether this subjectivity is dealt with by the apostolate of the pre-Easter disciples of Jesus. Harnack in particular is correct in his point that Paul's appeal to the apostolic authority of the Twelve is due to his sense of lack of apostolic recognition. But the idea that Paul created the apostolic authority for the Twelve is not persuasive. Seufert's view that the special sense of the apostolate was applied to the Twelve in reaction to the Pauline apostolate is also misleading. Schmithals' post-Pauline development of the apostolate of the Twelve is also untenable. They all reject the pre-Pauline apostolate of the Twelve, and fail to explain

---

61. Schmithals, *Office*, 21–95.
62. Ibid., 96–230.
63. Cf. F. Gogarten, *The Reality of Faith: The Problem of Subjectivism in Theology* (Philadelphia: Westminster Press, 1959).
64. Schmithals, *Office*, 229.
65. Ibid., 234.

how Paul's subjectivity problem is related to the pre-Easter apostleship. As we have shown above, Paul's concept of apostle is closely related to his re-reading of the Isaianic herald motif in the light of the Jesus-tradition of the mission discourse. So, it is more reasonable to speak of Paul's subjectivity problem, which seeks to corroborate his apostleship by "appealing" to the apostleship of the pre-Easter disciples which had already existed rather than by "creating" or "transmitting" the apostleship.

We, then, may suggest a line of thought regarding Paul's subjectivity problem in his apostleship and its relationship to that of the pre-Easter disciples: (1) Paul's lack of objectivity is due to his lack of connection to the pre-Easter Christ; (2) the apostolate of the pre-Easter disciples which was a *prima facie* fact in the pre-Pauline church as the tradition of the sending of the disciples was well preserved and even known to Paul, (3) even if, for Paul, the Risen Christ on the road to Damascus certainly is the very person who sent his disciples on the mission to the Jews, his lack of objectivity naturally led him to seek corroboration of his unmediated dominical origin of his apostolate by identifying his being sent by the Risen Lord with the pre-Easter disciples' being sent by the earthly Jesus, and (4) yet Paul's appeal in his letters to the sending of the disciples by the pre-Easter Christ is not explicit or developed. Since his outer form of calling is closer to the post-Resurrection appearances of Christ to the Twelve (and to others), his appeal is made only in an implicit or partial equation of his apostleship with that of the pre-Easter apostles.

4.2.3. Paul's Appeals to Other Apostles

4.2.3.1. Resurrection Appearance and Apostleship

Seyoon Kim observes that "Paul considers the Christophany on the road to Damascus to be of the same kind as the appearances of the risen Christ to his disciples, and therefore reckons himself among the witnesses to Christ's resurrection (1 Cor 15:5–11)"[66] and presupposes that "Paul's claim for the resurrection appearance to him is his claim for an apostleship."[67] Contrary to this view, R. Schnackenburg argues that, even if Paul does connect his

---

66. Kim, *Origin*, 55.
67. Ibid., 31.

Christophany, which is in nature different from the resurrection appearances of Jesus with the traditional formulae of the appearances to the disciples, Paul deliberately brings the idea that "it does not follow that the appearance of the risen Lord created the apostleship."[68] Which view, then, is correct? Does Paul equate his Christophany with the resurrection appearances to the other disciples for his apostolic claim by making himself one of them? Or does he deliberately undermine the implication of the current traditional formula which stands on the resurrection appearance? Before judging, we need to ask whether or not Paul suggests that the resurrection appearance of the risen Lord created the apostleship at least for those in the traditional formula (1 Cor 15:5–7) as both Kim and Schnackenburg[69] presuppose.

In 1 Corinthians 15, Paul's paraenetic concern for the Corinthians for their salvation is their sticking to (κατέχειν) what is preached by the apostle (εὐηγγελισάμην, v. 2): Christ's resurrection as the vindication of the apostolic preaching and the resultant faith of the saints (v. 14) and as the reason for the saints' life in pursuit of a life imperishable (ἄφθαρτος) (vv. 35–58). In this context, Paul's apostolic authority and the claim for it are the secondary issue.[70] Paul elucidates that he preached the message of the resurrection of Christ as *one* of the apostles who were the witnesses to the resurrection of Christ. It is because Paul saw the risen Christ that he could affirm that the gospel of the resurrection is true. With this consideration Paul is certainly making himself one of the witnesses of the risen Christ. However, the logic that the resurrection appearances made those people apostles is impossible here. It is unlikely that those five hundred brothers were apostles.[71] Moreover, Paul's final enumeration of the traditional formula that then [the Lord] appeared τοῖς ἀποστόλοις πᾶσιν (v. 7) already

---

68. Schnackenburg, "Apostles," 291–192.

69. Ibid., 291.

70. D. F. Watson, "Paul's Rhetorical Strategy in 1 Corinthians 15," in *Rhetoric and the New Testament: Essays from the 1992 Heidelberg Conference*, eds. S. E. Porter and T. H. Olbricht (Sheffield: Sheffield Academic Press, 1993), 238; J. H. Schütz, *Paul and the Anatomy of Apostolic Authority*, SNTSMS (London: Cambridge University Press, 1975), 102; A. Eriksson, *Traditions as Rhetorical Proof: Pauline Argument in 1 Corinthians*, (Stockholm: Almqvist & Wiksell International, 1998), 255.

71. Schnackenburg, "Apostles," 292.

presupposes apostleship of those witnesses of the appearance.[72] So, it is unlikely that Paul's enumeration suggests any indication of the resurrection appearance as the basis of an apostolic claim.[73] Rather, it is more likely that Paul simply enumerates different traditions of the appearances of the risen Lord to individuals and groups, whether apostles or not (cf. Luke 24:1ff) as the evidences of the fact that Christ is indeed resurrected to which Paul's own experience of the Damascus Christophany testifies as well. Having stated this, then Paul's apostolic claim (v. 9) comes into Paul's statement that it was "apostles" who preached the gospel (particularly of the resurrection of the Lord) that was believed by many others among whom are the Corinthians through Paul's preaching. In this observation neither Paul's apostleship nor that of other apostles is based on the resurrection appearance of the Lord. Paul simply equates his Damascus experience with other traditions of the resurrection appearances of the Lord for his claim that he is one of the witnesses of the resurrection of Christ.

So, while Kim is correct that Paul reckons himself among the witnesses to Christ's resurrection, Schnackenburg fails to see Paul's recognition of his Damascus experience as the same event as the Lord's post-Easter appearances to other disciples. But at the same time while Schnackenburg correctly observes that Paul does not work as an apostle on the basis that the resurrection appearance of the Lord created the apostleship,[74] Kim fails to observe that Paul's equation of his experience of the Damascus Christophany with the resurrection appearances of the Lord to others is

---

72. It is still possible to infer, however, that a previous resurrection appearance made them apostles and the current appearance was given to them again. But considering Paul's inclusion of the appearances to the five hundred brothers and James who could not be apostles for Paul militates against this view. "All the apostles" is likely to be another expression in a different tradition of "the Twelve." Murphy-O'Conner, "Tradition and Redaction in 1 Cor 15:3–7," *CBQ* 43 (1981): 582–589; R. P. Martin, *The Spirit and the Congregation: Studies in 1 Corinthians 12–15* (Grand Rapids: Zondervan, 1984), 338. See below Appendix C, 2.5.2.

73. O. Cullmann, *Peter: Disciple, Apostle, Martyr: A Historical and Theological Study* (London: SCM Press, 1953), 59–60, criticizes the uncritical identification of apostle with witness to the resurrection.

74. Note, however, that Schnackenburg works out this idea from an unlikely hypothesis that Paul's apostleship comes from the Antiochene missionary context (294–295).

no more than his claim to be a witness to the resurrection of Christ (rather than the claim of his apostleship).

Even if it is correct that Paul's experience of the Damascus Christophany is the *basis of his existence* as an apostle,[75] and he equates its *quality* with the Lord's resurrection appearances to many others, it does not necessarily indicate that Paul understands that apostleship was given by Christ through his resurrection appearance to both the other apostles and to himself. Rather, given the previous consideration that his mission to the Gentiles was regarded as the "extension" of the pre-Easter Christ's and his disciples' mission to the Jews, and that his subjectivity problem led him to seek historical corroboration for his direct appointment by Christ, the exclusive focus on the "post-Easter dominical appearance" for the reading of ὤφθη requires a corrective. It is to be noted that while Paul's use of ὤφθη technically signifies the Jesus whom Paul saw in the vision on the road to Damascus as the resurrection appearance of Christ to many others, in any case *for Paul* Jesus appeared to him in the event always bore two realities of one person (i.e. the pre-Easter earthly Jesus and the post-Easter exalted Christ),[76] and therefore, the Jesus whom he saw on the road to Damascus is the Jesus who had established the apostleship by appointing a number of apostles during his earthly ministry.[77] This point becomes clearer in 1 Corinthians 9:1.

4.2.3.2. οὐκ εἰμὶ ἀπόστολος; οὐχὶ Ἰησοῦν τὸν κύριον ἡμῶν ἑόρακα *(1 Cor 9:1)*

The above observation must be considered in one's exegesis of 1 Corinthians 9:1, in particular the reading of the active perfect verb ἑόρακα. Most exegetes' interest has been focused on whether Paul's language of ἑόρακα (and ὤφθη) describes a mere revelatory implication or word of the resurrected

---

75. Kim, *Origin*, 31.

76. Nevertheless, it is not to suggest that Paul's literary intent of ὤφθη here is as such, since Paul's logic is limited to the point that Jesus appeared to him just in the same way in which Jesus had appeared to many others.

77. *Contra* H. D. Betz, "Apostle," 310–311, who argues that Paul "reinterpret[ed]" the concept of apostle held by the church before him, and "effectively changed" these criteria: (1) having known the historical Jesus personally, (2) witnessing the resurrection, and (3) founding churches, by rejecting (1) as Betz believes 2 Cor 5:16 to support this view. For an alternative reading of 2 Cor 5:16 see above n.25.

Christ[78] or a specific and actual seeing of the resurrected Christ with the physical eyes.[79] However, whether Paul signifies a different reality of Jesus (i.e. of the pre-Easter) in what he saw on the road to Damascus other than the aspect of Jesus as the risen and exalted Christ is seldom asked.

Paul deals with the polemical situation caused by his exercise of apostolic freedom (i.e. *not* receiving financial support from the Corinthians) in 1 Corinthians 9. His assertion that he has apostolic freedom is made in a series of rhetorical questions that claim his apostolic authority, starting "Am I not an apostle?" (v. 1). And he directly goes on to ask "Have I not seen (ἑόρακα) Jesus our Lord?" This certainly indicates that the fundamental basis for Paul's apostleship is his personal contact with Jesus. And it is very natural to read ἑόρακα as referring to his personal contact with Jesus at the Damascus Christophany. However, we need to ask whether the active perfect verb ἑόρακα is to be taken purely as a technical term for Jesus' resurrection as in 1 Corinthians 15:5–8.

S. Kim effectively argues that what Paul saw on the road to Damascus was the *proleptic revelation* of the *parousia* of Christ (Gal 1:12, 16; Rom 1:4).[80] And this leads him to categorize 1 Corinthians 9:1 as one of the references to Paul's "Lord–christology."[81] But this may not be the full meaning of what Paul really pictures in ἑόρακα Ἰησοῦν τὸν κύριον ἡμῶν. For Paul God's Son (Gal 1:16), who gave him apostleship (cf. Rom 1:3–5), was also the earthly Jesus of Nazareth whom, and whose followers, Paul once severely persecuted (cf. 1 Cor 15:9). As Fee rightly observes Ἰησοῦς ὁ κύριος is unusual Pauline language (cf. Rom 4:24).[82] The case of Romans 4:24–25 may suggest that the juxtaposition of Ἰησοῦς and κύριος signify the two aspects

---

78. W. Michaelis, "ὁράω," *TDNT* 5. 335–360; W. Marxsen, *The Resurrection of Jesus of Nazareth* (London: SCM, 1970), 98–111.

79. K. H. Rengstorf, *Die Auferstehung Jesu: Form, Art und Sinn der urchristlichen Osterbotschaft*, (4th ed.; Witten: Ruhr, 1960), 48–92: J. Lindblom, *Gesichte und Offenbarungen: Vorstellungen von gottlichen Weisungen und ubernaturlichen Erscheinungen im altesten Christentum*, ARSHLL (Lund: Gleerup, 1968), 88; G. O'Collins, *The Resurrection of Jesus Christ* (Valley Forge, 1973), 7–9; J. D. G. Dunn, *Jesus and the Spirit: A Study of the Religious and Charismatic Experience of Jesus and the First Christians as Reflected in the New Testament* (London: SCM, 1975), 97–109; F. Kerr, "Paul's Experience: Sighting or Theophany?" *New Blackfriars* 58 (1977): 304–313; Kim, *Origin*, 71–72, n.1.

80. Kim, *Origin*, 56.

81. Ibid., 104.

82. Fee, *1 Corinthians*, 395, n.14.

of Jesus in one person: Jesus *before* glory and Jesus *after* glory.[83] If our reading is correct, it is hard to avoid the impression that Paul here wants to talk about the two aspects of Jesus: not only the one who was risen and exalted and appeared to Paul but also the one who was born and served and died for the restoration of Israel. Thus, when he speaks of having seen "Jesus the Lord" he can certainly imply the pre-Easter person Jesus, who appointed apostles among whom Paul certainly includes himself, but whom once he had zealously persecuted, but who was vindicated and exalted as the Lord (cf. ὁ κύριος ἡμῶν Ἰησοῦς Χριστός in Rom 4:25–5:1).[84]

This point is paradoxically supported in that Paul does not strongly stick to that claim (that he has seen *this* Jesus the Lord), since, as his very personal experience in the Damascus Christophany *interpreted* as such by Paul at any rate may not successfully convince others, he immediately goes onto corroborate the point he wants to make in his appeal to the visible outcome of apostolic work: the Corinthians themselves as the seal of Paul's apostleship (9:1d–2). It is not least due to the subjectivity problem inherent in his apostolic calling by Jesus the Lord. Nevertheless, in verse 5 Paul still has every reason to claim his apostleship by appealing to "other apostles, the brothers of the Lord, and Cephas" whose relationship to Christ and apostleship was all established *before* Easter and re-commissioned at the time of the post-Easter resurrection appearances.

The reason why Paul does not explicitly expound his point in detail is not easily explained. Nevertheless, on the basis of our consideration of Paul's subjectivity problem and his perception of his apostleship as the extension of the pre-Easter apostleship, it may be suggested that on the one hand the polemical situation regarding his apostleship, it would have been much worse if Paul had insisted on his apostleship as such and his opponents' misunderstanding of the point would have given them more reason to accuse him of being a megalomaniac let alone a less-qualified apostle.

---

83. If Paul's language is not accidental in 1 Cor 9:1, then, Paul's language is not only the reference to "Lord-christology" but also Servant-christology.

84. Paul's perception of the continuity between the pre-Easter Jesus and the exalted / vindicated Christ is further supported by Paul's perception of the bodily resurrection of Jesus. Cf. W. L. Craig, "The Bodily Resurrection of Jesus," in *Gospel Perspectives I: Studies of History and Tradition in the Four Gospels*, eds. R. T. France and D. Wenham (Sheffield: JSOT Press, University of Sheffield, 1980), 47–74.

But, on the other hand, insofar as his experience of the calling by Jesus the Messiah in the Christophany on the road to Damascus has the identical implication and the typological similarity with the resurrection appearances to the disciples and to the vocational calling of them as the heralds of Jesus, the connection between Paul and the pre-Easter disciples in terms of apostles and / or the eschatological heralds is not thoroughly eschewed but at times alluded to carefully.

4.3. Conclusion

In this chapter we have been concerned with the background for Paul's conception of mission, particularly in order to elucidate the influence of dominical tradition on the apostle's conception of the eschatological heralds and his self-conception as an apostle.

(1) It was shown that in 1 Corinthians 9 Paul exhibits his familiarity with the context and the contents of the Jesus-tradition of the mission discourse now preserved in the synoptic material. We argued that in 1 Corinthians 9 Paul's affirmation of the right to support as a dominical instruction and his eschewal of such right indicate not only his familiarity with a comprehensive dominical tradition of the mission discourse but also his interpretation and application of the tradition for his own self-conception as one of the gospel heralds. (2) Our consideration of Paul's apostolic self-conception in Romans 10:14–17 in relation to his citation of Isaiah 52:7 enabled us to appreciate that Paul re-interpreted the Isaianic herald motif; this provided him with a crucial theological background for his conception of the eschatological heralds in the light of the particular dominical tradition of the pre-Easter apostleship. (3) We went on to observe that, despite the significance of the pre-Easter apostleship in Paul's conception of the eschatological heralds and his self-conception as an apostle, his claim to be an apostle was complicated by the subjective nature of his conversion / call; we saw that in 1 Corinthians 9:1 Paul betrays his conception of apostleship by addressing implicitly his connection to the pre-Easter Jesus, and corroborates it by appealing to the traditions about the pre-Easter apostles.

All these observations aptly indicate that, while the prophets and the eschatological Servant / herald figure in the Jewish scriptures and traditions provided Paul with some formative backgrounds for his conception of the

eschatological heralds and apostles, dominical traditions, particularly the tradition about sending of Jesus' disciples played a very important role for the apostle's self-conception.

Having shown the influence of the dominical tradition for the one prong of Paul's bifurcated conception of mission, we must now go on to observe whether the dominical tradition influenced the other prong, and if so, which tradition(s).

CHAPTER 5

Paul's Mission-Conception of the Eschatological Community and the Jesus-Tradition

It was argued in the previous chapter that the Jesus-tradition of the mission discourse serves as an important background for Paul's concept of eschatological heralds and his apostolic self-conception. If Paul's knowledge of the particular tradition significantly influences the one half of his concept of mission, what about the other half? Did the Jesus-tradition influence Paul's missio-ecclesial understanding? This question leads us to turn our attention in this chapter to that other half (i.e. the eschatological event of the community of the people of God).

5.1. The Question of the Influence of the Jesus-Tradition on Paul's Missio-Ethical Understanding

5.1.1. The Influence of the Teachings of Jesus on Paul's Ethical Understanding

5.1.1.1. *The Probability of the Influence of Jesus' Ethical Teaching on Paul*

As we have observed already, Paul perceived the church's mission in terms of an ontological ethical vocation to live as the eschatological people of God. If such an ethical dimension was vital to Paul's missio-ecclesial understanding, the probability of the influence of Jesus' ethical teaching on

Paul's advanced by various scholarly discussions is conducive to our current discussion.

Despite the paucity of explicit indication of allusion to a dominical tradition – therefore the general difficulty in deciding any allusion – there is a general agreement that in Romans Paul's ethical teaching at times reflects the tradition about Jesus' teachings. For instance, Michael Thompson extensively explores Romans 12:1–15:13 carefully advancing various criteria for Paul's allusions and echoes.[1] While trying to avoid both maximalist over-argument and minimalist ignorance of dominical influence on Paul,[2] Thompson demonstrates at least three cases (12:14; 13:8–10; 14:14) where the influence of dominical teaching on Paul is "certain,"[3] a "highly probable" case (14:13a),[4] and various cases where Paul's echoing of dominical logia is "less certain but still probable" (12:9, 17–19; 13:7, 11–12; 14:13b, 17) and "possible" (12:3–8, 10, 18; 14:18–19).[5] While in view of the ultimate significance of the example of Jesus (e.g. Rom 15:3, 7) Thompson is careful not to exaggerate the role of dominical teaching for Paul's ethical understanding,[6] his analysis leads him to conclude that the "cumulative effect of the more probable echoes decisively favours the conclusion that dominical teachings significantly influenced Paul."[7]

While acknowledging a number of differences of emphasis between Jesus and Paul (i.e. Paul more negative about the law, more oriented to the Spirit, and less radical in social ethics),[8] David Wenham finds much in common between the two figures' ethical understanding particularly in terms of criticism of Jewish righteousness, speaking of the fulfillment of the law and of a superior righteousness, emphasis on love, and conception

---

1. Thompson, *Clothed*, 30–36.
2. Ibid., 240.
3. Ibid., 96–105, 121–140, 185–199.
4. Ibid., 161–173.
5. Ibid., 87–96, 112–120, 141–160, 174–184, 200–207.
6. Ibid., 240. While considering that Paul probably would not want to distinguish sharply between the example and teachings of Jesus, Thompson regards the former as ultimately carrying more significance for Paul since the apostle sees the "Christian goal as conformity to the *person* of Christ" (240, original emphasis).
7. Ibid., 238.
8. D. Wenham, *Follower*, 241.

of a radical social outlook.⁹ As Wenham further shows various possible and probable connections between Jesus and Paul regarding ethical issues, he demonstrates a considerable number of possible Pauline echoes of the synoptic discourses in general and of the sermon on the mount (e.g. salt, light, fulfilling the law, cutting off offending limbs, prohibition of oaths, love of enemies, not judging) in particular.¹⁰

Christopher L. Carter in his recent research on 1 Corinthians pays particular attention to the influence of the "Great Sermon tradition" on Paul's fiscal thought.¹¹ He attempts to deal with Paul's pecuniary thought, which is a stock of different but related ideas, in comparison with the dominical sermon tradition. Since he understands the authenticity issue of the Jesus-tradition not in terms of the authentic "words" of Jesus but the authentic "theology" of Jesus,¹² his focus is exclusively on thematic correspondences between Paul's fiscal thought and that of the Jesus-tradition. For the comparison he identifies from the Jesus-tradition of the great sermon a nexus of ideas expressing an "other worldly financial worldview" with four sub-categories: "reality, economic zone, rights and concerns; imperative; relational priority; and impending judgment."¹³ He demonstrates that in 1 Corinthians there appears an "apparent theological congruity" in a "significant degree of symmetry" with the nexus of ideas extracted from the sermon tradition: "reality" (1:26–28; 5:9–11), "economic zone" (13:3), "rights" (6:1–11; 9:1–27), "concerns" (7:29–31), "imperatives" (1:31; 5:11–13; 7:29–31; 11:27–34), "relational priority" (6:1–11; 9:19–23; 11:17–34) and "impending judgment" (5:13; 6:9–10; 9:24–27; 11:29–32).¹⁴

As these scholars' studies suggest, Paul's echoes of Jesus' ethical teaching seem to appear more extensively particularly in Romans and 1 Corinthians. Perhaps, there are some reasons behind this. However, if the influence of

---

9. Ibid., 215–241.
10. Ibid., 254–266.
11. C. L. Carter, *The Great Sermon Tradition as a Fiscal Framework in 1 Corinthians: Towards a Pauline Theology of Material Possessions*, LNTS (London: T. & T. Clark, 2010).
12. Ibid., 17–41.
13. Ibid., 73–105.
14. Ibid., 130–203.

Jesus' ethical teaching on Paul is highly probable and it was central to his christologically oriented ethics, Paul would not have overlooked Jesus' teaching when exhorting his converts, particularly for their Christian life as ones "in Christ" and as ones "called to be of Jesus Christ" (κλητοὶ Ἰησοῦ Χριστοῦ, Rom 1:6). Rather, it would be more natural and reasonable to expect such a dominical influence on Paul in his other letters.

5.1.1.2. Loving One Another: The Influence of Jesus' Teaching on Paul's Notion of Intra-Community Ethics

The probability that Paul's ethical understanding is significantly influenced by Jesus' teaching provides a very positive indication of the indebtedness of Paul's missio-ecclesial understanding to dominical tradition. However, since Paul's ethical dimension per se is only a part of Paul's missio-ecclesial concept, dominical influence on Paul's ethics does not automatically amount to dominical influence on Paul's missio-ethical view. As we have shown previously, Paul envisions the church's ontological-ethical vocation (that entails missional / evangelistic effect for the salvation of non-believers) in terms of a qualitative restoration of Israel by forming a loving community as the family of God. It was further observed that ethics of intra-community reciprocity (ἀλλήλοις / ἀλλήλων) is central to Paul's missio-ecclesial understanding as it is expressed in the love commandment (that fulfils the law or the law of Christ, Rom 13:8–10; Gal 5:13–14; 6:2).[15] In this regard, whether Paul's notion of the intra-community reciprocal love command is under dominical influence is a significant question for our current discussion. And there are indeed some good reasons to think it is.

It is often considered that the particular emphasis on reciprocity in the love commandment is absent from the synoptic gospels, and it only appears in John's gospel (John 13:34–35; 15:12, 17) and non-Pauline NT epistles (1 John 3:11, 23; 4:7, 11–12; 2 John 5; 1 Pet 1:22, cf. 1 Pet 4:9; 5:5, 14).[16] In view of such contrast between the two groups of the NT materials the dominical logion attributed to the Jesus of John's gospel and / or the mutual love commandment is often regarded as an idea coming from the primitive

---

15. See above chapter 3, 4.3.2.

16. Cf. Thompson, *Clothed*, 123, who observes that the same occurs also in the apostolic Fathers (Ign. *Magn.* 6:2; *Trall.* 13:2; *2 Clem.* 9.6). John's gospel makes it clear that such a command is from Jesus and 1 John 3:11 mentions its early origin (so 2 John 5).

Christian community without any basis in Jesus' own teaching.[17] However, while acknowledging the influence of the OT (Lev 19:18) and Jewish tradition on Paul's notion of the reciprocal love commandment,[18] Thompson considers the fundamental characteristic of the teaching of mutual love in early Christian catechism, the incredibility of Paul being ignorant of the early tradition as a well-travelled Christian, the centrality of Christ in Paul's theology, and most importantly the perception of the fulfillment of the law in the sense of moral renewal in the eschatological messianic aeon, an idea of which is seldom found in Judaism.[19] He concludes that "although the call for mutual love is not, in itself distinctively dominical, in the light of Paul's historical / theological context, the balance of probability favours an underlying influence of JT."[20]

While considering the link between the mutual burden-bearing love and "fulfilling the law" (Gal 6:2) as a significant indication of dominical influence on Paul, Wenham considers more seriously the possibility that Paul knows the dominical tradition that John records and that by "fulfilling the law of Christ" he refers to the teaching of Jesus.[21] According to Wenham, the contrast between the synoptists who broadly delineate the love command and the inward-looking love commandment in John's gospel must not be exaggerated, since the synoptists also have Jesus' teaching of special responsibility of in-community brotherly love (Matt 5:24; 18; Mark 9:42–50; Luke 6:32; 17:1–4) and the love of brother and the love of outsiders for Paul are a case of "both-and" rather than of "either-or" (1 Thess 3:12; 5:12; Gal 6:10; Rom 12; 1 Cor 7:15).[22] On the basis of these Wenham concludes "that 'loving one another' was an emphasis associated not only

---

17. Cf. R. Bultmann, *The Gospel of John. A Commentary* (Oxford: Blackwell, 1971), 525, 542.

18. Ibid., 123, 125. Thompson considers e.g. *T. Zeb.* 8:5; *T. Gad* 6:1; 7:7; *T. Jos.* 17.2; 1QS 8:2; CD 6:20–21; *m. 'Abot* 1:2; *War* 2.119.

19. Ibid., 125–137, 140.

20. Ibid., 125.

21. D. Wenham, *Follower*, 257.

22. Ibid., 258–259, 261.

with the Johannine church and that it probably had its roots in Jesus' own teaching."[23]

Wenham's proposal of Paul's "double perspective" on the love of brothers *and* the love of outsiders and the apostle's dependence for the mutual love command on the tradition in John 13:34 may be further supported by comparison between the logion attributed to Jesus in John 13:35 and what we have construed as Paul's missio-ethical understanding. First, the dominical logion in John 13:35 does not only command the mutual brotherly love but also envisions clearly outsiders' recognition of the messianic reality among those who obey Jesus' love command (γνώσονται πάντες ὅτι ἐμοὶ μαθηταί ἐστε, ἐὰν ἀγάπην ἔχητε ἐν ἀλλήλοις), an expectation probably oriented missiologically. Second, such a further interest in outsiders as a direct corollary of the mutual brotherly love is strikingly similar to Paul's missio-ecclesial vision, in which intra-community ethics bears prime significance for outsiders' salvation.

In view of the emphatic appearance of the mutual love command in various non-Pauline NT epistles,[24] the presence of special responsibility of in-community brotherly love as well as loving one's enemy in the synoptics, and such a striking affinity between Paul's missio-ecclesial vision and John 13:34–35, it becomes highly likely that behind Paul's two-way view of Jesus' love command and his understanding of the relation between the two dimensions of Christian ethics (intra-communal and universal) dominical influence played a significant role.

5.1.2. Paul's Missio-Ecclesial Vision in Philippians in Comparison with the Sermon on the Mount

5.1.2.1. Paul's Missio-Ecclesial Understanding as a Nexus of Ideas

The above observation that (1) Jesus' teaching significantly influenced Paul's ethical understanding in general and that (2) Jesus' mutual love command was a significant influence for Paul's conception of intra-community ethics, provides us with a good basis for our further discussion. Particularly

---

23. Ibid., 259, Wenham further considers 1 Thess 5:13 (cf. Mark 9:50); Col 3:12–14 (John 13:34; Matt 5:48; 18:23–35).

24. Cf. Ibid., 258, n.108.

the latter point provides a promising indication of Paul's indebtedness to the Jesus-tradition for his missio-ecclesial understanding. Nevertheless, we need to remember that Paul's missio-ecclesial understanding is much more complicated than Pauline ethics. It means for Paul that the church is itself an eschatological event in which and through which the inaugurated restoration of Israel is being fulfilled as it continues to actualize God's salvation by living out Christ's model / command of loving / serving one another.[25] It also means that, while the vocation of the church is primarily an ontological one, its missiological relationship with the world is also envisioned in terms of it demonstrating a quality of community life and so demonstrating the goodness of God and his people. Such a missio-ecclesial understanding is a complex set of ideas. The related ideas are spread around Paul's epistles and led us in the discussion of the earlier chapter to consider various texts to do with Paul's eschatological, ethical, and ecclesial understanding in relation to his missiological framework. The issue at stake, now, is to identify the influence of the Jesus-tradition, if there was any, on such a nexus of ideas.

5.1.2.2. Setting a Test Case Study: Paul's Missio-Ecclesial Vision in Philippians 1:6–11 and 1:27–2:18 in Relation to the Jesus-Tradition in Matthew 5:14–16

For this discussion we will not explore every related Pauline text to examine whether they are under the influence of the Jesus-tradition. Not only would such attempt be going beyond our purpose, but also it would not work. Methodologically, collecting and combining different "influences" from the Jesus-tradition on Paul only establishes Paul's knowledge of and dependence on various Jesus-traditions in general, yet still fails to show his indebtedness to a specific nexus of ideas.

Thus, with the promising indications for our current enquiry that we have observed in the previous section, we choose our further discussion to be a test case study of Philippians 1:27–2:18 (which has already been dealt with in our previous discussion in chapter 2 being seen as one of the most distinct passages that shows Paul's conception of the church as the eschatological community of the people of God whose primary vocation is to form a missio-ethical community) and 1:6–11 (which prefigures the

---

25. See chapter 3, 4.3.

similar thought) to examine whether behind the Pauline passages any influence of the Jesus-tradition can be observed.

Selecting the passages from Philippians has a particular relevance for our current question. Philippians 2:5–11, the so called the Christ-hymn, is a conspicuous example of Paul drawing on Jesus' example in teaching his congregation about Christian ethics.[26] And in Philippians 2:15 Paul specifically describes the role of the Christian community in terms that echo the Sermon on the Mount, particularly the Jesus-tradition preserved in Matthew 5:14–16.[27] Since the Jesus-tradition of the "Light and Lamp Saying" in Matthew 5:14–16 strongly exhibits a missio-ethical conception of community with ontological and teleological dimensions, we choose it for our comparison with the passages from Philippians.

Thus, in what follows we will argue for Paul's indebtedness to Jesus' teaching in Matthew 5:14–16 for his missio-ethical understanding by observing: (1) that the paraenetic section of Philippians 1:27–2:18; 1:6–11 generally corresponds with the sermon on the mount in terms of the same

---

26. See chapter 2, n.150, 151.

27. D. Wenham, *Follower*, 254. For many Matt 5:14–16 does not stand as a coherent block of authentic tradition but rather as a block in which Matthew carefully brings, edits and paraphrases different traditions and sources for his own "interpretation" of Jesus' teaching. For example, the salt saying ("you are the salt of the earth") in Matt 5:13 is Matthew's adaptation from the tradition behind Mark 9:49–50 / Luke 14:34–35 and the light saying ("you are the light of the world") in Matt 5:14a is Matthew's adaptation from the tradition in Mark 4:21–22 / Luke 14:34–35 (e.g. Davies and Allison, *Matthew*, 1.472–475; Nolland, *Matthew*, 211; U. Luz, *Matthew 1–7* (Minneapolis: Fortress Press, 2007), 247.); the City (set on a hill) saying in Matt 5:14b comes from a Jewish scriptural (Hagner, *Matthew 1–13*, WBC [Dallas: Word Books, 1993], 99) or proverbial tradition (Nolland, *Matthew*, 213). Scholars conclude that Jesus' sermon context in Matt 5:14–16 derived from Matthew, who has made use of earlier isolated traditions that had varying contexts and meanings. It is undisputable that Matthew is a skilful redactor. Nevertheless, Matthew's possible adaptation of language and ideas from different traditions and sources in Matt 5–7 does not conclusively rule out the possibility that Matthew is dealing with a single tradition in Matt 5:14–16 (Cf. H. D. Betz, *The Sermon on the Mount: A Commentary on the Sermon on the Mount, Including the Sermon on the Plain (Matthew 5.3–7.27 and Luke 6.20–49)* (Minneapolis: Fortress, 1995), avers that in the pre-synoptic stage the sermons existed separately but complete in contents. See also H. B. Green, *Matthew, Poet of the Beatitudes*, JSNT (Sheffield: Sheffield Academic Press, 2001), who suggests Luke's dependence on Matthew's version of the sermon. A more popular view is that of D. C. Allison, *The Jesus Tradition in Q* (Harrisburg: Trinity, 1997), 67–95 and of Lohfink, *Jesus and Community*, 35, who prefer "Q" behind Luke and Matthew with Luke preserving it intact and Matthew expanding it). Given the inconclusive nature of some critical discussion of the gospels, we should not assume redaction of other synoptic traditions when the evangelists may have been dependant on other dominical traditions.

Jewish apocalyptic dualistic framework; (2) that Philippians 1:6–11 parallels Matthew 5:16b in terms of conceptual and linguistic agreement in regard to the function of "good works; and (3) that Philippians 1:27–2:18 is connected with Matthew 5:14–16 in terms of collocation of verbal and thematic parallels.

5.2. Paul's Dependence for His Missio-Ethical Understanding in Philippians 1:6–11 / 1:27–2:18 on the Jesus-Tradition in Matthew 5:14–16

5.2.1. Correspondence in the Function of the Jewish Apocalyptic Eschatological Duality

5.2.1.1. Philippians 1:27–2:18

In Philippians 1:28 Paul juxtaposes "sign of destruction" (ἔνδειξις ἀπωλείας) and "[sign] of salvation" ([ἔνδειξις] σωτηρίας) as things simultaneously (μὲν . . . δέ)[28] manifest in the present world. Regardless of what the "sign" exactly refers to,[29] the contrast of destruction and salvation, meant to be directed respectively upon the Philippians and the persecutors of the community, certainly points to Paul's Jewish apocalyptic eschatological perception of the church in relation to the world.[30] Here, Paul clearly builds on

---

28. MVict Aug, D², P, Ψ, 075, 104, 1505*pc etc.* read αὐτοῖς μέν ἐστιν or ἐστιν αὐτοῖς μέν in the place of ἐστὶν αὐτοῖς (ℵ, Α, B, C, D*, F, G, 0278, 33, 81, 365, 1175, 1241ˢ, 1739, 1881, 1464, *pc,* lat). In any case, the simultaneous contrast remains.

29. The linguistic ambiguity raised by ἥτις in Phil 1:28 leads many scholars to different interpretations in regard to the meaning of the sign. But this does not necessarily affect our point of discussion.

30. Most commentators and English translations agree to read v. 28b as referring to the contrast and respective eschatological destinations upon the Philippians and their persecutors. Fowl, *Philippians,* 66–69, following Beare, *Philippians,* 67–68, argues that the contrast between destruction and salvation is to be read as the "opponents' evaluation" on the fate of the Christians, since αὐτοῖς ἔνδειξις is to be interpreted in a "psychologizing sense" (i.e. the opponents' awareness of the Philippians' destruction which is actually misconceived) as the transition of perception regarding Paul's own fate (Phil 3:18–20) is reflected in the Philippians' fate (1:28). However, this argument is not convincing, since the opponents' evaluation of the Philippians' fate is not necessary for and indeed not necessarily assumed in Paul's argument for the Philippians' steadfastness in the gospel (cf. O'Brien, *Philippians,* 155–156) and Paul in Phil 3:20 certainly mentions about the final ἀπώλεια of the enemies of the cross of Christ (cf. 1 Cor 1:18).

an eschatological setting in which duality in the temporal and spatial sense is unmistakable.

The christological material of Philippians 2:6–11 is also largely set in a strong dualistic frame: divinity vs humanity, humility (obedience) vs arrogance (disobedience), and more importantly heaven vs earth. Christ is presented as one who travels from heaven down to earth overcoming the dark half of the reality and is exalted to heaven again.[31] Again in 2:15 Paul presents the world being occupied by two contrasting groups of people, ἄμεμπτοι καὶ ἀκέραιοι, τέκνα θεοῦ ἄμωμα and γενεᾶ σκολιᾶς καὶ διεστραμμένης, existing simultaneously.

However, this contrast does not lead to *conflict* but to *mission*.[32] When observed in between community and the world outside the community in the present time frame, the duality functions not merely as a notable tension but more importantly as a ground for benefit (presumably salvation) for outsiders (i.e. community's missio-ethical ontology). The Philippians are admonished to *become* (ἵνα γένησθε) God's proper people (ἄμεμπτοι καὶ ἀκέραιοι, τέκνα θεοῦ ἄμωμα) in the midst of their opponents' world (ἐν οἷς φαίνεσθε) as the lights of the world (ὡς φωστῆρες ἐν κόσμῳ). As scholars rightly observe, Paul probably had in mind the Danielic reference to those who are prudent shining like lights of heaven and leading many to

---

31. Perhaps this argument begs the question of how the dualistic view of the world can be reconciled with the tripartite expression of the cosmos, "of things in heaven, and things in earth, and things under the earth" (ἐπουρανίων καὶ ἐπιγείων καὶ καταχθονίων) in Phil 2:10. In my opinion, while it is true that Paul and other ancient Jews and Christians often viewed the cosmos largely as tripartite (heaven-earth-Sheol, e.g. Ps 139:8) or even as quadripartite (heaven-earth-under the earth-sea, e.g. Rev 5:13), such a multipartite view of cosmos needs not be seen in tension with a bipartite view of the world (heaven above-earth below). Scholars, whom my fellow research student D. Kang introduced to me, such as P. Johnston, *Shades of Sheol: Death and Afterlife in the Old Testament* (Leicester: Apollos, 2002), 99–119; J. T. Pennington, "Dualism in Old Testament Cosmology: Weltbild und Weltanschauung," *SJOT* 18, no. 2 (2004): 226, point out that in Jewish thinking Sheol or the underworld has a similar semantic function to "earth" and "sea" as distinguished from "heaven." This view may explain the Pauline evidence. While Paul's use of καὶ καταχθονίων along with "of heaven and of earth" indicates his tripartite cosmology, he simply speaks thus to stress the entirety of the world and uses the two adjectives ἐπουράνιος and ἐπίγειος elsewhere only to juxtapose dual realities of the world: heaven above and earth below (1 Cor 15:40; 2 Cor 5:1; Phil 3:19, cf. John 3:12; Jas 3:15).

32. This point is best explained by a distinction between "inaugurated eschatology" and "Jewish apocalyptic eschatology" in which the most distinctive feature is the difference between "world-transforming" and "world-negating." Cf. Witherington, *End of the World*, 18.

righteousness (Dan 12:3) in the resurrection age.³³ The light Paul mentions is not a mere distinctive quality of the people of God in contrast to the world, but it has a beneficial character like that of a lighthouse. However, what is unmistakable is that the beneficial effect of the light is not a direct injunction,³⁴ but the result of a direct injunction (vv. 14–15: ποιεῖτε . . . ἵνα γένησθε ἄμεμπτοι καὶ ἀκέραιοι, τέκνα θεοῦ ἄμωμα). It is only made possible through the actualization of the direct admonition to become ontologically what God wants (vv. 14–15, cf. 1:16–11; 1:27–2:4).³⁵ When Paul juxtaposes God's people with the world in the present time frame (i.e. before the consummation of the kingdom of God) he expects the ontological luminosity (or goodness, cf. 1:6: ἐν ὑμῖν ἔργον ἀγαθὸν ἐπιτελέσει ἄχρι ἡμέρας χριστοῦ Ἰησοῦ) of the people of God to precipitate a mission effect in the world recognizing the glory of God (cf. 1:11: εἰς δόξαν καὶ ἔπαινον θεοῦ; 2:11: εἰς δόξαν θεοῦ πατρός).

5.2.1.2. Matthew 5:3–12, 14–16

This Jewish apocalyptic eschatological duality regarding different realms and the nature of their occupiers and the idea of the conduct of those in the one realm bringing benefit to those in the other is vividly expressed in Matthew 5:14–16 and its previous section, the Beatitudes (Matt 5:3–12).³⁶

Scholars often note that Matthew's (Luke's as well) beatitudes exhibit both present and future aspects of the kingdom of God: Matthew frames it with "present-ness" of the kingdom of God (ὅτι αὐτῶν ἐστιν ἡ βασιλεία τῶν οὐρανῶν, vv. 3, 10), while all other specific promises of blessing are in the future tense (vv. 4–9).³⁷ But the contrasting realities are not only temporal but also spatial, as the reign of God is implicitly contrasted with

---

33. Fee, *Philippians*, 247–248; Bockmuehl, *Philippians*, 158. Cf. Bruce, *Philippians*, 62; O'Brien, *Philippians*, 296.

34. Note the middle or passive φαίνεσθε.

35. Cf. chapter 2, 3.2.

36. Even if vv. 11–12 is often excluded from the Beatitudes since it changes persons (third to second) and reiterates themes with a slight modification, it perfectly summarizes the preceding verses and smoothly brings the latter sayings into the initiated theme of those "persecuted but blessed."

37. I. H. Marshall, *The Gospel of Luke*, NIGNTC (Exeter: Parternoster, 1978), 250; D. C. Allison, *The Sermon on the Mount: Inspiring the Moral Imagination* (New York: Crossroad, 1999), 42; Carter, *Great Sermon Tradition*, 77.

the earthly reign in which poverty (in spirit), mourning, and thirst and hunger for righteousness are the present realities. This spatial duality (i.e. heavenly kingdom vs earthly kingdom) becomes clearer in verses 11–12 where Matthew straightforwardly mentions great reward in "heaven" (ὁ μισθὸς ὑμῶν πολὺς ἐν τοῖς οὐρανοῖς, cf. Luke 6:23),[38] which is implicitly contrasted with "earth" where Jesus' disciples are persecuted.[39] It is into this context of duality that Matthew casts the three *ontological* images of Jesus' disciples.[40] By changing persons from third (vv. 3–10) to second in verses 11–12 and maintaining the second person in 13–16 ("you are . . ."), Matthew precisely brings the listeners of Jesus' sermon into the context of the beatitudes where such a duality prevails and situates those who are "blessed," "good" (cf. Mark 9:50: καλὸν τὸ ἅλας) and "shining" with heavenly grace in the midst of the present earthly reign and persecution.[41]

On the one hand, the spatial duality is maintained vividly in the explicit mentioning of the salt "of the earth" in verse 13 (τὸ ἅλας τῆς γῆς), but, on the other hand, the salt saying provides a solution to the tension caused by the duality, as the ontological and teleological goodness of salt is presented as *preserving the earth*. The following image of light (city / lamp) of the world in verses 14–15 intensifies this paradoxical setting in which, on the one hand, the duality becomes more emphatic (i.e. light vs darkness), on the other hand, the ontological and teleological nature of the light as having a positive function for its opposite becomes cosmological.[42] What is to

---

38. As Luke also uses heaven language (ἐν τῷ οὐρανῷ) in the parallel verse, it is less likely that heaven in Matt 5:12 is Matthean but rather traditional.

39. Cf. Goulder, *Midrash*, 282: "The reward of the persecuted is great in heaven: and to Matthew the pair for heaven is earth."

40. Cf. D. Wenham, "The Rock on Which to Build: Some Mainly Pauline Observations about the Sermon on the Mount," in *Built upon the Rock, Studies in the Gospel of Matthew*, eds. D. M. Gurtner and J. Nolland (Grand Rapids: Eerdmans, 2008), 198–202, who observes a certain paradoxical duality in which those "passively" weak and needy in the first four beatitudes (Matt 5:3–6) are transformed into "actively" able ones in "righteousness" given by the power and grace of the Kingdom of God in the later four beatitudes (Matt 5:7–10); the blessed ones who shall impress the world by their far excellent righteousness (Matt 5:13–20) in the face of worldly hostility (Matt 5:11).

41. Cf. Nolland, *Matthew*, 208–215.

42. Cf. Goulder, *Midrash*, 283: "The κόσμος accordingly makes [Matthew's] third: "the persecuted preserve the world, like salt [(earth)], and they also witness to the universe, like the sun [(heaven)]." The NT use of κόσμος is not always unambiguous in regard to its exact designation (e.g. the created order including non-earthly things or beings, the

be noticed is that Matthew, unlike other synoptists, emphasizes the *entirety* of the scope on which the positive role of the light affects. While Mark 4:21–22//Luke 8:16–17, 11:33 only focuses on the intrinsic visibility of light (and the folly of hiding it), Matthew in 5:15b focuses on the entirety of the scope of the visibility by adding "to *all* that are in the house" (πᾶσιν τοῖς ἐν τῇ οἰκίᾳ). Thus, the qualifier for light, τοῦ κόσμου is not merely used appositionally to the qualifier of salt, τῆς γῆς (v. 13), which signifies the contrast against heaven (v. 12), but together with the πᾶσιν accentuates the entirety of the scope of the light.[43] This entirety should help to interpret the enigmatic saying concerning the "City." What is to be seen is not only its obvious visibility of the city set on a high place to people's sight, but its unmistakability so that *every one* will see it and have to respond (cf. Phil 2:10–11: "πᾶν γόνυ"; "πᾶσα γλῶσσα").

In considering further this duality in verses 13–16, it must be noted that commentators' common limitation of the sense or meaning of the each image – salt, city, light (lamp) – to a mere "visibility" or "obviousness" of their intrinsic nature misses the real target at which Matthew aims, namely the *paradoxical impact* of a lowly and numerically small existence of the community of Jesus' disciples.[44] The listeners of Jesus' sermon who are still under the earthly reign and consequent persecution (due to their association with Jesus) are also meant to be paradoxically "able ones" who can lead outsiders to the glorification of God in heaven through their good works (v. 16). The two contrasting realities do not remain in ongoing tension, but are expected to be resolved by the visibility of the disciples' intrinsic nature (i.e. "righteousness") functioning as a benefit for outsiders.

This parallel may not be explained by Jesus' and Paul's contemporary Jewish eschatological hope for the restoration of a glorious Israel, in that restorationist tradition the negative half of the duality is very often

---

entire inhabited earthly realm, humanity). However, the most unmistakable sense of the expression is the world in its most inclusive sense or "of its sum total."

43. Cf. Ibid., 282–283, who interestingly considers Matthew's "triadic structure" (heaven-earth-world) as the stages where Jesus' disciples play by relating the third stage, "world" to the third setting ("under water") of the Decalogue. In this connection, it is interesting that the Pauline text in question also contains the triadic language (Phil 2:10: ἐπουρανίων καὶ ἐπιγείων καὶ καταχθονίων) to refer to the entire scope where Christological homage is made.

44. Lohfink, *Jesus and Community*, 67–69.

described as Israel's enemies receiving condemnation and final destruction (e.g. 1QM; *1 Enoch* 90:16–38; *Sib. Or.* 3:652–795) and being excluded from receiving the Law (e.g. Bar 4:1–3; 1 Macc 2:48; *War* 2.414).[45] Rather, this parallel is to be seen as an evidence for the thought relationship between the Jesus' movement which was reflected in the sermon tradition and Pauline mission in regard to their understanding of the role of the people of God in relation to the world.

5.2.2. Conceptual and Linguistic Agreement in Regard to the Function of "Good Works" between Philippians 1:6–11 and Matthew 5:16b

5.2.2.1. Eschatological Sense of ἔργον ἀγαθόν in Philippians 1:6–11

As we have seen above, Philippians 1:27–2:18 strongly exhibits outsider-conscious community ethics. This paraenetic theme governs the direction of the entire letter and is already prefigured in the introductory and greeting section (vv. 1–11). In verse 6 Paul expresses his confidence that God who began the "good work" (ἔργον ἀγαθόν) in the Philippians will complete it at the day of Christ Jesus. Our particular interest is in the meaning of ἔργον ἀγαθόν. Even if it is unspecified,[46] it could have something to do with the previously mentioned Philippians' financial assistance for the apostle and their contribution to the gospel proclamation through it.[47] However, it is less likely that Paul refers to only that specific action,[48] since Paul's focus has now shifted from the ground for thanksgiving (i.e. the Philippians' support and partnership for Paul) to his ground for "confidence" that is brought about through God's initiative and faithful completion. Moreover, this confidence has eschatological scope in scale (ἄχρι ἡμέρας Χριστοῦ Ἰησοῦ). Therefore, it is better to see that by ἔργον ἀγαθόν Paul is referring to what God has initiated (ἐνήρξατο) in the lives of the Philippians – his

---

45. Cf. Bird, *Jesus and the Origins*, 131–132.
46. Cf. Gundry Volf, *Paul and Perseverance*, 33.
47. See chapter 2, *2.2.2.3.* and n.78.
48. *Contra* Dickson, *Mission-Commitment*, 127, who identifies it with the Philippians' financial support.

"new creation"⁴⁹ or "salvation"⁵⁰ or "grace"⁵¹ – which he will complete at the *parousia*.

5.2.2.2. Socio-Ethical-Missiological Sense

However, the referential force of the expression, ἔργον ἀγαθόν is not limited to that God-initiated salvation in the Philippians, but extended to the *actual outcome* of that salvation that is to be *possessed by* the Philippians.⁵² Thus, Paul, in verses 9–11, is led to pray (προσεύχομαι) for the Philippians in the following two ἵνα clauses:

1) ἵνα ἡ ἀγάπη ὑμῶν ἔτι μᾶλλον καὶ μᾶλλον περισσεύῃ . . . εἰς τὸ δοκιμάζειν ὑμᾶς τὰ διαφέροντα;

2) ἵνα ἦτε εἰλικρινεῖς καὶ ἀπρόσκοποι . . . πεπληρωμένοι καρπὸν δικαιοσύνης . . . εἰς δόξαν καὶ ἔπαινον θεοῦ.

To be sure, Paul's prayer for the growth of excellence-discerning love (v. 9) and sincerity and purity being filled with the fruit of righteousness (vv. 10–11) is the *actualization* of and *explication* for the ἔργον ἀγαθόν that was initiated in the Philippians. Then, ἔργον ἀγαθόν does not merely refer to God-initiated salvation in the Philippians but also refers to the outcome (cf. καρπὸν δικαιοσύνης in v. 11)⁵³ through the communal life of the Philippians as Christ-followers.⁵⁴ And, more importantly, this outcome (i.e. the good works of the Philippians) ultimately purports to be εἰς δόξαν καὶ ἔπαινον θεοῦ.

What is important in our discussion is that Matthew 5:16b has a very similar idea of "the good works" (τὰ καλὰ ἔργα): "in order that people see your good works and glorify your father in heaven" (ὅπως ἴδωσιν ὑμῶν τὰ

---

49. O'Brien, *Philippians*, 64; Hawthorne, *Philippians*, 21.
50. Bruce, *Philippians*, 31–32; Martin, *Philippians*, 63.
51. Michael, *Philippians*, 13.
52. Cf. Hawthorne, *Philippians*, 13, 21, who rightly interprets ἐν ὑμῖν not only in a locative sense, but also in an instrumental sense.
53. Cf. O'Brien, *Philippians*, 81, who, while he limits the meaning of good works to God's new creation in the Philippians, yet rightly observes the meaning of the fruit of righteousness as "outcome" of the Philippians' life made right with God (righteousness).
54. My suggestion for the meaning of good works is, thus, *life in fidelity to the gospel* (cf. Phil 1:27: ἀξίως τοῦ εὐαγγελίου τοῦ Χριστοῦ πολιτεύεσθε). *Contra* Gundry Volf, *Paul and Perseverance*, 36–42, who argues that God is the only "mover" of good works.

καλὰ ἔργα καὶ δοξάσωσιν τὸν πατέρα ὑμῶν τὸν ἐν τοῖς οὐρανοῖς). Even if the linguistic correspondence is not precise, the overall verbal and thematic correspondence is unmistakable:

(Phil 1:6–11) ὅτι ὁ ἐναρξάμενος ἐν ὑμῖν **ἔργον ἀγαθὸν** ἐπιτελέσει ἄχρι ἡμέρας Χριστοῦ Ἰησοῦ . . . ἵνα ἦτε εἰλικρινεῖς καὶ ἀπρόσκοποι εἰς ἡμέραν χριστοῦ πεπληρωμένοι καρπὸν δικαιοσύνης τὸν διὰ Ἰησοῦ Χριστοῦ **εἰς δόξαν καὶ ἔπαινον θεοῦ**

(Matt 5:16b) ὅπως ἴδωσιν ὑμῶν **τὰ καλὰ ἔργα** καὶ **δοξάσωσιν τὸν πατέρα** ὑμῶν τὸν ἐν τοῖς οὐρανοῖς

However, this single case of thematic and linguistic correspondence may seem to be of little significance, since the paralleled theme itself (i.e. good works may glorify God) is too general to be regarded as denoting Paul's echoing of a dominical tradition which is preserved in Matthew 5:16b, particularly seen against the background of the first century Jewish religious milieu where the virtuous conduct of Israel is very naturally regarded as for God's glory. Moreover, the Pauline verse itself lacks any mention of outsiders while Matthew 5:16 explicitly does (ἔμπροσθεν τῶν ἀνθρώπων). Thus, while it is plain in Matthew 5:16 that it is outsiders who glorify God, it is unclear in Philippians 1:11 whether it is the good works themselves in the Philippians or those who observe it that glorifies God.

Nevertheless, we must not too quickly dismiss the parallel as irrelevant to our discussion. Since Paul's hope for the Philippians to be sincere and blameless (ἵνα ἦτε εἰλικρινεῖς καὶ ἀπρόσκοποι) in 1:10 reappears latter in 2:15 (ἵνα γένησθε ἄμεμπτοι καὶ ἀκέραιοι) in the form of an exhortation which clearly exhibits an interest in outsiders and in their eventual benefit, Paul must have presupposed in his prayer for the actualization of the good works in the Philippians such a setting in relation to the world. And of more importance is that as Paul's hope for the good works in the Philippians is based on their emulation of the master's attitude (2:6–11),[55]

---

55. Note that the "love" in knowledge and perception that leads to discerning excellence (1:9–10a) may be a reflection of Christ's *love-driven choice* of self-emptying which is not folly but indeed *excellence* (2:6–8). The characteristics (i.e. sincerity, purity, and other qualities expressed in the "fruit") that reflect the right relationship with God (righteousness) (1:10b–11a) and that lead to God's glory and praise (v. 11b) may be related to Christ's vindication and the world's recognition of his righteousness that leads to the glorification of God (2:9–11).

it is natural to expect their good works to result in the same effect, εἰς δόξαν θεοῦ πατρός (i.e. the world's recognition of their righteousness and the glorification of their God). Even if this sort of setting and effect is not specified in 1:6–11, it must be recognized that Paul presupposes in his prayer the setting and the function of the good works as comes out clearly in his later paraenesis (1:27–2:18).

Moreover, despite some similarity with the idea in Galatians 5:22, Paul's expression of "the fruit of righteousness" in verse 11 is a *hapax* in the NT,[56] while the idea of the (fruit of) righteousness (as an overall reference to good works in the Philippians)[57] that leads to God's glorification is strikingly similar to Matthew's point that the new relationship with God (i.e. righteousness) and its tangible and visible outcome should make other people glorify God. Paul's expression of the fruit of righteousness "that is through Jesus Christ" (τὸν διὰ Ἰησοῦ Χριστοῦ) may well reflect Paul's knowledge of what Jesus taught about his new righteous community, namely the tradition of the Sermon on the Mount,[58] as well as what Christ himself demonstrated (Phil 2:6–11).

5.2.3. The Collocation of Verbal and Thematic Parallels

A close observation of the paraenetic pericope of Philippians 1:27–2:18 in comparison with Matthew 5:14–16 leads us to find at least three sets of verbal and thematic correspondences:

(Phil 2:15) ἵνα γένησθε . . . ἄμωμα μέσον γενεᾶς σκολιᾶς καὶ διεστραμμένης, ἐν οἷς **φαίνεσθε ὡς φωστῆρες ἐν κόσμῳ**

(Matt 5:14–16) ὑμεῖς ἐστε τὸ φῶς τοῦ κόσμου . . . οὕτως λαμψάτω τὸ φῶς ὑμῶν ἔμπροσθεν τῶν ἀνθρώπων, ὅπως ἴδωσιν ὑμῶν τὰ καλὰ ἔργα

---

56. Another occurrence is the LXX Amos 6:12.
57. *Pace* O'Brien, *Philippians*, 80.
58. Cf. 1 Thess 4:1ff where Paul seems to use some tradition indicators (ἐν κυρίῳ Ἰησοῦ; διὰ τοῦ κυρίου Ἰησοῦ) which may imply Jesus' admonition on immorality and divorce which is a part of Matthean version of this sermon tradition.

(Phil 2:10–11) ἵνα ἐν τῷ ὀνόματι Ἰησοῦ πᾶν γόνυ κάμψῃ **ἐπουρανίων καὶ ἐπιγείων καὶ καταχθονίων** . . . **εἰς δόξαν θεοῦ πατρός**

(Matt 5:16) καὶ **δοξάσωσιν τὸν πατέρα ὑμῶν τὸν ἐν τοῖς οὐρανοῖς**

(Phil 1:27) Μόνον ἀξίως τοῦ εὐαγγελίου τοῦ Χριστοῦ **πολιτεύεσθε**

(Matt 5:14) οὐ δύναται **πόλις** κρυβῆναι ἐπάνω ὄρους κειμένη

5.2.3.1. Link via φαίνεσθε ὡς φωστῆρες ἐν κόσμῳ *and* λαμψάτω τὸ φῶς ὑμῶν (τὸ φῶς τοῦ κόσμου)

The similarity of language and idea between Philippians 2:15 and Matthew 5:14–16 is the most obvious among the three sets of parallels, so we look at it first. Paul exhorts the Philippians to "shine as stars in the world," while Matthew has Jesus exhorting the crowd to "let your light shine before people" since they are "the light of the world."

Not only is the verbal and thematic correspondence striking, but also the dissimilarity of the idea to the OT understanding of the eschatological luminosity of the people of God is remarkable. As we have already observed, it is unmistakable that the LXX Daniel 12:3a (φανοῦσιν ὡς φωστῆρες τοῦ οὐρανοῦ) is behind Philippians 2:15c. One obvious dissimilarity is between "world" and "heaven."[59] We understood this shift of idea in terms of Paul's inaugurated eschatology which is largely of "world-transforming" than "world-negating." Thus, the ethical exhortation naturally turns into a missiological instruction. The same shift of idea is also unmistakable in Matthew's wording. The listeners of Jesus' word are not the luminaries in the sky or heaven being detached from the earthly world, but the light of the world (τοῦ κόσμου): they should shine "in the face of people" (ἔμπροσθεν τῶν ἀνθρώπων) through the visible means of "good works" (ἴδωσιν ὑμῶν τὰ καλὰ ἔργα). It is doubtful whether such a missiological understanding of the eschatological people of God as an already inaugurated *entity in history* is congruent with other strands of Judaism contemporary to Paul (cf. e.g. 1QS 2:4–10) except for Jesus' movement.[60]

---

59. The Hebrew word is רָקִיעַ.
60. Cf. B. F. Meyer, *The Aims of Jesus*, 129–142, 212–213.

In Romans 2:17 and following, Paul clearly hints that contemporary Jews thought of themselves as a "light to those in the darkness" (φῶς τῶν ἐν σκότει, v. 19) as the bearer / teachers of the Torah. This Jewish idea is similar to Philippians 2:15 / Matthew 5:14-16. However, what Paul points out is that they misconceived of their function as a light, guide and teacher (v. 20) by not doing and even contradicting the teachings (vv. 21-23). Paul's final verdict on their wrong perception is striking, since they even dishonour (ἀτιμάζω, v. 24) and blaspheme (βλασφημέω, v. 25) God and his name. While echoes of Isaiah 52:5 and Ezekiel 36:22 are unmistakable, Paul's entire polemic and indictment of the Jewish self-conception also strongly recall the language and idea of Matthew 5:13-16 by way of a diametrical contrast. In view of this it may be held that Paul understood the socio-ethical role of the people of God missiologically being more conscious of such a dominical tradition than the traditional Jewish view of themselves.

5.2.3.2. Link via ἐπουράνιος-δόξα-πατήρ and δοξάζω-πατήρ-οὐρανοί

In the later part of Paul's christological section and in Matthew 5:16 we have a rather striking collocation of a cluster of key words: ἐπουράνιος-δόξα-πατήρ (Phil 2:10-11) which parallels δοξάζω-πατήρ-οὐρανοί (Matt 5:16). However, we need to admit a couple of difficulties in suggesting the parallel as a sound evidence of intertextuality between Paul and Matthew.[61]

First, because of the apparent linguistic connection between the language used for the christological homage in Philippians 2:10-11 and the LXX Isaiah 45:23-25 (i.e. κάμπτω; πᾶν γόνυ; ἐξομολογέω; πᾶσα γλῶσσα; δόξα; κύριος), the parallel we suggest, at first glance, may look artificial or accidental. It looks almost certain that Paul (or a pre-Pauline author) appropriates the homage to Israel's God in the LXX Isaiah 45:23-24a (ὅτι ἐμοὶ κάμψει πᾶν γόνυ καὶ ἐξομολογήσεται πᾶσα γλῶσσα τῷ θεῷ λέγων δικαιοσύνη καὶ δόξα πρὸς αὐτόν) to the homage to Jesus.[62] However, while the two actions (κάμπτω and ἐξομολογέω) and the two subjects of the

---

61. On how to methodologically deal with a cluster of theme words, see chapter 4, *1.1.1*.
62. L. C. Hurtado, *How on Earth Did Jesus Become a God?: Historical Questions about Earliest Devotion to Jesus* (Grand Rapids: Eerdmans, 2005), 91-95; O'Brien, *Philippians*, 243.

actions (πᾶν γόνυ and πᾶσα γλῶσσα) are explicitly adopted for the ones who profess homage to Christ (ὅτι κύριος Ἰησοῦς Χριστὸς), it is less likely that the verbal contents of the homage to God in Isaiah 45:24a (λέγων δικαιοσύνη καὶ δόξα πρὸς αὐτὸν) is the only background for Philippians 2:11c (εἰς δόξαν θεοῦ πατρός). Rather, regardless of the language in the Isaianic homage to God, ὅτι κύριος Ἰησοῦς Χριστὸς and εἰς δόξαν θεοῦ πατρός are already well developed Christian formulae. Therefore, the real issue is to what extent Paul (or a pre-Pauline author) is dependent on the Isaianic language for Philippians 2:10–11 and whether one can detect background other than Isaiah 45:23–25.

It is to be noted that, contrary to Martin[63] and Käsemann's[64] estimation, εἰς δόξαν θεοῦ πατρός is not an unnatural "tail-piece" nor a mere stylized (doxological) closing formula, but a very important part for the hymn and the letter.[65] As Hurtado rightly argues, Paul's use of the "story of Jesus" who humbly obeyed God (vv. 6–8) in the face of suffering and God's vindicating exaltation of Jesus as Christ (vv. 9–11b) leads to the "apex" point of God's own glorification (v. 11c).[66] Considering Paul's previous prayer for the Philippians to be filled with the fruits of righteousness through Jesus Christ "unto the glory and praise" (Phil 1:11) and the final doxological prayer for "unto our God and Father be the glory for ever and ever" (Phil 4:20), the motif of the final glorification of God is certainly one of the central motifs for Philippians.[67] On this interpretive point, we need to note that verses 9–11, if not explicitly, certainly bears Paul's paraenetic intent and perfectly serves not only as an additional part of the story of Jesus itself but also for Paul's hortatory purpose to encourage the Philippians to live their lives to reflect God's shining glory (cf. 2:15) in the midst of opposition and suffering (cf. 1:27–30) as in the case (or example) of Jesus Christ (vv. 6–11).

---

63. Martin, *Carmen Christi*, 272.
64. Käsemann, "Critical Analysis," 81–82.
65. Cf. Gnilka, *Der Philipperbrief*, 130; O'Brien, *Philippians*, 243, 250.
66. Hurtado, *Devotion to Jesus*, 90–91.
67. Cf. M. S. Park, *Submission within the Godhead and the Church in the Epistle to the Philippians* (London: T. & T. Clark, 2007), who emphasizes "God's sovereignty" throughout the letter.

If this point is sound, one must notice that εἰς δόξαν θεοῦ πατρός does not exclusively point to God's own sovereignty and faithfulness to his word and his people (Isa 45:23a), but rather assumes *a process* in which the good works of the people of God (i.e. Jesus explicitly and the Philippians implicitly), whose final vindication entails the world's confession of Christ's Lordship and the glorification of God.[68] As we have discussed in the previous section (2.2.2), the theme of good work (ἔργον ἀγαθόν) initiated by God in Christ and its relation to the glorification of God in 1:6–11 is now to be seen more clearly in this light: the good works of Christ (and in the Philippians) is to be seen by the people in the world (cf. Matt 5:16a: ἔμπροσθεν τῶν ἀνθρώπων) and the glory is to be ascribed to God by them who realize that their previous verdict on Jesus Christ (and on the Christians) was wrong. Then, it is to be seen that εἰς δόξαν θεοῦ πατρός is much closer in language and theme to that in Matthew 5:16 (ὅπως ἴδωσιν ὑμῶν τὰ καλὰ ἔργα καὶ δοξάσωσιν τὸν πατέρα ὑμῶν) in which the process is clearly in view than that of Isaiah 45:24–25 (λέγων δικαιοσύνη καὶ δόξα πρὸς αὐτὸν ἥξουσιν ... ἀπὸ κυρίου δικαιωθήσονται καὶ ἐν τῷ θεῷ ἐνδοξασθήσονται) in which the process is largely uninterested and muted.

Moreover, the hymn's direct connection of δόξα with θεοῦ πατρός suggests its proximity to Matthew 5:16 rather than Isaiah 45. While Matthew 5:16 has the direct connection of δοξάσωσιν with τὸν πατέρα ὑμῶν, the father (and mother) language in Isaiah 45:10 (τῷ πατρί ... [τῇ μητρί]) is distant from and indirect to the use of the δόξα language in Isaiah 45:24–25. While the direct connection of God with glory and the expression of God as father are not uncommon in the Jewish, Christian and Greco-Roman tradition,[69] the direct connection of Father language with glory (e.g. ἡ δόξα [θεοῦ] πατρός) is almost exclusively Christian. This may indicate that εἰς δόξαν θεοῦ πατρός reflects dominical tradition in which Jesus is presented

---

68. Scholars are generally divided into two regarding to which part (i.e. either the world's confession or Jesus Christ's being the Lord) εἰς δόξαν θεοῦ πατρός is connected. Each position has its own interpretive plausibility. However, the either / or debate somehow misses the point that the glorification of God is made finally by the world through the process of Christ's obedience and God's vindication of him.

69. Cf. *Diod. Sic.* 4.11.1: "Ζευς πατηρ."

as one with "Father's glory" (Cf. Rom 6:4; Phil 2:11; Matt 5:16, 16:27; Mark 8:38//Luke 9:26; John 8:54, 17:5, 22, 24).[70]

The second difficulty to be addressed is about our proposal of Paul's ἐπουράνιος to be linked to Matthew's οὐρανοί. Paul's ἐπουράνιος is used to describe the heavenly realm, being juxtaposed with other two adjectives "earthly" (ἐπίγειος) and "under the earth" (καταχθόνιος), where christological confession is made about Jesus by every knee and tongue, whereas Matthew's "heavens" at first hand refers to God's transcendent dwelling place.[71] Nevertheless, this external referential difference must not obscure the profound similarity of language. Even if we cannot be sure whether the triadic expression in verse 10 is Pauline or pre-Pauline,[72] the *existence* of the expression in the Pauline paraenetic section self evidently speaks for its Pauline nature. Paul's use of the adjective elsewhere may also bear some significance in understanding the use of it here. Paul always uses ἐπουράνιος elsewhere (1 Cor 15:40, 48f; cf. Eph 1:3, 20; 2:6; 3:10; 6:12; 2 Tim 4:18) in the sense of *celestial* realm or dimension in contrast to earthly realm. And the heavenly dimension is naturally assumed to be the place where Christ belongs (cf. 1 Cor 15:49; 2 Cor 3:18). Despite the lack of explicit heaven and departure language, the idea of heaven as the realm of glorious God and his glorious Son is naturally assumed in Philippians 2:6–8. And the idea is more clearly in view in verses 9–11 in which doxological language (ὑπερυψόω, v. 9) and explicit heaven language signify Christ's vindication as his restoration to the original place (i.e. his heavenly status).[73]

---

70. Cf. Reumann, *Philippians*, 359, who argues that Jesus' Lordship requires Paul to mention Father to distinguish God from Jesus.

71. Note that ὁ πατὴρ ὑμῶν ὁ ἐν τοῖς οὐρανοῖς is Matthew's favorite. However, this does not warrant that the idea and expression is Matthean. Cf. Mark 11:25.

72. Most recent scholarship tends to accept it as an original part of the hymn. Cf. W. Schenk, *Die Philipperbriefe des Paulus: Kommentar* (Stuttgart: W. Kohlhammer, 1984), 190–193, who suggests that vv. 6c, 8c, 9c, 11c are Paul's addition to the hymn that was originally composed by the Christians in Philippi themselves in response to what Paul had taught reflecting their own situation and understanding.

73. Pace J. D. G. Dunn, *Christology in the Making: A New Testament Inquiry into the Origins of the Doctrine of the Incarnation* (Philadelphia: Westminster, 1980), 114–121; cf. J. Murphy-O'Connor, "Christological Anthropology in Phil II.6–11," *RB* 83 (1976): 25–50; G. Howard, "Phil 2:6–11 and the Human Christ," *CBQ* 40 (1978): 368–387 – whose interpretation of the hymn according to the Adam Christology rules out the notion of the pre-existence of Christ, and presumably his heavenly status, from the outset. Such a suggestion basically assumes the equivalence between μορφή and דְּמוּת/צֶלֶם (Gen 1:26–27)

Moreover, as we have previously noted, if the triadic expression serves to emphasize the entirety of realms where christological homage is to be made and the proleptic harmony between heaven and earth, the ἐπουράνιος is not a mere constituent part of a three fold universe, but is the eschatological heaven where God is finally glorified by the whole creation. Then, the implicit similarity between Paul's ἐπουράνιος and Matthew's οὐρανοῖς is much bigger than apparent dissimilarity.

In the light of our consideration thus far, we see that the parallel between the cluster of key words found in Philippians 2:10–11, ἐπουράνιος-δόξα-πατήρ, and that of Matthew 5:16, δοξάζω-πατήρ-οὐρανοί is neither artificial nor accidental. Even if some linguistic and thematic influence from Isaiah 45 on the hymn is evident, the parallel that we propose is also unmistakable.

5.2.3.3. Link via πολιτεύομαι in Philippians 1:27 and πόλις in Matthew 5:14

Compared to the previous links the degree of external correspondence between πολιτεύομαι and πόλις is small. The external linguistic and stylistic differences between a straightforward imperative "live out one's citizenship in fidelity to the gospel of Christ" and a rather aphoristic statement about the unmistakable visibility of a "city" set on a hill are very considerable. The only similarity is the common root "πολι-."[74]

It is to be noted that the verb πολιτεύομαι is a *hapax* in the Pauline corpus,[75] whereas Paul's customary verb for Christian conduct or behaviour elsewhere is περιπατέω (e.g. Rom 6:4; 1 Cor 3:3; 2 Cor 5:7; Gal

---

which is not ontologically a divine or heavenly quality but something that is granted to the Adamic humanity. However, the proposed equivalence is not convincing since the LXX reads the Hebrew as εἰκών and there is no evidence that the Greek word is not equivalent to μορφή. Rather, since the noun ἁρπαγμός and the articular infinitive "τὸ εἶναι ἴσα θεῷ" (v. 6) stress the "equality" between God and Christ, we better understand the first part of the hymn as speaking of Christ's self-emptying / lowering from his divine and heavenly status. Cf. R. H. Hoover, "The HARPAGMOS Enigma: A Philological Solution," *HTR* 64 (1971): 95–119; O'Brien, *Philippians*, 206–216.

74. For the relationship between the cognates, see H. Srathmann, "πόλις," *TDNT* 6. 516–535.

75. The other occurrence is in Acts 23:1 in the sense of "to walk according to the course of a religious conviction." Cf. Esth 8:12; 2 Macc 6:1; 11:25; 3 Macc 3:4; 4 Macc 2:8, 23; 4:23; 5:16; Acts 23:1. For

5:16; Phil 3:17; 1 Thess 2:12; cf. Eph 2:2).[76] Considering 1 Thessalonians 2:12 (cf. Eph 4:1; Col 1:10) where Paul uses περιπατέω being directly modified by ἀξίως τοῦ θεοῦ τοῦ καλοῦντος ὑμᾶς, it strongly appears that Paul uses πολιτεύομαι in Philippians 1:27 in a full synonymous sense with περιπατέω.[77]

In view of this, scholars have widely agreed that Paul's unusual use of πολιτεύομαι instead of περιπατέω is not accidental. But the explanation for this varies. R. R. Brewer argues that the ideal of Greco-Roman cities where mutuality, interdependence and responsibility for the benefit of a city community are highly prized is reflected in Paul's verb.[78] Against Brewer's view of the Greco-Roman setting as the background of the choice of the verb, E. C. Miller observes that the term is used in the LXX and the pre-NT Hellenistic Jewish writings to denote the covenantal relationship shown in obedience to Torah, and concludes that Paul by the use of the verb in the Jewish sense exchanges the Torah with Christ, the new law, as do other post-Pauline NT writers.[79] However, despite the plausibility of these explanations, particularly in the Philippians' Greco-Roman city context, and despite the apostle's possible knowledge of the pre-NT Hellenistic Jewish use of πολιτεύομαι, and his possible theological application of it to his Christology, Brewer's and Miller's suggestions respectively fail to explain why the same verb is *not* used in other letters. Was the particular verb πολιτεύομαι irrelevant at any rate to the contexts of other Christian communities in other Greco-Roman cities?[80] Or was the Christological ap-

---

76. R. P. Martin and G. F. Hawthorne, *Philippians, Revised*, WBC (Nashville: Thomas Nelson, 2004), 69.

77. BAGD, 649. However, the LXX never uses περιπατέω in association with religious fidelity to the Torah or synonymously with πολιτεύομαι as Paul does. This may mean that the use of περιπατέω as such is either of Pauline origin or of pre-Pauline Christian origin.

78. R. R. Brewer, "The Meaning of *Politeuesthe* in Philippians 1:27," *JBL* 73 (1954): 76–83.

79. E. C. Miller, "Πολιτεύεσθε in Philippians 1.27: Some Philological and Thematic Observations," *JSNT* 15 (1982): 86–96. So O'Brien, *Philippians*, 147.

80. Paul's exhortation for Christian conduct with περιπατέω appears in all the undisputed and disputed letters except the letters to persons (i.e. Phlm, 1 Tim, 2 Tim, Titus).

propriation (in regard to Torah and Christ) expressed in the particular citizenship language not suitable for other church contexts?[81]

To account for the problem, other scholars appeal to the hypothesis that Philippi was characterized by the Roman citizens occupying a comparatively high proportion of the population and that the make-up of the church would have reflected this.[82] An example of this view is G. F. Hawthorne:

> [when Paul arrived] Philippi was inhabited predominantly by Romans, ... Its people were proud of their city, proud of their ties with Rome, proud to be Roman citizens (cf. Acts 16:21) ... By choosing this word [*politeuesthe*] Paul seems to be appealing to their pride as Roman citizens, and to be extending this idea now to the church, the new community to which they belong, and of which they must be responsible citizens, abiding by its law of love.[83]

This "dual citizenship" view of πολιτεύομαι (and πολίτευμα, 3:20) seems to be becoming something of a consensus. This view particularly of the composition of the church with "many citizens" in Philippi, however, is not free from criticism.[84] Peter Oakes admits the usefulness of scholars' suggestion that the unusual nature of the city (i.e. the assumption that the city was full of veteran soldiers) may be reflected in the church; but he argues that the number of veteran soldiers by the time of Paul's arrival was not high as scholars suppose, since most of veterans who were not originally from Philippi would have left the city as the city lost its military significance; ongoing veteran settlement from other places is not historically attested.[85] His consideration of historical evidence and sociological analysis of the likely pattern of the development of Philippi leads him to conclude that "the majority of the population of the town were

---

81. In Galatians and Romans where Paul's argument about Christ-Torah antithesis seems apparent, only περιπατέω is used to connote Christian conduct (cf. Gal 5:16; Rom 8:4).

82. Lightfoot, *Philippians*, 105; R. Roberts, "Old Texts in Modern Translatio, Philippians 1:27," *ExpTim* 49 (1937–38): 325–328; Beare, *Philippians*, 66; Loh and Nida, *Philippians*, 38; Fee, *Philippians*, 19, 24–26, 162.

83. Hawthorne, "Philippians, Letter to the," *DPL*, 707–708.

84. Oakes, *Philippians*; S. E. Fowl, *Philippians*, 61–62.

85. Oakes, *Philippians*, 50–54.

probably not Romans and not citizens."⁸⁶ Moreover, he suggests that the predominance of non-citizen Greeks in the city was probably amplified in the make-up of the church, given social groups within the city and Paul's pattern of evangelism.⁸⁷

If Oakes' reconstruction is seriously considered, scholars' assumption that πολιτεύομαι and πολίτευμα (3:20) are particularly chosen for the Philippians' own context is hazardous. If one cannot be sure whether or not the citizenship issue was relevant to the context of the church at Philippi, one more important consideration remains: *Paul's own letter writing context*. G. Fee observes a notable number of *hapaxes* in Philippians and attributes them not only to Paul's conscious awareness of the Roman provenance of their situations but also to *his* as well.⁸⁸ Somewhat different but not unrelated to this is, as M. Thompson argues, the likelihood that Paul's sudden change in literary activity (e.g. expression, grammar, vocabulary etc.) indicates conscious or unconscious allusion to a source.⁸⁹ Even if these suggestions may not be conclusive,⁹⁰ the importance of Paul's own letter writing context and the possibility of a literary source (written or oral) behind Paul's composition must not be ignored and legitimately allow us to consider further the apostle's possible background for the particular choice of the language.

In view of all the other evidences of Paul's dependence on the Sermon on the Mount tradition, it is an alternative possibility that Paul's unusual use of the verb reflects his own letter writing context (i.e. his dependence on a source for his composition of the letter) rather than his readers' social context (i.e. the assumption that the church at Philippi had a particular issue of citizenship while other churches did not!). In other words, the *hapax* verb reflects his literary dependence, whether consciously or subconsciously or unconsciously, on his source(s), which explains the choice of

---

86. Ibid., 54.
87. Ibid.
88. Fee, *Philippians*, 18–19.
89. Cf. Thompson, *Clothed*, 34.
90. Note that "Ephesian provenance" of Philippians is also a weighty argument against Roman provenance and that "Paul's source" is by and large conjectural.

the particular language including the citizenship language at this point in Paul's letter to the Philippians.[91]

That possibility is supported by a careful examination of the use of the words in their contexts; the common root πολι is plausibly seen as more than a mere accidental similarity. As commentators unanimously agree, Paul's πολιτεύομαι presupposes the Philippians' "heavenly citizenship" (cf. 3:20: πολίτευμα),[92] which provides them with a collective identity as people who belong to a distinguishable realm (cf. 1:28; 2:15), whether literally or spiritually.[93] Matthew's πόλις explicitly refers to both a literal realm in which people dwell and to its literal and ethical visibility to every one around. Moreover, both references are either directly or indirectly connected to the luminosity of the realms (or to be the collective luminosity of the dwellers of the realms[94]). Matthew explicitly and directly connects the existence of the city to their being "light of the world" (v. 14b). Despite the literary distinctness of the christological hymn in its context, the imperative verb, πολιτεύεσθε in the first verse of the paraenesis governs the entire paraenesis of Philippians 1:27–2:18 making everything in the pericope function as a modifier in some sense.[95] Φαίνεσθε ὡς φωστῆρες ἐν κόσμῳ (2:15), thus, is connected to πολιτεύεστε together with other

---

91. If Paul had or knew certain source(s) containing a particular cause for the citizenship language, our previous question as to why Paul did not use the verb πολιτεύομαι or cognates in other letters might be directed against our own hypothesis. Considering the relatively late date of the composition of Philippians – as I am inclined to the view that Philippians was written during Paul's imprisonment in Rome rather than Ephesus or elsewhere –, it is not impossible that Paul had access to a more developed tradition and reflected it in Philippians, while his earlier letters reflect only other earlier versions of tradition. However, whether this conjecture is correct or not does not nullify our hypothesis nor affect our conclusion, since our hypothesis only requires us to consider Paul's possible source behind his text.

92. While "Roman citizenship" may not be historically attested, Paul's point of heavenly citizenship is unmistakable.

93. Fee, *Philippians*, 162: "... new "polis" the believing community of which they are part . . . of which they are citizens and to which they have obligation."

94. Cf. R. T. France, *The Gospel of Matthew*, NICNT (Grand Rapids: Eerdmans, 2007), 171, n.3.

95. Cf. Martin, *Philippians*, 84; Martin and Hawthorne, *Philippians*, 66–68; O'Brian, *Philippians*, 143; Fee, *Philippians*, 155; Beare, *Philippians*, 66; Bockmuehl, *Philippians*, 96; Fowl, *Philippians*, 90, 125.

imperatives throughout the pericope.⁹⁶ Therefore, Paul's verb and Matthew's noun respectively denote the same privilege to dwell in the community of the people of God and the obligation to benefit the world in which their community exists as the community of the true followers of Jesus.

We, then, may suggest that the source for Paul's πολιτεύομαι has something to do with the Jesus-tradition of the "πόλις" saying which is preserved in Matthew 5:14b (οὐ δύναται πόλις κρυβῆναι ἐπάνω ὄρους κειμένη), and that the saying was not an isolated tradition but a part of a larger Jesus-tradition that talks about outsider-conscious community ethics as appearing in Matthew's context of Matthew 5:14–16: "You are the light that shines in (or to) the world (τὸ φῶς τοῦ κόσμου), as a city (πόλις) set on a hill never fails to be exposed to every eye, so let your good works (τά καλά ἔργα) lead people to glorify your father in heaven (δοξάζειν τὸν πατέρα ὑμῶν τὸν ἐν τοῖς οὐρανοῖς)."

5.3. Conclusion: The Influence of Jesus' Missio-Ethical Teaching on Paul's Conception of the Mission of the Eschatological Community

In this chapter we have investigated the paraenetic block of Philippians 1:27–2:18 (and Phil 1:6–11) in comparison with Matthew 5:14–16. We identified at least three important parallels between the two texts: (1) a correspondence in the function of eschatological duality in which both Paul and Matthew agree to locate the eschatological half, namely the restored people of God in a beneficial role in relation to the world, the other half of the duality; (2) a conceptual and linguistic agreement in regard to the function of "good works" as the missiological means *via* a glorification of God; and (3) at least three sets of verbal and thematic correspondences of varying plausibility.

---

96. It is certain that φαίνεσθε is best rendered as imperative (cf. K. Barth, *The Epistle to the Philippians* (London: SCM, 1962), 77; Fee, *Philippians*, 246, n.27; Reumann, *Philippians*, 392; Silva, *Philippians*, 147; O'Brien, *Philippians*, 296, with reservation), however, as Martin and Hawthorne, *Philippians*, 146, rightly observes ("it is unlikely that Paul is merely reminding the Philippians of what they are already doing"), Paul expects and implicitly commands them to continue to shine.

While the intertextuality between the two texts is unmistakable given the volume of the evidence of allusions and echoes, a consideration of the distinctiveness of the ideas suggests that the intertextuality is very likely to be the result of an influence of Jesus' own eschatological vision for the restoration of Israel over Paul and the evangelist.

Such a specimen study of the relationship between the apostle's missio-ecclesial understanding and Jesus' teaching only provides a small window, through which we can begin to see connections. Nonetheless, through the small window, we may aptly conclude that the nexus of ideas that constitute Paul's missio-ecclesial thought was not merely a result of his creative theologizing out of the buffet of various relevant ideas Jewish and Christian, but also likely to be the result of his familiarity with and ability to comprehend Jesus' teachings for Israel.

CHAPTER 6

Summary and Conclusions

The aim of this study has been to give a plausible description of Paul's conception of mission that explains what the apostle expected to be the role of the church in relation to his own mission. I began this study by seeking to delineate the current contours of the debate on the issue and by concluding: (1) scholars have aptly shown that the evidence in the Pauline letters is indicative of a certain *continuity* between the apostle and the church at least in terms of *intentionality* in relation to the salvation of others; (2) however, whether such a continuity was for the apostle merely a matter of sharing the same intentionality or also of sharing the same function is a still unsettled question requiring further investigation; and (3) the issue requires not only adequate exegesis of related Pauline texts but also more appropriate consideration of the definition of mission and of the background for the apostle's conception of mission. Next I addressed the inappropriateness of some scholars' discussions in which (a) Paul's conceptuality of mission tends to be dealt with exclusively in terms of working for conversion and (b) the background for Paul's conception of mission is viewed in terms of his indebtedness to pre-Christian "Jewish mission." After suggesting the usefulness of approaching Paul's conception of mission in terms of an "eschatological event" and the significance of post-conversion influences on the apostle, particularly of the Jesus-tradition, I went on (i) to examine whether Paul's letters indicate mission-functional continuity between the apostle and the church; (ii) to delineate his conceptuality of mission; and (iii) to identify the apostle's indebtedness to the Jesus-tradition for his conception of mission. I will now summarize my conclusions.

6.1 Summary of Conclusions

1. It is possible that texts such as Romans 15:19ff; 1 Corinthians 11:1; 2 Corinthians 5:20; Philippians 4:9; 1 Thessalonians 1:6; 2:14–16; Ephesians 2:19–22; 4:16 indicate Paul's expectation for the church's missiological impact on non-believers. These texts, nevertheless, do not state whether the missional impact involves a proactive evangelism by congregations or by individual evangelists, or whether through direct evangelism or through indirect attraction. While these texts may serve as an indication of a certain intentional continuity between Paul and the church, they are invalid or insufficient for the test of mission-functional continuity between Paul and the church.

2. 1 Thessalonians 1:8; Philippians 1:5; 1:14; 1:27–30; 2:16; Ephesians 6:15, 17b are often considered as evidence of Paul's implicit and explicit expectation for the church's organized and proactive evangelism. But none of these texts supports such a conclusion: (1) in 1 Thessalonians 1:8 Paul only speaks about the gospel having been preached by his own apostolic band as they had departed from the Thessalonians (cf. Phil 4:15; Rom 15:19b) and about the beneficial function of the report of their response and faith. (2) Linguistic and contextual considerations of Paul's κοινωνία language in Philippians 1:5 suggest that it cannot be seen as the Philippians' participation in Paul's ministry through direct evangelism; it only refers to their evangelistic contribution through sharing their material resources with the apostle for his further apostolic ministry. (3) οἱ ἀδελφοί in Philippians 1:14 are best understood as qualified by ἐν κυρίῳ and as referring to a distinguishable group of individuals from the church in the city of Paul's imprisonment. (4) Semantic parallelism in Philippians 1:27–30 and the ethical connotation in the adjacent verses strongly suggest that μόνον ἀξίως τοῦ εὐαγγελίου τοῦ Χριστοῦ πολιτεύεσθε is Paul's exhortation for the Philippians' perseverance and ethical behaviour in conformity with Christ's model. (5) ἐπέχοντες in Philippians 2:16a can hardly mean direct proclamation of the gospel even if it carries a dual meaning "holding fast" and "holding forth: by using the term along with other important terms and themes reflecting Daniel 12:2–3a and dominical logia (Matt 5:14b–16) in Philippians 2:15–16, Paul probably envisions the Philippians' socio-ethical fidelity to the gospel (i.e. "holding fast") as the primary sense, expecting

a missional impact from such a community life per se as a corollary (i.e. "holding forth"). (6) Evangelistic exhortation is not clearly in view in the expression "having the feet shod ἐν ἑτοιμασίᾳ τοῦ εὐαγγελίου τῆς εἰρήνης" in Ephesians 6:15. While "foundation" is the most natural sense of ἑτοιμασία /מָכוֹן, the appositional character of ἡ εἰρήνη, the repeated distinction between the gospel heralds and its recipients, and the emphatic exhortation to stand firm strongly suggest that the expression is a typical Pauline exhortation for socio-ethical fidelity to the gospel. (7) ἡ μάχαιρα τοῦ πνεύματος ὅ ἐστιν ῥῆμα θεοῦ in Ephesians 6:17b is best read as a reference to the same effect of the divine Spirit and Word. In view of the role of the Spirit (5:18–6:9) and the word (5:26) understood in terms of the community's maturity in obedient, sacrificial and loving caring Christian familial and social relationships, it is certain that the exhortation to take the weapons repeats the previous point as a socio-ethical exhortation. The investigation shows that (i) Paul is silent about the church's proactive evangelism (*contra* e.g. O'Brien, Marshall, Ware, Keown); but (ii) he certainly recognizes the church as a partaker in Paul's apostolic proclamation of the gospel.

3. Paul's missional horizon has its fundamental ground in Jewish restoration eschatology, which envisioned the New Age to come in which Israel is restored and Gentiles will have a place in salvation. Thus, while it was the futuristic hope for the eschatological restoration of Israel understood through a Pharisaic lens that Paul led to persecute the church, it was again the restoration of Israel, but being understood as inaugurated by the Christ-event, that Paul led to his post-conversion mission. In such a Christian worldview, what Paul perceived of as his task was his participation in God's inaugurated but ongoing salvation: (1) the restoration of Israel and (2) precipitated by that, the incoming of the Gentiles. This indicates that Paul's view of mission generally follows the traditional Jewish pattern of the pilgrimage of the Gentiles into Zion (*contra* Donaldson) following on from the restoration of Israel. Contrary to various scholars (e.g. Sanders), in Paul the order of the eschatological events was not inverted, since he maintained that restoration of Israel was inaugurated partly in the community of the people of God, *viz* the church, this restoration itself being the key to the ongoing incoming of the Gentiles.

4. The above consideration opens up a way by which Paul's conception of mission is best explicated in terms of *what* and *how*: if the restoration of Israel and the incoming of the Gentiles are the aim, i.e. the *what* of the apostle's mission, *how* is such a dual-task to be implemented? Paul expected this task to be implemented in two ways: (1) by apostolic work by the workers of the gospel, being the eschatological heralds, and (2) by the ontological / ethical mission of the church showing itself to be the people of God. This is demonstrated from Paul's use of gospel-language and various other texts which show that there are two parties in distinct but related (bifurcated or two-pronged) sub-eschatological events; these cohere together for the full implementation of God's eschatological salvation. Paul's silence about the church's proactive evangelism and his recognition of it as a partaker in his apostolic proclamation of the gospel is best explained by his conception of mission which sees two vocations, being separate but related, for the eschatological heralds on the one hand, and the eschatological community on the other.

5. While the nature of Paul's conception of the eschatological heralds is indebted to his Jewish eschatological worldview in general and to the scriptural / traditional restorative expectation for the future of Israel and the nations in particular, there are evidences that it is also indebted notably to the Jesus-tradition: (1) Paul's extensive knowledge of the dominical tradition of the mission discourse and skilful use of the related logion ("without payment," Matt 10:8b) in the polemical situation in 1 Corinthians 9 strongly indicate the significance of the dominical tradition for his conception of εὐαγγελιζόμενοι and his sense of purpose as one who is thoroughly devoted to the proclamation of the gospel. (2) In Romans 10:14–17 Paul reads Isaiah 52:7 in the light of the historical event of Jesus' sending of his disciples into mission, and this further indicates that (a) for Paul the Isaianic vision of the sending of the eschatological εὐαγγελιζόμενοι is fulfilled in the historical event of Jesus and his authorization / sending of his emissaries; (b) for Paul Jesus' sending (ἀποστέλλω) is vital to his understanding of ἀποστολή and the εὐαγγελιζόμενοι, and (c) Paul understands his own ἀποστολή as the extension of the pre-Easter apostleship. (3) In 1 Corinthians 9:1 the problem of subjectivity intrinsic to the nature of Paul's claim to be an apostle leads him to corroborate his apostleship not by creating a new concept of apostle

but by appealing implicitly to the pre-Easter apostles. All these evidences suggest that one half of Paul's conception of mission is deeply indebted to the dominical tradition of the sending of the disciples.

6. There is evidence that the other half of Paul's conception of mission, *viz* his missio-ecclesial understanding is deeply indebted to the Jesus-tradition. (1) This is positively indicated by the probability of the influence of Jesus' model and ethical teaching on Paul in general and particularly by the strong emphasis on love within the community being its hallmark. (2) It is further demonstrated by the evidence coming from a comparison between Philippians 1:6–11 / 1:27–2:18 and Matthew 5:14–16. (a) The nexus of ideas that undergirds Paul's missio-ecclesial understanding in Philippians 1:27–2:18 parallels that of the Beatitudes (Matt 5:3–12) and of the salt / light / city sayings (Matt 5:14–16). They reflect a Jewish apocalyptic eschatological duality, in which the eschatological superiority / luminosity of the vindicated is expected to be beneficial to the world as the children of God. (b) Regarding the "good works" that lead people to glorify God there appears an overall verbal and thematic correspondence between Philippians 1:6–11 and Matthew 5:16b. And (c) there appear further three sets of parallel: (i) a probable echo of Jesus' "lamp" logion (Matt 5:14–16) in Philippians 2:15a; (ii) a parallel between the cluster of key words in Philippians 2:10–11 (ἐπουράνιος-δόξα-πατήρ) and that in Matthew 5:16 (δοξάζω-πατήρ-οὐρανοί); and (iii) Paul's πολιτεύομαι Philippians 1:27 being reminiscent of Jesus' πόλις logion. All these positive indications and the cumulative effect of the varyingly close echoes of Jesus' logia strongly suggest that Paul's missio-ecclesial thought was not merely a result of his creative theologizing drawn from the buffet of various relevant ideas, Jewish and Christian; it was also probably the result of his familiarity with and understanding of Jesus' teachings for Israel.

6.2 Conclusion and Implications

The different arguments presented in this study lead to our final conclusion: Paul has a coherent concept of mission as a bifurcated or two-pronged eschatological event, one prong being the mission of eschatological heralds and the other that of the eschatological community. Even if such a conception of mission is profoundly indebted to the apostle's Jewish thought-world, each part of the bifurcated eschatological event is significantly indebted to the tradition about Jesus; such a conception of mission and the indebtedness to the Jesus-tradition are certainly the most probable reasons for Paul's being silent about the church's proactive evangelism while emphatically teaching them to be the real people of God.

The importance of this study for debates about Paul's view of his mission and that of the church may be summarized as follows: (1) We have shown that the exegetical arguments used by some scholars to prove that Paul saw the church as having a direct evangelistic role (comparable to his own role as an apostle) are unpersuasive. (2) Positively we have shown, by approaching Paul's conceptuality of mission not only in terms of contents but also in terms of context, the importance of ethics in relation to proselytism / conversion within Paul's missiological thinking. Ethics is too often relegated to a secondary position, or just seen as contributing to direct evangelism, that being what really matters. (3) We have seen that the continuity between Paul's mission and the Jewish thought-world / socio-historical context tends to be exaggerated, while the continuity with Jesus' ministry vision is not fully recognized.[1]

In all of these areas we have contributed, significantly we believe, to important debates in relation to Paul, debates which will no doubt continue vigorously in the future, and which will need to engage with the perspectives we have offered.

---

1. While this study has demonstrated the bifurcated nature of Paul's conception of mission and the profound *theological* influence from dominical traditions on each sub-concept, the further question as to whether dominical influence for Paul's conception of mission goes back to the historical person of Jesus himself, or whether Jesus' own *modus operandi* expressed the same bifurcated shape has not been addressed. Such historical Jesus issues are beyond the scope of this thesis.

APPENDIX A

Paul's Conception of Universal Evangelism?

An emphatic insistence on Paul expecting the church to have an involvement identical to his own has been recently suggested by Mark Keown. He believes that Paul's notion of an axiomatic imperative that "Christ is to be proclaimed" naturally indicates "universal evangelism."

A.1. "Χριστὸς καταγγέλλεται" in Philippians 1:18, a Theological Axiom of Unlimited Evangelism?

In favour of seeing evangelistic encouragement as a central theme in Philippians 1:18 and in the entire letter, Keown argues that "[the fact that in every way] Χριστὸς καταγγέλλεται" which is for Paul the ultimate joy, functions as a "strong stand-alone theological statement" within in the literary context of v. 18.[1] Keown's argument consists of two points: (1) παντὶ τρόπῳ (in every way) may not just be limited to the following εἴτε προφάσει εἴτε ἀληθείᾳ, but maybe taken as denoting "the totality of every way,"[2] namely, Paul implies all sorts of different agents or media (i.e. regardless of whether the general congregation or set-apart evangelists) to be used so that Χριστὸς καταγγέλλεται.[3] (2) The ground for point (1) is that Paul's εἴτε . . . εἴτε construction here is used to illustrate Paul's generic theological axiom (in any and every way Christ is proclaimed!), and this

---

1. Keown, *Congregational Evangelism*, 96.
2. Ibid., 95.
3. Ibid.

is applicable beyond the immediate literary context; in other words, Paul's affirmation of evangelism is not just regardless of motives, but also regardless of mode or evangelistic model. Keown argues that most other cases of the construction (Rom 12:6–8; 1 Cor 3:21–22; 8:5; 10:31; 12:13; 13:8; 14:7; 2 Cor 5:9–10; 12:1–3; Eph 6:8; Phil 1:18; 1:20; 1:27; Col 1:16; 1:20; 1 Thess 5:10; 2 Thess 2:15) that illustrate Paul's generic theological statement may be applicable in any context.[4] Based on these points, he goes on to conclude that Paul in verse 18 "hoped for evangelism from others without limitation" – "whether by me, or apostles, co-workers, evangelists, believing wives, believing husbands, prophets, elders, teachers, pastors, Apollos, *general believers*, by men or women."[5]

However, Keown's argument for Paul's notion of unlimited evangelism in Philippians 1:18 is methodologically inadequately based on a misleading reading of Paul's use of the εἴτε . . . εἴτε construction elsewhere in his letters. A closer reading shows that his treatment of Paul's use of the εἴτε . . . εἴτε construction does not justify παντὶ τρόπῳ as all-embracing language in the sense of "the totality of every way" and that Keown has confused "motives" with "ways" in the sense of means or agents of evangelism.[6]

To respond to Keown's argument for Paul's notion of unlimited evangelism in Philippians 1:18, we need to discuss whether Paul's εἴτε . . . εἴτε construction functions as a contextual illustrator of Paul's stand-alone axiomatic statement as Keown believes it to be; then, we will discuss how and in what sense Paul mentions Χριστὸς καταγγέλλεται in 1:18.

A.1.1. Does Paul's εἴτε . . . εἴτε Construction Always Come as a Universal Statement?

Paul's use of the εἴτε . . . εἴτε construction does not always signal that he is making a stand-alone theological statement. In fact, Paul very rarely uses the εἴτε . . . εἴτε construction to talk about an axiomatic statement which stands in all circumstances in relation to "all creation" (1 Cor 3:21–22, cf. Col 1:16, 20). In many other cases, however, Paul's εἴτε . . . εἴτε construction comes in connection with his immediate point which may not stand

---

4. Ibid., 96–98.
5. Ibid., 101 (my emphasis).
6. Ibid., 96.

on its own as a stand-alone theological statement unless contextual explanation is provided.[7] And in most cases, Paul's examples in εἴτε . . . εἴτε constructions are simply limited to a specific *category* of things to make Paul's point complete. For example, in Romans 12:6–8 and in 1 Corinthians 13:8 Paul uses the εἴτε . . . εἴτε construction to list spiritual gifts which, if definable, may be included within the category of spiritual gifts. But it is very unlikely that Paul would include other things of other categories (for example, the Philippians' financial gift to Paul) to make his current points ("the gift must be expressed whatever it is" and "love excels other spiritual gifts"). Paul is simply talking about important spiritual principles in relation to the spiritual gifts. Actually, Paul's main points may not make sense unless the εἴτε-introduced lists reflect his literary contexts. Similarly, Paul uses the same construction elsewhere (e.g. 1 Cor 8:5; 10:31; 14:7; 2 Thess 2:15 etc.) to embrace a variety of possible cases to which his main idea is applicable. In these cases again, his main point is completed only when his list of things in the εἴτε . . . εἴτε construction is provided: *there are so called gods at* "any possible location" (1 Cor 8:5), "any possible human behaviour" *must be performed for the glory of God* (1 Cor 10:31), "any lifeless instrument" *can make sounds* (1 Cor 14:7), and "any form of tradition transmitted by apostles" *must be held* (2 Thess 2:15).[8] If Paul had not provided the possible conditions or examples, his point may not stand or be lost. Therefore, we can safely confirm that Paul's use of the εἴτε . . . εἴτε construction does not constitute any exegetical ground for one to take it as a signal of a stand-alone theological statement by Paul.

A.1.2. Paul's Use of εἴτε . . . εἴτε Construction with Universal Statement

In some other cases it is difficult to decide whether Paul is bringing a stand-alone theological statement or as to whether the εἴτε . . . εἴτε construction implies an all-embracing possibility regardless of its immediate context (e.g. 2 Cor 5:9; Phil 1:18, 20 etc.). Nevertheless, even if Paul certainly brings quite a universal statement into his literary context, what he really

---

7. *Pace* Ibid.: "Almost exclusively the initial statements from which the εἴτε . . . εἴτε constructions flow are general, stand-alone theological axioms in their own right."

8. Italic denotes Paul's main part of his point, and double quotation the εἴτε . . . εἴτε construction.

wants to bring into his points must be sought and weighed by that literary context itself. For example, in 2 Corinthians 5:9 where Paul talks about his (or a Christian) aspiration to be acceptable to God (which sounds like a very universal statement) εἴτε ἐνδημοῦντες, εἴτε ἐκδημοῦντες (whether at home or absent), is this εἴτε . . . εἴτε construction to be taken as an all embracing condition as Keown takes it to be (whether in Corinth or Ephesus, male or female, any dual category)?[9] And is it Paul's point here that the Christians must please God in every circumstance?[10] It seems to me that Paul never intends other sorts of dual categories to come into this εἴτε-introduced phrase, except the Christian's[11] physical life mortal and the Christian's heavenly life eternal.

We must consider the context in that Paul talks about "earthly house of the tent" in the sense of a Christian's mortal body (or earthly and bodily life) and the hope to be clothed with the heavenly dwelling (τὸ οἰκητήριον) meaning "a resurrected body" (or heavenly life) in verses 1–4. On this, in verses 6–8, Paul certainly explains ἐκδημῆσαι and ἐνδημῆσαι exclusively in terms of the meaning of a Christian's physical life and death and their comparative meanings in relation to the presence of Christ (cf. 2 Cor 4:10–12). Moreover, in 4:16 and following Paul already has made his point that believers have no reason to lose heart because of earthly affliction which is given to the "outer man" (ὁ ἔξω ἄνθρωπος) in the sense of *physical existence*, since the affliction is only temporary and light compared to the big and eternal glory, since the Christians have an "inner man" (ὁ ἔσωθεν [ἄνθρωπος]) in the sense of *eternal existence* (4:16) and the "promise of mortality being swallowed up by the life" (5:4). Thus, in his confidence (cf. θαρρέω in vv. 6 and 8) in this Christian existential reality in Christ regarding the believer's physical life and death, even if Paul would prefer ἐκδημῆσαι from his body in the sense of *to die physically* (v. 8) (perhaps, so that he could avoid θλῖψις, with groaning (στενάζειν) imposed onto his

---

9. Ibid., 97.

10. Cf. Martin, *2 Corinthians*, 113–114.

11. Paul's first person plural in 2 Cor is sometimes unclear as to whether he is refering to himself and his apostolic band or to believers in general including himself. I regard Paul's ἡμῶν here to be referring to the latter. However, it is important to notice that Paul's apologetic overtone (cf. 2:17–4:15) may govern other uses of the first person plurals in 2 Cor, so that the primary application of it might be to Paul himself and his companions.

mortal being), he eventually sees himself as called to labour even in his less favourable situation, ἐνδημοῦντες [ἐν τῷ σώματι] (v. 9, cf. Phil 1:21–24). Then, to read εἴτε ἐνδημοῦντες, εἴτε ἐκδημοῦντες as something that might embrace other dual categories is unpersuasive. The sense "being at home as well as being away" is preferable. Moreover, if Paul would have wanted to exhort his readers to please God in any circumstance, a logical absurdity arises: could Paul expect a dead believer to conduct a God-pleasing life?[12] Perhaps, Paul uses εὐάρεστος here in a Jewish cultic sense in which a dead animal's body was normally accepted by God, but at the same time appropriates it to a Christian sense in which a "Christian's body" which is still alive (cf. Rom 12:1) is also made acceptable to God through the mysterious exchange with the vicarious death of Christ (cf. 2 Cor 4:11). Then, what is seen in both senses (εὐάρεστος) is that in both cases "death" makes the animal and the Christian acceptable to God. Perhaps, εὐάρεστος may be best read as "made acceptable" in a passive sense, rather than "pleasing" in an active sense here. εἴτε ἐκδημοῦντες, εὐάρεστοι αὐτῷ εἶναι may thus be easily understood without the unlikely notion of a dead Christian to perform God-pleasing conduct. So, εἴτε ἐνδημοῦντες, εἴτε ἐκδημοῦντες, εὐάρεστοι αὐτῷ εἶναι may not be understood to be carrying any parenetic intent for a universal imperative of "God-pleasing conduct in any circumstance," but rather as Paul's theological statement of what happened to the Christian existence in Christ regarding physical life and death. It is plain to Paul (and to all) that believers must please God in all circumstances, but our observation here shows us that such a notion is not in view and εἴτε ἐνδημοῦντες, εἴτε ἐκδημοῦντες simply serves as a re definer of Paul's literary context which might have been blurred, and prevents Paul's unclear point from being misunderstood.

A very similar example to the above is Philippians 1:20. Paul stresses his hope that Christ shall live in his body now as always εἴτε διὰ ζωῆς εἴτε διὰ θανάτου (whether by life or by death). Keown reads the phrase as denoting "any other life category" such as "in plenty," "want," "chains," "free,"

---

12. Cf. Martin, *2 Corinthians*, 113: "this strongly suggests that there is no chance of doing wrong in the intermediary state, which logically leads us to conclude that there is no way to displease Christ once we are at home."

"working or not" etc.[13] But this is an over interpretation. We must note that Paul here is talking about his "life and death situation" – whether to die (by beheading in prison?) or to be set free – though he concludes that he will live (σωτηρία in v. 19). In verses 21–22 he talks about profit both in his death (τὸ ἀποθανεῖν) and in his life in the flesh (τὸ ζῆν ἐν σαρκί) since τὸ ζῆν is Christ in him. Again, in the two following verses he talks about his hard pressed situation in between τὸ ἀναλῦσαι καὶ σὺν Χριστῷ εἶναι and τὸ δὲ ἐπιμένειν ἐν τῇ σαρκὶ (cf. 2 Cor 5:8–9).[14] It seems to me that Paul is now exclusively occupied by the ultimate reality of himself (or of a Christian) who is facing the *matter of physical life and death*, which will regardlessly lead to the glorification of Christ; in that he finds ultimate joy (1:18b,[15] cf. 2 Cor 5:1–9). So, it is more natural to read εἴτε διὰ ζωῆς εἴτε διὰ θανάτου as it reads without expecting other categories to come in.[16] Here again, although Paul seems to bring a broad notion (perhaps indeed an axiomatic statement) into his context, his point is strictly governed by the life and death issue which he has been stating previously and now redefined by εἴτε διὰ ζωῆς εἴτε διὰ θανάτου.

So we conclude that Paul's use of the εἴτε . . . εἴτε construction elsewhere does not provide Keown with any exegetical ground for taking παντὶ τρόπῳ in Philippians 1:18 to denote every possible means of evangelism. Rather, our discussion clearly shows us that Paul's εἴτε . . . εἴτε constructions in most cases function as a simple *re-definer* of his literary context or as a *literary supplement* to what he wants to point out. So, judging whether

---

13. Ibid., 98.
14. Cf. Martin and Hawthorne, *Philippians*, 54.
15. Many commentators rightly observe that Paul's joy in v. 18b is linked to the following clause rather than the preceding clause.
16. Another similar case is 1 Thess 5:10 in which Paul comforts the Thessalonians by writing that they are destined by God to obtain salvation through Christ who died for them, so that they should live whether they are awake or asleep (εἴτε γρηγορῶμεν εἴτε καθεύδωμεν). As Green, *Thessalonians*, 243, correctly observes, Paul's use of the verbs γρηγορέω and καθεύδω in v. 10 denote *physical life and death* rather than spiritual alertness or abstraction (vv. 6–7): "although the terminology in v. 10 is identical to that found in vv. 6–7, the sense is entirely different." It is absurd to take καθεύδω in v. 10 to mean "sleeping spiritually" since Paul uses it to classify unbelievers in v. 7 while he uses γρηγορέω for Christians. To be sure, Paul's εἴτε . . . εἴτε construction here is limited to the issue of physical life and death reflecting 1 Thess 4:13–15 where Paul talks about the destiny of the dead and living in Christ.

παντὶ τρόπῳ in Philippians 1:18 is limited by the immediate literary context reflected in the following εἴτε . . . εἴτε construction or whether it refers in a more universal sense must be decided by considering the literary context of the text in question.

A.1.3. Is "Χριστὸς καταγγέλλεται," a Theological Axiom of Unlimited Evangelism?

Paul's εἴτε . . . εἴτε construction in Philippians 1:18a does indeed function as a re-definer of his context which he has already mentioned, and illustrates what παντὶ τρόπῳ exactly means in the context. Paul refers εἴτε προφάσει εἴτε ἀληθείᾳ to the context where the impure motives of some evangelists were added to Paul's chain as an additional suffering (v. 17).[17] It is quite natural to infer that Paul took it very seriously, and this is expressed in verses 15–18a in which Paul reports the incident in a rhetorically articulated form:

A	διὰ φθόνον καὶ ἔριν	(v. 15a)
B	δι' εὐδοκίαν	(v. 15b)
B'	ἐξ ἀγάπης	(v. 16)
A'	ἐξ ἐριθείας, οὐχ ἁγνῶς, οἰόμενοι θλῖψιν ἐπιφέρειν	(v. 17)
A''	προφάσει	(v. 18a)
B''	ἀληθείᾳ	(v. 18a)[18]

The new sentence starting with τί γάρ (v. 18) must not be treated independently of the preceding part. Even if the τί γάρ carries a transitional force here, Paul's εἴτε . . . εἴτε construction is still governed by the previous incident and directly qualifies πλὴν ὅτι παντὶ τρόπῳ.[19] Thus, it is difficult to expect that Paul had in mind other categories of things than evangelists' motives. Perhaps, Paul could provide, in the εἴτε . . . εἴτε construction in

---

17. Paul's report section in Philippians seems to be intended to describe his suffering and his striving to overcome following the model that is found in Christ's suffering and victory (2:5–11), so that in the body of the letter the apostle could exhort the community in their suffering to emulate the models (Paul's, Christ's and perhaps, the two good brothers') who stood or are standing firm in the midst of suffering. On this understanding of the epistle, I take Paul's mentioning of the bad motives of some evangelists in 1:14–18 to have a double function: to describe his situation of suffering and to facilitate his exhortation to have one mind in Christ.

18. Martin and Hawthorne, *Philippians*, 45.

19. Cf. O'Brien, *Philippians*, 106.

verse 18, *other motives* which may be in the *category of Christian inner attitudes* (cf. Phil 2:1–14). So, it is more plausible to think that by "παντὶ τρόπῳ" the apostle means "in every case where people have different motives" (whether the motives are pure or even impure).

Another point to be made is that Keown unjustifiably downplays the significance of the theme of motivations among the evangelists at the cost of the unduly emphasized phrase, Χριστὸς καταγγέλλεται: "[t]hat is, Paul here notes that, compared to the cosmic imperative of preaching the gospel, motive is irrelevant."[20] If our discussion so far sufficiently proves that παντὶ τρόπῳ is limited to the evangelists' inner motives, on what basis can one take Χριστὸς καταγγέλλεται as "the cosmic imperative of preaching the gospel"? The passive voice certainly suggests that Paul takes it as an eventual result (ἐν τούτῳ) from the unexpected (or un desirable) situation (πλὴν ὅτι παντὶ τρόπῳ) where his suffering in chains was intensified by the impure motive (of rivalry) of the evangelists. Perhaps, he could take the eventual result that Χριστὸς καταγγέλλεται as a remedy or compensation for his θλῖψις. But this fact does not lead him to delight in impure motives in Christian brothers and sisters. Rather, he goes on to exhort the Philippians not to have "impure" motives (2:3)[21] and to think on whatsoever is pure (4:8). Moreover, it must be noted that Paul quickly changes to another reason for joy in 18b, ἀλλὰ καὶ χαρήσομαι. Many commentators have observed that Paul's joy here is linked with the following reason which is stated in a notably longer part (vv. 18b–26) rather than the preceding reason.[22] Paul has been describing the suffering not simply of his body in chains but also of his mind because of some brothers' rivalry, which eventually allowed him a rather *paradoxical joy* since even in that Christ is proclaimed, yet he immediately goes on to state his conviction and another reason for joy that his suffering will end up with his release (v. 19) and the exaltation of Christ in his *body* (v. 20). This is happening through the Philippians' prayers and the help of Christ's Spirit, in order that he can make another visit to the

---

20. Keown, *Congregational Evangelism*, 98.

21. Paul here uses exactly the same word ἐριθεία which is used in 1:17 to describe the nature of the impurity of some brothers' motive.

22. Martin and Hawthorne, *Philippians*, 48. Cf. O'Brien, *Philippians*, 108, who is sympathetic to those who deny the gap between v. 18a and v. 18b.

Philippians for their progress and *joy* in faith (v. 25). This strongly suggests that Paul's intended focus in this passage is not on Χριστὸς καταγγέλλεται but on εἴτε προφάσει εἴτε ἀληθείᾳ, which certainly describes Paul's situation of suffering which paradoxically ends up with joy. Therefore, Paul's mention of Χριστὸς καταγγέλλεται is to be seen as an expression of his *counter-spirit* which makes him always choose to rejoice even in suffering (cf. Phil 2:17; 2 Cor 6:10) (and may reflect his *loyalty to his task* as an apostle who is set apart for the furtherance of the gospel of Christ).

A.2. Conclusion

Our discussion has shown that Paul's use of the εἴτε . . . εἴτε construction elsewhere in his letters may not be taken as an exegetical ground for reading Paul as making an axiomatic theological statement and as having the same meaning in other contexts. Rather, Paul's εἴτε . . . εἴτε construction in most cases functions as a re-definer in the context and is related only to that particular context. Therefore, Keown's argument for reading παντὶ τρόπῳ in Philippians 1:18 as denoting every possible evangelistic method and agent and Χριστὸς καταγγέλλεται as Paul's universal imperative to preach the gospel παντὶ τρόπῳ turns out to be unpersuasive. Rather, it seems that Paul connects "Χριστὸς καταγγέλλεται" with his hortatory purpose, as a motive for rejoicing in the midst of suffering; as his suffering in chains and uncertainty of life and death will eventually end up with the exaltation of Christ and his release which will bring him the final joy (cf. 2:17), the Philippians should rejoice with the apostle (2:18). It is very plain to Paul that Christ must be proclaimed, but Χριστὸς καταγγέλλεται in Philippians 1:18 is not making that particular point, and does not indicate a notion of universal evangelism.

APPENDIX B

The Origin of the Pauline (or Christian) Apostolate

B.1. Pre-Pauline Nature of Apostolate

It has been widely agreed that the LXX and non-biblical use of the word ἀπόστολος is alien to the Christian use of it, thus the origin of Paul's (or the earliest Christians') use of the word is to be sought elsewhere.[1] One popular theory by K. H. Rengstorf seeks its origin in the later Jewish institution of שליח (juridical representative).[2] When it is considered that the NT applies ἀπόστολοι to those who were sent by Jesus (and by a community in Acts 14:4, 14) as the representatives and the authorized messengers of one who sends, the theory is persuasive. But, scholars such as J. Munck,[3] A. Ehrhardt,[4] and W. Schmithals[5] emphatically rejected the theory suggesting that, apart from formal and conceptual similarity between the Christian apostolate and the later Jewish institution of שליח, the theory suffers the lack of concrete historical evidence,[6] and true phenomenological

---

1. K. H. Rengstorf, "ἀπόστολος," *TDNT* 1. 407–413; J. A. Kirk, "Apostleship since Rengstorf," *NTS* 21 (1974–1975): 249–264 (250); Barnett, "Apostle," *DPL*, 45.

2. Rengstorf, "ἀπόστολος," 414–420. For a detailed survey on the studies on the question of the origin of Christian apostolate, see F. H. Agnew, "The Origin of the NT Apostle-Concept: A Review of Research," *JBL* 105 (1986): 76–96.

3. J. Munck, "Paul, the Apostles and the Twelve," *StTh* 3 (1950): 96–110.

4. A. Ehrhardt, *The Apostolic Succession in the First Two Centuries of the Church* (London: Lutterworth, 1953).

5. Schmithals, *Office*, 101–106.

6. Ehrhardt, *Apostolic Succession*, 17. Cf. Schmithals, *Office*, 101–103, who reserves the possibility that pre-institutional שליח convention might have influenced the NT use.

parallelism between the two.⁷ Considering that Paul, who was the first Christian writer, uses ἀπόστολος mostly in terms of mission, we may be safely led to conclude that Christian provenance (i.e. in the ministry of Jesus or the early church) is a more likely explanation in the search for the origin of the Christian apostolate.⁸

Against Rengstorf, a common (perhaps, the only) explanation that seeks the origin of the Christian use of ἀπόστολος in the Christian contexts is the *Pan-Antioch (Syria) theory*. According to this, it was Paul⁹ or at least the Christian community at Antioch¹⁰ that first coined the Christian use of ἀπόστολος. For example, Schmithals has suggested that Paul had never regarded the Twelve (of Jerusalem) as apostles, since Paul always puts them in a sharp contradistinction with ἀπόστολοι whom Schmithals believes to be the earliest missionary apostles in Antioch.¹¹ According to Schmithals, Paul drew his concept of apostle from the "the earthly redeemer-figure" found in the missionary office of Jewish or Jewish Christian Gnosticism whose homeland is not Jerusalem but Syria.¹² Similarly, while admitting that Paul knew some traditions (i.e. 1 Cor 15:5–7) to which *an apostolic concept* had already been attached in such a manner as to confine it to the Twelve who saw the resurrection appearance of Jesus around Jerusalem (and perhaps with a space for James the brother of the Lord), Schnackenburg believes that Paul brings into the tradition *another conception of apostle* which had been developed to accommodate those who were official missionaries who were not necessarily the witnesses to Christ's resurrection in

---

7. Munck, "Paul," 100; Schmithals, *Office*, 103–106.
8. Kirk, "Apostleship," 252.
9. H. von Campenhausen, "Der urkirchliche Apostelbegriff," *StTh* 2 (1948): 166; Munck, "Paul," 109; G. Klein, *Die zwölf Apostel: Ursprung und Gehalt einer Idee* (Göttingen: Vandenhoeck & Ruprecht, 1962), 112ff.
10. H. Mosbech, "Apostolos in the New Testament," *StTh* 2 (1948): 188–189; R. Schnackenburg, "Apostles Before and During Paul's Time," in *Apostolic History and the Gospel*, eds. W. W. Gasque and R. P. Martin (Grand Rapids: Eerdmans, 1970), 294; Schmithals, *Office*, 114–230. Cf. Rengstorf, "ἀπόστολος," 435, also suggests that Antioch was the first place where Hellenistic Christians first began to use ἀπόστολοι in relation to the missionary expedition, then to an individual (ἀπόστολος) perhaps having Paul particularly in mind.
11. Schmithals, *Office*, 21–95.
12. Ibid., 96–230.

the Hellenistic Christian mission context around Antioch.[13] This line of thought presupposes two things: (1) "two competing churches" or "Paul *versus* Peter" (or James as the head of the Jerusalem community) relationship at the time of Paul's mission[14] and (2) Antioch as the centre or birthplace of Pauline mission and theology.[15] However, this line of thought will not stand up in the light of certain important considerations.

First, it may be that the word ἀπόστολος is inextricably related to the mission context in Paul's thought.[16] But there is no confirming reason to believe that Paul's (or the Christian) concept of apostle *emerged* for the first time from the Hellenistic mission context in Antioch. Our available sources, Paul's own and Luke's, suggest that Paul's sense of apostolic calling was obtained through his Damascus experience of the revelation of the Son (Gal 1:15; Acts 9; 22; 26).[17] Even if we are careful not to confuse his sense of apostolic calling with his derivation of the use or conception of the word

---

13. Schnackenburg, "Apostles," 287–294. Cf. Räisänen, *Paul and the Law*, 251–263; Segal, *Paul the Convert*, 6–11, 26, 205, who argue that Paul's gentile mission was naturally taken for granted in the Gentile Christian "community" to which he joined.

14. For a recent argument in this direction see I. J. Elmer, *Paul, Jerusalem and the Judaisers: The Galatian Crisis in its Broadest Historical Context*, WUNT (Tübingen: Mohr Siebeck, 2009).

15. Among the scholars of the history-of-religions school particularly J. Becker, *Paulus: der Apostel der Völker* (Tübingen: Mohr Siebeck, 1989), 107f; W. Bousset, *Kyrios Christos: A History of the Belief in Christ from the Beginnings of Christianity to Irenaeus* (Nashville: Abingdon Press, 1970), 75. Cf. Hengel-Schwemer, *Between Damascus and Antioch*, 268–310, who emphatically reject this view.

16. Cf. Munck, "Paul," 100: "[t]he Christian apostles are part of something entirely new and dynamic in that the whole Christian religion is something to be spread abroad. It is not mere chance that this is stressed by a number of important terms: it is the gospel, the good news which must be announced (*kērysso*) by heralds . . . The word *apostolos* has been determined by this steady sending forth-the mission if one likes, so characteristic of Christianity."

17. The detailed implication of the Damascus experience to Paul regarding the revelation of the Son and Paul's sense of calling substantially varies according to scholars. However, the immediacy and the primary feature of the calling to be the apostle to the Gentiles in the Damascus Christophany are widely agreed: Stendahl, *Paul among Jews and Gentiles*, 7; Sanders, *Paul and Palestinian Judaism*, 152; Bruce, *Paul*, 75; Hengel-Schwemer, *Between Damascus and Antioch*, 47–50; Dunn, *Jesus, Paul and the Law*, 92; Kim, *Origin*, 57, 91–99; Kim, *Paul and the New Perspective*, 37–39; Barnett, *Paul*, 118–126. Contra A. Oepke and J. Rohde, *Der Brief des Paulus an die Galater* (5th ed; Berlin: Evangelisches, 1984), 33; W. D. Davies, "The Apostolic Age and the Life of Paul," in *Peake's Commentary on the Bible*, eds. H. H. Rowley and M. Black (London: T. Nelson, 1967), 874; B. Rigaux, *The Letters of St. Paul: Modern Studies* (Chicago: Franciscan Herald Press, 1968), 61; P. Gaechter, *Petrus und seine Zeit. Neutestamentliche Studien* (Innsbruck: Tyrolia-Verlag, 1958), 408–415.

ἀπόστολος,[18] it is likely that he entered the mission context and joined the community in Antioch with an already given apostolic identity. Some scholars have suggested that it is likely that Paul's visit to Arabia[19] and the return to Damascus (Gal 1:17) had a *mission purpose*.[20] So Paul's apostolic conception could have *interacted* with or even been *influenced* by that of the mission context or the community in Antioch (if there was one at all), but may have not *originated* from it.

Second, even if it is plausible to think that at the time of Paul's ministry in Asia and even in Macedonia and Achaia there was no uniform concept of apostleship,[21] otherwise, we would not have the situation in Paul's letters where people had doubt about Paul's apostleship and particularly in 2 Corinthians where Paul had to deal with the problem of "super-apostles"[22] and "false apostles."[23] Nevertheless, we certainly have an indication that for Paul apostleship is made possible through a *dominical connection* (1 Cor 9:1; 15:5–10). Peoples' doubts about Paul's apostleship were doubts about his dominical connection (e.g. the Corinthians' misguided perception of

---

18. Cf. Best, *Paul and His Converts*, 19.

19. For the related geographical identification issue see Riesner, *Paul's Early Period*, 256ff.

20. W. A. Meeks, *The First Urban Christians: The Social World of the Apostle Paul* (New Haven: Yale University, 1983), 10; Bruce, *Paul*, 81f; Oepke and Rohde, *Galater*, 62; Murphy-O'Connor, "Paul in Arabia," *CBQ* 55 (1993): 732–737; Hengel and Schwemer, *Between Damascus and Antioch*, 106–113. Cf. Riesner, *Paul's Early Period*, 258–260, who, while allowing the possibility of Paul's mission under the Jews living in the Nabataean territory, generally expresses doubts about Paul's mission in Arabia.

21. Cf. Hengel-Schwemer, *Between Damascus and Antioch*, 94.

22. I regard this expression as nothing more than the intruders' self–description or some Corinthians' appraisal of the intruders, the truth of which is not assumed by Paul as he made note of them. *Contra* M. E. Thrall, "Super-Apostles, Servants of Christ, and Servants of Satan," *JSNT* 6 (1980): 42–57, who argues that the "super-apostles" are no other than the primitive apostles in Jerusalem.

23. It seems to me that "false apostles" is Paul's own expression of his verdict on those "super-apostles," who are probably related to "false brothers" in 2 Cor 11:23 (cf. Gal 2:4) who disguised themselves as followers of Jesus or workers of Jesus (i.e. Messianic, but non-Christian – in Paul's perspective –, Jewish impeders of the Pauline gospel). See S. E. McClelland, "'Super-Apostles, Servants of Christ, and Servants of Satan': A Response," *JSNT* 14 (1982): 82–87. Cf. P. W. Barnett, "Opposition in Corinth," *JSNT* 22 (1984): 5, who plausibly suggests that ὑπερλίαν ἀποστόλων is Paul's deliberate sarcastic language which is reflected in his other ὑπερ-usages (10:14, 16; 12:7) which express criticism of the missionary imperialism of those intruders. *Contra* C. K. Barrett, "Paul's Opponents in II Corinthians," *NTS* 17 (1971): 233–254.

one's πρόσωπον as one's Χριστοῦ εἶναι in 2 Cor 10:7), and Paul's answer was also made in terms of it (Gal 1:1; 1:11–15; Rom 1:1).

The question of Paul's conception of apostle, then, is "which form or aspect of dominical connection does Paul appeal to or rely on for his apostolic claim?" This question is important, since it can be argued that apostleship is potentially open to anyone in Christ in all ages, insofar as those who are "in Christ" have a real dominical connexion at any rate (cf. Kirk's proposal of revelatory apostolic calling by the *ascended* Christ on a supra-historical basis[24] or Harnack's view of Providence of God who can freely choose anyone among those in Christ as apostle according to his own will[25]).

To this question, we propose an answer that Paul's apostolic conception stands on an *unmediated* dominical connection, understood in *historical* terms (i.e. apostolic calling as a historical and actual *event* rather than an ahistorical and theological *phenomenon*), which may not be repeated in time or transmitted to another person.[26] It must be noted that when Paul mentions apostles in terms of his "*belongingness*" to or "*independence*" from the apostles, he does appeal to *their history* (1 Cor 15:5, 7; Gal 1:17) along with *his own history* (1 Cor 15:8; Gal 1:15–16). This strongly indicates that Paul's apostolic self-conception is defined by the history of the pre and post-Easter Christ's appointment of his apostles, who were already to be found as a *history* in the church traditions (cf. παραδίδωμι / παραλαμβάνω in 1 Cor 15:1–3). And this sort of unmediatedness is, for Paul, not some kind of common trait to be shared with others in his missionary context in Antioch or elsewhere, but an exclusive quality having its decisive parallel in the OT tradition of the calling of the prophets (Gal 1:15), in the Jewish scriptural / traditional motif of the Isaianic eschatological heralds (Isa 41:27f; 52:7f, cf. 40:1–9; 61:1), and more importantly in the Jerusalem apostles (Gal 1:17–19), whose direct relationship to Christ is

---

24. Kirk, "Apostleship," 257.
25. Harnack, *Mission and Expansion*, 322.
26. The unmediated or charismatic nature of prophets and teachers (e.g. 1 Cor 12:28, cf. Eph 4:11) is unmistakable. However, it seems to me that for Paul what makes apostles different from other functionaries (despite similarlities in functions) is whether it is defined historically or ahistorically. This distinction according to historical significance may explain Paul's use of "apostles" in careful distinction from "διάκονοι" and "συνεργοί," despite their functional similarity. Cf. Hengel and Schwemer, *Between Damascus and Antioch*, 235.

naturally presupposed to be established already in the pre-Easter appointment / commission of the earthly Jesus (Luke 9, 10; Matt 10; Mark 6, cf. Matt 28; Luke 24).

If we are correct in the suggestion that Paul appealed to his dominical connection in terms of historical unmediatedness of this kind, then, Paul's conception of apostle probably had more to do with the earlier motifs of Jewish Palestinian origin rather than with thoughts developed in the Antiochene Hellenistic missionary context.

B.2. Ἀπόστολος Χριστοῦ and Jesus' שְׁלִיחִים

Those scholars who reject the connection of ἀπόστολος to the late Rabbinic convention of שְׁלִיח and attempt to find the origin of ἀπόστολος in Christian contexts other than the Jerusalem community do not provide a satisfactory explanation because of their highly unacceptable presuppositions. However, there is an alternative view maintaining the Christian provenance of ἀπόστολος by appealing to its *adaptation* of the concept from the OT and the Jewish sending convention which is expressed in the שׁלח/ἀποστέλλειν word group.[27]

It is to be noted that there are in the NT, even if it is rare, cases in which ἀπόστολος is used to refer to one who is sent in a general sense (John 13:16)[28] or more importantly in a non-dominical sense (2 Cor 8:23; Phil 2:25) by Paul himself.[29] This indicates that the early Christians used ἀπόστολος mostly in their totally new Christian perspective while maintaining its general and conventional sense as well. This general use may be taken to be of Jewish origin in which the root שׁלח in the OT gives the

---

27. J. B. Roloff, *Apostolat-Verkündigung-Kirche* (Gütersloh: Mohn, 1965), 9–15, 38–41, 272–274; Roloff, "Apostel/Apostolat/Apostolizität I. Neues Testament," in *Theologische Realenzyklopädie*, eds. G. Krause and G. Müller (Berlin: de Gruyter, 1978), 3, 432–433.

28. John interchangeably uses the verb ἀποστέλλω with πέμπω (e.g. John 1:6; 1:22; 3:17; 20:21, etc.). So, while John certainly means ἀπόστολος here of Jesus' disciples, he would have used the same noun for Jesus as well (cf. John 13:20; 20:21). Cf. Rengstorf, "ἀπόστολος," 421. The authenticity of the "sending" language (in Aramaic) on Jesus' lips is likely when the Israel-particularistic passages (Matt 10:2; 15:24) include such a language. Cf. B. Witherington, *The Christology of Jesus* (Minneapolis: Fortress Press, 1990), 124–125.

29. G. Schille, *Die urchristliche Kollegialmission* (Zürich: Zwingli-Verl, 1967), 13: F. Hahn, "Der Apostolat im Urchristentum: Seine Eigenart und seine Voraussetzungen," *KD* 20 (1974): 56.

specific sense of sending and being sent.[30] If we recognize this, it would be unnatural to regard Paul's technical Christian sense, as found on most occasions in his letters, as having a radically different sense or origin from that of the general use.[31] It is more likely that, with *a particular reason*, Paul's general Jewish conception of sending, which is naturally derived from scriptural and conventional[32] understanding of the שלח/ἀποστέλλειν word group, found a new way of application, namely the appellation of apostle in a solemn sense. Therefore, even if Rengstorf's theory of the "immediate" derivation of the Christian apostolate from the late Rabbinic convention of שליח cannot be proved, the Jewish background for Christian concept of apostle (perhaps, together with the later Rabbinic convention) is unmistakable.[33]

In this connection, we suggest that Paul's use of ἀπόστολος, regardless of its different levels of significance of meaning, does not necessarily show a radical divergence from the general Jewish sense of sending in order to bring a totally new Christian sense. As Gerhardsson correctly points out, a profound religious and theological sense always presupposes behind it a general juridical sense, and the apostles of God (or Christ) and the apostles of community are not far from each other.[34] Certainly Munck and Schmithals exaggerated the uniqueness of Christian use of ἀπόστολος in terms of mission distinguishing it from the general and juridical sense of שליח,[35] as a result they lost sight of the essential similarity. So, for Paul

---

30. Cf. Barnett, "Apostle," in *DPL*, 47, who suggests that Paul borrowed the idea from Jewish practice and applied it to his church; Witherington, *Christology*, 133, cites m. *Rosh Hash.* 1:3 and 4:9 speaking about pre-70 AD שליח with which the sending of the Twelve may be functionally identical; Harnack, *Mission and Expansion*, 327, has already suggested that even if Jewish officials bearing the title of apostle are unknown until 70 AD, it is very unlikely that no Jewish apostles previously existed before Christianity.

31. Cf. B. Gerhardsson, "Die Boten Gottes und die Apostel Christi," *SEÅ* 27 (1962): 89–131.

32. Paul's mention of accreditation letters (2 Cor 3:1ff) and Luke's description of Paul asking the high priest for that sort of letter (Acts 9:2) may indicate that Paul was familiar with the Jewish juridical practice of authorized sending with an accreditation letter. Cf. Hahn, "Apostolat," 64–65; Schille, *Kollegialmission*, 15–18.

33. Agnew, "Origin," 94.

34. Gerhardsson, "Apostel Christi," 109–110. Cf. n.9, n.10.

35. Munck, "Paul," 100: "The word apostolos has been determined by this steady sending forth-the mission if one likes, so characteristic of Christianity. Compared with this, the Jewish use of the apostolic idea is a rule as far removed from the Christian usage as a

ἀπόστολος simply denotes a *delegate* from a particular party. What makes Paul differentiate the level of use of the word is the party who sends the delegate. Therefore, for Paul there is no such concept as "*missionary* apostles"[36] since what makes one an apostle is not the function as missionary but the sender. If the Antiochene community would call any one an apostle, the apostle is not necessarily a missionary but a commissioned one (delegate) for a mission *by their church*. This conception is attested by Paul (2 Cor 8:23; Phil 2:24) and Luke (Acts 14:4, 14) where the apostles are the delegates of the Christian communities. But, when Paul mentions "apostle of Christ" it means a delegate appointed *by Christ in person*, given with his authority as opposed to a delegate appointed by man or men (cf. Gal 1:1).

Furthermore, if our suggestion is correct in that Paul's ἀπόστολος Χριστοῦ bears a general sense of delegate and what makes the delegate religiously and theologically solemn for Paul is Christ the sender, we may raise further questions as to whether Jesus ever had this concept of שליח/שליחים and applied it to himself and to his disciples.

Considering a number of the dominical traditions which are generally accepted as authentic (Mark 9:37; Matt 10:5, 40; 15:24; 18:5; Luke 4:18, 43; 9:48; John 12:44; 13:16, 20), it may be held that Jesus worked on the concept of שליח/שליחים regarding his own mission and his disciples' mission, even if it is difficult to decide whether the actual term was used.[37] Ben Witherington suggests that considering his sense of purpose and mission, Jesus certainly perceived himself as "the שליח of Yahweh" and understood his sending out of the disciples in terms of his שליחים.[38] If these considerations are sound, we cannot avoid the impression that ἀπόστολος Χριστοῦ in Paul's thought is strikingly similar to Jesus' שליחים.

---

diplomatic envoy is from a missionary to the heathen"; Schmithals, *Office*, 103–106.

36. *Pace* Schile, *Kollegialmission*, 56, who identifies the general category with "missionary apostles" to which he locates those of 1 Cor 15:7; Gal 1:17, 19, and those "false apostles" in e.g. 2 Cor 11:13; similarly H. D. Betz, "Apostle," *ABD* 1. 310, who sees Rom 16:7; Acts 13:2–4; 14:4, 14; 1 Thess 2:1–7 as the references to "missionary apostles"; Schnackenburg, "Apostles," 294–297, also reads "apostles of Christ" in 1 Thess 2:7 and 2 Cor 11:13c as "missionary apostles."

37. Cf. C. G. Kruse, "Apostle," in *DJG*, eds. J. B. Green, S. Mcknight, and I. H. Marshall (Leicester: IVP, 1992), 32–33. Cf. Rengstorf, "ἀπόστολος," 443–445.

38. Witherington, *Christology*, 124–127.

This observation is important for our particular discussion. Given our conclusion in the previous section that Paul knew the tradition of Christ's pre-Easter sending of his disciples in the form of a detailed tradition, we may suggest that the Jesus-tradition of mission instruction to the Twelve / Seventy (two) as the Messiah's שליחים certainly had influence on Paul in conceiving his apostolic self-conception expressed in ἀπόστολος Χριστοῦ.

APPENDIX C

The Scope of Apostles in Paul's Thought

C.1. The Question of the Scope of Apostles in Paul's Thought

According to scholars, Paul's understanding of the group of apostles is very elastic. Traditionally, Paul's concept of apostle was seen to consist of the Twelve plus Paul himself. However, since Lightfoot in an excursus to his commentary on Galatians suggested that Paul's concept of apostle is much wider than the narrow and rigid conception attributed to the Twelve,[1] the traditional view has lost its place in the academic discussion. Now we have generally three categorically different arguments about the scope of Paul's apostolic concept which may help our further discussion.

C.1.1. Paul's Apostleship as a Unique Category?

For G. Sass Paul's conception of apostle knows little more than the "individuality and uniqueness of Paul's eschatological-prophetic consciousness of his office" and there is "only one apostle who in unique sense, by God himself and by Christ, is determined to be an apostle, and that is Paul himself."[2] Even if Sass admits that Paul knew other apostles and their significance, he argues that Paul's missionary praxis and religious conviction "exclude the possibility that there could be even a single other apostle

---

1. Lightfoot, "The Name and Office of Apostle," in *St Paul's Epistle to the Galatians* (10th ed.; Grand Rapids: Zondervan, 1957 [1865]), 92–100.
2. G. Sass, *Apostelamt und Kirche*, (Munich: Kaiser, 1939), 113, 141.

beside himself (Paul) with the same tasks and authorizations from God as he himself possessed."[3] This view is shared with a number of scholars[4] and echoed by many by focusing on the unique (apocalyptic) eschatological nature of Paul and his ministry.[5] Paul's uniqueness in terms of eschatological and salvation historical significance is indeed essential for our discussion. Moreover, this view is useful to us in understanding Paul's apostolic self-conception as a historically oriented one rather than an ahistorical-functionary conception. Nevertheless, we do not accept taking Paul as the "supreme point" or "the second founder" of the primitive Christianity at the cost of οἱ πρὸ ἐμοῦ ἀπόστολοι (Gal 1:17) or οἱ λοιποὶ ἀπόστολοι (1 Cor 9:5). It is to be seen that Paul is best located *amongst* or *along with* other eschatological representatives of Jesus Christ, who initiated this eschatological apostolate for the restoration of Israel and its sequel salvation of mankind.[6] We will come back to this point later.

C.1.2. Paul, One among Many Christian Missionary Apostles Apart from the Twelve?

About a century ago, A. von Harnack surveyed the references in the NT and the early church Fathers to the word ἀπόστολος/ἀπόστολοι, concluding that in the primitive stage of the Christian church there were *two rival conceptions* of ἀπόστολος standing side by side: *a wider one* in which the number of apostles cannot be limited to the Twelve disciples of Jesus, and *a narrower one* that was created by Paul himself and does not allow any apostle other than the Twelve disciples of Jesus plus himself.[7] He suggested that in Paul the two conceptions were playing together, while Paul himself would remain in the former, later Christians gave prominence to

---

3. Ibid., 131.
4. See chapter 1, 3.2.2.
5. E.g. Käsemann, *Romans*, 306–307; E. Käsemann, "Justification and Salvation History in the Epistle to the Romans," in *Perspectives on Paul*, ed. E. Käsemann (Philadelphia: Fortress Press, 1971), 60–78; Sanders, *Palestinian Judaism*, 441–442; N. T. Wright, "The Paul of History and Apostle of Faith," *TB* 29 (1978): 61–88; P. R. Jones, "Paul the Last Apostle," *TB* 34 (1984): 3–34; Donaldson, *Paul*, 252.
6. Bowers, "Mission," 617.
7. Harnack, *Mission and Expansion*, 319–327, generally means "narrow conception of apostle" by "the circle of the Twelve," but he freely includes Paul in this conception when the early Fathers' use of ἀπόστολος/ἀπόστολοι is discussed.

the latter.[8] It would be redundant to cite the vast number of scholars who take this line of thought but with substantial divergence. However, what is generally agreed is that Paul did not belong to the apostolic category that described the Twelve alone, and there was an apostolic conception which was more encompassing and fluid than the rigid and narrow conception of the Twelve. The rigid or narrow conception of apostle is never to be seen as a dominical or the pre-Pauline conception, but at best as a development contemporary to or later than Paul.

This line of thought seems to be becoming something of a consensus for the discussion of the Christian apostolate. In its favour it may be seen as helping us make sense of Paul's unclear description of apostleship regarding the relationship of the Twelve with other figures (e.g. 1 Cor 9:1–6; 15:5–8; Gal 1:18–19).[9] Moreover, the unsettled stage in the development of the Christian conception of apostle may be seen as moving in this direction. Nevertheless, there are a number of considerations to take into account against this view.

This line of thought depends on the highly improbable view that the community which Paul initially joined developed a Christian mission theology and praxis in sharp contrast to that of the Jerusalem community. The necessary resultant thought of one apostolic concept struggling with another or stimulating the rise of a counter concept must remain in the realm of pure conjecture, unless such a conflict between the two churches is historically established. Then, one might suggest a development in Paul from a functional concept which Paul espoused at an early stage to a positional concept, or maybe from a wider concept to a narrower concept, while leaving or admitting many other apostles in the former category. However, such a conjecture will stand or fall according to how we read Paul's texts concerning how he sees (or addresses and describes) his other contemporary Christian missionaries or leaders; thus it remains open to debate. As Kirk points out, since Paul himself makes clear that the Twelve, or at least some of them, held a place and authority in the church which it would be impossible to account for on the grounds that Jerusalem borrowed it in a

---

8. Ibid., 327.
9. Cf. Kirk, "Apostleship," 257; Fee, *1 Corinthians*, 729.

counter spirit, there is no *a priori* reason for rejecting the development of the term from a more restricted to a more open sense.[10] Moreover, it turns out to be a weak suggestion since its natural connection to a functional conception of apostleship[11] turns out to be non-Pauline when it is compared with Paul's understanding of his own apostleship in terms of a *historically understood* apostleship. We will examine this in more detail below.

C.1.3. Paul, One of the Apostles Commissioned by the Risen Lord, Who Can Elect Apostles Even Today?

For Kirk, 1 Corinthians 15:5 and Galatians 1:17–19; 2:1–10 are sufficient evidence that Paul certainly recognized the special place of the Twelve as apostles in the primitive Jerusalem Christian community,[12] and that the origin of the term apostle derives from the first mission of the Twelve in the ministry of Christ.[13] However, Kirk believes that Paul's recognition of the Twelve as the primitive apostles does not create any distinction from later individuals (e.g. Paul himself, James, Barnabas and so on) whom Paul *broadly* recognizes as apostles according to their special commission by the Lord and their concomitant fruits of ministry since "the difference was based, not so much on dogmatic consideration as on different historical circumstances."[14] On this basis Kirk rejects the common presumption that Paul's *broad concept* of apostle differs from that of Luke, since each writer is faithful to the concept of apostle which is in continuity with the *sense of the apostolic commission by the Risen Christ* and which is discontinuous with the sense of *timing and form of the commission*, and therefore he can expects the same apostolic ministry in differing historical circumstances even today.[15]

---

10. Kirk, "Apostleship," 253, n.5. Cf. Barrett, *1 Corinthians*, 341.

11. Cf. Fee, *1 Corinthians*, 30, 174, who suggests that Paul's usage of ἀπόστολος is both functional and positional (official).

12. Kirk, "Apostleship," 257. *Contra* Schmithals, *Office*, 21–95; Munck, "Paul," 102–103.

13. Kirk, "Apostleship," 260.

14. Ibid.

15. Ibid., 264.

This view certainly has a merit since it remedies the improbable scepticism on the pre-Pauline nature of the apostolate of the Twelve.[16] However, Kirk makes Paul's apostolic conception ahistorical and his apostolic authority in the church "relative."[17] Moreover, even if Kirk recognizes a conflict between the "eschatological nature of apostleship" in the primitive stage which is linked with the consciousness of the imminence of the end-time and the "functional concept" which scholars tend to regard as the most primitive form of apostle(s),[18] he erroneously synthesizes or harmonizes the conflict between them (i.e. eschatological vs functional) in terms of "continuity" in the sense of supra-historical revelatory apostolic calling, into which he categorizes Paul's (and Luke's as well) apostolic concept.[19] This view is exactly opposite in scope to that of G. Sass and requires from us the same response that Paul must be located among those eschatological apostles to whom historical significance is firmly attached (1 Cor 15:5–8). Moreover, his highly functional view on Paul's apostleship[20] begs the question whether it is really coming from Paul himself.

C.2. Paul's Use of the Appellation Apostle

Given this preliminary discussion, now we go on to discuss Pauline apostle-passages where scholars see the postulated broad understanding of apostles in Paul's thought.

---

16. One example of improbable scepticism is Mosbech, "Apostolos," 191, who suggests that Paul's technical term apostle was first invented by Paul during the discussion with those of Jerusalem and then taken over by the twelve.

17. Barnett, "Apostle," 46.

18. Kirk, "Apostleship," 257.

19. Ibid., 256–259, 264.

20. Ibid., 261: "for Paul apostleship is proved, not by any exclusive claim, but by the fruits of those who exercise it."

C.2.1. Andronicus and Junia(s) (Rom 16:7)[21]

With many other modern exegetes,[22] Schnackenburg, though he argues that ἐπίσημοι ἐν τοῖς ἀποστόλοις can be rendered as "well known among the group of apostles" as it does not necessarily mean that they are apostles, concludes that in Romans 16:7 Paul introduces Andronicus and Junia(s) to the Roman congregation as ones who belonged to a group of apostles.[23] And he takes this exegesis as evidence to indicate Paul's different concept of apostle from the tradition he received and mentioned in 1 Corinthians 15:7–9:

> Andronicus and Junias, therefore, belonged to a group a group of "apostles" who were early and recognized heralds of the gospel, *without being able to lay claim to an appearance of the Risen Lord*. Paul grants them the designation "apostle," certainly not just because of his own understanding of apostleship, but also he had found this concept already present in the church. We may assume that this way of speaking of "apostles" was widespread among the Hellenistic Christian congregations, as also among the Jewish Christians of the Diaspora.[24]

Of course, Paul's use of substantives (adjectives and nouns) combined with the construction of "ἐν + a group of people" could be taken in two ways: (1) the person with the substantive belongs to the party of the ἐν construction

---

21. For a brief history of the debate on Rom 16:7 see M. H. Burer and D. B. Wallace, "Was Junia Really an Apostle? A Re-examination of Rom 16.7," *NTS* 47/1 (2001): 76–91.

22. Harnack, *Mission and Expansion*, 321; Ellis, "Co-Workers," 437–452; Barnett, "Apostle," 48; Cranfield, *Romans*, 2. 789; Moo, *Romans*, 924; Dunn, *Romans 9–16*, 894–895; Morris, *Romans*, 534; R. Bauckham, *Gospel Women: Studies of the Named Women in the Gospels* (London: T. & T. Clark, 2002), Fitzmyer, *Romans*, 739–740; Witherington, *Romans*, 390; Dickson, *Mission-Commitment*, 137, n.9; L. Belleville, "'Ἰουνιᾶν . . . ἐπίσημοι ἐν τοῖς ἀποστόλοις: A Re-examination of Romans 16.7 in Light of Primary Source Materials," *NTS* 51 (2005): 231–249; E. J. Epp, *Junia: The First Woman Apostle* (Minneapolis: Fortress Press, 2005). Scholars who do not maintain the apostleship of the two include E. H. Gifford, *The Epistle of St. Paul to the Romans: With Notes and Introduction* (London: William Clowes & Sons, 1886), 232; C. Hodge, *Commentary on the Epistle to the Romans* (Grand Rapids: Eerdmans, 1886), 449; Lenski, *Romans*, 906–907; J. Murray, *The Epistle to the Romans: The English Text with Introduction, Exposition and Notes, II* (Grand Rapids: Eerdmans, 1965), 230; Burer and Wallace, "Junia," 76–91; D. K. Huttar, "Did Paul Call Andronicus an Apostle in Romans 16:7?" *JETS* 52, no. 4 (2009): 747–778.

23. Schnackenburg, "Apostles," 293.

24. Ibid., 294 (my emphasis).

(e.g. 1 Cor 6:5; 11:30), and (2) the person with the substantive belongs to another party other than the party of the of the ἐν construction (e.g. 2 Cor 2:15). Paul could mean either (1) or (2) in the case of Romans 16:7. Then, Schnackenburg's argument for the Antiochene origin of Pauline apostolic conception may stand and collapse according to which exegesis of Romans 16:7 is to be taken. Our suggestion is that Romans 16:7 belongs to the case (2).

First, Paul's adjective ἐπίσημος here is used substantively (as predicative rather than attributive) and naturally linked with the previous substantives συγγενής (adjective) and συναιχμάλωτος (noun). Then, Paul's literary weight is laid on the adjective itself as carrying a substantive force (as "well known ones") rather than the qualifier ἐν τοῖς ἀποστόλοις. The qualifier may simply function to denote a passive perception of the information by the apostles: "to the apostles" or "in the eyes of the apostles."[25] If Paul wanted to mean "distinctive apostles" (i.e. to make ἐπίσημος carry attributive force), οἵτινές εἰσιν οἱ ἐπίσημοι ἀπόστολοι would have been more natural wording.[26]

Second, if Paul wanted to make the point of the two being apostles, it is rather an odd word order with him putting it later than his kinsmenship and the shared imprisonment experience. Moreover, in the list of the persons whom Paul wanted the Romans to greet, the two apostles

---

25. The NT use of ἐν + dative is rarely used to mean "by" (e.g. 2 Thess 1:10; Heb 1:1). The adjective ἐπίσημος is a word of perception which presupposes a perceptor. Then, it is natural to read ἐν τοῖς ἀποστόλοις as "in the apostles' perception" (cf. εὐωδία which is perceived in two ways ἐν τοῖς σῳζομένοις καὶ ἐν τοῖς ἀπολλυμένοις in 2 Cor 2:15).

26. Cf. Burer and Wallace, "Junia," who suggest to distinguish an "implied comparative sense" and an "elative sense" according to different adjuncts which modify ἐπίσημος: ἐπίσημος + genitive substantives as carrying implied comparative sense (e.g. Ἐλεαζαρος δέ τις ἀνὴρ ἐπίσημος τῶν ἀπὸ τῆς χώρας ἱερέων: Then a certain Eleazar, famous among the priests of the country in 3 Mac 6:1) and ἐπίσημος + ἐν datives genitive substantive as carrying elative sense (e.g. οἱ υἱοὶ καὶ αἱ θυγατέρες ἐν αἰχμαλωσίᾳ πονηρᾷ ἐν σφραγῖδι ὁ τράχηλος αὐτῶν ἐν ἐπισήμῳ ἐν τοῖς ἔθνεσιν: the sons and the daughters in painful captivity their neck in a seal were *a spectacle* among the Gentiles in *Pss. Sol.* 2:6). The point seems to agree with our alternative reading 2). However, this argument is weak. For example, they read ἐν ἐπισήμῳ ἐν τοῖς ἔθνεσιν in *Pss. Sol.* 2:6 as "a spectacle among the Gentiles" and suggest that the datives ἐν τοῖς ἔθνεσιν which follow the adjective ἐπίσημος can never be identical with οἱ υἱοὶ καὶ αἱ θυγατέρες or ὁ τράχηλος αὐτῶν and this lends support rendering Rom 16:7 in a similar way. But it is more plausible, as LXE *Pss. Sol.* 2:6; 17:30, suggest, to take ἐν ἐπισήμῳ as missing τόπῳ to mean a "conspicuous place," which has nothing to do with the status of the sons and the daughters (cf. LXE 1 Macc 11:37, 14:48).

(if they were) are listed after five other people.²⁷ In the light of Paul's emphatic mentioning of the apostleship which was given to apostles in God's *Heilsplan* in which the Romans were also called to belong to Jesus Christ (Rom 1:1–6), the third position in one's character and the sixth position in the list of important persons are difficult to explain. Again, if Paul had meant that the two were apostles, οἳ καὶ πρὸ ἐμοῦ γέγοναν ἐν Χριστῷ is redundant, since the apostles were always in Christ before Paul was (Gal 1:17, cf. 1 Cor 15:8).

Given these considerations, we may infer that Andronicus and Junia(s) were a Jewish Christian couple²⁸ of Hellenistic background who were staying in Jerusalem in the earliest times making themselves distinctive from other Christians in sharing the gospel and serving the church. Later on, perhaps with the persecution on Hellenists, they were dispersed from Jerusalem taking it as their opportunity to serve the Lord even at the cost of imprisonment. Further inference would be too imaginative.

Therefore, Schnackenburg's conclusion that Andronicus and Junia were missionary apostles in Antioch is not derived from the passage in question but rather from his assumption that the Christians in Antioch already had the appellation "apostles" for their recognized missionaries. He takes Luke's use of ἀπόστολοι (Acts 14:4, 14) as possible evidence for his theory.²⁹ But this case probably does not support his view, since Luke uses it for Paul and Barnabas only. We do not know any more concerning the title apostle apart from the two in Luke. Perhaps, Luke's use of ἀπόστολοι in the Antiochene mission context suggests a certain usage of ἀπόστολοι in the church in Antioch not necessarily in Schnackenburg's terms (i.e. missionary apostles) but in accordance with that of the Jerusalem church in which they had an Aramaic or Hebrew term for delegates (i.e. שליחים).³⁰ As Kirk rightly

---

27. Cf. Bauckham *Gospel Women*, 181, who suggests that before mentioning the others Paul first mentions those of "special personal significance to himself owing to their role in his Aegean mission."

28. Cf. R. R. Schulz, "Romans 16:7: Junia or Junias?" *ExpT* 98 (1987): 108–110. Even if the gender of Junia(s) does not affect our discussion, I am convinced that Ἰουνίαν is the accusative of Ἰουνία a woman's name: henceforth, not Junia(s) but Junia.

29. Schnackenburg, "Apostles," 294.

30. Note that in Acts 13:1ff it is not Barnabas and Saul who received the command of the Spirit but the group of the leaders in the Antiochene church (v. 2). Moreover, it was not the Spirit that sent the two but the group (ἀπέλυσαν, v. 3). The context itself makes it

observes, it is unlikely that a mainly Hellenistic congregation took a Greek word (ἀπόστολος) with a very different usage from their own convention using it for their own purpose in a truly creative and unique sense.[31] It is more likely that the abruptness has come about by translating a Jewish concept with an approximately equivalent Greek word. In this light we may infer that in Antioch ἀπόστολοι was the approximate equivalent for the שליחים of the Jerusalem church (cf. Gal 2:12; Acts 15:27–33) or of their own community (Acts 14:4, 14).[32] Then, ἀπόστολοι in Luke's description of Paul and Barnabas' mission under the Antiochene church's commission (laying hands and sending away) may be explained in this way. Paul's own, a rather striking, use of ἀπόστολος in connection with the brothers sent with Titus (2 Cor 8:23) and with Epaphroditus (Phil 2:25) may support our suggestion (a general use of ἀπόστολος as the rendering of שליח).[33]

For the moment, regarding Romans 16:7, we may conclude that Paul neither talks about Andronicus and Junia as his fellow apostles nor does he allude to the concept of missionary apostles to which he belongs, even if he can speak elsewhere of *apostles of church* apart from *apostles of Christ*.

C.2.2. Silvanus and Timotheus (1 Thess 2:7)

In the first letter to the Thessalonians, Paul, Silvanus and Timotheus are co-senders of the epistle. In 2:7 the co-senders are qualified with Χριστοῦ ἀπόστολοι. This has been one reason for many to maintain that "us, apostles of Christ" including Silvanus and Timotheus indicate Paul's broad understanding of apostleship. Schnackenburg takes up the plural as "real" to argue for his "Antiochene apostleship" (missionary apostles) which he wants to attribute to recognized missionaries, regardless of them seeing the risen Lord; he identifies the first person plural in 2 Corinthians 1:19 (the proclamation "through us") which includes Timotheus (who was Paul's

---

clear that Barnabas and Saul were in a sense the apostles of the church.

31. Kirk, "Apostleship," 259.

32. Cf. C. K. Barrett, "Shaliah and Apostle," in *Donum Gentilicium: New Testament Studies in Honour of David Daube*, eds. E. Bammel, C. K. Barrett and W. D. Davies (Oxford: Oxford University Press, 1978), 99.

33. Moo, *Romans*, 924, suggests that Paul calls Andronicus and Junia apostles in the general sense; so Witherington, *Romans*, 390. However, it is less likely that Paul does so, since the case is not specific as it is in 2 Cor 8:23 and Phil 2:25 (i.e. "of the churches" and "of yours").

co-preacher of the gospel but not one who had seen the Risen Lord) with that of 1 Thessalonians 2:7.³⁴ However, can this first person plural and the single instance of Χριστοῦ ἀπόστολοι testify that in Paul's view each person of Silvanus and Timotheus was an apostle of Christ as such Paul was (1 Cor 1:1; 2 Cor 1:1; Gal 1:1f)?

C.2.2.1. Timothy

Regarding Timothy, it has been widely agreed that it is difficult to include him in the group of Christ's apostles. Ellis observes his subordinate relationship to Paul and denies his apostleship.³⁵ Masson points to that in the later passage of 1 Thessalonians 3:2, when Paul sends Timothy alone, he avoids using ἀπόστολος but chooses, to call Timothy, ἀδελφός καὶ συνεργός.³⁶ Similarly, G. L. Green, pointing to 2 Corinthians 1:1, Philippians 1:1, and Colossians 1:1 where Timothy is never designated an apostle, suggests that Paul does not attribute the title of apostle to Timothy in 1 Thessalonians 2:7.³⁷ A similar observation is given by Harnack: "[i]n the greetings of the Thessalonian and Philippian epistles Paul does not call himself an apostle, since he is associating himself with Timothy, who is never given this title (1 Thess ii. 7 need not be taken as referring to him)."³⁸ This may be an important point to consider for our discussion. If Paul regarded Timothy as an apostle of Christ, then why did he need different designations ἀδελφός and συνεργός apart from ἀπόστολος to refer to him alone in the same letter?³⁹ Were ἀδελφός and συνεργός synonymous with ἀπόστολος for Paul?⁴⁰ Conversely, if Paul could call himself συνεργός (along

---

34. Schnackenburg, "Apostles," 294–295. See E. J. Richard, *First and Second Thessalonians* (Collegeville: The Liturgical Press, 1995), 109–110; E. Best, *The First and Second Epistles to the Thessalonians*, BNTC (London: Black, 1986), 99–100; F. F. Bruce, *1 and 2 Thessalonians*, WBC (Waco: Word Books, 1982), 31; Dickson, *Mission-Commitment*, 91, n.19.

35. Ellies, "Co-Workers," 439, n.5

36. C. Masson, *Les deux épîtres de saint Paul aux Thessaloniciens* (Paris: Delachaux & Niestle, 1957) cited in Schnackenburg, "Apostles," 294. n.2.

37. Green, *Thessalonians*, 126.

38. Harnack, *Mission and Expansion*, 321, n.4, my emphasis.

39. Cf. Ellis, "Co-Workers," 440–441, 445.

40. Paul only once referred to himself as an συνεργός in 1 Cor 3:9 and never used ἀδελφός for himself.

with Apollos)⁴¹ in the first letter to the Corinthians and could call himself by a number of designations elsewhere in his letters (e.g. 1 Cor 3:5; Rom 1:1; Phlm 17), then why did he continuously appeal to none other than the title ἀπόστολος when he spoke about his own ministerial authority? Therefore, we are clear that ἀδελφός and συνεργός and any other designation for Pauline co-workers cannot replace ἀπόστολος (Χριστοῦ). Even if Paul may call Timothy as an ἀπόστολος, the term would not refer to the same apostleship that Paul was often compelled to defend. It seems probable that, on the one hand, Paul preferred other designations than apostle when identifying himself with fellow Christian workers, who shared his work. On the other hand, he reserved the word ἀπόστολος confining it to a number of Christians who had been commissioned by the Lord *in person*.

Therefore, it is reasonable to think that Paul had not Timothy in mind when he referred to Χριστοῦ ἀπόστολοι, even if Timothy was obviously a recognized gospel-herald among the church,⁴² since he had not received the apostolic calling directly from the Lord in the way all the apostles, in Paul's conception, had received it.⁴³

C.2.2.2. Silvanus, שליח from the Jerusalem Church

What, then, about Silvanus? For those scholars who argue for the Antiochene conception of apostle (i.e. missionary apostles) he is counted as an apostle since, for them, Silvanus was a *missionary* in the Antiochene or Syrian mission context.⁴⁴ For others, he was already an apostle within the group of earlier⁴⁵ or higher⁴⁶ apostles. However, Silvanus' designation "apostle" by Paul may be explained otherwise.

Given the discussion above, it is likely that since Paul was familiar with the Jewish convention of שליח he could refer to church delegates (שליחים)

---

41. We do not suggest that Paul regarded Apollos as an apostle. We will discuss this point later.

42. *Contra* Dickson, *Mission-Commitment*, 91–92, 137, who concludes that ἀπόστολος for Paul connotes "one sent / commissioned" for the gospel regardless of source or origin of commission. Dickson certainly fails to recognize the huge importance of unmediatedness of calling in Paul overemphasizing the importance of "authorization."

43. See Wanamaker, *Thessalonians*, 99–100.

44. Typically Schnackenburg, "Apostles," 295.

45. Ollrog, *Mitarbeiter*, 19.

46. Dunn, *Romans 9–16*, 895.

such as Silvanus with the Greek word ἀπόστολος. This conjecture may be supported by the two instances where Paul uses the word when he refers to "the two brothers" as ἀπόστολοι ἐκκλησιῶν in 2 Corinthians 8:23 and to Epaphroditus, ὑμῶν ἀπόστολος in Philippians 2:25, while his apostleship is always qualified with "of Christ" in many cases or in Galatians 1:1 "neither from man nor through men" (to be sure "men" in the sense of "not by the church")[47]. In this sense, Paul's use of ἀπόστολος for Silvanus is rather natural even if his own apostleship may often be described differently. Luke's description of Silas (no doubt identical with "Silvanus" in Paul's letters) may support our suggestion. Acts tells us that Silas was one of the "leading men" (ἄνδρες ἡγουμένους) together with Judas Barsabas, and was chosen to be sent for the task of delivering a letter from the Jerusalem church to the church in Antioch (Acts 15:22–24). Here the picture of Silas (and Barsabas) being sent by the Jerusalem church to the church in Antioch reminds one of the practice in the Jewish convention of שליח. Even if Luke tells us that Silas was also a "prophet" so he exhorted (παρεκάλεσαν) the brethren in the Antioch church, the exhortation was not Silas' main task. Luke's general description of Silas' (and Barsabas') task at least in Antioch is not of being heralds of the gospel[48] but of being representatives of the Jerusalem Christian community. His main task with regard to the Antiochene church was "letter bearing" which was one of the common tasks of שליחים.[49]

It is difficult to think, thought not impossible, that the Greek word ἀπόστολοι in the sense of שליחים was used in the Jerusalem Jewish Christian community to refer to their delegates such as Silas and Barsabas. Luke's non-use of the word may indicate the linguistic situation in the community. However, it is reasonable to think that the community in Antioch needed a suitable Greek designation to refer to the two שליחים from Jerusalem. It is not impossible that the Jewish Christian leaders (cf. Acts 13:1) did not

---

47. Rengstorf, "ἀπόστολος," 441–442, who suggests that the church in Gal 1:1 is the Antioch church, and the man may be Barnabas. Cf. Longenecker, *Galatians*, 4, who takes the expression as referring to the Jerusalem church and the "apostles" there.

48. Cf. Acts 15:35: Paul and Barnabas' ministry as heralds of the gospel in Antioch is described as "διδάσκοντες καὶ εὐαγγελιζόμενοι."

49. Rengstorf, "ἀπόστολος," 417, talks about Paul's role in Acts 9:1ff as one of שליחים who were commissioned by a sending community to be representatives and bearers of letter of accreditation or communication.

bother to pick up a new word for שליחים other than ἀπόστολοι, which was already in the tradition a designation for those who were commissioned to be the gospel-heralds by the Lord, to refer to Silas and Barsabas who were also commissioned by the "church of God" in Jerusalem. Perhaps, since the Antiochene Christians had no confusion or dispute concerning one's apostleship, distinguishing designations with qualifiers such as ἀπόστολοι ἐκκλησιῶν (Ἱεροσολύμων) (cf. 2 Cor 8:23) and ἀπόστολοι Χριστοῦ (e.g. 1 Cor 1:1; 2 Cor 1:1) was not so necessary in the community.

For this reason, even if Paul had in mind a clear conceptual distinction between the apostles of Christ (i.e. delegates appointed by Christ in person) and the apostles (שלוחים) of the Jerusalem church, when Paul wrote the letter to the Thessalonians he was not very careful in the use of a qualifying genitive "Χριστοῦ" – at a later time he will have used with a greater care (e.g. 1 Cor 1:1) –, and so he freely included Silvanus and Timothy his mission companions under his solemn title the apostles of Christ.[50] Sometime later, when Paul, in the face of challenges to his apostleship, had to refer to "apostles before me" (Gal 1:17, 19) or "all the apostles" (1 Cor 15:7) to which he belongs, he would not have intended to include Silvanus or other church delegates who were also missionaries. We conclude that ἀπόστολοι in Antioch was not a designation for missionary apostles as many scholars argue, but for church delegates (cf. Acts 14:4, 14) whose conception was not of Antiochene origin but from Jerusalem or Palestine.

C.2.3. Apollos (1 Cor 3:5–4:13)

Apollos has often been taken as an evidence for Paul's wider or functional conception of apostle.[51] When one considers Paul's use of διάκονοι[52] (1 Cor

---

50. Barnett, "Apostle," 49, correctly suggests that at the time of Paul's composition of his letters to the Thessalonians there was no hint of Paul's apostleship being in dispute, he sees this as the reason for Paul to feel "free to bracket Silvanus and Timothy with himself on equal terms and to include them with him as 'apostles of Christ'".

51. E.g. Fee, *1 Corinthians*, 174; Ellis, "Co-Workers," 445, n.1. Cf. Harnack, *Mission and Expansion*, 321, n.4: "Apollos, too, is never called an apostle." Harnack also cites *1 Clem.* 47: 4 which discriminates Apollos as "δεδοκιμασμένος" from the two highly reputed apostles Cephas and Paul (Harnack, *Mission and Expansion*, 325).

52. Paul can use διάκονος to refer to either one who is in service of God's purpose or evil purpose (Rom 13:4: secular Gentile rulers; Rom 15:8, Gal 2:17 (negatively): Christ; Rom 16:1; 1 Cor 3:5; 2 Cor 3:6; 6:4; 11:23; Eph 3:7; 6:21; Phil 1:1; Col 1:7, 23, 25; 4:7; 1 Tim 3:8, 12; 4:6. Cf. 2 Cor 11:15: διάκονοι Σατανᾶν.

3:5) and συνεργοί (v. 9) in an equal fashion to refer to both Paul and Apollos, it looks as if Paul uses the two terms to describe the same quality for the workers of God in difficult service (κόπος and διακονία) for the Corinthians' faith.[53] The two terms strongly suggest that Paul and Apollos belong to the same category of specialized Christians in the service of preaching and teaching of the gospel. Numerous commentators' reading of the ambiguously abbreviated δι' ὧν ἐπιστεύσατε, καὶ ἑκάστῳ ὡς ὁ κύριος ἔδωκεν (v. 5b) as "through us (διάκονοι: Paul and Apollos) as God gave to each [task of διάκονος] you came to faith" seems to strengthen the impression of "equality" between Paul and Apollos as God-appointed ministers.[54] Moreover, regarding the subject and the purpose of Paul's argument, τίς οὖν ἐστιν Παῦλος, τίς δὲ Ἀπολλώς (3:5) and μετεσχημάτισα εἰς ἐμαυτὸν καὶ Ἀπολλὼ δι' ὑμᾶς (4:6), we have a strong impression that Paul includes Apollos in apostles when he mentions ἡμᾶς τοὺς ἀποστόλους ἐσχάτους (v. 9). So, do all these considerations point to Apollos' apostleship in Paul's view? Other important considerations veto Apollos' apostleship.

First, we need to ask what made Paul pick up the two other words apart from the straightforward ἀπόστολοι. It may be answered, as we have discussed already in the case of Timotheus, that Paul had no reason to call Apollos an apostle. It is likely that on the one hand, Paul could include himself in the designation διάκονοι together with Apollos since the nature of their works was identical, but on the other hand, he could not include Apollos in ἀπόστολοι. Even if E. E. Ellis admits Apollos' apostleship on the basis of an unlikely inference,[55] he rightly elucidates what makes Paul fail to use ἀπόστολος for Apollos:

> Just as diakonoi were a special class of workers, so "apostles" probably were regarded by Paul as a special class of diakonoi. Accordingly, they do the same work, preaching and teaching,

---

53. Ellis, "Co-Workers," 440–441.
54. Fee, *1 Corinthians*, 131.
55. Ellis, "Co-Workers," 445, n.1. He suggests Paul's functional conception of apostle by taking "us apostles of the last" in 1 Cor 4:9 as including Apollos, and Apollos' apostleship on the basis on Christ's pre-resurrection commission "in the style of those in Luke ix.59; x.1."

as the diakonoi, and Paul can, with reference to his apostolic labours, refer to himself as a diakonos.[56]

Second, against most commentators, a more natural reading of δι' ὧν ἐπιστεύσατε, καὶ ἑκάστῳ ὡς ὁ κύριος ἔδωκεν (3:5b) is "through us (διάκονοι: Paul and Apollos) you came to faith as God gave to each [of you Corinthians]." In other words ἑκάστῳ ὡς ὁ κύριος ἔδωκεν refers to "the faith" which was given to the Corinthians by God rather than to "the task" which was given to Apollos and Paul by God. This reading is strongly supported by the fact that Paul is now simply comparing their *mere mediatory role* as human agents compared to God and redirecting the misleading (or misled) Corinthians' perspective from man to God, the ultimate source of the grace of faith.[57] Paul's point here is that it is not the workers but God who gave the Corinthians the faith, thus the veneration either of Apollos or Paul is wrong! Paul never gives us any impression of "equality" between Apollos and himself as διάκονοι. The comparison is made between God and mere human agents but not at all between the two human agents. Moreover, regarding συνεργοί (3:9), there is no clear indication that Apollos is a co-worker "with" Paul, but it is explicit that each of them is respectively co-worker *with God*.[58] In Paul's two sentences, the two common designations are not intended to talk about their equal status or authority but only about the respective nature of their work for the Corinthians.

Third, we must consider the context of 1 Corinthians 1:10–4:21 in which Paul deals with a very sensitive issue (i.e. veneration of human wisdom to which the message of the cross stands opposed, misled adherence to Apollos at the cost of Paul, and party spirit) in a very unpredictable situation. In this situation, it is very reasonable to expect one like Paul

---

56. Ibid., 444–445.
57. Fee, *1 Corinthians*, 132.
58. Cf. 1 Thess 3:2; 2 Cor 6:1; Rom 16:3; Phil 1:24. See H. Conzelmann, *1 Corinthians: A Commentary on the First Epistle to the Corinthians* (Philadelphia: Fortress Press, 1975), 74–75; J. A. Fitzmyer, *1 Corinthians* (New Haven: Yale University Press, 2008), 195–196. *Contra* Barrett, *1 Corinthians*, 86; Bruce, *1 and 2 Corinthians* (London: Oliphants, 1971), 43; A. C. Thiselton, *First Corinthians: A Shorter Exegetical and Pastoral Commentary* (Grand Rapids: Eerdmans, 2006), 63; R. B. Hays, *First Corinthians* (Louisville: John Knox Press, 1997), 52–53; Banks, *Paul's Idea*, 159–160. If Paul wanted to point to synergic relationship between Paul and Apollos as co-workers for God, he would have put it like Rom 16:3, "τοὺς συνεργούς μου ἐν Χριστῷ Ἰησοῦ."

who was a skillful writer to be very careful in composing his sentences. In this connection, D. P. Ker's study on the relationship between Paul and Apollos is suggestive.[59] According to him when Paul refers to Apollos in 1 Corinthians 3 Paul does not only have in his mind Apollos and his misled adherents as the main problem of the Corinthian division (which is not unrelated to the issue of wisdom revolving around the comparison between Paul and Apollos) and as his main target of attack, but is also well aware that he must be careful in referring to Apollos who was highly esteemed by many among the congregation because an open criticism of Apollos may lead the volatile situation to backfire.[60]

It may be a false accusation against Paul if one suggests that his aim in the passages in question is simply a strategically hidden criticism of his rival. Nevertheless, Paul's nuanced attitude towards Apollos is unmistakable. This may explain why Paul does not start by explicitly comparing or differentiating himself and Apollos, but rather with the *nuanced* designation of διάκονοι and συνεργοί in response to his own rhetorical questions "Τί οὖν ἐστιν Ἀπολλῶς; τί δέ ἐστιν Παῦλος?" (1 Cor 3:5, 9). In this understanding of 1 Corinthians 3 and 4, it turns out to be that even if Paul uses first person plurals including Apollos, the logic towards Apollos is not always inclusive.

Rather it is carefully arranged – in order to avoid any unnecessary division which Paul has rebuked previously – to carry an "implicitly differentiating effect" particularly in the unclear section of 4:1–9. Even if ἡμᾶς in verse 1 is to be considered to definitely refer to general Christian leaders (ὑπηρέτας καὶ οἰκονόμοι) who are to be found faithful, to whom Apollos is naturally included, and Paul explicitly mentions Apollos pairing with himself in verse 6, the first person plurals play little part here and cannot hide Paul's exclusive attitude towards Apollos, since Paul immediately turns his focus from οἰκονόμοι to himself (ἐμοὶ δὲ in v. 3) and his prime argument

---

59. D. P. Ker, "Paul and Apollos-Colleagues or Rivals?" *JSNT* 77 (2000): 75–97. Cf. J. F. M. Smit, "'What Is Apollos? What Is Paul?' In Search for the Coherence of First Corinthians 1:10–4:21," *NovT* 44, no. 3 (2002): 231–251, who generally agrees with Ker.

60. Ker, "Paul and Apollos," 84. Whether the other Christ party and Cephas party were the actual objects of Paul's polemic is open to debate. However, considering that Paul resumes mentioning Cephas and Christ only after 3:22ff, it seems that Paul cites the two in order to soften his attack on Apollos party.

is not about quality required in οἰκονόμοι in general but is making other points: (1) the Corinthians' negative judgment on Paul (by implication in comparison with Apollos) was not made by faithfulness but by human wisdom, thus is irrelevant and unjustifiable (4:3–5). (2) Paul's figurative explanations regarding Paul and Apollos (i.e. gardening and building imageries in chapter 3)[61] are intended to teach the Corinthians not to forget the scriptural lesson (τὸ μὴ ὑπὲρ ὃ γέγραπται φρονεῖν) that God is going to turn their comparative evaluations of wisdom and folly upside down (1:19; 3:19–20)[62] so that they must stop their misguided boast in human wisdom in support of Apollos at the cost of Paul (μὴ εἷς ὑπὲρ τοῦ ἑνὸς φυσιοῦσθε κατὰ τοῦ ἑτέρου).[63] If this reading is correct, then it is very unlikely that Paul, when he speaks about ἡμᾶς τοὺς ἀποστόλους ἐσχάτους in 4:9 in a very depressed picture (4:9–13) and in a different mood from 4:8, would include Apollos, the venerated one by those puffed up whereas the apostles are *suffering* and *lowered*.

Moreover, Paul seems to imply that Apollos belongs among the Corinthians' numerous tutors in Christ in distinction from Paul who is the father of the community (v. 15), he does not suggest Apollos as one whose life is to be imitated, but instead Paul himself and his faithful son Timothy are recommended as Christian models (vv. 16–17). Another reference to Apollos in 1 Corinthians 16:12 (cf. Titus 3:13) may indicate Apollos' not totally independent authority in relation to Paul's ministry. Considering all these, the most natural reading of Paul's references to Apollos must prevent one from seeing Paul giving the title of apostle to Apollos.[64]

C.2.3.1. Luke's View on Apollos

Even if Luke's descriptions of the primitive Christian missionaries are often suspected of resulting from Luke's mission-theologically driven creativity, the description of Apollos in Acts may shed some light on our discussion.

---

61. Ker, "Paul and Apollos," 92; *Pace* D. R. Hall, "A Disguise for the Wise: μετευχηματισμός in 1 Corinthians 4.6," *NTS* 40 (1994): 144, who suggests that ταῦτα are "unnamed teachers."

62. W. Wuellner, "Haggadic Homily Genre in I Corinthians 1–3," *JBL* 89 (1970): 199–204, followed by Ker, "Paul and Apollos," 93.

63. Cf. Fee, *1 Corinthians*, 169–170.

64. *Pace* Rengtorf, "ἀπόστολος," 423.

Apollos is described by Luke as being a different type of preacher and teacher of the gospel compared to Paul. In Acts 14:4 and 14:14 Luke explicitly uses in reference to Paul (and Barnabas) the designation of apostle which is absent for Apollos, while Paul's apostolic authority is clearly and consistently described as given without human mediation but through a direct contact with Christ. Such an unmediated calling to apostolic work is lacking or at least unrecognizable in regard to Apollos.[65] Rather, according to Luke, Apollos' public ministry had to be redirected by Aquila and Priscilla's mentoring, and his ministry in Corinth was made possible through the Ephesian congregation's accreditation letter (Acts 18:24–28; cf. 2 Cor 3:1–6). Even if Luke's evaluation or interpretation of Apollos' missionary authority may not directly serve to understand Paul's conception of apostle, that Paul and Luke agree with each other in not giving the title apostle to Apollos is striking.

C.2.3.2. Clement's Comment on Apollos in 47:4

Clement's view on Apollos in *1 Clem.* 47:1–4 is also suggestive in our discussion. When Clement recalls Paul's time and the division among the Corinthian Christians, he calls Paul and Cephas "apostles already of high reputation" (ἀπόστολοι μεμαρτυρημένοι) and Apollos "a man whom they had approved" (ἀνήρ δεδοκιμασμένος παρ᾿ αὐτοῖς). Harnack considers Clement's discrimination of Apollos from the two apostolic figures to be due to the later development which goes against Paul's wider conception based on 1 Corinthians 15:7 and Romans 16:7.[66] However, our discussion so far may indicate another direction. Paul, Luke and Clement all alike do not count Apollos in the group of apostles. Do we, then, need to posit any development of the concept of apostle from Paul's wider one to Clement's narrow one at least in the case of Apollos?

C.2.4. Barnabas (1 Cor 9:6, cf. Acts 14:4, 14)

Despite Luke's description of Barnabas in Acts 14:4, 14 apparently as an apostle (along with Paul), the use of the appellation, as we have already seen, is better understood in the sense of the apostle of the church. What

---

65. *Pace* Ellis, "Co-Workers," 444–445.
66. Harnack, *Mission and Expansion*, 322. Cf. Schmithals, *Office*, 244–246.

is striking is that he is never exclusively referred to as an apostle by Paul. In Galatians 2:1 and following, Paul recalls his visit to Jerusalem "with Barnabas and taking Titus along" (μετὰ Βαρναβᾶ συμπαραλαβὼν καὶ Τίτον, v. 1). While Paul's words betrays Barnabas' status equal to Paul notably in a comparison with Titus, in the further account Paul leaves Barnabas to one side and emphasizes his own unique role for the gospel for the uncircumcised in relation to Peter for the circumcised.[67] What is explicit here is that while Bananas is sufficiently described as Paul's ministerial companion (v. 9), the apostleship (ἀποστολή, v. 8) is mentioned only for Paul himself.

A similar situation is observed in 1 Corinthians 9:1 and following. While Paul mentions Barnabas as his co-worker of the gospel who is legitimately entitled to the right to congregational aid (vv. 4–6), the apostleship issue is entirely limited to Paul himself (vv. 1–3). One could infer that this is because Barnabas' apostleship was rather well approved and did not need to be defended. However, this is not satisfactory since it was both Barnabas and Paul who did work for a living (vv. 6, 12) and presumably were under the same attack. If so both need defending. But Paul's argument only defends Barnabas' right to support (as "we" suggests in v. 12) by appealing to the Lord's command (v. 14), while he is compelled to defend his apostleship as well. This seems to suggest that what Paul argues for in 1 Corinthians 9:3–14 may not be termed "apostles' rights" but the rights to which a wider group of gospel-workers (including apostles) are entitled.

C.2.5. James (Gal 1:19; 1 Cor 15:5–7)

C.2.5.1. Galatians 1:19

Regarding whether Paul attributes the appellation of apostle to James, the brother of the Lord, we have two ambiguous references: Galatians 1:19 and 1 Corinthians 15:5–7. In the former, Paul writes ἕτερον δὲ τῶν ἀποστόλων οὐκ εἶδον εἰ μὴ Ἰάκωβον τὸν ἀδελφὸν τοῦ κυρίου, thus it can mean either (1) "I did not see other apostles, but [I did see] James, the brother of the Lord" in the sense of James as excluded from the group of "other apostles,"

---

67. Donaldson, *Paul*, 252, n.14.

if the exceptive phrase εἰ μή is taken to be relating only to οὐκ εἶδον,⁶⁸ or (2) "I did not see other apostles except James, the brother of the Lord" in the sense of James as the only apostle whom Paul saw apart from Cephas, when εἰ μή is taken to be referring to the whole preceding clause.⁶⁹

J. B. Lightfoot, who is one of the pioneers of the view of "wider circle of apostles" in modern NT scholarship, tries to resolve this ambiguity of the verse by emphasizing the syntactical ground of the sentence: "the sense of ἕτερον naturally links it with εἰ μή from which it cannot be separated without harshness, and ἕτερον carries τῶν ἀποστόλων with it."⁷⁰ Against this it must be said that in fact without such a "harshness" one can separate ἕτερον τῶν ἀποστόλων from εἰ μή, since Paul in Galatians 2:16 can state οὐ δικαιοῦται ἄνθρωπος ἐξ ἔργων νόμου ἐὰν μὴ διὰ πίστεως Ἰησοῦ Χριστοῦ. Here ἐὰν μή (εἰ μή) does not necessarily refer to the whole preceding clause, but rather refers to the contrasting aspect of the negative verb.

In objection to this possible grammatical parallel to the alternate reading (1), however, Bruce argues that "where the exception [εἰ μή] only relates to the negative verb, the context makes this clear, as in Galatians 2:16 ... [but] There is nothing in the present context to suggest that here the exception relates to οὐκ εἶδον only."⁷¹ Rather, he suggests that 1 Corinthians 1:14 which reads εὐχαριστῶ [τῷ θεῷ] ὅτι οὐδένα ὑμῶν ἐβάπτισα εἰ μή Κρίσπον καὶ Γάϊον is a good grammatical parallel to the construction in question.⁷² However, the fact is that the construction of 1 Corinthians 1:14 is not exactly identical to that of Galatians 1:19. While the former is the *positive* accusative (being qualified by the genitive τῶν ἀποστόλων) + the *negative* verb and an εἰ μή construction, the latter is the *negative* accusative (being qualified by the genitive ὑμῶν) + the *positive* verb and an εἰ μή construction. We need to notice that in 1 Corinthians 1:14 Paul gives the

---

68. Betz, *Galatians*: 78; T. Zahn, *Der Brief des Paulus an die Galater* KNT 9 (Leipzig: Deichert, 1905). Cf. H. Conzelmann, *1 Corinthians: A Commentary on the First Epistle to the Corinthians* (Philadelphia: Fortress Press, 1975), 251–260.

69. Lightfoot, *Galatians*, 84–85; J. Blinzler, *Die Brüeler und Schwestern Jesu*, SBS 21 (Stuttgart: Katholisches Bibelwerk, 1967), 119ff; Bruce, *Galatians*, 101–102; Longenecker, *Galatians*, 38.

70. Lightfoot, *Galatians*, 84–85.

71. Bruce, *Galatians*, 100.

72. Ibid.

negative force to his accusative rather than his verb to make his point clear that the two exceptional individuals (i.e. Crispus and Gaius) belong to the assumed party in the accusative, and that the positive verb naturally relates to both the parties. But in Galatians 1:19 the positive accusative construction ἕτερον τῶν ἀποστόλων does actually limit Paul's negative action as (οὐκ ὁράω) relating only to itself and requires one to assume another positive action for the party in the εἰ μὴ construction. Therefore, Bruce's suggestion of 1 Corinthians 1:14 as a grammatical parallel to Galatians 1:19 does not strongly support the alternative reading (2).

Arguments depending on other Pauline constructions which are thought to be grammatically parallels to Galatians 1:19 do not justify any alternative reading and cannot effectively remove the ambiguity residing in the sentence in question, unless we had some clarifying element such as "οὐδένα."[73]

Another important consideration, however, is whether Paul uses the adjective ἕτερος here as an attributive to qualify "the apostles": in the sense of ἄλλος (cf. 1 Cor 9:12) or λοιπός (cf. 1 Cor 9:5) to mean "other apostles or the rest of apostles." It is obvious that Paul uses the adjective ἕτερον here as *substantive* (the accusative case) being qualified by the genitive construction (τῶν ἀποστόλων). Therefore, the direct object of the verb (οὐκ) ὁράω is ἕτερον rather than τῶν ἀποστόλων. If Paul wanted to mean "any other one who is one of the apostles" (except Cephas), this construction is unusual. The natural construction is ἕτερον + accusative as almost all the OT (LXX), the Apocryphal, and the NT Greek use of the adjective ἕτερος suggest: ἕτερον as a direct object of a verb has the same case (i.e. accusative) to qualify it or to be qualified by it as the identical person or thing with the ἕτερος.[74] In other words, Paul should have used the accusatives τούς ἀποστόλους after or before the ἕτερον. Paul certainly keeps to this grammatical principle elsewhere in his letters (cf. Rom 7:23; 2 Cor 11:4; Gal 1:6), whereas in Galatians 1:19 Paul uses the genitives rather than the

---

73. Some other manuscripts such as D*, F, G, G^lat read "εἶδον οὐδένα," and P[51 vid], E read "οὐκ εἶδον οὐδένα" instead of οὐκ εἶδον.

74. Gen 4:25; 26:21f; 30:24; 37:9; 43:22; Exod 22:4; 26:17, 28; 30:9; Lev 14:42; Num 14:24; 2 Sam 18:26; 1 Chr 16:20; Jdt 8:20; Tob 7:15; 2 Macc 10:3; Ps 104:13; Wis 19:3; *Pss. Sol.* 4:12; Jer 18:4; 43:28, 32; Ezek 12:3; Dan 4:37; Dat. 7:6, 8; Acts 12:17; 17:7; Rom 7:23; 13:8; 2 Cor 11:4; Gal 1:6; Heb 7:11; Jud 1:7.

accusative to qualify the substantive ἕτερος. So, no one could confidently claim that Paul here refers to the "other apostles" that he did not see at the time of his visit to Jerusalem.

L. P. Trudinger observes this and concludes that the ἕτερος with the genitives in Galatians 1:19 is to be read as "[one who is] other than" since it carries "comparative force" which differentiates it from the following genitive construction.[75] He suggests in support of his reading two cases which parallel Galatians 1:19 from classical Greek literature: "φίλους ποιεῖσθαι . . . ἑτέρους τῶν νῦν ὄντων" (Thuc. *Hist.* 1.28); aether as "στοιχεῖον οὖσαν ἕτερον τῶν τεσσάρων, ἀκήρατόν" (Arist. *Op. Omnia* 3:623).[76]

Against this view, G. Howard argues that even if ἕτερος in each instance makes a comparison, still it makes the comparisons "between persons or objects of the same class of things," and goes on to add "the τερους [ἑτέρους] belong to the same species of beings as the former, that is, both are *friends* . . . "being an element other than the four," still it is an *element* along with the four."[77] Rather, he suggests that to carry the force of comparison (i.e. "other than") ἕτερος must be neuter or in combination with παρά, ἤ or the dative case as is in the case of Arist. *Pol.* 1294a; Plato *Prot.* 333a; Diog. Laert. 3:53; Xen. *Cyr.* I.6:2.[78]

However, Howard's argument is highly irrelevant to Trudinger's, since Trudinger's point about ἕτερος is not related to "class" or "species" but to its "belongingness" to the class assumed in the genitives. φίλους ποιεῖσθαι strongly indicates that ἑτέρους at the time of mentioning (νῦν) are those who are *not currently friends*. And even if aether is an element (material) as are the four materials, it does not belong to "the four, indestructible" things. Moreover, the use of ἕτερος in combination as such is other ways or more specific ways of making ἕτερος carry the comparative force, thus it

---

75. L. P. Trudinger, "ΕΤΕΡΟΝ ΔΕ ΤΩΝ ΑΠΑΣΤΟΛΩΝ ΟΥΚ ΕΙΔΟΝ ΕΙ ΜΗ ΙΑΚΩΒΟΝ: A Note on Galatians 1:19," *NovT* 17 (1975): 200–202.

76. Ibid., 201.

77. G. Howard, "Was James an Apostle?: A Reflection on a New Proposal for Gal. I 19," *NovT* 19 (1977): 63.

78. Ibid., 64.

may not be posited as a strict grammatical rule.⁷⁹ Therefore, insofar as the precise grammatical parallels which Trudinger suggests (i.e. the constructions of ἕτερος whether masculine and neuter + genitive) make the ἕτερος carry differentiative or comparative force, it is fair and reasonable to read ἕτερον τῶν ἀποστόλων in Galatians 1:19 as "one who is other than the apostles" despite the possible otherwise reading.⁸⁰

If a strict grammatical rule may not be applied in deciding the meaning of ἕτερον δὲ τῶν ἀποστόλων, a further consideration is possible. As J. Bligh suggests, the εἰ μή clause certainly gives us an impression that for Paul James is "thrown in as an afterthought": "I saw none of the other apostles – unless you count James as an apostle."⁸¹ In this case, regardless of whether ἕτερος is to be read as "other" or "other than," James remains as some one who is to be considered more or less otherwise than the apostles or any other category (cf. "elders" in e.g. Acts 11:30; 15:6, 22, 23).⁸²

If Paul's main intention in his first visit to Jerusalem (Gal 1:18) was to meet up with Peter and the other apostles and to discuss with them, his encounter with James could have been something unexpected, but of importance if James was having growing influence in the Jerusalem church.⁸³ But Paul's description of James at his latter visit to Jerusalem (Gal 2:1ff) certainly indicates the fully acknowledged leadership of James in the Jerusalem community (perhaps as the leading one of οἱ δοκοῦντες στῦλοι). So, it is likely that Paul's current evaluation of James is reflected in his retrospective account on his first encounter with James, who at first

---

79. Trudinger's case of "φίλους ποιεῖσθαι ... ἑτέρους τῶν νῦν ὄντων" certainly shows us that the masculine ἑτέρους can carry a comparative force. Cf. Longenecker, *Galatians*, 38, who follows Howard's unlikely explanation.

80. A very similar construction with Gal 1:19 is found in Matt 8:21: "ἕτερος (nominative) δὲ τῶν μαθητῶν [αὐτοῦ] εἶπεν αὐτῷ." Given our consideration, it is possible to read it as "one who is other than the disciples."

81. J. Bligh, *Galatians in Greek: A Structural Analysis of St. Paul's Epistle to the Galatians, with Notes on the Greek* (Detroit: University of Detroit Press, 1966), 96.

82. Cf. Hengel and Schwemmer, *Between Damascus and Antioch*, 245, who suggest the connection of the brothers from James in Gal 2:12 with the Christian "elders" who start to appeal in Acts 11:30.

83. As the most historical reconstructions of the Jerusalem community in the first two decades agree, James' ascendancy as the leader of the community must have taken place after the persecution under Agrippa I (cf. Acts 12:1ff) around 42 CE. On this see Hengel and Schwemmer, *Between Damascus and Antioch*, 244–245; Riesner, *Paul's Early Period*, 117–123.

had less prominence (Gal 1:19) but was now the leader of the Jerusalem community, exercising influence on other churches outside Jerusalem and Palestine even on Peter (Gal 2:12). James' prominence, however, does not indicate his apostleship in Paul's view. Rather, as εἰ μὴ suggests, it is likely that Paul had in mind some Christians' who were regarding James as an apostle by his supreme leadership even over the two of the original apostles. Nevertheless, as 1 Corinthians 9:5 suggests, it is to be noted that Paul certainly distinguishes James (if "the brothers of the Lord" refers to James and his other brothers) from other apostles.[84]

C.2.5.2. *1 Corinthians 15:5–7*

To argue for Paul's inclusion of James in the apostolic band (and for a wider circle of apostles in Paul's mind), Bruce suggests that in 1 Corinthians 15:5–7 Paul "links the appearance to Cephas with a following appearance to "the twelve" (to whose number Cephas belonged), his linking of the appearance to James with a following appearance to 'all the apostles' suggests that he included James among 'all the apostles.'"[85] However, whether one can posit the two pairs of connection (i.e. Cephas – the Twelve and James – all the apostles) which may indicate James' belongingness to the wider circle of apostles is a questionable reading of the much debated pericope of verses 3b–8.[86]

---

84. So Fitzmyer, *1 Corinthians*, 358–359.

85. Bruce, *1 and 2 Corinthians*, 100–101; Barrett, *1 Corinthians*, 48. This view is postulated by other scholars in favour of "Peter *versus* James theory": e.g. Harnack, *Die Verklärungsgeschichte Jesu, der Bericht des Paulus I Kor 15, 3 ff. und die beiden Christusvision des Petrus*, SAB (Berlin: Walter de Gruyter, 1922), 62–80, who argues that the core of the appearance list was the conflation of two credential formulas of two rival leaders of Jewish Christianity (i.e. Cephas-his followers *versus* James-his followers); U. Wilckens, *Die Missionsreden der Apostelgeschichte: Form und traditionsgeschichtliche Untersuchungen*, WMAN 3, (Neukirchen: Neukirchner Verlag, 1960); Wilckens, "The Tradition-history of the Resurrection of Jesus," in *The Significance of the Message of the Resurrection for Faith in Jesus Christ*, ed. C. F. D. Moule (Naperville: Alec R. Allenson, 1968), 51–76; Wilckens, *Resurrection, Biblical Testimony to the Resurrection: An Historical Examination and Explanation* (Atlanta: John Knox, 1978), 6–15; G. Lüdemann, *Opposition to Paul in Jewish Christianity* (Minneapolis: Fortress Press, 1989), 49; G. Lüdemann, *The Resurrection of Jesus: History, Experience, Theology* (Minneapolis: Fortress, 1994), 37.

86. For brief summaries of the debate regarding the history and the form of the pre-Pauline formula see J. S. Kloppenborg, "An Analysis of the Pre-Pauline Formula in 1 Cor 15:3b–5 in Light of Some Recent Literature," *CBQ* 40 (1978): 351–367; R. H. Fuller, *The Formation of the Resurrection Narratives* (New York: Macmillan, 1971); R. M. Price,

Our reasons for believing this are, first, because of the literary break made by the formulaic character of the repeated ὅτι and εἶτα / ἔπειτα between ὅτι ὤφθη Κηφᾷ and εἶτα τοῖς δώδεκα. This suggests that the block beginning with εἶτα is Paul's addition of other traditions to the original creedal formula, being constructed with the four ὅτι-clauses:[87]

A   ὅτι Χριστὸς ἀπέθανεν ὑπὲρ τῶν ἁμαρτιῶν ἡμῶν κατὰ τὰς γραφὰς (death of Christ)

B   καὶ ὅτι ἐτάφη (witness to the death of Christ)

A′   καὶ ὅτι ἐγήγερται τῇ ἡμέρᾳ τῇ τρίτῃ κατὰ τὰς γραφὰς (resurrection of Christ)

B′   καὶ ὅτι ὤφθη Κηφᾷ[88] (witness to the resurrection of Christ)

C   εἶτα τοῖς δώδεκα
ἔπειτα ὤφθη ἐπάνω πεντακοσίοις ἀδελφοῖς ἐφάπαξ . . .
ἔπειτα ὤφθη Ἰακώβῳ
εἶτα τοῖς ἀποστόλοις πᾶσιν (additional available evidences of the resurrection)

B″   ἔσχατον δὲ πάντων ὡσπερεὶ τῷ ἐκτρώματι ὤφθη κἀμοί (Paul's witness to the resurrection)

"Apocryphal Apparitions: 1 Corinthians 15:3–11 as a Post-Pauline Interpolation," *JHC* 2, no. 2 (1995): 69–99.

87. P. Stuhlmacher, *Das paulinische Evangelium. I. Vorgeschichte*, FRLANT 95 (Göttingen: Vanderhoeck und Ruprecht, 1968), 274, suggests that the Pauline list is carefully formulated developing from a bipartite proclamation of death and resurrection to include, initially, the scriptural proof, then the burial and the appearance to Peter, then those to the other witnesses including Paul's own. Cf. Fee, *1 Corinthians*, 723, n.52, points out that if εἶτα τοῖς δώδεκα were a part of the creedal formula, it would have been with καί rather than εἶτα; J. Weiss, *Der erste Korintherbrief* (Göttingen: Vandenhoeck und Ruprecht, 1910), 330; idem, *The History of Primitive Christianity* (New York: Wilson-Erickson, 1937), 24, who argues that the reference to the Twelve is a scribal gloss to harmonize the list with the Gospels.

88. W. Michaelis, "ὁράω," *TDNT* 5, 358f, argues that the original formula would have lacked Κηφᾷ. However, considering the tradition preserved in Luke 24:34; Matt 16:16ff (cf. Gerhardsson, *Memory*, 300), it is more likely that the prominence of Peter was established very early and the reference to Cephas belonged to the pre-Pauline traditional formula in the question.

As the above arrangement shows, each part of the traditions that Paul reiterates has a different degree of importance or rhetorical function in Paul's argument.[89] Thus, it is to be noted that Paul primarily focuses on the two major points: (1) Christ surely died and (2) Christ was surely raised.[90] Quite apart from the contextual hints in verse 12 and verses 20–22, this is suggested by the fact that κατὰ τὰς γραφὰς is attached only to the first and the third ὅτι-clause. Then, ὅτι ἐτάφη and ὅτι ὤφθη Κηφᾷ serve to corroborate the truthfulness of Christ's death and resurrection respectively.[91] Then, it seems that Paul's enumeration of the different resurrection appearances starting with the temporal adverbs εἶτα or ἔπειτα is plainly intended to function as additional evidences of the resurrection of the Lord, which is initially corroborated by the original part of the creedal formula (i.e. ὅτι ὤφθη Κηφᾷ). This observation of the rhetorical structure of the pericope hardly allows the symmetry or literary pairings of "Cephas – the Twelve" and "James – all the apostles." Rather, considering Paul's conscious paralleling himself with Peter elsewhere (Gal 2:8), it is more plausible that the tradition of the resurrection appearance to Peter (B′) is effectively linked to that of Paul who *closes* (ἔσχατον) the chronology of the witnesses to the resurrection appearance of the Lord (B″).

Second, as "Cephas – the Twelve" and "James – all the apostles" links are improbable, to assume that "all the apostles" is different or bigger than "the Twelve" is unnecessary.[92] This point is supported by scholars' observation of 1 Corinthians 15:1–7 (even v. 8 as well) as reflecting the Rabbinic method of handling traditions.[93] B. Gerhardsson suggests that 1 Corinthians 15:3–8 sets out as a series of "סימנים" which is the Rabbinic

---

89. Cf. Gerhardsson, *Memory*, 299: "He *needs* only this part of the tradition in question" (original emphasis).

90. Cf. A. Eriksson, *Traditions as Rhetorical Proof: Pauline Argument in 1 Corinthians*, (Stockholm: Almqvist & Wiksell International, 1998), 253, who plausibly suggests that Paul here uses the pre-Pauline baptismal instruction which highlights Christ's death and resurrection into which Christians are united through baptism.

91. *Pace* C. F. Evans, *Resurrection and the New Testament* (London: SCM, 1970), 50–51, who argues that the "formula has little influence on the rest of the chapter." Similarly Price, "Apocryphal Apparitions," argues that the whole pericope 3–11 is a post-Pauline interpolation which anachronistically contains the Peter vs James relationship.

92. *Pace* Fitzmyer, *1 Corinthians*, 358, 551.

93. J. Jeremias, *The Eucharistic Words of Jesus* (Oxford: Blackwell, 1955), 129; E. Ellis, "Traditions in 1 Corinthians," *NTS 32* (1986): 481; Gerhardsson, *Memory*, 299–300.

term for titles or headings which summarize a piece of tradition or teaching in a key-word or catch-word.[94] If this memorization technique for longer and detailed contents of different traditions is applicable to the block of the four εἶτα / ἔπειτα clauses, it is reasonable to assume that the condensed traditions remain distinguishable from each other for effective chronological enumeration. So, the puzzling question of the identity of "all the apostles" in the final enumeration of the traditions regarding the previous tradition of the Twelve must not cause over-interpretation. As J. Murphy-O'Connor plausibly suggests, the identity of the all the apostles is no other than the Twelve.[95] In other words, the last tradition of the Lord's appearance to all the apostles means another appearance to the Twelve. If the enumeration of סימנים (if Paul had used this Rabbinic term) or "credos" (in Stuhlmacher's term) contained the same titles (i.e. "the Lord appeared to the Twelve" in the first enumeration of the traditions and again "the Lord appeared to the Twelve" in the last enumeration of the traditions), there would have been no point in practicing mnemonic technique. Different headings are naturally required for chronologically different events despite the same characters playing in them. Therefore, attempts to establish James' apostleship (which might have belonged to the wider circle of apostles) based on the Pauline texts turn out to be unconvincing.

C.3. Conclusion

In summary, our exegesis of the Pauline apostle-passages has shown that Paul's conception of apostle may not be explained in terms of a "functional concept" or a "wider concept" which many scholars have favoured often.[96] Rather, it shows that Paul does not admit any recognized missionary figure

---

94. Gerhardsson, *Memory*, 143ff, 153ff, 299. Similarly, Roloff, "Apostel," 48; P. Stuhlmacher, *Das Paulinische Evangelium: I Vorgeschichte*, FRLANT 95 (Göttingen: Vandenhoeck & Ruprecht, 1968), 266–276.

95. J. Murphy-O'Connor, "Tradition and Redaction in 1 Cor 15:3–7," *CBQ* 43 (1981): 582–589, suggests that the postposition of "all" indicates Paul's addition to the tradition of the second appearance of the Lord to the Twelve to effectively include himself. See R. P. Martin, *The Spirit and the Congregation: Studies in 1 Corinthians 12–15* (Grand Rapids: Zondervan, 1984), 338.

96. Even if a scholarly view of the "indefinable" or "contingent" nature of Pauline apostleship due to the contingent Pauline epistolary contexts may be noted, this view is automatically dismissed once a coherent conception is established.

as an "apostle of Christ," nor does he modify (widen or narrow down) the concept in varying contexts, apart from his general use of "apostle of church." Paul's expressed or worked out concept (if it underwent a development) of the "apostle of Christ" is certainly and consistently a narrowly defined one which is always applied to a limited number of special figures of Jesus' own delegates, who at first were expected to be found in Jerusalem (Gal 1:17–18) and later in a mobile mission context (1 Cor 9:5).

If our observation here is sound, it is difficult to avoid the impression that for Paul שליח/ἀπόστολος and מְבַשֵּׂר/εὐαγγελιζόμενος are not understood identically. It is more plausible to think that though the two concepts are closely interwoven forming a coherent concept of the eschatological heralds in Paul's mind, the apostle understood ἀπόστολοι (in a solemn sense) as a special group within εὐαγγελιζόμενοι (perhaps, in the sense of the Twelve + Paul himself).

Bibliography

1. Primary Sources

Aland, K. et al., ed. *Novum Testamentum Graece*. 27th ed. Stuttgart: Deutsche Bibelgesellschaft Stuttgart, 1993.

Apostolic Fathers, The. *The Loeb Classical Library Edition: The Apostolic Fathers*. Translated by B. D. Ehrman. 2 vols. LCL. Cambridge: Harvard University Press, 2003.

Aristotle. *The Loeb Classical Library Edition of Aristotle*. Translated by H. Rackham et al. 23 vols. LCL. Cambridge: Harvard University Press, 1926–1991.

Charlesworth, J. H., ed. *The Old Testament Pseudepigrapha*. 2 vols. New Haven: Yale University Press, 2010.

Diodorus Siculus. *The Loeb Classical Library Edition of Diodorus Siculus*. Translated by C. H. Oldfather et al. 12 vols. LCL. Cambridge: Harvard University Press, 1933–1967.

Diogenes Laertius. *The Loeb Classical Library Edition of Diogenes Laertius*. Translated by R. D. Hicks. 2 vols. LCL. Cambridge: Harvard University Press, 1925.

Elliger, K., and W. Rudolf, eds. *Biblia Hebraica Stuttgartensia*. Stuttgart: Deutsche Bibelgesellschaft Stuttgart, 1990.

Josephus. *The Loeb Classical Library Edition of Josephus*. Translated by H. St. J. Thackeray et al. 10 vols. LCL. Cambridge: Harvard University Press, 1926–1965.

Martínez, F. G., and E. J. C. Tigchelaar, eds. *The Dead Sea Scrolls Study Edition*. 2 vols. Leiden: Brill, 1997–1998.

Philo. *The Loeb Classical Library Edition Philo*. Translated by F. H. Colson and G. H. Whitaker. 12 vols. LCL. Cambridge: Harvard University Press, 1929–1962.

Plato. *The Loeb Classical Library Edition Plato*. Translated by H. N. Fowler et al. 12 vols. LCL. Cambridge: Harvard University Press, 1914–1935.

Rahlfs, A., ed. *Septuaginta*. Stuttgart: Deutsche Bibelgesellschaft Stuttgart, 1979 (1935).

Thucydides. *The History of the Peloponnesian War.* Translated by R. Warner. Middlesex: Penguin Books, 1952.

Xenophon. *The Loeb Classical Library Edition Xenophon.* Translated E. C. Marchant et al. 7 vols. LCL. Cambridge: Harvard University Press 1918–1925.

2. General Works

Abbott, T. K. *A Critical and Exegetical Commentary on the Epistles to the Ephesians and to the Colossians.* ICC. Edinburgh: T. & T. Clark, 1899 (1897).

Achtemeier, P. J. "An Apocalyptic Shift in Early Christian Tradition: Reflections on Some Canonical Evidence." *CBQ* 45 (1983): 231–248.

———. "Apropos the Faith of/in Christ: A Response to Hays and Dunn." In *Pauline Theology Vol. 4: Looking Back, Pressing On,* edited by E. E. Johnson and D. M. Hay, 82–92. Atlanta: Scholars Press, 1997.

———. *Paul and the Jerusalem Church: An Elusive Unity.* Eugene: Wipf & Stock, 1987.

Ådna, J., and H. Kvalbein, eds. *The Mission of the Early Church to Jews and Gentiles.* WUNT. Tübingen: Mohr Siebeck, 2000.

Ådna, J., S. J. Hafemann and O. Hofius, eds. *Evangelium, Schriftauslegung, Kirche: Festschift Für Peter Stuhlmacher Zum 65. Geburtstag.* Göttingen: Vandenhoeck & Ruprecht, 1997.

Agnew, F. H. "The Origin of the NT Apostle-Concept: A Review of Research." *JBL* 105 (1986): 76–96.

Allen, R. *Missionary Methods: St. Paul's or Ours?* London: World Dominion Press, 1962 (1912).

Allison, D. C. "The Eschatology of Jesus." In *The Encyclopedia of Apocalypticism,* edited by J. J. Collins, vol. 1, 267–302. New York: Continuum, 1998.

———. *The Jesus Tradition in Q.* Harrisburg: Trinity, 1997.

———. "The Pauline Epistles and the Synoptic Gospels: the Pattern of the Parallels." *NTS* 28 (1982): 1–32.

———. *The Sermon on the Mount: Inspiring the Moral Imagination.* New York: Crossroad, 1999.

Allison, D. C., and W. D. Davies. *A Critical and Exegetical Commentary on the Gospel according to Saint Matthew.* ICC. 3 vols. Edinburgh: T. & T. Clark, 1988–1997.

Allo, E. B. *Saint Paul: Second épître aux Corinthiens.* 2nd ed. Paris: Études Bibliques, 1956.

Arnold, C. E. *Ephesians: Power and Magic; the Concept of Power in Ephesians in Light of Its Historical Setting*. SNTSMS. Cambridge: Cambridge University Press, 1989.

———. *Powers of Darkness: A Thoughtful, Biblical Look at an Urgent Challenge Facing the Church*. Downers Grove: InterVarsity Press, 1992.

Augustine. *St. Augustine's Confessions*. Cambridge/London: Harvard University Press/Heinemann, 1960.

Aune, D. E. "Eschatology (Early Christian)." In *ABD*, edited by D. N. Freedman, vol. 2, 594–609. New York: Doubleday, 1992.

———. "Jesus and Cynics in First-Century Palestine: Some Critical Considerations." In *Hillel and Jesus*, edited by J. H. Charlesworth and L. Johns, 176–192. Minneapolis: Fortress, 1997.

———. *Prophecy in Early Christianity and the Ancient Mediterranean World*. Grand Rapids: Eerdmans, 1983.

Baird, W. "Pauline Eschatology in Hermeneutical Perspective." *NTS* 17 (1971): 314–327.

Bammel, E., C. K. Barrett and W. D. Davies, eds. *Donum Gentilicium: New Testament Studies in Honour of David Daube*. Oxford: Oxford University Press, 1978.

Banks, R. J. *Paul's Idea of Community: The Early House Churches in their Cultural Setting*. Peabody: Hendrickson, 1994.

Barclay, J. M. G. *Obeying the Truth: Paul's Ethics in Galatians*. Edinburgh: T. & T. Clark, 1988.

———. "Paul among Diaspora Jews: Anomaly or Apostate?" *JSNT* 60 (1995): 92–111.

Barnett, P. W. "Apostle." In *DPL*, edited by G. F. Hawthorne and R. P. Martin, 45–51. Downers Grove: InterVarsity Press, 1993.

———. "Opposition in Corinth." *JSNT* 22 (1984): 3–17.

———. *Paul, Missionary of Jesus*. Grand Rapids: Eerdmans, 2008.

Barram, M. *Mission and Moral Reflection in Paul*. New York: Peter Lang, 2006.

Barrett, C. K. *A Commentary on the First Epistle to the Corinthians*. HNTC. London: Black, 1968.

———. *A Commentary on the Second Epistle to the Corinthians*. BNTC. London: Black, 1986, c1973.

———. *The Epistle to the Romans*. BNTC. Peabody: Hendrickson, 1991.

———. "The Gentile Mission as an Eschatological Phenomenon." In *Eschatology and the New Testament: Essays in Honor of George Raymond Beasley-Murray*, edited by H. Gloer, 65–75. Peabody: Hendrickson Publishers, 1988.

———. "Paul's Opponents in II Corinthians." *NTS* 17 (1971): 233–254.

———. "Paulus als Missionar und Theologe." *ZTK* 86 (1989): 18–32.

———. "Shaliah and Apostle." In *Donum Gentilicium: New Testament Studies in Honour of David Daube,* edited by E. Bammel, C. K. Barrett and W. D. Davies, 88–102. Oxford: Oxford University Press, 1978.

Barth, K. *The Epistle to the Philippians.* London: SCM, 1962.

Barth, M. *Ephesians.* Vol. 2, AB. Garden City: Doubleday, 1974.

———. *The People of God.* JSNTSup. Sheffield: JSOT Press, 1983.

Bassler, J. M., ed. *Pauline Theology.* Vol. 1. Minneapolis: Fortress, 1991.

Bauckham, R. *Gospel Women: Studies of the Named Women in the Gospels.* London: T. & T. Clark, 2002.

Baumgarten, A. I. "Rivkin and Neusner on the Pharisee." In *Law in Religious Communities in the Roman Period: The Debate over Torah and Nomos in Post-biblical Judaism and Early Christianity,* edited by P. Richardson and S. Wilfrid, 109–126. SCJ. Waterloo: Published for the Canadian Corporation for Studies, 1991.

Beale, G. K. *The Temple and the Church's Mission: A Biblical Theology of the Dwelling Place of God.* Downers Grove: InterVarsity Press; Leicester, England: Apollos, 2004.

Beare, F. W. "The Epistle to the Ephesians." In *The Interpreter's Bible Commentary,* vol. 10. New York/Nashville: Abingdon, 1953, 597–749.

———. *Philippians.* London: Black, 1959.

Becker, J., H. Conzelmann and G. Friedrich. *Die briefe an die Galater, Epheser, Philipper, Kolosser, Thessalonicher und Philemon.* Göttingen: Vandenhoeck & Ruprecht, 1990.

———. *Paul: Apostle to the Gentiles.* Louisville: Westminster John Knox Press, 1993.

Beckwith, J. *Early Christian and Byzantine Art.* 2nd ed. New Haven: Yale University Press, 1986.

Beker, J. C. *Heirs of Paul: Paul's Legacy in the New Testament and in the Church Today.* Minneapolis: Fortress, 1991.

———. *Paul's Apocalyptic Gospel: The Coming Triumph of God.* Philadelphia: Fortress Press, 1982.

———. *Paul the Apostle: The Triumph of God in Life and Thought.* Philadelphia: Fortress Press, 1980.

Bell, R. H. *The Irrevocable Call of God: An Inquiry into Paul's Theology of Israel.* Tübingen: Mohr Siebeck, 2005.

Belleville, L. "'Ἰουνιᾶν . . . ἐπίσημοι ἐν τοῖς ἀποστόλοις: A Re-examination of Romans 16:7 in Light of Primary Source Materials." *NTS* 51 (2005): 231–249.

Bellinger Jr., W. H., and W. R. Farmer, eds. *Jesus and the Suffering Servant: Isaiah 53 and Christian Origins.* Harrisburg: Trinity, 1998.

Berger, K. *Die Gesetzesauslegung Jesu: ihr historischer Hintergrund im Judentum und im Alten Testament*. Neukirchen-Vluyn: Neukirchener Verlag, 1972.
Best, E. *A Critical and Exegetical Commentary on Ephesians*. ICC. Edinburgh: T. & T. Clark, 1998.
———. *Ephesians*. JSNTSup. Sheffield: JSOT Press, 1993.
———. *The First and Second Epistles to the Thessalonians*. BNTC. London: Black, 1986.
———. *Paul and His Converts: The Sprunt Lectures 1985*. Edinburgh: T. & T. Clark, 1988.
Betz, H. D. "Apostle." In *ABD*, edited by D. N. Freedman, vol. 1, 309–311. New York: Doubleday, 1992.
———. *Galatians: A Commentary on Paul's Letter to the Churches in Galatia*. Philadelphia: Fortress Press, 1979.
———. *The Sermon on the Mount: A Commentary on the Sermon on the Mount, Including the Sermon on the Plain (Matthew 5.3–7.27 and Luke 6.20–49)*. Minneapolis: Fortress, 1995.
Betz, O. "Jesus and Isaiah 53." In *Jesus and the Suffering Servant: Isaiah 53 and Christian Origins*, edited by W. H. Bellinger, Jr. and W. R. Farmer, 70–87. Harrisburg: Trinity, 1998.
Bingham, D. J. "Justin and Isaiah 53." *Vigiliae Christianae* 54 (2000): 248–261.
Bird, M. F. *A Bird's-eye View of Paul: The Man, His Mission and His Message*. Nottingham: InterVarsity Press, 2008.
———. *Crossing Over Sea and Land: Jewish Missionary Activity in the Second Temple Period*. Peabody: Hendrickson, 2010.
———. *Jesus and the Origins of the Gentile Mission*. London: T. & T. Clark, 2006.
Blauw, J. *The Missionary Nature of the Church: A Survey of the Biblical Theology of Mission*. Guildford: Lutterworth Press, 1974.
Bligh, J. *Galatians in Greek: A Structural Analysis of St. Paul's Epistle to the Galatians, with Notes on the Greek*. Detroit: University of Detroit Press, 1966.
Blinzler, J. *Die Brüeler und Schwestern Jesu*. SBS 21. Stuttgart: Katholisches Bibelwerk, 1967.
Blomberg, C. *Contagious Holiness*. Downers Grove: InterVarsity Press, 2005.
Bloomquist, L. G. *The Function of Suffering in Philippians*. JSNTSup. Sheffield: JSOT Press, 1993.
Bockmuehl, M. N. A. *A Commentary on the Epistle to the Philippians*. BNTC, 4th ed. London: Black, 1997.
———. *Revelation and Mystery in Ancient Judaism and Pauline Christianity*. Tübingen: Mohr Siebeck, 1990.

Borgen, P., V. K. Robbins, and D. B. Gowler, eds. *Recruitment, Conquest, and Conflict: Strategies in Judaism, Early Christianity and the Graeco-Roman World*. Atlanta: Scholars, 1998.

Bormann, L., K. D. Tredici, and A. S. Standhartinger, eds. *Religious Propaganda and Missionary Competition in the New Testament World: Essays Honoring Dieter Georgi*. NovTSup. Leiden: Brill, 1994.

Bornkamm, G. "The Missionary Stance of Paul in 1 Corinthians 9 and in Acts." In *Studies in Luke-Acts*, edited by E. Keck and J. L. Martyn, 194–207. Philadelphia: Fortress, 1980.

———. *Paul*. London: Hodder and Stoughton, 1971.

Bosch, D. J. *Transforming Mission: Paradigm Shifts in Theology of Mission*. New York: Orbis, 1991.

Bousset, W. *Kyrios Christos: A History of the Belief in Christ from the Beginnings of Christianity to Irenaeus*. Nashville: Abingdon Press, 1970.

Bowers, W. P. "Church and Mission in Paul." *JSNT* 44 (1991): 89–111.

———. "Fulfilling the Gospel: The Scope of the Pauline Mission." *JETS* 30 (1987): 185–198.

———. "Mission." In *Dictionary of Paul and His Letters*, edited by Gerald F. Hawthorne, Ralph P. Martin, and Daniel G, Reid, 608–619. Downers Grove: InterVarsity Press, 1993.

———. "Paul and Religious Propaganda in the First Century." *NovT* 22, no. 4 (1980): 316–323.

———. "Studies in Paul's Understanding of His Mission." PhD dissertation, Cambridge University, 1976.

Bowker, J. *Jesus and the Pharisees*. Cambridge: University Press, 1973.

Bowman, J. W. "The Term Gospel and Its Cognates in Palestinian Syriac." In *New Testament Essays: Studies in Memory of T. W. Manson*, edited by A. J. B. Higgins, 54–67. Manchester: Manchester University Press, 1959.

Boyarin, D. *A Radical Jew: Paul and the Politics of Identity*. Contraversions; Berkeley: University of California Press, 1994.

Branick, V. P. "Apocalyptic Paul?" *CBQ* 47 (1985): 664–675.

Bratcher, R. G. *A Translator's Guide to Paul's Second Letter to the Corinthians*. London: United Bible Societies, 1983.

Brewer, R. R. "The Meaning of *Politeuesthe* in Philippians 1:27." *JBL* 73 (1954): 76–83.

Brotherton, D. O. "An Examination of Selected Pauline Passages concerning the Vocational Missionary: An Interpretive Basis for Critiquing Contemporary Missiological Thoughts." PhD dissertation, Southwestern Baptist Theological Seminary, 1986.

Brown, J. P. "Synoptic Parallels in the Epistle and Form History." *NTS* 10 (1963): 27–48.

Brown, R. E., J. A. Fitzmyer, and R. E. Murphy, eds. *The Jerome Biblical Commentary*. Englewood Cliffs: Prentice-Hall, 1968.
Broyles C. C., and C. A. Evans. "Gospel (Good News)." In *DJG*, edited by J. B. Green, S. McKnight and I. H. Marshall, 282–286. Downers Grove: InterVarsity Press, 1992.
———. *Writing and Reading the Scroll of Isaiah Vol. 2: Studies of an Interpretive Tradition*. VTSup. Leiden: Brill, 1997.
Bruce, F. F. *1 and 2 Corinthians*. NCBC. London: Oliphants, 1971.
———. *1 & 2 Thessalonians*. WBC. Waco: Word Books, 1982.
———. *The Epistle to the Galatians*. NIGTC. Grand Rapids: Eerdmans / Bletchley: Paternoster, 1982.
———. *Epistles to the Colossians, to Philemon, and to the Ephesians*. NICNT. Grand Rapids: Eerdmans, 1984.
———. *Paul: Apostle of the Heart Set Free*. Grand Rapids: Eerdmans, 1991 (1977).
———. *Philippians*. NIBC. Peabody: Hendrickson Publishers, 1989.
———. "St. Paul in Macedonia: 3. The Philippian Correspondence." *BJRL* 63 (1981): 260–286.
Bryan, S. M. *Jesus and Israel's Traditions of Judgement and Restoration*. SNTSMS. Cambridge: Cambridge University Press, 2002.
Bultmann, R. *The Gospel of John: A Commentary*. Oxford: Basil Blackwell, 1971.
———. *Glaube und Verstehen*. Tübingen: Mohr Siebeck, 1933.
———. "History and Eschatology in the New Testament." *NTS* 1 (1954/1955): 5–16.
———. *Primitive Christianity in Its Contemporary Setting*. London: Thames and Hudson, 1956.
———. *Theology of the New Testament*. New York, 1951–1955.
Burer, M. H., and D. B. Wallace, "Was Junia Really an Apostle? A Re-examination of Rom 16.7." *NTS* 47:1 (2001): 76–91.
Burke, T. J., and B. S. Rosner, eds. *Paul as Missionary: Identity, Activity, Theology, and Practice*. LNTS. London: T. & T. Clark, 2011.
Burrows, M. "The Origin of the Word Gospel." *JBL* 44 (1925): 21–33.
Burton, E. de W. *A Critical and Exegetical Commentary on the Epistle to the Galatians*. ICC. Edinburgh: T. & T. Clark, 1921.
Buscarlet, A. F. "The 'Preparation' of the Gospel of Peace." *ExpTim* 9, no. 1 (1897): 38–48.
Byrne, B. *Romans*. Collegeville: Liturgical Press, 1996.
Caird, G. B. *Principalities and Powers: A Study of Pauline Theology*. Oxford: Clarendon Press, 1956.
Carleton Paget, J. "Jewish Proselytism at the Time of Christian Origins: Chimera or Reality?" *JSNT* 62 (1996): 65–103.

Calvin, J. *The Epistles of Paul the Apostle to the Galatians, Ephesians, Philippians, Colossians*. Translated by T. H. L. Parker. Grand Rapids: Eerdmans / Carlisle: Paternoster Press, 1996.

Campbell, W. S. "Israel." In *DPL*, edited by G. F. Hawthorne and R. P. Martin, 441–446. Downers Grove: InterVarsity Press, 1993.

———. *Paul and the Creation of Christian Identity*. London: T. & T. Clark, 2008.

———. "Paul's Missionary Practice and Policy in Romans." *IBS* 12 (1990): 2–25.

———. "Salvation for Jews and Gentiles: Krister Stendahl and Paul's Letter to the Romans." *Studia Biblica* 3 (1978): 65–72.

Carr, W. *Angels and Principalities: The Background, Meaning and Development of the Pauline Phrase hai archai kai exousiai*. SNTSMS. Cambridge: Cambridge University Press, 2005.

Carrez, M. "Le 'Nous' en 2 Corinthiens." *NTS* 26 (1979–1980): 474–486.

Carter, C. L. *The Great Sermon Tradition as a Fiscal Framework in 1 Corinthians: Towards a Pauline Theology of Material Possessions*. LNTS. London: T. & T. Clark, 2010.

Cerfaux, L. *Christ in the Theology of St. Paul*. New York: Herder and Herder, 1959.

Chae, D. "Paul." In *Dictionary of Mission Theology: Evangelical Foundation*, edited by J. Corrie, 277–278. Nottingham: InterVarsity Press, 2007.

Charlesworth, J. H., and L. Johns, eds. *Hillel and Jesus*. Minneapolis: Fortress, 1997.

Chester, A. "Jewish Messianic Expectations and Mediatorial Figures and Pauline Christology." In *Paulus und das antike Judentum*, edited by M. Hengel and U. Heckel, 17–78. WUNT. Tübingen: Mohr Siebeck, 1991.

Collange, J.-F. *Enigmes de la deuxième épître de Paul aux Corinthiens: étude exégétique de 2 Cor. 2:14–7:4*. SNTSMS. Cambridge: Cambridge University Press, 1972.

———. *The Epistle of Saint Paul to the Philippians*. London: Epworth Press, 1979.

Collins, J. J. *The Apocalyptic Imagination: An Introduction to Apocalyptic Literature*. 2nd ed. Grand Rapids: Eerdmans, 1998.

———, ed. *The Encyclopedia of Apocalypticism Vol. 1: The Origins of Apocalypticism in Judaism and Christianity*. London: Continuum, 2000.

Conzelmann, H. *1 Corinthians: A Commentary on the First Epistle to the Corinthians*. Philadelphia: Fortress Press, 1975.

———. "Die Brief an die Epheser." In *Die briefe an die Galater, Epheser, Philipper, Kolosser, Thessalonicher und Philemon*, edited by J. Becker, H. Conzelmann, G. Friedrich. Göttingen: Vandenhoeck & Ruprecht, 1990.

Corley, B. "The Jews, the Future and God." *SJT* 19 (1976–1977): 42–56.

Corrie, J., ed. *Dictionary of Mission Theology: Evangelical Foundation.* Nottingham: Inter-Varsity Press, 2007.

Craddock, F. B. *Philippians.* Atlanta: John Knox Press, 1985.

Craig, W. L. "The Bodily Resurrection of Jesus." In *Gospel Perspectives I: Studies of History and Tradition in the Four Gospels*, edited by R. T. France and D. Wenham, 47–74. Sheffield: JSOT Press, University of Sheffield, 1980,

Cranfield, C. E. B. *The Epistle to the Romans.* ICC. 2 vols. Edinburgh: T. & T. Clark, 1975.

Cross, F. L., ed. *Studies in Ephesians.* London: Mowbray, 1956.

Cullmann, O. "Der eschatologische Charakter des Missionsauftrags und dea apostolischen Selbstbewußtseins bei Paulus." In *Vorträge und Aufsätze, 1925–1962*, edited by O. Cullmann, 305–336. Tübingen: Mohr, 1966.

———. "Le caractère eschatologique du devoir missionnaire et de la conscience apostolique de S. Paul: Étude sur le κατέχον (-ων) de 2 Thess. 2.6–7." *RHPR* 16 (1936): 210–245.

———. *Peter: Disciple, Apostle, Martyr: a Historical and Theological Study.* London: SCM Press, 1953.

———. *Vorträge und Aufsätze, 1925–1962.* Tübingen: Mohr, 1966.

Dahl, N. A. "Der Name Israel: Zur Auslegung von Gal 6,16." *Judaica* 6 (1950): 161–170.

———. *Studies in Paul: Theology for the Early Christian Mission.* Minneapolis: Augsburg, 1977.

Daube, D. *The New Testament and Rabbinic Judaism.* London: Athlone Press, 1956.

Davies, W. D. "The Apostolic Age and the Life of Paul." In *Peake's Commentary on the Bible*, edited by H. H. Rowley and M. Black, 870–881. London: T. Nelson, 1967.

———. *Paul and Rabbinic Judaism: Some Rabbinic Elements in Pauline Theology.* London: SPCK, 1948, 4th1981.

de Boer, M. C. "Paul and Apocalyptic Eschatology." In *The Encyclopedia of Apocalypticism*, edited by J. J. Collins, vol. 1, 345–383. London: Continuum, 2000.

de Vos, C. S. *Church and Community Conflicts: The Relationships of the Thessalonian, Corinthian and Philippian Churches with their Wider Civic Communities.* SBLDS. Atlanta: Scholars, 1997.

Deissmann, A. *Light from the Ancient East.* Translated by L. R. M. Strachan. New York: George H. Doran Co., 1927.

———. *St. Paul: A Study in Social and Religious History.* London: Hodder & Stoughton, 1912.

Dennison, W. "Indicative and Imperative: The Basic Structure of Pauline Ethics." *CTJ* 14 (1979): 55–78.

Dewey, A. J. "ΕΙΣ ΤΗΝ ΣΠΑΝΙΑΝ: The Future and Paul." In *Religious Propaganda and Missionary Competition in the New Testament World: Essays Honoring Dieter Georgi*, NovTSup, edited by L. Bormann, K. D. Tredici and A. Standhartinger, 321–349. Leiden: Brill, 1994.

Dibelius, M. *A Fresh Approach to the New Testament and Early Christian Literature.* London: Nicholson & Watson, 1936.

Dickson, J. P. *Mission-Commitment in Ancient Judaism and in the Pauline Communities: The Shape, Extent and Background of Early Christian Mission.* WUNT. Tübingen: Mohr Siebeck, 2003.

Dinter, P. "Paul and the Prophet Isaiah." *BTB* 13 (1983): 48–52.

Dodd, C. H. *The Apostolic Preaching and Its Developments: Three Lectures with an Appendix on Eschatology and History.* London: Hodder & Stoughton, 1936.

———. *The Mind of Paul: II in New Testament Studies.* Manchester: University Press, 1953.

Donaldson, T. L. "The 'Curse of the Law' and the Inclusion of the Gentiles: Galatians 3, 13–14." *NTS* 32 (1986): 94–112.

———. "Israelite, Convert, Apostle to the Gentiles: The Origin of Paul's Gentile Mission." In *The Road from Damascus: The Impact of Paul's Conversion on His Life, Thought, and Ministry*, edited by R. N. Longenecker, 62–83. Grand Rapids: Eerdmans, 1997.

———. *Paul and the Gentiles: Remapping the Apostle's Convictional World.* Minneapolis: Fortress, 1997.

———. "Proselytes or 'Righteous Gentiles'? The Status of Gentiles in Eschatological Pilgrimage Patterns of Thought." *JSP* 7 (1990): 3–27.

Donfried, K. P., ed. *The Romans Debate.* Edinburgh: T. & T. Clark, 1991, 47.

Downs, D. J. *The Offering of the Gentiles: Paul's Collection for Jerusalem in Its Chronological, Cultural, and Cultic Contexts.* WUNT. Tübingen: Mohr Siebeck, 2008.

Drane, J. W. "Patterns of Evangelization in Paul and Jesus: A Way Forward in the Jesus-Paul Debate?" In *Jesus of Nazareth: Lord and Christ: Essays on the Historical Jesus and New Testament Christology*, edited by J. B. Green and M. Turner, 281–296. Grand Rapids: Eerdmans, 1994.

Dungan, D. *The Sayings of Jesus in the Churches of Paul: The Use of the Synoptic Tradition in the Regulation of Early Church Life.* Oxford: B. Blackwell / Philadelphia: Fortress Press, 1971.

Dunn, J. D. G. *Beginning from Jerusalem: Christianity in the Making.* Grand Rapids: Eerdmans, 2009, 322–335.

———, ed. *The Cambridge Companion to St Paul.* Cambridge: Cambridge University Press, 2003.

———. *Christology in the Making: A New Testament Inquiry into the Origins of the Doctrine of the Incarnation.* Philadelphia: Westminster, 1980.

———. *Jesus and the Spirit: A Study of the Religious and Charismatic Experience of Jesus and the First Christians as Reflected in the New Testament*, NTL. London: SCM, 1975.

———. *Jesus, Paul and the Law: Studies in Mark and Galatians*. London: SPCK, 1990, 97–98.

———. *Jesus Remembered. Christianity in the Making*. Grand Rapids: Eerdmans, 2003.

———. "'A Light to the Gentiles': The Significance of the Damascus Road Christophany for Paul." In *The Glory of Christ in the New Testament: Studies in Christology in Memory of George Bradford Caird*, edited by L. D. Hurst and N.T. Wright, 91–98. Oxford: Clarendon Press, 1987.

———. "The Relationship between Paul and Jerusalem according to Galatians 1 and 2." *NTS* 28 (1982): 461–478.

———. *Romans 1–8*. WBC. Nashville: Thomas Nelson, 1988.

———. *Romans 9–16*. WBC. Nashville: Thomas Nelson, 1988.

———. *The Theology of Paul the Apostle*. Edinburgh: T. & T. Clark, 1998.

———. *Unity and Diversity in the New Testament: An Inquiry into the Character of Earliest Christianity*. 3rd ed. London: SCM, 2006.

———. "Was Judaism Particularist or Universalist?" In *Judaism in Late Antiquity*, Part 3, Vol. 2, edited by J. Neusner and A. J. Avery-Peck, 57–74. Leiden: Brill, 1995.

Eckert, J. "Indikativ und Imperativ bei Paulus." In *Ethik Im Neuen Testament*, edited by K. Kertelge, 168–189. Freiburg: Herder, 1984.

Ehrhardt, A. *The Apostolic Succession in the First Two Centuries of the Church*. London: Lutterworth, 1953.

Ellicott, C. J. *A Critical and Grammatical Commentary on St. Paul's Epistle to the Philippians, Colossians, and to Philemon with a Revised Translation*. London: J. W. Parker, 1861.

Ellis, E. E. "Paul and Co-workers." *NTS* 17 (1971): 437–452.

———. *Prophecy and Hermeneutics in Early Christianity*. WUNT. Tübingen: Mohr Siebeck, 1978.

———. "Traditions in 1 Corinthians." *NTS 32* (1986): 481–502.

Elmer, I. J. *Paul, Jerusalem and the Judaisers: The Galatian Crisis in Its Broadest Historical Context*. WUNT. Tübingen: Mohr Siebeck, 2009.

Engberg-Pederson, T. "The Hellenistic *Öffentlichkeit*: Philosophy as a Social Force in the Greco-Roman World." In *Recruitment, Conquest, and Conflict: Strategies in Judaism, Early Christianity and the Graeco-Roman World*, edited by P. Borgen, V. K. Robbins, and D. B. Gowler, 16–37. Atlanta: Scholars, 1998.

Epp, E. J. *Junia: The First Woman Apostle*. Minneapolis: Fortress Press, 2005.

Eriksson, A. *Traditions as Rhetorical Proof: Pauline Argument in 1 Corinthians*. Stockholm: Almqvist & Wiksell International, 1998.

Evans, C. A., and S. E. Porter, eds. *Dictionary of New Testament Background*. Downers Grove: InterVarsity Press, 1993.

Evans, C. A., and J. A. Sanders, eds. *Paul and the Scriptures of Israel*. JSNTSup. Sheffield: JSOT Press, 1993.

Evans, C. A. "From Gospel to Gospel: The Function of Isaiah in the New Testament." In *Writing and Reading the Scroll of Isaiah Vol. 2: Studies of an Interpretive Tradition*, VTSup, edited by C. C. Broyles and C. A. Evans, 651–691. Leiden: Brill, 1997.

———. "Paul and the Prophets." In *Romans and the People of God: Essays in Honor of Gordon D. Fee on the Occasion of His 65th Birthday*, edited by S. V. Soderlund and N. T. Wright, 115–128. Grand Rapids: Eerdmans, 1999.

———. "Preacher and Preaching: Some Lexical Observations." *JETS* 24, no. 4 (1981): 315–322.

———. "Prophet, Paul as." In *DPL*, edited by G. F. Hawthorne and R. P. Martin, 762–765. Downers Grove: InterVarsity Press, 1993.

Evans, C. F. *Resurrection and the New Testament*. London: SCM, 1970.

Evans, O. E. "New Wine in Old Skins: XIII. The Saints." *ExpTim* 86 (1975): 196–200.

Everts, J. M. "Conversion and Call of Paul." In *DPL*, edited by G. F. Hawthorne and R. P. Martin, 156–163. Downers Grove: InterVarsity Press, 1993.

Farmer, W. R., ed. *Crisis in Christology: Essays in Search of Resolution*. Livonia: Dove Booksellers, 1995.

Fee, G. D. *The First and Second Letters to the Thessalonians*. NICNT. Grand Rapids: Eerdmans, 2009.

———. *The First Epistle to the Corinthians*. NICNT. Grand Rapids: Eerdmans, 1987.

———. *God's Empowering Presence: The Holy Spirit in the Letters of Paul*. Peabody: Hendrickson Publishers, 1994.

———. *Paul's Letter to the Philippians*. NICNT. Grand Rapids: Eerdmans, 1995.

———. "Philippians 2:5–11: Hymn or Exalted Pauline Prose?" *BBR* 2 (1992): 29–46.

Fitzmyer, J. A. *1 Corinthians: A New Translation with Introduction and Commentary*. New Haven: Yale University Press, 2008.

———. "The Letter to the Philippians." In *The Jerome Biblical Commentary*, edited by R. E. Brown, J. A. Fitzmyer, and Roland E. Murphy, 249. Englewood Cliffs: Prentice-Hall, 1968.

———. *Romans: A New Translation with Introduction and Commentary*, AB. New York: Doubleday, 1993.

Fjärstedt, B. *Synoptic Tradition in 1 Corinthians: Themes and Clusters of Theme Words in 1 Corinthians 1–4 and 9.* Uppsala: Teologiska Institutionen, 1974.

Forbes, C. "Pauline Demonology and/or Cosmology? Principalities, Powers, and the Elements of the World in Their Context." *NSNT* 85 (2002): 51–73.

———. "Prophecy and Inspired Speech in Early Christianity and Its Hellenistic Environment." PhD dissertation, Macquarie University, 1987.

Fowl, S. E. *Philippians.* THNTC. Grand Rapids: Eerdmans, 2005.

France, R. T., and D. Wenham, eds. *Gospel Perspectives 1: Studies of History and Tradition in the Four Gospels.* JSNTSup. Sheffield: JSOT Press, 1980.

———. *Gospel Perspectives 2: Studies of History and Tradition in the Four Gospels.* JSNTSup. Sheffield: JSOT Press, 1981.

France, R. T. *The Gospel of Matthew.* NICNT. Grand Rapids: Eerdmans, 2007.

Fredriksen, P. *Jesus of Nazareth, King of the Jews: A Jewish Life and the Emergence of Christianity.* New York: Vintage Books, 2000.

Freedman, D. N., ed. *The Anchor Bible Dictionary.* 6 vols. New York: Doubleday, 1992.

Fridrichsen, A. "Eglise et Sacrement dans le Nouveau Testament." *RHPR* 17 (1937): 338–347.

Friedrich, G. "εὐαγγελίζομαι, εὐαγγέλιον, προευαγγελίζομαι, εὐαγγελιστής." In *TDNT*, edited by G. Kittel and G. Friedrich, vol. 2, 707–737. Grand Rapids: Eerdmans, 1964–1976.

Fuller, R. H. *The Formation of the Resurrection Narratives.* New York: Macmillan, 1971.

Fung, Y. K. *The Epistle to the Galatians.* NICNT. Grand Rapids: Eerdmans, 1988.

Funk, R. W. and G. Ebeling, ed. *God and Christ: Existence and Province.* New York: Harper, 1968.

Furnish, V. P. *1 and 2 Thessalonians.* ANTC. Nashville: Abingdon, 2007.

———. *II Corinthians*, AB. New York: Doubleday, 1984.

———. "Prophets, Apostles and Preachers: A Study of the Biblical Concept of Preaching." *Interpretation* 17, no. 1 (1963): 48–60.

———. *Theology and Ethics in Paul.* Nashville: Abingdon Press, 1968.

Gadenz, P. T. *Called from the Jews and from the Gentiles: Pauline Ecclesiology in Romans 9–11.* WUNT. Tübingen: Mohr Siebeck, 2009.

Gaebelein, F., ed. *EBC.* Vol. 11/12. Grand Rapids: Zondervan, 1978.

Gaechter, P. *Petrus und seine Zeit. Neutestamentliche Studien.* Innsbruck: Tyrolia-Verlag, 1958.

Gager, J. G. *Kingdom and Community: The Social World of Early Christianity.* Englewood Cliffs: Prentice-Hall, 1975.

———. *The Origins of Anti-semitism: Attitudes toward Judaism in Pagan and Christian Antiquity.* New York: Oxford University Press, 1985.

Garland, D. E. "Philippians 1:1–26: The Defense and Confirmation of the Gospel." *RevExp* 77 (1980): 329–330.
Gasque, W. W., and R. P. Martin, eds. *Apostolic History and the Gospel.* Grand Rapids: Eerdmans, 1970.
Gaston, L. *No Stone on Another: Studies in the Significance of the Fall of Jerusalem in the Synoptic Gospels.* NovTSup. Leiden: Brill, 1970.
———. *Paul and the Torah.* Vancouver: University of British Columbia Press, 1987.
Gaventa, B. R. *From Darkness to Light: Aspects of Conversion in the New Testament.* Philadelphia: Fortress Press, 1986.
Gensichen, H.-W. *Glaube für die Welt: Theologische Aspekte der Mission.* Gütersloh: Gerd Mohn, 1971.
Georgi, D. *The Opponents of Paul in Second Corinthians: A Study of Religious Propaganda in Late Antiquity.* Philadelphia: Fortress Press, 1986.
Gerhardsson, B. "Die Boten Gottes und die Apostel Christi." *SEÅ* 27 (1962): 89–131.
Gifford, E. H. *The Epistle of St. Paul to the Romans: With Notes and Introduction.* London: William Clowes & Sons, 1886.
Gloer, H., ed. *Eschatology and the New Testament: Essays in Honor of George Raymond Beasley-Murray.* Peabody: Hendrickson Publishers, 1988.
Gnilka, J. *Der Philipperbrief.* HTKNT. Freiburg: Herder, 1968.
———. *Theologie des Neuen Testaments.* Freiburg: Herder, 1994.
Godet, F. *Commentary on St Paul's Epistle to the Romans.* Vol. 1. Edinburgh: T. & T. Clark, 1892.
Gogarten, F. *The Reality of Faith: The Problem of Subjectivism in Theology.* Philadelphia: Westminster Press, 1959.
Goodman, M. *Mission and Conversion: Proselytizing in the Religious History of the Roman Empire.* Oxford: Oxford University Press, 1994.
Goulder, M. *Luke: A New Paradigm.* JSNTSup. Sheffield: JSOT Press, 1989.
———. *Midrash and Lection in Matthew.* London: SPCK, 1974.
Green, G. L. *The Letters to the Thessalonians.* PNTC. Grand Rapids: Eerdmans / Leicester: Apollos, 2002.
Green, H. B. *Matthew, Poet of the Beatitudes.* JSNT. Sheffield: Sheffield Academic Press, 2001.
Green, J. B., and M. Turner, eds. *Jesus of Nazareth: Lord and Christ: Essays on the Historical Jesus and New Testament Christology.* Grand Rapids: Eerdmans, 1994.
Green, J. B., S. Mcknight, and I. H. Marshall, eds. *Dictionary of Jesus and the Gospels.* Nottingham: Inter-Varsity Press, 1992.
Greeven, H. "Die missionierende Gemeinde nach den Apostolischen Briefen." In *Sammlung und Sendung - Vom Auftrag der Kirche in der Welt: Eine*

Festgabe für D. Heinrich Rendtorff zu seinem 70. Geburtstag am 9. April 1958, edited by J. Heubach and H.-H. Ulrich, 59–71. Berlin: Christlicher Z-Verlag, 1958.

Grudem, W. A. *The Gift of Prophecy in 1 Corinthians.* Lanham: University Press of America, 1982.

Guelich, R. A. *Mark*, WBC. Nashville: Thomas Nelson, 1989.

Gundry Volf, J. M. *Paul and Perseverance: Staying In and Falling Away.* WUNT. Tübingen: Mohr Siebeck, 1990.

Gurtner, D. M., and J. Nolland, eds. *Built upon the Rock, Studies in the Gospel of Matthew.* Grand Rapids: Eerdmans, 2008.

Guthrie, D. *New Testament Theology.* Nottingham: Inter-Varsity Press, 1981.

Guthrie, D., and R. P. Martin. "God." In *DPL*, edited by G. F. Hawthorne and R. P. Martin, 354–369. Downers Grove: InterVarsity Press, 1993.

Hagner, D. A. *Matthew 1–13.* WBC. Dallas: Word Books, 1993.

Hahn, F. "Der Apostolat im Urchristentum: Seine Eigenart und seine Voraussetzungen." *KD* 20 (1974): 54–77.

———. *Mission in the New Testament.* London: SCM, 1965.

Hall, D. R. "A Disguise for the Wise: μετεσχημάτισμος in I Corinthians 4.6." *NTS* 40 (1994): 143–149.

Halliday, M. A. K. *Introduction to Functional Grammar.* London: Arnold, 1985.

Hansen, G. W. *The Letter to the Philippians*, PNTC. Grand Rapids: Eerdmans / Nottingham: Apollos Press, 2009.

Hanson, P. D. "Apocalypse, Genre and Apocalypticism." In *IDB: Supplementary Volume*, edited by K. Crim, 27–34. Nashville: Abingdon, 1976.

Harnack, A. *Die Verklärungsgeschichte Jesu, der Bericht des Paulus (1 Kor 15, 3 ff.) und die beiden Christusvision des Petrus.* Sitzungberichte der Preussischen Akademie der Wissenschaften. Berlin: Walter de Gruyter, 1922.

Harvey, A. E. "'The Workman Is Worthy of His Hire': Fortunes of a Proverb in the Early Church." *NovT* 24 (1982): 209–221.

Hauck, F. "κοινός, κοινωνός, κοινωνέω, κοινωνία, συγκοινωνός, συγκοινωνέω, κοινωνικός, κοινόω." In *TDNT*, edited by G. Kittel and G. Friedrich, vol. 3, 789–821. Grand Rapids: Eerdmans, 1964–1976.

Hawthorn, T. "'Philippians i.12–19.' With Special Reference to vv. 15.16.17." *ExpTim* 62, no. 10 (1951): 314–317.

Hawthorne, G. F. "Philippians, Letter to the." In *DPL*, edited by G. F. Hawthorne and R. P. Martin, 707–713. Downers Grove: InterVarsity Press, 1993.

———. *Philippians.* WBC. Waco: Word Books, 1983.

Hawthorne, G. F., and R. P. Martin, eds. *Dictionary of Paul and his Letters.* Downers Grove: InterVarsity Press, 1993.

Hays, R. B. "Christology and Ethics in Galatians: The Law of Christ." *CBQ* 49 (1987): 268–290.

———. *Echoes of Scripture in the Letters of Paul.* New Haven: Yale University Press, 1989.

———. *The Faith of Jesus Christ.* 2nd ed. Grand Rapids: Eerdmans, 2002.

———. *First Corinthians.* Louisville: John Knox Press, 1997.

———. *The Moral Vision of the New Testament: Community, Cross, New Creation.* San Francisco: Harper, 1996.

———. "Who Has Believed Our Message?: Paul's Reading of Isaiah." In *SBL 1998 Seminar Papers*, 205–225. Atlanta: Scholars Press, 1998.

———. "ΠΙΣΤΙΣ and Pauline Christology: What Is at Stake?" In *Pauline Theology Vol. 4: Looking Back, Pressing On*, edited by E. E. Johnson and D. M. Hay, 35–60. Atlanta: Scholars Press, 1997.

Helyer, L. R. "The Necessity, Problems, and Promise of Second Temple Judaism for Discussions of New Testament Eschatology." *JETS* 47, no. 4 (2004): 597–615.

Hendrickson, W. *Philippians.* NTC. Edinburgh: Banner of Truth, 1962.

Hengel, M., and A. M. Schwemer. *Paul between Damascus and Antioch: The Unknown Years.* Translated by J. Bowden. London: SCM, 1997.

Hengel, M. "Jesus, the Messiah of Israel: The Debate about the 'Messianic Mission' of Jesus." In *Crisis in Christology: Essays in Search of Resolution*, edited by W. R. Farmer, 217–240. Livonia: Dove Booksellers, 1995.

Hengel, M., and U. Heckel, eds. *Paulus und das antike Judentum.* WUNT. Tübingen: Mohr Siebeck, 1991.

Hengel, M. *Between Jesus and Paul: Studies in Earliest History of Christianity.* London: SCM, 1983.

———. *The Pre-Christian Paul.* London: SCM / Philadelphia: Trinity Press International, 1991.

Heubach, J., and H.-H. Ulrich, eds. *Sammlung und Sendung - Vom Auftrag der Kirche in der Welt: Eine Festgabe für D. Heinrich Rendtorff zu seinem 70. Geburtstag am 9. April 1958.* Berlin: Christlicher Z-Verlag, 1958.

Higgins, A. J. B., ed. *New Testament Essays: Studies in Memory of T. W. Manson.* Manchester: Manchester University Press, 1959.

Hodge, C. *Commentary on the Epistle to the Romans.* Grand Rapids: Eerdmans, 1886.

Hofius, O. "'All Israel Will Be Saved': Divine Salvation and Israel's Deliverance in Romans 9–11." *PSB*, Supplementary Issue 1 (1990): 19–39.

———. "Das vierte Gottesknechtslied in den Briefen des Neuen Testaments." In *Der leidende Gottesknecht: Jesaja 53 und seine Wirkungsgeschichte mit einer Bibliographie zu Jesaja 53*, FAT, edited by B. Janowski and P. Stuhlmacher, 107–127. Tübingen: Mohr Siebeck, 1996.

———. "Paulus-Missionar und Theologe." In *Evangelium Schriftsauslegung Kirche: Festschrift Für Peter Stuhlmacher Zum 65. Geburtstag*, edited by J. Ådna, S. J. Hafemann, and O. Hofius, 224–237. Göttingen: Vandenhoeck, 1997.

Hollander, H. W., and M. de Jonge. *The Testaments of the Twelve Patriarchs*. Leiden: Brill, 1985.

Holloway, P. A. *Consolation in Philippians: Philosophical Sources and Rhetorical Strategy*. SNTSMS. Cambridge: Cambridge University Press, 2001.

Holmgren, F. H. *With Wings as Eagles: An Interpretation*. Chappaqua: Biblical Scholars Press, 1973.

Holzbrecher, F. *Paulus und der histrische Jesus: Darstellung und Analyse der bisherigen Forschungsgeschichte*. Tübingen: Francke, 2007.

Hooker, M. D. A Book Review of "*Paul: Follower of Jesus or Founder of Christianity?* by David Wenham." *JBL* 115, no. 4 (1996): 756–758.

———. *Jesus and the Servant*. London: SPCK, 1959.

Hoover, R. H. "The HARPAGMOS Enigma: A Philological Solution." *HTR* 64 (1971): 95–119.

Horrell, D. G. "'The Lord Commanded . . . But I Have Not Used . . .' Exegetical and Hermeneutical Reflections on 1 Cor 9.14–15." *NTS* 43 (1997): 587–603.

Houlden, J. H. *Paul's Letters from Prison: Philippians, Colossians, Philemon and Ephesians*. Harmondsworth: Penguin, 1970.

Howard, G. *Paul: Crisis in Galatia: A Study in Early Christian Theology*. SNTSMS. Cambridge: Cambridge University Press, 1979.

———. "Phil 2:6–11 and the Human Christ." *CBQ* 40 (1978): 368–387.

———. "Was James an Apostle?: A Reflection on a New Proposal for Gal. I 19." *NovT* 19 (1977): 63–64.

Hübner, H. *Gottes Ich und Israel: zum Schriftgebrauch des Paulus in Römer 9–11*. FRLANT. Göttingen: Vandenhoeck & Ruprecht, 1984.

Hughes, P. E. *Paul's Second Epistle to the Corinthians: The English Text with Introduction, Exposition and Notes*. London: Marshall, Morgan & Scott, 1962, c1961.

Hultgren, A. J. *Paul's Gospel and Mission: The Outlook from his Letter to the Romans*. Philadelphia: Fortress Press, 1985.

———. *Paul's Letter to the Romans: A Commentary*. Grand Rapids: Eerdmans, 2011.

Hurst, L. D., and N. T. Wright, eds. *The Glory of Christ in the New Testament: Studies in Christology in Memory of George Bradford Caird*. Oxford: Clarendon Press, 1987.

Hurtado, L. C. *How on Earth Did Jesus Become a God?: Historical Questions about Earliest Devotion to Jesus*. Grand Rapids: Eerdmans, 2005.

Hurtado, L. W. "The Jerusalem Collection in Galatians." *JSNT* 5 (1979): 46–62.

———. "Jesus as Lordly Example in Philippians 2:5–11." In *From Jesus to Paul: Studies in Honour of Francis Wright Beare*, edited by P. Richardson and J. C. Hurd, 113–126. Waterloo: Wilfrid Laurier University Press, 1984.

Huttar, D. K. "Did Paul Call Andronicus an Apostle in Romans 16:7?" *JETS* 52, no. 4 (2009): 747–778.

Hvalvik, R., "In Word and Deed." In *The Mission of the Early Church to Jews and Gentile*, WUNT, edited by J. Ådna and H. Kvalbein, 277–280. Tübingen: Mohr Siebeck, 2000.

———. "A 'Sonderweg' for Israel: A Critical Examiniation of a Current Interpretation of Romans 11.25–27." *JSNT* 38 (1990): 87–107.

———. *Struggle for Scripture and Covenant: The Purpose of the Epistle of Barnabas and Jewish-Christian Competition in the Second Century*. WUNT. Tübingen: Mohr Siebeck, 1996.

Hyatt, J. P., ed. *The Bible in Modern Scholarship*. Nashville: Abingdon, 1965.

James, W. *The Varieties of Religious Experience*. New York: Coller MacMillan, 1961.

Janowski, B., and P. Stuhlmacher, eds. *Der leidende Gottesknecht: Jesaja 53 und seine Wirkungsgeschichte mit einer Bibliographie zu Jesaja 53*, FAT. Tübingen: Mohr Siebeck, 1996.

Jeremias, J. *The Eucharistic Words of Jesus*. Oxford: Blackwell, 1955.

———. *Jesus' Promise to the Nations*. London: SCM, 1958.

———. *Unknown Sayings of Jesus*. London: SPCK, 1964.

Jervell, J. "The Mighty Minority." *Studia Theologia* 34 (1980): 13–38.

Jewett, R. "The Agitators and the Galatian Congregation." *NTS* 17 (1971): 198–212.

———. "Conflicting Movements in the Early Church as Reflected in Philippians." *NovT* 12 (1970): 361–390.

———. "The Epistolary Thanksgiving and the Integrity of Philippians." *NovT* 12 (1970): 40–53.

Johnson, E. E., and D. M. Hay, eds. *Pauline Theology Vol. 4: Looking Back, Pressing On*. Atlanta: Scholars Press, 1997.

Johnson, L. T. "A Historiographical Response to Wright's Jesus." In *Jesus and the Restoration of Israel: A Critical Assessment of N. T. Wright's Jesus and the Victory of God*, edited by C. C. Newman, 212–216. Carlisle: Paternoster, 1999.

———. "Paul's Ecclesiology." In *The Cambridge Companion to St Paul*, edited by J. D. G. Dunn, 119–211. Cambridge: Cambridge University Press, 2003.

Johnston, P. *Shades of Sheol: Death and Afterlife in the Old Testament*. Leicester: Apollos, 2002.

Jones, P. R. "Paul the Last Apostle." *TB* 34 (1984): 3–34.

Judge, E. A. "St. Paul and Classical Society." *JAC* 15 (1972): 19–36.

Käsemann, E. *Commentary on Romans*. Grand Rapids: Eerdmans, 1980.

———. "A Critical Analysis of Philippians 2:5–11." In *God and Christ: Existence and Province*, JTC 5, edited by R. W. Funk, 45–88. New York: Harper, 1968.

———. "Justification and Salvation History in the Epistle to the Romans." In *Perspectives on Paul*, edited by E. Käsemann, 60–78. Philadelphia: Fortress Press, 1971.

———. *Perspectives on Paul*. Philadelphia: Fortress Press, 1971.

Kaylor, R. D. *Paul's Covenant Community*. Atlanta: John Knox Press, 1988.

Keck, L. E., and J. L. Martyn, eds. "Paul and Apocalyptic Theology." *Interpretation* 38 (1984): 254–267.

———. *Romans*, ANTC. Nashville: Abingdon Press, 2005.

———. *Studies in Luke-Acts*. Philadelphia: Fortress, 1980.

Kehl, A. "Gewand (de Seele)." *RAC* 10 (1978): 945–1025.

Kent Jr., H. A. "Philippians." In *EBC*, edited by F. Gaebelein, vol. 11/12, 93–159. Grand Rapids: Zondervan, 1978.

Keown, M. J. *Congregational Evangelism in Philippians: The Centrality of an Appeal for Gospel Proclamation to the Fabric of Philippians*. Carlisle, Cumbria: Paternoster, 2008.

Ker, D. P. "Paul and Apollos-Colleagues or Rivals?" *JSNT* 77 (2000): 75–97.

Kerr, F. "Paul's Experience: Sighting or Theophany?" *New Blackfriars* 58 (1977): 304–313.

Kerrigan, A. "Echoes of Themes from the Servant Songs in Pauline Theology." In *Studiorum Paulinorum Congressus 1961*, 217–228. Rome: Pontifical Biblical Institute, 1963.

Kerteleg, K., ed. *Ethik Im Neuen Testament*. Freiburg: Herder, 1984.

———, ed. *Mission Im Neuen Testament*. Freiburg: Herder, 1982.

Kijne, J. J. "We, Us and Our in I and II Corinthians." *NovT* 8 (1966): 171–179.

Kim, S. *The Origin of Paul's Gospel*, WUNT. Tübingen: Mohr Sieback, 1984.

———. *Paul and the New Perspective: Second Thoughts on the Origin of Paul's Gospel*, WUNT. Tübingen: Mohr Siebeck, 2002.

———. "Paul as an Eschatological Herald." In *Paul as Missionary: Identity, Activity, Theology, and Practice*, LNTS, edited by T. J. Burke and B. S. Rosner, 9–24. London: T. & T. Clark, 2011.

Kirk, J. A. "Apostleship since Rengstorf." *NTS* 21 (1974–1975): 249–264.

Kistemaker, S. J. *Exposition of the Second Epistle to the Corinthians*, NTC. Grand Rapids: Baker Book House, 2002.

Kittel, G. "λέγω, λόγος, ῥῆμα, λαλέω, λόγιος, λόγιον, ἄλογος, λογικός, λογομαχέω, λογομαχία, ἐκλέλομαι, ἐκλογή, ἐκλεκτός." In *TDNT*, edited by G. Kittel and G. Friedrich, vol. 4, 69–143. Grand Rapids: Eerdmans, 1964–1976.

Klausner, J. *From Jesus to Paul*. London: Allen & Unwin, 1946.

———. *The Messianic Idea in Israel: From Its Beginning to the Completion of the Mishnah*. London: Allen and Unwin, 1956.

Klein, G. *Die zwölf Apostel: Ursprung und Gehalt einer Idee*. Göttingen: Vandenhoeck & Ruprecht, 1962.

———. "Paul's Purpose in Writing the Epistle to the Romans." In *The Romans Debate*, edited by K. P. Donfried, 32–49. Edinburgh: T. & T. Clark, 1991.

Kloppenborg, J. S. "An Analysis of the Pre-Pauline Formula in 1 Cor 15:3b–5 in Light of Some Recent Literature." *CBQ* 40 (1978): 351–367.

Knight, J. *Jesus: An Historical and Theological Investigation*. London: T. & T. Clark, 2004.

Knox, J. "Romans 15:14–33 and Paul's Conception of His Apostolic Mission." *JBL* 83 (1964): 1–11.

Koch, D.-A. "Crossing the Border: The Hellenists' and Their Way to the Gentiles." *Neot* 39, no. 2 (2005): 289–312.

Koester, H. "Paul and Hellenism." In *The Bible in Modern Scholarship*, edited by J. P. Hyatt, 187–195. Nashville: Abingdon, 1965.

Kohler, K. *The Origin of the Synagogue and the Church*. New York: Macmillan, 1929.

Köstenberger, A. J., and P. T. O'Brien. *Salvation to the Ends of the Earth: A Biblical Theology of Mission*. Leicester: Apollos, 2001.

Krause, G., and G. Müller, eds. *Theologische Realenzyklopädie*. Berlin: de Gruyter, 1978.

Kreitzer, L. J. "Eschatology." In *DPL*, edited by G. F. Hawthorne and R. P. Martin, 253–269. Downers Grove: InterVarsity Press, 1993.

———. *Jesus and God in Paul's Eschatology*, JSNTSup. Sheffield: JSOT Press, 1987.

Kruse, C. G. "Apostle." In *DJG*, edited by J. B. Green, S. Mcknight, and I. H. Marshall, 27–33. Downers Grove: InterVarsity Press, 1992.

Kummel, W. G. *Römer 7 und die Bekehrung des Paulus*. Leipzig: Hinrichs, 1929.

Lane, A. N. S., ed. *The Unseen World: Christian Reflections on Angels, Demons and the Heavenly Realm*. Cumbria: Paternoster Press, 1996.

Larsson, E. *Christus als Vorbild: eine Untersuchung zu den paulinischen Tauf- und Eikontexten*. Uppsala: C. W. K. Gleerup, 1962.

Lee, J. H. "Against Richard B. Hays's 'Faith of Jesus Christ.'" *JGRChJ* 5 (2008): 51–80.

Lenski, R. C. H. *The Interpretation of St Paul's First and Second Epistles to the Corinthians*. Minneapolis: Augsburg Publishing House, 1963.

Lightfoot, J. B. "The Name and Office of Apostle." In *St Paul's Epistle to the Galatians*, edited by J. B. Lightfoot, 92–101. 10th ed. Grand Rapids: Zondervan, 1957 (1865).

———. *Saint Paul's Epistle to the Philippians: A Revised Text with Introduction, Notes, and Dissertations*. 4th ed. with slight alterations. London: Macmillan, 1898.

Lim, K. Y. *"The Sufferings of Christ Are Abundant in Us": A Narrative Dynamics Investigation of Paul's Sufferings in 2 Corinthians*. London: T. & T. Clark, 2009.

Lincoln, A. T. *Ephesians. Word Biblical Commentary*. Dallas: Word Books, 1990.

Lindblom, J. *Gesichte und Offenbarungen: Vorstellungen von gottlichen Weisungen und ubernaturlichen Erscheinungen im altesten Christentum*, ARSHLL. Lund: Gleerup, 1968.

Lippert, P. *Leben als Zeugnis: Die werbende Kraft Christlicher Lebensführung nach dem Kirchenverständnis neutestamentlicher Briefe*. Stuttgart: Katholisches Bibelwerk, 1968.

Litfin, D. *St. Paul's Theology of Proclamation: 1 Corinthians 1–4 and Greco-Roman Rhetoric*, SNTSMS. Cambridge: Cambridge University Press, 1994.

Loh, I. J., and E. A. Nida. *A Translator's Handbook on Paul's Letter to the Philippians*. London: United Bible societies, 1977.

Lohmeyer, E. *Der Brief an die Philipper*, KEKNT. Göttingen: Vandenhoeck & Ruprecht, 1964.

Lohmeyer, E. *Grundlagen Paulinischer Theologie. Beiträge Zur Historischen Theologie*. Tübingen: J.C.B. Mohr, 1929.

Longenecker, B. W. *Eschatology and the Covenant: A Comparison of 4 Ezra and Romans 1–11*, JSNTSup. Sheffield: JSOT Press, 1991.

Longenecker, R. N. *Galatians*, WBC. Dallas: Word Books, 1990.

———. "The Nature of Paul's Early Eschatology." *NTS* 31 (1985): 85–95.

———. *Paul, Apostle of Liberty*. New York: Harper & Row, 1964.

———, ed. *The Road from Damascus: The Impact of Paul's Conversion on His Life, Thought, and Ministry*. Grand Rapids: Eerdmans, 1997.

Lüdemann, G. *Opposition to Paul in Jewish Christianity*. Minneapolis: Fortress Press, 1989.

———. *The Resurrection of Jesus: History, Experience, Theology*. Minneapolis: Fortress, 1994.

Luz, U. *Matthew 1–7*. Minneapolis: Fortress Press, 2007.

Lyttelton, G. *Observations on the Conversion and Apostleship of St. Paul: By Lord George Lyttleton; with an Introductory Essay by Henry Rogers*. London: R. Dodsley, 1747.

Macaskill, G. *Revealed Wisdom and Inaugurated Eschatology in Ancient Judaism and Early Christianity*, SupJSJ. Leiden: Brill, 2007.

Malherbe, A. J. *The Letters to the Thessalonians*, AB. New York: Doubleday, 2000.

Manson, S. "Pharisees." In *DNTB*, edited by C. A. Evans and S. E. Porter, 782–787. Downers Grove: InterVarsity Press, 1993.

Mare, W. H. "Zion." In *ABD*, edited by D. N. Freedman, vol. 6, 1096–1097. New York: Doubleday, 1992.

Marshall, I. H. *The Gospel of Luke*, NIGNTC. Exetrer: Parternoster, 1978.

———. "A New Understanding of the Present and the Future: Paul and Eschatology." In *The Road from Damascus: The Impact of Paul's Conversion on His Life, Thought, and Ministry*, edited by R. N. Longenecker, 43–61. Grand Rapids: Eerdmans, 1997.

———. "Who Were the Evangelists?" In *The Mission of the Early Church to Jews and Gentile*, WUNT, edited by J. Ådna and H. Kvalbein, 253–264. Tübingen: Mohr Siebeck, 2000.

Marshall, P. *Enmity in Corinth: Social Conventions in Paul's Relations with the Corinthians*, WUNT. Tübingen: Mohr Siebeck, 1987.

Martin, R. P. *2 Corinthians*, WBC. Waco: Word Books, 1986.

———. *Carmen Christi: Philippians II 5–11 in Recent Interpretation and in the Setting of Early Christian Worship*, SNTSMS. Grand Rapids: Eerdmans, 1983 (c1967).

———. *Philippians*, TNTC. Leicester: IVP / Grand Rapids: Eerdmans, 1991.

———. *The Spirit and the Congregation: Studies in 1 Corinthians 12–15*. Grand Rapids: Zondervan, 1984.

Martin, R. P., and G. F. Hawthorne, *Philippians*, revised, WBC. Nashville: Thomas Nelson, 2004.

Martyn, J. L. *Galatians*, AB. New York: Doubleday, 1997.

Marxsen, W. *The Resurrection of Jesus of Nazareth*. London: SCM, 1970.

Masson, C. *Les deux épîtres de saint Paul aux Thessaloniciens*. Paris: Delachaux & Niestle, 1957.

McClelland, S. E. "'Super-Apostles, Servants of Christ, and Servants of Satan': A Response." *JSNT* 14 (1982): 82–87.

McDonald, J. I. H. *Kerygma and Didache: The Articulation and Structure of the Earliest Christian Message*, SNTSMS. Cambridge: Cambridge University Press, 1980.

McKnight, S. *A Light Among the Gentiles: Jewish Missionary Activity in the Second Temple Period*. Minneapolis: Fortress Press, 1991.

Mearns, C. L. "Early Eschatological Development in Paul: The Evidence of I and II Thessalonians." *NTS* 27 (1981): 137–157.

Meeks, W. A. *The First Urban Christians: The Social World of the Apostle Paul*. New Haven: Yale University, 1983.

Meier, J. P. *A Marginal Jew, Vol.2: Rethinking the Historical Jesus*. New York: Doubleday, 1994.

Meyer, B. F. *The Aims of Jesus*. London: SCM, 1979.

———. *The Early Christians: Their World Mission and Self-Discovery*. Wilmington: Michael Glazier Inc., 1986.

Meyer, H. A. W. *Critical and Exegetical Handbook to the Epistles to the Philippians and Colossians*, CECNT. Edinburgh: T. & T. Clark, 1875.

———. *Critical and Exegetical Handbook to the Epistle to the Ephesians and the Epistle to Philemon*, CECNT. Edinburgh: T. & T. Clark, 1895.

Michael, J. H. *The Epistle of Paul to the Philippians (Moffatt New Testament Commentary*. London: Hodder and Stoughton, 1939.

Michaelis, W. "ὁράω, εἶδον, βλέπω, ὀπτάνομαι, θεάομαι, θεωρέω, ἀόρατος, ὁρατός, ὅρασις, ὅραμα, ὀπτασία, αὐτόπτης, ἐπόπτης, ἐποπτεύω, ὀφθαλμός, καθοράω, προοράω, προεῖδον." In *TDNT*, edited by G. Kittel and G. Friedrich, vol. 5, 315–382. Grand Rapids: Eerdmans, 1964–1976.

Miller, E. C. "Πολιτεύεσθε in Philippians 1.27: Some Philological and Thematic Observations." *JSNT* 15 (1982): 86–96.

Milligan, G. *St. Paul's Epistles to the Thessalonians: The Greek Text with Introduction and Notes*. London: Macmillan, 1908.

Mitton, C. L. *The Epistle to the Ephesians*. Oxford: Clarendon Press, 1951.

Moffatt, J. *The First Epistle of Paul to the Corinthians*, MNC. London: Hodder and Stoughton, 1938 (1930).

Moo, D. J. *The Epistle to the Romans*, NICNT. Grand Rapids: Eerdmans, 1996.

Morgan, R., ed. and trans. *The Nature of New Testament Theology: The Contribution of William Wrede and Adolf Schlatter*. London: SCM, 1973.

Moritz, T. *A Profound Mystery: The Use of the OT in Ephesians*, NovTSup. Leiden: Brill, 1996.

Morris, L. *The Epistle to the Romans*. Nottingham: Inter-Varsity Press, 1988.

———. *The First and Second Epistles to the Thessalonians*, NICNT. Grand Rapids: Eerdmans, 1991.

Mosbech, H. "Apostolos in the New Testament." *StTh* 2 (1948): 166–200.

Motyer, A. *The Message of Philippians: Jesus Our Joy*. 2nd ed. Nottingham: Inter-Varsity Press, 1997.

Moule, C. F. D. *An Idiom Book of New Testament Greek*. 2nd ed. Cambridge: University press, 1959.

———, ed. *The Significance of the Message of the Resurrection for Faith in Jesus Christ*. Naperville: Alec R. Allenson, 1968.

Moule, H. C. G. *The Epistle of Paul the Apostle to the Philippians*. Cambridge: Cambridge University Press, 1923.

Moulton, J. H., and G. Milligan. *The Vocabulary of the Greek Testament: Illustrated from the Papyri and Other Non-literary Sources*. London: Hodder and Stoughton, 1930.

Moyise, S., and M. J. J. Menken, eds. *Isaiah in the New Testament*. London/New York: T. & T. Clark, 2005.

Müller, U. B. *Der Brief des Paulus an die Philipper*, THKNT. 2nd ed. Liepzig: Evangelische Verlagsanstalt, 2002.

Munck, J. *Christ and Israel: An Interpretation of Romans 9–11*. Minneapolis: Fortress Press, 1967.
———. *Paul and the Salvation of Mankind*. London: SCM Press, 1959.
———. "Paul, the Apostles and the Twelve." *StTh* 3 (1950): 96–110.
———. *Paulus und die Heilsgeschichte*. Copenhagen: Ejnar Munksgaard, 1954.
Murphy-O'Connor, J. "Christological Anthropology in Phil II.6–11." *RB* 83 (1976): 25–50.
———. "Paul in Arabia." *CBQ* 55 (1993): 732–737.
———. "Tradition and Redaction in 1 Cor 15:3–7." *CBQ* 43 (1981): 582–589.
Murray, J. *The Epistle to the Romans: The English Text with Introduction, Exposition and Notes, II*. Grand Rapids: Eerdmans, 1965.
Mussner, F. *Galaterbrief*, HTKNT. Freiburg: Herder, 1974.
———. "Ganz Israel wird gerettet werden (Röm 11. 26)." *Kairos* 18 (1976): 245–253.
Nanos, M. D. *The Mystery of Romans: The Jewish Context of Paul's Letter*. Minneapolis: Fortress, 1996.
Neirynck, F. "Paul and the Sayings of Jesus." In *L'Apôtre Paul: Personnalité, style et conception du ministère*, edited by A. Vanhoye, 265–321. Leuven: University Press, 1986.
Neusner, J., and A. J. Avery-Peck. *Judaism in Late Antiquity*. Part 3, vol. 2. Leiden: Brill, 1995.
Neusner, J. *From Politics to Piety: The Emergence of Pharisaic Judaism*. Englewood Cliffs: Prentice-Hall, 1973.
———. *The Rabbinic Traditions about the Pharisees before 70*. 3 vols. Leiden: Brill, 1971.
Newman, C. C., ed. *Jesus and the Restoration of Israel: A Critical Assessment of N.T. Wright's "Jesus and the Victory of God"*. Carlisle: Paternoster, 1999.
Nickelsburg, G. W. E. *Jewish Literature between the Bible and the Mishnah: A Historical and Literary Introduction*. Philadelphia: Fortress Press, 1981.
Nickle, K. F. *The Collection: A Study in Paul's Strategy*. London: S.C.M. Press, 1966.
Nineham, D. E. "The Case against the Pauline Authorship." In *Studies in Ephesians*, edited by F. L. Cross, 21–35. London: Mowbray, 1956.
Nock, A. D. *Conversion: The Old and the New in Religion from Alexander the Great to Augustine of Hippo*. Oxford: Clarendon Press, 1933.
Nolland, J. *Gospel of Matthew: A Commentary on the Greek Text*, NIGTC. Grand Rapids: Eerdmans / Bletchley: Paternoster, 2005.
———. "Proselytism or Politics in Horace, *Satires* I, 4, 138–143?" *VC* 33 (1979): 347–355.
O'Brien, P. T. *Consumed by Passion: Paul and the Dynamic of the Gospel*. Homebush West: Anzea, 1993.

———. *The Epistle to the Philippians*, NIGTC. Grand Rapids: Eerdmans / Bletchley: Paternoster, 1991.

———. *Gospel and Mission in the Writings of Paul: An Exegetical and Theological Analysis*. Carlisle: Paternoster, 1995.

———. *Introductory Thanksgivings in the Letters of Paul*, NovTSup. Leiden: Brill, 1977.

———. *The Letter to the Ephesians*, PNTC. Leicester: Apollos, 1999.

———. "Principalities and Powers: Opponents of the Church (20th-Century Interpretations)." *ERT* 16 (1992): 353–384.

O'Collins, G. *The Resurrection of Jesus Christ*. Valley Forge: Judson Press, 1973.

Oakes, P. *Philippians: From People to Letters*, SNTSMS. Cambridge: Cambridge University Press, 2001.

Ochenmeier, E. "The Great Commission (Matt. 28.19-20) in History and Today or Why the Great Commission Is Not the Duty of All Believers." Paper Presented at the New Testament Study Group of the *Tyndale Fellowship*, Cambridge (UK), July (2011).

Oepke, A., and J. Rohde. *Der Brief des Paulus an die Galater*. 5th ed. Berlin: Evangelisches, 1984.

———. "ἐν." In *TDNT*, edited by G. Kittel and G. Friedrich, vol. 2, 537–543. Grand Rapids: Eerdmans, 1964–1976.

Ollrog, W.-H. *Paulus und seine Mitarbeiter: Untersuchungen zu Theorie und Praxis der paulinischen Mission*. Neukirchen-Vluyn: Neukirchener Verlag, 1979.

Orlinsky, H. M., and N. H. Snaith. *Studies on the Second Part of the Book of Isaiah*, VTSup. Leiden: Brill, 1977.

Osiek, C. *Philippians, Philemon*, ANTC. Nashville: Abingdon Press, 2000.

Pahl, M. W. D. *Discerning the 'Word of the Lord': The Word of the Lord in 1 Thessalonians 4:15*, LNTS. London: T. & T. Clark, 2009.

Park, M. S. *Submission within the Godhead and the Church in the Epistle to the Philippians*. London: T. & T. Clark, 2007.

Parsons, M. "Being Precedes Act: Indicative and Imperative In Paul's Writing." In *Understanding Paul's Ethics: Twentieth Century Approaches*, edited by B. S. Rosner, 217–247. Carlisle: Paternoster Press, 1995.

Pennington, J. T. "Dualism in Old Testament Cosmology: Weltbild und Weltanschauung." *SJOT* 18, no. 2 (2004): 260–277.

Peterman, G. W. "Giving and Receiving in Paul's Epistles: Greco-Roman Social Conventions in Philippians and in Other Pauline Writings." DPhil dissertation, King's College, London, 1992.

———. *Paul's Gift from Philippi: Conventions of Gift-Exchange and Christian Giving*, SNTSMS. Cambridge: Cambridge University Press, 1997.

Pfitzner, V. C. *Paul and the Agon Motif: Traditional Athletic Imagery in the Pauline Literature*, NovTSup. Leiden: Brill, 1967.

Pietersma, A., and C. Cox, eds. *De Septuaginta: Studies in Honour of John William Wevers on His Sixty-Fifth Birthday.* Toronto: Benben, 1984.

Pitre, B. *Jesus, the Tribulation, and the End of the Exile: Restoration Eschatology and the Origin of the Atonement,* WUNT. Tübingen: Mohr Siebeck, 2005.

Plummer, R. L. "Imitation of Paul and the Church's Missionary Role in 1 Corinthians." *JETS* 44, no. 2 (2001): 234–235.

———. *Paul's Understanding of the Church's Mission: Did the Apostle Paul Expect the Early Christian Communities to Evangelize?* Carlisle, Cumbria: Paternoster, 2006.

———. "A Theological Basis for the Church's Mission in Paul." *WTJ* 64 (2002): 253–271.

Polhill, J. B. "Paul: Theology Born of Mission." *RevExp* 78 (1981): 233–247.

Porter, S. E., ed. *Paul and His Opponents.* Leiden: Brill, 2005.

———. "Paul's Concept of Reconciliation, Twice More." In *Paul and His Theology,* edited by S. E. Porter, 134–144. Leiden: Brill, 2006.

Porter, S. E., and T. H. Olbricht, eds. "Reconciliation as the Heart of Paul's Missionary Theology." In *Paul as Missionary: Identity, Activity, Theology, and Practice,* LNTS, edited by T. J. Burke and B. S. Rosner, 172–176. London: T. & T. Clark, 2011.

———. *Rhetoric and the New Testament: Essays from the 1992 Heidelberg Conference.* Sheffield: Sheffield Academic Press, 1993.

Price, R. M. "Apocryphal Apparitions: 1 Corinthians 15:3–11 as a Post-Pauline Interpolation." *JHC* 2, no. 2 (1995): 69–99.

Räisänen, H. *Paul and the Law,* WUNT. Tübingen: Mohr Siebeck, 1987.

Refoulé, F. '... *Et ainsi tout Israël sera sauvé': Romains 11.25–32.* Paris: Le Cerf, 1984, 56–61.

Renan, E. *Saint Paul.* Paris: Calmann Lévy, 1883.

Rengstorf, K. H. "ἀποστέλλω (πέμπω), ἐξαποστέλλω, ἀπόστολος, ψευδαπόστολος, ἀποστολή." In *TDNT,* edited by G. Kittel and G. Friedrich, vol. 1, 398–447. Grand Rapids: Eerdmans, 1964–1976.

———. *Die Auferstehung Jesu: Form, Art und Sinn der urchristlichen Osterbotschaft.* 4th ed. Witten: Ruhr, 1960.

Reumann, J. *Philippians: A New Translation with Introduction and Commentary,* AYB. New Haven: Yale University Press, 2008.

Richard, E. J. *First and Second Thessalonians.* Collegeville: The Liturgical Press, 1995.

Richardson, A. *An Introduction to the Theology of the New Testament.* London: SCM, 1958.

Richardson, P., and J. C. Hurd, eds. *From Jesus to Paul: Studies in Honour of Francis Wright Beare.* Waterloo: Wilfrid Laurier University Press, 1984.

Richardson, P., and S. Wilfrid. *Law in Religious Communities in the Roman Period: The Debate over Torah and Nomos in Post-biblical Judaism and Early Christianity.* Waterloo: Published for the Canadian Corporation for Studies, 1991.

Richardson, P. *Israel in the Apostolic Church*, SNTSMS. Cambridge: Cambridge University Press, 1969.

Ridderbos, H. N. *Paul: An Outline of His Theology.* Grand Rapids: Eerdmans, 1975.

Riesner, R. *Paul's Early Period: Chronology, Mission Statement, Theology.* Grand Rapids: Eerdmans, 1998.

———. "A Pre-Christian Jewish Mission?" In *The Mission of the Early Church to Jews and Gentile*, WUNT, edited by J. Ådna and H. Kvalbein, 221–250. Tübingen: Mohr Siebeck, 2000.

Rigaux, B. *The Letters of St. Paul: Modern Studies.* Chicago: Franciscan Herald Press, 1968.

Roberts, R. "Old Texts in Modern Translation, Philippians 1:27." *ExpTim* 49 (1937–1938): 325–328.

Robertson, A. T. *A Grammar of the Greek New Testament in the Light of Historical Research.* 3rd ed. New York: Hodder & Stoughton, 1919.

Robinson, D. W. B. "The Distinction between Jewish and Gentile Believers in Galatians." *ABR* 13 (1965): 29–44.

Robinson, J. R. "ΠΩΡΩΣΙΣ and ΠΗΡΩΣΙΣ." *JTS* 3 (1902): 81–93.

Roels, E. D. *God's Mission: The Epistle to the Ephesians in Mission Perspective.* Franeker: T. Wever, 1962.

Roloff, J. B. *Apostolat-Verkündigung-Kirche.* Gütersloh: Mohn, 1965.

———. "Apostel/Apostolat/Apostolizität I. Neues Testament." In *Theologische Realenzyklopädie*, edited by G. Krause & G. Müller, 430–445. Berlin: de Gruyter, 1978.

Rosner, B. S., ed. "Paul's Ethics." In *The Cambridge Companion to St. Paul*, edited by J. D. G. Dunn, 212–223. Cambridge: Cambridge University Press, 2003.

———. *Understanding Paul's Ethics: Twentieth Century Approaches.* Carlisle: Paternoster Press, 1995.

Rowland, C. *Christian Origins: An Account of the Setting and Character of the Most Important Messianic Sect of Judaism.* 2nd ed. London: SPCK, 2002.

———. *The Open Heaven: A Study of Apocalyptic in Judaism and Early Christianity.* London: SPCK, 1982.

Rowley, H. H., and M. Black, eds. *Peake's Commentary on the Bible.* London: T. Nelson, 1967.

Russell, D. S. *The Method and Message of Jewish Apocalyptic, 200 BC–AD 100.* London: SCM, 1964.

Saldarini, A. J. "Pharisees." In *ABD*, edited by D. N. Freedman, vol. 5, 289–303. New York: Doubleday, 1992.
Sanders, E. P. *Jesus and Judaism*. London: SCM, 1985.
———. *Jewish Law from Jesus to the Mishnah: Five Studies*. London: SCM; Philadelphia: Trinity Press International, 1990.
———. *Judaism: Practice and Belief, 63 BCE–66 CE*. London: SCM; Philadelphia: Trinity Press International, 1992.
———. *Paul and Palestinain Judaism*. London: SCM, 1977.
———. "Paul's Attitude toward the Jewish People." *USQR* 33 (1978): 180–183.
———. *Paul, the Law, and the Jewish People*. Philadelphia: Fortress Press, 1983.
Sandnes, K. O. *Paul-One of the Prophets?: A Contribution to the Apostle's Self-Understanding*, WUNT. Tübingen: Mohr Siebeck, 1991.
Sass, G. *Apostelamt und Kirche*. Munich: Kaiser, 1939.
Schaller, B. "'ΗΞΕΙ ΕΚ ΣΙΩΝ Ο ΡΥΟΜΕΝΟΣ.' Zur Textgestalt von Jes 59:20f. in Röm 11:26f." In *De Septuaginta: Studies in Honour of John William Wevers on His Sixty-Fifth Birthday*, edited by A. Pietersma and C. Cox, 201–206. Toronto: Benben, 1984.
Schenk, W. *Die Philipperbriefe des Paulus: Kommentar*. Stuttgart: W. Kohlhammer, 1984.
Schiffman, L. H. *The Eschatological Community of the Dead Sea Scrolls: A Study of the Rule of the Congregation*, SBLMS. Atlanta: Scholars Press, 1989.
Schille, G. *Die urchristliche Kollegialmission*. Zürich: Zwingli-Verl, 1967.
Schlier, H. *Der brief an die Galater*, KEKNT. Göttingen: Vandenhoeck & Ruprecht, 1962.
———. *Der Römerbrief: Kommentar*, HTKNT. Freiburg im Breisgau: Herder, 1977.
Schmidt, K. L., and M. A. Schmidt. "παχύνω, πωρόω (πηρόω), πώρωσις (πήρωσις), σκληος, σκληρότης, σκληροτράχηλος, σκληρύνω." In *TDNT*, edited by G. Kittel and G. Friedrich, vol. 5, 1022–1031. Grand Rapids: Eerdmans, 1964–1976.
Schmidt, K. L. "καλέω, κλῆσις, κλητός, ντικαλέω, ἐγκαλέω, γκλημα, εἰσκαλέω, προκαλέω, συρκαλέω, ἐπικαλέω, προσκαλέω, ἐκκλησία." In *TDNT*, edited by G. Kittel and G. Friedrich, vol. 3, 487–536. Grand Rapids: Eerdmans, 1964–1976.
Schmithals, W. *The Office of Apostle in the Early Church*. London: SPCK, 1971.
Schnabel, E. J. "Beginnings of the Mission to the Gentiles." In *Jesus of Nazareth: Lord and Christ: Essays on the Historical Jesus and New Testament Christology*, edited by J. B. Green and M. Turner, 37–58. Grand Rapids: Eerdmans, 1994.
———. *Early Christian Mission*. 2 vols. Downers Grove: InterVarsity Press, 2004.

Schnackenburg, R. "Apostles Before and During Paul's Time." In *Apostolic History and the Gospel*, edited by W. W. Gasque & R. P. Martin, 287–303. Grand Rapids: Eerdmans, 1970.

———. *The Epistle to the Ephesians*. Edinburgh: T. & T. Clark, 1991.

Schnelle, U. *Gerechtigkeit und Christusgegenwart: vorpaulinische und paulinische Tauftheologie*. Göttingen: Vandenhoeck & Ruprecht, 1983.

Schoeps, H. J. *Paul: The Theology of the Apostle in the Light of Jewish Religious History*. London: Lutterworth Press, 1961.

Schreiner, T. R. *Romans*, BECNT. Grand Rapids: Baker, 1998.

Schrenk, G. "Der Segenwunsch nach der Kampfepistel." *Judaica* 6 (1950): 170–190.

Schubert, P. *Form and Function of the Pauline Thanksgivings*. Berlin: Alfred Töpelmann, 1939.

Schulz, R. R. "Romans 16:7: Junia or Junias?" *ExpTim* 98 (1987): 108–110.

Schürer, E. *The History of the Jewish People in the Age of Jesus Christ*. New English version. Edinburgh: T. & T. Clark, 1986.

Schütz, J. H. *Paul and the Anatomy of Apostolic Authority*, SNTSMS. London: Cambridge University Press, 1975.

Schwarz, H. *Eschatology*. Grand Rapids: Eerdmans, 2000.

Schweitzer, A. "The Church as the Missionary Body of Christ." *NTS* 8 (1961/62): 1–11.

———. *Church Order in the New Testament*. London: SCM, 1961.

———. *The Mysticism of Paul the Apostle*. London: A. & C. Black, 1931.

———. *The Quest for the Historical Jesus: A Critical Study of Its Progress from Reimarus to Wrede*. 2nd ed. London: Adam and Charles Black, 1911.

Scobie, C. H. H. "Jesus or Paul? Origin of the Universal Mission." In *From Jesus to Paul: Studies in Honour of Francis Wright Beare*, edited by P. Richardson and J. C. Hurd, 47–60. Waterloo: Wilfrid Laurier University Press, 1984.

Scott, J. M. *Paul and the Nations: The Old Testament and Jewish Background of Paul's Mission to the Nations with Special Reference to the Destination of Galatians*, WUNT. Tübingen: Mohr Siebeck, 1995.

———. "Paul's Use of Deuteronomic Tradition." *JBL* 112, no. 4 (1993): 645–665.

———. "Restoration of Israel." In *DPL*, edited by G. F. Hawthorne and R. P. Martin, 799–805. Downers Grove: InterVarsity Press, 1993.

———. *Restoration: Old Testament, Jewish and Christian Perspectives*, JSJSup. Leiden: Brill, 2001.

Seesemann, H. *Der Bergriff KOINWNIA im Neuen Testament*. Giessen: Verlag von Alfred Toepelmann, 1933.

Segal, A. F. *Paul the Convert: The Apostolate and Apostasy of Saul the Pharisee*. New Haven: Yale University Press, 1990.

Senior, D., and C. Stuhlmueller. *The Biblical Foundations for Mission*. London: SCM, 1983.

Seufert, W. *Der Ursprung und die Bedeutung des Apostolates in der christlichen Kirche der ersten zwei Jahrhunderte*. Leiden: Brill, 1887.

Silva, M. "Old Testament in Paul." In *DPL*, edited by G. F. Hawthorne and R. P. Martin, 630–642. Downers Grove: InterVarsity Press, 1993.

———. *Philippians*, WEC. Chicago: Moody Press, 1988.

Sim, D. C. "Matthew and the Pauline Corpus: A Preliminary Intertextual Study." *JSNT* 31 (2009): 401–422.

Smit, J. F. M. "'What Is Apollos? What Is Paul?' In Search for the Coherence of First Corinthians 1:10–4:21." *NovT* 44, no. 3 (2002): 231–251.

Snaith, N. H. "A Study of the Teaching of the Second Isaiah and Its Consequences." In *Studies on the Second Part of the Book of Isaiah*, VTSup, edited by H. M. Orlinsky and N. H. Snaith, 155–157. Leiden: Brill, 1977.

Soderlund, S. V., and N. T. Wright, eds. *Romans and the People of God: Essays in Honor of Gordon D. Fee on the Occasion of His 65th Birthday*. Grand Rapids: Eerdmans, 1999.

Srathmann, H. "πόλις, πολίτης, πολιτεύομαι, πολιτεία, πολίτευμα." In *TDNT*, edited by G. Kittel and G. Friedrich, vol. 6, 516–535. Grand Rapids: Eerdmans, 1964–1976.

Stanley, C. D. *Paul and the Language of Scripture: Citation Technique in the Pauline Epistles and Contemporary Literature*, SNTSMS. Cambridge: Cambridge University Press, 1992.

———. "The Redeemer Will Come ἐκ Σιών' Romans 11.26–27 Revisited." In *Paul and the Scriptures of Israel*, JSNTSup, edited by C. A. Evans and J. A. Sanders, 118–142. Sheffield: JSOT Press, 1993.

Stanton, G. N. *Jesus of Nazareth in New Testament Preaching*, SNTSMS. Cambridge: Cambridge University Press, 1974.

Stendahl, K. "The Apostle Paul and the Introspective Conscience of the West." In *Paul among Jews and Gentiles*, edited by K. Stendahl, 78–96. Philadelphia: Fortress, 1976.

———. *Final Account: Paul's Letter to the Romans*. Minneapolis: Fortress, 1995.

———. *Meanings: The Bible as Document and as Guide*. Philadelphia: Fortress Press, 1984.

———. *Paul among Jews and Gentiles, and Other Essays*. London: SCM Press, 1977.

Stettler, H. "Colossians 1:24 in the Framework of Paul's Mission Theology." In *The Mission of the Early Church to Jews and Gentiles*, WUNT, edited by J. Ådna and H. Kvalbein, 185–208. Tübingen: Mohr Siebeck, 2000.

Stewart, J. S. *A Man in Christ: The Vital Element of St. Paul's Religion*. London: Hodder & Stoughton, 1947.

Stowers, S. K. "Friends and Enemies in Politics of Heaven: Reading Theology in Philippians." In *Pauline Theology*, edited by J. M. Bassler, vol. 1, 105–121. Minneapolis: Fortress, 1991.

Strelan, J. G. "Burden-Bearing and the Law of Christ: A Re-Examination of Galatians 6.2." *JBL* 94 (1975): 266–276.

Stuhlmacher, P. *Biblische Theologie des Neuen Testaments I*. Göttingen: Vandenhoeck & Ruprecht, 1992.

———. *Das Paulinische Evangelium: I Vorgeschichte*, FRLANT. Göttingen: Vandenhoeck & Ruprecht, 1968.

———, ed. *The Gospel and the Gospels*. Grand Rapids: Eerdmans, 1991.

———. "The Pauline Gospel." In *The Gospel and the Gospels*, edited by P. Stuhlmacher, 156–165. Grand Rapids: Eerdmans, 1991.

———. *Paul's Letter to the Romans: A Commentary*. Edinburgh: T. & T. Clark, 1994.

———. "Zur Interpretation von Römer 11.25–32." In *Probleme Biblischer Theologie: Gerhard Von Rad Zum 70. Geburtstag*, edited by H. W. Wolff, 555–570. München: Kaiser, 1971.

Sumney, J. L. *Identifying Paul's Opponents: The Question of Method in 2 Corinthians*, JSNTSup. Sheffield: JSOT Press, 1990.

Talbert, C. *Romans*, SHBC. Macon: Smyth & Helwys, 2002.

Taylor, N. *Paul, Antioch and Jerusalem: A Study in Relationships and Authority in Earliest Christianity*, JSNTSup. Sheffield: JSOT Press, 1992.

Theissen, G., and D. Winter. *The Quest for the Plausible Jesus: The Question of Criteria*. Louisville: Westminster John Knox Press, 2002.

Theissen, G. *Psychological Aspects of Pauline Theology*. Edinburgh: T. & T. Clark, 1987.

———. *The Social Setting of Pauline Christianity: Essays on Corinth*. Philadelphia: Fortress Press, 1982.

Thiselton, A. C. *First Corinthians: A Shorter Exegetical and Pastoral Commentary*. Grand Rapids: Eerdmans, 2006.

Thompson, M. *Clothed with Christ: The Example and Teaching of Jesus in Romans 12.1–15.13*, JSNTSup. Sheffield: JSOT Press, 1991.

Thrall, M. E. *A Critical and Exegetical Commentary on the Second Epistle to the Corinthians*, ICC. 2 vols. Edinburgh: T. & T. Clark, 1994–2000.

———. "Super-Apostles, Servants of Christ, and Servants of Satan." *JSNT* 6 (1980): 42–57.

Tomson, P. J. *Paul and the Jewish law: halakha in the Letters of the Apostle to the Gentiles*. Assen: Fortress Press; Minneapolis: Van Gorcum, 1990.

Towner, P. H. "Households and Household Codes." In *DPL*, edited by G. F. Hawthorne and R. P. Martin, 417–419. Downers Grove: InterVarsity Press, 1993.

Trafton, J. L. "The Psalms of Solomon: New Light from the Syriac Version?" *JBL* 105 (1986): 227–237.
Troeltsch, E. *The Absoluteness of Christianity and the History of Religions.* Westminster: John Knox Press, 2005.
Trudinger, L. P. "ΕΤΕΡΟΝ ΔΕ ΤΩΝ ΑΠΟΣΤΟΛΩΝ ΟΥΚ ΕΙΔΟΝ ΕΙ ΜΗ ΙΑΚΩΒΟΝ: A Note on Galatians 1:19." *NovT* 17 (1975): 200–202.
Tuckett, C. M. "Paul and the Synoptic Mission Discourse?" *ETL* 60 (1984): 376–381.
Turner, N. *Grammatical Insights into the New Testament.* Edinburgh: T. & T. Clark, 1965.
van der Horst, P. W. "Only Then Will All Israel Be Saved: A Short Note on the Meaning of *kai houtōs* in Romans 11.26." *JBL* 119 (2000): 521–539.
van Swigchem, D. *Het missionair karakter van de Christelijke gemeente volgens de brieven van Paulus en Petrus.* Kampen: Kok, 1955.
Vanhoye, A., ed. *L'Apôtre Paul: Personnalité, style et conception du ministère.* Leuven: University Press, 1986.
Vincent, M. R. *A Critical and Exegetical Commentary on the Epistles to the Philippians and to Philemon,* ICC. Edinburgh: T. & T. Clark, 1897.
———. *Word Studies in the New Testament.* Vol. 3. Peabody: Hendrickson, 1888.
von Campenhausen, H. F. "Der urkirchliche Apostelbegriff." *StTh* 2 (1948): 96–130.
von Harnack, A. *The Mission and Expansion of Christianity in the First Three Centuries.* Gloucester: Peter Smith, 1972 (1902).
von Soden, H. "ἀδελφός, ἀδελφή, ἀδελφότης, φιλάδελφος, φιλαδελφία, ψευδάδελφος." In *TDNT*, edited by G. Kittel and G. Friedrich, vol. 1, 144–146. Grand Rapids: Eerdmans, 1964–1976.
von Weizsäcker, C. *The Apostolic Age of the Christian Church.* London: Williams and Norgate, 1894–1895.
Vos, G. *The Pauline Eschatology.* Grand Rapids: Eerdmans, 1979 (1953).
Wagner, J. R. "The Heralds of Isaiah and the Mission of Paul: An Investigation of Paul's Use of Isaiah 51–55 in Romans." In *Jesus and the Suffering Servant: Isaiah 53 and Christian Origins,* edited by W. H. Bellinger and W. R. Farmer, 193–222. Harrisburg: Trinity, 1998.
———. *Heralds of the Good News: Isaiah and Paul "in Concert" in the Letter to the Romans,* NovTSup. Leiden: Brill, 2002.
———. "Isaiah in Romans and Galatians." In *Isaiah in the New Testament: The New Testament and the Scriptures of Israel,* edited by S. Moyise and M. J. J. Menken, 117–132. London: T. & T. Clark, 2005.
Walter, N. "Paul and the Early Christian Jesus-Tradition." In *Paul and Jesus,* edited by A. J. M. Wedderburn, 51–80. London: T. & T. Clark, 1989.

Wanamaker, C. A. *The Epistles to the Thessalonians: A Commentary on the Greek Text*, NIGTC. Exeter: Paternoster Press; Grand Rapids: Eerdmans, 1990.

———. "'Like a Father Treats His Own Children': Paul and the Conversion of the Thessalonians." *JTSA* 92 (1995): 46–55.

Ware, J. P. "'Holding Forth the Word of Life': Paul and the Mission of the Church in the Letter to the Philippians in the Context of Second Temple Judaism." PhD dissertation, Yale University, 1996.

———. *The Mission of the Church in Paul's Letter to the Philippians in the Context of Ancient Judaism*, NovTSup. Leiden: Brill, 2005.

———. "The Thessalonians as Missionary Congregation: 1 Thessalonians 1.5–8." *ZNW* 83 (1992): 126–132.

Warneck, G. *Evangelisch Missionslehre: Ein missionstheoretischer Versuch*. Gotha: Friedrich Andreas Perthes, 1892–1903.

Warneck, J. *The Living Forces of the Gospel: Experiences of a Missionary in Animistic Heathendom*. Edinburgh: Oliphant, Anderson & Ferrier, 1909.

Watson, D. F. *Paul, Judaism and the Gentiles: A Sociological Approach*, SNTSMS. Cambridge: Cambridge University Press, 1986.

———. "Paul's Rhetorical Strategy in 1 Corinthians 15." In *Rhetoric and the New Testament: Essays from the 1992 Heidelberg Conference*, edited by S. E. Porter and T. H. Olbricht, 231–249. Sheffield: Sheffield Academic Press, 1993.

Weadors, E. P. *Jesus the Messianic Herald of Salvation*, WUNT. Tübingen: Mohr Siebeck, 1995.

Weaver, J. A. *Theodoret of Cyrus on Romans 11:26: Recovering an Early Christian Elijah Redivivus Tradition*. New York: Peter Lang Publishing, 2007.

Wedderburn, A. J. M., ed. *Paul and Jesus*. London: T. & T. Clark, 1989.

———. "Paul and Jesus: Similarity and Continuity." In *Paul and Jesus*, edited by A. J. M. Wedderburn, 117–143. London: T. & T. Clark, 1989.

———. "Paul and the Story of Jesus." In *Paul and Jesus*, edited by A. J. M. Wedderburn, 161–189. London: T. & T. Clark, 1989.

Weima, J. A. D. "Gal. 6:11–18: A Hermeneutical Key to the Galatian Letter." *CTJ* 28 (1993): 90–107.

Weiss, J. *Der erste Korintherbrief*. Göttingen: Vandenhoeck und Ruprecht, 1910.

———. *The History of Primitive Christianity*. New York: Wilson-Erickson, 1937.

Wenham, D. "Paul and the Synoptic Apocalypse." In *Gospel Perspectives 2: Studies of History and Tradition in the Four Gospels*, JSNTSup, edited by R. T. France and D. Wenham, 345–375. Sheffield: JSOT Press, 1981.

———. *Paul: Follower of Jesus or Founder of Christianity*. Grand Rapids: Eerdmans, 1995.

———. "The Rock on Which to Build: Some Mainly Pauline Observations about the Sermon on the Mount." In *Built upon the Rock, Studies in the*

Gospel of Matthew, edited by D. M. Gurtner and J. Nolland. Grand Rapids: Eerdmans, 2008.

———. "The Story of Jesus Known to Paul." In *Jesus of Nazareth: Lord and Christ: Essays on the Historical Jesus and New Testament Christology*, edited by J. B. Green and M. Turner, 297–311. Grand Rapids: Eerdmans, 1994.

Wernle, P. *The Beginnings of Christianity*. Vol. 1. London: Williams & Norgate, 1903.

———. *Paulus als Heidenmissionar*. Freiburg/B: Mohr, 1899.

Whiteley, D. E. H. *The Theology of St. Paul*. Oxford: Blackwell, 1964.

Wilckens, U. *Der Brief an die Römer*. Vol. 2. EKKNT. 3rd ed. Zürich: Bebziger Verlag, 1993.

———. *Die Missionsreden der Apostelgeschichte: Form und traditionsgeschichtliche Untersuchungen*, WMANT 3. Neukirchen: Neukirchner Verlag, 1960.

———. *Resurrection, Biblical Testimony to the Resurrection: An Historical Examination and Explanation*. Atlanta: John Knox Press, 1978.

———. "The Tradition-history of the Resurrection of Jesus." In *The Significance of the Message of the Resurrection for Faith in Jesus Christ*, edited by C. F. D. Moule, 51–76. Naperville: Alec R. Allenson, 1968.

Wiles, G. P. *Paul's Intercessory Prayers: The Significance of the Intercessory Prayer Passages in the Letters of St Paul*, SNTSMS. Cambridge: Cambridge University Press, 1974.

Wilk, F. "Isaiah in 1 and 2 Corinthians." In *Isaiah in the New Testament*, edited by S. Moyise and M. J. J. Menken, 133–158. London/New York: T. & T. Clark, 2005.

Willis, W. L. "An Apostolic Apologia? The Form and Function of 1 Corinthians 9." *JSNT* 24 (1985): 33–48.

Wilson, S. G. *The Gentiles and the Gentile Mission in Luke-Acts*. Cambridge: Cambridge University Press, 1973.

Wink, W. *The Powers That Be: Theology for a New Millennium*. Garden city: Doubleday, 1998.

Witherington, B. *The Christology of Jesus*. Minneapolis: Fortress Press, 1990.

———. *Conflict and Community in Corinth: A Socio-rhetorical Commentary on 1 and 2 Corinthians*. Grand Rapids: Eerdmans, 1994.

———. *Friendship and Finances in Philippi: The Letter of Paul to the Philippians*. Valley Forge: Trinity Press International, 1994.

———. *Jesus, Paul, and the End of the World: A Comparative Study in New Testament Eschatology*. Carlisle, Cumbria: Paternoster Press, 1992.

———. *The Paul Quest: The Renewed Search for the Jew of Tarsus*. Nottingham: Inter-Varsity Press, 1998.

———. *Paul's Letter to the Philippians: a Socio-rhetorical Commentary*. Grand Rapids: Eerdmans, 2011.

———. *Paul's Letter to the Romans: A Socio-rhetorical Commentary.* Grand Rapids: Eerdmans, 2004.

Wolff, C. "Humility and Self-denial in Jesus' Life and Message and in the Apostolic Existence of Paul." In *Paul and Jesus*, edited by A. J. M. Wedderburn, 145–160. London: T. & T. Clark, 1989.

———. "True Apostolic Knowledge of Christ: Exegetical Reflections on 2 Cor 5.12ff." In *Paul and Jesus*, edited by A. J. M. Wedderburn, 92–97. London: T. & T. Clark, 1989.

———. "True Apostolic Knowledge of Christ." In *Paul and Jesus*, edited by A. J. M. Wedderburn, 85–98. London: T. & T. Clark, 1989.

Wolff, H. W., ed. *Probleme Biblischer Theologie: Gerhard Von Rad Zum 70. Geburtstag.* München: Kaiser, 1971.

Woodbridge, P. "Did Paul Change His Mind? – An Examination of Some Aspects of Pauline Eschatology." *Themelios* 28, no. 3 (2003): 5–18.

Wrede, W. *Paul.* London: P. Green, 1907.

———. "The Task and Methods of 'New Testament Theology.'" In *The Nature of New Testament Theology: The Contribution of William Wrede and Adolf Schlatter*, edited and translated by R. Morgan, 68–116. London: SCM, 1973.

Wright, C. J. H. "Family." In *ABD*, edited by D. N. Freedman, vol. 2, 761–769. New York: Doubleday, 1992.

Wright, N. T. *The Climax of the Covenant: Christ and the Law in Pauline Theology.* Edinburgh: Clark, 1991.

———. *Jesus and the Victory of God (Christian origins and the question of God).* London: SPCK, 1996.

———. "The Messiah and the People of God: A Study in Pauline Theology with Particular Reference to the Argument of the Epistle to the Romans." PhD dissertation, University of Oxford, 1980.

———. *The New Testament and the People of God.* London: SPCK, 1992.

———. *Paul: In Fresh Perspective.* Minneapolis: Fortress Press; London: SPCK, 2005.

———. "The Paul of History and Apostle of Faith." *TB* 29 (1978): 61–88.

Wuellner, W. "Haggadic Homily Genre in I Corinthians 1–3." *JBL* 89 (1970): 199–204.

Yeung, M. W. *Faith in Jesus and Paul: A Comparison with Special Reference to "Faith That Can Remove Mountains" and "Your Faith Has Healed/Saved You,"* WUNT. Tübingen: Mohr Siebeck, 2002.

Yinger, K. L. "A Book Review of John P. Dickson, 'Mission-Commitment in Ancient Judaism and in the Pauline Communities . . .'" *JSNT* 27 (2004): 116–118.

Young, E. M. "'Fulfill the Law of Christ': An Examination of Galatians 6.2." *StBT* 7 (1977): 31–42.

Zahn, T. *Der Brief des Paulus an die Galater*, KNT 9. Leipzig: Deichert, 1905.

Zeller, D. *Juden und Heiden in der Mission des Paulus: Studien zum Römerbrief.* Stuttgart: Katholisches Bibelwerk, 1973.

———. "Theologie der Mission bei Paulus." In *Mission Im Neuen Testament*, edited by K. Kertelge, 164–189. Freiburg: Herder, 1982.

Reference Index

1. Hebrew Bible / Old Testament

Genesis
1:26–27 *276*
4:25 *331*
10:32 *206*
12:1 *206*
12:3 *206*
17:4–14 *200*
17:10 *201*
24:38 *206*
26:21f *331*
30:24 *331*
37:9 *331*
43:22 *331*

Exodus
6:14 *206*
15 *132*
16:31 *203*
19:6 *135*
22:4 *331*
26:17 *331*
26:28 *331*
30:9 *331*
31:2 *206*

Leviticus
10:6 *203*
14:42 *331*
19:17 *203*
19:18 *259*
20:5 *206*
22:13 *206*

Numbers
1:2 *206*
1:3 *184*
1:4 *206*
2:2 *206*
11:1–6 *102*
14:1–4 *102*
14:24 *331*
20:2 *102*
20:29 *203*
21:4–5 *102*
25:6ff *132*

Deuteronomy
1:23 *206*
4:10 *184*
7:6 *189*
15:3 *203*
15:11 *203*
15:12 *203*
17:15 *203*
21:23 *51*
22:1 *203*
22:21 *206*
23:1–3 *184*
24:10 *203*
29:17 *206*
32 *42, 98, 154*
32:5 *102, 154*
32:5–20 *98*
32:6 *103*
32:7 *104*
32:21 *154, 209, 213, 215*
32:29 *104*
32:43 *156, 215*
33:2 *189*

Joshua
2:12 *206*
6:23 *206*
9:2 *184*

Judges
6 *132*
6:15 *206*
18:1 *206*

Ruth
4:11 *203*

**1 Samuel /
1 Kingdoms**
2:31 *206*
7:2f *203*
9:21 *206*

**2 Samuel /
2 Kingdoms**
1:12 *203*
5:7 *216*
6:15 *203*
12:8 *203*
16:3 *203*
18:26 *331*
24:14 *220*

1 Kings / 3 Kingdoms
8:1 *216*
8:50 *220*
12:21 *203*

1 Chronicles
9:22 *91*
11:5 *216*
14:22 *91*
16:20 *331*

Ezra
2:68 *116*
3:3 *116*
9:6–15 *215*

Nehemiah
1:11 *220*
9:5–37 *215*

Psalms
2:6 *216*
2:7 *203*
9:11 *216*
9:14 *216*
9:38 (LXX) *111, 115*
10:17 *115*
14:2 *104*
15:3 *189*
18:7ff *132*
18:49 *156*
21:22 *184*
23:1–2 *228*
47:6–9 *143*
50:2 *216*
53:2 *104*
64:10 *116*
68:17 *220*
68:30–32 *143*
76:2 *216*
88:15 *116*
89:5 *189*
89:7 *189*
104:13 *331*
114:2 (LXX) *115*
115:12 *203*
117:1 *156*
133:3 *216*
135:19 *203*
139:8 *264*

Isaiah
2:2–3 *156*
2:2–4 *143*
2:3 *161*
5:7 *203*
6:7 *242*
8:14 *216*
8:18 *216*
9:2–7 *99, 109*
10:16 *132*
10:22 *146*
11 *121, 122*
11:4 *122*
11:5 *122*
11:6–10 *143*
11:10 *156*
14 *143*
14:2 *203*
18:7 *143, 216*
19:23 *143*
25:6–10a *143*
27:9 *209, 215*
28:14ff *132*
28:16 *216*
29:5ff *132*
40:1–9 *162, 305*
40:9 *216*
40:12 *159*
41:27f *162, 305*
42:1 *161*
42:1–9 *159, 162*
42:1–12 *143*
42:4 *161*
42:6 *161*
42:6–7 *99, 109, 242*
42:7–9 *161*
44:18–25 (LXX) *98*
45 *98, 275, 277*
45:10 *275*
45:10–11 *203*
45:14 *143*
45:22 *98*
45:23a *275*
45:23ff *148*
45:23–24a *273*
45:23–25 *273, 274*
45:24a *274*
45:24–25 *275*
46:3 *203*
49 *156*
49:1 *161, 242*
49:1ff *211*
49:1–6 *159*
49:1–13 *171*
49:2–3 *162*
49:4 *159, 173, 242*
49:4a *172*
49:4b *172*
49:4–8 *172*
49:5 *158, 242*
49:6 *99, 109, 242*
49:6–13 *172*
49:8 *159, 187*
49:8a *172*
50:4–9 *159*
50:20 *154*
52:5 *273*
52:7 *111, 112, 113, 118, 119, 159, 162, 164, 165, 216, 235, 239, 252, 288*
52:7f *162, 305*
52:13 *160*
52:13–53:12 *159, 162*
52:14–53:12 *98*
52:15 *160*
52:15b *162*
52:19 *104*
53 *160*
53:1 *159, 238*
54:1 *159*

56:6–8 *143*
57:19 *165*
58:8–10 *99, 109*
59:7 *112*
59:15ff *132*
59:17–21 *123*
59:20 *153, 215, 216*
59:20–21 *30, 209*
59:21 *123*
60:11 *143*
61:1 *162, 236, 305*
63:7 *203*
63:16 *203*
64:7 *203*
66:18–20 *143*

Jeremiah
1:5 *158, 242*
3:17 *143*
16:19 *143*
18:4 *331*
43:28 *331*
43:32 *331*

Lamentations
2:8 *216*

Ezekiel
2:3 *242*
12:3 *331*
36:22 *273*
37:11 *203*
37:16 *203*
39:12 *203*
39:22f *203*
39:25 *203*
39:29 *203*
40:4 *203*

43:7 *203*
43:10 *203*
44:6 *203*
44:12 *203*
44:22 *203*
45:17 *203*
45:6 *203*
45:8 *203*

Daniel
3:38 *215*
4:13 *189*
4:37 *331*
7 *190*
7:13–27 *189*
7:22 *190*
8:13 *189*
9:4–19 *215*
9:24 *215*
9:25 *239*
11:7 *116*
11:20–21 *116*
12:2 *104*
12:2–3 *104*
12:2–3a *286*
12:3 *99, 100, 104, 107, 108, 140, 165, 189, 265*
12:3a *103, 107, 110, 272*
12:3b *104, 107, 109*

Hosea
1:6 *203*
5:1 *203*
6:10 *203*
11:1 *203*

11:12 *203*

Joel
2:32 *237*
3:5 (LXX) *237, 239*
3:17 *216*

Amos
5:1 *203*
5:3f *203*
5:25 *203*
6:1 *203*
6:12 (LXX) *271*
6:14 *203*
7:10 *203*
9:9 *203*

Micah
1:5 *203*
3:1 *203*
3:9 *203*
4:1–3 *143*
4:2ff *217*
4:8 *216*
7:17 *143*

Nahum
2:1 (LXX) *235*
2:4 *116*

Haggai
2:7 *143*

Zechariah
5:11 *116*
8:13 *203*
8:20–23 *143*
14:5 (LXX) *189*
14:16 *143*

2. New Testament

Matthew
3:10 *42*
4:16 *109*
5:3 *265*
5:3–6 *266*

5:3–10 *266*
5:3–12 *265, 289*
5:4–9 *265*
5:7–10 *266*
5:10 *265*

5:11 *266*
5:11–12 *265, 266*
5:12 *266*
5:13 *262, 266*
5:13–16 *266, 273*

5:13–20 *266*
5:14 *272, 277*
5:14–15 *266*
5:14–16 *99, 109, 261, 262, 263, 265, 271, 273, 282, 289*
5:14a *108, 262*
5:14b *262, 282*
5:14b–16 *108, 286*
5:15b *267*
5:16 *270, 272, 273, 276, 277, 289*
5:16a *275*
5:16b *263, 268, 269, 270, 289*
5:24 *259*
5:30 *42*
5:48 *260*
5–7 *262*
7:19 *42*
8:17 *160*
8:21 *333*
10 *306*
10:2 *306*
10:5 *236, 308*
10:5–6 *40*
10:5–8 *236*
10:6–7 *238*
10:7 *236*
10:8b *231, 232, 241, 288*
10:9-10a *231*
10:40 *308*
11:1 *231*
11:2–6 *40*
11:4–6 *226*
13:41 *189*
13:49 *189*
15:24 *40, 306, 308*
16:16ff *335*
16:27 *276*
18 *259*

18:5 *308*
18:8 *42*
18:23–35 *260*
19:28 *190*
20:28 *160*
24:14 *29*
25:14–30 *229*
28 *18, 306*
28:20 *20, 230*

Mark
1:14–15 *40*
1:15 *95*
2:16 *135*
3:13–19 *236*
4:21–22 *262, 267*
6:7 *236*
6:9 *231*
6:12 *230, 236*
6:32–44 *228*
8:38 *189, 276*
9:37 *308*
9:42–50 *259*
9:49–50 *262*
9:50 *260, 266*
10:10 *226*
10:43–45 *234*
10:45 *160*
11:25 *276*
13:10 *29*
13:27 *189*

Luke
1:38 *238*
1:78–79 *109*
3:9 *42*
3:10–14 *229*
4:17–18 *40*
4:18 *308*
4:42 *101*
4:43 *308*
5:5 *238*
6:23 *266*
6:32 *259*
7:18–23 *40*

7:22–23 *226*
8:16–17 *267*
9 *306*
9:1 *229, 236*
9:2 *229, 236*
9:3 *231*
9:6 *229, 236*
9:26 *276*
9:48 *308*
10 *229, 306*
10:1 *229*
10:3 *229*
10:4 *231*
10:7 *226, 229, 241*
10:8 *229*
10:9 *229*
10:10 *229*
10:11 *229*
10:16 *229*
10:19 *229*
11:33 *267*
13:7 *42*
14:34–35 *262*
14:7 *101*
17:1–4 *259*
17:7–10 *229*
20:9–19 *229*
22:28–30 *190*
24 *306*
24:1ff *248*
24:34 *335*

John
1:4–5 *99*
1:6 *306*
1:22 *306*
1:29 *160*
3:12 *264*
3:17 *306*
3:32–36 *229*
8:12 *99, 109*
8:54 *276*
9:5 *99*
12:38 *160*

12:44 *308*
12:46 *99*
13:16 *306, 308*
13:20 *306, 308*
13:34 *260*
13:34–35 *258, 260*
13:35 *260*
14:2ff *206*
15:12 *258*
15:17 *258*
17:22 *276*
17:24 *276*
17:5 *276*
20:21 *306*

Acts
1:21ff *245*
2:14ff *10*
2:44–47 *10*
3:5 *101*
3:12ff *10*
3:13 *160*
5:20 *238*
6:1ff *10*
6:7 *91, 130*
6:8ff *10*
6:8–8:3 *130*
8:3 *130, 185*
8:5ff *10*
8:25 *62*
8:32–35 *160*
9 *303*
9:1ff *322*
9:1–2 *34, 130*
9:1–9 *44*
9:2 *307*
9:10–17 *241*
9:15 *238*
11:30 *333*
12:1ff *333*
12:17 *331*
12:34 *62*
13:1 *322*
13:1ff *20, 318*

13:2–4 *308*
13:44 *62*
13:48 *62*
14:4 *301, 308, 318, 319, 323, 328*
14:14 *301, 308, 318, 319, 323, 328*
15:6 *333*
15:9 *91*
15:22–23 *333*
15:22–24 *322*
15:27–33 *319*
15:35 *322*
15:35–36 *62*
16:3 *39*
16:5 *91*
16:21 *279*
17–18 *64*
17:1–10 *64*
17:5–10 *64*
17:7 *331*
17:13 *64*
18:24–28 *328*
19:10 *62*
19:22 *101*
19:32–41 *184*
22 *303*
22:4–11 *44*
22:12–16 *241*
23:1 *277*
23:6 *130*
26 *303*
26:5 *130*
26:9–18 *44*

Romans
1:1 *163, 168, 305, 321*
1:1ff *35*
1:1–3 *235*
1:1–6 *158, 163, 234, 239, 318*
1:1–7a *188*
1:1–17 *8*
1:2–5 *141*

1:3 *51, 233*
1:3–5 *250*
1:4 *250*
1:5 *91, 163, 174, 185, 217, 234*
1:5ff *179*
1:5–17 *91*
1:6 *190, 258*
1:7 *80, 174, 189, 195*
1:8 *61, 65*
1:9 *68, 73, 163, 168*
1:10 *74*
1:12 *197*
1:13 *195*
1:14–15 *168*
1:15 *164, 168, 173, 174*
1:16 *147, 211*
1:17 *93*
1:27 *197*
2:5ff *214*
2:10 *147*
2:15 *197*
2:16 *163, 180, 193*
2:17 *273*
2:17ff *214*
2:19 *273*
2:24 *164*
2:28–29 *41, 154*
2:29 *214*
3:9 *164*
3:11 *104*
3:15 *112*
3:17 *113*
3:20 *91*
3:21ff *41*
3:22–30 *91*
3:25 *95*
3:26 *91*
3:31 *92*
3–10 *211*
4:9–20 *91*
4:14 *195*

4:17 *151, 187*
4:20 *91*
4:24 *250*
4:24–25 *250*
4:25–5:1 *160, 251*
5:1–2 *91*
5:2 *91*
5:11 *171*
5:12 *150*
5:12–21 *166*
6:1–11 *139*
6:4 *89, 276, 277*
6:4–5 *139*
6:6 *133*
6:12 *174*
6:13 *151*
6:16 *174*
7:1 *195*
7:6 *214*
7:23 *331*
8:1 *89*
8:1ff *41*
8:1–27 *214*
8:4 *89, 279*
8:12 *195*
8:12–17 *195*
8:14 *194*
8:14ff *207*
8:16 *194*
8:17 *195*
8:19 *194*
8:21 *194*
8:27 *189*
8:28 *188*
8:29 *194, 195*
8:38 *83*
9:1–8 *41*
9:4f *166*
9:5 *51, 217, 233*
9:6–10:13 *217*
9:6–29 *154*
9:8 *136, 194, 216*
9:24–26 *187*

9:24ff *216*
9:26b *216*
9:27 *146*
9:30–32 *91*
9:32 *207*
9:33 *154, 216*
9:33b *216*
9–11 *41, 156, 214, 235*
10:1 *195*
10:4 *149, 233*
10:5–13 *158*
10:5–21 *164*
10:8 *120, 163, 164*
10:9 *91*
10:9–21 *235*
10:13 *237*
10:13–18 *237*
10:14 *163, 235*
10:14ff *235*
10:14–16 *164*
10:14–17 *234, 240, 252, 288*
10:14–18 *113*
10:15 *113, 119, 159, 163, 164, 165, 176, 235, 236*
10:15–16 *169*
10:15–17 *10*
10:16 *159, 174, 235*
10:17 *121*
10:18 *65*
10:18–21 *164*
10:19 *148, 151, 152, 154*
10:19–21 *237*
10:21 *235*
11 *150, 151, 154, 208, 213, 218, 220*
11:1ff *187*
11:1–17 *146*
11:4–5 *151*
11:5 *146*

11:6 *181*
11:6–13 *203*
11:7 *146*
11:7ff *205*
11:11 *148, 151, 152*
11:11ff *154*
11:11–12 *41, 146, 149*
11:12 *38, 146*
11:12–15 *145*
11:13–32 *41*
11:14 *148*
11:15 *38, 151*
11:16–17 *146*
11:17 *67, 70*
11:17ff *149*
11:17–18 *155*
11:18–22 *42*
11:20 *91*
11:24 *42*
11:25 *144, 146, 149, 151, 195, 209*
11:25b *149, 150*
11:25–26 *30*
11:25–27 *41, 147*
11:25–32 *239*
11:25ff *137*
11:25b–26 *180*
11:25b–26a *148*
11:26 *150, 153, 156, 208, 217*
11:26a *150, 151*
11:26b *218, 221*
11:26b–27 *215, 218*
11:29 *151, 187*
11:30–31 *146, 151, 220*
11:32–36 *220*
11:34 *159*
11:36 *221*
12 *220, 259*
12:1 *195, 220, 295*
12:1–15:7 *221*
12:1–15:13 *256*

12:3–8 *256*
12:4–13 *221*
12:4–5 *166, 193*
12:5 *197*
12:6–8 *292, 293*
12:9 *256*
12:10 *196, 197, 256*
12:11 *214*
12:13 *66, 70, 72, 80, 189*
12:14 *256*
12:14–13:7 *221*
12:16 *197*
12:17–19 *256*
12:18 *196, 256*
12–15 *220*
13:4 *323*
13:7 *256*
13:8 *197, 331*
13:8–10 *221, 256, 258*
13:11–12 *256*
13:13 *89*
13:14 *221*
14:1 *91*
14:1–15:13 *156, 221*
14:1–18 *221*
14:4 *94*
14:10 *195*
14:10ff *189, 214*
14:13 *195, 197*
14:13a *256*
14:13b *256*
14:13–18 *214*
14:14 *82, 256*
14:15 *89, 195*
14:16 *221*
14:17 *214, 256*
14:18 *221*
14:18–19 *256*
14:19 *197, 221*
14:21 *195*
15:1–8 *234*
15:1–13 *214*

15:2 *221*
15:3 *221, 256*
15:5 *197, 221*
15:7 *197, 256*
15:7–12 *187*
15:7–13 *156*
15:8 *51, 195, 221, 323*
15:8–19 *239*
15:12 *156*
15:14 *83, 197*
15:14–15 *195*
15:16–20 *162, 163*
15:17–20 *168*
15:18 *174*
15:19 *214*
15:19b *64, 286*
15:19ff *58, 286*
15:20 *164, 181*
15:20b *165, 169*
15:20ff *64*
15:20–21 *160*
15:21 *104*
15:25 *80*
15:25–26 *189*
15:25–28 *214*
15:26 *66, 70, 80, 196*
15:27 *66, 70, 146*
15:30 *195*
15:31 *80, 189*
16 *84*
16:1 *177, 195, 323*
16:1–5 *80*
16:2 *80, 82, 87, 89, 189*
16:3 *11, 325*
16:5 *11, 195*
16:5ff *177*
16:7 *177, 308, 316, 317, 319, 328*
16:8 *82*
16:9 *11*
16:11 *82*
16:11ff *82*

16:12f *11*
16:13 *195*
16:14 *78, 85, 195*
16:14–15 *80*
16:15 *80, 189*
16:16 *80, 197*
16:17 *174, 195*
16:19 *174*
16:22 *82*
16:23 *80, 189, 195*
16:25 *163*
16:26 *91, 174*

1 Corinthians
1:1 *26, 188, 189, 320, 323*
1:2 *80, 189*
1:2b *190*
1:3 *195*
1:8 *180, 193*
1:9 *66, 69, 70, 187*
1:10 *195*
1:10–4:21 *326*
1:11 *195*
1:14 *330, 331*
1:16 *195*
1:17 *164, 168, 174, 232*
1:18 *263*
1:19 *327*
1:23 *51*
1:24 *188*
1:26 *187, 195*
1:26–28 *257*
1:31 *82, 257*
2:1 *195*
2:6 *139*
2:14 *124*
3 *326*
3:1 *195*
3:3 *89, 277*
3:5 *177, 195, 321, 324, 326*
3:5ff *11*

3:5–4:13 *323*
3:5–10 *161*
3:6–9 *181*
3:8 *179*
3:9 *177, 320, 324, 326*
3:9a *172*
3:9–17 *193*
3:13 *180, 193, 214*
3:16–17 *214*
3:19–20 *327*
3:21–22 *292*
4 *326*
4:1 *177*
4:1–2 *195*
4:1–9 *326*
4:3 *326*
4:3–5 *327*
4:6 *195, 326*
4:8 *327*
4:9 *324, 327*
4:9–13 *327*
4:15 *163, 181, 195, 327*
4:16 *60*
4:16–17 *327*
4:17 *11, 51, 82*
4–6 *329*
5:5 *180, 193*
5:9–11 *257*
5:10 *196*
5:11 *189, 195*
5:11–13 *257*
5:13 *257*
6:1 *80*
6:1–11 *257*
6:2 *80, 190*
6:3 *190*
6:4 *80*
6:5 *189, 195, 317*
6:6 *195*
6:8 *195*
6:9–10 *257*
6:15 *193*

7:5 *196*
7:7–40 *139*
7:10 *230*
7:12 *195, 230*
7:15 *187, 195, 259*
7:16 *18, 19, 183*
7:17 *80, 89, 150, 185*
7:17–18 *187*
7:17–20 *39*
7:20 *187*
7:20–22 *187*
7:22 *82*
7:24 *187, 195*
7:29 *195*
7:29–31 *139, 257*
7:36 *150*
7:39 *82*
8:5 *292, 293*
8:6 *195*
8:11 *195*
8:12 *79, 195*
8:13 *195*
9 *228, 229, 230, 240, 245, 250, 252, 288*
9:1 *141, 229, 241, 243, 249, 250, 252, 288, 304, 329*
9:1f *82*
9:1–2 *44, 243*
9:1–3 *329*
9:1–6 *313*
9:1–14 *169*
9:1–27 *257*
9:2 *229, 243*
9:3 *232*
9:3ff *231*
9:3–14 *329*
9:4 *226, 229*
9:4–6 *329*
9:4–14 *227*

9:5 *51, 161, 195, 229, 312, 331, 334, 338*
9:5ff *11*
9:6 *229, 328, 329*
9:7 *229*
9:7–13 *175*
9:11 *229*
9:12 *226, 229, 329, 331*
9:12–23 *163*
9:13 *229*
9:14 *51, 168, 175, 176, 179, 226, 227, 229, 230, 241, 329*
9:15 *175, 227*
9:15ff *227*
9:16 *30, 164, 229, 241*
9:16–22 *141*
9:17 *195, 229*
9:18 *164, 229, 231, 232, 241*
9:19–23 *23, 183, 257*
9:23 *67, 70*
9:24–27 *257*
9:27 *229*
10:1 *195*
10:1–13 *103, 166*
10:5 *86*
10:11 *139*
10:16 *66, 70*
10:17 *166*
10:18 *67, 203*
10:20 *67*
10:27 *187, 229*
10:31 *292, 293*
10:31–11 *10*
10:31–11:1 *8, 18, 19, 23, 183*
10:32 *80, 189*
11:1 *51, 58, 60, 286*
11:2 *100*

11:6 *185*
11:11 *82*
11:17–34 *257*
11:18 *185*
11:22 *189, 195*
11:23–25 *51*
11:27–34 *257*
11:28 *150*
11:29 *166*
11:29–32 *257*
11:30 *317*
11:33 *195, 197*
11:34 *195*
12:1 *195*
12:12–27 *177, 193*
12:12ff *166*
12:13 *292*
12:25 *197*
12:28 *177, 185, 305*
12:28a *179*
12:28ff *10*
13:3 *257*
13:8 *292, 293*
14:6 *195*
14:6ff *159*
14:7 *292, 293*
14:14–15 *19*
14:20 *195*
14:22–25 *183*
14:23–25 *18, 57*
14:25 *57, 150*
14:26 *195*
14:33 *80, 189*
14:33–34 *185*
14:35 *185, 195*
14:39 *195*
15 *247*
15:1 *163, 164, 195*
15:1–3 *305*
15:1–7 *336*
15:2 *100, 106, 247*
15:3 *160, 240*
15:3b–8 *334*

15:3–8 *336*
15:3–11 *169*
15:5 *305, 314*
15:5–7 *247, 302, 329, 334*
15:5–8 *250, 313, 315*
15:5–10 *243, 304*
15:5–11 *246*
15:6 *86, 195*
15:7 *247, 305, 308, 323, 328*
15:7–9 *316*
15:8 *234, 305, 318*
15:8–11 *44*
15:8–12 *243*
15:9 *130, 185, 187, 189, 243, 250*
15:9–11 *168*
15:9f *243*
15:11 *150*
15:11–12 *163*
15:12 *106*
15:14 *247*
15:20–23 *139*
15:22 *166*
15:23–28 *136*
15:28 *68*
15:31 *195*
15:35 *106*
15:35–58 *247*
15:40 *264, 276*
15:45 *166*
15:48f *276*
15:49 *276*
15:50 *195*
15:51–52 *139*
15:58 *82, 195*
16:1 *80, 189, 196*
16:11f *195*
16:12 *327*
16:13 *92, 94*
16:15 *80, 189, 195*
16:15f *11*

16:19 *80, 82, 185, 189, 195*
16:20 *189, 195, 197*
19:19–23 *39*

2 Corinthians
1:1 *80, 189, 195, 320, 323*
1:2 *195*
1:4 *73*
1:7 *67*
1:8 *195*
1:12–14 *170*
1:12–15 *105*
1:14 *180, 193*
1:15–16 *106*
1:19 *11, 163, 319*
1:21–22 *170*
1:21a *170*
1:21b *170*
1:22 *170*
1:24 *92*
2 *233*
2:3 *83*
2:6 *180, 193*
2:12 *67, 82, 163*
2:13 *195*
2:14–7:4 *170*
2:15 *171, 317*
2:17–4:15 *294*
3:1ff *307*
3:1–6 *328*
3:3 *19*
3:6 *195, 323*
3:7–18 *166*
3:18 *276*
4:1–5 *168*
4:2 *89*
4:3 *163, 169, 171*
4:5 *163*
4:6 *44*
4:7 *171*
4:10–12 *294*
4:11 *295*

4:15 *86*	9:3 *195*	1:2 *78, 80, 85, 185,*
4:16–5:5 *193*	9:5 *195*	*189, 195*
5 *171*	9:6ff *197*	1:3 *195*
5:1 *264*	9:12 *80, 189*	1:4 *51, 139*
5:1–9 *296*	9:12–13 *70*	1:6 *187, 331*
5:1–10 *139*	9:13 *66, 67, 68, 70, 71*	1:6–9 *169*
5:7 *89, 277*	9:13b *67*	1:7 *204*
5:8–9 *296*	10:2f *89*	1:8 *161*
5:9 *293, 294*	10:5–6 *174*	1:8–9 *165, 169*
5:9–10 *292*	10:7 *305*	1:11 *163, 164, 195*
5:10 *214*	10:8 *181*	1:11ff *49*
5:15 *171*	10:12 *104*	1:11–15 *305*
5:16 *49, 233, 249*	10:14 *163*	1:11–17 *10*
5:16–17 *171*	10:16 *169*	1:11–2:10 *159*
5:16–20 *171*	10:17 *82*	1:12 *250*
5:17 *35, 133, 139,*	11:4 *124, 163, 331*	1:13 *80, 130, 136,*
193, 234	11:5 *243*	*185, 189*
5:17–6:2 *172*	11:7 *163, 164, 232*	1:13–14 *130*
5:18–6:2 *18*	11:8 *80, 185*	1:13–16 *44*
5:18–19 *171*	11:9 *78, 85, 195*	1:14 *135*
5:19–20 *187*	11:12 *42*	1:15 *187, 211, 303,*
5:20 *58, 171, 172, 286*	11:13 *244, 308*	*305*
5:20b *171*	11:15 *195, 323*	1:15–16 *44, 168, 305*
5:21 *171*	11:23 *195, 304, 323*	1:15–16a *158*
6:1 *124, 172, 187*	11:28 *185*	1:15–16b *161*
6:1–10 *158, 160*	12:1–10 *159*	1:15ff *242*
6:2 *35, 156, 159, 187*	12:1–3 *292*	1:16 *136, 141, 164,*
6:4 *177, 195, 323*	12:11 *243*	*250*
6:10 *100, 299*	12:12 *243*	1:17 *304, 305, 308,*
6:14 *66*	12:13 *185*	*312, 318, 323*
6:16 *193*	12:18 *89, 195*	1:17–18 *338*
7:4 *73*	12:19 *181*	1:17–19 *305, 314*
7:13 *63*	13:5 *91*	1:18 *240, 333*
7:15 *174*	13:10 *181*	1:18–19 *313*
8:1 *80, 185, 189, 195*	13:11 *195*	1:19 *195, 308, 323,*
8:4 *66, 70, 80, 189*	13:12 *80, 189, 197*	*329, 330, 331,*
8:17 *124*	13:13 *66*	*332, 333*
8:18 *163, 195*	13:14 *70*	1:22 *80, 95, 185*
8:19–24 *185*	**Galatians**	1:23 *91*
8:22f *195*	1:1 *63, 195, 305, 308,*	2:1 *329*
8:23 *67, 306, 308,*	*322*	2:1ff *333*
319, 322, 323	1:1f *320*	2:1–10 *314*
9:1 *80, 189*		2:2 *141, 163*

2:4 *196, 304*
2:5 *68*
2:7 *163, 169*
2:7–8 *234*
2:7–9 *137*
2:8 *217, 336*
2:8ff *39*
2:9 *66, 69*
2:10 *89*
2:12 *197, 319, 334*
2:16 *91, 96, 198, 204, 207, 330*
2:16ff *200*
2:17 *195, 323*
2:18 *181*
2:20 *139, 204*
3:1 *51, 204*
3:1ff *200*
3:1–5 *204, 205*
3:1–18 *205*
3:2 *204, 207*
3:5 *204, 207*
3:6ff *200*
3:7 *204*
3:8 *198, 204*
3:9 *204*
3:10 *207, 214*
3:10–14 *166*
3:11 *204*
3:12 *204*
3:13ff *51*
3:14 *204*
3:15 *195*
3:15ff *200*
3:19 *149, 233*
3:19–29 *205*
3:22 *198, 204*
3:23 *204*
3:23ff *200*
3:24 *204*
3:25 *204*
3:26 *95, 194, 204*
3:26–28 *198*

3:29 *195, 200*
4:1ff *200*
4:4 *51, 233*
4:4ff *207*
4:5 *234*
4:6 *195*
4:8–11 *204, 205*
4:9 *205*
4:12 *195*
4:13 *164*
4:14 *124*
4:21 *204, 205*
4:21ff *200, 207*
4:21–31 *166*
4:26 *154*
4:27 *159*
4:28 *195*
4:31 *195*
5:1 *94*
5:1–12 *204, 205*
5:1–4 *207*
5:1–6:10 *204*
5:2ff *200, 207*
5:3 *205*
5:4 *205*
5:5 *204, 207*
5:6 *39, 204*
5:8 *187*
5:10 *82*
5:11 *17, 38, 39, 195*
5:13 *187, 195, 196, 197*
5:13–14 *258*
5:13–26 *196*
5:13–6:10 *199, 204, 205, 207*
5:14 *214*
5:15 *197*
5:16 *89, 133, 278, 279*
5:16–26 *207*
5:17 *197*
5:22 *271*
5:22–23 *205*

5:26 *197*
6 *197*
6:1 *195*
6:1–10 *196, 197*
6:2 *150, 196, 197, 198, 205, 206, 214, 258, 259*
6:6 *66, 69, 70, 176, 177, 179*
6:6–8 *197*
6:7–8 *197*
6:10 *194, 196, 197, 199, 204, 208, 259*
6:10a *196*
6:10b *197, 199, 203, 204*
6:12–16 *204*
6:15 *139, 234*
6:16 *41, 136*
6:18 *195*

Ephesians
1:1 *189*
1:2 *195*
1:3 *276*
1:4 *190*
1:15 *95, 189*
1:16 *73, 74*
1:18 *187, 189*
1:20 *276*
1:21 *234*
1:22 *186*
1:22–2:22 *186*
1:23 *193*
2:1–6 *119*
2:2 *89, 278*
2:6 *276*
2:10 *89*
2:11–19 *118, 119*
2:13 *186*
2:13–14 *117*
2:14–19 *186*
2:16 *118, 186*

2:17 *111, 112, 118, 119, 165, 169*
2:17–19 *117*
2:17–20 *118*
2:19 *189, 194, 197, 203*
2:19–22 *58, 193, 286*
2:20 *119, 179*
2:21 *82, 119*
2:21–22 *118*
3:1 *189*
3:1–13 *117, 119*
3:2 *195*
3:7 *195, 323*
3:8 *168, 189*
3:10 *276*
3:14–19 *119*
3:17 *119*
3:20 *117*
4:1 *82, 87, 89, 187, 278*
4:1–16 *186*
4:2 *197*
4:4 *187*
4:11 *178, 305*
4:11ff *10*
4:12 *166, 178, 189*
4:13–16 *119*
4:16 *58, 286*
4:17 *82, 89*
4:17–24 *119*
4:25 *197*
4:30 *180, 193*
4:32 *197*
5:1 *60*
5:2 *89*
5:3 *189*
5:8 *82, 89*
5:11 *66*
5:15 *89*
5:17 *104*
5:18 *124*
5:18–6:9 *287*
5:21 *197*
5:26 *287*
6:1 *82*
6:8 *292*
6:10 *82*
6:10–19 *186*
6:10–20 *8, 19, 110*
6:11 *110*
6:11–17 *115*
6:12 *110, 124, 276*
6:13 *110, 114*
6:14 *111, 114, 122*
6:14–17a *121*
6:15 *58, 110, 111, 112, 113, 116, 118, 119, 120, 286, 287*
6:17 *111, 120*
6:17b *58, 120, 121, 122, 123, 286, 287*
6:18 *189*
6:19 *163*
6:20 *171*
6:21 *81, 84, 189, 195, 323*
6:23 *195*

Philippians
1:1 *80, 82, 189, 195, 320, 323*
1:1–11 *268*
1:2 *195*
1:3 *73, 75, 76, 77*
1:3b *73*
1:3–4 *73*
1:3–6 *77*
1:3–8 *65*
1:3–11 *100*
1:4 *75, 76, 90*
1:5 *8, 58, 65, 66, 67, 68, 71, 72, 75, 77, 78, 97, 100, 286*
1:5b *77*
1:5–7 *163*
1:6 *19, 75, 76, 83, 102, 106, 110, 180, 193, 268*
1:6–11 *261, 262, 263, 268, 270, 271, 275, 282, 289*
1:7 *11, 67, 70, 72, 84, 97, 100*
1:7c *77*
1:9–10a *270*
1:9–11 *102, 106, 269*
1:10 *180, 193, 270, 276*
1:10b–11a *270*
1:11 *270, 274*
1:12 *67, 79, 84, 85, 86, 91, 97, 100, 163, 195*
1:12–14 *79, 81, 85*
1:12–18 *84, 86*
1:12–18a *14, 100*
1:12–26 *88*
1:13 *84, 86*
1:14 *58, 77, 79, 81, 82, 83, 85, 86, 88, 100, 195, 286*
1:14–18 *8, 11, 297*
1:15 *100*
1:15b *140*
1:15–18 *84, 85*
1:15–18a *297*
1:16 *85, 97, 100, 163*
1:16b *173*
1:17 *84, 85, 100, 298*
1:17–18 *166*
1:18 *84, 86, 100, 291, 292, 293, 297, 299*
1:18a *298*
1:18b *298*
1:18b–26 *298*
1:18b–2:11 *14*

1:19 *91, 105, 298*
1:19–20 *88*
1:20 *292, 293, 295, 298*
1:21 *139*
1:21–24 *295*
1:22 *100*
1:23 *105, 139*
1:24 *325*
1:25 *83, 93, 105, 299*
1:26 *105*
1:27 *8, 67, 86, 88, 94, 95, 96, 97, 100, 103, 105, 272, 277, 278, 289, 292*
1:27a *88, 89, 94, 95, 107*
1:27b *105*
1:27c *73, 87, 90, 91, 93, 94, 95, 107*
1:27–2:18 *97, 261, 262, 263, 268, 271, 281, 282, 289*
1:27–28 *106*
1:27–29 *165*
1:27–30 *58, 86, 87, 97, 100, 274, 286*
1:28 *88, 91, 92, 103, 106, 110, 263, 281*
1:28–29 *93*
1:28–30 *95*
1:29 *86, 166*
1:30 *8*
1–2 *108*
2:1 *66, 70*
2:1–4 *95, 96*
2:1–14 *298*
2:3 *93, 197, 298*
2:4 *93*
2:5 *96*

2:5–11 *100, 160, 262, 297*
2:6c *276*
2:6–11 *96, 98, 270, 271, 274*
2:6–8 *96, 270, 274, 276*
2:6–9 *98*
2:8c *276*
2:9 *276*
2:9–11 *270, 274, 276*
2:9–11b *274*
2:9c *276*
2:10 *267*
2:10ff *148*
2:10–11 *98, 267, 272, 273, 274, 277, 289*
2:11 *98, 195, 276*
2:11b *270*
2:11c *274, 276*
2:12 *102, 103, 174*
2:12–15 *103*
2:12–16 *139*
2:12–18 *14, 102*
2:14 *93, 102, 106, 109*
2:14b *281*
2:14–16 *166*
2:14–17 *18, 19*
2:15 *98, 102, 108, 154, 167, 194, 262, 264, 270, 271, 272, 274, 281*
2:15–16 *167, 286*
2:15–16a *107*
2:15–16b *105*
2:15a *289*
2:15b *110, 165*
2:15c *103, 107, 110, 272*
2:16 *8, 58, 73, 98, 99, 100, 101, 106,*

159, 180, 189, 193, 214, 286
2:16a *100, 102, 107, 109, 110, 286*
2:16b *102, 105, 107, 160*
2:16b–18 *166*
2:17 *299*
2:18 *299*
2:19 *82*
2:22 *11, 67, 97, 100, 163, 195*
2:24 *82, 308*
2:25 *11, 72, 76, 177, 189, 195, 306, 319, 322*
2:29 *82*
2:30 *11*
3:1 *82, 195*
3:2 *93*
3:3 *82*
3:4 *82*
3:5 *130*
3:5–9 *44*
3:6 *80, 130, 185*
3:7–8 *44, 136*
3:8–12 *103*
3:9 *91*
3:10 *66, 70*
3:13 *195*
3:14 *187*
3:17 *195, 278*
3:17f *89*
3:18–20 *263*
3:19 *264*
3:20 *89, 263, 279, 280, 281*
3–4 *73*
4:1 *92, 93, 94, 195*
4:1f *82*
4:2 *93*
4:2–3 *73*
4:3 *11, 97, 100, 163*

4:4 *82*
4:5 *139, 165*
4:8 *195, 298*
4:9 *58, 286*
4:10 *76, 82*
4:10ff *71, 76*
4:10–20 *72, 76, 77*
4:14 *66, 72, 77*
4:14–18 *72, 73, 76*
4:15 *64, 66, 70, 72, 77, 80, 97, 100, 163, 286*
4:15–18 *77*
4:16 *72*
4:17 *72*
4:17–19 *77*
4:18 *72, 77*
4:20 *274*
4:21 *78, 80, 176, 189, 195*
4:21–22 *80*
4:21b *80*
4:22 *80, 189, 195, 198*
4:22a *80*
6–11 *96*

Colossians
1:1 *189, 320*
1:1f *195*
1:2 *81, 189, 195*
1:4 *95, 189*
1:5–6 *8, 68*
1:7 *195, 323*
1:10 *87, 89, 278*
1:12 *189*
1:16 *292*
1:18 *166, 186, 193*
1:20 *292*
1:20–22 *186*
1:23 *91, 120, 163, 195, 323*
1:23–27 *168*
1:24 *29, 193*
1:25 *195, 323*

1:26 *189*
2:6 *89*
2:7 *91*
2:18–19 *186*
2:19 *193*
3:7 *89*
3:9 *197*
3:12 *189, 190, 220*
3:12–14 *260*
3:13 *197*
3:15 *187*
3:18 *82*
3:20 *82*
4:5 *89*
4:6 *112*
4:7 *81, 84, 195, 323*
4:9 *195*
4:10 *124*
4:15 *195*
4:17 *82*

1 Thessalonians
1:1 *80, 185, 189, 195*
1:2 *73, 74*
1:4 *195*
1:5 *8, 10, 68, 122, 163, 169*
1:6 *58, 59, 60, 62, 124, 286*
1:6–7 *59, 60*
1:6–10 *59, 62*
1:7 *60*
1:8 *11, 13, 18, 19, 58, 59, 65, 286*
1:8a *59*
1:8b *59*
1:8c *59*
1:9a *59*
1:9f *139*
1:9–10 *59, 60, 143*
2:1 *65, 195*
2:1–7 *308*
2:1–12 *11*
2:2 *163*

2:2–4 *159, 169, 170*
2:3 *65*
2:4 *163, 168*
2:6 *169*
2:7 *308, 319, 320*
2:8 *163*
2:8–9 *169*
2:9 *163, 170, 195*
2:12 *87, 89, 187, 278*
2:13 *124*
2:14 *60, 80, 189, 195*
2:14–16 *58, 286*
2:15–16 *214*
2:17 *195*
3:2 *11, 163, 169, 195, 320, 325*
3:4 *159*
3:6 *63, 74, 174*
3:6–9 *76*
3:7 *73, 195*
3:8 *82, 94*
3:9 *74*
3:12 *19, 196, 197, 259*
3:13 *80, 189*
4:1 *82, 89, 195*
4:1ff *271*
4:1–8 *26*
4:6 *195*
4:7 *187*
4:9 *196, 197*
4:10 *79, 195*
4:11–12 *176*
4:11f *176*
4:12 *89, 196*
4:13 *195*
4:13ff *214*
4:13–14 *189*
4:13–15 *296*
4:13–5:11 *139*
4:15 *62*
4:17 *150*
4:18 *197*
5:1 *195*

5:1ff *214*
5:1–8 *180, 193*
5:4 *195*
5:6–7 *296*
5:7 *296*
5:10 *292, 296*
5:11 *196, 197*
5:12 *82, 195, 259*
5:13 *260*
5:14 *176, 195*
5:15 *196, 197*
5:21 *100*
5:23 *93*
5:24 *187*
5:25ff *195*
5:26 *80*
5:27 *80, 176*

2 Thessalonians
1:1 *80*
1:1–2 *195*
1:3 *197*
1:7 *189*
1:8 *174*
1:10 *180, 189, 193, 317*
1:11 *187*
2:6–7 *29*
2:10 *124*
2:13 *8*
2:14 *169, 170, 187*
2:15 *292, 293*
3:1 *62, 63*
3:1–2 *8*
3:4 *82*
3:6 *89*
3:6–15 *176*
3:7 *60*
3:9 *60*
3:11 *89*
3:14 *174*
4:21 *195*

1 Timothy
1:2 *195*

1:11 *163*
1:11–17 *19*
2:1–4 *19*
2:7 *163*
3:4 *195*
3:5 *195*
3:7 *19*
3:8 *195, 323*
3:12 *195, 323*
3:15 *194*
4:6 *195, 323*
4:16 *101*
4:19 *198*
5:1 *195*
5:4 *195*
5:8 *198*
5:10 *189*
5:13 *195*
5:17 *198*
5:17b *177*
5:18 *176, 179*
5:22 *66*
6:2 *195*
6:12 *187*
6:18 *67*

2 Timothy
1:2 *195*
1:3 *73*
1:8 *163, 169*
1:9 *187*
1:11 *163*
1:16 *195*
2:8 *163*
2:11 *163*
2:21 *111*
3:6 *195*
3:10 *91*
4:5 *19*
4:8 *180, 193*
4:13 *198*
4:18 *276*
4:19 *195*
4:21 *195*

Titus
1:4 *195*
1:7 *195*
1:10 *198*
1:11 *195*
1:13 *91*
2:2 *91*
2:3–5 *19*
2:10 *18*
3:3 *197*
3:7 *195*
3:13 *327*

Philemon
1 *195*
2 *80, 177, 195*
3 *195*
4 *73, 74*
5 *189*
5–6 *65*
6 *66, 70*
7 *189, 195*
10 *195*
13 *11*
16 *82, 195, 198*
17 *67*
20 *82, 195*

Hebrews
1:1 *317*
1:3 *238*
4:2 *91*
4:12 *122*
7:11 *331*
11:3 *238*

James
3:15 *264*

1 Peter
1:22 *258*
3:15 *111*
4:9 *258*
5:5 *258*
5:9 *91*
5:14 *258*

2 Peter
1:5 *91*
2:10 *198*
3:2 *238*

1 John
3:11 *258*
3:23 *258*

4:7 *258*
4:11–12 *258*

2 John
5 *258*

3 John
6 *87, 89*

Jude
3 *91*
14–15 *189*
20 *91–93*

Revelation
5:13 *264*
19:15 *121*

3. Old Testament Apocrypha and Pseudepigrapha

Baruch
1:15–3:8 *215*
2:34–35 *215*
4:1–3 *268*
5:5 *74*

1 Esdras
8:73–74 *215*

2 Esdras
9:7 *215*

Judith
8:20 *331*

1 Maccabees
1:43–53 *42*
1:62–64 *42*
2:48 *268*
3:15–19 *42*
7:9 *42*
7:22 *42*
9:5–6 *42*
9:23–27 *42*
9:51 *42*
11:37 *317*
14:48 *317*

2 Maccabees
6:1 *277*
10:3 *331*
11:25 *277*
14:10 *149*

3 Maccabees
3:4 *277*

4 Maccabees
2:8 *277*
2:23 *277*
4:23 *277*
5:16 *277*
17:5 *108*

Sirach
4:10 *203*
14:11 *89*
22:13 *42*
36:1–17 *215*
36:13 *42*
36:14 *215*

Tobit
7:15 *331*
13:3–6 *40*
13:11–13 *143*
14:5 *215*
14:6–7 *143*

Wisdom
2:12–5:13 *166*
2:19 *165*
5:17–20 *115*
5:18 *115*
7:15 *89*
13:12 *113, 114, 116*
16:1 *89*
19:3 *331*

2 Baruch
1:4 *40*
8:33 *42*
17:2–3 *133*

17:4 *133*
24:1–25:24 *42*
29:3–30:3 *42*
29–30 *136*
40 *136*
41:3 *42*
41:4 *40*
51:3 *108*
68:5 *143*
68:5–7 *215*
72–74 *136*
77:2–6 *42*

1 Enoch
5:6–9 *42*
10:16 *42*
10:21 *143*
16:1 *133*
37–71 *136*
38:1–4 *108*
38:4–5 *189*
48:5 *143*
53:1 *143*
80:2–8 *42*
81:7–9 *42*
83:8 *42*
89:51 *215*
89:73 *42, 215*
90:16–38 *268*
90:26–30 *42*
90:28–33 *215*
90:33 *143*
91–104 *133*
91:11–17 *133*
91:12–17 *134, 136*

93 *134*
93:1–10 *136*
93:3–10 *133*
94:4 *42*
99:10 *42*

2 Enoch
66:7 *108*

4 Ezra
3:5–7 *133*
3:11–17 *42*
3:20–21 *133*
3:36 *42*
7:22–24 *42*
7:50 *133*
7:50–61 *42*
7:97 *108*
7:112–119 *133*
7:125 *108*
8:1 *133*
8:2–3 *42*
8:14–18 *42*
9:8–12 *42*

Damascus Document
CD 1:3–5 *42*
CD 1:4–10 *40*
CD 1:12–2:12 *42*
CD 2:6–7 *40*
CD 3:19–20 *42*
CD 6:20–21 *259*

Thanksgiving Hymns[a]
1QH[a] 22:10–15 *40*

War Scroll
1QM 1:9–10 *40*
1QM 4:12 *40*
1QM 10:9 *42*
1QM 12:13–14 *143*
1QM 13:8 *42*
1QM 13.9–12 *133*
1QM 14:8–9 *42*

13 *136*
13:12 *143*

Jubilees
1:12 *215*
1:27–29 *136*
15:34 *42*
23:19 *42*
23:26–29 *134*
23:26–31 *136*

Psalms of Solomon
2:6 *317*
4:12 *331*
8:15–20 *42*
10:6 *42*
10:9 *42*
12:6 *42*
13:5–10 *42*
17:26–46 *42*
17:30 *317*
17:31 *143*

Sibylline Oracles
3:652–795 *268*

4. Dead Sea Scrolls

Commentary on Nahum
1QpNah 3:2–3 *42*

Community Rule
1QS 1:18–24 *133*
1QS 2:4-10 *272*
1QS 3:17–4:1 *133*
1QS 4:11–14 *42*
1QS 4:18-19 *133*
1QS 5:13 *189*
1QS 5:22 *42*
1QS 8:2 *259*
1QS 8:4 *42*
1QS 8:17–23 *189*
1QS 11:13–14 *143*

3:702–731 *143*
3:767–795 *143*

Testament of Asher
1:3–5 *133*

Testament of Benjamin
9:2 *143*

Testament of Gad
6:1 *259*
7:7 *259*

Testament of Joseph
17:2 *259*

Testament of Judah
20:1–5 *133*

Testament of Moses
4:8 *42*
10:9 *108*

Testament of Zebulon
8:5 *259*

Rule of the Congregation
1QSa 1:6 *42*

Ages of Creation
4Q181 *42*

Messianic Apocalypse
4Q521 *40, 162, 226*

Melchizedek Document
11Q13 *40, 162*
11Q13 18 *239*

5. Philo and Josephus

Philo
Every Good Man
  138 *184*
On the Life of Moses
  1.149 *40*
On the Special Laws
  2.44 *184*

Josephus
Jewish Antiquities
  2.101 *102*
  4.35 *184*
  4.309 *184*
  20.43 *38*
  20.145 *102*
The Jewish War
  1.654 *184*
  1.666 *184*
  2.119 *259*
  2.414 *268*
  2.462 *101*
  3.487 *101*
  4.442 *101*
  5.186 *101*
  5.303 *101*
  5.543 *101*
  6.180 *101*
The Life of Flavius Josephus
  268 *184*

6. Mishnah, Talmud and Targumic Texts

Babylonian Talmud
b. Pesah. 87b *40*
b. Shab. 31a *40*

Mishnah
m. 'Abot 1:2 *259*
m. 'Abot 4:1 *133*
m. Rosh Hash. 1:3 *307*
m. Rosh Hash. 4:9 *307*

Targum to Isaiah
Tg. Isa. 16:1 *143*

7. Early Christian, Classical and Hellenistic Writers and Sources

Didache
11:4 *179, 185*
11–13 *231*
13 *179*

1 Clement
16 *160*
47:1–4 *328*
47:4 *323*

2 Clement
9.6 *258*

Augustine
Confessions
  8:12 *45*

Ignatius
Letter to the Magnesians
  6:2 *258*
Letter to the Trallians
  13:2 *258*

John Chrysostom
Homilies on Philippians
  62.244 *100*

Justin Martyr
1 Apology
  50–51 *160*
Dialogue with Trypho
  13.32 *160*

Aristotle
Opera Omnia
  3:623 *332*
Politica
  1294a *332*

Diodorus Siculus
4.11.1 *275*

Diogenes Laertius
3:53 *332*

Plato
Protagoras
  333a *332*

Thucydides
The History of the Peloponnesian War
  1.28 *332*
  1.139 *184*
  1.187 *184*
  6.8 *184*
  8.69 *184*

Xenophon
Cyropaedia
  I.6:2 *332*

Author Index

Abbott, T. K. 111, 122
Achtemeier, P. J. 96, 140, 242
Ådna, J. 2, 5, 20, 29, 181
Agnew, F. H. 301, 307
Allen, R. 2, 59
Allison, D. C. 134, 228-229, 231, 262, 265
Allo, E. B. 233
Arnold, C. E. 110, 112, 115, 120
Aune, D. E. 32, 140, 159
Avery-Peck, A. J. 143
Baird, W. 139
Bammel, E. 319
Banks, R. J. 58, 117, 184-185, 193-196, 203, 325
Barclay, J. M. G. 32, 204-205
Barnett, P. 3, 17, 40, 130, 234, 243, 301, 303-304, 307, 315-316, 323
Barram, M. 3, 5, 23, 55, 57, 101, 174, 182-183, 193
Barrett, C. K. 2, 67, 86, 144, 146, 150, 152, 190, 192, 304, 314, 319, 325, 334
Barth, K. 282
Barth, M. 111-113, 122, 143
Bassler, J. M. 93
Bauckham, R. 316, 318
Baumgarten, A. I. 134
Beale, G. K. 58
Beare, F. W. 78, 90, 97, 99, 108, 122, 263, 279, 281
Becker, J. 32, 122, 303
Beckwith, J. 116
Beker, J. C. 33-35, 45, 129-130, 133, 139-140, 146, 150-151, 185
Belleville, L. 316
Bellinger, Jr, W. H. 160
Bell, R. H. 45
Berger, K. 227
Best, E. 59, 112, 117, 169, 181, 304, 320
Betz, H. D. 182, 197-198, 249, 262, 308, 330
Betz, O. 160
Bingham, D. J. 161
Bird, M. F. 7, 17, 32, 39, 43, 131-132, 176, 192, 225, 268
Black, M. 303
Blauw, J. 192
Bligh, J. 333
Blinzler, J. 330
Blomberg, C. 135
Bloomquist, L. G. 78
Bockmuehl, M. N. A. 66, 73, 76-78, 81, 87, 89, 99, 105, 108, 150, 265, 281
Boer, M. C. de 133, 139
Borgen, P. 32
Bormann, L. 2
Bornkamm, G. 2, 181
Bosch, D. J. 1, 3, 30, 58, 141
Bousset, W. 303
Bowers, W. P. 2, 4-13, 16-19, 22, 24-27, 30, 32, 37, 57-58, 61, 64, 101, 106, 129, 137-138, 143, 174, 223, 232, 234, 312
Bowker, J. 135
Bowman, J. W. 167
Boyarin, D. 45

Branick, V. P. 139
Bratcher, R. G. 86
Brewer, R. R. 278
Brotherton, D. O. 2
Brown, J. P. 175, 226
Brown, R. E. 66
Broyles, C. C. 167
Bruce, F. F. 59, 66-67,
    81, 85, 98-99,
    102, 108, 117,
    169, 202, 205,
    211, 230, 265,
    269, 303-304,
    320, 325, 330-
    331, 334
Bryan, S. M. 43
Bultmann, R. 31, 49,
    161, 168, 233,
    259
Burer, M. H. 316-317
Burke, T. J. 3, 40, 160,
    171
Burrows, M. 167
Burton, E. 201-202
Buscarlet, A. F. 112
Byrne, B. 146, 173
Caird, G. B. 46, 110
Campbell, W. S. 1-2,
    33, 144, 211,
    214
Campenhausen, H. F.
    von 302
Carleton Paget, J. 27
Carrez, M. 170
Carr, W. 110
Carter, C. L. 257, 265
Cerfaux, L. 242
Chae, D. 5
Charlesworth, J. H. 32
Chester, A. 162
Collange, J.-F. 73, 92,
    170
Collins, J. J. 132-134

Conzelmann, H. 122,
    227, 325, 330
Corley, B. 150
Corrie, J. 5
Cox, C. 153
Craddock, F. B. 78, 81
Craig, W. L. 251
Cranfield, C. E. B.
    146-148, 150-
    151, 190, 214,
    219, 235, 316
Cross, F. L. 182, 186,
    232-233, 263,
    325
Cullmann, O. 29, 248
Dahl, N. A. 2, 146,
    150, 203
Daube, D. 200, 319
Davies, W. D. 33, 45,
    187, 192, 231,
    262, 303, 319
Deissmann, A. 45, 190
Dennison, W. 182
Dewey, A. J. 2
Dibelius, M. 182
Dickson, J. P. 3, 5, 7,
    11-13, 15-17,
    21, 23, 26-28,
    39-40, 60,
    62-63, 65-66,
    68, 71, 74-76,
    79, 82-83, 85,
    87, 91, 99-102,
    106-107, 112-
    113, 115-116,
    123-124, 126,
    161-162, 167-
    169, 173, 176,
    183, 193, 201,
    223, 235, 238-
    239, 268, 316,
    320-321
Dinter, P. 160-161

Dodd, C. H. 31, 140,
    168
Donaldson, T. L. 1,
    16, 32, 35-39,
    41-42, 45, 47,
    144-145, 147,
    154-156, 201,
    287, 312, 329
Donfried, K. P. 173
Downs, D. J. 242
Drane, J. W. 52
Dungan, D. 175, 227,
    230-231
Dunn, J. D. G. 33, 41,
    44-46, 48-50,
    96, 131, 133-
    134, 143-144,
    146-148, 151,
    162, 167, 174,
    182, 184-187,
    189-190, 195,
    208, 211, 217,
    219, 221, 227,
    234-235, 239,
    250, 276, 303,
    316, 321
Ebeling, G. 97
Eckert, J. 182
Ehrhardt, A. 301
Ellicott, C. J. 66, 81
Ellis, E. E. 79, 86,
    169, 176-177,
    179, 195, 316,
    320, 323-324,
    328, 336
Elmer, I. J. 242, 303
Engberg-Pederson, T.
    32
Epp, E. J. 316
Eriksson, A. 247, 336
Evans, C. A. xvi, 154,
    158-159, 162,
    173, 215, 242

Author Index

Evans, C. F. 336
Evans, O. E. 189
Everts, J. M. 46
Farmer, W. R. 160, 181
Fee, G. D. 61-62, 66, 73, 75, 78, 81-83, 85, 87, 89, 96-97, 99, 109, 120-122, 124, 158, 178, 185, 189-190, 227, 230, 250, 265, 279-282, 313-314, 323-325, 327, 335
Fitzmyer, J. A. 66, 144, 146, 150, 217, 316, 325, 334, 336
Fjärstedt, B. 175, 228-229, 231
Forbes, C. 78, 110
Fowl, S. E. 97, 263, 279, 281
France, R. T. 251, 281
Fredriksen, P. 49
Freedman, D. N. xv
Fridrichsen, A. 185
Friedrich, G. xviii, 111, 122, 167, 235
Fuller, R. H. 334
Fung, Y. K. 158, 242
Funk, R. W. xvi, 97
Furnish, V. P. 61, 65, 67, 168, 182, 184, 233
Gadenz, P. T. 131
Gaebelein, F. 78
Gaechter, P. 303
Gager, J. G. 192, 210

Garland, D. E. 66, 78, 81
Gasque, W. W. 242, 302
Gaston, L. 47, 146, 203, 210
Gaventa, B. R. 45
Gensichen, H. W. 4
Georgi, D. 2, 242
Gerhardsson, B. 230, 240, 307, 335-337
Gifford, E. H. 316
Gloer, H. 192
Gnilka, J. 66, 68, 73, 79, 81, 85, 87, 90, 99, 187, 274
Godet, F. 174
Gogarten, F. 245
Goodman, M. 17, 27, 32
Goulder, M. 50, 230, 266
Gowler, D. B. 32
Green, G. L. 59, 61, 169, 296, 320
Green, H. B. 262
Green, J. B. xvi, 52, 126, 192, 308
Greeven, H. 4
Grudem, W. A. 159
Guelich, R. A. 236
Gurtner, D. M. 266
Guthrie, D. 185-187, 206
Hafemann, S. J. 2, 181
Hagner, D. A. 262
Hahn, F. 2, 17, 30, 143, 306-307
Hall, D. R. 327
Halliday, M. A. K. 84
Hansen, G. W. 92

Hanson, P. D. 133
Harnack, A. von 2, 58, 234, 244-245, 305, 307, 312, 316, 320, 323, 328, 334
Harvey, A. E. 227
Hauck, F. 65, 69-70
Hawthorne, G. F. xvi, 66, 73, 76, 78, 81, 85, 87, 91, 109, 269, 278-279, 281-282, 296-298
Hay, D. M. 95-96
Hays, R. B. 42, 95-96, 143, 154, 160, 182, 184, 204, 213, 325
Helyer, L. R. 133
Hendrickson, W. 7, 58, 66, 78, 112, 120, 144, 192
Hengel, M. 1, 3, 33, 130, 159-160, 192, 240, 304-305, 333
Heubach, J. 4
Hodge, C. 316
Hofius, O. 2, 144, 146, 150, 160, 181, 210
Hollander, H. W. 131
Holloway, P. A. 73
Holmgren, F. H. 171
Holzbrecher, F. 51, 227
Hooker, M. D. 50, 161
Hoover, R. H. 277
Horrell, D. G. 226-227, 231

Horst, P. W. van der 150
Houlden, J. H. 78
Howard, G. 201, 276, 332-333
Hübner, H. 213
Hughes, P. E. 233
Hultgren, A. J. 2, 4, 143, 146-147
Hurd, J. C. 97, 143
Hurst, L. D. 46
Hurtado, L. C. 97, 196-198, 203, 273-274
Huttar, D. K. 316
Hvalvik, R. 20, 24, 26, 40, 211
Hyatt, J. P. 33
James, W. 45
Janowski, B. 161
Jeremias, J. 49, 63, 336
Jervell, J. 150
Jewett, R. 74, 79, 85, 200-201, 205
Johns, L. 32
Johnson, E. E. 95-96
Johnson, L. T. 41, 135, 184-185
Johnston, P. 264
Jones, P. R. 243, 312
Jonge, M. de 131
Judge, E. A. 33
Käsemann, E. 97, 144, 146, 150-152, 164, 173, 219, 238, 274, 312
Kaylor, R. D. 143
Keck, L. E. 2, 139, 146
Kehl, A. 192
Kent, Jr, H. A. 78

Keown, M. J. 5, 7, 13, 20-22, 65-66, 68-69, 73, 75-76, 78-79, 83, 85-88, 99-100, 102, 105-106, 109-110, 112-114, 121-122, 287, 291-292, 294-296, 298-299
Ker, D. P. 326-327
Kerr, F. 250
Kerrigan, A. 160
Kijne, J. J. 170-171
Kim, S. 41, 46, 48, 130, 141, 150, 160, 170, 230, 242, 246-250, 303
Kirk, J. A. 243, 301-302, 305, 313-315, 318-319
Kistemaker, S. J. 68
Kittel, G. xviii, 72
Klausner, J. 45, 135
Klein, G. 173, 302
Kloppenborg, J. S. 334
Knight, J. 43
Knox, J. 2, 181
Koch, D. A. 130
Koester, H. 33
Kohler, K. 34
Köstenberger, A. J. 143, 160-161
Krause, G. 306
Kreitzer, L. J. 136
Kruse, C. G. 308
Kvalbein, H. 5, 20, 29
Lane, A. N. S. 110
Larsson, E. 160, 173
Lee, J. H. 96

Lenski, R. C. H. 67, 316
Lightfoot, J. B. 66, 68-69, 78, 81, 90, 93, 279, 311, 330
Lim, K. Y. 30
Lincoln, A. T. 113, 115, 117-118, 121-122
Lindblom, J. 250
Lippert, P. 4
Litfin, D. 168-169, 173
Loh, I. J. 66, 76, 78, 81, 90, 104, 110, 279
Lohmeyer, E. 90, 158
Longenecker, B. W. 143
Longenecker, R. N. 32, 39, 130, 139, 176, 194, 196, 198, 201-202, 205, 322, 330, 333
Lüdemann, G. 334
Luz, U. 262
Lyttelton, G. 44
Macaskill, G. 134
Malherbe, A. J. 59
Manson, S. 134
Mare, W. H. 216
Marshall, I. H. xvi, 5, 8, 18-20, 59, 62, 99, 139-140, 233, 265, 287, 308
Marshall, P. 72
Martin, R. P. xvi, 63, 66-67, 74, 76, 78, 86, 97, 99, 102, 106, 108,

Author Index

172, 185, 206, 242, 248, 269, 274, 278, 281-282, 294-298, 302, 337
Martyn, J. L. 2, 239
Marxsen, W. 250
Masson, C. 320
McClelland, S. E. 304
McDonald, J. I. H. 168
McKnight, S. xvi, 17, 26-27, 308
Mearns, C. L. 140
Meeks, W. A. 304
Meier, J. P. 49, 236
Menken, M. J. J. 164, 172
Meyer, B. F. 43, 192, 272
Meyer, H. A. W. 104, 117
Michaelis, W. 250, 335
Michael, J. H. 66, 78, 85, 90, 99, 269
Miller, E. C. 278
Milligan, G. xvii, 63, 72
Mitton, C. L. 122, 186
Moffatt, J. 227
Moo, D. J. 144, 151, 154, 203, 210-211, 217, 316, 319
Morgan, R. 49
Moritz, T. 115
Morris, L. 59, 152, 163, 174, 190, 219-220, 234, 238, 316
Mosbech, H. 242, 302, 315
Motyer, A. 78

Moule, C. F. D. 86, 334
Moule, H. C. G. 78
Moulton, J. H. xvii, 72
Moyise, S. 164, 172
Müller, G. 306
Müller, U. B. 73
Munck, J. 1, 29, 33, 38, 45, 137-138, 143-144, 146, 151, 196, 208, 210, 219, 238, 301-303, 307, 314
Murphy-O'Conner, J. 248
Murphy, R. E. 66
Murray, J. 316
Mussner, F. 202, 210
Nanos, M. D. 146, 148-150, 210-212, 216-219, 221
Neusner, J. 134-135, 143
Newman, C. C. 135
Nickelsburg, G. W. E. 131
Nickle, K. F. 196
Nida, E. A. 66, 76, 78, 81, 90, 104, 110, 279
Nineham, D. E. 186
Nock, A. D. 45
Nolland, J. xiii, 231, 262, 266
Oakes, P. 92, 279-280
O'Brien, P. T. 5, 7-10, 13, 23, 58-60, 66-71, 73-76, 78, 80-81, 84-90, 99, 101-102, 104, 106,

109-113, 115-118, 121-122, 143, 160-161, 166-167, 175, 185, 189, 263, 265, 269, 271, 273-274, 277-278, 282, 287, 297-298
Ochenmeier, E. 20
O'Collins, G. 250
Oepke, A. 82, 84, 303-304
Olbricht, T. H. 247
Ollrog, W.-H. v, 4, 6, 10-13, 23, 76, 79, 169, 321
Orlinsky, H. M. 172
Osiek, C. 92
Pahl, M. W. D. 63
Park, M. S. 274
Parsons, M. 182
Pennington, J. T. 264
Peterman, G. W. 66, 72, 74, 76-77
Pfitzner, V. C. 86-87, 90
Pietersma, A. 153
Pitre, B. 43
Plummer, R. L. 1, 3-5, 7, 9-10, 12, 58-60, 62, 66, 69, 78, 85, 99, 112-113
Polhill, J. B. 3
Porter, S. E. xvi, 171, 242, 247
Price, R. M. 334, 336
Räisänen, H. 32, 47, 303
Refoulé, F. 215
Renan, E. 4

Rengstorf, K. H. 158, 243, 250, 301-302, 306-308, 322
Reumann, J. 74, 78, 83, 85, 87, 276, 282
Richard, E. J. 59, 169, 320
Richardson, A. 192
Richardson, P. 97, 134, 143, 150, 202, 211
Ridderbos, H. N. 4, 150, 185
Riesner, R. 2, 17, 27, 34, 39-40, 64, 160, 242, 304, 333
Rigaux, B. 303
Robbins, V. K. 32
Robertson, A. T. 117
Roberts, R. 279
Robinson, D. W. B. 202
Robinson, J. R. 146
Roels, E. D. 112-113, 115-116
Rohde, J. 303-304
Roloff, J. B. 306, 337
Rosner, B. S. 3, 40, 160, 171, 182
Rowland, C. 131-134, 136
Rowley, H. H. 303
Russell, D. S. 133
Saldarini, A. J. 134
Sanders, E. P. 1, 32-33, 42-43, 45, 47, 49, 131, 135, 143-144, 147, 150, 157, 192, 200, 211, 217-218, 287, 303, 312
Sanders, J. A. 154
Sandnes, K. O. 117, 159, 242
Sass, G. 311, 315
Schaller, B. 153
Schenk, W. 74, 99, 276
Schiffman, L. H. 35
Schille, G. 306-307
Schlier, H. 192, 219
Schmidt, K. L. 146, 185, 187
Schmidt, M. A. 146
Schmithals, W. 242, 245, 301-302, 307-308, 314, 328
Schnabel, E. J. 2, 5, 8, 10, 17, 19-20, 57, 59, 62, 64, 66, 78, 99, 112-113, 121, 130, 192
Schnackenburg, R. 117, 122, 242, 246-248, 302-303, 308, 316-321
Schoeps, H. J. 143
Schreiner, T. R. 150, 174, 217
Schrenk, G. 202
Schubert, P. 74
Schulz, R. R. 318
Schürer, E. 131
Schütz, J. H. 247
Schwarz, H. 31
Schweitzer, A. 30-31, 33, 137-140, 143-145, 192
Schweizer, E. 58, 186
Schwemer, A. M. 159, 240, 304-305
Scobie, C. H. H. 143-144, 192
Scott, J. M. 42-43, 131-132, 136, 143, 214
Seesemann, H. 65, 71
Segal, A. F. 46-47, 211, 303
Senior, D. 1, 141
Seufert, W. 242, 244-245
Silva, M. 66, 76, 78, 81, 99, 105, 107, 282
Sim, D. C. 50
Smit, J. F. M. 326
Snaith, N. H. 172
Soden, H. von 81
Soderlund, S. V. 158
Standhartinger, A. S. 2
Stanley, C. D. 154, 215
Stanton, G. N. 233
Stendahl, K. 1, 3, 32, 45-46, 144, 210-211, 303
Stettler, H. 29, 137, 160
Stewart, J. S. 45
Stowers, S. K. 93
Strelan, J. G. 196
Stuhlmacher, P. 2, 144, 146, 150, 161-162, 167, 181, 190, 211, 217, 235, 238-239, 335, 337
Stuhlmueller, C. 1, 141
Sumney, J. L. 242

Author Index

Swigchem, D. van 4, 59, 86
Talbert, C. 150
Taylor, N. 242
Theissen, G. 33, 45, 227
Thiselton, A. C. 325
Thompson, M. 221, 227, 256, 258-259, 280
Thrall, M. E. 68, 233, 304
Tomson, P. J. 47
Towner, P. H. 195-196
Trafton, J. L. 134
Tredici, K. D. 2
Troeltsch, E. 3-4
Trudinger, L. P. 332-333
Tuckett, C. M. 227-230
Turner, M. 52, 126, 192
Turner, N. 174
Ulrich, H. H. 4
Vincent, M. R. 74, 78, 85, 87, 112
Vos, C. S. de 92
Vos, G. 150
Wallace, D. B. 316-317
Walter, N. 50, 233
Wanamaker, C. A. 46, 61, 321
Ware, J. P. 4-5, 7, 9, 13-16, 20-21, 32, 59-60, 62, 65-66, 78-81, 83, 86-88, 98-101, 105, 108-110, 125, 143, 160, 165-167, 173, 176, 287

Warneck, G. 3
Warneck, J. 1
Watson, D. F. 46, 174, 235, 247
Weadors, E. P. 226
Weaver, J. A. 150
Wedderburn, A. J. M. 50-52, 130, 171, 232-233
Weima, J. A. D. 202, 204
Weiss, J. 335
Weizsäcker, C. von 1-2
Wenham, D. i, xiii, 50, 63, 108, 126, 175, 190, 221, 226, 228-231, 233-234, 240, 251, 256-257, 259-260, 262, 266
Wernle, P. 1, 4
Whiteley, D. E. H. 185-186
Wilckens, U. 146, 217, 334
Wiles, G. P. 73
Wilfrid, S. 97, 134, 143
Wilk, F. 160, 172
Willis, W. L. 227
Wilson, S. G. 192
Wink, W. 110
Winter, D. 33
Witherington, B. 32, 68, 70, 74-78, 89, 91-92, 105, 139-140, 144, 150-151, 154, 159, 196-199, 202, 217, 264, 306-308, 316, 319

Wolff, C. 52, 171, 233
Wolff, H. W. 217
Woodbridge, P. 140
Wrede, W. 4, 9, 49, 192
Wright, C. J. H. 196, 206
Wright, N. T. xiii, 32-33, 37-38, 42-43, 46-47, 97, 131-132, 134-135, 139, 143, 146, 149-151, 156, 158, 166, 211, 215, 217, 233-235, 312
Wuellner, W. 327
Yeung, M. W. 50
Yinger, K. L. 27
Young, E. M. 196
Zahn, T. 330
Zeller, D. 2, 151, 173

Langham Literature and its imprints are a ministry of Langham Partnership.

Langham Partnership is a global fellowship working in pursuit of the vision God entrusted to its founder John Stott –

> *to facilitate the growth of the church in maturity and Christ-likeness through raising the standards of biblical preaching and teaching.*

Our vision is to see churches in the majority world equipped for mission and growing to maturity in Christ through the ministry of pastors and leaders who believe, teach and live by the Word of God.

Our mission is to strengthen the ministry of the Word of God through:
- nurturing national movements for biblical preaching
- fostering the creation and distribution of evangelical literature
- enhancing evangelical theological education

especially in countries where churches are under-resourced.

Our ministry

Langham Preaching partners with national leaders to nurture indigenous biblical preaching movements for pastors and lay preachers all around the world. With the support of a team of trainers from many countries, a multi-level programme of seminars provides practical training, and is followed by a programme for training local facilitators. Local preachers' groups and national and regional networks ensure continuity and ongoing development, seeking to build vigorous movements committed to Bible exposition.

Langham Literature provides majority world preachers, scholars and seminary libraries with evangelical books and electronic resources through publishing and distribution, grants and discounts. The programme also fosters the creation of indigenous evangelical books in many languages, through writer's grants, strengthening local evangelical publishing houses, and investment in major regional literature projects, such as one volume Bible commentaries like *The Africa Bible Commentary* and *The South Asia Bible Commentary*.

Langham Scholars provides financial support for evangelical doctoral students from the majority world so that, when they return home, they may train pastors and other Christian leaders with sound, biblical and theological teaching. This programme equips those who equip others. Langham Scholars also works in partnership with majority world seminaries in strengthening evangelical theological education. A growing number of Langham Scholars study in high quality doctoral programmes in the majority world itself. As well as teaching the next generation of pastors, graduated Langham Scholars exercise significant influence through their writing and leadership.

To learn more about Langham Partnership and the work we do visit **langham.org**

www.ingramcontent.com/pod-product-compliance
Lightning Source LLC
Chambersburg PA
CBHW061703300426
44115CB00014B/2547